Allyn & Bacon's **MyLabSchool—www.mylabschool.com**

Allyn & Bacon's MyLabSchool VideoLab for Reading Methods includes 15 segments—over a full hour—of real classroom video footage on the following 9 topics:

- Module 1: Early Literacy
- Module 2: Word Recognition and Phonics
- Module 3: Vocabulary
- Module 4: Writing and Reading Connection
- Module 5: Comprehension
- Module 6: Content Area Reading
- Module 7: Using Literature
- Module 8: Assessment
- Module 9: Diversity and Special Needs

The VideoLab includes an *Observation Guide* (available for easy download in PDF format) to help your students analyze the material they encounter in the videos. Post-viewing activities are included to strengthen the connection between the material and real classrooms.

To order *Literacy for Life* with MyLabSchool Access Code Card, use ISBN 0-205-49926-0.

Literacy
for
Life

Donna E. Norton   *Texas A&M University*

PEARSON

Boston   New York   San Francisco

Mexico City   Montreal   Toronto   London   Madrid   Munich   Paris

Hong Kong   Singapore   Tokyo   Cape Town   Sydney

Executive Editor: Aurora Martínez Ramos
Editorial Assistant: Lynda Giles
Development Editor: Christien Shangraw
Executive Marketing Manager: Krista Clark
Production Editor: Janet Domingo
Editorial Production Service: Publishers' Design and Production Services, Inc.
Composition Buyer: Linda Cox
Manufacturing Buyer: Megan Cochran
Electronic Composition: Publishers' Design and Production Services, Inc.
Interior Design: Debbie Schneck
Photo Researchers: Annie Pickert and Naomi Rudov
Cover Administrator: Joel Gendron

For related titles and support materials, visit our online catalog at www.ablongman.com.

Between the time web site information is gathered and then published, it is not unusual for some sites to have closed. Also, the transcription of URLs can result in typographical errors. The publisher would appreciate notification where these errors occur so that they may be corrected in subsequent editions.

ISBN is on file at the Library of Congress.

ISBN: 0-205-39438-8

Printed in the United States of America

10 9 8 7 6 5 4 3 2 1 RRD-OH 10 09 08 07 06

Photo credits:

Page xxx, Courtesy of Donna E. Norton; **p.** 8, Michael Newman/PhotoEdit; **p.** 13, EyeWire/Photodisc/Getty Images; **p.** 20, Stockbyte/Getty Images; **pp.** 25, 26, 27, 28, 29, 30, Courtesy of Donna E. Norton; **p.** 33, Pearson Learning Photo Studio; **p.** 37, Lindfors Photography; **p.** 37, mult- Leanne Temme/Photolibrary.com; **p.** 39, Lindfors Photography; **p.** 44, Ruth Jenkinson/Dorling Kindersley; **p.** 46, Silver Burdett Ginn; **p.** 47, Photodisc/Getty Images; **p.** 48, Digital Vision/Getty Images; **p.** 51, Ellen B. Senisi/The Image Works; **p.** 55, Comstock Royalty Free Division; **p.** 60, Chris Ware/The Image Works; **p.** 62, David Mager/Pearson Learning Photo Studio; **p.** 67, Corbis Royalty Free Division; **p.** 75, Andy Crawford/Dorling Kindersley; **p.** 79, Comstock Royalty Free Division; **p.** 82, IPNstock.com; **p.** 92, Elizabeth Crews; **p.** 93, Jules Frazier/Photodisc/Getty Images; **p.** 97, Photodisc/Getty Images; **p.** 99, Frank Siteman;

Photo credits continue on page 545, which constitutes a continuation of the copyright page.

Brief Contents

1 ■ Changing Trends in Literacy Education 1

2 ■ Emergent Literacy, Language Development, and Cognitive Development 50

3 ■ Assessment and Evaluation in the Reading and Writing Program 98

4 ■ Phonics and Phonemic Awareness 136

5 ■ Vocabulary Development 174

6 ■ Developing Approaches for Fluency and Comprehension 214

7 ■ Reading, Writing, and Literature in the Content Areas: Kindergarten through Fourth Grades 256

8 ■ Reading, Writing, and Literature in the Content Areas: Fourth through Eighth Grades 308

9 ■ The Reading and Writing Connection 354

10 ■ Literacy Instruction for ELL Students, Multicultural Education, and Students with Special Needs 404

11 ■ Computer-Assisted Instruction and Reading and Writing 456

12 ■ Putting It All Together: Literacy Instruction That Works 480

Contents

Features at a Glance   xiv

Preface   xvii

About the Author   xxix

1

Changing Trends in Literacy Education   1

Models of the Reading Process   7

Bottom-Up Model   8

Top-Down Model   9

Interactive Model   9

Approaches to Reading Instruction   11

Balanced Reading Approaches   11

Phonics Approaches   12

Sub-Skills Approaches   13

Whole Language Approaches   15

Literature-Based Approaches   16

Theories of Learning Related to Reading Instruction   19

Behaviorist Theory of Learning   20

Cognitive Development Theory of Learning   20

Sociolinguistic Theory of Learning   21

Reader Response Theory of Learning   22

A History of Basal Reading   24

Silver, Burdett Series (1902)   25

McGuffey's Eclectic Reader (1921) and Elson Basic Readers (1931)   27

Reading with Phonics Series (1948)   30

McGraw-Hill Reading Series (2001)   31

Instructional Techniques   32

Ability Groupings   32

Literature Circles   33

Uninterrupted Sustained Silent Reading (USSR)   33

Recreational Reading Groups   34

Focus or Thematic Units   34

Reading Assessment in the Classroom   35

Mandated Tests   35

Consequences of Mandated Tests   36

A History of Requirements for Teachers of Reading   38

Summary   40

Extend Your Reading   41

For Further Reading   42

References   42

2

Emergent Literacy, Language Development, and Cognitive Development   46

Emergent Literacy   50

Creating an Environment for Emergent Literacy   53

Characteristics of Language Development in Early Childhood   54

Techniques That Enhance Language Development in Early Elementary Grades   56

   Informal Conversations   57

   Reading Aloud to Children   58

   Storytelling   61

   Creative Drama   64

   Creating a "Best Books" List for Emergent Literacy Students   66

Children's Cognitive Development in Lower Elementary Grades   68

   Cognitive Development for Social Studies in Lower Elementary Grades   71

Language Development and Cognitive Development in the Middle and Upper Elementary Grades   73

   Characteristics of Language Development in Middle And Upper Elementary Grades   73

   Techniques That Enhance Language Development in Middle and Upper Elementary Grades   74

   Characteristics of Cognitive Development in Middle and Upper Elementary Grades   78

Cognitive Development for Social Studies in the Upper Elementary and Middle School   79

   Summary   83

   Extend Your Reading   84

   For Further Reading   86

   References   86

3

Assessment and Evaluation in the Reading and Writing Program   92

Standardized Tests   98

   Provisions of No Child Left Behind That Relate to Reading Instruction   98

   Reactions to No Child Left Behind   100

Assessment in the Classroom That Leads to Instructional Planning   102

   National Assessment of Educational Progress (NAEP)   103

   Principles of Assessment   104

   Relating Assessment to Instructional Approaches   106

   Assessment through Observation   108

   Diagnostic Reading Inventories and Informal Tests in Reading   109

   Running Records   117

   Miscue Analysis   119

   Cloze Assessment   122

   Portfolio Assessment   123

   Additional Types of Informal Testing in the Reading Program   124

   Summary   132

   Extend Your Reading   133

   For Further Reading   134

   References   134

4

Phonics and Phonemic Awareness 136

The Importance of Phonemic Awareness   139

What Is Phonemic Awareness?   140

Building Foundations for Reading through Phonemic Awareness   141

Phonics Instruction   149

Phonics and Stages of Word Knowledge Development   151

Phonics Instruction for Stages of Word Knowledge Development   152

Integrating Phonics Skills in a Whole Language Classroom   158

Phonics and Spelling Connections   160

Using Students' Papers to Assess Phonics Skills and Spelling Errors   161

Choosing Spelling Words   162

Word Analysis Extended to Upper Grades (4–8)   164

Summary   169

Extend Your Reading   170

For Further Reading   171

References   171

5

Vocabulary Development 174

Guidelines for Vocabulary Development   178

Vocabulary Development in the Pre-K through Fourth Grades   179

Instructional Strategies and Activities That Relate Vocabulary to Personal Experience   180

Developing Word Walls   181

Expanding Vocabulary Knowledge by Oral Reading   182

Identifying Vocabulary Words for Comprehension   183

Using Webbing for Vocabulary Development   183

Developing Individualized Dictionaries and Vocabulary Notebooks   185

Vocabulary Development in the Fourth through Eighth Grades   187

Webbing and Plot Structures for Vocabulary Development (Grades 4–8)   187

Vocabulary in the Content Areas   190

Using Precise Vocabulary to Enhance Cognitive Development   191

Vocabulary Development for Underachieving Urban Students   193

Teaching Contextual Analysis   194

Definition and Illustration   195

Comparison   196

Author Summary   197

Familiar Expressions   197

Experience   198

Synonym   198

Building Student Responsibility for Vocabulary Development   202

Vocabulary Development in the Content Areas   203

Semantic Feature Analysis   204

Summary   208

Extend Your Reading   209

For Further Reading   210

References   211

6

Developing Approaches for Fluency and Comprehension 214

Schema Theory   218

Mental Imagery   221

Graphic Organizers   223
Semantic Maps   223
Improving Comprehension through Time Lines   229

Using Modeling Techniques   232

Using Questioning Strategies   238
Literal Recognition   238
Inference   238
Evaluation   239
Appreciation   240
Questioning Strategies to Use While Reading   240

Predicting Outcomes to Improve Comprehension   243

Developing Fluency in Reading   245
Guided Repeated Oral Reading   246
Independent Silent Reading   247

Summary   251
Extend Your Reading   252
For Further Reading   253
References   253

7

Reading, Writing, and Literature in the Content Areas: Kindergarten through Fourth Grades 256

Reading and Literature in English/Language Arts   261
Teaching the Literature Content for English/Language Arts   262
Developing Knowledge of Literary Genres   269

Reading and Literature in Social Studies   282
Using Different Parts of a Book   283
Differences between Fiction and Nonfiction   284
Similarities and Differences between Versions of a Folktale   284

Reading and Literature in Science   288
Connections between Science Centers and Literature   288
Analyzing Organization of Science Literature   289

Reading and Art 292
Illustrations That Depict the Literary Elements   292
Reinforcing Emergent Literacy by Examining Illustrations in Alphabet Books   293
Comparing Illustrators' Interpretations of the Same Story   294
Using Art to Develop Book Reports   295
Using Art Books to Teach Following Directions   296
Art Lessons Using Caldecott Books   296

Summary   300
Extend Your Reading   301
For Further Reading   302
References   303

8

Reading, Writing, and Literature in the Content Areas: Fourth through Eighth Grades   308

Reading and Literature in English/Language Arts   312

Applying Analytical Reading Skills to a Book   313

Teaching Authentication of Setting in English/Language Arts   315

Developing Research Skills for Reading in Content Areas   317

Choose a Topic and Formulate Questions   317

Plan   317

Gather   318

Sort   319

Synthesize and Organize   319

Evaluate   319

Present/Report   319

Developing Reading Skills in the Content Areas   319

Reading in Social Studies and History   319

Reading and Science   331

Reading and Art   333

Reading and Writing Connections in the Content Areas   339

Summary   348
Extend Your Reading   349
For Further Reading   350
References   350

9

The Reading and Writing Connection   354

Current Attitudes toward Writing Instruction Related to Reading   358

How Should Writing Be Taught?   360

Three Types of Writing That Relate to Reading   363

Expressive Writing   364

Imaginative Writing   364

Expository Writing   365

Expository Writing and Emergent Literacy   365

Labels in the Classroom   365

Charts Listing Daily Activities   366

The Writing Center   366

Language Experience Activities   366

Imaginative Writing   367

Imaginative Writing for Emergent Literacy   367

Imaginative Writing through Poetry Appreciation and Writing Workshops   370

Expository Writing   382

Expository Writing in Emergent Literacy   382

Teaching Reading and Writing through Expository Writing Workshops   383

Reading and Writing an Opinion Article   390

Understanding Viewpoints through Expository Writing   393

Summary   396

Extend Your Reading   397

For Further Reading   399

References   399

10

Literacy Instruction for ELL Students, Multicultural Education, and Students with Special Needs   404

Programs for Students Whose First Language Is Not English   408

ESL Programs   409

Bilingual Programs   409

Issues in the Selection of Programs   410

The Most Effective Programs for Teaching ELL Students   410

Oral Language and Vocabulary Development   411

Reading Materials and Approaches for Comprehension   414

Developing Family Support with ELL Students   419

Extending Phonemic Awareness   420

Multicultural Education through Multicultural Literature   420

Examples of Literature for Native American Study Presented by Phases   423

Examples of Literature for African American Study Presented by Phases   426

Examples of Literature for Latino Study Presented by Phases   428

Examples of Literature for Asian American Study Presented by Phases   430

Instructional Strategies Used with Multicultural Literature   431

Using Technology to Learn about the Latino Culture   436

Students with Special Needs in Reading   437

Characteristics of Students with Special Needs in Reading and Approaches for Intervention   438

Intervention Strategies for Specific Special Needs   439

Summary   446

Extend Your Reading   448

For Further Reading   449

References   450

11

Computer-Assisted Instruction and Reading and Writing   456

Taxonomy for Using Technology in the Classroom   460

Media for Communication   460

Media for Expression   461

Media for Inquiry   461

Media for Construction   461

Research Studies Connecting Reading and Technology   461

Using Technology in the Reading Curriculum 462

Using Technology to Enhance Word Recognition and Vocabulary 462

Using Technology to Enhance Reading Comprehension 463

Using Technology to Enhance Literary Research 465

Evaluating Software for Reading Comprehension 467

The Reading and Writing Connection and Technology 468

Designing Classrooms for Writing through Technology 469

Writing Software 470

Teaching Students the Meaning of and Consequences of Plagiarism 471

Summary 476

Extend Your Reading 477

For Further Reading 477

References 478

12

Putting It All Together: Literacy Instruction That Works 480

Balanced Literacy 483

Balance between Published Reading Programs and Trade Books 486

Balancing between Prescribed Instruction and Instruction Based on Individual Learners 493

Balance between Teacher-Guided Instruction and Independent Reading 493

Balance between Teacher-Directed Instruction and Center-Based Discoveries 495

Balance That Integrates Listening, Speaking, Reading, and Writing 498

Grouping Arrangements for Reading Instruction 502

Reading Aloud to Students 502

Ability Level Groupings 503

Reading Interest Groups 504

Book Clubs 505

Shared Reading Groups 506

Shared Writing Groups 508

Partner Reading Groups 509

Coaching Groups 509

Flexibility and Transitioning between Groups 512

Organizing the Classroom 513

Summary 518

Extend Your Reading 519

For Further Reading 520

References 521

Appendix: International Reading Association (IRA), Standards for Reading Professionals 523

Glossary 527

Index 531

Features at a Glance

Chapter	Up for Discussion	Lesson Plan
1	p. 37	
2	p. 79	*Frog and Toad Are Friends*, p. 70
3	The Role of National Tests, p. 124	Informal Assessment, p. 128
4	p. 151	
5	How Should Vocabulary Be Taught?, p. 203	▪ Searching for Teaching Context Clues, p. 198 ▪ Understanding Context Clues, p. 200
6	p. 244	▪ Developing Schema for *Crispin: The Cross of Lead*, p. 200 ▪ Developing a Time Line from Russell Freedman's *Franklin Delano Roosevelt*, p. 230 ▪ Modeling Similes with Lower Elementary Students, p. 233 ▪ Modeling Inferencing Characterization with Students in the Upper Grades, p. 236
7	Declining Reading Habits, p. 291	
8	Censorship, p. 344	
9	p. 392	
10	Issues Related to Multicultural Literature, p. 437	Developing Background Knowledge and Respect for Cultural Literacy, p. 418
11	The Current State of Technology in the Classroom, p. 471	Thematic Unit: Literature, Movies, and Technology, p. 472
12	Readability versus Leveling, p. 510	

Focus Unit/Activity	Differentiating Instruction
	p. 39
	p. 80
Developing a Diagnostic Test, p. 129	p. 131
	p. 167
	p. 207
Comparing Variants of the "Little Red Riding Hood" Tale, p. 224	p. 248
■ Choral Reading of Nursery Rhymes, p. 280 ■ Comparing Different Versions of "Cinderella," p. 285	p. 297
■ A Study of World War II, p. 321 ■ Teaching Point of View in Social Studies and History, p. 328 ■ Developing a Unit around Conservation Programs, p. 331 ■ Understanding the Writing Techniques of an Award-winning Biographer, p. 342	p. 346
■ Feature Focus Unit, p. 376 ■ Critical Evaluation of African American Literature, p. 389	p. 394
A Multicultural Literature Study, p. 432	p. 444
Reading Strategies for Computer-Based Classrooms, p. 467	p. 474
Putting It All Together through a Study of Democracy, p. 499	p. 517

Preface

The theme of this text is right in its title: *Literacy for Life*. I believe we are literacy learners throughout our lives, and that a strong, early foundation in reading skills is among the most valuable gifts a teacher can impart. *Literacy for Life* is designed for use in pre-service reading and literacy courses, as well as by in-service elementary classroom teachers. It will help students understand the theoretical and research underpinnings of literacy education, and apply this understanding in teaching a balanced approach to literacy.

Why a "balanced approach" to reading and literacy? Both the International Reading Association (IRA) and the National Council of Teachers of English (NCTE) stress the need for highly qualified teachers who know *what* to teach, as well as *how* to teach. Teachers need strategies to meet the needs of all of their students. Only a balanced approach to literacy instruction meets these goals. For example, this text meets the policy guidelines of the NCTE by providing:

- a wide knowledge of effective reading methods
- assessment strategies that help teachers design and implement effective programs
- approaches for teaching literacy through literature applications from a range of genres
- approaches for teaching reading through writing
- critical-thinking approaches that lead to effective decision making, and
- technologies that help students succeed in the contemporary world.

College students frequently ask me why I use so much multicultural literature when I teach reading and writing. I encountered one excellent response to this question in a May 10, 2006, headline in the *Washington Post*: "Of U.S. Children Under 5, Nearly Half Are Minorities." The article suggests that these minority numbers have broad implications for the nation's schools. I have given hundreds of in-service presentations, conducted many research studies, and written numerous articles on selecting and using reading materials and literacy methodologies that motivate minority students and improve their literacy skills. Consequently, this text is designed to help you be an effective literacy teacher for all students in your classroom.

Literacy for Life is also designed to meet the requirements of different types of college classes. The content provides the coverage found in traditional reading courses as well as the coverage needed in a reading/language arts block course. There is an emphasis on reading and writing, and also on reading and literature. If your classes are divided according to reading in kindergarten through fourth grade or reading in the fourth through eighth grades, there are specific portions of chapters—and even whole chapters—that focus on the needs of these specific courses.

Special Features of This Text

CHAPTER **OUTLINE**

Standardized Tests
  Provisions of No Child Left Behind That Relate to Reading Instruction
  Reactions to No Child Left Behind
Assessment in the Classroom That Leads to Instructional Planning
  National Assessment of Educational Progress (NAEP)
  Principles of Assessment
  Relating Assessment to Instructional Approaches
  Assessment through Observation
  Diagnostic Reading Inventories and Informal Tests in Reading
  Running Records
  Miscue Analysis
  Cloze Assessment
  Portfolio Assessment
  Additional Types of Informal Testing in the Reading Program

Chapter Outlines

Chapter Outlines appear before each chapter to give students and professors a clear picture of what will be covered.

Focus Questions

Focus Questions demonstrate the goals of each chapter, indicating, "After reading this chapter, you will be able to answer the following questions. . . ."

FOCUS QUESTIONS

After reading this chapter you will be able to answer the following questions:

1. What content might be included in a scope and sequence for reading in the content area?
2. What are some strategies that are effective for teaching reading in English/language arts?
3. What are effective strategies for teaching reading in social studies and history?
4. What inquiry processes could be useful for improving research skills when teaching reading in science?
5. What are some strategies for teaching reading in science?
6. What are effective strategies for teaching reading in art?
7. What are some reading and writing connections in the content areas?

Read All About It!

Read All About It! demonstrates that reading is a current and dynamic field of study—and one relevant to teachers' and students' daily lives—through current articles culled from numerous publications. This feature is always accompanied by **Critical Thinking Questions** to activate discussion on the issues presented.

Read All About It!

"Summer Reading List Blues"

by Barbara Feinberg, *New York Times*, July 18, 2004

I don't remember exactly what books were on the summer reading list handed out on the last day of school when I was 10—more than 30 years ago—but I do recall that they were merely "suggested reading." I can remember scraps of stories: children making kooky inventions; a lonely girl making a Japanese doll house out of bright fabric; something about a fat little witch afraid of Halloween.

But mostly it's the easy feeling I remember when I picture reading that summer. I imagine myself sitting under a broad, shady tree, surrounded by distant hills, turning pages of a crinkly covered library book. There is a breeze high in the branches. I might never have actually sat under such a tree then; we lived in the city, and it's u...

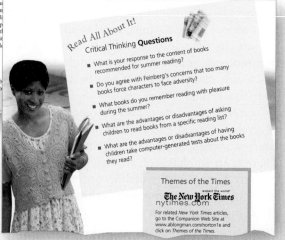

Read All About It!

Critical Thinking **Questions**

- What is your response to the content of books recommended for summer reading?
- Do you agree with Feinberg's concerns that too many books force characters to face adversity?
- What books do you remember reading with pleasure during the summer?
- What are the advantages or disadvantages of asking children to read books from a specific reading list?
- What are the advantages or disadvantages of having children take computer-generated tests about the books they read?

Themes of the Times

The New York Times
nytimes.com

For related *New York Times* articles, go to the Companion Web Site at www.ablongman.com/norton1e and click on *Themes of the Times*.

Running Records

Running records are a form of informal assessment. According to Marie Clay (1989), running records allow teachers to evaluate a child's oral reading while the student is reading from the basal texts or student's self-selected books used in the classroom. A running record for text reading according to Carolyn A. Denton, Dennis J. Ciancio, and Jack M. Fletcher (2006) is a method for recording oral reading of connected text. They identify the following types of recordings used to analyze student responses: "(a) correctly read words, (b) miscues, (c) repetitions, (d) self-corrections, (e) appeals from the child for help, and (f) words told by th[e] records are then analyzed to identify patterns kinds of reading skills and strategies that st[u] duct the running record, the teacher stands be student reads correctly and makes notes of a[ ] ning records are beneficial because the teache dents read a text of a specific difficulty or g revealed from the reading, and group studen in that area. This grouping may be for shor[ ] Teachers may date running records, therefor[ ]

readers' theater Students read a script out loud often through a staged performance.

reading aloud Reading appropriate books and other materials out loud to children in order to model reading behaviors and develop interest in topics and responses to books.

reading interest groups Dividing students for instruction according to specific interests in reading.

receptive vocabulary The vocabulary used in reading and listening.

running records An assessment technique in which the teacher notes words read correctly and errors made while a student reads orally.

schema theory A cognitive theory that emphasizes the importance of prior knowledge in the development of reading comprehension.

self-contained, heterogeneous classes Teachers teach all of the subjects to students of differen[t]

Key Terms

Key Terms are set in bold throughout the text, indicating their inclusion in the end-of-text glossary.

Lesson Plans

Lesson Plans are a unique and important feature of *Literacy for Life*. They are clear, concise examples of how a master teacher systematically creates a lesson plan. They are based on specific books and include headings such as Purpose, Materials, Grade Level, Book Summary, and Procedures.

LESSON PLAN:
Frog and Toad Are Friends

PURPOSE	1. To develop higher thought processes. 2. To develop an understanding of theme. 3. To identify evidence in a story that will support a theme.
MATERIALS	Arnold Lobel's *Frog and Toad Are Friends* (1970)
GRADE LEVEL	Early Elementary (first–second grades)
BOOK SUMMARY	The book includes five short stories about the adventures of Frog and Toad. "The Story," the second story, will be used for theme. It is about Frog not feeling well and asking Toad for a story. Toad cannot

Up for Discussion

On international tests for geography and history, students in the United States do poorly, consistently ranking below students in European and Canadian schools. Why do you think our test scores are so low?

After reading and analyzing the social studies skills recommended for upper elementary students, do you believe that students in the United States have the knowledge base or are they lacking this knowledge base? Use your own experiences with these subjects to help you answer the question. What recommendations do you have for improving understandings of geography and history? How might improvements in reading comprehension influence the test scores of students? Share your recommendations with your class.

A teacher uses a map to help students understand geographic locations in texts and to read the visual aids found in many content materials.

Up for Discussion

Up for Discussion is a feature that appears in every chapter of the text. It is designed to activate a conversation on contemporary issues facing literacy teachers. There are no right or wrong answers to the questions; students are encouraged to bring their own experience and understanding to bear on the discussion.

A History of Requirements for Teachers of Reading 39

DIFFERENTIATING INSTRUCTION

Meeting the instructional needs of all students is a major undertaking and a worthy goal of all teachers. Within heterogeneous classrooms are students who read at different levels and require modifications in instruction. For example, you may be teaching a fourth-grade class that includes students who are reading at second-, fourth-, and ninth-grade levels. Modifications in instruction are required in order to teach reading to this group because a student reading at a second-grade level requires different instructional materials and instructional strategies than a student reading at a ninth-grade level.

Modifying instruction when appropriate to meet the different reading needs of students in the classroom is called **differentiating instruction**. According to C. A. Tomlinson (1999), instruction can be differentiated according to content, process, or product. When differentiating according to content, students are given reading materials that match their instructional needs. Differentiating through process means that teachers modify their instructional strategies and their teaching so that all students are able to learn. This modification may mean that some children receive individualized instruction when they fail to grasp a concept, or it may mean that teachers need to use totally different reading instructional strategies with those students.

When differentiating instruction through product, the assignment following a lesson may be differentiated to reflect the ability levels of different students. Mary C. McMackin and Nancy L. Witherell (2005) assert that

> It is not realistic or even advisable for teachers to develop individual or small-group lessons for every instructional task. It is feasible, however, to meet individual needs by creating leveled, or tiered, follow-up activities to reinforce whole class instruction. (p. 243)

Differentiating instruction also includes instruction for students whose first language is not English. The editors of *Language Arts* (Short et al., 2006) state: "Multilingual classrooms present teachers with significant opportunities, such as exploring multiple perspectives and preparing students to live in a diverse world, but they also present significant challenges" (p. 287). Within this textbook we consider both the

Excellent teachers help all students read by modifying instruction when necessary.

Differentiating Instruction

Differentiating Instruction is a strong and unique feature of *Literacy for Life*, one students and professors will not find in other literacy texts. Because diverse learners have diverse needs, this end-of-chapter feature provides relevant, practical material on: English Language Learners (ELLs); Struggling Readers and Writers; and Gifted and Accelerated Readers and Writers.

Reflect on Your Reading

Reflect on Your Reading is a recurring feature that allows the reader to pause and reflect on how their new knowledge might be put to practical use in a classroom.

Reflect on Your Reading

What approach do you think would be the most beneficial for teaching phonics in an upper elementary class? Consider how you might use your students' papers to assess phonics skills.

Extend Your Reading

1. After reading the descriptions of these effective classrooms, develop an inventory of a room or school environment that you could use to evaluate the environment for emergent literacy. You might use an inventory similar to the following "Inventory to Evaluate Environment for Emergent Literacy":

Inventory to Evaluate Environment for Emergent Literacy

The inventory could include some of the following topics:

	high quality	average quality	low quality
1. The room has a library corner with a variety of reading materials, both fiction and nonfiction.	___	___	___

Extend Your Reading

Extend Your Reading is an explanatory list of particular strategies for teaching reading with authentic children's literature.

For Further Reading

For Further Reading is a bibliographical listing of recommended readings related to the chapter content.

For Further Reading

1. If you are focusing on lower elementary grades, choose and read one of the references identified by Strickland and Feeley in "Development in the Elementary School Years" (2003, pp. 339–356). The authors focus on studies associated with "The Learner Develops," "Oral Language Development," "Language and Thought," "Oral Language in the Classroom," "Written Language Development," "Primary Years (K–2)," and "Literary Development." Report your findings to your class.

2. If you are focusing on middle and upper elementary grades, choose and read one of the references identified by Simmons and Carrol

Young Adolescents," "Characteristics of Young Adolescents," "Adolescent and Young Adult Literature," "Censorship," "Language," "Reading," "Writing," and "Assessment/ Evaluation." Report your findings to your class.

3. Search for and read the information on the Web sites for some of the authors included in this chapter including:

   Joseph Bruchac: www.josephbruchac.com
   Eric Carle: www.eric-carle.com
   Joy Cowley: www.joycowley.com
   Jane Yolen: www.janeyolen.com

4. To learn more about involving families of ELL students in their literacy educations read

References/Children's Literature References

References/Children's Literature References is unique to *Literacy for Life*. Donna Norton's expertise on children's literature has so strongly influenced the choice of reading matter featured in the text, that it became important to distinguish the children's literature references from the other (varied and extensive) research material referenced at the end of each chapter.

Sulzby, Elizabeth. (1989). "Assessment of Writing and of Children's Language While Writing." In L. Morrow & J. Smith (Eds.) *The Role of Assessment and Measurement in Early Literacy Instruction.* Englewood Cliffs, NJ: Prentice Hall, pp. 83–89.
Tingle, Tim. (2002). "Presentation for Storyteller in Residence." College Station: Texas A&M University.

Trostle, S., & Hicks, S. J. (1998). "The Effects of Storytelling versus Story Reading on Comprehension and Vocabulary Knowledge of British Primary School Children." *Reading Improvement, 35,* 127–136.
Warren, Lynne. (2002) "Snowy Owls." *National Geographic, 202,* 104–118.

Children's Literature References

Andersen, Hans Christian. (2004). *The Emperor's New Clothes.* Retold by Marcus Sedgwick. Illustrated by Alison Jay. Chronicle Books.
Andersen, Hans Christian. (2004). *The Little Mermaid.* Translated by Anthea Bell. Illustrated by Lisbeth Zwerger. Penguin.
Andersen, Hans Christian. (2004). *Thumbelina.* Retold and Illustrated by Brad Sneed. Dial Press.
Andersen, Hans Christian. (2004). *Thumbelina.* Illustrated by J. Brian Pinkney. Diane Publishing.
Andersen, Hans Christian. (2004). *The Ugly Duckling.* Translated by Anthea Bell. Illustrated by Robert

Bredsdorff, Bodil. (2004). *The Crow Girl.* Farrar, Straus & Giroux.
Brenner, Barbara. (1994). *If You Were There in 1776.* Bradbury.
Brown, Monica. (2005). *My Name Is Gabriela/Me llamo Gabriela: The Life of Gabriela Mistral/la vida de Gabriela.* Illustrated by John Parra. Luna Rising Press.
Bruchac, Joseph. (1997). *Tell Me A Tale.* Harcourt.
Bunting, Eve. (1999). *Butterfly House.* Illustrated by Greg Shed. Scholastic.
Busby, Peter. (2003). *First to Fly: How Wilbur and*

Organization of This Text

CHAPTER 1

"Changing Trends in Literacy Instruction," introduces the foundations for literacy and reading and how reading instruction is influenced by reading models, approaches to reading, and theories about reading. The chapter presents a history of basal reading, from 1902 into the early 2000s. This foundation chapter introduces various instruction techniques, the importance of reading assessment in the classroom, and a history of the requirements for teachers of reading.

CHAPTER 2

"Emergent Literacy, Language Development, and Cognitive Development," stresses the importance of these components in literacy development. The chapter stresses the effect of different environments on fostering emergent literacy and language development throughout the elementary grades. By studying children's cognitive development, we discover the various characteristics of successfully literate children; we understand the need for effective instruction that develops the mental skills and abilities—including reasoning, concept understanding, and developing memory— that are so important to becoming a successful reader. Tables include general characteristics of language and cognitive development, and the implications for instruction. The recommendations of authentic literature, which are included for each age level, have been field tested with appropriate age children.

CHAPTER 3

"Evaluation in Reading and Writing Programs," discusses the consequences of high-stakes testing resulting from the No Child Left Behind legislation. The chapter emphasizes the authentic assessment situated in real classroom situations focusing on children's learning and the instructional goals of the curriculum. Assessment choice based on instructional approaches such as phonics, sub-skills, whole language, literature-based, and balanced instruction are discussed. The chapter includes the tests that many teachers use throughout the year to discover the effectiveness of their instruction, including diagnostic reading inventories, running records, miscue analysis, cloze assessments, and portfolio assessment.

CHAPTER 4

"Phonics and Phonemic Awareness," presents strategies—such as auditory awareness and auditory discrimination—for building foundations for reading through phonemic awareness. The chapter extends phonemic awareness to phonics instruction that stresses the stages of word knowledge, and includes material directed at the needs of emergent readers, beginning readers, and advanced readers. The chapter includes ways to integrate phonics skills into whole language and spelling instruction.

CHAPTER 5

"Vocabulary Development," provides general guidelines for vocabulary development including both instruction in reading vocabulary and indirect approaches for vocabulary development that emphasize the extensive reading of a broad range of materials. Research-based vocabulary instruction emphasizes teaching students to learn independently, teaching students the meanings of specific words by emphasizing synonyms or definitions, pre-teaching critical vocabulary, and helping students develop an appreciation for words by experiencing enjoyment in their use. Vocabulary development is divided between pre-K through fourth grade, and fourth through eighth grades. This division allows students to understand how effective vocabulary development changes with grade levels. An important section of this chapter emphasizes teaching vocabulary through contextual analysis.

CHAPTER 6

"Developing Approaches for Fluency and Comprehension," emphasizes comprehension as the primary goal of most reading programs. The chapter introduces the importance of schema theory, stressing the necessity of activating prior knowledge and filling in the information gaps before students read a selection. Mental imagery is one example of a method for improving memory of—and comprehension for—what is read. The chapter emphasizes the importance of graphic organizers, such as semantic maps or webs, for developing concepts and interests. Modeling techniques are described because they are considered one of the most important techniques for improving comprehension. Two modeling lessons are developed, focusing on different age levels. All teachers and instructional materials advocate questioning students to evaluate comprehension. The chapter includes questioning strategies that evaluate literal recognition, inference, evaluation, and appreciation.

CHAPTER 7

"Reading, Writing, and Literature in the Content Areas: Kindergarten through Fourth Grades," includes the best practices identified by the position statement of the International Reading Association: studying high-quality literature, taking part in literacy experiences for various reasons, using multiple texts to expand concepts, building background knowledge, and balancing direct instruction with reading that promotes independent reading. The chapter discusses reading and literature in English/Language Arts through strategies such as developing knowledge of literary elements and literary genres. The chapter extends reading into the content areas through reading and literature in social studies, science, and art. These areas are especially important because most lower-elementary teachers teach all of these subjects. The subjects provide ways for students to improve their reading ability as well as ways to improve their knowledge about this important content. Numerous examples of literature are included to help the teacher.

CHAPTER 8

"Reading, Writing, and Literature in the Content Areas: Fourth through Eighth Grades," extends the subject matter developed in Chapter 7 into the upper elementary grades. The topics include those that are especially crucial if older students are to master the important concepts required for literacy development in the upper grades. Strategies such as applying analytical reading skills and authenticating literature are developed with detailed examples using real books. The text provides guidelines for developing research skills for reading in the content areas. There is an emphasis for developing reading ability through writing in the content areas, and numerous examples of literature are included in the chapter.

CHAPTER 9

"The Reading and Writing Connection," emphasizes current attitudes toward writing instruction related to reading and how writing should be taught. The chapter includes topics such as expressive writing and emergent literacy, imaginative writing, and expository writing. The chapter details examples of developing reading and writing through writing workshops that develop both literature appreciation and writing ability. Examples of workshops include poetry writing to develop imaginative writing and expository writing workshops. These workshops were all field tested with teachers and public school students.

CHAPTER 10

"Literacy Instruction for ELL Students, Multicultural Education, and Students with Special Needs," emphasizes three very important subjects for elementary teachers.

The ELL (English Language Learners) section emphasizes the development of effective programs designed to teach reading to students whose first language is not English. The research indicates that helping learners build background knowledge is one of the most important ways for increasing comprehension for what is read. When students draw upon their cultural identities and take part in interactive learning they begin to make connections. Using multicultural literature is a proven way to improve comprehension of reading for students from that specific culture. The five-phase study of the literature developed in the chapter is a result of my extensive research on the topic. The chapter concludes with teaching reading to students with special needs. The chapter includes characteristics of children with special needs in reading and approaches for intervention including students who show weakness in comprehension, word meaning, and background knowledge as well as students who lack linguistic sophistication and have deficiencies in memory that cause difficulties in organizing materials.

CHAPTER 11

"Computer-Assisted Instruction and Reading and Writing," includes a taxonomy for using technology in the classroom and research studies that show connections between reading and technology. Specific strategies are developed that relate reading and technology by using technology to enhance word recognition and vocabulary, reading comprehension, and literary research. The chapter includes a discussion about the meaning and consequences of plagiarism. Plagiarism has become an especially important topic since the Internet has made copying very easy for students.

CHAPTER 12

"Putting It All Together: Literacy Instruction That Works," provides guidelines for developing a balanced approach for teaching reading and literacy. The balanced literacy section includes information on how to strike especially well the balance between published basal reading series, trade books, and other reading materials, between prescribed instruction and instruction based on individual learners, and between teacher-directed instruction and center-based discoveries. I describe how to attain an integrated balance of listening, speaking, reading, and writing. The chapter discusses various grouping arrangements for reading instruction and shows classroom diagrams that emphasize different types of instruction, such as a traditional classroom and a classroom designed for inquiry learning.

A Complete Teaching and Learning Package

Literacy for Life is accompanied by an extensive supplements package, including print, digital, and online resources to support both teachers and learners.

Instructor's Manual and Test Bank

The combined Instructor's Manual and Test Bank is a comprehensive resource available to adopting instructors. It includes Teaching Tips, Classroom Management Strategies, and Sample Syllabi correlated to the text for both reading methods and the block course of reading/language arts methods. It also contains for each chapter:

Learning Objectives, At-a-Glance Grids, Chapter Summary, Detailed Lecture Outlines, Key Terms, Lecture Launchers and Discussion Topics, Demonstrations/Activities, Web links, Media Resources, and Additional Readings. The manual also contains a print version of the Computer Test Bank.

Computerized Test Bank

This computerized version of the Test Bank contains, multiple-choice, T/F, essay, and Case Study questions. It is available to adopters in CD-ROM for both PC and Macintosh computers. Please ask your Allyn & Bacon representative for details.

Companion Web Site at www.ablongman.com/norton1e

This dynamic, interactive Companion Web Site includes: Chapter Learning Objectives; multiple choice, essay and true/false study questions with text page references; "live" links to relevant web sites; "Themes of the Times" articles from the *New York Times;* field activities; and additional enrichment material on a chapter-by-chapter basis.

Instructor Resource Center

The Instructor Resource Center allows convenient online access to a variety of print and media resources in downloadable, digital format. As a registered faculty member, you can log in directly to download resource files directly to your computer. In addition to text-specific resources, you will find access to Research Navigator™ (see description below), and access and instructions for downloading a Blackboard® cartridge, or WebCT® e-Pack or for creating your own CourseCompass® course.

ResearchNavigator™ (with ContentSelect Research Database) (Access Code Required)

Research Navigator™ (researchnavigator.com) is the easiest way for students to start a research assignment or research paper. Complete with extensive help on the research process and three exclusive online databases of credible and reliable source material including EBSCO's ContentSelect™ Academic Journal Database, *New York Times* Search by Subject Archive, and "Best of the Web" Link Library, Research Navigator™ helps students quickly and efficiently make the most of their research time. Research Navigator™ is free when packaged with the textbook and requires an Access Code.

MyLabSchool

MyLabSchool is a collection of online tools for student success in the course, in licensure exams, and the teaching career. Visit www.mylabschool.com to access the following: **video footage** of real-life classrooms, with opportunities for students to reflect on the videos and offer their own thoughts and suggestions for applying theory to practice; an extensive archive of **text and multi-media cases** that provide valuable perspectives on real classrooms and real teaching challenges; Allyn & Bacon's **Lesson and Portfolio Builder** application, which includes an integrated state standards correlation tool; help with your research papers using **Research Navigator**™, which provides access to three exclusive databases of credible and reliable source material including EBSCO's ContentSelect Academic Journal Database, *New York Times*

Search by Subject Archive, and "Best of the Web" Link Library. MyLabSchool also includes a **Career Center** with resources for Praxis exams and licensure preparation, professional portfolio development, job search, and interview techniques.

Acknowledgments

My first acknowledgment for support and guidance in writing this textbook must be of the hundreds of undergraduate and graduate students I have taught at Texas A&M University. They have allowed me to hone and clarify the material in this textbook. They have tested the ideas with real students in real classrooms. My graduate students tested and expanded on the research base for literacy instruction. I especially want to thank four of my current Ph.D. students: Corrine Wickens, Mary Beth Tierce, Norma Garcia, and Sherry Smith for their work in various areas of literacy. Corrine is currently researching the content of literature for middle school students; Mary Beth, a Texas Teacher of the Year, is conducting research on effective literacy approaches used throughout the state; Norma is researching the use of multicultural materials with mostly Latino students and their teachers; and Sherry is exploring the use of highly illustrated texts with underachieving readers.

I would like to thank the teachers at the International Schools in Geneva, Switzerland, for their exciting K–8 instruction, which encouraged my study-abroad students to enjoy a totally integrated approach to teaching literacy. I would also like to thank the teachers who took part in numerous writing and literacy workshops that Mark Sedowski and I taught. They took the ideas from the workshops, developed instruction approaches, and tested these materials with real students and reported their findings. They found that by using the many approaches detailed in this text, they were able to improve both reading and writing scores of their students.

In addition to students and teachers, I am indebted to both university and public librarians who provided insights into current issues that influence the selection of literacy materials. Texas A&M librarians Jane Smith, Director, Education Reference Library, and Halbert Hall, Senior Scholar and Bibliographer, were especially helpful in suggesting the most up-to-date references and clarifying educational issues. The librarians at the Cooperative Children's Book Center at the University of Wisconsin, Madison were especially helpful through their insightful discussions of books. These librarians include Kathleen T. Horning, Merri V. Lindgren, Hollis Rudiger, and Megan Schliesman. Children's Librarians at the Madison, Wisconsin Public Library provided expert assistance in identifying materials that they believe are effective with children. These librarians include Linda Olson, Director of Children's Division, Kelly Verheyden, Amy Brandt, Carolyn Forde, Alice Oakey, Jill Olig, and Bridget Zinn. The storytellers at the Pitkin Public Library in Aspen, Colorado, and their hundreds of eager listeners provided insight into how to motivate literacy and develop children who would hopefully become life-long learners.

I would also like to acknowledge several people who motivated my constant search for authentic texts and the need to teach students to authenticate materials including historical and biographical texts and the values and beliefs in folklore that are authentic for a culture. Sonja von Romatowski Seward, born December 9, 1924 in Berlin is a survivor of Hitler's Germany. She and her true story taught me the importance of authenticating the literature written about World War II and to share with students why they need to examine the truth in the literature and to be able to identify the authors' viewpoints that influence material. Tim Tingle, a member of the Choctaw tribe, a nationally recognized storyteller and a descendant of the Choctaws who walked the Trail of Tears, taught me to respect the peoples' cultural values and to teach my students to authenticate the folklore and other materials about Native Americans.

This text also benefited greatly from the suggestions provided by its outstanding reviewers, who each put their expertise to work by offering close, critical readings of the developing manuscript. Thank you all for your generous professional assistance: Glenda Allen-Jones, Governors State University; Kelly Anderson, University of North Carolina at Charlotte; Carrie Birmingham, Pepperdine University; Beverly Boulware, Western Kentucky University; Carol L. Butterfield, Central Washington University; Laurie J. Curtis, Kansas State University; Neva Ann Medcalf Davenport, St. Mary's University; Margaret Davis, Eastern Kentucky University; Deborah Doty, Northern Kentucky University; George Font, Purdue University, West Lafayette; Dorothy L. Gottshall, Stephen F. Austin State University; Susan Hall, University of the Incarnate Word; Dottie Kulesza, University of Nevada, Las Vegas; Isaac Larison, Xavier University; Debbie Ann Murzyn, Indiana University at Bloomington; Mary Napoli, Penn State Harrisburg; Margaret Policastro, Roosevelt University; Andrea Rosenblatt, Barry University; Lorae Roukema, Campbell University; Nina Rynberg, Lake Superior State University; Ramon Serrano, St. Cloud State University; Andrea Sledge, Central Washington University; Kim Truesdell, Buffalo State College; Jacqueline Valadez, St. Mary's University; Staci Walton-Duggar, Florida State University, Tallahassee; Shelley Hong Xu, California State University, Long Beach.

And of course the personnel at Allyn & Bacon provided extraordinary and ongoing support for this book over the course of its development, production, and publication: Aurora Martínez Ramos, Executive Editor; Sonny Regelman and Christien Shangraw, Development Editors; Janet Domingo, Production Editor; Denise Botelho, and Publishers' Design and Production Services. Thank you!

About the Author

Donna E. Norton is a Professor of Reading and Children's Literature at Texas A&M University, where she is a member of the graduate faculty in the Department of Teaching, Learning and Culture. She is the award-winning author of *Through the Eyes of a Child: An Introduction to Children's Literature*. Her other literacy-related textbooks include *Multicultural Children's Literature*, *The Effective Teaching of Language Arts*, and *Language Arts Activities for Children*.

CHAPTER

1

Changing Trends in Literacy Instruction

CHAPTER **OUTLINE**

Models of the Reading Process
  Bottom-Up Model
  Top-Down Model
  Interactive Model

Approaches to Reading Instruction
  Balanced Reading Approaches
  Phonics Approaches
  Sub-Skills Approaches
  Whole Language Approaches
  Literature-Based Approaches

Theories of Learning Related to Reading Instruction
  Behaviorist Theory of Learning
  Cognitive Development Theory of Learning
  Sociolinguistic Theory of Learning
  Reader Response Theory of Learning

A History of Basal Reading
  Silver, Burdett Series (1902)
  McGuffey's Eclectic Reader (1921) and Elson Basic Readers (1931)
  Reading with Phonics Series (1948)
  McGraw-Hill Reading Series (2001)

Instructional Techniques
  Ability Groupings
  Literature Circles
  Uninterrupted Sustained Silent Reading (USSR)
  Recreational Reading Groups
  Focus or Thematic Units

Reading Assessment in the Classroom
  Mandated Tests
  Consequences of Mandated Tests

A History of Requirements for Teachers of Reading

After reading this chapter you will be able to answer the following questions:

1. What are the models of the reading process that have influenced how reading should be taught?
2. What are the approaches to reading instruction and how do models of reading relate to the approaches?
3. How do theories of reading instruction influence the development of reading and the approaches to reading?
4. How have basal readers changed from the beginning to the end of the twentieth century?
5. What are some of the instructional techniques that add excitement to the reading curriculum?
6. How does the type of assessment used influence reading instruction? What are the consequences of mandates for assessment such as No Child Left Behind?

Read All About It!

"Who Needs Education Schools?"

by Anemona Hartocollis, *New York Times Education Life*, July 31, 2005

The whistle-stop town of Emporia, Kansas (population 27,000), has two claims to fame: William Allen White, the Pulitzer Prize–winning newspaper editor and confidant of Theodore Roosevelt, and turning out teachers.

Emporia State University was established as a "normal" school—dedicated solely to the training of teachers—in 1863, two years after Kansas became a state. The esteem in which teaching is held there can be seen in the one-room schoolhouse maintained as a kind of shrine at the edge of campus.

The National Teachers Hall of Fame is in Emporia, and tourists come to see the dollhouse models of classrooms from the early seventeenth century onward and to read the plaques of inductees—70, so far.

"Teacher education on this campus is one of the more rigorous majors," says Teresa Mehring, dean of the teachers' college, pulling out the ACT scores of entering students to prove a point that most education deans would be hard-pressed to make and defend.

A visit to classes suggests that raw material is not the only difference. The Emporia State curriculum is heavy on traditional courses like "Using Children's Literature in the Elementary Classroom" and "Reading for the Elementary Teacher." The college's plain-spoken mission statement: "To develop the professional: critical thinker, creative planner and effective practitioner."

If Emporia State is a throwback to an earlier time, when preparing teachers for the classroom was a high calling, it is also a reminder of how many teachers' colleges have strayed from the central mission of the normal school. For decades, education schools have gravitated from the practical side of teaching, seduced by large ideas like "building a caring learning community and culture" and "advocating for social justice."

Today, education schools face pressure to improve from all directions. The soul-searching has accelerated with the federal No Child Left Behind Act,

which demands a highly qualified teacher—state certified, with a bachelor's degree and proven knowledge of subject—in every classroom by the end of this coming school year.

In fact, No Child Left Behind, with its emphasis on standards and hard data, has placed national policy in direct conflict with the prevailing approach of many colleges, where the John Dewey tradition of progressive education holds sway, marked by a deep antipathy toward testing.

Just what do education schools teach?

"One of the biggest dangers we face is preparing teachers who know theory and know nothing about practice," acknowledges Arthur Levine, president of Teachers College at Columbia, one of the leading avatars of progressive education. Historians note that Dewey himself had such concerns in the 1920s. But, Dr. Levine says, that is not what happens at strong—and philosophically diverse—education schools like Stanford, the University of Virginia, Alverno College in Milwaukee, and Emporia State.

"They have a clarity of mission," says Dr. Levine, who is conducting a two-year study on the quality of education schools that will be published in November. "They know what they're trying to do. Their definition of success is tied to student learning in classes taught by those teachers."

It used to be that if you wanted to become a teacher, you went to an education school. Now a growing movement holds that these schools have become irrelevant, especially in urban areas.

Alternative programs to certification are now offered in 47 states and the District of Columbia. Organizations like Teach for America, a Peace Corps model that puts new college graduates in troubled schools for two-year stints, and the New York City Teaching Fellows, which promotes teaching as a second career, are taking it upon themselves to train teachers. Recruits with no experience are given a quick and dirty version of education school—a few weeks of classroom management, learning theory, literacy (the teaching of reading and writing), diversity training—then placed in the classroom, with coaching from mentors. People who enter through such routes are not exempt from state requirements, like a master's degree in education in New York; the advantage is they can teach and study for the degree at the same time.

Commercial organizations are also getting into the act. Harold O. Levy, the former New York City schools chancellor who helped found the Teaching Fellows, has developed an online teaching college for Kaplan Inc, the test-prep company. Similarly, David Levin, co-founder and superintendent of the KIPP schools, a network of 38 charter schools from Houston to the South Bronx, is working on a teacher-training program meant to produce the kind of teachers he needs in his schools.

"That would be our dream, to credential our own teacher," says Mr. Levin, who adds that he has found "a sizable gap between what people are learning in schools of education and what they need in public schools." Where education schools fall short, he argues, is in conveying the skills you might learn in business school: how to manage time, how to build motivation and evaluation into every lesson. "You need whatever the theory is, and you need to put it into practice," he says. "There needs to be immediate feedback on that practice."

At Emporia State, undergraduates spend their entire senior year in surrounding school districts, including Olathe, Topeka, and Kansas City. They are assigned to observe or teach classes during regular school hours. They take college classes after hours in the districts they are assigned to, not on campus. By the second semester, they are expected to function as head teachers. Supervising professors know the curricula of those districts as well as any district employee. "I know Olathe's program inside out," says Tara Azwell, a professor who until recently supervised students there. "I could step into any classroom and teach it."

Emporia State classes strive to balance the theoretical with the practical. Professors not only talk about the theories behind reading, writing and literature, but also demonstrate in painstaking detail how to teach specific lessons.

In an introductory reading class last spring, Professor Azwell urged her students to listen to the language of children's literature. Her enthusiasm for the books she had selected to pass out to her students was contagious. Of "The Ghost-Eye Tree," she said, "It's a great scary story for little kids." Of "Flossie and the Fox," she said, "I love this one because it uses wonderful dialect. One character speaks Southern dialect, and the other one speaks very literary language, so the contrast is great."

She tells her students what a professor once told her: that a teacher should know at least three hundred children's books intimately and be able to pick the right book for the right child at the right moment.

Ms. Azwell says she believes in whole language, the system of teaching children to read by exposure to literature, but she does not reject phonics. The politics of teaching reading, she says, has turned whole language into a caricature of how she learned to teach reading. "To me, phonics was never not a part of whole language," she says. "I was taught all the language cueing systems: graphophonics, sound-symbol relationships; semantic, the meaning system; syntactic, the language structure system. So phonics is an integral part of that."

The college's plain-spoken mission statement: "To develop the professional: critical thinker, creative planner and effective practitioner."

While Ms. Azwell has been teaching for a long time and can balance theory and practice, the article concludes with concerns that a group of new teachers in training expressed after their first experiences in a classroom. Their questions include: What is balanced literacy? How do I adjust to the latest curriculum shift that includes balanced literacy? When should children stop using invented spelling and spell by the rules? What is guided reading and how do I accomplish it? How do I integrate reading and social studies? And, How do I integrate reading and writing?

Read All About It!

Critical Thinking Questions

- What are your concerns, fears, and hopes as you become a reading teacher in training?

- What do you believe should be the major emphasis in college classes that prepare reading teachers? What experiences do you believe you should have that would prepare you to be like Ms. Azwell and be able to step into any classroom and teach reading?

- Think back to your own experience with reading in school. What made the experiences memorable? Describe a reading teacher who had an impact on you.

- What are some of the advantages and disadvantages to the different methods for teacher certification discussed in the article?

To read for understanding, to express educated opinions on a subject, and to apply our reading ability and knowledge to new situations are certainly long-range goals of any reading and literacy program. Educators through the centuries have debated how we reach these goals and produce readers who have these abilities. For example, the sixteenth-century philosopher and scholar, Francis Bacon, recommended an approach established by classical scholars. He divided reading into a three-part process: first, gaining basic knowledge of the subject by developing a foundation of information; second, taking the knowledge into your own understanding by evaluating it to decide if it is valid; and, third, folding the information into your own understanding in order to form your own opinions and reactions to the reading.

Susan Wise Bauer (2003) emphasizes that Bacon's three-stage process is equally valid when approaching reading education because "To tackle a course of reading successfully, we have to retrain our minds to grasp new ideas by first understanding them, then evaluating them, and finally forming our own opinions" (p. 19).

In this textbook, we will think of teaching reading as a way to develop these three processes that educated adults use so effectively. We will consider the building blocks, the foundations of reading. These building blocks include children's abilities to sound out the words they are reading and to comprehend the words when they are combined into sentences, paragraphs, and stories. The foundations of reading stress students' growing vocabularies, their understandings of sight words, and their understandings of grammatical structures and spelling patterns. The building blocks include basic knowledge in the content areas of social studies and science that are frequently related to reading in the early grades.

The second stage emphasizes critical thinking and analytical skill at all ages. Reading methodologies use the foundational knowledge of recognizing words, understanding the meaning of the words and sentences, and basic content knowledge to help students critically evaluate what they read. They are taught to use the background knowledge they learned as part of their building blocks.

For example, when reading texts with a setting related to Pioneer America such as Laura Ingalls Wilder's *Little House in the Big Woods,* Carol Ryrie Brink's *Caddie Woodlawn,* and Patricia MacLachlan's *Sarah, Plain and Tall,* students in fourth- and fifth-grade classes discover they can use prior information learned in social studies to evaluate the authenticity and accuracy of the setting developed by the author. Students ask questions such as: Are the dates accurate? Are the activities correct for the time period and the location? Is the geography description accurate? And, is the conflict in the story one that actually occurred during Pioneer America? To obtain a better understanding of the prairie environment, students can view Jim Arnosky's illustrations in *Grandfather Buffalo* (2006). The illustrations depict not only the possible harshness of the prairies as depicted in *Sarah, Plain and Tall* but also the wonderful expanse of the tall grass.

During the final stage, reading methodologies help students form their own opinions about what is read. They are taught to consider carefully, to form their own opinions after they have grasped new ideas and evaluated those ideas. After critically evaluating the Pioneer America setting, for example, students can use their educated understandings to form their own opinions. Now they are ready to respond to questions such as: What does the author want me to believe about Pioneer America? Am I convinced that this is true about Pioneer America? Why or Why not? And, What would I do if I lived in Pioneer America and experienced these same problems? This final level of reading is frequently developed through writing assignments that teach reading through writing.

Before proceeding with this reading methods textbook, think about your own reading process. What foundations and background knowledge do you have that help you understand a subject? How do you use this knowledge to help you evaluate what you read? What information do you use before you develop and state an opinion about what you read? Remember that the students you will be teaching need to develop the ability to use this same process.

As you consider your own reading process and how you would like to teach reading, remember that teaching of reading is a complex subject that is also influenced by the literacy achievement of your students as a consequence of national and state reading tests. One of the most influential groups is the National Assessment Governing Board (2004). This board oversees the National Assessment of Educational Progress (NEP), a federally funded, large-scale testing program that tests reading achievement across the United States and uses the results to make comparisons among students.

This governing board provides the framework for the NAEP 2009 reading assessment. By reading the board's definition for reading proficiency, teachers also discover what components of reading they are expected to teach. For example, Taffy E. Raphael and Kathryn H. Au (2005) have reviewed this 2009 framework and draw the following conclusions about what is considered reading proficiency:

> [S]tudents will be expected to read comfortably across genres within fiction, nonfiction, procedural texts, and poetry. They will be required to successfully answer questions, 70% to 80% of which call for the integration, interpretation, critique, and evaluation of texts read independently. . . . Over half of the higher-level questions will require students to provide a short or extended written response rather than simply to select from multiple-choice options. (p. 206)

In addition, a student judged proficient when reading fiction must be able to think about and write responses to questions about themes, elements of plot structures, and various points of view. When reading nonfiction, they must understand text organizations, descriptions, relationships, and logical connections as well as identify details found in the reading materials, graphs, and photographs.

Throughout this textbook, we will focus on reading methodologies that develop reading proficiency by encouraging students to read various genres of literature with understanding, that develop higher levels of thinking through interpretation and critical analysis of what is read, and that encourage students to think deeply and to write using responses that focus on different types and levels of comprehension.

As we proceed in this methods text, we discover that, just as there is no one type of child in the reading classroom, there is not one approach to the teaching of reading. Consequently, teachers need to understand how and when to use the various approaches. In this chapter we discover that there are many influences on the way that teachers teach reading. In the section "Models of the Reading Process," for example, we discover that there are three models of the reading process that influence the instructional materials to be used and the way that reading is taught. There are advocates who endorse each of these models. In the section "Approaches to Reading Instruction," we relate the models of the reading process to the major approaches to reading instruction. We discover that approaches such as balanced-reading approaches, phonics approaches, sub-skills approaches, whole language approaches, and literature-based approaches are related to the models of the reading process.

In the section "Theories of Learning Related to Reading Instruction," we discover how these models and approaches to reading instruction relate to different theories about how children learn. In the section "A History of Basal Reading," we trace changes in basal readers, the sequentially developed reading series designed to teach reading, by providing examples of basal readers published during the past hundred years. This discussion also highlights how different theories of reading and definitions of reading influenced how reading was taught during the time periods.

In the section "Instructional Techniques," we introduce the various instructional techniques that are used to teach children various reading skills and comprehension abilities. Instructional techniques are discussed in chapters throughout the text. The section "Reading Assessment in the Classroom," presents a brief discussion of assessment. An in-depth discussion of assessment is covered in Chapter 3, "Assessment and Evaluation in the Reading and Writing Program."

The section "A History of Requirements for Teachers of Reading," emphasizes the changes in contemporary classrooms, especially the impact of students with limited English proficiency also called English Language Learners (ELL). An in-depth discussion of this topic is found in Chapter 10, "Literacy Instruction for ELL Students, Multicultural Education, and Students with Special Needs." As a consequence of the diversity in today's classrooms, each chapter concludes with a section titled "Differentiating Instruction." This section emphasizes how teachers may modify instruction for ELL students, gifted students, and struggling readers and writers.

This chapter on changing trends in literacy instruction concludes with a brief history of the changing requirements for teachers of reading. When we realize that teacher preparation has progressed from requiring prospective teachers to attend two-year normal schools in the early twentieth century to the current full four-year and master's-degree specialization in reading, we also realize that teacher preparation is considered a serious topic. Before you read further, it is worthwhile to restate the Standards 2003 requirements recommended by the International Reading Association that concludes this chapter. These standards state that teachers of reading require knowledge about foundations of reading; instructional strategies and curricular materials; assessment, diagnosis, and evaluation; creating a literature environment; and professional development. Why do you believe that the International Reading Association emphasizes each of these standards as important for teaching reading? How would knowledge of each of the standards make a difference in the way reading is taught? How would knowledge of the standards make a difference in the reading achievement of the students in the classroom?

Models of the Reading Process

While most educators and the general public agree that the quality of instruction makes a difference in student learning, there is considerable disagreement about the way students learn and the best way to improve their instruction. This is especially true for reading instruction. Millions of dollars have been spent on research designed to identify how students process information as they read.

A teacher provides background information as students are involved in literacy activities.

Reading educators and researchers have identified at least three models of reading that influence the way reading is taught: bottom-up (text-based); top-down (reader-based); and interactive (a combination of the two).

Bottom-Up Model

The **bottom-up model** of the reading process is a text-based model because it focuses on the information provided by the text rather than input from the readers' experiences or previous knowledge. In this model, reading begins with the sound of the letter and progresses upward from the single letter to the combination of letters that form words. Figure 1.1 shows a diagram of this bottom-up model. As the letters are sounded out, the letters are formed into words, the words into sentences, and the sentences into paragraphs. A first-grade teacher using the bottom-up approach would teach the sounds of the beginning consonants such as *b* and *c*. After learning a few consonant sounds, the students would be introduced to word families, such as *at*. The students would combine the consonants with the word families to create words such as *bat* and *cat*. The words are then introduced within a phrase, such as *a round bat* or *the fat cat* and then within a sentence, such as *The fat cat sat on the round bat*. When using this model with older students, teachers tell students to first focus on the sounding out of the word and then consider the meaning of the word. This model has a controlled vocabulary text where students master one skill at a time. In this model, rules for word patterns and sounding out words are more important than understanding longer texts.

As Mary Gove (1983) describes, "Bottom-up models assume that the translation process begins with print, that is, letter or word identification, and proceeds to progressively larger linguistic units, phrases, sentences, [and so on], ending in meaning" (p. 262). Mastery of these small parts is assumed to lead to competency in reading.

In this model, learning problems are considered to be caused by the inability to decode the small parts.

Top-Down Model

The **top-down model** of the reading process is a reader-based model because the reader brings his or her own knowledge, culture, and experiences to the interpretation of the text. In this model concepts held in the mind of the reader trigger information during reading. The reader's knowledge and expectations for language as well as the reader's prior experiences help the reader comprehend material. This model presumes that the reader has considerable prior knowledge that he or she will use to help comprehend word identification, the meanings of vocabulary words, and plot structures. Figure 1.1 shows a diagram of this top-down model, called *top-down* because reading is believed to begin as the reader uses background knowledge to generate hypotheses and predictions about what is read. The reader uses cues in the materials such as letters and words to test these hypotheses.

In the top-down model, the reader's knowledge about words in a sentence helps the reader make predictions and hypotheses about the direction of the story. For example, when students hear or read, "Once upon a time, in a land far away, there lived a King with his three daughters. Two daughters were selfish and cruel, the third was beautiful and kind," the top-down model assumes that students' prior experiences of listening to or reading folktales have prepared them to visualize the setting for the story, the types of characters who will be in the story, and the plot structure.

If they have had experience listening to or reading folktales, students immediately know that "Once upon a time, in a land far away" places the story in the distant past in a magical location where the extraordinary is possible. The phrase, "there lived a king" places the story in a castle and a kingdom that may be enchanted. The phrase "Two daughters were selfish and cruel, the third was beautiful and kind" prepares students for conflict between characters. It also introduces students to a familiar plot structure where the kind daughter will overcome problems and there will be a "happily ever after" ending.

In the top-down model, readers might not understand specific vocabulary words or pronounce them correctly, but they have an understanding of the story as a whole. This prior knowledge helps the reader make sense of the actions of the story and the motivations of the characters. The focus on prior knowledge in the top-down model emphasizes the need for a curriculum that introduces students to a wide range of knowledge and experiences in the classroom.

As shown in Figure 1.1, the bottom-up model begins at the bottom with the sounds of the letters and progresses up to the top or the meaning of the text. In contrast, the top-down model, also seen in Figure 1.1, begins with reader's background knowledge and proceeds through hypotheses, testing, and making predictions to get meaning. The goal of both bottom-up and top-down models is comprehension, but how it is achieved differs.

Interactive Model

The **interactive model** of the reading process is a combination of the bottom-up (text-based) and top-down (reader-based) models. In this model, reading comprehension is

FIGURE 1.1
Models of the Reading Process

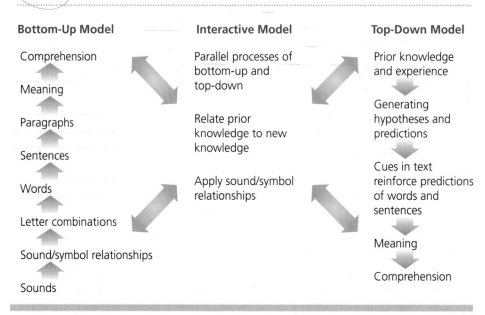

seen as an interactive process in which both text and reader's knowledge play key roles. It is called an interactive model because the reader begins by looking at the print and decoding words and sentences and then uses prior knowledge to predict what will happen in the story and comprehend the text. David Rumelhart (1976) was one of the early advocates of using this model for teaching reading. According to Rumelhart, top-down and bottom-up processing occur simultaneously.

Burns, Roe, and Smith (2002) state: "An interactive model assumes parallel processing of information from print and information from background knowledge. Recognition and comprehension of printed words and ideas are the result of using both types of information" (p. 17). Most educators and researchers now agree that a combination of both models is necessary for the successful teaching of reading and for reading comprehension.

Harry Singer (1985) outlines implications for teaching with an interactive model that includes both bottom-up and top-down strategies. From the bottom-up (text-based) model, for example, Singer suggests that teachers select texts that are well-organized and explain causes for the actions in the text. He recommends that teachers relate a student's prior knowledge to new knowledge found in the text and teach students to process and recall information by using the organizational features found in the text, such as when an author introduces a sequence of actions using *first, second,* and *third.* From the top-down (reader-based) model, Singer suggests teachers teach students the necessary knowledge structures and frameworks for comprehending texts, such as by explicitly stating, "The structure of a folktale is . . ." Singer encourages teachers to realize that different cultural backgrounds are likely to foster different ways of interpreting texts.

The consequences of using only one model are clear when we identify how each model makes assumptions about students who are failing in reading. The bottom-up model, for example, assumes that struggling students have failed to learn to apply correct sounds to their corresponding symbols (letters, words, sentences, and stories), provides additional training in how students are to use these sounds and symbols, and tests reading according to the student's ability to apply sound-symbol relationships. The students may be taught to ignore their own knowledge and experiences and focus only on the words. In contrast, the top-down model assumes that struggling readers lack the knowledge and experiences needed to comprehend the text. Students may be taught with strategies that discourage them from using the strong sound-symbol relationships found in the language and to not use these sound-symbol relationships when they are unable to identify words.

These implications relate to the characteristics of each of the models as seen in Figure 1.1. The instructional strategies, however, show the importance of using parallel strategies in the interactive model that balances the best components from both models. As you can see, teaching strategies that leave out one of the models could result in misunderstanding and lack of comprehension.

In the next section, we will consider the major approaches for reading instruction and identify how the approaches relate to the models of reading processing.

Reflect on Your Reading

In this section we have discussed three models of reading: bottom-up (text-based), top-down (reader-based), and interactive (a combination of the two). Think of two texts you have read recently. One of the texts covers a subject that you know little about. The vocabulary is not in your usual background. The other text is about a subject that is very familiar to you. The words and their meanings are in your natural vocabularies. Think about or reread portions of each text aloud. What reading models are you using to gain comprehension of each text?

Approaches to Reading Instruction

Approaches to reading instruction are the methods being used for teaching reading. These approaches exemplify how reading is actually defined and taught in the classroom. Advocates of each approach define reading in ways that match the philosophy and objectives of each approach. The objectives and philosophy of the approach usually specify how reading is taught, the materials that are used for reading instruction, and the types of instructional techniques used to teach reading. In this section, we will relate the previously identified models of the reading process to the following approaches of reading instruction: balanced reading approaches, phonics approaches, sub-skills approaches, whole language approaches, and literature-based approaches.

Balanced Reading Approaches

The discussion of various approaches begins with the balanced reading approach because it is considered one of the most beneficial approaches for the teaching of reading. The **balanced reading approach** emerged in the 1990s as an alternative to programs that used either mainly bottom-up (text-based) models of the reading process with their heavy use of sound-symbol relationships to master reading (phonics approaches) and the top-down (reader-based) models of the reading process that emphasized that readers could comprehend even if they were unable to identify each word (whole language). Either approach, when used exclusively, was believed to produce readers who lacked important reading capabilities. Consequently, many educators now advocate teaching an approach that combines phonics and sub-skills instruction with reading and responding to real literature.

In a balanced reading approach, skills are taught by the teacher both directly and indirectly as students read texts and develop their own understandings. The instructional materials in the classroom may use texts with more controlled vocabulary as well as numerous examples of fiction and nonfiction literature. For example, a fifth-grade class might read a short story about endangered species and then gain more in-depth knowledge about the subject by reading Phillip Hoose's *The Race to Save the Lord God Bird,* about the ivory-billed woodpecker, or Lola M. Schaefer's *Arrowhawk* about an endangered bird of prey. Now, students can compare and evaluate information using several sources.

D. Ray Reutzel and Robert B. Cooter (2000) observe that

> Each day in balanced literacy classrooms, one typically sees oral reading by teachers and children alike, direct skill instruction and practice in guided reading groups, a great deal of independent reading by students in books they enjoy. . . . Balanced literacy teachers rely on strategic and ongoing assessment, and their carefully planned classrooms provide a language-rich environment for the learners. (p. 5)

Three components found in an exemplary reading program identified by International Reading Association (2000) highlight the requirements for a balanced reading approach:

1. Teachers should meet the needs of individual students by adapting various methods of early instruction to meet those needs.

2. Teachers need to provide wide access to books and encourage voluntary reading because students who read more read better.

3. Teachers should use reading assessment to identify students' strengths and weaknesses to determine which instructional activities will foster their individual learning.

As seen by these effective components of an exemplary reading program, there is no single reading approach that meets the needs of all students. The balanced approach, to be effective, requires careful analysis of each child in the classroom.

Phonics Approaches

Phonics approaches are emphasized in the bottom-up model of reading in which reading progresses from the parts to the whole. Phonics approaches focus on instruction that proceeds from consonant sounds, to blending consonant and vowel sounds, to reading and writing stories that are phonetically regular. Vocabulary words such as *man* and *tan,* for example, are phonetically regular. Students can sound out the words as soon as they learn the sounds of *m* and *t* and the word family *an*. In contrast, words such as *comb* and *live* as in *I live in the United States* are not phonetically regular. They must be taught as sight words (words that cannot be sounded out) rather than decoded (sounded out) by the rules associated with sound-symbol relationships. The materials selected for phonics approaches are usually written with words, sentences, and stories designed for reading phonetically regular patterns. For example, a mostly phonetically regular sentence such as *The cat liked to dig in the sand* might be part of a story about animal pets. *The* is the only word that must be taught independently as a sight word.

Phonics approaches are based on the belief that reading requires considerable instruction in the sound-symbol relationships within language. Phonics approaches, at least for younger readers, suggest that mastering and applying these sound-symbol relationships leads to comprehension of text materials. This belief is apparent when viewing the instructional materials for beginning readers. These materials show that beginning readers spend considerable time learning the sounds of letters and sounding out individual lists of words. When reading is tested at this beginning level, the tests focus on sound-symbol relationships. A more detailed discussion of phonics approaches is covered in Chapter 4.

Sub-Skills Approaches

In **sub-skills approaches** to reading, educators believe that there is a set of sub-skills that must be mastered in order for students to read proficiently. These sub-skills include a set of discreetly identifiable skills that are considered the building blocks for reading that is taught and tested. It is closely related to the bottom-up model.

S. J. Samuels (1994) points out that within a sub-skills approach, teachers teach these skills until they become automatic. Automatic reading of the sub-skills is believed to be related to reading comprehension.

Richard Smith (1970), one of the early advocates of the sub-skills approach, identifies the following specific sub-skills that are part of reading:

1. Word attack, including identifying rhyming elements in words, knowing sight words, and understanding letter sounds;

Reading for pleasure is an important part of literacy for life.

2. Comprehension, including listening skills, context clues, and understanding whole stories;

3. Study skills, including following directions, using dictionaries and encyclopedias, and organizing information;

4. Self-directed reading, including recreational reading, conducting research, and enjoying a variety of literature;

5. Interpretive skills, including reacting to stories, recognizing implied ideas, and reaching conclusions on the basis of information in a text;

6. Creative skills, including engaging in dramatic play, participating in choral speaking, and composing original story poems.

These sub-skills may become the focus for individual lessons that are isolated for instruction. For example, vocabulary words may be taught as a lesson before first-, second-, and third-grade students read them in a story. Or, third-grade student's may be taught how to search for main ideas before they are asked to read a longer story and identify the main idea.

A sub-skills approach usually includes a scope and sequence chart. This chart includes a statement of the skills and objectives that will be taught and tested at each grade level. Figure 1.2 shows an example of a scope and sequence chart for phonic analysis that would be used in kindergarten through third-grade classrooms. This scope and sequence chart identifies several components of phonic analysis that would be taught, specific to each grade.

Looking at Smith's list of sub-skills, we also see that some of the sub-skills require a top-down model. For example, under interpretive skills, a third-grade student reading E. B. White's *Charlotte's Web* should be able to recognize and analyze subtle emotional reactions and motives of

FIGURE **1.2**

Examples of a Scope and Sequence Chart for Phonic Analysis: Kindergarten through Grade Three

....

Kindergarten	Listens for rhyming elements in words (*man—pan*)
	Recognizes rhyming words in a nursery rhyme (*Little Miss Muffet, sat on a tuffet*)
Grade One	Recognizes beginning and ending consonants (*bin ball-boy, tin bat-hut*)
	Recognizes consonant blends (*bl, cr, gr*)
	Identifies short vowels (*u* in *duck*)
Grade Two	Identifies and pronounces long vowel sounds (*a* in *take*)
	Knows short vowel rules (*a* in *pat, i* in *pin*)
	Identifies consonant digraphs (*ch, sh*)
Grade Three	Identifies three-letter consonant blends (*spr, scr*)
	Knows principles of silent letters (*k* in *knight*)

characters, such as identifying with Fern's fear that her father will kill the pig and Charlotte's love for Wilbur that allows her to save the pig.

Whole Language Approaches

The **whole language approach** is the closest reading approach to the top-down model of reading. The whole language philosophy is based on the belief that reading is a natural process like speech, and since children naturally acquire speech by exposure to the spoken language, in a similar fashion they will naturally become literate as long as they are exposed to whole texts, rather than isolated words, sound, or vocabulary-controlled stories. This approach emphasizes that a child's language should be the basis for all reading instruction. Consequently, children should not be taught basic skills such as sound-symbol relationships in isolation. Instead, reading processing requires highly integrated learning experiences in the classroom.

Kenneth S. Goodman (1998), an advocate of the whole language approach, stipulates that children learn best in an environment in which they read and respond to whole literature selections rather than to the smaller building blocks identified in the phonics approach.

The whole language classroom is defined by Dahl, Scharber, Lawson, and Grogan (2003) as having the following five characteristics:

1. The curriculum is child-centered and focuses on instruction that addresses the learner's processes of reading and writing.

2. The teaching approach is one in which reading and writing are taught as meaning-centered processes. Learning proceeds from the whole text to part of the text rather than from part to whole.

3. The materials used to teach reading include a wide selection of children's literature, a variety of print sources, and children's writing.

4. The classroom is a literature environment where reading and writing are considered tools for learning. There is sustained time for children to read self-selected books and to write about topics of their choice.

5. There is a collaborative environment in which children are encouraged to exchange information and work together.

Emphasis in the whole language classroom is not placed on reading precision and accuracy, but on overall comprehension of the text as a whole. Students read to identify words from context clues rather than sounding out words. With this approach, students are not expected to read a text word-for-word. They are allowed to leave out, insert, or substitute words as long as the understanding of the text as a whole is sustained.

A reading classroom using the whole language approach might look like this:

■ A large classroom library of reading materials as well as access to the school library where reading material has a heavy emphasis on the top-down model of the reading process;

■ Books with larger print so students see and understand the connection between spoken and written words;

- Books with predictable stories that use repeated language patterns so that new vocabulary is easily understood in the context of the story;

- Shared reading experiences that allow students to listen to a story;

- Opportunities for students to talk about the story, retell the story, dictate the story to the teacher or to another student, and illustrate the story;

- Interest centers such as a writing center with writing materials, an illustration center with supplies for illustrating stories, and a book-making center with materials for students to turn stories into books.

Because the whole language approach allows students more control over the content and language used in the stories, this approach is particularly effective for students who speak English as a second language and for any other students who have minimal English proficiency. One of the techniques used with students who have minimal English proficiency or English Language Learners (ELL) is the language experience approach. The approach is especially worthwhile because it allows students to see the connections between oral and written language. According to Susanne F. Peregoy and Owen F. Boyle (2001) the language experience approach is recommended for ELL students because the students provide the text through dictation; this text then becomes the source for reading instruction. Consequently, the resulting material is tailored to the students' language proficiency, background knowledge, interests, and cultural strengths. In addition, when a teacher is directly involved when a student dictates and reads a story, the teacher is able to gain diagnostic insight into the student's specific reading difficulties (Waugh, 1993). An example of a language experience approach is developed in Chapter 10: "Literacy Instruction for ELL Students, Multicultural Education, and Students with Special Needs.

Literature-Based Approaches

Literature-based approaches use quality literature as a basis for reading instruction. The whole language and literature-based approaches to reading have several characteristics in common: both use literature as the primary source of material in the reading program, both emphasize reading whole books rather than short selections that have been abridged, and both see the need for an environment that is rich in books and other print materials. There are other characteristics that make the programs very different. While whole language classes rarely use teacher-directed, explicit skill instruction, the teacher using a literature-based approach frequently provides instruction in such reading-related comprehension skills as inferring the main idea of a story, evaluating cause-and-effect relationships, and judging the authenticity of a piece of literature.

While the whole language approach is basically a top-down (reader-based) model of reading, the literature-based approach is closely related to the interactive model, a combination of bottom-up (text-based) and top-down (reader-based) models of the reading process. As students read, parallel processes occur that include identifying words and sentences and then using background knowledge to make hypotheses and predictions in order to comprehend the literature. When teachers teach specific skills related to literature, such as identifying the characteristics of theme, students are learning one of the building blocks for comprehending literature that would be required in a bottom-up (text-based) model. These skills are not taught in isolation, however, as might occur in the bottom-up model. By introducing students to a variety of story structures, genres of literature, and styles of writing, teachers are providing background information and literature experiences that allow readers to make predictions and hypotheses about reading that are emphasized in the top-down model.

In a literature-based approach, reading is not the acquisition of a set of isolated skills. Instead, reading is the ability to read all types of literature with understanding, appreciation, and enjoyment. In this approach, literature can be used to develop or support the reading curriculum, to teach or reinforce reading skills, and to introduce students to a variety of good books and authors (Norton, 2007).

The instructional materials for a classroom that emphasizes a literature-based approach are, of course, literature. Literature, however, may be selected and taught in different ways. Some teachers, for example, use class sets of specific titles of literature where students within a group all read the same selection. There would be introductory lessons that prepare the students to read the selection. This introduction might include background information necessary to understand the historic time period, the conflict in the book, or the characteristics of the genre of literature being read. While the students read the book, the teacher might include guided discussions that focus on comprehending the literary elements such as characterization, conflict, theme, and point of view. The discussions and follow-up activities focus on the strengths of the literature.

Other teachers who use a literature-based approach may ask students to select their reading from a list of recommended sources. If the class is studying Latino culture, values, and beliefs as expressed in folktales, for example, the teacher would collect as many folktales from the genre as possible. Examples of these texts could include Tomie DePaola's *The Lady of Guadalupe,* Lois Ehlert's *Cuckoo: A Mexican Folktale,* and Barbara Knutson's *Love and Roast Chicken: A Trickster Tale from the Andes Mountains.* Then each student would read a different book and share the knowledge he or she gained about the culture from reading the book. Together, the students compile their discoveries. This approach has advantages because each student reads a book at his or her own level of reading ability.

Encouraging various reading responses is a major part of the literature-based approach. A. Purves and Diane Monson (1984) identify six types of responses that are encouraged in the literature-based curriculum:

1. A descriptive response is encouraged when students are asked to retell a story, identify the characters, or describe the illustration.

2. An analytical response results when students examine the style or point of view in a selection.

3. A classifying response is found when readers place work in an historical context within a genre of literature.

4. A personal response is encouraged when readers describe their reactions to the work and how the work triggers memories and emotions.

5. An interpretive response is required when readers are asked to make inferences about the work and relate the work to other literature.

6. An evaluative response is required when readers judge the work's merit using various literary criteria.

When teachers encourage students to use these various types of responses, they are also showing students how to use an interactive process that requires both bottom-up (text-based) and top-down (reader-based) models of the reading processes.

Literature and literature-related activities historically have had a strong place in the U.S. reading curriculum, although educators have often disagreed about which literature to read and what type of activities should accompany it.

A review of the place of literature in the curriculum explains some of the disagreements: for example, three structures emerged during the nineteenth and twentieth centuries for teaching literature-based curricula (Purves & Monson, 1984). In the late 1800s and early 1900s, students read and discussed classical literature. Early advocates such as Mathew Arnold (1895), argued that a core of literature exists, which educated people should read and recognize for its literary and historical excellence. Such literature is seen as a way to transmit the culture and historical values of the society to the children. As part of this theory, a "canon" of literature that students should read can be identified and be used to acquire standards of excellence by which they judge other books.

A second structure for choosing literature for reading programs identified by Purves and Monson is cognitive or analytic and based on the work of literary critics such as Northrop Frye (1964). In this approach, students are taught to analyze, criticize, and classify literature. Literature activities stress the development of critical thinking abilities as students practice comprehending, analyzing, and responding to literature.

The third structure identified by Purves and Monson is psychological and influenced by early psychologists and educators such as Sigmund Freud and John Dewey. This approach to reading through literature encourages students to respond directly and personally to what they read. Louise Rosenblatt (1968) is one of the main advocates of a reader response theory. Reading activities using this structure stress individual growth through responding to the literature.

These three structures are found in many literature-based programs today. If a literature-based curriculum incorporates aspects of all three structures, teachers choose books and other materials that encourage students to read and enjoy a wide variety of examples. The curriculum includes class examples of each genre as well as contemporary works that students might use for comparisons, criticisms, and evaluations. Exposure to a variety of books and other written materials encourages students to develop their own knowledge about literature and literature structures. Some of the books are used for formal instruction, while many others are used for recreational reading and incidental learning. Additional discussions of literature-based approaches are found in Chapter 7 and Chapter 8.

Developing an approach to reading instruction for today's students that allows them to use a variety of skills and to read the materials that are necessary in our contemporary world is a challenge that teachers in the twenty-first century must meet. Table 1.1 provides comparisons of the various reading approaches, how each approach relates to the reading process, how each approach emphasizes comprehension, how reading instruction proceeds, and the types of teaching materials used. This textbook presents all of the techniques and approaches associated with reading instruction. (See Chapter 12 for an expanded discussion of balanced reading approaches.)

Reflect on Your Reading

What do you believe is the impact of each approach to reading instruction discussed in this section? Think back to your own elementary reading instruction. Can you identify any of the approaches that might have influenced your reading? Try to remember how your teachers taught reading. What approaches might have influenced them?

TABLE 1.1

Comparisons of Reading Approaches

	Balanced	Phonics	Sub-Skills	Whole Language	Literature-Based
Reading Process	Interactive	Bottom-Up	Bottom-Up	Top-Down	Interactive
How Students Learn to Comprehend	Reading is divided between skills and more holistic approaches that compliment each other	Analyzing sound-symbol relationships leads to comprehension	Analyzing defined sets of sub-skills develops reading ability	Students' background and language lead to comprehension	Story structures, genres and writing styles allow students to make predictions and comprehend
How Instruction in Reading Proceeds	Reading may begin with sounding out words and rapidly uses prior knowledge to comprehend	Small parts to whole as words are sounded out	Sub-skills to whole as words are decoded	Whole to parts Reading initiated by informed guesses and proceeds through verification	Lessons prepare readers how to read various genres
Teaching Materials	Both basal materials that teach a sequence of skills and high quality literature that encourages students to apply the skills	Worksheets, workbooks and controlled vocabulary materials that teach sound-symbol relationships	Materials that teach sub-skills and are controlled for words that apply to sub-skills	Begin with student's own language and stories that are within student experiences	High quality literature that illustrates literary elements and characteristics of genres of the literature

Theories of Learning Related to Reading Instruction

At this point you may be wondering why there are so many different models of the reading process and why these models suggest so many different approaches to how reading should be taught. These models and approaches are related to different theories about how children learn. The influences of these theories have changed over time. In this section we will discuss the following learning theories related to reading instruction: behaviorist, cognitive, sociolinguistic, and reader response.

These theories provide the underpinnings of all reading instruction. Just as students require prior knowledge to comprehend a text, teachers must have a knowledge of the theories that influence the reading approaches they will be using. Reading theories provide a belief system that is important for anyone going into teaching and particularly reading instruction as a profession. Teachers need to be able to explain and defend the theories that have influenced the instructional approaches they are using in their classrooms.

Behaviorist Theory of Learning

The **behaviorist theory of learning** became popular in the 1960s with the work of B. F. Skinner (1968). Behaviorist theorists stipulate that students learn to read by being taught a sequence of skills that form the building blocks of reading. They also believe that a student can be taught to perform any task successfully if the unit of learning is small enough. The behaviorist theory has influenced educators who adhere to the bottom-up (text-based) model of the reading process where students learn to read by proceeding from the parts to the whole.

To apply this behaviorist theory in the classroom, teachers drill students on the skills, use worksheets that reinforce the skills, and teach with materials in which the students practice these skills. Students who have difficulty reading, according to this theory, have not been able to show mastery with these skills.

Cognitive Development Theory of Learning

The consequences for literacy for life are reflected when adults show their love for reading.

The **cognitive development theory of learning** considers the changes that occur in children's mental skills. Jean Piaget's theory of cognitive development (Piaget & Inhelder, 1969) has had a powerful impact on reading instruction. He believed that children go through stages of cognitive development that influence their abilities to learn. More detail about the characteristics of and implications for each stage in cognitive development can be found in Chapter 2.

Piaget maintains that learning occurs when students modify their cognitive structure or schemata. **Schema theory** falls under the cognitive theory of learning. According to schema theory, the basis for comprehension, learning, and remembering the ideas in texts is the reader's schema, or organized knowledge of the world. In this theory, readers create meaning using their prior knowledge of various texts, their knowledge of the world, and the cues supplied by the texts.

According to schema theory (Anderson, 1985), our schema, with its sets of knowledge and expectations, provide the scaffolding that allows us to assimilate new information. When new information fits into prior sets of knowledge, it is readily learned. When the information does not fit into our prior sets of knowledge, it is neither easily understood nor readily learned. Prior knowledge and past experiences are important when comprehending texts. Students who hear stories read aloud, for example, learn to develop schema for story structures, vocabulary, and other literary elements. Stories read aloud are important at all grade levels because many of the story structures are difficult for students to read independently. The cognitive development theory, including schema theory, relates to both top-down and interactive models of the reading process. As in the top-down models, prior knowledge is necessary for developing understanding. As in the interactive models, children are active learners as they relate new information to prior knowledge and develop comprehension of the text.

Lesley Mandel Morrow (1996) describes an early childhood curriculum following Piaget's theories of cognitive development as one that uses real-life materials that allow children to play, explore, and experiment. The curriculum emphasizes decision making, problem solving, and goal setting.

Sociolinguistic Theory of Learning

The **sociolinguistic theory of learning** emphasizes that learning develops within each person at an individual level, but also as a result of interactions and relationships with others. Consequently, sociolinguists such as Lev Vygotsky (1981), who pioneered the role of social interactions in the development of cognitive abilities, maintain that learning to read is a social activity because it reflects the culture of the children and the communities in which they live. Children learn by internalizing the culture around them, incorporating the behaviors and knowledge found in their culture, and using these social interactions when learning new information. In the sociolinguistic theory, teachers provide scaffolds for students that help them make connections between their background knowledge and new experiences. As in the top-down model of the reading process, students bring their backgrounds, culture, and experiences into the reading act to help them comprehend. As in the interactive model, students use parallel processing in order to interpret the text.

Vygotsky's theory of sociolinguistics emphasizes that social interactions influence all types of learning in the classroom. Robin Fogarty (2001) describes what this could look like in the classroom:

> This belief in the socialization process of idea-making permeates the essence of the interactive classroom. Student-to-student engagement ranges from small groups of children bent over a map of Antarctica, deep in discussion of human survival, to pairs of students going head-to-head as they debate the most efficient way to solve a problem. (p. 145)

If we take this into the reading classroom, we see students reading to each other and interacting in both small groups and larger groups. We see students using knowledge from their cultural and social backgrounds to comprehend a text and to share this information with other students. We see teachers making use of the sociolinguistic theory as they relate new information to children's backgrounds in order to develop comprehension for the new ideas. For example, in a fifth-grade class, when reading and discussing a story about new immigrants to the United States, teachers could use literature such as Kashmira Sheth's *Blue Jasmine* or Pegi Deitz Shea's *Tangled Threads: A Hmong Girl's Story*. Both texts cover the subject of dislocation. The two texts are interesting comparisons because in *Tangled Threads* the family is dislocated for political reasons, while in *Blue Jasmine*, a father moves his family to Iowa from India in order to become a university professor. Both books develop the theme that even though the experiences are challenging, it is possible to live in two cultures without giving up the cultural traditions that are important to a family. In using these texts, the teacher could have students discuss their personal experiences of moving, of dislocation, or of having immigrant family members and relate them to the experiences of the characters in the book. The teacher could also ask students how they struggle to maintain personal and cultural beliefs within their families. Both of these books have positive messages that are enhanced through a sociolinguistic theory of learning.

Elizabeth Dutro, Elham Kazemi, and Ruth Balf (2005) emphasizes discussion topics that engage fourth- and fifth-grade students to think about issues of race as part of the literacy classroom. For example, after reading multiracial books such as Adoff Arnold's *Black Is White Is Tan* (1973) or Alma Flor Ada's *I Love Saturdays y Domingos* (2002) students take part in critical discussions that consider:

- Who benefits from the situation in this text?
- Whose interest is reflected in statements or policies in the book?
- What was the purpose of the of the practice described in the text?
- How might someone else have experienced this situation?
- What beliefs or values about race are reflected in this situation?
- What would you have done in the same situation?
- Have you ever experienced a similar situation? Why or why not?
- What language do we use in our classroom to talk about these issues?

Reader Response Theory of Learning

A **reader response theory** suggests that meaning results when there is an interaction between the reader and the text. Educators who emphasize the reader response theory consider how readers respond emotionally to texts, connect texts to their own experiences and beliefs, and interpret and evaluate texts. Proponents of the reader response learning theory argue that reading activities should stress individual growth by encouraging students to respond directly and individually to what they read.

Reader response theory emphasizes that readers bring their emotional, cultural, and scholastic backgrounds to the reading task. Readers approach a text with their previous knowledge of the subject, their purposes for reading the text, and their various strategies for gaining meaning from the text. Each reader, therefore, can gain quite different meanings from the same text. Consequently, the interpretation of the text is a complex task. Interpretations require personal responses that allow readers to connect experiences, emotions, and text; to understand and appreciate the unique requirements associated with different literary elements and genres of books; and to apply various strategies to gain meaning and to comprehend numerous examples of texts.

Louise Rosenblatt (1968, 1985, 2003) is one of the major proponents of a reader response theory. She distinguishes between two types of meaning related to text: efferent and aesthetic. Rosenblatt (1985) distinguishes between the two when she states that efferent reading focuses attention on "actions to be performed, information to be retained, conclusions to be drawn, solutions to be arrived at, analytical concepts to be applied, propositions to be tested" (p. 70). Aesthetic reading, according to Rosenblatt, focuses on "what we are seeing and feeling and thinking, on what is aroused within us by the very sound of the words, and by what they point to in the human and natural world" (p. 70).

When describing a reader response theory, Robert Probst (1989) uses the terms *reading for information* and *reading for experience*. In reading for information, readers respond by drawing on evidence in the text; to make inferences about what they read they must pay close attention to the text and find justifications for their answers and positions. In contrast, reading for experience requires that students are encouraged to attend to their own experiences that include "emotions, associations, memories, and thoughts that are evoked during the reading of the work" (p. 180).

For example, consider how a teacher could include both efferent (reading for information) and aesthetic (reading for experience) responses to Jim Murphy's *An American Plague: The True and Terrifying Story of the Yellow Fever Epidemic of 1793*. This book is a likely candidate for reading in the upper grades because it won the Robert F. Sibert Medal, the Newbery Honor Award, and is a National Book Award Finalist. When leading a discussion about the efferent meaning, questions might focus on the *who, what, when, where,* and *why* of this informational book. For example, *what* questions might include: What is the chronological order developed by the author? What is the significance of writing this book in chronological order? And, What are the medical beliefs and practices of the time and conditions that helped the disease spread so rapidly? An additional activity about efferent meaning might ask students to read one of the sources recommended at the back of Murphy's book and compare the facts in both books.

Aesthetic response questions using the same book could ask: How did you respond emotionally when you read that barbers drew blood in an effort to treat the plague? How would you respond if your doctor offered to use this technique on you? What image or incident from the book was meaningful to you? And, How do you respond to the author's statement that "yellow fever is a modern-day time bomb" (p. 125)? This reader response theory is closely related to literature-based approaches.

Some general types of questions that may be used with most reading materials include:

- What is your first response or reaction to the text?
- What emotions did you feel as you read the text?
- What ideas or thoughts were suggested by the text?
- How did you respond emotionally to the text? Did you feel involved with the text or did you feel distant from the text?
- What did you focus on within the text? What word, phrase, image, or idea caused this focus?
- If you were to write about your reading on what would you focus? Would you choose an association or memory, an aspect of the text, something about the author, or something else about the text?

- Describe an image that was called to your mind by the text.
- What in the text or in your reading caused you the most trouble?
- Do you think that this is a good text? Why or why not?
- What memories do you have after reading the text: memories of people, places, sights, events, smells, feelings, or attitudes?
- What sort of person do you think the author is?
- How did your reading of the text differ from that of your classmates? How was your reading similar?
- What did you observe about others as they read or discussed the text?
- Does the text remind you of any other literary work such as a poem, a play, a film, a story, or another genre? If it does, what is the text and what connection do you see between the two works?

Notice that the types of questions developed for a reader response theory emphasize how the reader responds and reacts emotionally, socially, and intellectually to the text. These questions could be used with many different examples of fiction, poetry, and biography. The questions do not require, or should not demand, the same answer from every reader. Consequently, teachers may choose to select texts that are meaningful to individual children or to groups of children. Not all children respond to the same text in the same way. For example, many of the books discussed in the section "Multicultural Literature" in Chapter 10 develop either positive or negative personal reactions when read by students who are members of that culture.

It is the belief that meaning results when there is an interaction between the reader and the text that makes the reader response theory appropriate for many ELL students. If the materials are carefully selected, the students comprehend the subject when they make connections between their cultural understandings and the content of the text.

> **Reflect on Your Reading**
>
> Consider the four theories we have discussed: behaviorist, cognitive, sociolinguistic, and reader response. Which of these theories have the greatest appeal for you? Why?

A History of Basal Reading

At some time in your elementary education, you were probably taught to read using a series of books called **basal readers**. Basal readers are a published sequentially developed reading series that progress from prereading materials through upper-elementary and middle-school grades. Basal readers follow a sequence of reading and skill development that is believed to be the most effective by authors of the series. Consequently, different basal publishers may reflect different philosophies about how reading should be taught, the order of skills to be taught, and the types of materials printed in the basal readers. Most basal readers, however, provide a framework for reading development that progresses from the teaching of prereading competencies, such as listening to rhyming elements in words, distinguishing shapes and letters, and learning the sounds of letters, to higher levels of reading competencies found in upper grades, such as identifying points of view in an argument and writing a paper that presents a logical point of view.

The philosophy behind the basal reading series is that if students follow a specific skill sequence they will learn to read. Different authors of basal readers may present slightly different skill sequences. A basal series usually includes workbooks and worksheets designed to teach various reading skills, a textbook designed to have students practice the skills, and a teachers' manual that tells teachers how to teach the series. The textbooks include stories that the students are to read and discuss. The teachers' manuals provide explicit instructions, such as lesson plans that accompany each story. Many basal series include tests that accompany the basal and are to be administered to students following each unit of study. Basal readers can be influenced by models of the reading process, approaches to reading instruction, and learning theories. Techniques for teaching the basal readers are covered in Chapter 12.

Because basal series have been used for so many years, a history of basal reading provides insights into the changing trends in reading education. How have basal reading series changed? To answer this question we will draw examples from books written for students over the past hundred years. We will make comparisons between a basal series published in 1902, two series published in the 1920s and 1930s, a series published in 1948, and a series published in 2001. As you read each of these examples, try to identify a model of reading that would influence how the teachers teach reading and how the students would approach reading.

Silver, Burdett Series (1902)

In 1902, the Silver, Burdett Company introduced *Stepping Stones to Literature: Second Reader* and *Stepping Stones to Literature: Third Reader,* written by Sarah Louise Arnold and Charles B. Gilbert. The series stresses that the materials are centered around children's interests. The preface to the second-grade reader states that the aim of the book is to lead children to a love of literature by having them read the world's best books because "a taste for good things, developed now, will lead the pupils to demand good things when free to choose" (p. v). The preface recommends that teachers read to children especially the poems of Henry Wadsworth Longfellow. The basal reader includes language lessons which the teacher is to relate to the reading selections. The text includes pictures, as wells as lessons, which "should be studied until some appreciation of their meaning is gained. Artists' names should become as familiar to the children as are the names of poets" (p. vii). There is also a "Manual for Teachers," with additional suggestions for teaching.

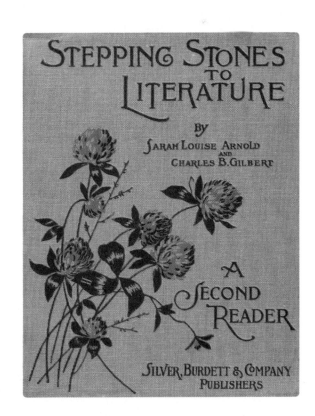

A SECOND READER.   31

SAVED.   *Sir Edwin Landseer.*

Tell the story which this picture tells you.

STUDY.   *Answer the questions.*

You have read the story of the good dog Hero. This fine picture has told you another story. Can you not tell or write the story of some dog that you know?

What kind of dog is he? Where does he live?

What is his name? What can he do?

For this second-grade series many of the stories are taken from fables such as "The Fox and the Crow" and "The Town Mouse and the Country Mouse." Poems include titles such as "The Old Love" by Charles Kingsley, "A Child's Prayer" by M. Bentham-Edwards, and "Lady Moon" by Lord Houghton. The lessons that follow the selections include vocabulary and questions about the readings. Art appreciation is included through reproductions of color and black-and-white paintings. Writing activities and language expansion activities are suggested.

The preface for the third-grade reader continues the objectives for developing a love of literature and reading. In addition, every lesson provides suggestions for outside reading and additional study. For example, "[t]he story of 'Columbus' opens the way to events of history and facts of geography. The children's questions point the way. The value of the lessons as reading lessons will be increased a hundred fold if they are reinforced by language exercises suggested by the text" (p. vi). The text teaches the vocabulary by placing the words after the story and not before because "[i]t is believed that the mastery of the new word is most easily achieved when the word is studied as it occurs in the text rather than apart from it. Let the children, in their own study, learn to select the hard words which demand special effort" (p. vi). As in the second-grade reader, this third-grade reader recommends that teachers read to students, familiarizing them with the best poems and literature.

The selections of stories in this third-grade reader include numerous traditional tales, modern fantasy, and poems. Examples of stories include "Diamonds and Toads" by Charles Perrault, Greek myths such as "Hercules and the Lazy Man," fantasy such as "The Daisy and the Lark" and "The Ugly Duckling" by Hans Christian Andersen, and poems such as "The Rime of the Ancient Mariner" by Samuel Taylor Coleridge and "Under the Greenwood Tree" by William Shakespeare.

A SECOND READER.   35

Study without help.

THE KID AND THE WOLF.

A little kid stood on the roof of a house.

As he looked down, he saw a wolf passing by.

"Oho!" he cried, "who cares for the wolf?"

The wolf smiled as he said, "It is the roof that makes you so brave, my fine fellow. If you were in the field, how you would run!"

HELP IN STUDY.

pass	o-ho	smile
passing	oho	smiled
fell	piece	gave
fellows	field	brave

How did the roof make the little kid brave?

Why is a kid afraid of a wolf?

McGuffey's Eclectic Reader (1921) and Elson Basic Readers (1931)

These two basal reading series are among the most popular and well-known series used in elementary schools during the time periods. For this comparison we will consider books written for fifth- and sixth grade students. The McGuffey Readers were first introduced in 1879 and continued in new editions until this one was published in 1921. The McGuffey Readers begin with "Elocution" drills that are divided under the following heads: "Articulation," "Inflection," "Accent and Emphasis," "Reading Verse," "The Voice," and "Gesture." Each of these sections includes a definition of the terms such as "Emphasis consists in uttering a word or phrase in such a manner as to give it force and energy, and to draw the attention of the hearer particularly to the idea expressed" (p. 34). The section on emphasis includes examples for students to practice reading, with emphasis placed on certain words. Consequently, developing appropriate speech when reading or speaking is an important goal of this series: "The business of training youth in elocution, must be commenced in childhood. The first school is the nursery. There, at least, may be formed a distinct articulation, which is the first requisite for good speaking. How rarely is it found in perfection among our orators" (p. 57).

The reader continues with selections written by leading authors who reflect "the best English and American literature" (p. iii). Each reading selection includes explanatory notes that help students understand a selection and a biographical sketch of the author. The text also includes examples of art. The authors provide the following reasons for these features:

> In the absence of a large number of books of reference, explanatory notes are absolutely necessary, in some cases, for the intelligent reading of the piece; and it is

---

72   *ECLECTIC SERIES.*

V. AFTER THE THUNDERSTORM.

James Thomson, 1700–1748, the son of a clergyman, was born in Scotland. He studied at the University of Edinburgh, and intended to follow the profession of his father, but never entered upon the duties of the sacred office. In 1724 he went to London, where he spent most of his subsequent life. He had shown some poetical talent when a boy; and, in 1826, he published "Winter," a part of a longer poem, entitled "The Seasons," the best known of all his works. He also wrote several plays for the stage; none of them, however, achieved any great success. In the last year of his life, he published his "Castle of Indolence," the most famous of his works excepting "The Seasons." Thomson was heavy and dull in his personal appearance, and was indolent in his habits. The moral tone of his writings is always good. This extract is from "The Seasons."

As from the face of heaven the shattered clouds
Tumultuous rove, the interminable sky
Sublimer swells, and o'er the world expands
A purer azure.

Through the lightened air
A higher luster and a clearer calm,
Diffusive, tremble; while, as if in sign
Of danger past, a glittering robe of joy,
Set off abundant by the yellow ray,
Invests the fields; and nature smiles revived.

'T is beauty all, and grateful song around,
Joined to the low of kine, and numerous bleat
Of flocks thick-nibbling through the clovered vale:
And shall the hymn be marred by thankless man,
Most favored; who, with voice articulate,
Should lead the chorus of this lower world?

Shall man, so soon forgetful of the Hand
That hushed the thunder, and serenes the sky,
Extinguished feel that spark the tempest waked,
That sense of powers exceeding far his own,
Ere yet his feeble heart has lost its fears?

believed that in all cases they will add largely to the interest and usefulness of the lessons. The biographical notices, if properly used, are hardly of less value than the lessons themselves. They have been carefully prepared, and are intended not only to add to the interest of the pieces, but to supply information usually obtained only by the separate study of English and American literature. The illustrations are presented as specimens of fine art. They are the work of the best artists and engravers that could be secured for the purpose in this country. (p. iv)

The co-author of the *Elson Basic Readers*, William S. Gray, is regarded as one of the leading reading experts of his time. The "Preface" to the reader presents the philosophy of the authors by stressing the features that are considered the most valuable: "Among these features are (a) an authorship group of recognized standing, (b) variety in the types of material presented, (c) definite organization of the selections into parts, each part focusing on a specific aspect of social environment or child in-

---

LINDBERGH, PIONEER AIR SCOUT   59

honors upon Lindbergh, he went to visit New York City where they planned the biggest celebration ever given any visiting hero!

When the festivities were over in New York, Lindbergh was invited to St. Louis. This was his home city —the city for which his monoplane, the *Spirit of St. Louis*, had been named. It was also the city in which money had been raised to pay for the making of the airplane and for other expenses of the trip. St. Louis could not turn out so many millions of people to see Lindbergh as did New York City. But there was a hearty welcome and a spirit of pride for what Charles Lindbergh had been able to do.

Paris, Brussels, London, Washington, New York, St. Louis, Chicago! Why did so many cities do their best to honor Lindbergh? This is easy to answer. Charles Lindbergh was brave; he had skill and good health; he was friendly and kind to other people and knew how to make them friendly toward him. Charles Lindbergh was ready to do a great work, and when the time came, the great work was done.

NOTES AND QUESTIONS

1. How far did Lindbergh fly?
2. How many hours was he in the air?
3. Was he in the air about one day, a day and a half, or two days?
4. Give four dangers that Lindbergh faced on his flight.
5. How is a compass helpful in guiding a person?

---

60   THE ELSON BASIC READERS—BOOK V

6. What land across the ocean did he first see?
7. What message did Lindbergh carry to the people of Europe?
8. Here is a list of nine words, and nine sentences with letters in them. Write the letters (a) to (i) on your paper. After each letter write the word that belongs where that letter is in the sentence.

overcast   hangars   uproar
cockpit   airway   throng
beacons   flares   skill

....(a).... means being able to do something very well.
When the sky is cloudy, we say it is ....(b)....
Airplanes are kept in ....(c)....
Lights to guide people at night are called ....(d).... or ....(e)....
A crowd of people is called a ....(f)....
The route over which airplanes travel is called an ....(g)....
An aviator sits in the ....(h).... of his plane.
A mixture of many loud noises is called an ....(i)....

9. On a map of the world find New York, Nova Scotia, Newfoundland, Ireland, England, the English Channel, Cherbourg, and Paris. Be ready to show on a wall map just where Lindbergh flew.

You will enjoy reading "New York to Paris," Lindbergh (in *We*); "Through the Storm," Collins (in *Skyward Ho!*, Mathiews); *Picture Book of Flying*, Dobias.

terest, (d) definite helps for the teacher and the pupil" (p. 3). Further insights into the authors' philosophy are reflected in the features emphasized in this latest edition:

1. The present book contains an ample and carefully selected body of informational material, the product of writers well known in the fields which they discuss.

2. The content is marked by greater simplicity in concepts, sentence structure, and vocabulary.

3. The selections provide for a far wider range of pupil interest and present a broader introduction to the many phases of environment.

4. Illustrations occupy a very prominent place throughout the book and are made a valuable adjunct of comprehension, as well as of interest. (p. 4)

> ### A BACKWARD LOOK
>
> Airplanes, radios, dog-teams, horses, trains—we have read about all these ways of carrying men or sending messages. We perhaps understand a little better how man has made the world smaller. There are other ways, too.
>
> Make a list of all the ways men send messages.
> Make another list of the ways they travel.
> Write down the different ways you have traveled and sent messages.
> Your class might like to gather pictures of ways of traveling and sending messages. These pictures could be put on a bulletin board.
>
> There was a time when traveling almost always meant danger—danger from wild animals, from cold and hunger and thirst, from savage people. Now in most parts of the world we travel in comfort and safety, and our messages speed on their way to our friends. But there are still parts of the world where travel is hard, and where men wait days and even weeks for news they are eager to get.
> Name five places where this is true. One of the stories in this Part tells you of such a place.
>
> The four stories you have just read are only a few of many just as interesting. How men have dug canals for boats, strung thousands of miles of wire for messages, built roads over and through mountains for trains, wagons, and automobiles, spent long hours of patient, careful study and work to invent the radio and the airplane—these are things you may like to read about. And men have written them down for you and for me in many books. You will find some very interesting ones in the list on page 431.
>
> 62

Each of the reading selections includes text to be read, illustrations, notes and questions to be answered, and additional reading. The text is divided into eight units in which the stories are written about a common theme. For example, one of the selections in "Skyways and Highways" is "Lindbergh, Pioneer Air Scout" by Laura Antoinette Large. The selection is divided by subtitles that help focus the reading such as "Off to Paris," "Crossing the Atlantic," "Paris at Last—Messages of Good-Will," and "America Honors the Hero." Following the selection is a list of questions, a list of nine words and nine sentences that test vocabulary, an activity in which students use a map to show Lindbergh's route, and a listing of three books that can be read to discover more information about Lindbergh. This section on "Skyways and Highways" concludes with a poem, "Air Mail" by Gordon Hillman that emphasizes the role of airplanes and "A Backward Look" that summarizes information from Part One of the text, "Skyways and Highways." The "Backward Look" includes additional class activities such as preparing a bulletin board showing pictures to illustrate ways of traveling and sending messages and reading additional books on the subject. Fifteen "Good Books to Read" are listed.

Reflect on Your Reading

Based on this information about the reading series published in the earlier 1900s, what were the objectives for teaching reading through these readers? Which model of the reading process would be associated with each of these series? If asked to provide a definition of reading, what definition would you give? What are differences between the earlier series and the one published in 1946? What model of reading would support the *Reading with Phonics* series?

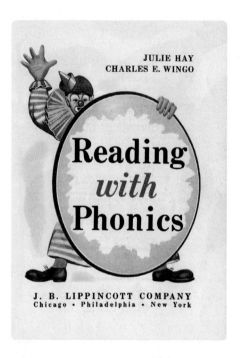

Reading with Phonics Series (1948)

In 1948 Hay and Wingo wrote *Reading with Phonics*, published by Lippincott. In this basal reading series, the authors first develop the reasons for teaching reading through phonics by indicating that 87 percent of English words are phonetically regular and only 13 percent are not. In addition, the child will be able to sound out 62 percent of the syllables when he or she recognizes short vowel blends. The authors also identify how teachers should provide instruction in phonics by first listening to the sounds and then looking at the symbols. These two approaches are described in full under auditory discrimination (sound) and visual discrimination (sight). According to the preface of this basal reader, "[s]ight and sound are being matched constantly as pupils grow in reading ability. Suggestions for adequate seat work related to any given unit of work

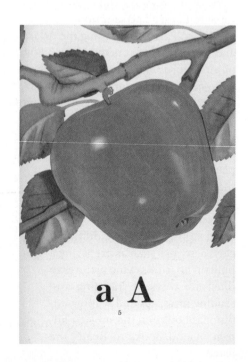

provide ample opportunity for a teacher to work with a class on any kind of group division that seems desirable" (p. 10).

The children's basal materials begin with pictures that show specific sound and letter relationships such as *a* is for *apple* and *e* is for *elephant*. The lessons then proceed as students blend consonant and vowel sounds such as *met, miss, men, mop, map, mad,* and *mud*. After presenting these words, the text provides sentences for students to read, such as "Miss Muff sat on the mat. Miss Mop sat on the mat too" (p. 21).

As students gain these phonetic abilities, teachers are instructed to encourage students to write their own stories with the caveat: "At each stage of development the teacher must keep the vocabulary within the children's phonetic power, using as few unphonetic words as possible" (p. 90). The teacher's manual provides examples of stories that include words that are phonetically regular.

McGraw-Hill Reading Series (2001)

The McGraw-Hill series is a typical series of basal readers used in contemporary classrooms. (See Chapter 12 for an example of a typical basal reader.) The first-grade reader includes a pretest for phonics by testing sound-symbol relationships, phonics blending, and high-frequency words. The materials provide lessons in beginning consonants, vowels, and high-frequency words. The first of these stories to be read by students is called "Dad has Sam!" Each section progresses through a specific sequence of activities. For example, a series of lessons beginning with "Duke the Ant" teaches using the phonics approach that includes rhyme. The story to be read by the class is "The Knee-High Man," a play adapted from an African American folktale, which is followed by a series of questions and activities. Questions include literal-level questions, such as "What did Bob tell Sam to do?" and more evaluative questions in which students need to apply prior knowledge, such as "How is a play different from a story?" The activities also ask students to find out more. For example, "'The Knee-High Man' is a folktale. It teaches a lesson. Find another folktale that teaches a lesson" (p. 93). The lessons conclude with a "Study Skills" chart and a test that covers the skills taught throughout the section.

The series continues using a similar format. By third grade, students are reading different types of literature and responding to art, for example, Japanese and Chinese tales, a nonfiction story about the family, several science nonfiction articles, historical fiction, and biographies. Each series begins with a reproduction of art related to the topic and then includes story questions and activities, study skills, and a test. The section focusing on a biography about Benjamin Franklin, for example, begins by asking students to respond to both "Franklin's Experiment in Electricity" and a painting by Currier and Ives. The text suggests that the teacher have students

- answer questions about the story
- create a brochure describing some of Franklin's inventions
- conduct an experiment similar to one conducted by Franklin
- make a book of sayings similar to the one written by Franklin
- research another of Franklin's inventions
- conduct a simple science experiment in which they must follow directions
- take a test covering the content

In addition, each of the units in the series includes a connection with another subject in the curriculum such as language arts, social studies, art, science, math, or music.

Instructional Techniques

Within the various reading approaches are instructional techniques that you may use to teach, to reinforce, and to review children's reading skills and comprehension abilities. In this section, we will briefly describe a few of these instructional techniques so that you begin to appreciate that teaching reading is an exciting and rewarding profession. In addition, these instructional techniques can create excitement, enthusiasm, and the enjoyment of reading among students in the classroom.

This section also introduces some of the instructional techniques that allow you choices in grouping students and selecting instructional materials. These alternative groupings provide ways of dividing students beyond the ability groupings that usually accompany the basal readers discussed in the previous section and in Chapter 12. The following groupings provide an interesting alternative in literacy classrooms.

Ability Groupings

Grouping students by their abilities to read and their reading instructional needs are probably the most common reading groupings found in schools. In a report of elementary reading instruction practices (Baumann, Hoffman, Duffy-Hester, & Ro, 2000) researchers found that the majority of teachers teach in self-contained, heterogeneous classes, use a balanced approach that uses both basals and literature, and provide explicit instruction in skills such as phonic analysis and comprehension.

A self-contained, heterogeneous classroom means that teachers are teaching students with a wide range of reading abilities. Ability groupings allow the teacher to divide the class into smaller groups according to the various reading abilities found within the class. Ability groupings are usually formed following assessment of reading. Students are now placed into groups in which students read at approximately the same levels and require approximately the same type of instruction. Many teachers use basal reading approaches that lend themselves to ability groupings because the material is directed at certain grade levels. Many classrooms include low ability, average ability, and high ability groups for reading instruction.

Ability groupings are related to the reading assessment strategies discussed in Chapter 3, "Assessment and Evaluation in the Reading and Writing Program." For example, the "Informal Reading Inventory" discussed in the chapter uses graded reading passages and comprehension checks to identify students' independent, instruction, and frustration levels of reading. These levels can be used to select appropriate reading materials and to divide students into various levels of instruction. Now students receive appropriate reading instruction for areas such as word recognition and comprehension. This level of instruction is usually at the student's instructional reading level.

Educators are also concerned, however, that students have many opportunities to read with students who are reading at different reading levels. Consequently, teachers use a variety of groupings that encourage students to read and discuss topics with children who are reading at other ability levels. The groupings that follow are found in many heterogeneous classes.

Literature Circles

Literature circles include small groups of three or four students who read a particular book or story, develop their own questions about the reading, and discuss the stories. They may compare the story with other stories or relate the stories to their own experiences. These literature circles are usually less formal than groups divided according to reading ability. For example, a group of first-graders who are just learning to read might form a literature circle to read and discuss easy-to-read books such as Dr. Seuss's *The Cat in the Hat* (1957) or Arnold Lobel's *Frog and Toad Are Friends* (1970). They could discuss their reactions to the humorous illustrations, read orally the rhyming dialogue or turn the text from *Frog and Toad Are Friends* into a play and take turns reading the parts.

Literature Circles provide interactions among students who help each other during the reading process. This group interaction enhances a sociolinguistic theory of learning, and responding to literature enhances a reader response theory of learning. Literature circles can enhance instruction in all of the reading approaches. Reading the rhyming words in *The Cat in the Hat* and *Frog and Toad Are Friends* enhances phonics and sub-skills approaches. Responding to the language and enacting the dialogue enhances reader response theories of learning and literature-based approaches.

Uninterrupted Sustained Silent Reading (USSR)

Uninterrupted Sustained Silent Reading, USSR for short, is an instructional strategy used to increase independent reading in all the classes of a school or in individual classrooms. Teachers who use this approach allow about 30 minutes each day or several periods during the week in which students silently read self-selected books. If the entire school is involved, everyone employed by the school stops normal duties and reads self-selected materials. The beliefs behind this approach are that self-selected materials are motivating, that students gain from seeing other students enjoying reading, and that the more one reads the better one reads. This strategy is supported especially by balanced reading approaches because the students have opportunities to balance more skills approaches with literature approaches and interactive models. Motivation is also a major emphasis in Piaget's cognitive development theory.

Recreational Reading Groups

Recreational reading groups encourage students to select reading materials of their choice around a specific theme or topic and include opportunities for students and teachers to discuss and respond to their reading experiences. Students select books of their own choosing from a wide range of literature, or teachers provide a narrower range of topics, genres, or characteristics of literature such as poetry or folklore from a specific culture. If topics are the focus, students are grouped according to interest in those topics rather than by their reading achievement levels. Consequently, teachers usually include a range of materials that meets reading levels of all the students in the group. For example, a recreational reading group in fifth grade could be formulated around fantasy where the students choose books by J. K. Rowling, such as *Harry Potter and the Sorcerer's Stone* (1998) or *Harry Potter and the Half-Blood Prince* (2005), or any other book of fantasy, such as J. R. R. Tolkien's *The Hobbit* (1938), Alan Armstrong's *Whittington* (2005), Susan Cooper's *The Dark Is Rising* (1973), Cornelia Funke's *Dragon Rider* (2004), Christopher Paoline's *Eragon* (2003) or *Eldest* (2005), or Kate Dicamillo's *The Miraculous Journey of Edward Julane,* (2006).

They can read the books while in the group. They might each read a chapter in their book and then share parts that are especially appealing, such as a character who accomplishes something they wish they could do, or a setting that was so believable they thought it was true.

Recreational reading groups have the benefit of motivating students to read and share something they enjoy. Sharing in a group motivates students to read. Group interaction enhances a sociolinguistic theory and responding to literature enhances a reader response theory. Reading and sharing books of one's own choosing is related to the whole language approach and to the top-down model of reading instruction. Reading and discussing books from a specific genre and developing appreciation for the reading of those books supports a literature-based approach to reading.

Focus or Thematic Units

Many teachers who use a basal series for reading instruction stop periodically to teach through focus, or thematic, units. This teaching strategy allows students to develop in-depth studies of a topic that may not be possible to cover in the more content-controlled basal readers. Focus or thematic units are especially important because they increase interaction among areas such as language arts, reading, science, and social studies. Units encourage students to apply their reading and language arts skills, search for information, work together in interest or research groups, share enthusiasm about topics, increase knowledge in other content areas, and share their findings in creative ways. Examples of focus units can be found in most chapters in this textbook.

Units are related to the cognitive development theory through their emphasis on developing research skills and problem-solving. Working within groups during the unit activity is supported by sociolinguistic theories. The activities developed within the unit usually require interactive models of reading. The unit also encourages a balanced reading approach through the interaction with other areas of the curriculum. A discussion of other instructional strategies related to groupings such as reading interest groups, book clubs, shared reading groups, shared writing groups, partner-reading groups, and coaching groups can be found in Chapter 12.

Reading Assessment in the Classroom

A major question that accompanies the use of any of the models of the reading process and approaches to reading is "How well do the children read as a result of the reading program?" To answer this question, teachers and school districts use various reading tests or assessment procedures to evaluate the effectiveness of the reading curriculum.

This testing may take the form of standardized tests given to all students. Standardized tests are tests that have been constructed, tested, interpreted, and revised by experts. After the tests are administered, the scores are collected and they are interpreted to reflect how well individuals, classes, and students in school districts as a whole are reading.

Reading assessment may also take the form of informal tests used by teachers to help them determine an individual child's strengths and weaknesses and to help teachers design reading lessons that will help the child learn to read. Such informal assessments may include Informal Reading Inventories, running records, and miscue analysis, which are discussed in Chapter 3.

The reading teacher needs to decide what assessment he or she will use in the classroom, the purposes for the assessment, and how the assessment matches the objectives of the reading approach chosen.

Mandated Tests

Federal and state controls of reading are now determining what form of assessment will be used in many schools. This control is exemplified by tests mandated under the **No Child Left Behind** legislation signed into law in January 2002. This act states that reading achievement must be measured at the end of specified grade levels. The law stipulates that schools develop high standards in reading and annual assessments must be geared to evaluate whether students have met the standards. The law rewards schools for meeting the standards by providing bonus funds. Conversely, the law punishes schools that fail to make adequate yearly progress by removing portions of their administrative funds.

The consequences of policies that emphasize reduced funds and may place schools and teachers on probation until reading scores improve have considerable impact on the reading curriculum. Teachers may, for example, "teach to the test" and teach students only to master reading skills they know will be tested. This approach may develop an unbalanced approach to reading. When visiting a fifth-grade reading class, I asked the teacher to describe how she taught poetry to her class and how she fostered a love of poetry. Her response was, "I don't teach poetry anymore. It is not on the test. This is disturbing to me because I always loved teaching poetry and my students got so much out of it, but the principal wants us to focus on reading skills that are measured on the test." This is an example of how the No Child Left Behind legislation may influence and even mandate what is taught in the reading curriculum.

Consequences of Mandated Tests

Currently, there is considerable interest in, criticism of, and discussions about the consequences resulting from the tests required by the federal government under No Child Left Behind legislation. An example of such criticism is Donald H. Graves's (2002) comment, "Instead of preparing children for tests, teachers need to be teaching the skills that will, in fact, make them better readers" (p. 20). The title of an article in *The Council Chronicle,* published by the National Council of Teachers of English, states the concern of many educators: "NCTE Members Seek to Influence NCLB Reauthorization" (Harris, 2006). This organization of educators urges that the reauthorization of No Child Left Behind should:

> Include the respected voices of English language arts teachers and teacher educators as advisors at every stage of the reauthorization process; support policies that reward rather than punish teachers who choose to work in the nations most challenging schools; abandon impoverished assessment systems and support the development of multiple tools that measure the complexity of student literacy and learning; and shift the focus from packaged reading programs to initiatives that respect teachers' expertise in educating all children to read and write. (Harris, 2006, p. 1)

Contradictions when reporting results are also consequences of mandatory testing. For example, a *New York Times* article called "Gains in Houston Schools: How Real Are They?" (Schemo & Fessenden, Dec. 3, 2003, p. 1) reports research that compares the Houston districts test results for fourth, eighth, and tenth grades that used two different tests of assessment—the Stanford Achievement Test and the Texas Assessment of Academic Skills. The Stanford Achievement Test is a national test, while the Texas Assessment of Academic Skills is a state-mandated test given only to students in Texas. According to the article, there are sizable differences in the outcomes of the two tests. These results show that the same students who performed poorly on the Stanford Achievement Test performed at a higher rate on the Texas Assessment of Academic Skills, raising questions about which tests to use in evaluating a school's reading program and what tests conclude about the effectiveness of the reading program.

An article about testing in New York public schools by Michael Winerip (2005) stresses other results of mandated tests. The mayor cites the rise in the city's 2005 fourth-grade test results, which were up 10 percentage points in English, as proof that the school reading program is a success. A school principal reports, however, that the 2005 test was easier than the 2004 test, citing evidence such as longer passages with words unfamiliar to urban children in the 2004 test and pointing out that the 2005 test was shorter, simpler, and included content familiar to urban children. Educators debate these results. How important is the content of the test when testing urban children or children who have minimal English language abilities? Winerip quotes Ykehonela Ortiz, an experienced fourth-grade teacher who stresses the importance of knowing the format of the test: "We know the test now. We start preparing them in September. When I go through a lesson, I always connect it to what's in the exam. We know there's always letter-writing, so we give more of that. We know there's nonfiction, so we make sure we do it before the test" (p. A23). Ortiz says that when she gives a writing assignment she now sets a timer for ten minutes to stimulate testing conditions. Winerip ends the article by asking, "Does it mean students are getting smarter and teachers better?" Ms. Ortiz answers, "I do not know." This article emphasizes concerns about influences of the test content as well as concerns about teaching students to take the test. Do students benefit when they are taught to read specific areas that will be covered on the test? What happens to the reading of content that is not covered on the test?

Reflect on Your Reading

Consider your own experiences as a student in reading classrooms. Do you think standardized tests and other forms of assessment influenced the way you were taught? Why, or why not?

There can be both negative and positive consequences of reading instruction through the No Child Left Behind legislation. Negative consequences include reduced funds for schools that do not meet the standards, increased time spent on preparing students to take the test, decreased time spent on reading skills that are not measured by the test, and a control of the reading curriculum that does not develop a balanced approach for reading. Positive consequences include an increased focus on reading instruction in schools that have slighted or completely ignored reading instruction in the past, more teaching of reading to students who have difficulty learning to read, and additional training for teachers of reading.

Discussions of high stakes testing, different types of assessments in reading, developing and using informal assessments of reading, running records, miscues analysis, and lesson plans for informal assessment can be found in Chapter 3.

Up for Discussion

Those who have chosen teaching as a profession, and reading teachers in particular, face pressures from their students, parents, principals, school districts, and state and federal laws. This chapter presents the theoretical framework behind reading instruction. Why is it important that this textbook begins with a discussion of the reading process, the approaches to reading instruction, and the theories of learning? Why is it important that reading teachers know the differences among the reading approaches? When might reading teachers need to apply this knowledge in and out of a reading classroom?

Now, respond to this statement: "Reading teachers need to be empowered with knowledge of the theoretical framework behind reading as they face pressures from principals, school district, state and federal laws, and parents."

A teacher motivates students' interest when the students respond to a story.

A History of Requirements for Teachers of Reading

Teacher education programs have changed dramatically in the past hundred years. Programs have progressed from a few courses in reading and language arts to the current complete set of standards in reading education endorsed by the International Reading Association (IRA). In the early twentieth century, most elementary teachers gained their education by attending two-year normal schools with programs designed for teacher training that lacked course work in reading and English language arts (Squire, 2003).

In the 1950s and 1960s there was increased interest in school reforms and in strengthening the teaching of subject matter such as reading and language arts. Large research studies like "First Grade Reading Studies" (Bond & Dykstra, 1967) provided information about how reading was being taught. These large studies also provided grounds for advocates of teacher reform.

In the 1960s and 1970s there was a decline in interest in teacher education. Centers for research in reading became less common. Laboratory schools, which were connected to universities, closed. The purpose of these laboratory schools had been to provide a location where teachers in training could develop and practice their teaching skills while university educators conducted research. Teacher training moved into the public school classroom so that teacher training became more "realistic." At this point, a renewed concern about the quality of reading teachers led to calls for reforms in teacher education.

Concerns about the quality of teachers are fueled by current studies that compare students' reading scores across grade levels, states, and countries. Politicians and those interested in educational reform often use results from large-scale testing to argue for changes in teacher education and teacher certification.

Reflect on Your **Reading**

As you begin your studies in reading education, what are your thoughts about teacher reform?

Currently, there are numerous calls for teacher reform and for changes in not only the education of teachers, but also in teacher certification. These calls for reform can be found in professional educational journals as well as in professional reading organizations. Headlines in two articles in the *Chronicle of Higher Education,* for example, highlight current concerns. One recommends the need for a major overhaul of teacher education and calls for teaching to be treated as a modern, clinical profession, complete with a two-year "residency" program that is similar to the residency program in medicine (Fogg, 2002). Another cites problems resulting from both a critical teacher shortage and inadequate training and preparation (Gregorian, 2001). The latter article identifies problems related to teachers who lack college majors or even minors in the subjects they teach and calls for increased standards for teachers, use of highly qualified university faculty in the teaching of students, and higher standards for state licensing of teachers.

It is interesting to note that while some states are in the process of lowering certification requirements in order to attract more teachers, professional associations such as the International Reading Association are increasing the standards for teachers of reading. *Standards 2003,* for example, lists five essential requirements for reading professionals: essential knowledge about the foundations of reading; instructional strategies and curricular materials; assessment, diagnosis, and evaluation; creating a literature environment; and professional development.

DIFFERENTIATING INSTRUCTION

Meeting the instructional needs of all students is a major undertaking and a worthy goal of all teachers. Within heterogeneous classrooms are students who read at different levels and require modifications in instruction. For example, you may be teaching a fourth-grade class that includes students who are reading at second-, fourth-, and ninth-grade levels. Modifications in instruction are required in order to teach reading to this group because a student reading at a second-grade level requires different instructional materials and instructional strategies than a student reading at a ninth-grade level.

Modifying instruction when appropriate to meet the different reading needs of students in the classroom is called **differentiating instruction**. According to C. A. Tomlinson (1999), instruction can be differentiated according to content, process, or product. When differentiating according to content, students are given reading materials that match their instructional needs. Differentiating through process means that teachers modify their instructional strategies and their teaching so that all students are able to learn. This modification may mean that some children receive individualized instruction when they fail to grasp a concept, or it may mean that teachers need to use totally different reading instructional strategies with those students.

When differentiating instruction through product, the assignment following a lesson may be differentiated to reflect the ability levels of different students. Mary C. McMackin and Nancy L. Witherell (2005) assert that

> It is not realistic or even advisable for teachers to develop individual or small-group lessons for every instructional task. It is feasible, however, to meet individual needs by creating leveled, or tiered, follow-up activities to reinforce whole class instruction. (p. 243)

Differentiating instruction also includes instruction for students whose first language is not English. The editors of *Language Arts* (Short et al., 2006) state: "Multilingual classrooms present teachers with significant opportunities, such as exploring multiple perspectives and preparing students to live in a diverse world, but they also present significant challenges" (p. 287). Within this textbook we consider both the

Excellent teachers help all students read by modifying instruction when necessary.

educational opportunities and the ways teachers can approach these challenges, especially ways that teachers of literacy can bring children's linguistic and cultural backgrounds into the classroom.

Each chapter of this book ends with recommendations for differentiating instruction for the topic covered in the chapter. Each section on differentiated instruction includes proven classroom methods for modifying instruction for English language learners (ELL), struggling readers and writers, and gifted and accelerated readers and writers.

Reflect on Your Reading

How might a teacher and a school develop an environment that meets the needs of all students? Think back to your own elementary school experiences. How did the teachers differentiate instruction according to content, process, and product? Which of these modifications were most successful?

Summary

Reading instruction is influenced by the models of the reading process advocated by different educators. The bottom-up (text-based) model proceeds from parts to the whole as students proceed from letter-sound relationships to the comprehension of whole texts. The top-down (reader-based) model proceeds from reading whole texts in which readers use informed guesses and proceed to parts as they verify their guesses. An interactive (a combination of bottom-up and top-down) model visualizes readers as using parallel processes that use both skills and more holistic approaches.

These models of the reading process influence the approaches to reading instruction. Both the phonics and sub-skills approaches have characteristics found in the bottom-up models. The whole language approach emphasizes both a child's language and background knowledge in an approach that is similar to the top-down model. The literature-based approach uses quality literature to teach students to analyze and respond to their reading. A balanced approach is an interactive model that balances reading instruction between the best components of skills and literature approaches.

Theories of learning provide the underpinnings for the various reading processes and approaches. These influential theories of learning include behaviorist theory, cognitive development theory, sociolinguistic theory, and reader response theory.

Basal reading instruction has changed over the past century. The basal readers reflect different philosophies about how reading should be taught.

A history of basal reading series provides insights into changing trends in reading education. Within each approach to reading there are instructional techniques that are used to enhance children's reading skills and comprehension abilities.

Reading assessment is an important consideration especially when the No Child Left Behind legislation mandates that reading achievement will be assessed and schools will be held accountable for providing quality reading instruction. One of the consequences for mandates on reading is teacher reform.

We are currently living in a time when there are numerous disagreements about how reading is taught. There is also considerable diversity in the classroom. It is also an exciting time for teachers as they prepare readers to face the challenges of the twenty-first century.

Key Terms

bottom-up model, p. 8

top-down model, p. 9

interactive model, p. 9

balanced reading approaches, p. 11

phonics approaches, p. 12

sub-skills approaches, p. 13

whole language approaches, p. 15

literature-based approaches, p. 16

behaviorist theory of learning, p. 20

cognitive development theory of learning, p. 20

schema theory, p. 20

sociolinguistic theory of learning, p. 21

reader response theory, p. 22

basal readers, p. 24

No Child Left Behind, p. 35

differentiating instruction, p. 39

> For authentic classroom videos, online case studies, and grade-level appropriate classroom activities, go to Allyn & Bacon's MyLabSchool.com, and choose your course from among Reading Methods, Language Arts, Content Area Reading, or one of the many others.

Extend Your Reading

1. Search through current newspapers and locate articles that discuss issues of teaching reading in your city or state. Share these articles with your reading class.

2. Search the Internet for examples of requirements for teachers of reading in your state and community. What standards are recommended by the administrators in your state? How do these standards match recommendations by the International

Reading Association? What standards do you believe are necessary for your own education?

3. Compare a basal series that uses considerable reading through literature with a basal series that teaches through a phonics approach. How is beginning reading taught in each basal? What do you feel are the strengths and weaknesses of each basal?

For Further Reading

1. To gain an international perspective on the history of reading read John Dixon's article (2003) "Historical Considerations: An International Perspective," in James Flood, Diane Lapp, James R. Squire, & Julie M. Jensen (Eds.), *Handbook of Research on Teaching the English Language Arts*, 2nd ed. Mahwah, NJ: Lawrence Erlbaum, 18–23.

2. To develop an understanding of the impact of education reforms read Margaret Taylor Stewart's article (2004), "Early Literacy Instruction in the Climate of No Child Left Behind," in *The Reading Teacher*, 57, 732–743.

3. To develop an understanding of reader response theory as it relates to multicultural literature, read Janice Hartwick Dressel's article (2005), "Personal Response and Social Responsibility: Responses of Middle School Students to Multicultural Literature," in *The Reading Teacher*, 58, 750–764.

4. To discover more about the issues associated with assessment, read Marcia A. Invernizzi, Timothey J. Landrum, Jennifer L. Howell, and Heather P. Warley's (2005), "Toward the Peaceful Coexistence of Test Developers, Policymakers, and Teachers in an Era of Accountability," in *The Reading Teacher*, 58, 610–618.

REFERENCES

Anderson, Richard C. (1985). "Role of Reader's Schema in Comprehension, Learning, and Memory." In Harry Singer & Robert B. Ruddell (Eds.), *Theoretical Models and Processes of Reading*, 3rd ed. Newark, DE: International Reading Association, pp. 372–384.

Arnold, Mathew. (1895). *The Study of Poetry, Essays in Criticism: Second Series*. London: Macmillan.

Arnold, Sarah, & Gilbert, Charles B. (1902). *Stepping Stones to Literature: A Second Reader*. New York: Silver Burdett.

Bacon, Francis. (1625). "Of Studies." *Essayes or Counsels*. London.

Bauer, Susan Wise. (2003). *The Well-Educated Mind: A Guide to the Classical Education You Never Had*. New York: W.W. Norton.

Baumann, James F., Hoffman, James V., Duffy-Hester, Ann M., & Ro, Jennifer Moon. (July/August/September 2000). "The First R Yesterday and Today: U.S. Elementary Reading Instruction Practices Reported by Teachers and Administrators." *Reading Research Quarterly*, 35, 338–377.

Bond, Guy, & Dykstra, Robert. (1967). "The Cooperative Research Programs in First-Grade Instruction." *Reading Research Quarterly*, 2, 5–7.

Burns, Paul C., Roe, Betty D., & Smith, Sandy H. (2002). *Teaching Reading in Today's Elementary Schools*. Boston: Houghton Mifflin.

Dahl, Karin L., Sharer, Patricia L., Lora, L., & Grogan, Patricia R. (2003). "Student Achievement and Classroom Case Studies in Phonics in Whole Language First Grades." In James Flood, Diane Lapp, James R. Squire, & Julie M. Jensen (Eds.), *Handbook of Research on Teaching the English Language Arts,* 2nd ed. Mahwah, NJ: Lawrence Erlbaum.

Dutro, Elizabeth, Kazemi, Elham, & Balf, Ruth. (November 2005). "The Aftermath of 'You're Only Half': Multiracial Identities in the Literacy Classroom." *Language Arts, 83,* 96–106.

Elson, William H., & Gray, William S. (1931). *Elson Basic Readers, Book Five*. Chicago: Scott Foresman.

Fogarty, Robin. (2001). "Our Changing Perspective of Intelligence: Master Architects of the Intellect." In Arthur L. Costa (Ed.), *Developing Minds: A Resource Book for Teaching Thinking,* 3rd ed. Alexandria, VA: Association for Supervision and Curriculum Development, pp. 144–149.

Fogg, Piper. (19 September, 2002). "Carnegie Corporation Calls for Major Reforms in Teacher Education." *The Chronicle of Higher Education, 4.*

Frye, Northrop. (1964). *The Educated Imagination*. Bloomington: Indiana University Press.

Goodman, Kenneth S., ed. (1998). *In Defense of Good Teaching: What Teachers Need to Know about Reading Wars*. York, ME: Stenham.

Gove, Mary. (1983). "Clarifying Teachers' Beliefs about Reading. *The Reading Teacher, 37,* 261–268.

Graves, Donald H. (April/May 2002). "When Testing Lowers Standards." *Reading Today,* 19–20.

Gregorian, V. (2001). "Teacher Education Must Become Colleges' Central Preoccupation." *The Chronicle of Higher Education.* Accessed online at http://chronicle.com/weekly/v47/i49/49b00701.htm.

Harris, Peggy. (March 2006). "NCTE Members Seek to Influence NCLB Reauthorization." 15, 1, 4.

Hartocollis, Anemona. (21 July, 2005). "Who Needs Education Schools?" *New York Times Education Life,* pp. 24–28.

Hay, Julie, & Wingo, Charles E. (1948). *Reading with Phonics*. Philadelphia: J. B. Lippincott.

Hoffman, James, & Pearson, P. David. (January/February/March 2000). "Reading Teacher Education in the Next Millennium: What Your Grandmother's Teacher Didn't Know That Your Granddaughter's Teacher Should." *Reading Research Quarterly, 35,* 28–44.

Lenters, Kimberly. (December 2004/January 2005). "No Half Measures: Reading Instruction for Your Second-Language Learners." *The Reading Teacher, 58,* 328–336.

McGuffey. (1921). *McGuffey's Sixth Eclectic Reader*. New York: American Book Company.

McMackin, Mary C., & Witherell, Nancy L. (November 2005). "Different Routes to the Same Destination: Drawing Conclusions with Tiered Graphic Organizers." *The Reading Teacher, 59,* 242–252.

Morrow, Lesley Mandel. (1996). *Literacy Development in the Early Years,* 3rd ed. Boston: Allyn & Bacon.

National Assessment Governing Board. (2004). *Reading Framework for the 2009 National Assessment of Educational Progress*. Washington, DC: American Institutes for Research.

Norton, Donna E. (2007). *Through the Eyes of a Child: An Introduction to Children's Literature,* 7th ed. Upper Saddle River, NJ: Merrill/Prentice Hall.

Peregoy, Suzanne F., & Boyle, Owen F. (2001). *Reading, Writing, and Learning in ESL,* 3rd ed. New York: Longman.

Piaget, Jean, & Inhelder, B. (1969). *The Psychology of the Child*. New York: Basic Books.

Probst, Robert. (1989). "Teaching the Reading of Literature." In James Flood, Diane Lapp, & N. Farnan (Eds.), *Content Reading and Learning: Instructional Strategies*. Englewood Cliffs, NJ: Prentice Hall, pp. 179–186.

Purves, A., & Monson, Diane. (1984). *Experiencing Children's Literature*. Glenview, IL: Scott Foresman.

Raphael, Taffy E., & Au, Kathryn H. (November 2005). "QAR: Enhancing Comprehension and Test Taking Across Grades and Content Areas." *The Reading Teacher, 59,* 206–221.

Reutzel, D. Ray, & Cooter, Robert B. (2000). *Making a Difference Means Making It Different: Honoring Children's Rights to Excellent Reading Instruction*. Newark, DE: International Reading Association.

Rosenblatt, Louise. (1968). *Literature as Exploration*. New York: Noble and Noble.

Rosenblatt, Louise. (1985). "Language, Literature, and Values," In S. N. Tichudi (Ed.), *Language, Schooling, and Society*. Upper Montclair, NJ: Boyton/Cook, pp. 64–80.

Rosenblatt, Louise. (2003). "Literary Theory." In James Flood, Diane Lapp, James R. Squire, & Julie M. Jensen (Eds.), *Handbook of Research on Teaching the English Language Arts,* 2nd ed. Mahwah, NJ: Lawrence Erlbaum.

Rumelhart, David. (1976). *Toward an Interactive Model of Reading*. San Diego: University of California Center for Human Information Processing.

Samuels, S. J. (1994). "Toward a theory of automatic information processing in reading, revisited." In R. B. Ruddell, M. R. Ruddell, & H. Singer (Eds.), *Theoretical*

Models and Processes of Reading, 4th ed. Newark, DE: International Reading Association, pp. 816–837.

Schemo, Diana Jean, & Fessenden, Ford. (3 December, 2003). "Gains in Houston Schools: How Real Are They?" *New York Times,* A1, A27.

Short, Kathy G., Schroeder, Jean, Kauffman, Gloria, & Kaser, Sandy. (March 2006). "Thoughts from the Editors." *Language Arts,* 83, 287.

Singer, Harry. (1985). "A Century of Landmarks in Reading Research." In Harry Singer & Robert B. Ruddell (Eds.), *Theoretical Models and Processes of Reading,* 3rd ed. Newark, DE: International Reading Association, pp. 8–12.

Skinner, B. F. (1968). *The Technology of Teaching.* New York: Appleton-Century Crafts.

Smith, Richard, & Otto, Wayne. (1970). *Administering the School Reading Program.* Boston: Houghton Mifflin.

Squire, James R. (2003). "The History of the Profession." In James Flood, Diane Lapp, James R. Squire,

& Julie M. Jensen (Eds.), *Handbook of Research on Teaching the English Language Arts,* 2nd ed. Mahwah, NJ: Lawrence Erlbaum, pp. 3–17.

Tharp, R. (1997). *From At-Risk to Excellence: Research Theory and Principles for Practice.* Santa Cruz, CA: Center for Research on Education, Diversity and Excellence.

Tomlinson, C. A. (1999). *The Differentiated Classroom: Responding to the Needs of All Learners.* Alexandria, VA: Association for Supervision and Curriculum Development.

Vygotsky, Lev. (1981). "The Genius of Higher Mental Functions," in J. J. Wertch (Ed.), *The Concept of Activity.* White Plains, NY: M. E. Sharpe.

Waugh, Joyce Clark. (1993). "Using LEA in Diagnosis." *Journal of Reading,* 37, 56–57.

Winerip, Michael. (5 October, 2005). "Secret to Better Scores: Making the Reading Tests Easier." *New York Times,* A23.

Children's Literature References

Armstrong, Alan. (2005). *Whittington.* Illustrated by S. D. Schindler. Random House.

Arnold, Adoff. (1973). *Black Is White Is Tan.* Harper & Row.

Alexander, Lloyd. (1964). *The Book of Three.* Henry Holt.

Arnosky, Jim. (2006). *Grandfather Buffalo.* Putnam.

Brink, Carol Ryrie. *Caddie Woodlawn.* (1935). Illustrated by Trina Schart Hyman. Macmillan.

Cleary, Beverly. (1975). *Ramona the Brave.* Illustrated by Alan Tiegreen. William Morrow.

Cleary, Beverly. (1979) *Ramona and Her Father.* Illustrated by Alan Tiegreen. William Morrow.

Cooper, Susan. (1973). *The Dark Is Rising.* Atheneum.

dePaola, Tomie. (1980). *The Lady of Guadalupe.* Holiday House.

Dicamillo, Kate. (2006). *The Miraculous Journey of Edward Tulane.* Illustrated by Begram Ibatoulline. Candlewick.

Ehlert, Lois. (1997). *Cuckoo: A Mexican Folktale.* Translated into Spanish by Gloria de Aragon Andujar. Harcourt.

Funke, Cornelia. (2004). *Dragon Rider.* Scholastic.

Grahame, Kenneth. (1908, 1940). *The Wind in the Willows.* Scribners.

Hoose, Phillip. (2004). *The Race to Save the Lord God Bird.* Farrar, Straus & Giroux.

Knutson, Barbara. (2004). *Love and Roast Chicken: A Trickster Tale from the Andes Mountains.* Carolrhoda.

Lobel, Arnold. (1970). *Frog and Toad Are Friends.* Harper & Row.

MacLachlan, Patricia. (1985). *Sarah, Plain and Tall.* Harper & Row.

Murphy, Jim. (2003). *An American Plague: The True and Terrifying Story of the Yellow Fever Epidemic of 1793.* Clarion.

Nesbit, E. (1907). *Beautiful Stories from Shakespeare, a Facsimile of the 1907 Edition.* Weathervane Books.

Packer, Tina. (2004). *Tales from Shakespeare.* Scholastic.

Paolini, Christopher. (2005). *Eldest.* Knopf.

Paolini, Christopher. (2003). *Eragon.* Knopf.

Rowling, J. K. (2005) *Harry Potter and the Half-Blood Prince.* Scholastic.

Rowling, J. K. (1998). *Harry Potter and the Sorcerer's Stone.* Scholastic.

Schaefer, Lola M. (2004). *Arrowhawk.* Illustrated by Gabi Swiakowska. Henry Holt.

Seuss, Dr. (1957). *The Cat in the Hat.* Random House.

Shea, Pegi Deitz. (2003). *Tangled Threads: A Hmong Girl's Story*. Clarion.

Sheth, Kashmira. (2004). *Blue Jasmine*. Hyperion.

Tolkien, J. R. R. (1938). *The Hobbit*. Houghton Mifflin.

White, E. B. (1952). *Charlotte's Web*. Illustrated by Garth Williams. Harper & Row.

Wilder, Laura Ingalls. (1932). *Little House in the Big Woods*. Harper & Row.

Emergent Literacy, Language Development, and Cognitive Development

CHAPTER **OUTLINE**

Emergent Literacy
  Creating an Environment for Emergent Literacy

Characteristics of Language Development in Early Childhood

Techniques That Enhance Language Development in Early Elementary Grades
  Informal Conversations
  Reading Aloud to Children
  Storytelling
  Creative Drama
  Creating a "Best Books" List for Emergent Literacy Students

Children's Cognitive Development in Lower Elementary Grades
  Cognitive Development for Social Studies in Lower Elementary Grades

Language Development and Cognitive Development in the Middle and Upper Elementary Grades
  Characteristics of Language Development in Middle and Upper Elementary Grades
  Techniques That Enhance Language Development in Middle and Upper Elementary Grades
  Characteristics of Cognitive Development in Middle and Upper Elementary Grades

Cognitive Development for Social Studies in the Upper Elementary and Middle School

After reading this chapter you will be able to answer the following questions:

1. What is emergent literacy and what are the characteristics of an environment that fosters emergent literacy?
2. What are the characteristics of language development in the early grades and what are the techniques that enhance this development?
3. What are the characteristics of cognitive development in the early grades and what are the techniques that enhance this cognitive development?
4. What are the characteristics of language development in middle and upper elementary grades (fourth through eighth grades) and what are the techniques that enhance this development?
5. What are the characteristics of cognitive development in middle and upper elementary grades (fourth through eighth grades) and what are the techniques that enhance this development?

Read All About It!

"We're Bookworms! Madison, in recent study, ranks fourth in nation for having outstanding reading culture"

by Brenda Ingersoll, *Wisconsin State Journal*, Madison Wisconsin, August 4, 2004

Madison is a reading town where "books are still important," city Library Director Barbara Dimick said Tuesday after hearing that Madison, Wisconsin, ranks fourth in the nation for having a vibrant reading culture.

The new study—America's Most Literate Cities 2004—ranked the nation's seventy-nine cities with populations of 200,000 or more. Compiled by Jack Miller, Chancellor of the University of Wisconsin—Whitewater, the study looked at five factors: citizens' educational attainment, newspaper circulation rates, library resources, the number of magazines and journals published, and number of booksellers to develop each city's reading profile. Madison was fourth after Minneapolis, Seattle, and Pittsburgh.

"We measure reading in this country almost exclusively by school test scores, rather than looking at the real goal of whether we're encouraging life-long reading habits in people," Miller says. "This study looks at a city's overall investment in that goal, and many things, like library resources, are factors they can control. . . ."

But Greg Markle, executive director of the Madison Area Literacy Council, says the study is flawed because it doesn't examine literacy levels. "Literacy is measured by a person's ability to read, write and understand the language, and a better measurement of literacy in a community is the functional literacy rate of its individuals," says Markle.

Miller responds that the study was not intended to be a measure of functional literacy. "It's a study not of whether people can read, but whether they do," he says. "I agree with Markle wholeheartedly that there are a lot of adults out there who can't read."

The library's Dimick says the study is no surprise. "We do our own studies and compare our library's performance with libraries in cities of comparable size. We're always way up there in terms of library visits per capita."

And Madison parents know it's important to read to their children, Dimick says. "People here understand the importance of establishing a love of books early in life, so they read to their children and bring them to story time at the public library" (p. 1, A7).

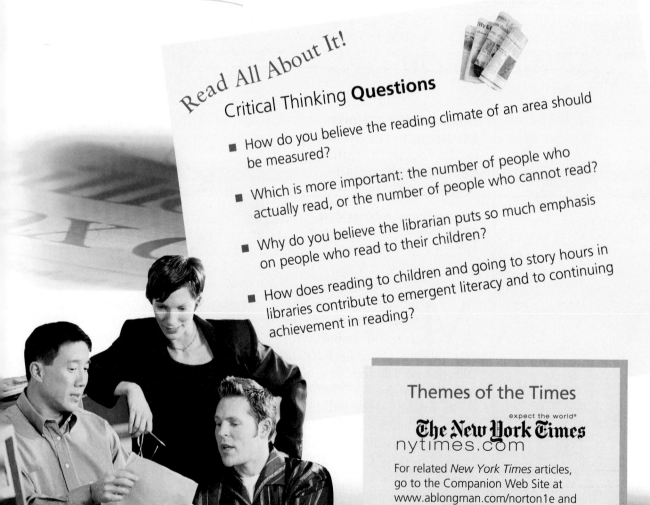

Read All About It!

Critical Thinking **Questions**

- How do you believe the reading climate of an area should be measured?

- Which is more important: the number of people who actually read, or the number of people who cannot read?

- Why do you believe the librarian puts so much emphasis on people who read to their children?

- How does reading to children and going to story hours in libraries contribute to emergent literacy and to continuing achievement in reading?

The "Read All About It" article emphasizes the importance of developing a climate that encourages even young children to appreciate reading and writing and to understand the importance of language. When reviewing the building blocks essential for effective reading instruction discussed in the previous chapter, we discover the importance of creating a climate that develops both language skills and cognitive capabilities. These building blocks are the foundations of reading that include children's abilities to sound out words and to comprehend the meaning of the words when they are combined into sentences, paragraphs, and stories. To create these building blocks requires the nurturing of language growth. This foundational knowledge ideally expands into students' critical thinking and analytical skills as they use their language and background knowledge to help them recognize words, understand the meanings of the words and sentences, and critically evaluate what they read. It is their cognitive development that influences their ability to learn and to make decisions about what they read, or in the case of young children, what they hear and see.

Young children begin to develop language and cognitive skills long before they start formal reading instruction in school. They learn to speak and increase their vocabularies as adults reinforce their growing language capabilities by talking to them, by reading stories aloud that highlight word meanings and provide models for language development, and by encouraging them to ask questions and to think about the world around them.

Educators of young children who focus on development from birth to lower elementary grades use the term **emergent literacy** to emphasize the process associated with gaining the concepts and knowledge base required for reading and writing. Researchers have spent considerable time identifying children's language and cognitive development related to specific age levels and stressing the types of instructional activities that nurture the development of literacy.

Many educators who develop instructional programs designed to increase children's emergent literacy emphasize the importance of understanding both children's language and cognitive development. Patrick Finn (1985), for example, maintains that language learning should not be conducted in isolation, but should allow children to grow in both their use of language and their ability to understand concepts and ideas. Cathy Collins Block (2001) emphasizes that instructional programs in reading should foster parallel development in thinking and reading.

Marie M. Clay (2002) makes the connection between language and cognitive development when she emphasizes that the foundations for language acquisition are laid long before children enter school. In her view, "Preschoolers use it [language] to code cognitive stores of information and acquire processes for accessing that information. They devise order and structure for language from massively different and diverse samples, test and refine their values for production, and are barely conscious of any of these processes" (p. 47). Clay makes further connections between language and cognitive development when she relates children's processing strategies to Piaget's theory of cognitive development and the development of schemas.

Effective classrooms create environments that encourage students to have positive attitudes toward books and reading and to gain awareness about the nature of and the purposes for written language. Language development is important at all levels of education, from the preschool child learning to understand words and using the rules of language to the upper elementary child using complex sentences in both speaking and writing. Fostering cognitive development is equally important, from the preschool child who is discovering ways to organize and classify words to the upper elementary child who is able to apply reasoning to abstract problems. In this chapter we will first focus on the child from birth through lower elementary grades and consider how to foster emergent literacy, especially through children's language and cognitive development. We will then consider how language and cognitive development are nurtured in the middle and upper elementary grades.

Emergent Literacy

Emergent literacy involves children's understanding that text conveys language, print has meaning, spoken language can be represented through print, written language has consistent letter sound relationships, and stories have structures such as beginnings, middles, and endings. Obtaining these understandings, however, is not automatic for all children. To learn more about emergent literacy, educators investigate both the characteristics of children's early home life that promote literacy and the characteristics of young children at various age levels. They try to identify literacy behaviors that are found in most children at approximate stages in their development. These types of studies are important for the teachers of young children.

To learn more about the importance of the environment on emergent literacy, educators may search for characteristics of parental interactions with children and home environments that promote literacy. Pia Rebello Britto, Jeanne Brooks-Gunn, and Terri M. Griffin (2006) summarize studies that show that parent-child interactions in the home are associated with school readiness. For example, these studies suggest that (1) children who are exposed to a rich verbal environment demonstrate better vocabulary skills in early childhood; (2) shared book reading between parents and children is associated with language development, reading ability, and school achievement; and (3) interactions that emphasize problem solving are associated with school readiness.

The second type of investigation into emergent literacy searches for examples of the reading and writing behaviors of young children that precede literacy. Educators who study early literacy frequently define the period of emergent literacy as infancy to about age seven. They study children's responses during literacy development and identify literacy characteristics. For example, Elizabeth Sulzby (1991) investigated emergent literacy behaviors connected with storybook reading and writing. She found that storybook reading behaviors of young children include pretending to read and turning pages as they "read." They may recognize some of the letters of the alphabet and begin to identify words on familiar labels such as names of cereals and signs such as stop signs. One of the most effective activities to foster emergent literacy of reading is to read orally to children. Consequently, sharing books orally is a major technique developed in this chapter.

When emergent literacy begins in writing, children may make scribbling motions that they call writing. Sulzby's studies identified the sequence in emergent writing as proceeding from scribbling, drawing, nonphonetic letterstrings, invented spelling, and finally to conventional spelling. Sulzby found that scribbling begins between twelve and eighteen months. Drawing and writing that resembles scribbling begins between two and three years. Sometime between the ages of three and four children begin to write with letters. Invented spellings appear (children create their own spellings by using their own understandings of the sounds of words) during kindergarten and first grade.

Catherine E. Snow, M. Susan Burns, and Peg Griffin (2001) review research that indicates the accomplishments that a successful learner is likely to exhibit during the preschool years. They observe that the accomplishments shown in Table 2.1 "capture many highlights of the course of literacy acquisition that have been revealed through several decades of research. Needless to say, the timing of these accomplishments will to some extent depend on maturational and experiential differences between children" (p. 60). Table 2.1 summarizes the results of their research.

By reviewing these accomplishments of successful learners we gain insight into the importance of creating a learning environment that enhances both language and cognitive development. Language development is enhanced, for example, by allowing children to enjoy rhyming language, listen to stories, attend to beginning or rhyming sounds in words, and show interest in books and reading. **Cognitive development** is enhanced when children label objects, comment on the qualities of characters in books, understand that pictures in books are symbols for real objects, understand that different text forms are used for different functions of print, follow oral directions, make connections between events in a story and life experiences, and understand literal meanings in stories.

Creating an environment that fosters emergent literacy enhances both emergent storybook reading and emergent writing. Consequently, we will consider how to create this environment and then discuss some observational guidelines that may be used to assess emergent literacy in young children.

A rich environment for emergent literacy provides many opportunities for reading and other literacy activities.

TABLE 2.1

Developmental Accomplishments of Literacy Acquisition

Birth to Three-Year-Old Accomplishments

- Recognizes specific books by cover.
- Pretends to read books.
- Understands that books are handled in particular ways.
- Enters into a book-sharing routine with primary caregivers.
- Vocalization play in crib gives way to enjoyment of rhyming language, nonsense word play, etc.
- Labels objects in books.
- Comments on characters in books.
- Looks at picture in book and realizes it is a symbol for real object.
- Listens to stories.
- Requests/commands adult to read or write.
- May begin attending to specific print such as letters in names.
- Uses increasingly purposive scribbling.
- Occasionally seems to distinguish between drawing and writing.
- Produces some letter-like forms and scribbles with some features of English writing.

Three- and Four-Year-Old Accomplishments

- Knows that alphabet letters are a special category of visual graphics that can be individually named.
- Recognizes local environmental print.
- Knows that it is the print that is read in stories.
- Understands that different text forms are used for different functions of print (e.g., list for groceries).
- Pays attention to separable and repeating sounds in language (e.g., Peter, Peter, Pumpkin Eater, Peter Eater).
- Uses new vocabulary and grammatical constructions in own speech.
- Understands and follows oral directions.
- Is sensitive to some sequences of events in stories.
- Shows an interest in books and reading.
- When being read a story, connects information and events to life experiences.
- Questions and comments demonstrate understanding of literal meaning of story being told.
- Displays reading and writing attempts, calling attention to self. "Look at my story."
- Can identify 10 alphabet letters, especially those from own name.
- "Writes" (scribbles) message as part of playful activity.
- May begin to attend to beginning or rhyming sound in salient words.

Creating an Environment for Emergent Literacy

Notice in the following description of an effective classroom for reading instruction how Patricia Cunningham and Richard Allington (2003) characterize learning in a classroom for lower elementary students:

> Walk into a classroom where all the children are destined to succeed in learning to read and write and what do you see? There will be lots of books and other reading materials, along with evidence that the teacher and the children read and write. . . . Ask yourself, "How much time will the teacher and the children spend reading and writing real things?" Notice that the teacher reads a variety of real things to the children at different points in the day—not just a story after lunch. (p. 1)

These authors continue to describe an environment that is rich in books and that includes captions under pictures and labels on items. The books are available to be read to children and for self-selected reading. Children introduce and discuss books they are reading. Their writings are displayed throughout the room.

Another description of **literacy-rich environment** is found in the Primary Years Program (ages three to nine) for the International schools (2003). This description indicates a language-rich environment that fosters inquiry up through age nine:

> The Primary Years language classroom is a place where language is clearly in evidence in all its forms. There is a busy hum of discussion. The observer is tempted by the inviting book corner which is well stocked with reference books, picture books, story books, poetry books, students' self-made books and books in a variety of languages. Displays include a wide variety of print including students' writing, author of the month, questions, information and artifacts from the current unit of inquiry, posters, charts, calendars, memoranda, and instructions. The listening center is freely accessible, with a range of high-quality fiction and non-fiction audiocassettes. The clearly labeled writing center has a variety of materials and equipment, a word processor and printer, different types of paper, envelopes, blank forms, cards, bookbinding tape and ready-made blank books. (p. 2.3)

The Primary Years Program also describes student actions as younger students are involved in reading and independent writing while older students are involved in the writing process, which includes drafting, revising and editing imaginative stories, expressive poetry, science reports, personal journals, and reading responses.

The teachers in the Primary Years Program use a range of teaching strategies including individual, group, and whole-class instruction. Literature is an integral part of the curriculum. Books are read as author studies, fairy tales become part of social studies units, biographies are used to introduce science investigations, counting stories are used to reinforce mathematics, and comparisons are made of illustration techniques that encourage art skills as well as higher-level thinking abilities. Books are to be enjoyed, discussed, analyzed, created, compared, and contrasted.

Reflect on Your Reading

Based on these two descriptions of effective classrooms, what are the characteristics that make them effective? What are the characteristics of children who are fortunate enough to be in these classrooms? What knowledge and understanding about literacy are they gaining? What skills and understandings are required by the teacher in order to create this learning environment?

Characteristics of Language Development in Early Childhood

Promoting **language development** in children is considered one of the most vital goals of early childhood education. Researchers such as Dorothy Strickland and Joan T. Feeley (2003) believe that

> teachers' knowledge about language learning is a major source of empowerment. It enables them to take control over methods and materials and to make informed curricular decisions. . . . It is our belief that a better understanding of children as language learners will lead to improved classroom instructional practices. (p. 339)

The first few years of life produce dramatic changes in language development. During this time children progress from vocalizing sounds to creating meaningful language. Children usually speak their first word at about one year of age. At about eighteen months, they usually place two words together. By age three they have added adverbs, pronouns, and prepositions to their vocabularies. A three-year-old enjoys playing with the sounds of words. By four, most children produce sentences that are grammatically correct. The four-year-old usually asks many questions and wants to understand why and how.

Walter Loban's (1976) **longitudinal study** of language is considered by many to be the most extensive and useful study of language in school-age children. Loban examined the stages in language development of children over an extended period of time. He identified differences between students who ranked high in language proficiency and those who ranked low, and stressed the benefits of using taped oral language samples rather than published language tests. (Taped oral samples are recordings that show exactly how children speak in a variety of situations.)

Loban's findings related to differences between high and low proficiency in children's language provide guidance for teachers who are evaluating children's language development and providing instruction. First, children who demonstrated high language proficiency excelled in their abilities to express ideas. Both speech and writing showed consistency in planning. They spoke freely and fluently. The high group had reached a level of oral proficiency in first grade that the lower group did not obtain until the sixth grade. The lower group's oral communication was characterized by rambling and limited vocabulary.

In writing, students in the high group expressed their ideas with fluidity, used more words per sentence, and showed a richer vocabulary. The fourth-grade level of proficiency shown by the high group was not shown by the low group until the tenth grade. Children who were superior in oral language in kindergarten and first grade excelled in both reading and writing in the sixth grade. Consequently, instruction that emphasizes oral language in the early grades is beneficial for all students.

Although the rate of language development differs, Table 2.2 will help you visualize the approximate language development common to many children at specific age levels and identify some of the books that help foster language development.

Reflect on Your Reading

Consider the differences among the different age levels. What happens as a child's language development matures? Look at the characteristics of the books recommended for the youngest levels (ages two to three) and compare them with the characteristics of books recommended for older levels (ages eight to nine). Why are there such differences in the characteristics of the books recommended for language development?

TABLE 2.2

General Language Characteristics and Implications

Preschool: Ages 2–3: Very rapid language growth. Vocabularies of about 900 words. They use simple and compound sentences and understand tense and numerical concepts such as *many* and *few.* They learn to identify actions in pictures and large and small body parts.

Implications for Teaching Emergent Literacy: Encourage children to identify, describe, and imitate actions in real life and in picture books such as Denise Fleming's *In the Tall, Tall Grass* (1991), Joy Cowley's *Mrs. Wishy-Washy's Scrubbing Machine* (2005), Julie Markes's *Shhhh! Everybody's Sleeping* (2005) and Julian Russell's *Busy Dog* (2005).

Preschool: Ages 3–4: Vocabularies have increased to about 1,500 words. The verb past tense appears. Children understand numerical concepts such as *one, two,* and *three.* They use more adjectives, adverbs, pronouns, and prepositions.

Implications for Teaching Emergent Literacy: Allow children to listen to and interact with nursery rhymes, poetry, and riddles. Discuss what children did yesterday and allow them to tell about their environments. Read and discuss books such as Kevin Henkes's *Kitten's First Full Moon* (2004). Suse MacDonald's illustrations of Edward Lear's *A Was Once An Apple Pie* (2005), Lauren Thompson's *Polar Bear Night* (2004), Rosemary Wells's *Bunny Mail: A Max and Ruby Lift-Flap Book* (2004), Mo Willems's *Knuffle Bunny: A Cautionary Tale* (2004), and Jean Van Leewen's *Benny & Beautiful Delilah* (2006).

Preschool: Ages 4–5: Language is more abstract and children produce grammatically correct sentences. Vocabularies include about 2,500 words. They understand prepositions such as *over, under, in* and *out.* They enjoy asking questions about why things happen and how things work.

Implications for Teaching Emergent Literacy: Share and discuss books with more complex plots, have them retell folktales, and provide opportunities to tell stories from wordless books such as Barbara Lehman's *The Red Book* (2004), Laura Vaccaro Seeger's *Lemons Are Not Red* (2004) and David Wiesner's *Free Fall* (1988) and *Tuesday* (1991). Read and discuss books that allow children to search for answers to questions such as Millicent E. Selsam and Joyce Hunt's *A First Look at Caterpillars* (1987).

Preschool–Kindergarten: Ages 5–6: Most children use complex sentences. They understand about 6,000 words and begin to use correct pronouns and verbs. The average number of words per oral sentence is 6.8. They are curious about the written appearance of language and they enjoy taking part in dramatic play.

Implications for Teaching Emergent Literacy: Read and discuss books such as Jane Dyer's *Little Brown Bear Won't Go To School* (2003), Wanda Gag's *Millions of Cats* (1928, 1977), Dr. Seuss's *And to Think That I Saw It on Mulberry Street* (1937), and Rosemary Wells's *Yoko's World of Kindness: Golden Rules for a Happy Class* (2005). Write chart stories that allow children to see their stories placed into written form. Have children reread the chart stories.

Early Elementary: Ages 6–7: Children are speaking in complex sentences that use adjective clauses. They begin to use conditional clauses beginning with *if.* Their language is more symbolic. They begin to read, write, and understand concepts of time and seasons. The average sentence length is 7.5 words. They add many new words to their vocabularies.

Implications for Teaching Emerging Literacy: Read stories to and allow students to read stories independently that provide models for their expanding vocabularies and sentence structures such as Monica Brown's *My Name Is Gabriela: The Life of Gabriela Mistral* (2005), Kevin Henkes's *So Happy!* (2005), and Robert McCloskey's *Make Way for Ducklings* (1941). Encourage children to read easy-to-read books that expand their growing reading abilities such as Kate DiCamillo's *Mercy Watson to the Rescue* (2005), Doug Cushman's *Inspector Hopper's Mystery Year* (2003), Jean Little's *Emma's Strange Pet* (2003) and Cynthia Rylant's *Poppleton* (1997).

(Continued)

TABLE 2.2

(Continued)

Early Elementary: Ages 7–8: Children use relative pronouns. Most children use complex sentences. The average number of words per oral sentence is 7.6. The reading levels among children in second and third grades may vary dramatically. Some children are just beginning to read with understanding while other children are reading independently books appropriate for middle elementary grades.

Implications for Teaching Emerging Literacy: Continue reading books orally to children to provide models for language and reading. Read books such as Kelly Cunnane's *For You Are a Kenyan Child* (2006), Carolyn Curtis's *I Took the Moon for a Walk* (2004), Doreen Cronin's *Duck for President* (2004), Jill Esbaum's *Ste-e-e-e-eam Boat A Comin'!* (2005) and Meilo So's *Gobble, Gobble, Slip, Slop: A Tale of a Greedy Cat* (2004). Allow extensive free reading time during which children select and discuss books of their own choosing. Provide reading instruction that is based on the needs of the students.

Middle Elementary: Ages 8–9: Children begin to relate concepts to general ideas. Fifty percent of the children use the subordinating connector *although*. The average number of words in an oral sentence is 9.0. The range of reading abilities and interests continues to expand.

Implications for Teaching Emerging Literacy: Continue to read books orally to children in order to model reading and language. Many Newbery Award books such as Patricia MacLachlan's *Sarah, Plain and Tall* (1985), Cynthia Kadohata's *Kira-Kira* (2004), and classics in literature such as Natalie Babbitt's *Tuck Everlasting* (1975) provide sources for reading orally. Discuss children's interests and provide books that motivate and expand the interests. Use techniques such as modeling, drawing plot structures, and webbing to enhance comprehension. (These techniques are developed later in this text.)

Source: This table was compiled from studies by Bartel (1995), Brown (1973), Hendrick (1996), Loban (1976), and Norton (2004).

Techniques That Enhance Language Development in Early Elementary Grades

Classrooms that nurture emergent literacy through language development are rich in oral language activities that encourage children to use and expand their language. In this climate children need many different types of language activities that allow them to practice communication and to gain confidence in their language development (Barr, 2002; Jewel, 2002). In language-rich classrooms children are asked to actively think about their language. Oral language is enhanced, according to Gay Su Pinnell and Angela M. Jaggar (2003), by activities such as informal conversation, storytelling, creative dramatics (including pantomime and puppetry), role playing, and improvisation.

Notice in this list of effective activities that there are also close connections between speaking and listening. Consequently, to be effective learners students also need to be in classrooms that promote children's abilities to listen for specific purposes, such as to retell a story read by the teacher or to role-play a character. This section will consider how teachers can develop strategies for informal conversations, reading aloud to children, storytelling by both teachers and children, creative dramatics, and role-playing.

Informal Conversations

This type of oral language activity enhances the social interactions among children and offers them opportunities to talk about things that are important to them. The conversations may be something that children do in a group such as in "Show and Tell" or may be between two children as in "Telephone Conversations."

SHOW AND TELL   This type of conversation is usually conducted in a circular or semicircular arrangement with the children sitting on chairs or on the floor. Show and Tell develops both the role of the speaker and the role of the listener. The speaker tells something of importance to him or her. The listeners learn to listen politely, but also to ask questions of the speaker.

Teachers may provide some structure to Show and Tell by asking students to bring an object such as a favorite toy from home, or a drawing of a toy they would like. Now each child, in turn, introduces the object and tells something about the object. If the child has difficulty talking about the object, the teacher may prompt additional conversations by asking questions such as, "What is the name of your toy? Who gave you the toy? Where does the toy stay when you come to school?" Children who are listening in the group may be invited to ask their own questions. In one kindergarten class this activity led to additional conversations when two children each brought teddy bears. They created conversations between the two bears that extended into recess.

Teachers may use many creative ideas to accompany Show and Tell. For example, in autumn children could bring and describe a colored leaf they found on the way to school. They might bring a favorite book from home or the library. Or, they might share a favorite game. After students have had several opportunities to share in a group led by the teacher, they can divide into smaller group and take turns being the leader of the group who also asks the prompting questions.

TELEPHONE CONVERSATIONS   The two teddy bears example in the previous Show and Tell activity also led to conversations between the two characters on play telephones located in the classroom. These conversations may require role-playing as students practice how they might make a phone call to the fire department or to the police department in a time of emergency. In this type of conversation they discover the importance of giving details or asking questions about *who, what,* and *where.*

Some telephone conversations may be very imaginative as children role-play possible conversations with their favorite storybook characters such as "Winnie-the-Pooh" or "Little Red Riding Hood." These conversations are unstructured as children let their imaginations decide how they will respond when they play the different roles. For example, two very imaginative five-year-olds decided that they wanted to call "The Three Little Pigs" and warn them that the wolf was coming and to tell them what the wolf intended to do to the pigs' homes. Through their telephone conversation they became problem solvers and decided on novel solutions for the pigs' dilemma.

Reading Aloud to Children

Reading aloud to children encourages language development in both preschool and elementary level children. By reading orally to children, parents and teachers introduce children to the sounds of language, to the structures of literature, to the joys of reading and listening, and to the vast literary heritage that is found within the covers of books.

Steven Herb (1997) reviews research findings related to language development and reading to children and concludes that "Children's early experiences with books directly relate to their success in learning to read in school," and that "storybook reading is a more effective influence on literacy development when children have opportunities to engage in conversation about the story" (p. 23). June Brown (1999) emphasizes that because younger children's listening level is greater than their reading level, "reading aloud can build background knowledge, teach new words, and provide a positive role model. It also hooks children on quality literature, demonstrates the pleasure involved in the process, and motivates them to read alone" (p. 520).

When identifying best practices in elementary classrooms, Patricia M. Cunningham and Richard L. Allington (2003) identify oral reading to children as an important component for increasing literacy. They identify the following four types of materials that should be read to children daily: (1) informational material that is found in newspapers and nonfiction books; (2) literature that will become favorite choices for reading; (3) poetry, especially poems that encourage listeners to join in with rhyming elements and refrains; and (4) easy-to-read books that show reluctant readers the joy they will gain from reading.

SELECTING THE MATERIALS   By using these four types of literature, teachers will develop a balance in the materials read aloud. A selection of informational materials could include articles in children's magazines such as *Ranger Rick,* published by the National Wildlife Federation. Adult nonfiction magazines with excellent photographs are also favorites with many teachers. For example, almost any location being studied in social studies, geography, or a setting in a book can be found in *National Geographic.* Teachers in my classes have used *National Geographic* articles to accompany a reading and discussion of John Steptoe's *Mufaro's Beautiful Daughters* (1987). The photographs and text in "After Rhodesia, a Nation Named Zimbabwe" by Charles E. Cobb Jr. (November 1981) and "Rhodesia, a House Divided" by Alban C. Fisher (May 1975) provide photographs that could be compared with those illustrated by Steptoe. Lynne Warren's "The Magic of Snowy Owls" (December 2002) provides additional information for a study of owls, and John Hare's "Surviving the Sahara" (December 2002) provided pictorial descriptions of desert environments.

Many informational books may be read to children in the early elementary grades. Books such as Eve Bunting's *Butterfly House* (1999), Joy Cowley's *Red-Eyed Tree Frog* (1999), and Steve Jenkins's *Almost Gone: The World's Rarest Animals* (2006) appeal to younger listeners and introduce the excitement of listening to and reading informational books.

Examples of the second type of material that should be read daily include attractive picture story books for younger children such as Jane Yolan's

Owl Moon (1987) and the various Dr. Seuss books. Folktales such as Ed Young's *I, Doko: The Tale of a Basket* (2004), Barbara Knutson's *Love and Roast Chicken: A Trickster Tale from the Andes Mountains* (2004); and Nelson Mandela's *Nelson Mandela's Favorite African Folktales* (2005) add a multicultural understanding to reading aloud.

Poetry is the third source for daily reading aloud. Poetry was written to be read, reread, and shared aloud. The sounds, the rhythms, the vivid words, and the unexpected phrases lend themselves to oral reading. Poetry is available in collections by single poets such as Jack Prelutsky and Shell Silverstein. These often humorous and rhythmic poems are favorites of many younger children. Anthologies such as *Knock at a Star: A Child's Introduction to Poetry* (1999) and *Talking Like the Rain: A First Book of Poems* (1992) selected by X. J. and Dorothy M. Kennedy include poems to accompany many types of moods and subjects. Poems such as those found in Sharon Creech's *Who's That Baby?: New-Baby Songs* (2005) Eloise Greenfield's *In the Land of Words* (2004), and Jane Yolen's *This Little Piggy: Lap Songs, Finger Plays, Clapping Games, and Pantomime Rhymes* (2005) are especially good for reading to younger children. Creech's poetry celebrates love felt within the family when a new baby arrives. It lends itself to considerable conversations as children share their own experiences with babies. Greenfield's text includes poems such as "Nathaniel's Rap" that encourage children to interact with the poem by acting out the actions or repeating the rhyming words. Yolen's text includes simple musical arrangements for guitar and piano.

The final category of books to read aloud includes easier-to-read books that motivate children to try reading themselves. Arnold Lobel's easy-to-read books such as *Frog and Toad Are Friends* (1970), Sharleen Collicott's *Mildred and Sam* (2003), and Dr. Seuss's *The Cat in the Hat* (1957) are especially appealing to younger reluctant readers.

PREPARING TO READ ALOUD   Many teachers make the mistake of picking up a book to read to children without first reading the story aloud without an audience. Words that are difficult to pronounce, misinterpreting the mood of the story, or concepts that are too difficult for children to understand can cause embarrassment for the reader. Adults can read in front of a mirror or read into a tape recorder and then listen in order to practice and perfect their story reading style.

Poet Lee Bennett Hopkins (1987) provides the following suggestions for preparing and reading poetry to an audience:

1. Before reading a poem to an audience, read it aloud several times to get the feel of the words and the rhythm. Mark the words and phrases that you would like to emphasize.

2. Read the poem naturally, following the rhythm of the poem. Allow the physical appearance of the poem to dictate the rhythm and mood of the words. Some poems are meant to be read softly and slowly; others must be read at a more rapid pace.

3. Make pauses that make sense and that please you.

4. When reading a poem aloud, speak in a natural voice. Read a poem as though you were interested in the subject.

READING ALOUD   There are several guidelines that will help when developing the reading aloud experience. First, include eye contact between the reader and the audience. Second, read with expression rather than in a monotonous tone. Third, to improve an understanding of the vocabulary in the story, point to meaningful words or pictures in the book as it is being read rather than merely reading the story and showing the pictures. Fourth, select picture books that are large enough so children can see the text and the illustrations.

One method for adding interest to a reading aloud experience is to encourage children to join in the reading by asking them to join in during repetitive language or to fill in rhyming words. Texts such as "Slither-slee, slither, see, Down the branch and round the tree" (unnumbered) from Jane Yolen's *Off We Go!* (2000) are fun for joining in reciting the language. Phrases such as "Tip-toe, tippity toe," or "Scritch-scratch," encourage children to act out the story about going to Grandma's house. You can search for other picture books that encourage acting out the text, such as Lloyd Moss's *Zin! Zin! Zin! A Violin* (1995) and Helen Cooper's *Pumpkin Soup* (1999) and *A Pipkin of Pepper for the Pumpkin Soup* (2005).

Younger children also enjoy responding to the rhythms and sounds of poetry. Active poems such as jump-rope rhymes encourage them to become physically involved in the movement suggested by the poem. Read the rhyme first, asking the students to listen to the rhythm and the sound of the rhyme. Then read the rhyme again, asking the students to join in with movement and words.

Furthermore, children enjoy accompanying reading aloud with creative dramatizations. Such interactions heighten the levels of children's involvement with the text. Interaction also improves comprehension and listening ability. For example, while reading Michael Rosen's *We're Going on a Bear Hunt* (1989) to kindergarten or first-grade students, emphasize the repetitive language and the descriptive words. Show the students that the illustrator, Helen Oxenbury, places the repetitive verses on black-and-white backgrounds and the descriptive action words on colored back-

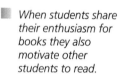

When students share their enthusiasm for books they also motivate other students to read.

grounds. Ask the students, "Why would an illustrator choose both black-and-white and colored backgrounds in the same book" and "How should we read this story to show the differences between black-and-white and colored backgrounds?" On the colored action pages, ask them to predict the sounds that the family will make as they go through each obstacle. Ask them to notice that each action is repeated three times and that each line increases in size. Ask the students, "Why would an author increase the size of the letters? How could we use our voices and actions to show this increasing size?" Then have the students read with you and act out the lines. Another book of poetry that encourages students to both listen carefully and respond to the meanings of the rhyming text is Shel Silverstein's *Runny Babbit* (2005).

Oral poetry reading also lends itself to dramatization. Narrative poems such as Clement Moore's "The Night Before Christmas" or "A Visit from St. Nicholas" include numerous scenes and passages that can be acted out. Tasha Tudor's illustrated version of *The Night before Christmas* (1999) appeals to elementary children. Robert Browning's "The Pied Piper of Hamelin" is also an enjoyable poem to dramatize.

Storytelling

Storytelling, the technique of telling a story orally without reading from a text, is part of an oral tradition in which for centuries, long before recorded history, groups shared their traditions and values. Native Americans developed mythologies expressing reverence for the earth and the animals that live on the continent. In Latin and South America, storytellers of the Yucatan Peninsula and the Andes chronicled the rise of the Mayan, Aztec, and Inca empires. Across Africa, highly respected storytellers developed a style that encouraged audiences to interact with the storytellers. In ancient cultures of Asia, early myths and folktales were eventually incorporated into tenets of Confucianism, Hinduism, and Buddhism. In Europe, the earliest oral traditions of the Celts, Saxons, and Danes could be heard through the stories of minstrels and bards. The mythologies of ancient Greece and Rome became influential as the Roman Empire expanded over much of the European continent.

These early stories were powerful means for people to pass on the values, beliefs, and histories of their people. Anthropologists, linguists, folklorists, historians, educators, and even business executives study the power of stories told rather than read. Researchers have found that storytelling improves comprehension and vocabulary knowledge. A study done in England (Trostle & Hicks, 1998) found that elementary students who were told stories scored higher on tests of vocabulary and comprehension. As a result of their research, they recommend that storytelling be used in classrooms to improve language and literacy development. They also recommend that storytelling should be part of the training for both teacher in-service and teacher preparation programs.

Storytelling may be so valuable because it improves comprehension and vocabulary knowledge as well as attention, writing ability, and interest in stories. A variety of storytelling techniques and styles such as felt boards, puppetry, and story maps are recommended for storytelling presentations.

The power of storytelling for both children and adults is seen in the rapid expansion of storytelling programs. The "Spellbinders Program," for example, is a community program that connects storytellers, community volunteers, libraries, and children. The National Storytelling Network of Jonesborough, Tennessee, sponsors festivals that attract thousands of storytellers and large audiences. The bimonthly *Storytelling Magazine* magazine includes articles on creating and crafting oral stories. Texas A&M University conducts a Storyteller in Residence program during which professional storytellers tell stories and provide guidance for teachers in training who would like to become storytellers.

CHOOSING A STORY   Stories selected by teachers for oral storytelling should be appropriate for the interests, ages, and experiences of the audience. Younger children like stories about familiar subjects such as animals, children, or home life. They respond to repetitive language in cumulative tales and enjoy joining in with stories such as "Henny Penny." Simple folktales such as "The Three Bears," "The Three Little Pigs," and "The Three Billy Goats Gruff" are excellent for kindergarten and first-grade children. The longer plots in tales such as the Native American "Spider Woman" or the African American tales about "Brer Rabbit" are appropriate for second- through fourth-grade students. These older students enjoy tall tales, ghost and scary stories, and stories associated with historical personages. Docents in one of the presidential libraries make history come alive for children by dressing as historical characters and telling stories as if they are the characters.

Flora Joy (2002) recommends examining the motif indexes in libraries to gain information about possible sources and studying the research about folktales written by experts in the field. Her advice is "READ, READ, READ, and READ some more of the numerous traditional folktales and fairy tales. Become familiar with the styles of writing, the plots, the characters, and all other story elements. In addition to reading, listening to recordings also helps fulfill this goal" (p. 15).

Numerous sources provide guidance in selecting, preparing, and sharing stories. Ramon Royal Ross's *Storyteller* (1996), David Holt and Bill Mooney's *Read-to-Tell* (1994), Joseph Bruchac's *Tell Me a Tale* (1997), and Paula Gaj Sitarz's *Story Time Sampler: Read Alouds, Booktalks, and Activities for Children* (1997) offer suggestions for teachers and other adults who are developing storytime activities.

PREPARING THE STORY   Storyteller Patti Hubert (Norton, 2003) recommends a sequence of steps in preparing a story such as those found in Figure 2.1.

SHARING THE STORY   Professional storytellers frequently introduce their stories by using artifacts from the culture of the story or by presenting background information about the story. Tim Tingle, a professional Choctaw storyteller, uses authentic musical instruments to introduce and often accompany his Native American stories (Tingle, 2002), for example. And Susan Klein introduces each of her stories with background information about the culture and the authenticity of the story.

Artifacts may or may not be used depending on the appropriateness to the story. If the story is from a published source, show the book jacket or develop a display of the books used as sources. This technique increases children's interests in reading the books and even preparing them for their own retelling. If retelling various Hans Christian Andersen stories, the book jackets could be displayed. *The Emperor's New Clothes,* retold by Marcus Sedgwick (2004); *Thumbelina,* illustrated by Brad Sneed (2004); *The Little Mermaid,* illustrated by Lizbeth Zwerger (2004); *The Princess and the Pea,* adapted by Lauren Child (2006); *The Ugly Duckling,* illustrated by Robert Ingpen (2005); *Thumbelina,* illustrated by

FIGURE 2.1

Sequence of Steps in Preparing a Story

1. Read the story completely through about three times.
2. List mentally the sequence of events. You are giving yourself a mental outline of the important happenings.
3. Reread the story, noting the events you did not remember.
4. Go over the main events again and add details that you remember. Think about the meaning of the events and ways to express that meaning, rather than memorize the words in the story.
5. When you believe that you know the story, tell the story to a mirror.
6. After you have practiced two or three more times, the wording will improve, and you can change vocal pitch to different characters.
7. Change your posture or hand gestures to represent different characters.
8. Do not be afraid to use pauses or to separate scenes.
9. Identify background information, share information about hearing the story for the first time, or share an object related to the story.

Brian Pinkney (2003), and *The Wild Swans*, illustrated by Anne Yvonne Gilbert (2005), all Andersen stories, provide excellent book jackets as well as stories for retelling. Travel posters may be used to enhance a setting. Puppets may depict various characters, or feltboard characters may enhance the plot of the story.

David Holt and Bill Mooney (1994) retell a story told by Susan Klein and provide suggestions for student involvement following telling the story. Klein recommends that the story, "The Wise Judge—A Story from Japan," be introduced by asking children to listen carefully so that they will be able to help solve the mystery at the end of the story. After telling the story, she asks questions and encourages numerous answers. In addition, Klein recommends the following types of exercises that can accompany a storytelling:

1. After telling a story, have a group discussion during which students try to solve a problem presented by the story and the initial question.
2. Have each listener do his or her own deductive thinking by writing a response to the story.
3. Have students, individually or in small groups, create stories that are similar to the story that is told.
4. Research the folklore and fairy tale sections of the library to find similar examples of tales from the culture.
5. Assign parts and dramatize the story.

As part of any storytelling activity, encourage children to become storytellers. The techniques for helping students learn the stories are similar to those identified for adults. When children first become storytellers, they may feel more comfortable if they use prompts such as feltboard characters to help them remember a sequence of events.

Creative Drama

Various types of creative dramatic activities help stimulate children's imaginations and language development as they learn to respond to language and various emotions through pantomime. Puppetry is a form of creative dramatics that encourages both oral language and creativity as students develop the puppets and tell a story. Puppetry also encourages listening development as children listen to the puppetry production and provide enthusiastic responses.

PANTOMIME   Pantomime is frequently used as an introduction to drama because it allows children to explore various body movements and to use their imaginations to depict the movements. Pantomime may be motivated by asking children to pantomime common actions and emotions or to pantomime a story or poem read by the teacher. For example, when pantomiming actions teachers may ask students to form a circle and pretend to toss a ball from one to the other within the circle. Students can choose what type of ball they will toss (baseball, football, volley ball, tennis ball, etc.). The person throwing the ball makes decisions about how the ball will be thrown that depend on size, heft, and shape. The child catching the ball needs to pay close attention to decide how to catch the ball. The actions continue until each child has an opportunity to throw and catch the ball. This activity may be varied by telling the students that the ball may have different proportions or characteristics such as hot, cold, sticky, or very light. Now, they need to watch carefully to identify how they will catch the ball. They can also change the characteristics of the ball before it is passed to the next child.

Students may choose partners, face each other, and take part in a pantomime activity called mirrors. This activity is excellent for developing cooperation and concentration. One student is the leader and acts out various motions and even facial expressions. The student's partner imitates the actions. Students then exchange roles and the other student does the imitation.

Pantomime may also accompany the reading of a story or poem. Now children pantomime all of the roles in the story including people and animals or even inanimate objects. Stories such as "The Three Little Pigs" provide opportunities to be each of the pigs, the big bad wolf, and even the various houses as they are blown down or stand strong.

PUPPETRY   Professional storytellers frequently use puppets to introduce their stories or use more elaborate puppet theaters with a cast of characters who tell the whole story. Children can make their own puppets or use ready-made puppets that may be placed in a storytelling center. When children make their own puppets they are learning about art. When they create a play from their own improvisations they are nurturing language development and creativity. When they retell a literature story they are developing interpretive and comprehension skills.

Begin a puppetry activity by sharing several different types of easily made puppets such as sock puppets, paper plate puppets, paper bag puppets, and cardboard container puppets. Let the children manipulate the puppets and experiment how they would use their own voices to make the puppets seem alive.

Extend the initial puppetry activity by allowing children to make their own puppets out of easily accessible materials. Figure 2.2 illustrates easy-to-make puppets.

FIGURE 2.2
Easy-to-Make Puppets

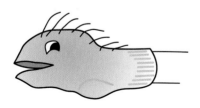

Sock Puppet

Cylinder Puppet

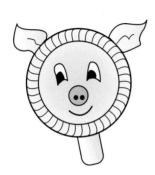

Paper-Plate Puppet

Paper-Bag Puppet

Box Puppet

Stick Puppet

After students have made simple puppets, let them use the puppets for improvisations for which they make up their own dialogues. They may make their puppets even more lifelike by adding hair with yarn, strips of construction paper, or scraps of material. Let children use their imaginations as they add hats and other characteristics such as whiskers for a lion or a trunk for an elephant.

Now the students are ready to select a play they would like to dramatize or make up their own plots and situations. For situations that are close to the students' experiences, the short stories in Rosemary Wells's *Yoko's World of Kindness: Golden Rules for a Happy Classroom* (2005) are easily dramatized. The characters are various animals including a kitten, mother cat, and the classmates who are animals, including a dog and a mouse. These characters are easily made from paper bags, boxes, paper plates, or cardboard cans. Because this book includes six short stories featuring the same characters, students can be divided into small groups so that each one can be part of a puppet scene. The story selected should be read a number of times so that each student can vocalize his or her puppet's character. Students can improvise by adding their own situations.

The puppet play should then be rehearsed so students can practice manipulating their characters. This type of puppet production can also be presented as a pantomime. Now the teacher reads the script and the students use their puppets to pantomime their roles. Beginning with a pantomime production provides the practice and self-confidence that many children need before they try creating their own dialogue.

Creating a "Best Books" List for Emergent Literacy Students

Each year the *School Library Journal* selects the books that a group of adult reviewers believe are the best books published for children during a specific year. The December 2004 issue includes sixty titles that were among the more than 4,400 books reviewed by the organization in 2004. This type of activity encourages students to become personally involved in the evaluation of books that have been identified by adults. For this activity, explain to the students that they will become critics for the books published for kindergarten through second grade. They will also have an opportunity to present their own opinions about the books. Would they identify the books as the best for the year? If so, why do they believe that the books are the best?

Before doing this activity, ask students to list some of the criteria that they look for when selecting and evaluating a book. This list might emphasize the quality of the illustrations, a story that attracts their attention, the development of appealing characters, a story that means something to them, a story that makes them laugh, and the use of language that makes them want to repeat lines. You may place the criteria on a chart. After each book is read orally by the teacher, allow the students to evaluate the book according to their criteria, to discuss the book with their peers, and to read or look at the book independently.

Collect as many of the books listed in Figure 2.3 as possible and place them in an attractive display. (School and public librarians frequently use these highly recommended lists of books when ordering new books. Consequently, the books should be available. Teachers can also become proactive and ask librarians to order specific books. All of the books are 2004 publications.)

Explain to the students that they will become evaluators and critics of the books that they see on the display. They will be able to decide if they agree with the panel of people who chose these books for the "Best Books" published during 2004. Over the next few days or weeks, read orally each of the books. Ask students to use their criteria and evaluate each of the books. Allow time for group discussion. Explain to

FIGURE 2.3

Best Books Identified for Kindergarten through Second Grade

Frank Asch, *Mr. Maxwell's Mouse*

Barbara Bottner and Gerald Kruglik, *Wallace's Lists*

Nina Crews, *The Neighborhood Mother Goose*

Doreen Cronin, *Duck for President*

Karen English, *Hot Day on Abbott Avenue*

Paul Fleischman, *Sidewalk Circus*

Bob Graham, *Tales from the Waterhole*

Kevin Hendes, *Kitten's First Full Moon*

Deborah Hopkinson, *Apples to Oregon*

Harry Horse, *Little Rabbit Goes to School*

Alison McGhee, *Mrs. Watson Wants Your Teeth*

Miriam Moss, *Don't Forget I Love You*

Kevin O'Malley, *Lucky Leaf*

Doris Orgel, *The Bremen Town Musicians and Other Animal Tales from Grimm*

James Rumford, *Sequoyah: The Cherokee Man Who Gave His People Writing*

Judy Sierra, *Wild About Books*

Martin Waddell, *Tiny's Big Adventure*

Ian Whybrow, *The Noisy Way to Bed*

Mo Willems, *Knuffle Bunny: A Cautionary Tale*

the students that everyone in the class does not need to agree on the quality of each book. This information can be placed on charts or if the children are able to write, they can use individual journals to respond to each of the books. At the conclusion of this activity, students can develop their own list of "Best Books."

A similar activity may be developed for older students. The sixty titles from the *School Library Journal* include books recommended for grades four through six and grades six and up. Older readers could also categorize the books according to genre or summarize characteristics of books that appeal to specific ages.

If desired, collect "Best Books" from other years of publication. These lists are found in the December issues of *School Library Journal*. Another comparative activity includes searching for the reviews of each of the books and then comparing the published reviews with those developed by the children. Remember that the children's opinions are just as important as those developed by adults. The December issues of *School Library Journal* also include "The Book Review: Cumulative Author/Illustrator Index."

Another language and literacy activity can accompany the reading of *The Art of Reading: Forty Illustrators*

Reflect on Your **Reading**

Think back to your own educational experiences. What strategies did your elementary teachers use in your classrooms? Which ones did you feel were the most effective and influential?

Celebrate RIF's 40th Anniversary (2005), compiled by Reading Is Fundamental. The forty illustrators each identify the book that most motivated them from their childhood. The text identifies the illustrator, presents a short essay by the illustrator, and includes a new illustration that is motivated by the book. Students may read or listen to the comments and compare the current illustration with the ones that are in the original source, such as Pat Cummings's illustration for C. S. Lewis's *The Lion, the Witch and the Wardrobe* from the Chronicles of Narnia series. Students can do a similar activity by thinking about a book that motivated them to read, tell why the book influenced them, and then create their own illustration to accompany the book.

Children's Cognitive Development in Lower Elementary Grades

Cognitive development, according to child development authority David Shaffer (1989), "refers to the changes that occur in children's mental skills and abilities" (p. 306). Activities that help children develop and interpret these mental skills are an important part of any classroom instruction and are required throughout all stages of development.

Two topics are usually related to cognitive development—physical knowledge and logicomathematical ability. Physical knowledge is gained through observing properties of objects within the child's experience. The child learns about the physical environment through observation and experimentation. Logicomathematical ability includes the ability to classify or group objects, to arrange objects according to size or quantity, to compare likenesses and differences among objects in the same category, to understand spatial relations, to understand relationships in terms of directions and distance, and to perceive time sequences. All of these cognitive abilities also relate to children's ability to read and to comprehend what is read.

As in language development, stages in children's cognitive development change with age. To help children advance in these important areas of cognitive development, an understanding of the typical cognitive development for children of a certain age is essential. It is also important for teachers to understand the educational implications for children in each of these stages of cognitive development. They need to understand what types of instructional activities may be used to encourage and enhance cognitive development.

Table 2.3 presents characteristics of children's cognitive development and implications for instructional practices.

The lesson plan that appears here using *Frog and Toad are Friends* was developed and taught by Ashley O'Connor (2003) to a group of first- and second-grade students. Notice how the lesson plan develops higher thought processes by requiring students to provide evidence in a story that supports a theme. The book is also an easy-to-read book designed to help younger students develop their reading skills. Notice that this book is listed in Table 2.3 as an implication for teaching cognitive skills to ages six to eight.

TABLE 2.3

Characteristics of Cognitive Development in Early Elementary Grades and Implications for Instruction

Preschool: Ages 3–4: Children begin to classify items according to color, size, shape, and use. They begin to understand how objects relate to number and amount. They begin to compare things according to bigger and smaller.

Implications for Teaching Cognitive Skills: Allow children to classify and group real objects. Have them classify objects in pictures such as in Eric Carle's *10 Little Rubber Ducks* (2005).

Preschool: Ages 4–5: Children can retell a short story if presented in a meaningful sequence. They increase their ability to group items. They pretend to tell time but do not understand the concept.

Implications for Teaching Cognitive Skills: Use flannel boards and pictures in stories to help children organize stories before they tell them. Stories such as "Three Billy Goats Gruff" and "The Gingerbread Boy" provide easier sequences that can be remembered. Share many concept books such as Saxton Freymann's *Food for Thought: Shapes, Colors, Numbers, Letters, Opposites* (2005) and allow children to group items and describe the characteristics of each group.

Preschool–Kindergarten: Ages 5–6: Children learn to follow one type of classification. They count to ten and identify primary colors. They require trial and error before arranging items from smallest to biggest. They still have vague concepts of time.

Implications for Teaching Cognitive Skills: Encourage activities that allow children to group, classify, and count objects. Use books such as Steve Jenkins's *Big and Little* (1996) to introduce and reinforce size concept and books such as Lois Ehlert's *Leaf Man* (2005) to encourage the development of observation and classification skills.

Early Elementary: Ages 6–8: Children are learning to read and want to demonstrate their new abilities. They are learning to write and want to create their own stories. Children's increased attention spans allow them to enjoy longer stories. Many children understand relationships among categories.

Implications for Teaching Cognitive Skills: Provide easy-to-read books such as Arnold Lobel's *Frog and Toad Are Friends* (1970) and Sharleen Collicott's *Mildred and Sam* (2003) to allow children to practice their reading skills. Allow children to write, illustrate, and share their own books. Children should read longer storybooks and chapter books such as Julius Lester's *The Last Tales of Uncle Remus* (1994). If ready, provide opportunities for children to read and discuss more difficult concept books such as Bruce McMillan's *Eating Fractions* (1991) and nonfiction such as Peter Busby's *First to Fly: How Wilbur and Orville Wright Invented the Airplane* (2003), and Frank Keating's biography *Theodore* (2006).

The characteristics and implications are based on research by Maxim (1997); Mussen, Conger, and Kagan (1989); Piaget and Inhelder (1969); and Norton (2007).

LESSON PLAN:
Frog and Toad Are Friends

PURPOSE	1. To develop higher thought processes. 2. To develop an understanding of theme. 3. To identify evidence in a story that will support a theme.
MATERIALS	Arnold Lobel's *Frog and Toad Are Friends* (1970)
GRADE LEVEL	Early Elementary (first–second grades)
BOOK SUMMARY	The book includes five short stories about the adventures of Frog and Toad. "The Story," the second story, will be used for theme. It is about Frog not feeling well and asking Toad for a story. Toad cannot think of one, so he tries some activities to help him think of a story.

PROCEDURES	1. Introduce or review the concept of theme. Share with students that theme is an important message that an author is trying to tell through the story. "What is the author trying to tell us that would make a difference in our lives?" Or, "What proof do we have in the book?"
	2. Ask the students to think about a story that they know, such as "Snow White and the Seven Dwarfs." Ask them to review the story and try to identify a message or a theme that the author is trying to convey. Students usually identify two contrasting themes: kindness is good and cruelty is bad. Ask them what happens in the story to help them understand that these are the themes of the book.
	3. Remind the students that they can discover theme through such things as the character's actions, the character's thoughts, and how the story ends. Sometimes the author tells us the theme of the story while the illustrations add to and support the theme.
	4. Next, introduce the book *Frog and Toad Are Friends*. As students listen to the story, they should ask questions such as "What is the author trying to tell us that would make a difference in our lives?" Write the theme or themes identified by the students on the board.
	5. Write a list of proofs under each theme: For example themes might include:
	    "The story told by Frog is very important:"
	    ▪ Toad banged his head against the wall.
	    ▪ Frog told Toad a story.
	    ▪ Toad told Frog that he should lie down.
	    ▪ Toad had to think of a story for Frog.

"Friendship is important."
- Toad took care of Frog.
- Toad tried to tell a story to Frog.
- Frog then told Toad a story.
- Frog took care of Toad.
6. Discuss how each of these proofs adds to the theme.

Cognitive Development for Social Studies in Lower Elementary Grades

The reading and social studies curriculums are closely related in lower elementary grades. The same teacher frequently teaches reading, language arts, and social studies. Consequently, teachers need to understand the cognitive skills that students need in order to comprehend social studies concepts in the lower elementary grades. In addition, many states have developed lists of "Essential Knowledge and Skills in Social Studies." These knowledge and skills may be tested as part of either state of school district mandated tests. The following implications for social studies were developed by the Social Studies Center for Educational Development. Norton (2007) identified the implications for literature.

As you read the following list of knowledge and skills for kindergarten, grade two, and grade four, consider what you, the teacher, would need to teach in order to help students master these skills. The following includes a few of the examples identified for each grade:

Kindergarten

History: Students understand that holidays are celebrations of specific events. They identify contributions of historic figures and ordinary people who shaped the community and understand the concept of chronological order.

Book example: James Cross Giblin's *George Washington: A Picture Book Biography* (1998)

Geography: Students understand concepts of location through terms such as *over, under, near, far, left,* and *right.*

Book example: Keith Baker's *Hide and Snake* (1991)

Economics: Students understand that basic human needs are met in many ways and that jobs are important.

Book example: Martin Waddell's *Farmer Duck* (1992)

Culture: Students understand similarities and differences among people and that people learn about themselves through family customs and traditions.

Book example: Jamie Lee Curtis's *Tell Me Again About the Night I Was Born* (1996)

Social Studies Skills: Students apply critical-thinking skills, gain information through visual sources, sequence and categorize information, identify main ideas, and express ideas orally.

Book example: Leo Lionni's *Swimmy* (1963) to evaluate problem solving

Grade Two

History: Students understand the historic significance of landmarks and celebrations; understand that various sources provide information about the past; compare interpretations of the same time period; and create and interpret timelines.

Book example: Barbara Brenner's *If You Were There in 1776* (1994)

Geography: Students use simple geographic tools, identify major landforms, understand how physical characteristics of places and regions affect activities and settlement patterns, and understand ways in which people modify the physical environment.

Book example: Jack Knowlton's *Geography from A to Z: A Picture Glossary* (1988)

Economics: Students understand the importance of work and are able to trace the development of a product from a natural resource to a finished product.

Book example: Dav Pilkey's *The Paper Boy* (1996)

Government: Students understand the purposes of government and the role of public office.

Book example: Emily Arnold McCully's *The Ballot Box Battle* (1998)

Social Studies Skills: Students create written and visual materials, use problem- solving process and decision-making skills to gather information and predict consequences.

Book example: Roni Schotter's *Nothing Ever Happens on 90th Street* (1997)

Grade Four

History: Students understand the similarities and differences among Native American groups in the Western Hemisphere and the causes and effects of European exploration and colonization.

Book examples: See list of Native American books in Chapter 6 and 10; Jean Fritz's *Around the World in a Hundred Years: From Henry the Navigator to Magellan* (1994)

Geography: Students use geographic tools to collect, analyze, and interpret data. They understand the concepts of regions, the location patterns of settlement, and how people adapt to and modify their environments.

Book examples: Jonathan D. W. Kahl's *Weather Watch: Forecasting the Weather* (1996) and Jim Brandenburg's *An American Safari: Adventures on the North American Prairie* (1997)

Citizenship: Students understand the importance of customs, symbols, and celebrations and effective leadership in a democratic society.

Book example: Bill Martin Jr. and Michael Sampson's *I Pledge Allegiance* (2002)

Social Studies Skill: Students apply critical thinking skills and use problem-solving and decision-making skills. By fourth grade students can conduct research into authentication of biographies, informational books, and folklore.

Reflect on Your Reading

Choose a grade level from the previous list of social studies knowledge and skills. As you read the essential knowledge and skills for kindergarten, grade two, and grade four, consider what you, as the teacher, would need to teach in order to help students master these skills. How are these skills related to the reading curriculum and the development of cognitive abilities?

Book examples: Numerous nonfiction sources such as Sally M. Walker's *Secrets of a Civil War Submarine: Solving the Mysteries of the H. L. Huntley* (2005) and biographies such as Michael Dooling's *Young Thomas Edison* (2006).

Language Development and Cognitive Development in the Middle and Upper Elementary Grades

Literacy development is not completed by third or fourth grades. Instead, the materials for reading become more demanding and higher levels of cognitive development are required. Writing and research skills become an increasing part of the curriculum. In addition, children's interests become more divergent. Consequently, it is necessary to provide many opportunities for independent reading and expanding reading skills.

As is true for students in the lower elementary grades, students in the middle and upper elementary grades vary in their levels of language and cognitive development. Education forms a continuum in which students eventually reach levels of literacy that one hopes are adequate for high school completion and employment or advancement into college. Catherine E. Snow, M. Susan Burns, and Peg Griffin (2001) conclude that reading ability is acquired quite easily for children who:

> have normal or above average language skills; have had experiences in early childhood that fostered motivation and provided exposure to literacy in use; are given information about the nature of print . . . and the contrasting nature of spoken and written language; and attend schools that provide coherent reading instruction and opportunities to practice reading. (p. 315)

They also identify the following three stumbling blocks that can negatively influence the acquisition of reading skills:

1. Difficulty in understanding and using the alphabetic principal, so students do not understand that written spellings represent the sounds of spoken words.
2. Failure to acquire and use comprehension skills and strategies.
3. Lack of motivation.

According to Snow, Burns, and Griffin, these three obstacles are related because "Difficulties mastering sound-letter relationships or comprehension skills can easily stifle motivation, which in turn hampers instructional efforts" (p. 316).

Characteristics of Language Development in Middle and Upper Elementary Grades

Numerous experiences with literacy provide most children with opportunities to expand their language development. Table 2.4 identifies characteristics of language development and implications for instruction.

TABLE 2.4

Characteristics of Language Development and Implications for Instruction

Middle Elementary: Ages 9–10 Children start to use the subordinating connector *although*. The present participle active and perfect participle appear.

Implications for Teaching Language: Use written and oral models of literature and other written materials to help children master their language skills. Allow numerous opportunities for children to share their interests and their opinions about what they read and write. Include all genres of literature in the curriculum. For example, Shannon Hale's *The Goose Girl* (2003) and Katherine Hannigan's *Ida B . . . and Her Plans to Maximize Fun, Avoid Disaster, and (Possibly) Save the World* (2004).

Upper Elementary: Ages 10–12 Children use complex sentences with subordinate clauses of concession introduced by *nevertheless* and *in spite of*. Auxiliary verbs *might, could,* and *should* appear. Many children have difficulty distinguishing among past, past perfect, and present perfect tenses. The average number of words in an oral sentence is 9.5.

Implications for Teaching Language: Use books and other written materials that model more complex sentence structures such as found in Bodil Bredsdorff's *The Crow Girl* (2004), Russell Freedman's *The Voice That Challenged a Nation: Marian Anderson and the Struggle for Equal Rights* (2004), E. L. Konigsburg's *The Outcasts of 19 Schuyler Place* (2004), Kathleen Krull's *Isaac Newton* (2006), Gary D. Schmidt's *Lizzie Bright and the Buckminster Boy* (2004), and Philip Pullman's *The Golden Compass* (1995), *The Subtle Knife* (1997), and *The Amber Spyglass* (2000). Provide many opportunities for students to conduct research and to write longer papers.

Techniques That Enhance Language Development in Middle and Upper Elementary Grades

Many of the techniques described for students in the lower elementary grades are still appropriate for students in grades four through eight. The selection of materials, vocabularies, and discussions related to the techniques must, however, be appropriate for the advancing interests and capabilities of the students.

READING ALOUD When adults read orally to students in the middle and upper elementary grades and in middle school, they can select works that expand students' understanding of vocabulary and provide important background knowledge. Some of the books are longer texts in which one or two chapters are read during each experience, while other books are shorter, illustrated texts. Teachers can discuss unusual vocabulary, highlight important meanings, and emphasize relationships developed through the literature.

Books that have vivid descriptions of setting encourage students to visualize these settings and to understand why authors need to select words carefully if they want to set the stage for their books. One of my favorite techniques is to ask students to close their eyes and listen to a passage. As they listen to the passage, they try to visualize the setting and then describe what they see. For example, while reading Natalie Babbitt's *Tuck Everlasting* (1974), ask the students to visualize the description of the setting that is described on pages 5 and 6.

After listening to the passage, ask students to describe their visions in as much detail as possible. "What does it look like to be uncomfortably hot, to be surrounded by oppressive dust and meager grass, and to see grass that is ragged and forlorn? What does the 'touch-me-not' house look like? What does grass look like if it is cut painfully to the quick? How did you visualize the gallows?" Ask students if they noticed the technique the author uses to make the setting seem real and vivid, encourage them to identify the author's use of personification, giving human emotions and characteristics to objects. Ask them to consider why the author describes the setting in personified terms. If they have not noticed the terms, read the paragraph a second time, have them note these terms, and ask them if the personification makes a difference in their ability to visualize the setting. Also, note that the word *gallows* helps readers identify the setting as taking place in an earlier time period. Notice that this type of activity also provides interest in and motivation for reading the book.

To provide additional background knowledge about Natalie Babbitt's book, read Betsy Hearne's "Circling Tuck: An Interview with Natalie Babbitt" (2000). Babbitt tells us that writing the book was easy

> because of the setting, which is a real place. . . . Everything about the place in the book is true, including the mouse living in the drawer. . . . Everything about the pond, about the toads—there were a lot of toads there—and frogs, everything is exactly the way it is in real life. All I had to do was fit my characters into the setting. (p. 153)

Hearne's article provides additional areas that students might focus on while reading or listening to *Tuck Everlasting,* for example, students might discuss how Babbitt uses the images of circles such as wheels circling, sun circling, weather cycling, ring of trees around the pond, rings in the water, a music box that circles back over the same song, and the plot that circles from the toad at the beginning of the story to the toad at the conclusion of the book. When reading books aloud to older students, take advantage of opportunities to model (see Chapter 6) in order to show students how you used your own thought processes to understand the meanings in the literature.

Poetry is another strong choice for reading orally to older students. There are some quite sophisticated illustrated books that are more appropriate for older students than they are for younger children. When reading heavily illustrated books such as Blaise Cendrars's *Shadow* (1982), for example, teachers can point out how Marcia Brown's illustrations reinforce the spooky mood of the poem in which a shadow staggers, steals back like a thief, and sprawls on the ground. Students can discuss how the poet's choice of words and use of language are heightened by the collage illustrations, especially the ones in which black silhouettes are on the same page with white ghostly images. After reading *Shadow,* teachers can read Edward Lear's *The Scroobious Pip* (1968), pointing out the effect of the soft pastel drawings on the mood of the poem. Students can focus on Lear's style of writing and discuss whether the pastel drawings are more appropriate for this poem than would be the predominantly black shapes found in *Shadow.* Highlighting moods created by illustrations helps students develop backgrounds for texts and analyze the appropriateness of relationships between the authors' choice of words and the illustrators' choice of drawings.

As texts become harder and more complex, teachers should take special care to point out difficult concepts and vocabulary. A similar visualization technique, as described for *Tuck Everlasting,* can be used to help students focus on unusual words, figurative meanings, and important relationships. The vocabularies in books such as Jamake Highwater's *Anpao: An American Indian Odyssey* (1977) might seem deceptively easy at first glance. But because the author uses considerable simile, metaphor, personification, and mythological symbolism, many readers might not comprehend the story or fully appreciate how the author's techniques add to the enjoyment of the story unless a teacher points out these features. For example, after providing background information about the book, teachers can ask students to close their eyes and visualize the first paragraph of the chapter:

In the Days of Plenty

In the days before the people fled into the water, the wind held leaves aloft in the sky like dragonflies. There was no war and people were at peace. The buffalo people lived in the world of the sweet grass below, and the sky above was filled with birds of many colors and of many songs. The air was blue and the earth was green and each thing rested upon the other. In the forest the leaves fell slowly. There was no fear. The birds did not leap into flight when the cats awoke. And the wild flowers changed colors to amuse themselves. (p. 15)

After reading the paragraph orally, ask the students to describe their visualization in as much detail as possible. Ask them how they visualized the time period as reflected in "before the people fled into the water." If the students have not studied Native American mythology, they might not know that this is an allusion to an earlier period in the beginning of Native American mythological history. Ask the students how they visualized the people who lived in this early time. "Who are the buffalo people?" Again, they might not be aware that the buffalo people belonged to one of the Great Plains tribes who lived in harmony with the buffalo. The buffalo provided food and other necessities for the people. These understandings can improve students' abilities to visualize the setting. How do leaves appear if they are compared to dragonflies? What does a setting look and sound like if the author describes *sweet grass below, colorful birds singing in the sky,* and *leaves falling slowly?* How is the visualization of the setting influenced by the description of birds that are not afraid of the cats? How did they visualize wildflowers that change colors to amuse themselves?

This is not a text that should be read rapidly. Instead, it should be savored for the language and the effect of the comparisons on the listener and the reader. Students' enjoyment and comprehension of the text is enhanced if teachers highlight the importance of similes, personification, and mythological symbolism as they read. Teachers can point out and discuss comparisons developed by the author and why these comparisons are appropriate in a text based on Native American legend and mythology.

Another excellent example of Native American symbolism and figurative language that can be read orally and discussed is Jan Hudson's *Sweetgrass* (1989). This historical fiction book is set in the northern prairies of the nineteenth century. Again, the author's frequent use of similes, metaphors, and mythological beliefs should be pointed out as students listen to the reading.

STORYTELLING   Storytelling in the upper grades and middle school is a very effective learning tool. Teachers can introduce storytelling by explaining that Stephen Denning, Program Director of the World Bank, discovered and used the power of storytelling to motivate organizational change. Notice how Denning explains the importance of using storytelling as a motivational tool, even with adults. When asked "why storytelling?" Denning (2001) replied,

> Nothing else worked. Charts left listeners bemused. Prose remained unread. Dialogue was just too laborious and slow. Time after time, when faced with the task of persuading a group of managers or front-line staff in a large organization to get enthusiastic about a major change, I found that storytelling was the only thing that worked. (p. xiii)

Denning stresses the need to develop and use what he terms a "springboard story" that allows listeners to grasp an idea. A teacher can easily use the characteristics of a successful springboard story. Denning states that a successful story needs to have a predicament that is familiar to the particular audience, have a degree of strangeness or incongruity for the listeners so that it captures their attention and stimulates their imaginations, but it also needs to be plausible. (I attended a two-day workshop conducted by Denning at the Smithsonian Institution. His ideas excited the audience, many of whom were business people.)

School, community, and even world problems could easily be the source for developing springboard stories. Ask students to brainstorm a list of problems that could be presented and even solved through stories. They should consider how they would use the interactions of the audience to the stories to help them ignite action and solve a problem. Sources for the problems and the stories could relate to specific issues and problems at school. Or, the problems and issues might come from a newspaper or television or radio news. For example, a highly recommended source for daily reading is a newspaper. By reading local or national newspapers students can identify problems that would be sources for springboard stories.

The following problems were identified by a group of middle school students after they searched several weeks of the *New York Times*:

- There is a shortage of people in the nursing and teaching professions.
- Problems related to global warming are increasing and may affect animals, fish, water supplies, and the weather.
- There are both advantages and disadvantages of oil exploration in national wildlife refugees.
- Deforestation is increasing in national parks and in wildlife sanctuaries.
- Using cell phones while driving a car can cause accidents. Should there be a law against using cell phones while driving?
- There may be considerable oil shortages. What should be done to prevent oil shortages?
- What are scientific issues for the nation and the world and how should we deal with these issues? (January 4, 2003 p. 27)

If students can locate real stories about incidents in other places, they can develop those stories for use in the new situation. This type of storytelling could easily be related to a content field such as geography or social studies. Allow students time

Reflect on Your Reading

How would language and cognitive development differ if you were teaching upper elementary grades versus teaching lower elementary grades? What are the implications for this difference on your instruction?

to develop their springboard stories, either in groups or individually, and share their stories with the class or with a community organization whose problems relate to the springboard story.

Storytelling is also an excellent way to increase understanding of other cultures. For example, a group of students in grades six through eight developed a "Multicultural Storytelling Festival." They selected stories that reflected the cultures they were studying, prepared the stories for telling, and told the stories to an appreciative audience of both fellow students and adults. The students also prepared posters and other visuals, as well as displays of books that accompanied the cultures and the stories. This type of festival can be duplicated in any school or community.

Characteristics of Cognitive Development in Middle and Upper Elementary Grades

Table 2.5 presents characteristics of children's cognitive development and implications for instructional practices.

TABLE 2.5

Characteristics of Cognitive Development and Teaching Implications

Middle Elementary: Ages 9–10 Children's reading skills improve rapidly. Within any one grade there is a considerable range of reading ability. A child's level of interest may still be above his or her reading ability. Many children can set purposes for reading and instruction.

Implications for Teaching Cognitive Skills: Provide many books that are at an appropriate level of reading. Encourage children to share their experiences with peers, teachers, and family members. Laura Ingalls Wilder's *Little House in the Big Woods* (1932, 1953) is a good choice for independent reading. Continue providing a story time for oral reading. Books such as Blue Balliett's *Chasing Vermeer* (2004) encourage readers to follow clues and solve a mystery. Linda Sue Park's *Project Mulberry* (2005) provides an excellent book in which listeners can hypothesize about what happened next.

Upper Elementary: Ages 10–12 Children develop an understanding of the chronological order of events. Many are now able to apply logical rules, reasoning, and formal operations to abstract problems. Interests expand and many children enjoy researching subjects related to the content fields. Hobbies and sports become very important to many students.

Implications for Teaching Cognitive Skills: Reading and discussing historical fiction, biographies and informational books will help students order events. Read and discuss James Cross Giblin's *The Century That Was: Reflections on the Last One Hundred Years* (2000) and Richard B. Stolley's *Life: Our Century in Pictures for Young People* (2000). Develop timelines of important events. Allow students to investigate the lives of people who are active in their hobbies or sports.

The characteristics and implications on this table are based on research by Maxim (1997); Mussen, Conger, and Kagan (1989); Piaget and Inhelder (1969); and Norton (2007).

Up for Discussion

On international tests for geography and history, students in the United States do poorly, consistently ranking below students in European and Canadian schools. Why do you think our test scores are so low?

After reading and analyzing the social studies skills recommended for upper elementary students, do you believe that students in the United States have the knowledge base or are they lacking this knowledge base? Use your own experiences with these subjects to help you answer the question. What recommendations do you have for improving understandings of geography and history? How might improvements in reading comprehension influence the test scores of students? Share your recommendations with your class.

A teacher uses a map to help students understand geographic locations in texts and to read the visual aids found in many content materials.

Cognitive Development for Social Studies in the Upper Elementary and Middle School

The reading materials and the teaching strategies used to teach social studies skills in the fourth through eighth grades present challenges for both teachers and students. The reading and comprehension demands related to the materials require students to use higher levels of reasoning abilities in order to solve problems. Kendall and Marzano (2000) analyzed the national standards published by the National Council of Teachers of English (NCTE) and the International Reading Association (IRA) to discover specific skills and abilities expected of students. They discovered the following six thinking and reasoning skills that were identified in the majority of content areas:

1. Identifying similarities and differences
2. Solving problems
3. Developing arguments
4. Making decisions
5. Testing hypothesis and engaging in scientific inquiry
6. Using logic and reasoning

Teachers need to consider how they might teach each of these thinking and reasoning skills, and the materials they might use in the upper grade levels. Table 2.6 includes social studies skills for grades six and eight.

Reflect on Your Reading

Read the list of skills and implications for teaching. Notice how closely the implications for teaching are related to the skills and abilities identified by the National Council of Teachers of English and the International Reading Association. Also, think about the interesting units that could be developed under each of the topics.

TABLE 2.6

Social Studies Skills for Grades Six and Eight and National Standards

Knowledge and Skills	Implications for Teaching	National Standards
Grade Six		
History: Historical events influence contemporary events and groups contribute to cultures.	Develop units that allow students to investigate how historical events influence our world today.	Identify similarities and differences.
Geography: Use maps, globes, graphs, charts, models, and data bases to answer questions.	Study how scientists gather information and conduct research to answer questions.	Solve problems, make decisions, test hypothesis.
Culture: Understand similarities and differences within and among cultures and religions.	Develop units that allow students to study various cultures and world religions. Relate art and music to cultures.	Identify similarities and differences, develop arguments, use logic and reasoning
Social Studies Skills: Apply critical-thinking skills and use problem-solving and decision-making skills.	Develop group and individual research and inquiry projects. Use writing process to draw and defend conclusions.	Solve problems, develop arguments, make decisions, test hypothesis, engage in scientific inquiry.
Grade Eight		
History: Understand economic and political issues of Revolutionary Era and Western movement.	Develop units about the American Revolution and Western expansion.	Identify similarities and differences. Solve problems, test hypothesis using logic and reasoning.
Government: Understand the processes of changing United States Constitution and impact on American society.	Study books such as Jaffe's *Who Were the Founding Fathers* (1996), Fleming's *Ben Franklin's Almanac* (2003).	Solve problems, develop arguments using logic and reasoning.
Culture: Understand relationships among the arts and times they were created and relationships among racial, ethnic, and religious groups.	Research connections between art and music of a time period. Study the contributions of racial, ethnic, and religious groups.	Identify similarities and differences, engage in scientific inquiry, use logic and reasoning.

DIFFERENTIATING INSTRUCTION

ELL Students

Robert W. Ortiz and Rosario Ordoñez-Jasis (2005) use Vygotsky's sociocultural theories to argue that literacy development is a sociocultural activity because it relates to education and how learning is shaped by children, parents, and teachers. They stress that especially when involving Latino parents, teachers and schools need to "broaden the role families have in their children's learning and establish home school relationships based on mutual respect and trust that support the attainment of literacy skills and goals" (p. 115).

To accomplish these broader goals, teachers need to use parent surveys, individual interviews, and focus groups to obtain background information from both parents; include multicultural literature that reflects diverse interests and richness of the culture; involve parents in children's **oral language development** through such sources as rhymes, songs, oral history, poems, and folklore; and use a variety of approaches to communicate with parents so that parents can be involved. Communication may require using the parents' native language or scheduling conference times that accommodate working parents; and link literacy activities to the home and community environments.

Jim Cummins, Patricia Chow, and Sandra R. Schecter (2006) describe a Canadian project that supports a "Community-as-Resource Policy." They administered a parental survey in which parents were asked about their children's reading experiences and habits, the sources for obtaining children's literature, and the parents willingness to share their cultural and language experiences. Following the survey they concluded: "Parents expressed an interest in a program that would support their children both in acquiring English and in maintaining their first language and culture" (p. 301).

The program includes a curriculum in which dual-language books are used so that children can take the books home where non-English speaking parents can read the books to their children in their own language while they expand the values, ideas, and concepts developed in the books. Additional activities include having children create their own dual-language books by using parental help in translation, being involved in dual-language storytelling, and writing narratives in two languages that allow the children to express their ideas about their experiences and their growing understandings of self.

Struggling Readers and Writers

Numerous research studies support the benefits of reading aloud to children and involving them in discussions during and after listening to a story. Research also supports the benefits of active learning in which students hear, use, manipulate, and play with the language. Active learning strategies are especially beneficial for children with minimal vocabularies who are less likely to acquire new vocabularies through incidental experiences.

Camille L. Z. Blachowicz and Connie Obrochta (2005) describe a reading aloud approach that begins with helping students activate their prior knowledge about the subject of the book and asking the students to contribute words. These words are placed on a chart and may explore the senses related to the book to be read. If the book is about a storm, for example, students may talk about what they would hear, see, and feel during a storm. While listening to the book being read, students are asked to become active listeners by participating in activities such as putting their thumbs up when they hear one of the new words.

Focus groups of ELL parents provide assistance to parents who are involved in literacy instruction with their children.

After the oral reading, the students discuss what they have learned and add any new words to the chart. They add information that reflects their own personal knowledge and write or dictate a short story that relates to the oral reading.

Gifted and Accelerated Readers and Writers

By the time gifted and accelerated readers are in the middle and upper elementary grades they are usually able to read aloud with both a faster rate and considerably greater accuracy than struggling readers. Gifted and accelerated readers enjoy learning new words and trying different approaches. They may enjoy learning about a linguistic term, *prosody*, which describes the rhythmic and tonal aspects of speech. Prosodic reading means that the reader reads with expression by stressing variations in intonation and stress patterns that contribute to reading. Roxanne F. Hudson and her colleagues (2005) emphasize the link between prosody and reading achievement because prosodic reading demonstrates evidence that the reader comprehends and understands the deeper meanings associated with what is read.

To improve expression during oral reading teachers can use strategies such as reading with recorded books, creating Readers' Theater from scripts that include rich dialogue, and adding sound effects to the reading as might be found in early radio dramas. It is interesting to note that *McGuffey's Sixth Eclectic Reader* (1879, 1896, 1907, 1921), one of the basal readers discussed in Chapter 1, taught students to read with expression as part of their reading instruction, urging them to use tones of voice that correspond with the moods and content of what is being read. An example of this approach taken from *McGuffey's Sixth Eclectic Reader* follows. Notice that the excerpts are taken from various types and genres of literature.

Examples

Passion
and
Grief
{
"Come back! Come back!" he cried, in grief,
   "Across this stormy water;
And I'll forgive your Highland chief,
   My daughter! O, my daughter!"

Plaintive {
I have lived long enough: my way of life
Is fallen into the sear, the yellow leaf:
And that which should accompany old age,
As honor, love, obedience, troops of friends,
I must not look to have.

Calm {
A very great portion of this globe is covered
With water, which is called sea, and is very distinct
from rivers and lakes.

Fierce
Anger {
Burned Marmion's swarthy cheek like fire,
And shook his very frame for ire;
And—"This to me!" he said,—
"An 't were not for thy hoary beard.
Such hand as Marmion's had not spared
To cleave the Douglas' head!"

Passion
and
Grief {
"Even in thy pitch of pride,
Here, in thy hold, thy vassals near,
I tell thee, thou 'rt defied!
And if thou said'st I am not peer
To any lord in Scotland here,
Lowland or Highland, far or near,
Lord Angus, thou hast lied!" (p. 54)

Reflect on Your Reading

Think back over your own elementary education. Consider instances in which teachers differentiated instruction to meet the needs of ELL students, struggling readers and writers, and gifted and accelerated readers and writers. Identify teaching strategies your teachers may have used that would have been effective for these three groups of students.

Summary

Emergent literacy, language development, and cognitive development are all important for developing reading ability. Environments need to foster emergent literacy and language development throughout the elementary grades. Reading to children and storytelling are both important for developing literacy. Motivational activities are important for developing interest in reading, and they encourage students to express their opinions about books. Reading activities that focus on easy-to-read books are important for children who are beginning to read.

By studying children's cognitive development we discover characteristics of children and implications for instruction that help develop the mental skills and abilities including reasoning, concepts, and memory that are so important for successful reading. Cognitive development for social studies includes essential knowledge and skills as well as implications for instruction. The national standards published by the National Council of Teachers of English and the International Reading Association provide lists of specific skills and abilities expected of students. Many of these skills and abilities may be taught through reading activities that are also important for the social studies curriculum.

Key Terms

emergent literacy, p. 49

cognitive development, p. 51

literacy-rich environments, p. 53

language development, p. 54

longitudinal studies, p. 54

reading aloud, p. 58

storytelling, p. 61

oral language development, p. 81

For video clips of authentic classroom instruction on **Emergent Literacy**, go to Allyn & Bacon's MyLabSchool.com. In MLS courses, click on Reading Methods, go to MLS Video Lab, and select **Module 1**.

Extend Your Reading

1. After reading the descriptions of these effective classrooms, develop an inventory of a room or school environment that you could use to evaluate the environment for emergent literacy. You might use an inventory similar to the following "Inventory to Evaluate Environment for Emergent Literacy":

Inventory to Evaluate Environment for Emergent Literacy

The inventory could include some of the following topics:

	high quality	average quality	low quality
1. The room has a library corner with a variety of reading materials, both fiction and nonfiction.	____	____	____
Comments:			
2. The room is attractive and reflects a love of learning and literacy.	____	____	____
Comments:			
3. Writing is displayed throughout the classroom. The children share their reading and writing.	____	____	____
Comments:			
4. The reading materials reflect the needs of the various content areas.	____	____	____
Comments:			
5. The main school library attracts students to select and read books.	____	____	____
Comments:			

6. The teacher and librarian provide book talks to motivate students. _____ _____ _____

Comments:

7. The students are excited about their learning. _____ _____ _____

Comments:

2. Consider the differences in language characteristics described in Table 2.1. Discuss these differences and implications of the differences with your reading methods class. If possible, observe several classes of children. What are the language characteristics of the children? How would you use information from your observation to enhance the literacy levels of the children?

3. Select, prepare, and share a book for oral reading. Ask your peers to evaluate the oral reading experience. To increase understanding, select a group of books that follow a theme or a subject. If possible, share the oral reading with an appreciative group of lower elementary students.

4. Develop a lesson plan that encourages students to classify and compare objects.

5. Develop a lesson plan that encourages students to organize stories with the help of a flannel board.

6. Review the charts for language development or cognitive development presented in this chapter. With a group of your peers, identify additional books that could be used to enhance language or cognitive development for a specific grade. Provide your reasons for choosing those specific books. Share your reasons with your class.

7. Select, prepare, and share a book for reading orally that is appropriate for students in middle and upper grades. Decide what you will emphasize to help students understand either the language or the illustrations. With a group of your peers, develop a file of sources that are appropriate for reading orally.

8. Start a portfolio of paragraphs from books or other materials that could be used to help students visualize settings.

9. Select a culture for a storytelling festival. Investigate the culture and stories that are appropriate for the culture. Prepare the story for presentation. Prepare an introduction to the story that provides background information and several purposes for listening. If possible, present the story to a group of children or present your story to your reading methods class. What books might you include in a display that motivates reading and extends understanding of the culture?

10. After you have read the list of knowledge and skills for social studies (Table 2.6, Social Studies Skills for Grades Six and Eight and National Standards), divide into groups for a specific grade. As a member of the group, evaluate how these competencies relate to reading skills. What are the units of instruction that you believe would be beneficial? What levels of reading comprehension are necessary for students to develop the social studies knowledge and skills and to learn the specific skills and abilities identified by the National Council of Teachers of English and the International Reading Association? Present your findings and recommendations to your reading class.

For Further Reading

1. If you are focusing on lower elementary grades, choose and read one of the references identified by Strickland and Feeley in "Development in the Elementary School Years" (2003, pp. 339–356). The authors focus on studies associated with "The Learner Develops," "Oral Language Development," "Language and Thought," "Oral Language in the Classroom," "Written Language Development," "Primary Years (K–2)," and "Literary Development." Report your findings to your class.

2. If you are focusing on middle and upper elementary grades, choose and read one of the references identified by Simmons and Carrol in "Today's Middle Grades: Different Structures, Students, and Classrooms" (2003, pp. 357–392). The authors include studies associated with "The Middle Grades and Young Adolescents," "Characteristics of Young Adolescents," "Adolescent and Young Adult Literature," "Censorship," "Language," "Reading," "Writing," and "Assessment/Evaluation." Report your findings to your class.

3. Search for and read the information on the Web sites for some of the authors included in this chapter including:

   Joseph Bruchac: www.josephbruchac.com
   Eric Carle: www.eric-carle.com
   Joy Cowley: www.joycowley.com
   Jane Yolen: www.janeyolen.com

4. To learn more about involving families of ELL students in their literacy educations read Jeanne G. Fain and Robin Horn's "Family Talk About Language Diversity and Culture" (2006, pp. 310–320).

REFERENCES

Barr, Myra. (2002). "The Reader in the Writer." *The Reading Hall of Fame.* San Francisco: International Reading Association.

Bartel, Nettie. (1995). "Assessing and Remediating Problems in Language Development." In Donald Hammill and Nettie Bartel (Eds.), *Teaching Children with Learning and Behavior Problems,* third edition. Boston: Allyn & Bacon.

Blachowicz, Camille L. Z., & Connie Obrochta. (November 2005). "Vocabulary Visits: Virtual Field Trips for Content Vocabulary Development." *The Reading Teacher,* 59, 262–268.

Block, Cathy Collins. (2001). "Improving Thinking Abilities through Reading Instruction." In Arthur L. Costa (Ed.), *Developing Minds: A Resource Book for Teaching Thinking,* 3rd ed. Alexandria, VA: Association for Supervision and Curriculum Development, pp. 292–297.

Brause, Rita S., & Mayher, John S. (2003). "Who Really Goes to School? Teaching and Learning for the Students We Really Have." In James Flood, Diane Lapp, James R. Squire, & Julie M. Jensen (Eds.), *Handbook of Research on Teaching the English Language Arts,* second edition. Mahwah, NJ: Lawrence Erlbaum.

Britto, Pia Rebello, Brooks-Gunn, Jeanne, & Griffin, Terri M. (January/February/March 2006). "Maternal Reading and Teaching Patterns: Associations with School Readiness in Low-Income African American Families." *Reading Research Quarterly,* 41, 68–89.

Brown, June. (1999). "Critical Questions." *The Reading Teacher,* 52, 520–521.

Brown, Roger. (1973). *A First Language: The Early Stages.* Cambridge, MA: Harvard University Press.

Clay, Marie M. (2003). "Child Development." In James Flood, Diane Lapp, James R. Squire, & Julie M. Jensen (Eds.), *Handbook of Research on Teaching the English Language Arts,* 2nd ed. Mahwah, NJ: Lawrence Erlbaum, pp. 46–52.

Cobb, Charles E. Jr. (1981). "After Rhodesia, A Nation Named Zimbabwe." *National Geographic,* 160, 616–651.

Cole, Jill E. (2002/2003). "What Motivates Students to Read? Four Personalities." *The Reading Teacher,* 56, 326–336.

Collins, R., & Cooper, P. J. (1997). *The Power of Storytelling: Teaching through Storytelling,* 2nd ed. Scottsdale, AZ: Gorsuch Scarisbrick.

Column, Carolyn (1999). *The Storytime Sourcebook,* 2nd ed. New York: Neal-Schuman.

Cummins, Jim, Chow, Patricia, & Schecter, Sandra R. (March 2006). "Community as Curriculum." *Language Arts,* 83, 297–307.

Cunningham, Patricia M., & Allington, Richard L. (2003). *Classrooms That Work: They Can All Read and Write,* 3rd ed. Boston: Allyn & Bacon.

Denning, Stephen. (2001). *The Springboard: How Storytelling Ignites Action Knowledge-Era Organizations.* Portsmouth, NH: Butterworth, Heinemann.

Fain, Jeanne G., & Horn, Robin. (March 2006). "Family Talk About Language Diversity and Culture." *Language Arts,* 83, 310–320.

Finn, Patrick. (1985). *Helping Children Learn to Read.* New York: Random House.

Fisher, Allan C. Jr. (May 1975). "Rhodesia, a House Divided." *National Geographic GEO News Handbook* (11–17 November 1990), 7.

Hare, John. (2002). "Surviving the Sahara." *National Geographic,* 202, 54–77.

Hearne, Betsy. (March/April 2000). "Circling Tuck: An Interview with Natalie Babbitt." *Horn Book,* 153–161.

Hendrick, Joanne. (1996). *The Whole Child,* 5th ed. Upper Saddle River, NJ: Merrill/Prentice Hall.

Herb, Steven. (1997). "Building Blocks to Literacy: What Current Research Shows." *School Library Journal,* 43, 23.

Holt, David, & Mooney, Bill. (1994). *Ready-to-Tell.* Little Rock, AR: August House.

Hopkins, Lee Bennett. (1987). *Pass the Poetry, Please!* New York: Harper & Row.

Hudson, Roxanne F., Lane, Holly B., & Pullen, Paige C. (May 2005). "Reading Fluency Assessment and Instruction: What, Why, and How." *The Reading Teacher,* 58, 702–714.

Ingersoll, Brenda, (4 August 2004). "We're Bookworms!" *Wisconsin State Journal,* 1.

Jewel, Connie (2002). "The Importance of Preschool and Kindergarten Language Development in Reading Acquisition." In *Reading Hall of Fame.* San Francisco: International Reading Association.

Jones, Trev, Toth, Luann, Charnizon, Marlene, Grabarek, Daryl, & Fleishhacker, Joy (2002). "Best Books 2002." *School Library Journal,* 48, 40–45.

Joy, Flora. (2002). "Suggestions for Recrafting Folktales/Fairy Tales." *Storytelling Magazine,* 14, 14–18.

Kendall, J. S., & Marzano, R. J. (2000). *Content Knowledge: A Compendium of Standards and Benchmarks for K-12 Education,* 3rd ed. Alexandria, VA: Association for Supervision and Curriculum Development.

Klein, Susan. (2002). "Spellbinders Programs." Aspen, CO: Pitkin Library.

Loban, Walter. (1976). *Language Development: Kindergarten through Grade Twelve.* Urbana, IL: National Council of Teachers of English.

Loban, Walter. (1986). "Research Currents: The Somewhat Stingy Story of Research into Children's Language." *Language Arts,* 63, 608–616.

Maxim, George (1993). *The Very Young: Guiding Children from Infancy through the Early Years.* Upper Saddle River, NJ: Merrill/Prentice Hall.

McGuffey Editions. (1879, 1896, 1907, 1921). *McGuffey's Sixth Eclectic Reader.* New York: American Book Company.

Merritt, D., & Culatta, B. (1998). *Language Intervention in the Classroom.* San Diego: Singular.

Mussen, Paul Henry, Conger, John Jeneway, & Kagan, Jerome. (1989). *Child Development and Personality.* New York: Harper & Row.

Norton, Donna E. (2004). *The Effective Teaching of Language Arts,* 6th ed. Upper Saddle River, NJ: Merrill/Prentice Hall.

Norton, Donna E. (2005). *Multicultural Children's Literature: Through the Eyes of Many Children,* 2nd ed. Upper Saddle River, NJ: Merrill/Prentice Hall.

Norton, Donna E. (2007). *Through the Eyes of a Child: An Introduction to Children's Literature,* 7th ed. Upper Saddle River, NJ: Merrill/Prentice Hall.

Ortiz, Robert W., & Ordoñez-Jasis, Rosario. (October 2005). "Leyendo Juntos (Reading Together): New Directions for Latino Parents' Early Literacy Involvement." *The Reading Teacher,* 59, 110–121.

Piaget, Jean, & Inhelder, B. (1969). *The Psychology of the Child.* New York: Basic Books.

Pinnell, Gay Su, & Jaggar, Angela (2003). "Oral Language: Speaking and Listening In Elementary Classrooms." In James Flood, Diane Lapp, James R. Squire, & Julie M. Jensen (Eds.), *Handbook of Research on Teaching the English Language Arts,* 2nd ed. Mahwah, NJ: Lawrence Erlbaum, pp. 881–913.

Ross, Ramon Royal. (1996). *Storyteller,* 3rd ed. Little Rock, AR: August House.

Shaffer, David. (1989). *Developmental Psychology: Childhood and Adolescence,* 2nd ed. Pacific Grove, CA: Brooks/Cole.

Sitarz, Paula Gaj. (1997). *Story Time Sampler: Read Alouds, Booktalks, and Activities for Children.* Englewood, CO: Libraries Unlimited.

Snow, Catherine E., Burns, M. Susan, & Griffin, Peg, eds. (2001). *Preventing Reading Difficulties in Young Children.* Washington, DC: National Academy Press.

Strickland, Dorothy S., & Feeley, Joan T. (2003). "Development in the Elementary School Years." In James Flood, Diane Lapp, James R. Squire, & Julie M. Jensen (Eds.), *Handbook of Research: Teaching the*

English Language Arts, 2nd ed. Mahwah, NJ: Lawrence Erlbaum, pp. 339–356.

Sulzby, Elizabeth. (1991). "Assessment of Emergent Literacy: Storybook Reading." *The Reading Teacher,* 44, 498–500.

Sulzby, Elizabeth. (1989). "Assessment of Writing and of Children's Language While Writing." In L. Morrow & J. Smith (Eds.) *The Role of Assessment and Measurement in Early Literacy Instruction.* Englewood Cliffs, NJ: Prentice Hall, pp. 83–89.

Tingle, Tim. (2002). "Presentation for Storyteller in Residence." College Station: Texas A&M University.

Tompkins, Gail E., & Tway, Eileen. (2003). "Elementary School Classroom." In James Flood, Diane Lapp, James R. Squire, & Julie M. Jensen (Eds.), *Handbook of Research on Teaching the English Language Arts,* 2nd ed. Mahwah, NJ: Lawrence Erlbaum.

Trostle, S., & Hicks, S. J. (1998). "The Effects of Storytelling versus Story Reading on Comprehension and Vocabulary Knowledge of British Primary School Children." *Reading Improvement,* 35, 127–136.

Warren, Lynne. (2002) "Snowy Owls." *National Geographic,* 202, 104–118.

Children's Literature References

Andersen, Hans Christian. (2004). *The Emperor's New Clothes.* Retold by Marcus Sedgwick. Illustrated by Alison Jay. Chronicle Books.

Andersen, Hans Christian. (2004). *The Little Mermaid.* Translated by Anthea Bell. Illustrated by Lisbeth Zwerger. Penguin.

Andersen, Hans Christian. (2004). *Thumbelina.* Retold and Illustrated by Brad Sneed. Dial Press.

Andersen, Hans Christian. (2004). *Thumbelina.* Illustrated by J. Brian Pinkney. Diane Publishing.

Andersen, Hans Christian. (2004). *The Ugly Duckling.* Translated by Anthea Bell. Illustrated by Robert Ingpen. Penguin.

Andersen, Hans Christian. (2005). *The Wild Swans.* Translated by Naomi Lewis. Illustrated by Anne Yvonne Gilbert. Barefoot Press.

Andrews-Goebel, Nancy. (2002). *The Pot That Juan Built.* Illustrated by David Diaz. Lee & Low.

Appelt, Kathi. (2002). *Bubba and Beau, Best Friends.* Illustrated by Arthur Howard. Harcourt.

Asch, Frank. (2004). *Mr. Maxwell's Mouse.* Illustrated by Devin Asch. Kids Can Press.

Aylesworth, Jim. (1992). *Old Black Fly.* Illustrated by Stephen Gammell. Henry Holt.

Babbitt, Natalie. (1975). *Tuck Everlasting.* Farrar, Straus & Giroux.

Balliett, Blue. (2004). *Chasing Vermeer.* Illustrated by Brett Helquist. Scholastic.

Baker, Keith. (1991). *Hide and Snake.* Harcourt.

Banks, Kate. (2002). *Close Your Eyes.* Illustrated by George Hallensleben. Farrar, Straus & Giroux.

Bash, Barbara. (1990). *Urban Roosts: Where Birds Nest in the City.* Little, Brown.

Bottner, Barbara, & Gerald Kruglik. (2004). *Wallace's Lists.* Illustrated by Olaf Landstrom. Katherine Tegen Books.

Brandenburg, Jim. (1997). *An American Safari: Adventures on the North American Prairie.* Walker.

Bredsdorff, Bodil. (2004). *The Crow Girl.* Farrar, Straus & Giroux.

Brenner, Barbara. (1994). *If You Were There in 1776.* Bradbury.

Brown, Monica. (2005). *My Name Is Gabriela/Me Ilamo Gabriela: The Life of Gabriela Mistral/la vida de Gabriela.* Illustrated by John Parra. Luna Rising Press.

Bruchac, Joseph. (1997). *Tell Me A Tale.* Harcourt.

Bunting, Eve. (1999). *Butterfly House.* Illustrated by Greg Shed. Scholastic.

Busby, Peter. (2003). *First to Fly: How Wilbur and Orville Wright Invented the Airplane.* Illustrated by David Craig. Crown.

Carle, Eric. (2005). *Ten Little Rubber Ducks.* Harper-Collins.

Cendrars, Blaise. (1982). *Shadow.* Illustrated by Marcia Brown. Scribners.

Child, Lauren, adapted by. (2006). *The Princess and the Pea.* Photographs by Polly Borland. Hyperion.

Collicott, Sharleen. (2003). *Mildred and Sam.* Harper-Collins.

Cooper, Hellen. (2005). *A Pipkin of Pepper for the Pumpkin Soup.* Farrar, Straus & Giroux.

Cooper, Hellen. (1999). *Pumpkin Soup.* Farrar, Straus & Giroux.

Cowley, Joy. (2005). *Mrs. Wishy-Washy's Scrubbing Machine.* Illustrated by Elizabeth Fuller. Philomel.

Cowley, Joy. (1999). *Red-Eyed Tree Frog.* Photographs by Mic Bishop. Scholastic.

Creech, Sharon. (2005). *Who's That Baby?: New-Baby Songs.* Joanna Cotler.

Crews, Nina. (2004). *The Neighborhood Mother Goose.* Amistad.

Cronin, Doreen. (2004). *Duck for President.* Simon & Schuster.

Cronin, Doreen. (2002). *Giggle, Giggle, Quack.* Illustrated by Betsy Lewin. Simon & Schuster.

Cummings, Pat, ed. (1992, 1997). *Talking with Artists.* Bradbury/Simon & Schuster.

Cunnane, Kelly. (2006). *For You Are a Kenyan Child.* Illustrated by Ana Juan. Simon & Schuster.

Curtis, Carolyn. (2004). *I Took the Moon for a Walk.* Illustrated by Alison Jay. Barefoot.

Curtis, Jamie Lee. (1996). *Tell Me Again about the Night I Was Born.* Illustrated by Laura Cornell. HarperCollins.

Cushman, Doug. (2003). *Inspector Hopper's Mystery Year.* HarperCollins.

DiCamillo, Kate. (2005). *Mercy Watson to the Rescue.* Illustrated by Chris Van Dusen. Candlewick.

DiCamillo, Kate. (2003). *The Tale of Despereaux.* Illustrated by Timothy Basil Ering. Candlewick.

Dooling, Michael. (2006). *Young Thomas Edison.* Holiday.

Dunrea, Olivier. (2002). *Gossie.* Houghton Mifflin.

Dyer, Jane. (2003). *Little Brown Bear Won't Go To School.* Little, Brown.

Ehlert, Lois. (2005). *Leaf Man.* Harcourt Children's Books.

English, Karen. (2004). *Hot Day on Abbott Avenue.* Illustrated by Javaka Steptoe. Clarion Books.

Esbaum, Jill. (2005). *Ste-e-e-e-eam Boat A Comin'!* Illustrated by Adam Rex. Farrar, Straus & Giroux.

Fleischman, Paul. (2004). *Sidewalk Circus.* Illustrated by Kevin Hawkes. Candlewick.

Fleming, Candace. (2003). *Ben Frankin's Almanac.* New York: Atheneum.

Fleming, Denise. (1991). *In the Tall, Tall Grass.* Henry Holt.

Freedman, Russell. (2002). *Confucius: The Golden Rule.* Illustrated by Frederic Clement. Levine/Scholastic.

Freedman, Russell. (2004). *The Voice That Challenged A Nation: Marian Anderson and the Struggle for Equal Rights.* Clarion.

Freymann, Saxton. (2005). *Food for Thought: Shapes, Colors, Numbers, Letters, Opposites.* Scholastic.

Fritz, Jean. (1994). *Around the World in a Hundred Years: From Henry the Navigator to Magellan.* Illustrated by Anthony Bacon Venti. Putnam.

Fritz, Jean. (1986). *Make Way for Sam Houston.* Illustrated by Elise Primavera. Putnam.

Gag, Wanda. (1928, 1977). *Millions of Cats.* Coward McCann.

Gay, Marie-Louise. (2002). *Stella, Fairy of the Forest.* Groundwood.

Giblin, James Cross, ed. (2000). *The Century That Was: Reflections on the Last One Hundred Years.* Atheneum.

Giblin, James Cross, ed. (1998). *George Washington: A Picture Book Biography.* Illustrated by Michael Dooling. Scholastic.

Graham, Bob. (2004). *Tales from the Waterhole.* Candlewick.

Greenfield, Eloise. (2004). *In the Land of Words.* Illustrated by Jan Spivey Gilchrist. HarperCollins.

Hale, Shannon. (2003). *The Goose Girl.* Bloomsbury.

Hanningan, Katherine. (2004). *Ida B. . . . and Her Plans to Maximize Fun, Avoid Disaster, and (Possibly) Save the World.* Greenwillow.

Henkes, Kevin. (2004). *Kitten's First Full Moon.* Greenwillow.

Henkes, Kevin. (2005). *So Happy!* Illustrated by Anita Lobel. Greenwillow.

Highwater, Jamake. (1977). *Anpao: An American Indian Odyssey.* Lippincott.

Hopkinson, Deborah. (2004). *Apples to Oregon.* Illustrated by Nancy Carpenter. Atheneum.

Horse, Harry. (2004). *Little Rabbit Goes to School.* Peachtree Publishers.

Hudson, Jan. (1989). *Sweetgrass.* Philomel.

Jaffe, Steven H. (1996). *Who Were the Founding Fathers? Two Hundred Years of Reinventing American History.* Henry Holt.

Jenkins, Steve. (1996). *Big and Little.* Houghton Mifflin.

Jenkins, Steve. (2006). *Almost Gone: The World's Rarest Animals.* HarperCollins.

Kahl, Jonathan D. W. (1996). *Weather Watch: Forecasting the Weather.* Lerner.

Kadohata, Cynthia. (2004). *Kira-Kira.* Atheneum.

Kalman, Maira. (2002). *Fireboat: The Heroic Adventures of the* John J. Harvey. Putnam.

Keating, Frank. (2006). *Theodore.* Illustrated by Mike Wimmer. Simon & Schuster.

Kennedy, X. J., & Kennedy, Dorothy M., eds. (1999). *Knock at a Star: A Child's Introduction to Poetry.* Illustrated by Karen Lee Baker. Little, Brown.

Kennedy, X. J., & Kennedy, Dorothy M., eds. (1992). *Talking Like the Rain: A First Book of Poems.* Illustrated by Jane Dyer. Little, Brown.

Ketchum, Liza. (1996). *The Gold Rush.* Little, Brown.

Knowlton, Jack. (1988). *Geography from A to Z: A Picture Glossary.* Illustrated by Harrie Barton. HarperCollins.

Knutson, Barbara. (2004). *Love and Roast Chicken: A Trickster Tale from the Andes Mountains.* Carolrhoda.

Konigsburg, E. L. (2004). *The Outcasts of 19 Schuyler Place.* Atheneum.

Krull, Kathleen. (2006). *Isaac Newton.* Illustrated by Boris Kulikov. Viking.

Kurtz, Jane, & Kurtz, Christopher. (2002). *Water Hole Waiting.* Illustrated by Lee Christiansen. Greenwillow.

Lasky, Kathryn. (1997). *The Most Beautiful Roof: Exploring the Rainforest Canopy.* Illustrated by Christopher G. Knight. Harcourt.

Lawrence, John. (2002). *This Little Chick*. Candlewick.

Lear, Edward. (2005). *A Was Once An Apple Pie*. Illustrated by Suse MacDonald. Orchard Books.

Lear, Edward. (1968). *The Scroobious Pip*. Illustrated by Nancy Ekholm Burkert. Harper & Row.

Lehman, Barbara. (2004). *The Red Book*. Houghton Mifflin.

Lester, Julius. (1994). *The Last Tales of Uncle Remus*. Illustrated by Jerry Pinkney. Dial Books.

Lillegard, Dee. (2002). *Tiger, Tiger*. Illustrated by Susan Guevara. Putnam.

Little, Jean. (2003). *Emma's Strange Pet*. Illustrated by Jennifer Plecas. HarperCollins.

Lionni, Leo. (1963). *Swimmy*. Pantheon.

Lobel, Arnold. (1970). *Frog and Toad Are Friends*. Harper & Row.

MacLachlan, Patricia. (1985). *Sarah, Plain and Tall*. HarperCollins.

Maestro, Betsy. (1996). *The Story of Religion*. Illustrated by Erika Weihs. Clarion.

Major, John S. (1995). *The Silk Route: 7,000 Miles of History*. Illustrated by Stephen Fieser. HarperCollins.

Mandela, Nelson. (2005). *Nelson Mandela's Favorite African Folktales*. W. W. Norton.

Markes, Julie. (2005). *Shhhhh! Everybody's Sleeping*. Illustrated by David Parkins. HarperCollins.

Martin, Bill Jr., & Michael Sampson. (2002). *I Pledge Allegiance: The Pledge of Allegiance*. Candlewick.

McClintock, Barbara. (2002). *Dahlia*. Farrar, Straus & Giroux.

McCloskey, Robert. (1941). *Make Way for Ducklings*. Viking.

McCully, Emily Arnold. (1998). *The Ballot Box Battle*. Random House.

McGhee, Alison. (2004). *Mrs. Watson Wants Your Teeth*. Illustrated by Harry Bliss. Harcourt.

McMillan, Bruce. (1991). *Eating Fractions*. Scholastic.

McMullan, Kate. (2002). *I Stink*. Illustrated by Jim McMullan. HarperCollins.

Moore, Clement C. (1999). *The Night Before Christmas*. Illustrated by Tasha Tudor. Little, Brown.

Moss, Lloyd. (1995). *Zin! Zin! Zin! A Violin*. Illustrated by Margorie Priceman. Simon & Schuster.

Moss, Miriam. (2003). *Don't Forget I Love You*. Illustrated by Anna Currey. Dial Books.

Newman, Marjorie. (2002). *Mole and the Baby Bird*. Illustrated by Patrick Benson. Bloomsbury.

O'Malley, Kevin. (2004). *Lucky Leaf*. Walker Books for Young Readers.

Orgel, Doris. (2004). *The Bremen Town Musicians and Other Animal Tales from Grimm*. Illustrated by Bert Kitche. Roaring Brook Press.

Park, Linda Sue. (2005). *Project Mulberry*. Clarion.

Park, Linda Sue. (2001). *A Single Shard*. Houghton Mifflin.

Pilkey, Dav. (1996). *The Paperboy*. Orchard.

Pullman, Philip. (2000). *The Amber Spyglass*. Knopf.

Pullman, Philip. (1995). *The Golden Compass*. Knopf.

Pullman, Philip. (1997). *The Subtle Knife*. Knopf.

Reading Is Fundamental. (2005). *The Art of Reading: Forty Illustrators Celebrate RIF's 40th Anniversary*. Dutton.

Romero, Martza. (1997). *Henry Cisneros: A Man of the People*. Rosen.

Root, Phyllis. (2002). *Oliver Finds His Way*. Illustrated by Christopher Denise. Candlewick.

Rosen, Michael. (1989). *We're Going on a Bear Hunt*. Illustrated by Helen Oxenbury. Little Simon.

Rumford, James. (2004). *Sequoyah: The Cherokee Man Who Gave His People Writing*. Houghton Mifflin.

Ryan, Pam Munoz. (2002). *When Marian Sang*. Illustrated by Brian Selznick. Scholastic.

Rylant, Cynthia. (1997). *Poppleton*. Illustrated by Mark Teague. Scholastic.

Schmidt, Gary D. (2004). *Lizzie Bright and the Buckminster Boy*. New York: Clarion.

Schotter, Roni. (1997). *Nothing Ever Happens on 90th Street*. Illustrated by Kyrsten Brooker. Orchard.

Seeger, Laura Vaccaro. (2004). *Lemons Are Not Red*. Roaring Brook Press.

Selsam, Millicent E., & Hunt, Joyce. (1987). *A First Look at Caterpillars*. Illustrated by Harriett Springer. Walker.

Seuss, Dr. [Theodore Weisel] (1937, 1989). *And to Think That I Saw It on Mulberry Street*. Random House.

Seuss, Dr. [Theodore Weisel] (1957). *The Cat in the Hat*. Random House.

Sewall, Marcia. (1990). *People of the Breaking Day*. Atheneum.

Shannon, David. (2002). *Duck on a Bike*. Scholastic.

Sierra, Judy. (2004). *Wild About Books*. Illustrated by Marc Brown. Knopf.

Silverstein, Shel. (2005). *Runny Babbit*. HarperCollins.

So, Meilo. (2004). *Gobble, Gobble, Slip, Slop: A Tale of a Greedy Cat*. Knopf.

Steptoe, Jon. (1987). *Mufaro's Beautiful Daughters: An African Tale*. Lothrop, Lee & Shepard.

Stojic, Manya. (2002). *Snow*. Knopf.

Stolley, Richard B., ed. (2000). *Life: Our Century in Pictures for Young People*. Little, Brown.

Sturges, Philemon. (1998). *Bridges Are to Cross*. Illustrated by Giles Laroche. Putnam.

Thompson, Lauren. (2004). *Polar Bear Night*. Illustrated by Stephen Savage. Scholastic.

Van Allsburg, Chris. (1985). *The Polar Express*. Houghton Mifflin.

Van Leewen, Jean. (2006). *Benny & Beautiful Baby Delilah*. Illustrated by Le Uyen Pham. Dial.

Waddell, Martin. (1992). *Farmer Duck*. Illustrated by Helen Oxenbury. Candlewick Press.

Waddell, Martin. (2004). *Tiny's Big Adventure*. Illustrated by John Laurence. Candlewick Press.

Walker, Sally M. (2005). *Secrets of a Civil War Submarine: Solving the Mysteries of the H. L. Hunley.* Carolrhoda.

Wells, Rosemary. (2004). *Bunny Mail: A Max and Ruby Lift-the-Flap Book*. Viking.

Wells, Rosemary. (2005). *Yoko's World of Kindness: Golden Rules for a Happy Class.* Hyperion.

Whybrow, Ian. (2004). *The Noisy Way to Bed*. Illustrated by Tiphanie Beeke. Arthur A. Levine.

Wiesner, David. (1988). *Free Fall*. Lothrop, Lee & Shepard.

Wiesner, David. (1991). *Tuesday*. Clarion.

Wilder, Laura Ingalls. (1932/1953). *Little House in the Big Woods*. Illustrated by Garth Williams. Harper & Row.

Willems, Mo. (2004). *Knuffle Bunny: A Cautionary Tale.* Hyperion.

Williams, Vera B. (1990). *More More More Said the Baby*. Greenwillow.

Yep, Laurence. (1993). *Dragon's Gate*. HarperCollins.

Yolen, Jane. (2000). *Off We Go!* Illustrated by Laurel Molk. Little, Brown.

Yolen, Jane. (1987). *Owl Moon*. Illustrated by John Schoenherr. Philomel.

Yolen, Jane. (2005). *This Little Piggy: Lap Songs, Finger Plays, Clapping Games, and Pantomime Rhymes.* Illustrated by Will Hillenbrand. Candlewick.

Young, Ed. (2004). *I, Doko: The Tale of a Basket.* Philomel.

Assessment and Evaluation in the Reading and Writing Program

CHAPTER **OUTLINE**

Standardized Tests
   Provisions of No Child Left Behind That Relate to Reading Instruction
   Reactions to No Child Left Behind

Assessment in the Classroom That Leads to Instructional Planning
   National Assessment of Educational Progress (NAEP)
   Principles of Assessment
   Relating Assessment to Instructional Approaches
   Assessment through Observation
   Diagnostic Reading Inventories and Informal Tests in Reading
   Running Records
   Miscue Analysis
   Cloze Assessment
   Portfolio Assessment
   Additional Types of Informal Testing in the Reading Program

After reading this chapter you will be able to answer the following questions:

1. What are the issues related to high-stakes testing?
2. What is the role of formal, standardized tests in the reading program?
3. What is the role of informal tests, especially informal reading inventories, in the reading program?
4. How can teachers develop lesson plans and units that emphasize diagnostic tests?

Read All About It!

"U.S. Says Language Exam Does Not Comply With Law"

by David M. Herszenhorn, *The New York Times,* July 11, 2006

The federal Department of Education has found that New York State's methods for testing the annual progress of disabled students and students with limited English proficiency do not comply with the No Child Left Behind law and that the state must correct the problems within a year or risk losing $1.2 million in federal school aid.

The finding was issued in a letter late last month to the state education commissioner, Richard P. Mills. In the letter, Henry L. Johnson, the assistant secretary for elementary and secondary education, told Mr. Mills that the New York State English as a Second Language Achievement Test "is not sufficiently comparable to the regular English language arts assessment" for use as "a substitute language arts assessment."

Mr. Johnson also said that tests for special education students were not suitable for their grade or age.

State officials said they were already working on the problems related to testing special education students. But they said the finding could have serious consequences for the state's nearly 175,000 non-English speaking students, including about 145,000 in New York

City, by requiring them to take the regular annual state reading exam.

A large number of these students would likely fail the test and, as a result, hundreds more schools could be branded as needing improvement under provisions of No Child Left Behind. The law requires annual testing and schools can be sanctioned if groups of students, like racial minorities or disabled children, fail to make adequate progress.

To help formulate its response to the federal government, the state education department later this week is convening a group of experts on bilingual education.

Other possible solutions include forcing non-English speakers to take both the regular test and the test they have been taking, or for the state to devise an entirely new test, which could cost millions of dollars. In the school year that just ended, 173,434 non-English speaking students statewide took the existing exam, known by its acronym, Nyseslat. Students are typically required to take the regular state English exam after three years in school in New York.

Mr. Mills, in a statement, said that it was too soon to describe specific remedies but that he expected to address regulators' concerns. "We are going to resolve these issues," he said. "We will work with educators from across the state to arrive at a solution. This will include members of the bilingual and special education communities."

David Cantor, a spokesman for Schools Chancellor Joel I. Klein, said it was premature for the city to comment.

New York was one of 36 states whose accountability systems under No Child Left Behind were found by federal reviews to have substantial problems and deemed "pending approval." Only 10 states won approval, while two, Maine and Nebraska, had their testing systems rejected.

Local experts on bilingual education said the federal government's complaint was just the latest example of non-English speaking children being an afterthought in American school systems.

Maria Neira, a first vice president of the state teachers' union, New York State United Teachers, said it was "unfair" of the federal government to expect newly arrived immigrant students to take the same exam as native English speakers.

"Of course, the tests are not comparable, they are not comparable because they are not developed to measure the same skills," she said. "One is language acquisition, the other is English language skills. What's going to happen is you are not going to have our English language learner students showing any progress. This is a big dilemma for us."

Lillian Rodríguez-López, the president of the Hispanic Federation, said the government should focus first on the programs offered to non-English speakers.

"What they really need to look at are the resources, the funding that they put into No Child Left Behind," she said. "There are not enough certified teachers, the curriculum is not strong enough. We need a solid set of standards that are being followed across the state."

Critical Thinking **Questions**

- How might the provisions of No Child Left Behind impact the education of students with special needs and students whose first language is not English?

- What is the national impact on reading assessment and reading curricula when 36 states "were found by federal reviews to have substantial problems and deemed 'pending approval'"?

- What are the arguments related to assessment presented by bilingual educators?

- What is your response to Lillian Rodríguez-López's solutions for enhancing programs for non-English speakers? Why does she emphasize resources, funding, adequate numbers of certified teachers, a strong curriculum, and a solid set of standards?

Themes of the Times

expect the world®

The New York Times
nytimes.com

For related *New York Times* articles, go to the Companion Web Site at www.ablongman.com/norton1e and click on *Themes of the Times.*

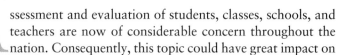

ssessment and evaluation of students, classes, schools, and teachers are now of considerable concern throughout the nation. Consequently, this topic could have great impact on you as a teacher. Many educators are searching for alternatives to high-stakes accountability while at the same time reading scores in many schools are not as high as educators desire.

Reading teachers need to decide what assessment they will use in the classroom, the purposes of the assessment, and how the assessment matches the objectives of the reading approach they have chosen. A mismatch between instructional approach and the assessment occurs when a test is chosen that does not match the skills that are taught through the reading approach used in the classroom. For example: what happens when students who are taught with a whole language approach or a top-down model of reading are tested with materials that focus primarily on the students' abilities to decode text using sound-symbol relationships? And, what happens when students are taught to read with a strong phonics approach or a bottom-up model of reading, but are tested with material that focuses on comprehension abilities that have not been covered in the instructional program? This chapter presents various ways to assess and improve reading.

Assessment refers to the gathering of data in order to understand the reading strengths and weaknesses of the student or the total reading program. Assessment includes many different types of both formal and informal tests as well as observations. The purpose for assessment is to evaluate students' performance in reading and to guide their instruction. The term **diagnosis** suggests a process similar to that used by medical doctors. Doctors first take tests and ask questions, check the results of the tests, and then give a diagnosis or recommend a course of treatment for the medical problem. Diagnosis in reading refers to gathering data and selecting appropriate tests for the students, administering the tests, and using the results of the tests to plan appropriate instruction.

Just as in the medical model, there are different levels of diagnosis in reading. A doctor may give a patient a yearly physical that includes an eye exam, blood pressure check, and blood tests. These are *survey levels of diagnosis*. At the survey level of diagnosis, the teacher examines the reading levels of all the students in a class in order to evaluate the success of the total reading program, to determine areas in which the whole class needs corrective instruction, and to identify students who require more specific levels of diagnosis. This level of diagnosis also helps the teacher identify a student's individual reading level and to identify how he or she compares with other students. The tests required for No Child Left Behind, introduced in Chapter 1, are survey level tests.

Survey levels of diagnosis in reading are the standardized tests, or survey tests. These are published tests that have been constructed by experts, administered to large groups of students, and scored according to stated criteria. These tests are given to large total populations of students in order to evaluate the success of the reading program for the school district, for the state, and for the nation. Among the most common standardized tests are the Iowa Test of Basic Skills, the Stanford Achievement Test, the Metropolitan Achievement Test, and the California Achievement Test. Standardized or survey-level test results are the test results that make the news headlines and are used to compare reading achievement among school districts.

Another type of test usually discussed with the survey level of diagnosis is the *norm-referenced test*. Norm-referenced tests are used to compare performance on the test with a representative sample, or norming group, of students. Norm-referenced tests establish levels of skill knowledge so that comparisons can be made. They are the most common tests used to measure a school's progress in reading achievement.

If these survey tests identify any reading difficulties or comprehension problems, the teacher may administer additional tests, usually in the form of non-standardized tests, to try to discover why the student is having difficulties with comprehension. These *specific levels of diagnosis* include tests to evaluate sub-skills of reading such as phonics and sight word vocabulary, tests to evaluate oral reading ability, and tests to evaluate a student's reading ability to comprehend at the independent, instructional, or frustration levels of comprehension. These levels are discussed later in the chapter under "Informal Reading Inventories." A type of test usually discussed with the specific level of diagnosis is the *criterion-referenced test,* which compares a student's performance with criteria identified by experts in the field. For example, the students will be able to identify 90 percent of the words on a sight-word vocabulary test and that would be the criterion the students taking the test would need to meet.

If there are still difficulties in diagnosing the problem, just as the doctor usually sends the patient to a specialist, a teacher sends the student to a reading specialist who is trained in advanced assessment skills. This becomes an *intensive level of diagnosis* in which the reading specialist uses all of his or her capabilities and advanced tests to identify the problem and plan a course of education that will remedy the problem and lead to reading success. This intensive level of diagnosis is usually reserved for students with severe reading disabilities. The tests given at an intensive level of diagnosis may include eye exams, physical exams, intensive diagnostic reading tests, intelligence tests, and observations related to emotional and behavioral characteristics. A reading specialist may write a case report that includes a tentative diagnosis, a prognosis for rate of reading gains, and a proposal for treatment. This case report is usually shared with teachers in order to help them provide instruction for the student. The case study may also be used to provide evidence that a student needs intensive remediation or special programs.

To be an effective reading teacher, it is necessary to continually evaluate the reading process. **Evaluation** includes considering test results and making decisions about the effectiveness of the instruction. In the medical model, when doctors evaluate the effectiveness of their treatment and make recommendations, they periodically check the progress of the patient and make decisions about whether medications must be changed or more intensive medical procedures are required. The same is true when evaluating children's reading progress. Teachers collect various types of test data and evaluate the effectiveness of instruction. Evaluation may suggest that students' needs have changed and they may require different approaches to learning to read or have not mastered one of the skills required to succeed in the specific reading program used by the teacher.

In this chapter, we discuss reading assessment according to two types of assessment that influence the reading teacher and how reading may be taught. We begin with standardized tests because they are the tests that schools are required to give and the results usually make headlines for the school districts involved and are mentioned in articles such as the one in "Read All About It." The chapter then discusses assessment in the classroom that includes measures that relate to instructional approaches and that may be referred to as informal tests because they are not standardized through administering to large populations. These informal tests, however, are the ones that most reading teachers use to make decisions about individual students and their reading needs.

Standardized Tests

Using standardized tests to evaluate schoolwide programs has received support as well as considerable criticism as a strategy for improving public education. A **standardized test** is a published test constructed by experts and then administered, scored, and interpreted according to specific criteria. The use of standardized tests has escalated over the past few years. Laura Hamilton and Daniel Koretz (2002) found that using such large-scale testing dates back to the nineteenth century in American education. The tests were used to evaluate the effectiveness of instructional programs and to compare schools and teachers. As Hamilton and Koretz point out, "the first standardized achievement test battery, the Stanford Achievement Test, was originally published in 1923, and the role of standardized testing grew markedly over the following years. It has been a fixture of elementary and secondary education ever since" (p. 14). The test results can be reported in a number of ways, such as percentile rankings or grade equivalent scores. In percentile rankings, student scores are compared with a national percentile rank, such as 50 percent of all students tested scored at this level. In grade equivalent scores, the student's performance is compared with all students tested at a specific grade level. Schools and state and federal agencies use the results of standardized tests to evaluate schoolwide reading programs.

These test results have serious consequences for students, reading teachers, and school systems because they are used for comparing and evaluating students' reading scores. Educators refer to these standardized tests as **high-stakes tests** because results of the reading test scores may cause schools and teachers to be rewarded or punished. Rewards for high reading scores may give reading teachers salary bonuses and recognition. Conversely, punishment for low reading scores may result in loss of jobs and the closing of schools. "In some states, low-performing schools can be taken over by the state, teachers and principals can lose their jobs, or teachers may be required to take competency tests to demonstrate their ability to teach" (Jones, Jones, & Hargrove, 2003). As a result of the No Child Left Behind Act, signed into law in January 2002, there is an increased focus on using standardized tests to evaluate a school's reading program. (Arenson, 2006)

Provisions of No Child Left Behind That Relate to Reading Instruction

A discussion of the legislation and accompanying testing surrounding No Child Left Behind is important because this legislation has so much impact on teachers and students across the United States. The law has produced both accolades for the legislation and concerns about the educational consequences resulting from the legislation. Provisions of No Child Left Behind (2002) that relate directly to the teaching and testing of reading include:

1. Achieving excellence through high standards and accountability
2. Improving literacy by putting reading first
3. Improving teacher quality
4. Moving limited English proficient students to English fluency
5. Promoting parental options and innovative programs
6. Enhancing education through technology
7. Encouraging freedom and accountability

The portions of the legislation that are most closely related to assessment and evaluation in reading are the issues of accountability and high standards, annual reading assessments, and the consequences for schools that fail to educate all students including those with special educational needs.

The policy statement begins with ways that education will be improved by "Closing the Achievement Gap" between successful and unsuccessful students through the following areas:

1. *Accountability and High Standards:* Accountability requires that all states, school districts, and schools must be accountable for reaching and maintaining high academic standards for all students. States must develop a system of sanctions and rewards to hold schools accountable.

2. *Annual Academic Assessments:* Reading and math must be assessed so that parents have the information they need to know how well their children do in school and how well the school is educating their children. States may select and design assessments of their choosing. A sample of students from each state will be tested each year using the National Assessment of Education Progress (NAEP) for fourth- and eighth-grade assessment in reading and math.

3. *Consequences for Schools That Fail to Educate Disadvantaged Students:* Schools that fail to make adequate yearly progress will come under corrective action if they fail to make adequate yearly progress for three consecutive years. Disadvantaged students may use Title I funds to transfer to a higher-performing public or private school, or receive supplemental educational services.

The legislation requires that all states, school districts, and schools must be accountable for high standards in reading, meaning that they accept responsibility for students' successes or failures in learning how to read. To prove that they are accountable, schools are required to assess students in reading and math. Although states may select and design assessments of their choosing, a sample of students from each state will be tested each year using the National Assessment of Education Progress (NAEP) for fourth- and eighth-grade assessment in reading and math.

The proposals under "Achieving Equality through High Standards and Accountability" also relate to assessment and evaluation in reading programs. The law indicates that schools develop rigorous accountability by setting high standards in reading and continually adding challenging contents in history and science. The annual assessments related to accountability are geared to evaluate whether or not students have met the standards. The law also requires progress reports on all students and that the results must be reported to the public "by race, gender, English language proficiency, disability, and socioeconomic status" (p. 8).

The law includes rewards for states and schools that narrow the achievement gaps by providing school bonus funds, and it includes consequences for schools that fail to make adequate yearly progress by removing portions of their administrative funds. Specifically, the legislation asserts, "Sanctions will be based on a state's failure to narrow the achievement gap in meeting adequate yearly progress requirements in math and reading in grades 3 through 8. Progress on state assessments will be confirmed by state results on an annual sampling of 4th and 8th grade students on the National Assessment of Educational Progress (NAEP) in math and reading" (p. 9).

In addition to requiring student success, No Child Left Behind has stipulations for improving teacher quality by establishing high standards for professional development, promoting innovative teacher reforms, expecting teacher quality to improve, and empowering parents with teacher quality information. The accountability and evaluation enters into teacher quality by holding states accountable for ensuring that all children are taught by effective teachers. This accountability includes reforming teacher certification or licensing and providing alternative certification, as well as merit-based teacher performance and bonus pay for teachers in high-need subject areas such as reading in high-poverty school districts.

Reactions to No Child Left Behind

Newspapers, educational journals, and books include many articles in which authors reflect on the advantages and disadvantages and the issues that arise from No Child Left Behind legislation and high-stakes testing. Understanding these reactions is important for anyone entering education.

The various national organizations for teacher educators are currently reviewing the mandates under No Child Left Behind and reporting the consequences of those mandates as well as recommendations for any changes to the education act that applies through 2007. For example, Peggy Harris (2006), clarifying the National Council of Teachers of English 2005 "Resolution on Reauthorization of the Elementary and Secondary Education Act", states why an understanding of No Child Left Behind is important to educators: "In all my years in education I have never felt such a high level of tension as exists today because of No Child Left Behind. In many of the schools and districts we serve, teachers have been bombarded with mandates and scripted programs that prevent them from using their professional knowledge and skill to respond to the needs of their students" (p. 1).

Harris's article includes interviews with educators across the United States. These interviews include both positive and negative consequences of No Child Left Behind that are important to teachers. For example, Michael L. Shaw, professor of literacy at St. Thomas Aquinas College in New York, quotes a superintendent of schools who maintains that the law allows him to increase time spent teaching literacy, to provide extra support for struggling readers, and to bring in consultants who help improve the curriculum. Shaw also identifies negative consequences such as teachers who state that it is unfortunate that all students are expected to learn through the same approaches, even though those approaches may not be the best for the students. Evan Robb, principal of a middle school in Virginia, questions the use of mandated assessment measures that encourage teachers to teach to the test rather than use formative and holistic assessment, which looks for growth and progress over a school year. Laura Robb, a professor and author of reading text books, believes that the mandated tests cause children to develop test anxiety because both parents and teachers are stressing the importance of the tests. Reba Wadsworth, a principal of an elementary school in Alabama, believes the answer is to rely on highly-skilled teachers who have the knowledge base to teach literacy. Paul Crowley, a professor of reading and language education at Sonoma State University in California, stresses the need for teachers to teach with strategies and materials that they know will work with their students, rather than mandated teaching materials.

As we progress in this chapter we will try to understand why educational organizations and individual educators are so concerned about both the positive and negative issues associated with the high-stakes testing required with No Child Left Behind.

ISSUES RELATED TO DEFINING ACCOUNTABILITY   One of the terms used in the legislation for No Child Left Behind is *accountability*. How will students prove that they are accountable for learning how to read? How will teachers prove that they are accountable for teaching students how to read? Katherine Ryan (2003) responds to issues related to accountability by asking the question, "What constitutes acceptable performance?" Several issues must be considered before there is reliable accountability. School systems and state agencies need to consider:

- Why are assessments given particular weights? What is more important or less important when testing?

- What parts of the reading program should be assessed?

- When should tests be given (all grades or selected grades)?

- How should performance be assessed (multiple-choice tests, performance assessments, portfolios, etc.)?

The answers to any of these questions will influence how reading is defined, how it is tested, and how it is taught. According to Ryan, these questions involve "consideration of accountability goals, levels, standard of accountability, and how much emphasis is given to current performance and how much to improvement over time" (p. 456).

ISSUES RELATED TO CONSEQUENCES OF NO CHILD LEFT BEHIND   The unintended consequences of high-stakes testing are summarized in a study by Gail Jones, Brett Jones, and Tracy Hargrove (2003), who divide them into four categories: educational resources, students, teachers, and instruction.

Consequences for educational resources include:

- increased funds spent for developing and giving tests

- increased scores in tested subjects

- increased funds for rewards

- increased funds spent on student remediation for tests

- increased student dropout rates

- increased numbers of grade level retention and referrals for special education programs.

Consequences for the students may include:

- increased testing of young children
- increased cheating on tests
- pressure from teachers and principals
- decreased graduation rates
- decreased confidence
- decreased love for learning.

Consequences for teachers may include:

- decreased teacher autonomy and teacher creativity
- increased levels of stress
- increased teacher turnover as teachers leave lower performing schools for the schools where students get higher scores
- increased professional development focused on assessment programs
- increased "teaching to the test"

Reflect on Your Reading

How do you think the stipulations of the No Child Left Behind Act will influence testing of reading, instructions in reading, and teacher effectiveness in teaching reading? How might the provisions in the law influence the reading curriculum? What do you believe are the major advantages and disadvantages of the law?

Consequences for instruction may include:

- a decrease in subjects if the subjects are not tested (for example, art and foreign languages)
- a decrease in creative writing
- less time spent on instruction
- a decrease in developmentally appropriate instructional practices
- increased external control of curriculum
- increased focus on lower-level skills
- increased time spent taking tests
- increased time spent on test-taking skills

Assessment in the Classroom That Leads to Instructional Planning

While standardized tests are extremely influential when evaluating total reading programs and identifying schools that are meeting specified standards in reading or are failing to meet those reading standards, standardized tests are not the most useful tools to help a teacher identify a student's specific strengths and weaknesses or to develop a reading program that meets the student's needs.

Alfie Kohn (2000) reminds us, "Standardized tests can't measure initiative, creativity, imagination, conceptual thinking, curiosity, effort, irony, judgment, commitment, nuance, good will, ethical reflection. . . . What they can measure and count are isolated skills, specific facts and functions, the least interesting and least significant aspects of learning" (p. 17).

National Assessment of Educational Progress (NAEP)

What happens when reading test results are compared between the state-developed reading assessments mandated under No Child Left Behind and federal tests that are also mandated under No Child Left Behind? The NAEP is one federally funded testing program that uses the same test to test reading and mathematics capabilities of students throughout the United States. Instead of allowing each state to develop and administer its own test, the NAEP is developed and regulated by the National Assessment Governing Board. Consequently, all students across the United States take the same reading assessment examination.

Issues related to reading proficiency result when reading scores of students are compared on the state mandated tests and the NAEP results. Sam Dillon (2005) reports major discrepancies between reading results on the reading tests developed by individual state tests and on the NAEP exams and concludes:

> Such discrepancies have intensified the national debate over testing and accountability, with some educators saying that numerous states have created easy exams to avoid the sanctions that President Bush's centerpiece education law *No Child Left Behind* imposes on consistently low-scoring schools. (p. 1A)

Dillon compares the reading test results of fourth- and eighth-grade results on state and federal exams in several states. In Mississippi, for example, 86 percent of fourth-graders performed at or above proficiency on the state reading tests, compared with 18 percent of the students who performed at the proficiency level on the federal reading tests. The differences in Texas are 79 percent proficiency on fourth-grade state tests compared with 29 percent on the NAEP test. Differences in New York showed 70 percent proficiency on state tests versus 34 percent on the NAEP test. Similar discrepancies are reported between eighth-grade state exams and NAEP reading exams. For example, 75 percent of students in Connecticut are proficient on state exams versus 34 percent proficient on NAEP exams. Dillon quotes several educators who maintain that the discrepancies over reading test results can be overcome only if all students take the same nationally administered reading test.

Why are there such large discrepancies in the reading scores between students who take their state tests and students who take the national tests? One of the ways to draw some conclusions is to discover what is being tested on the national test and how reading is measured on the test. For example, the National Assessment Governing Board (2004) reports the framework for the NAEP 2009 reading assessment. This framework defines what is expected in reading for students to measure proficiency in reading.

To be proficient in reading on the 2009 NAEP test, students will be expected to read across genres of literature including fiction, nonfiction, and poetry. They will be required to answer questions that demand that they integrate information, interpret text, and critique and evaluate texts they read. Over one-half of the questions on the test will be higher-level questions that require written responses rather than multiple-choice responses. To be proficient when reading fiction, students need to demonstrate understanding of themes, plot structures, and point of view. To be proficient when reading nonfiction, students need to recognize causal relationships and logical connections, and must identify details in texts, graphs, and photographs. Taffy E. Raphael and Kathryn H. Au (2005) analyze NAEP sample passage questions by giving an example of a question, showing the format that answering the question requires (e.g., multiple choice, short answer written response, or extended written response), and identifying the type of comprehension strategy needed to answer the question. They categorize these strategies as:

- "On My Own," in which students must activate prior knowledge about areas such as genre or authors or make connections with the topic.

- "Right There," in which they scan text to locate information, use notetaking strategies to support information, or use context clues to create definitions.

- "Think and Search," in which they identify important information, summarize information, make comparisons and contrasts, visualize settings and moods, use context to describe symbols and figurative language, clarify information, and make inferences.

- "Author and Me," in which students make predictions, visualize, develop simple and complex inferences, distinguish fact from opinion, and make connections between the text and self.

Table 3.1 presents Raphael and Au's analysis of NAEP sample passage questions.

Principles of Assessment

When developing a plan for assessing reading, educators use many different types of tests, but educators also need to remember that the ultimate goal in evaluating any reading program should be the improvement of instruction (Farr & Beck, 2003). Consequently, educators such as Robert B. Ruddell (2002) advocate that assessment should be based on real classroom learning experiences. This type of assessment is called **authentic assessment** because it requires that teachers evaluate reading while children are taking part in actual classroom reading activities. Ruddell identifies the following seven principles for authentic assessment:

1. Observation provides one of the most reliable assessments because teachers observe and take notes on students as they are engaged in classroom reading and writing tasks.

2. The focus of assessment should be on children's learning and the instructional goals of the curriculum. This focus allows teachers to identify students' strengths and instructional needs.

3. Assessment needs to be continuous as teachers base observations over a substantial period of time. Continuous observations allow teachers to note individual students' progress and growth.

TABLE 3.1

Analysis of NAEP Sample Passage Questions

Question	Format	QAR and Strategies
1. This article mostly describes how . . .	Multiple choice	Think & Search: ■ Identifying important information ■ Summarizing ■ Making simple inferences
2. Where do wombats live?	Multiple choice	Right There ■ Scanning to locate information
3. Describe one way in which wombats and koalas are similar and one way in which they are different.	Short constructed response	Think & Search ■ Visualizing ■ Identifying important information ■ Summarizing
4. Use the information in this passage to describe marsupials.	Short constructed response	Think & Search ■ Visualizing ■ Identifying important information ■ Using text organization to identify relevant information ■ Summarizing
5. Where do wombats usually live?	Multiple choice	Right There ■ Scanning to locate information
6. Choose an animal, other than a koala, that you know about and compare it to the wombat.	Short constructed response	Author & Me ■ Visualizing ■ Making simple and complex inferences (to compare) ■ Making text-to-self connections
7. Why are wombats not often seen by people?	Multiple choice	Right There ■ Scanning to locate information
8. Describe the sleeping area of wombats.	Short constructed response	Right There ■ Scanning to locate information ■ Note-taking to support easier recall
9. To get food, the wombat uses its . . .	Multiple choice	Right There ■ Scanning to locate information
10. What would a wombat probably do if it met a person?	Multiple choice	Author & Me ■ Predicting ■ Making simple and complex inferences
11. Why has Australia set up animal reserves to protect the wombat?	Short constructed response	Think & Search ■ Identifying important information ■ Using text organization to identify relevant information ■ Making simple inferences
12. Give two reasons why people should not have wombats as pets. Use what you learned in the passage to support your answer.	Extended constructed response	Author & Me ■ Identifying important information ■ Making complex inferences ■ Visualizing

Source: Analysis of NAEP Sample Passage Questions—Questions retrieved June 14, 2005 from http://nces.ed.gov/nationsreportcard/ITMRLS/search.asp?picksdsubi=Reading.

Reflect on Your Reading

As you read through these sample questions taken from a nonfiction selection, identify how these questions relate to the NAEP goal of demonstrating high levels of literacy when reading nonfiction. Remember that to be proficient students must draw on their knowledge of text organization including description, causal relationships, and logical connections, to identify important details in the text. What should your reading curriculum include so that students are proficient in reading nonfiction texts and answering questions about the texts?

4. Whatever the assessment, it should be equitable and take into account the diversity of students' culture, language, and special needs.

5. Assessment should include the active participation of children. This type of assessment includes Literature Response Journals that allow both student and teacher to write responses to literature in a journal. Students need opportunities to be involved in their own evaluation of reading and writing.

6. Assessment needs to be based on observations from many sources rather than on one assessment approach.

7. Assessment should be knowledge-based and reflect current understanding of reading and writing processes.

As Ruddell points out, observations of students when they are involved in classroom reading is one of the most reliable assessments because teachers take notes that describe a student's reading behaviors while he or she actually reads. Notes might include the literature students select for reading circles or recreational reading groups. Or, notes might focus on the types of errors students make when they read selections aloud.

Relating Assessment to Instructional Approaches

To help us understand the importance of matching assessment to the models of the reading process and the reading approaches discussed in Chapter 1, consider the characteristics of each approach defined in Table 1.1. In his principles of authentic assessment, Robert Ruddell emphasizes that the focus of assessment should be on children's learning and the instructional goals of the curriculum. Let us consider what types of assessment could be used to measure the instructional goals of phonics, sub-skills, whole language, literature-based, and balanced reading approaches.

PHONICS ASSESSMENT Phonics approaches are related to bottom-up models of reading processing that emphasize the importance of analyzing sound-symbol relationships. Consequently, beginning reading proceeds from sounds of letters, to patterns in words, to meaning. Teachers can easily develop their own tests to analyze students' abilities in phonics.

At the beginning level of awareness, assessment includes informal tests to measure whether students can identify rhyming elements in words. For example, the teacher can pronounce a series of words such as *mat/pat, ten/men,* and *fed/fad* and ask students to identify the words that rhyme and those that do not rhyme. At the first-grade level or beginning reading stage, a test of phonic analysis skills can measure a student's ability to identify the sounds of letters when the teacher holds up alphabet cards and assess a student's ability to identify whether two words such as *bat/bet, cat/get,* and *pen/pick* do or do not begin with the same sound or words such as *sit/six, tell/fill,* and *dog/rug* end with the same sound when the words are said by the teacher. Texts such as *Words Their Way: Word Study for Phonics, Vocabulary, and Spelling Instruction* (Bear and Colleagues, 2000) provide detailed examples of ways of testing phonics. There are also assessments available that test students' phonics abilities for example, J. K. Torgesen and B. R. Bryant's *Test of Phonological Awareness* (1994).

SUB-SKILLS ASSESSMENT   Sub-skills instruction is based on teaching identifiable sub-skills related to reading such as word attack skills, ways to identify vocabulary, and components of comprehension. The tests for sub-skills are frequently stated in performance objectives. A teacher-constructed test for testing third-graders for their knowledge of sight words vocabulary, for example, might include: "when given a two-second exposure per word, the student is able to recognize 130 words from the Dolch Basic Sight Vocabulary List of 220 words." The teacher would use such test results to identify students who have mastered this sub-skill and students who need additional instruction in sight words. Basic sight vocabulary tests are also included in the *Ekwall/Shanker Reading Inventory* discussed later in this chapter.

WHOLE LANGUAGE ASSESSMENT   The whole language approach is a top-down model of the reading process that emphasizes that students' backgrounds and language lead them to comprehension. Yetta Goodman (2003) recommends that teachers use checklists, inventories, and interviews that allow teachers to see changes in their students and to answer questions that focus on "students' attitudes about language, the kinds of materials they read, and the range of topics they write about" because these "provide insight into students' beliefs about the powers of language and its influence on their lives" (p. 604).

The miscue analysis, which is discussed later in this chapter, is one of the primary assessment approaches recommended by whole language advocates because teachers learn more about the students' reading processes when they listen to students read and analyze words within a whole story. Another type of assessment recommended by whole language advocates is taking notes on students as teachers observe them engaged in actual reading activities. (Various types of observational assessments are discussed later in the chapter.)

LITERATURE-BASED ASSESSMENT   Literature-based approaches emphasize the interactive reading process as students read and respond to literature. Knowledge of story structures, genres, and various writing styles develops schema for making predictions about the stories and comprehending texts. Because the students read using both teacher-directed activities with the literature and self-selected literature, informal "interest inventories" that identify their special interests and favorite authors are helpful. An example of an informal interest inventory is found later in this chapter.

Because students read from examples of literature selections, the portion of an **informal reading inventory** that identifies students' reading levels according to **independent reading level, instructional reading level,** and **frustration reading level** is very useful. At the instructional level teachers provide instruction using a literature selection; at the independent level students select books on their own for recreational reading. The frustration reading level identifies books that are too difficult for students to read.

Cloze tests, discussed more fully later in this chapter, assess students' abilities to read particular materials. An example of a cloze test is a text that leaves out every fifth word from an actual reading passage and has the student complete the text. These tests are very good for predicting a student's ability to read that text.

Consequently, the cloze technique is closely related to literature-based reading because students read passages taken directly from their reading materials. A cloze test with information on how to construct it and score it to provide instructional levels, independent levels, and frustration levels is shown later in this chapter.

BALANCED INSTRUCTION ASSESSMENT   The balanced instruction approach to assessment is another interactive approach that combines the best features of the skills approaches, as in phonics and sub-skills and reading quality literature, in a literature-based approach. Consequently, the assessments already discussed, especially the informal reading inventories, the cloze tests, and the tests for phonics analysis, are all important in a balanced reading approach. Table 3.2 includes a summary of the various types of assessments that match the instructional approaches.

Assessment through Observation

Observing of students while they are engaged in actual reading activities is one of the most reliable and easily used types of assessment. Yetta Goodman (2003) calls such observations "Kid-watching" because teachers step back from the instructional role, observe students, and take notes about what they see and how the students are interacting with the reading process.

Teresa M. McDevott and Jeanne Ellis Ormond (2004) identify several areas of observation that may be used to help teachers assess emergent literacy in young children. To discover children's attitudes toward books and literature, for example, a teacher could observe whether they are attentive and interested when listening to books being read to them. Teachers can also observe to see if children talk about the stories after they read them and see if they choose to look at books rather than choose other activities. These kinds of observations are very important for success in a literature-based approach.

The observable behavior children show when they interact with books is important because their attitudes toward books reflect their previous experiences with books. Children who have considerable experience are usually ready for successful reading instruction. Consider how the child holds a book. Is it held correctly? Is the child curious about the content of books? Does the child use pictures in the book to construct meaning or try to read the book? Using pictures to gain meaning is related to a top-down model of reading and to the whole language approach.

Observing how a child approaches word recognition is another way to judge readiness to read and possible success in a phonics approach. Does the child recognize letters? And does he or she try to sound out the letters and recognize words?

Teachers gain considerable information from observation that allows them to assess how students in the lower elementary grades are progressing within a specific approach to reading. For example, when you are observing students reading aloud, are they attending to the sounds of the letters when sounding out words? Are they using the meaning of the context of the sentence—the meaning of the words around the unknown word—to try to identify the unknown word? If they are not using both sound and meaning, they may require a balanced approach to reading that teaches them how to use both cueing systems.

One of my favorite observational approaches is to observe students as they tell a story they retell after "reading" a wordless book such as Barbara Lehman's *The*

TABLE 3.2

Assessment Related to Instructional Reading Approaches

	Phonics	Sub-Skills	Whole Language	Literature-Based	Balanced
Reading Process	Bottom-Up (Parts to whole)	Bottom-Up (Sub-parts to whole)	Top-Down (Whole to parts)	Interactive	Interactive
Types of Assessment	Tests that identify rhyming elements	Tests that identify and apply sub-skills that make up reading	Tests that evaluate use of language	Interest Inventories	Tests of phonics and sub-skills
	Tests consonant sounds	Tests knowledge of sight words	Miscue analysis	Comprehension portions of Informal Reading Inventories	All parts of Informal Reading Inventories
	Tests ability to blend sounds into words	Sub-skill tests on Informal Reading Inventories	Observational assessments	Cloze tests	Cloze tests
				Tests knowledge of literary elements	Observations
	Word attack portions of Informal Reading Inventories		Comprehension portions of Informal Reading Inventories		

Red Book or Paul Fleischman's *Sidewalk Circus*. To develop this observation, teachers can tell students they will have an opportunity to become authors and tell the story that accompanies the pictures. Teachers need to allow students plenty of time to look through the book and think about the story they will tell. When students are ready, ask them to tell the story that accompanies the book—they may use the book to prompt their story. The teacher writes down each student's story word-for-word.

These dictated stories give teachers several types of information. Does the student watch as the words are written, pace the dictation according to the teacher's ability to write the story, pause at the end of a sentence, or attempt to read the story back to the teacher? This information is especially important when assessing beginning readers because teachers are able to determine how much knowledge students have about print and the relationship between words and writing. Teachers can also assess the stories themselves to determine whether the students have developed a logical sequence, provided details associated with the setting, described characters, or expressed themselves through a vivid and well-developed vocabulary. Table 3.3 represents an observation profile that accompanies the retelling of a wordless book.

Diagnostic Reading Inventories and Informal Tests in Reading

In this next section, we will discover the role of informal tests in reading, how to develop and apply the findings from these tests, and how to develop individual portfo-

TABLE 3.3

Observation Profile
To Accompany a Retelling of a Wordless Book

	YES	Sometimes	NO
1. Watches while teacher writes story	___	___	___
2. Pauses at the end of sentences	___	___	___
3. Tries to read the story	___	___	___
4. Uses complete sentences	___	___	___
5. Tells story in logical order	___	___	___
6. Describes setting	___	___	___
7. Describes characters	___	___	___
8. Uses rich vocabulary	___	___	___
9. Is able to give a title that suggests a main idea	___	___	___
10. The story shows background knowledge	___	___	___

Examples of sentences

_____

_____

_____

_____

lios for assessing reading. We will also discover the role of observant reading teachers as they assess and evaluate the students during all types of instruction.

Educators who stress using assessment to make discoveries about the instructional needs of children emphasize using tests that are not large-scale standardized assessments. Lorna M. Earl (2003) believes "Educators need to think about the various purposes for assessment and make choices about the purposes that they believe are important and how to realize these purposes every day in their classrooms" (p. 13). She cites research by the Assessment Reform Group (1999) that argues, "Assessment that is explicitly designed to promote learning is the single most powerful tool we have for raising standards and empowering life-long learning" (p. 43). This type of assessment focuses on important aspects of the subject, gives students opportunities to practice skills and consolidate learning, and guides further instructional and learning activities.

Tests identified as diagnostic tests of reading ability rather than **standardized tests** that evaluate reading achievement of total programs are among the most useful tests. These tests provide specific information that teachers may use to guide instruction and diagnose areas such as a student's oral reading ability, word recognition and vocabulary skills, and comprehension. The tests may be developed by the teacher using instructional materials from the classroom, commercially published tests, or tests that accompany a reading series.

Suzann F. Peregoy and Owen F. Boyle (2001) provide a useful chart for identifying the reading levels of students, instruments that might be used, what is evaluated

A teacher uses an informal assessment of reading ability as she completes a running record while the child reads.

in each test, and what might be learned from the results. This chart (see Table 3.4) is equally beneficial for testing students who are in English as a Second Language (ESL) programs.

Although standardized tests usually identify each student's grade equivalency, this does not mean that a student's instructional reading level is at the same level. For example, one student may have been shown to have a grade equivalency of 2.5 to signify the middle of the second grade. Another student taking the same test may have a grade equivalency of 5.5 to signify the middle of the fifth grade; but this is not accurate for an instructional level because the student did not actually read passages at the fifth-grade level—but simply reading better than the child who tested at 2.5 using the same test.

Patricia Cunningham and Richard Allington (2003) point out:

> If your class average score is 2.5, you can be pretty sure that your class reads as well as the average class of second-graders on which the test was normed. Standardized scores give us information about groups of children, but give us only limited information about the reading levels of individual children. To determine the reading level of a child, we must listen to that child read and retell and find the highest levels at which they can do both with approximately 95 percent of word accuracy and 75 percent comprehension. Unfortunately, no shortcut will get us where we need to go." (p. 104)

Mary Lynn Woods and Alden J. Moe (1995) emphasize that an informal reading inventory allows teachers to gain important information about a student's reading ability because the informal reading inventory "is given in a one-to-one observation-and-response style," and because it "renders specific information about how the reader processes print, the examiner will be collecting quantitative data that [give] a general overview of the level of performance and qualitative data that [reveal] specific information about the strategies the reader uses to read texts. The very

TABLE 3.4

Reading Assessment Chart

Reading Level	Instrument that might be used	What is tested	What might be learned
Beginning Readers: usually early grades, but can be later grades as well.	Running Records: as student reads, the teacher checks off words that student reads correctly and codes those students has trouble with.	Student reading fluency and ability to process print: decoding, syntax, use of context, etc.	Whether students have basic ability to recognize words automatically so that they can concentrate on comprehension.
Intermediate Readers: students who have learned how to read but may still be having difficulties with processing text.	Miscues Analysis: student reads material while you are listening or tape recording: words are coded by you and comprehension questions are asked or student recalls information.	Student strategies for processing print: possible difficulties with print: and comprehension of information as given in recall or answering questions.	What student knows or doesn't know based upon oral reading. Whether student is "barking at print" or actually comprehending.
Advanced Readers: readers who have basic abilitiy to process print automatically and who focus on comprehension.	Comprehension Checks: looking at student's ability to understand both narrative and expository texts: e.g., GRI (Groups Reading Inventory).	Student ability to comprehend materials at high levels including: factual, inferential, and applicative.	Student's sophistication in reading various levels and genres of print.
Appropriate for all readers whether struggling or gifted.	Informal Reading Inventory (IRI): used leveled reading passages and comprehension checks, you can establish reading levels of your students.	Student ability to comprehend and process text at Independent, Instructional, and Frustration levels.	How student is able to read and comprehend passages written at various grade levels.
Appropriate for all readers and writers.	Portfolio Assessment: teacher and student together collect in a portfolio various examples of student's reading and writing.	How students perceive their literacy ability, general progress.	How student has developed over time. How student perceives work. What might be done next to assist moving the student to the next level of development.

Source: Suzann F. Peregoy and Owen F. Boyle (2001), *Reading, Writing, and Learning in ESL.* New York: Addison Wesley Longman, p. 378.

specific information learned from the qualitative analysis provides teachers with what they need to know to form an instructional plan" (p. 2).

By administering an informal reading inventory, teachers gain information about the student's level of word recognition, strengths and weaknesses the student shows during word recognition, oral and silent reading performance, comprehension strengths, and difficulties shown while reading at the independent reading level, instructional reading level, frustration reading level, and listening level.

There are several published informal reading inventories that allow the teacher to gain this important information about an individual student's reading abilities and to identify the reading levels of the student. For example, we will proceed through the components of one such inventory, called the *Ekwall/Shanker Reading Inventory,* Fourth Edition (2000). This inventory includes the following list of sub-tests:

1. A graded word list for quick assessment of reading

2. Reading passages designed to evaluate a student's oral reading

3. Silent reading and listening comprehension levels

4. Emergent literacy tests that assess phonemic awareness, concepts about print, and letter knowledge

5. Basic sight vocabulary tests

6. Phonics tests

7. Structural analysis tests

8. Reading interests survey

This list of sub-tests meets the requirements for most approaches to reading instruction. For example, phonics tests, structural analysis tests, basic sight words, and emergent literacy are found as part of the phonics, sub-skills, and balanced reading approaches. The reading interest survey may be very important in whole language, literature-based, and balanced reading approaches. The graded passages that give independent, instructional, and frustration levels of reading are required for all approaches.

GRADED WORD LISTS   To begin administering this inventory, the teacher is asked to have the students respond to a *graded word list*. Table 3.5 shows Test 1 of the San Diego Quick Assessment or Graded Word List (GWL). Notice that word lists extend from pre-primer level to ninth grade. Teachers begin the inventory with this test in order to obtain a quick estimate of the student's independent, instructional, and frustration reading levels; to determine a starting level for the oral reading passages, and to obtain initial diagnosis for sight vocabulary, phonics, and structural analysis skills. The sheet with the words is placed before the students. They are asked to begin at the pre-primer level (PP) and read all of the words aloud even if they are not sure of the words. As the students read, the teacher records the reading on the scoring sheet. A word pronounced correctly receives a "+" on the sheet. All incorrect responses should be written as read by the student. The student continues to read until he or she makes three or more errors on any one list. To establish levels on the graded word list, the teacher marks the highest level at which one or no words are missed to identify the level on which students can read with no help, or the *independent reading level*. The level at which two are missed is the *instructional reading level* and the lowest level at which three or more words are missed is the *frustration level*. The results are then tallied to give an independent, instructional, and frustration reading level on this part of the test.

READING PASSAGE TESTS   The teacher uses the information obtained from grading the word list for the next assessment called *reading passage tests*. This section in the reading inventory includes oral and silent reading passages. The teacher is asked to have the student begin reading a passage that is one level below the student's independent reading level as designated at the bottom of the word list test. The teacher tells the students to read the passage aloud and to try to read any unknown words.

TABLE 3.5

Test 1: San Diego Quick Assessment or Graded Word List (GWL)

Graded Word List (GWL) Scoring Sheet

Name _____   Date _____

School _____   Tester _____

PP		P		1.	
see	_____	you	_____	road	_____
play	_____	come	_____	live	_____
me	_____	not	_____	thank	_____
at	_____	with	_____	when	_____
run	_____	jump	_____	bigger	_____
go	_____	help	_____	how	_____
and	_____	is	_____	always	_____
look	_____	work	_____	night	_____
can	_____	are	_____	spring	_____
here	_____	this	_____	today	_____

2.		3.		4.	
our	_____	city	_____	decided	_____
please	_____	middle	_____	served	_____
myself	_____	moment	_____	amazed	_____
town	_____	frightened	_____	silent	_____
early	_____	exclaimed	_____	wrecked	_____
send	_____	several	_____	improved	_____
wide	_____	lonely	_____	certainly	_____
believe	_____	drew	_____	entered	_____
quietly	_____	since	_____	realized	_____
carefully	_____	straight	_____	interrupted	_____

TABLE 3.5

(Continued)

5. ⬚⬚

scanty	_____
buisness	_____
develop	_____
considered	_____
discussed	_____
behaved	_____
splendid	_____
acquainted	_____
escaped	_____
grim	_____

6. ⬚⬚

bridge	_____
commercial	_____
abolish	_____
trucker	_____
apparatus	_____
elementary	_____
comment	_____
necessity	_____
gallery	_____
relativity	_____

7. ⬚⬚

amber	_____
dominion	_____
sundry	_____
capillary	_____
impetuous	_____
blight	_____
wrest	_____
enumerate	_____
daunted	_____
condescent	_____

8. ⬚⬚

capacious	_____
limitation	_____
pretext	_____
intrique	_____
delusion	_____
immaculate	_____
ascent	_____
acrid	_____
binocular	_____
embankment	_____

9. ⬚⬚

conscientious	_____
isolation	_____
molecule	_____
ritual	_____
momentous	_____
vulnerable	_____
kinship	_____
conservatism	_____
jaunty	_____
inventive	_____

Results of Graded Word List

Independent Reading Level	Grade _____	Highest level at which one or no words were missed
Instructional Reading Level	Grade _____	Level at which two words were missed
Frustration Reading Level	Grade _____	Lowest level at which three or more words were missed

Source: From Margaret LaPray and Ramon Ross, "The Graded Word List: Quick Gauge of Reading Ability," *Journal of Reading* (January 1969), pp. 305–307. Reprinted with permission of the International Reading Association and the authors.

TABLE 3.6

Reading Passage Test Scoring Sheet

Jan *has* a dog.
The dog's name *is* Pat.
He can run fast.
One day Pat *ran away.*
Jan looked *for him.*
The dog wanted *to eat.*
Soon he came home.

(31 Words) (Number of word recognition errors _____) (*19 Dolch Words*)

Questions:

F 1. _____ What does Jan have? (A dog)

F 2. _____ What is the dog's name? (Pat)

F 3. _____ What can the dog do? (Run or run fast)

F 4. _____ What did Jan do when the dog ran away? (She looked for him)

F 5. _____ What did the dog want? (To eat)

Number of Questions Missed	Number of Word Recognition Errors				Reading Level	
	0	1	2–3	4		
0	+	•	•	×	+ Independent	
1	•	•	×	×	• Instructional	
2	•	×	×	×	× Frustration	
3	×	×	×	×		
4	×	×	×	×		
5+	×	×	×	×		

_____ Check here if this passage was used for the Listening Comprehension Test.

Listening Comprehension result: (*70 percent or higher to pass*)
_____ Percent _____ Passed _____ Failed

Source: From James L. Shanker and Eldon Ekwall, *Ekwall/Shanker Reading Inventory,* 4/e.
Published by Allyn & Bacon, Boston, MA. Copyright © 2000 by Pearson Education. Reprinted by permission of the publisher.

The student is also told that there will be questions to answer after each passage is read. While the passage is being read, the teacher uses the scoring sheet to record the student's errors while reading. Table 3.6 shows the Reading Passage Test Scoring Sheet that follows Test 1 (shown in Table 3.5). When giving this test, it is helpful to use a tape recorder so all errors are identified. When the student has completed the passage, the teacher asks questions related to the passage, records the answers, and identifies the reading level indicated on the scoring sheet.

After scoring this passage, the teacher has the student continue the test by reading the next higher passage. This procedure continues until the student reaches his or her frustration level. The inventory provides guidance for marking and scoring the oral reading passages and test summary sheets.

In addition to the Graded Word List and the Reading Passage Test, the inventory includes additional tests the teacher may use, such as "Emergent Literacy Tests," which assess phonemic awareness through rhyming, initial sound recognition, phoneme blending, and concepts about print; "Basic Sight Words and Phrases," such as phonics tests, which assess application in context, initial consonants, vowels, and blending; and "Structural Analysis Tests," which assess application in context, word parts, compound words, and dividing words into syllables. The Test Summary Sheet places all of this information on one source along with information gained from giving the "Reading Interest Survey."

After completing this reading inventory, the teacher knows at what level the student can read independently—that is, the level at which he or she can read a book with word recognition at 99 percent or more and with 90 percent comprehension; at what level most of the instructional material should be with 95 percent or more word recognition and 60 percent or more comprehension; and the frustration level, where the word recognition level is 90 percent or less and the comprehension level is 50 percent or less. If the other tests are administered, the teacher also acquires knowledge of important instructional implications for the reader's strengths and weaknesses.

Running Records

Running records are a form of informal assessment. According to Marie Clay (1989), running records allow teachers to evaluate a child's oral reading while the student is reading from the basal texts or student's self-selected books used in the classroom. A running record for text reading according to Carolyn A. Denton, Dennis J. Ciancio, and Jack M. Fletcher (2006) is a method for recording oral reading of connected text. They identify the following types of recordings used to analyze student responses: "(a) correctly read words, (b) miscues, (c) repetitions, (d) self-corrections, (e) appeals from the child for help, and (f) words told by the tester" (p. 11). The resulting running records are then analyzed to identify patterns of the student reading behaviors and the kinds of reading skills and strategies that students use when reading a text. To conduct the running record, the teacher stands behind the reader and writes the words the student reads correctly and makes notes of any errors read by the student. These running records are beneficial because the teacher can use the results to evaluate how students read a text of a specific difficulty or genre, identify specific types of problems revealed from the reading, and group students according to their need of instruction in that area. This grouping may be for short-term help or longer term remediation. Teachers may date running records, therefore monitoring student's progress.

To conduct a running record, select a passage of between one hundred and two hundred words that the student will read orally. The reading source may be a textbook or a selection of literature that the student is reading independently. The teacher listens to the reading and uses observations to signify the types of errors made and check marks to indicate words read correctly. For example, the following abbreviations are useful and are a fast way to record the reading:

✔	Means the word is read correctly.
T	Means the teacher told the child the word.
word work	Means the incorrect word is written above the correct word.
SC	Means the child self-corrects the word after making the error.
back black	Record self-correction because it gives hints as to what cues the reader is using to create meaning. Self-corrections are not counted as errors.
cal-log catalog	The child attempts to pronounce the word, but is unable to accomplish this. Include the sounds the child makes in the attempt.
	These errors also provide information about the reading process.
R	R written alongside the words or sentences means the child has repeated the reading. Repetitions are not counted as errors. They should be noted, however, as they may indicate that the child is not focusing on the reading.
———	Indicates that the child has skipped a word. Skipped words are counted as errors.
record word Λ	Indicates that the child has added words. Record any inserted words. Again, insertions may suggest that the child has added meaning or descriptive words to the text.

Teachers find running records are easily made when children are reading orally in small groups. Conducting a running record is not difficult, but it does require practice. Some teachers use a tape recorder to record students' readings for their initial time with running records. Recording makes it easier to go back to the text.

After completing a running record, calculate the number and types of errors. The percentage of errors indicates the student's approximate reading level. For example, if the reader makes 5 percent or fewer errors, the text is at the student's independent reading level, at which 95 percent to 100 percent of the words are known. If there are 6 percent to 10 percent errors, the student is reading at the instructional level, at which 90 percent to 95 percent of the words are known. When the percentage of known words falls below 90 percent the material is considered at the frustration level and too difficult for a student to read without considerable prereading help and assistance while reading. Table 3.7 is an example of a running record completed with a second-grade student reading "The Dog and His Image," a fable taken from an Aesop collection.

The 90 percent accuracy shown from this running record indicates that the student is reading at his instructional level. An analysis of the student's strength and weaknesses indicates that he has a good sight vocabulary of high-frequency words. He also sounds out unknown words by using his knowledge of beginning consonant blends as in *drop* for *dropped*, *green* for *greedy* and his identifying the *br* blends in *bridge* and *brook*. He has not yet mastered the *-ed* ending. He needs to pay more attention to the context of unknown words because the errors he makes when he replaces words such as *pec* for *piece*, *age* for *image*, and *green* for *greedy* do not make sense. Minilessons that focus on using a combination of known phonics principles (see Chapter 4) and context of a sentence (see Chapter 5) to gain meaning would be helpful.

TABLE 3.7

Running Record "The Dog and His Image"

Text	Running Record
Once upon a time, a dog	✔ ✔ ✔ ✔ ✔ ✔
found a large piece of meat.	✔ ✔ ✔ pec/piece ✔ ✔
"Ah," he said to himself, "that	✔ ✔ ✔ ✔ ✔ ✔
is fine! I will take it home and	✔ ✔ ✔ ✔ ✔ ✔ ✔ ✔
eat it by myself." So he ran	✔ ✔ ✔ ✔ ✔ ✔ ✔
off with it in his mouth.	✔ ✔ ✔ ✔ ✔ I/mouth
As he crossed the bridge over	✔ ✔ ✔ ✔ br-/bridge ✔
the brook, he looked down into	✔ br-/brook ✔ ✔ ✔ ✔
the water and saw his image.	✔ ✔ ✔ ✔ ✔ age/image
He thought it was another dog	✔ ✔ ✔ ✔ ✔ ✔
with another piece of meat; so he	✔ ✔ pec/piece ✔ ✔ ✔ ✔
jumped into the water to get it.	✔ ✔ ✔ ✔ ✔ ✔ ✔
He dropped what he already had,	✔ drop/dropped ✔ ✔ ✔ ✔
and found too late that there was	✔ ✔ ✔ ✔ ✔ ✔ ✔
nothing to gain. He was punished	✔ ✔ ✔ ✔ ✔ punched/punished
for being greedy.	✔ ✔ green/greedy

Calculation: 100 words

9 errors = 90% accuracy

Running Record: Instructional Level

Miscue Analysis

The **miscue analysis** is another form of informal assessment and is based on work by Kenneth Goodman (1967). According to Goodman, miscues or errors in reading provide direct insights into the reading process when comparing how the miscues differ from the expected reading response. Goodman believes: "Such insights reveal not only weaknesses, but strengths as well, because the miscues are not simple errors but the results of the reading process having miscarried in some minor or major ways" (p. 12).

The importance of analyzing miscues is revealed when teachers listen to students read and then the teachers analyze what caused students to make their errors. For example, if the text reads, "The *CAT* ran up the tree" and the student reads "The *CAN* ran up the tree" without correcting the error, the teacher knows that the child is paying attention to the beginning sound of the word and not to the contextual meaning of the word. Table 3.8 presents the Miscue Analysis Terminology along with examples of the forms of each miscue.

To complete the miscue analysis, the teacher has a copy of the text to be read by the student. Again, a tape recorder is helpful for this assessment. As the student reads, the teacher marks the errors and identifies the type of error it is according to the category of error identified in Table 3.8. Now, the teacher has a better understanding about how the reader uses the various functions of language to process text. Teachers may point out to students how they can use these functions of language to gain meaning from what they read.

Reading authorities who emphasize the importance of the miscue analysis contend that words in sentence structures that mirror the syntactic and semantic forms of the language increase the child's opportunities to detect errors and develop error-correcting strategies. This philosophy maintains that words alone do not carry precise meaning until they are placed in the structural and intonation systems of the English language.

Yetta Goodman (1972) stresses not only the importance of words in context for the oral reading analysis, but also the necessity for the reader to read a whole story. She hypothesizes that the reader uses different reading strategies when reading an isolated passage than when reading the same passage within its total literary setting. Kenneth Goodman (1967) observes, "Perhaps the most significant factor in analyzing any miscue is whether or not it is corrected. The analysis of which miscues are corrected and under what circumstances has been most revealing" (p. 19).

TABLE 3.8

Miscue Analysis Terminology

Term	Meaning	Example	
Miscue	Reader's response is different from expected response in the text.	Text:	Close the *door*.
		Miscue:	Close the *down*.
Graphic Proximity	Relationship between the actual letter appearance of the miscue and the intended word. Error compares with the shape and sequence of the real word.	Text:	*monkey*
		Miscue:	*money*
Phonic Proximity	Relationship between actual sounds of miscue and sound in the intended word.	Text:	The *cat* ran up the tree.
		Miscue:	The *can* ran up the tree.
Grammatical Function	Relationship between the function (noun, verb, adjective) of the miscue and the intended word	Text:	The boy *swam* in the river.
		Miscue:	The boy *fell* in the river (both verbs)
Semantic Acceptability	The miscue does not distort the meaning of the text.	Text:	The man *yelled* at the dog
		Miscue:	The man *shouted* at the dog. (does not distort meaning)
Non-word Miscue	Miscue is a nonsense word.	Text:	*balloon*
		Miscue:	*binth*
Corrected Miscue	Reader rereads and corrects the error.	Any correction that matches the text.	

Table 3.9 shows how a fifth-grade student read a nonfiction selection from *Elison Basic Readers* used in schools in the earlier part of the 1900s. (This basal series is discussed in Chapter 1). The selection is from *Balto, the Best Lead-Dog in Alaska,* by Margaret Frances Fox. The selection was used as part of a science unit that studied the contemporary dangers associated with a possible bird flu pandemic.

How does the miscue analysis differ from the previous running record? A running record of this student identifies nine errors out of 121 words. The accuracy rate of 93 percent places the student at the instructional level. The errors would be categorized as attempted pronunciations and incorrect words. The major errors are a result of not knowing how to attack multiple-syllable words.

Word analysis resulting from the miscue analysis shows that this student uses two types of cueing systems as he or she attacks unknown words: phonics or sounds of the language; and semantics, or the meaning of the text. These are strengths that the teacher needs to point out to the student. When he is having difficulty he needs to read the text and use his understanding of context clues to gain meaning. Also, the substitutions he used show that he understands the meaning of the text.

TABLE 3.9

Miscue Analysis

epidic (phonic proximity/non-word)   diptha (phonic proximity/non-word)
It was mid-winter, and an <u>epidemic</u> of <u>diphtheria</u> had broken out in Nome.

sickness (semantic acceptability)
They called it the "Black Death" up there, for the <u>disease</u> carried off not only the

children but their fathers and mothers. Indeed, whole families were swept away

terrible (syntactic acceptability   sickness (syntactic acceptability
semantic acceptability)   semantic acceptability)
during the time of that <u>dreadful</u> sickness. If the <u>disease</u> could not be stopped in

terrain (syntactic acceptability/semantic acceptability)
Nome, it was likely to spread over all the <u>territory</u> of which the city was the center—

Arc (phonic proximity/non-word)
to the east one thousand miles, and north even as far as the <u>Arctic</u> Ocean. In this

land (syntactic acceptability/semantic acceptability)
<u>region</u> there lived eleven thousand people. To care for them there was in Nome

but one doctor, who with his little band of nurses belonged to the United States

Pulic (non-word/phonic proximity)
<u>Public</u> Health Service

This is also an example that demonstrates the importance of providing background before students read unfamiliar content. Teaching concepts and associated words related to epidemics and diphtheria would have brought this text close to the student's independent level of reading.

Cloze Assessment

Cloze assessments are used to assess a student's ability to read particular materials. The cloze technique is closely related to literature-based approaches to reading because students read passages taken directly from their reading materials (Norton, 1992). Teachers can construct a cloze test by selecting a passage of 250 to 300 words. Passages should be selected from the front of the book so that the content is not loaded with concepts that will be developed later in the book. The first and last sentences of the passage should be left whole. Throughout the remainder of the passage, every fifth word should be deleted, leaving about fifty blanks to be completed by the student.

Before the student completes a cloze activity, allow him or her to practice using another example. After the student has finished the practice passage, give him or her the prepared passage. Allow as much time as the student needs to complete the passage. Grade the passage by counting the number of exact word replacements (some educators allow synonyms). Scores of 44 percent to 57 percent correct mean that the materials are at the student's instructional level. Scores of 58 percent and above signify an independent reading level. Scores of 43 percent and below reflect a frustration reading level.

Cloze tests have several advantages. Teachers can develop them using the exact literature that students will be reading. Tests can be constructed easily from all types of literature, can be group-administered, and are easy to grade. Teachers can develop cloze tests from a variety of literature selections, can keep the test results in students' portfolios, and evaluate changes in reading comprehension according to changes in cloze results over time.

The following example of a cloze test using a narrative text is taken from Lewis Carroll's *Through the Looking-Glass, and What Alice Found There,* first published in 1872:

"Do you know, I was so angry, Kitty," Alice went on, as soon as they were comfortably settled again, "When I saw all the mischief you had been doing, I was very nearly opening the window, and putting you out into the snow! And you'd have deserved _____ , you little mischievous darling!_____ have you got to _____ for yourself? Now don't _____ me!" she went on,_____ up one finger. "I'm _____ to tell you all _____ faults. Number one: you _____ twice while Dinah was _____ your face this morning. _____ you can't deny it, _____ : I heard you! What's _____ you say?! (pretending that _____ kitten was speaking.) "Her _____ went into your eye? _____, that's your fault, for _____ your eyes open—if _____ shut them tight up, _____ wouldn't have happened. Now _____ make any more excuses, _____ listen! Number two: you _____ Snowdrop away by the _____ just as I had _____ down the saucer of _____ before her! What, you _____ thirsty, were you? How _____ you know she wasn't _____ too? Now for number _____: you unwound every bit _____ worsted while I _____ looking!

    "That's three faults, _____. and you've not been _____ for any of them _____. You know I'm saving _____ all your punishments for _____ week—suppose they had _____ up all my punishments!" _____ went on, talking more _____ herself than the kitten. "_____ would they do at _____ end of a year? _____ should be sent to _____, I suppose, when the _____ came. Or—let me _____ —suppose each punishment was _____ be going without a _____: then, when the miserable _____ came, I should have _____ go without fifty dinners _____ once! Well, I shouldn't _____ that much! I'd far rather go without them than eat them! (p. 4)

Teachers can develop cloze tests to accompany different genres of literature or different levels of books. Students also improve their ability to use context clues and to notice sentence structures.

Portfolio Assessment

A portfolio is a collection of a student's work over a period of time. In a **portfolio assessment**, students and teachers first decide what is going to go into the portfolio—this could be a sampling of the student's work chosen by the student and teacher together or samples of the best work. When teachers and students are considering the development of a portfolio, it is helpful if they imagine themselves in a profession in which portfolios have been popular and extremely useful; for example, they might think of themselves as artists, photographers, or authors who want to demonstrate their talents and breadth of experience. They might ask, "What examples would best show my talents?" and "What examples might show how I have progressed in my chosen field?" Then they can think about what might be included in a portfolio of reading to illustrate their growing understanding of reading and appreciation for books.

    The contents of the portfolios should be related to the goals for instruction. They can include samples of work, teacher's observational notes, and the student's self-evaluations. The portfolio could include results from classroom tests, written responses to literature, scoring sheets from informal reading inventories, results of cloze assessments, and audio or video tapes. What is selected should relate closely to the instructional goals. For example, if understanding literary elements and plot structures are important goals, then literary webs and plot diagrams should be included in the portfolios. (These are presented in more detail in later chapters.)

    By stating the goals and priorities for instruction, teachers can select samples that reflect these goals; by assessing continuously, teachers can collect and assess several indicators related to reading; and by collecting both required evidence and supporting evidence, teachers can look

Reflect on Your Reading

As you read about these different types of informal assessments, try to visualize how you would assess the important knowledge and skills that you would like to include in your reading curriculum. For example, what would be in a portfolio that reflects what you want your students to learn? How will you know that the students have learned what you want them to learn? How would your choice of assessment influence your teaching?

systematically at the progress of the students and the effectiveness of the reading program.

Portfolios are also excellent sources for student-teacher conferences. Students and teachers can meet every few weeks to discuss progress, add notes, and decide what additional materials should be in the portfolios. These portfolios also provide excellent sources to use during parent-teacher conferences. Teachers can show parents what the students are doing and the progress they are making, or teachers can make recommendations for homework and recreational reading that can be accomplished away from school.

Additional Types of Informal Testing in the Reading Program

According to the International Baccalaureate Organization and the Language Scope and Sequence for the International Schools Primary Years Program (2003) there are three questions that should be used to formulate a school curriculum: (1) What do we want students to learn? (2) How best will students learn? (3) How will we know what students have learned? (The first two questions are covered elsewhere in the text in the chapters that focus on strategies and techniques for teaching reading.)

The Role of National Tests

There is considerable controversy over the role of high-stakes testing such as that required by the No Child Left Behind legislation. How do you think teachers and school districts should be evaluated for reading achievement? What should be the consequences if schools do not show adequate improvement in reading? What is the alternative to teaching to the test? What type of tests provide the greatest guidance for teachers who are developing effective reading programs? How should the school respond if students fail to reach the desired achievement in reading? What is your response to the rating of articles that are positive or negative when writing about No Child Left Behind? Why do you believe that the latest National Assessment of Education Progress (NAEP) found "the achievement gap for all three ages (9, 13, and 17) in both reading and math was smaller in 2004 than it was in 1971. The average reading score at age 13 had not significantly changed since 1999, the last year the test was given, but it was higher than 1971" (p. 1)?

These students are taking standardized tests as part of their formal assessment of reading.

Source: "Long-Term NAEP Scores Show Solid Gains." (August/September 2005). Reading Today, 23, pp. 1–6.

TABLE 3.10

Recommendations for Assessment

Preschool –Kindergarten ....

1. Students can retell a story in sequential order.

    (assessing story structures)

2. Using a wordless book, students create a story that is clear and logical.

    (assessing story structures)

3. Students demonstrate knowledge of the alphabet when "reading" alphabet books.

    (assessing knowledge of alphabet)

4. Students can predict what a book will be about after looking at the cover.

    (assessing cognitive ability)

5. Students contribute to group lists with understanding.

    (assessing subjects)

6. Students tell/write and illustrate their own stories.

    (assessing use of language)

7. Students add to their writing folders, date their work, and are interested in their own progress.

    (assessing student's self-motivation)

8. Students create their own alphabet books by matching pictures of objects with letters associated with the objects.

    (assessing phonemic awareness)

Ages Five to Seven ....

1. Students listen for sounds, identify sounds, and classify or group the sounds.

    (assessing sound-symbol relationships)

2. Students ask effective questions and consider what makes questions effective.

    (assessing overall comprehension)

3. Students predict what they believe will happen next in a story.

    (assessing cognitive skills)

4. Students use appropriate language when talking about the characters, settings, and events in a story.

    (assessing literary elements)

5. Students present information from a nonfiction book in chart or graph format.

    (assessing comprehension of nonfiction texts)

6. Students demonstrate their ability to use dictionaries.

    (assessing research skills)

7. Students demonstrate interest in authors and want to read additional books written by the authors.

    (assessing interest in literature)

8. Students demonstrate their ability to draw a plot diagram showing beginning, middle, and end incidents in a plot.

    (assessing ability to comprehend plot structures)

9. Students demonstrate their ability to identify similarities and differences between books.

    (assessing ability to make inferences)

TABLE 3.10

(Continued)

10. Students identify accurate details when reporting a story.

    (assessing reading for literal information)

11. During writing, students show their ability to use various strategies to develop ideas and to write various forms of writing.

    (assessing logical ideas)

12. Students can identify and respond to different forms of poetry.

    (assessing knowledge of poetic elements)

Ages Seven to Nine

1. Students can predict what a story will be about, retell the story, paraphrase the main ideas, and identify important details.

    (assessing higher level thought processes)

2. Students can group and categorize vocabulary according to a theme or idea.

    (assessing cognitive abilities)

3. Students ask relevant questions and stay on topic when listening to a presentation.

    (assessing knowledge of main ideas)

4. Students are able to use various search systems to locate resources.

    (assessing research skills)

5. After reading a book, students can identify the literary elements associated with characters, setting, plot, and theme.

    (assessing knowledge of literary elements)

6. Students can explain why they might use a specific reading technique to comprehend a story.

    (assessing comprehension strategies)

7. Students give detailed instructions that allow peers to follow directions and make a product.

    (assessing following directions)

8. Students are able to classify texts and state their reasons for the classifications.

    (assessing cognitive skills)

9. Students can write a narrative paragraph that includes a topic sentence, sequential order, details, and a closing sentence.

    (assessing understanding of narrative structures)

10. Students' writing reflects an understanding of the writing process.

    (assessing knowledge of writing process)

11. Students are able to self-correct their writing and to respond to suggestions for writing.

    (assessing knowledge of writing process)

12. Students write their own poetry after reading poetry in class.

    (assessing knowledge of poetic elements)

13. Students are able to present findings during a unit study to the class.

    (assessing research and summary abilities)

TABLE 3.10

(Continued)

14. Students show ability to read maps, charts, and graphs by creating their own examples to accompany a unit.

    (assessing cognitive skills)

Ages Nine to Twelve

1. Students show ability to generate and answer questions that demonstrate higher thinking skills.

    (assessing higher cognitive skills)

2. Students present arguments that reflect different points of view.

    (assessing ability to understand points of view)

3. Students develop and defend their preferences for selecting certain books or references.

    (assessing critical evaluation)

4. Students write effective summaries of plots.

    (assessing summarization abilities)

5. Students can give specific criteria for various genres of literature and categorize books according to the criteria.

    (assessing critical evaluation and cognitive skills)

6. Students can identify appropriate works that fit under specific genres.

    (assessing knowledge of literary genres)

7. Students can discuss the appropriateness of the character's responses in a specific story.

    (assessing forms of characterization and criticizing characterization)

8. Students can evaluate different purposes for writing such as to entertain, to persuade, and to inform and evaluate an author's effectiveness for each purpose for writing.

    (assessing purposes for writing)

9. Students can assess the reliability of the information they read or hear.

    (assessing ability to authenticate texts and judge sources)

10. Students are able to assess information using several sources.

    (assessing research and library skills)

11. Students writing folders show desired progress and they are able to set goals for their own improvement.

    (assessing self-motivation responses)

12. Students are able to distinguish differences in writing styles in literature.

    (assessing appreciation and identification of writing styles)

13. Students recognize and choose appropriate writing strategies during writing workshops.

    (assessing students' understanding of writing process)

14. Students are able to edit their own work and take part in peer editing.

    (assessing students' application during writing process)

15. Students produce poems that reveal an understanding of various poetic forms.

    (assessing understanding of and applications related to poetic elements)

According to the International Schools Primary Years Program, this third question—How will we know what students have learned?—is answered when teachers develop assessment that allows students to demonstrate their understanding of the specific expectations for the learning that is desired. In this assessment program, each assessment technique is highly related to the activity that is being taught in the classroom. The recommendations for assessment in Table 3.10 are a few of the suggestions included in the *Primary Years Programme: Language Scope and Sequence* (2003). As you read these assessment strategies, notice how closely the assessments are related to the desired student outcomes for learning and the strategies that are being used in the classroom to develop those outcomes for learning.

LESSON PLAN:
Informal Assessment

The following lesson plan might follow a series of activities in which students are taught to predict the content of a story, retell the story, paraphrase the main ideas, and identify important details. The lesson is used to evaluate the effectiveness of the previous instruction.

OBJECTIVES

1. To evaluate students' abilities to predict content of a story.
2. To evaluate students' ability to retell the story.
3. To evaluate students' ability to paraphrase main ideas.
4. To evaluate students' ability to identify important details.
5. To evaluate students' ability to respond through higher thinking skills.

MATERIALS

Choose short illustrated books that can be read to or by students. The books should include pictures that encourage prediction. The example in this lesson plan is Mordicai Gerstein's *The Man Who Walked between the Towers* (2004 Caldecott Medal).

GRADE LEVELS   Second through fourth grades

PROCEDURES

1. Introduce the book by asking students to look at the cover and predict what they think the book will be about by viewing the illustration and reading the title. If possible ask students to write their answers.
2. Either ask the students to read the book or read the book to the students. Ask the students to retell the story by writing responses or by orally retelling.
3. Ask the students to paraphrase the main ideas found in the book.
4. Ask the students to identify the important details in this book that tells the story of a real incident.

5. To evaluate students' ability to relate the story to a current incident, ask them to respond to the illustration on the final page. Why did the illustrator draw a picture showing the twin towers as silhouettes? Why does he state, "But in memory, as if imprinted on the sky, the towers are still there" (final page)?

6. Evaluate each child's ability to perform the objectives. If students are not able to provide responses for any of the questions, provide additional instruction in these important comprehension abilities.

FOCUS ACTIVITY:
Developing a Diagnostic Test

OBJECTIVES

1. To develop a diagnostic test that evaluates students' prior knowledge about a topic
2. To understand literary elements and literary genres

GRADE LEVEL

Students and teachers in the upper grades and middle school

PROCEDURES

1. Brainstorm to identify the important knowledge and understandings that should influence how you will teach a topic.
2. A diagnostic test such as the one found in Table 3.11 helps teachers identify what students have learned about the topic during prior classes.
3. As you read the test questions, identify what is considered important when using literature in the reading program. (The original test includes forty questions.)
4. Share your diagnostic test with your class.
5. You may choose to develop a diagnostic test that measures prior knowledge of any area related to reading and literacy or to a unit of study that you will teach.
6. Develop a similar unit as a group project.

TABLE 3.11

Diagnostic Test: Children's Literature and Literacy

Name: _____

Literary Elements Knowledge

1. To develop the order of events in a biography, an author probably organizes the narrative in which of the following ways?

    a. chronological order

    b. flashbacks

    c. problem and solution

    d. cause and effect

2. What is the usual source for plots in literature?

    a. characterization

    b. point of view

    c. conflict

    d. setting

3. Which of the following is the theme of the story?

    a. The story's location in time and place.

    b. The sequence of events in the story.

    c. The resolution of the conflict.

    d. The underlying idea that ties the plot, characters, and setting together.

4. The repetition of initial sounds in a line of poetry is called

    a. assonance

    b. alliteration

    c. hyperbole

    d. metaphor

5. "The moon this night is like a silver sickle," includes

    a. metaphor

    b. hyperbole

    c. simile

    d. idiom

6. Virginia Lee Burton's *The Little House* is an example of

    a. personification

    b. family life fantasies

    c. satire

    d. realistic situations

Knowledge of Literary Genres

7. Five-line poems in which the first, second, and last lines rhyme are

    a. haiku.

    b. cinquains.

    c. ballads.

    d. limericks.

8. The "willing suspension of disbelief" is important in

    a. fable.

    b. biography.

    c. realistic fiction.

    d. modern fantasy.

9. The term *contemporary realistic fiction* implies that everything in the story

    a. happened in our contemporary world.

    b. could happen in our contemporary world.

    c. is told from the viewpoint of a real person.

    d. is true.

10. What is the most important literary element in biography?

    a. plot

    b. characterization

    c. setting

    d. style

11. What is probably the most important criterion in evaluating information books?

    a. accuracy of facts

    b. author's creativity

    c. interesting story

    d. imaginative text

12. Anthropomorphism means

    a. writing fictitious dialogue for biographical characters.

    b. describing the life cycle of an animal.

    c. giving human emotions to animals.

    d. using stereotypes to describe females.

DIFFERENTIATING INSTRUCTION

The focused anecdotal assessment of reading adds to teachers' knowledge about all students including ELL, struggling readers and writers and gifted and accelerated readers and writers. Consequently, it may effectively be used with students who are among any of these groups. Paul Boyd-Batstone (2004) defines the procedure and presents guidelines for its use.

Authentic assessment is an activity in which the teacher plays an active role as he or she takes notes while a student is reading or taking part in another literary activity. These notes record information that relates to each child's literacy actions. Boyd-Batstone recommends that teachers first compile a list of meaningful verbs they will use when observing and writing anecdotal records. Table 3.12 is an example of his terms.

Before observing a student, create a form with the student's name and a listing of different dates on which observations will be made, with room for the observation and an example to support the observation. Table 3.12 highlights areas that are excellent for observation under reading strategies the student uses, listening capabilities, writing skills, reading abilities, and speaking. Notice that these terms clarify aspects of a total literacy program.

Teachers observe students frequently during literacy activities, periodically analyze the records of each student, and use the information to make recommendations.

TABLE 3.12

Meaningful Verbs for Writing Anecdotal Records

Strategies	Listening	Writing	Reading	Speaking
Uses (strategies)	Distinguishes	Writes	Blends	States
Organizes	Determines	Prints (legibly)	Reads	Describes
Generates	Recognizes	Spells	Tracks	Shares (information)
Classifies	Identifies	Illustrates	Decodes	Recites
Compares	Responds	Capitalizes	Follows words	Represents
Contrasts	Asks	Defines	Rereads	Relates
Matches	Questions	Indents	Uses references	Recounts
Plans	Clarifies	Describes	Studies	Retells
Provides	Discerns	Summarizes	Highlights	Reports
Connects (ideas)	Analyzes	Organizes		Concludes
Arranges	Follows directions			Quotes
Supports	Reacts			Delivers
Confirms	Points out			Requests
Selects	Points to			Asks
Chooses	Gestures			Indicates
Demonstrates				Confirms
Presents				
Clarifies				

Source: Based on data from Paul Boyd-Batstone, "Assessment: A Tool for Standards-based, Authentic Assessment," *The Reading Teacher, 58,* November 2004, p. 232.

Boyd-Batstone (2004) recommends analyzing the records every six to eight weeks and emphasizes task-oriented instruction:

As part of differentiating instruction, the teacher writes anecdotal records that accompany an individual student's reading.

Reflect on Your Reading

Consider the different types of and purposes for assessment in the classroom. Why does a teacher need to use differentiated instruction to modify the reading assessment to meet the needs of all the students in the classroom? What would be the consequences of using assessment that does not allow for any modifications, especially for ELL students and struggling readers and writers?

Once the anecdotal records are summarized in terms of strengths and needs, student-specific recommendations can be made. In essence, the teacher is customizing instruction and support for the individual. To be effective and practical; the recommendation should be task oriented. . . . Without a task associated to the strategy, the recommendation can be meaningless. (235)

This is also the place for teachers to write recommendations for specific tasks that students can do at home, such as sorting words into families of *and, up,* and *at,* retelling a story read independently, or following directions when using a recipe.

Summary

High-stakes testing has serious consequences for students, teachers, schools, and school systems. The No Child Left Behind legislation has produced both accolades for the legislation and concerns about the educational consequences resulting from the legislation. Authentic assessment is considered one of the most important characteristics of effective evaluation. Authentic assessment is situated in real classroom situations that focus on children's learning and the instructional goals of the curriculum. Observational approaches are among the most useful assessment tools for assessing emergent literacy in your children. Schools use both formal, standardized, and informal reading tests to evaluate reading. Diagnosis in reading includes the survey level, the specific level, and the intensive level as well as the diagnostic reading inventories and informal tests in reading. Informal reading inventories include graded word lists and passages designed for oral and silent reading. Other informal reading tests include running records, miscue analysis, and various types of evaluations that assess the effectiveness of previous instruction. When selecting and administering tests, teachers should ask: (1) What do we want students to learn? (2) How best will students learn? (3) How will we know what students have learned?

Key Terms

assessment, p. 96

diagnosis, p. 96

evaluation, p. 97

standardized tests, p. 98

high-stakes tests, p. 98

authentic assessment, p. 104

informal reading inventory, p. 107

independent reading level, p. 107

instructional reading level, p. 107

frustration reading level, p. 107

running records, p. 117

miscue analysis, p. 119

cloze assessment, p. 122

portfolio assessment, p. 123

For video clips of authentic classroom instruction on **Assessment**, go to Allyn & Bacon's MyLabSchool.com. In MLS courses, click on Reading Methods, go to MLS Video Lab, and select **Module 8**.

Extend Your Reading

1. Analyze the assessment components provided by published basal reading series such as McGraw-Hill Reading "Diagnostic/Placement Evaluation." (University libraries and school districts are good sources for locating reading series.) What types of reading skills are being assessed? Do the tests provide guidelines for teaching reading that are associated with the results of the tests?

2. Compare the content in two informal reading inventories. You might compare the content, directions, and scoring approaches and stated philosophies in *Analytical Reading Inventory,* by Mary Lynn Woods and Alden J. Moe, with the *Ekwall/Shanker Reading Inventory* described in this chapter.

3. Read a newspaper article that discusses how No Child Left Behind has or will influence testing of reading, instructions in reading, and teacher effectiveness. How is the law being interpreted in your own state or school district? How much impact on education has the law had?

4. Choose one of the assessment and evaluation techniques discussed in this chapter and use the assessment with a student. What are the strengths and weaknesses of each type of assessment? What abilities do you need in order to either give the test or to interpret the test? What types of tests provide you with the most information for evaluating the reading capabilities of the student?

5. Conduct an informal reading test using a running record or a miscue analysis. Select a child who is reading a story, such as one found in a basal reader, or is reading a short selection from literature. You may choose to record the child's reading. Using a tape recorder to record the experience helps you identify any

errors and to analyze the errors by replaying the oral reading. Use either a running record or a miscue analysis to analyze the child's reading. Try to answer the following questions: What information do you discover about the child's reading ability? If the child self-corrects reading errors, what are the circumstances that cause the self-correction? If the child ignores errors, what are the circumstances that result in the continuation of errors. If using a miscue analysis, analyze the errors to discover if the child uses graphic proximity, phonic proximity, grammatical function, or syntactic acceptability to help identify words. What did you discover about the child's reading by analyzing corrected miscues and miscues that are not corrected? Share your findings with your class. Do you have any suggestions about how you might help the child you tested become a better reader?

For Further Reading

1. Lorin W. Anderson, *Classroom Assessment: Enhancing the Quality of Teacher Decision Making.* Mahwah, NJ: Lawrence Erlbaum, 2003. The text includes chapters on classroom assessment, assessing student achievement, assessing classroom behavior, and interpreting assessment results.

2. Patricia M. Cunningham, and Richard L. Allington, "Chapter 6, Assessment," in *Classrooms That Work: They Can All Read and Write,* 3d ed., Boston: Pearson, 2003. The chapter includes: "What Is Assessment?, Determining Student Reading Level, Identifying Good Literacy Behaviors, and Documenting Progress."

3. Gary DeCoker, ed., *National Standards and School Reform in Japan and the United States.* New York: Teachers College Press, 2002. Sections include the creation of national standards and implementing and reacting to educational policy.

4. Peter Dewitz, and Pamela K. Dewitz, "They Can Read the Words, But They Can't Under-

stand: Refining Comprehension Assessment." *The Reading Teacher,* 56 (February 2003) pp. 422–435. According to the authors, "Comprehension problems can be difficult to detect and treat. Here are some suggestions for catching these problems and addressing students' shortcomings" (p. 422).

5. Patricia D. Hunsader, "Mathematics Trade Books: Establishing Their Value and Assessing Their Quality." *The Reading Teacher,* 57 (April 2004) pp. 618–629. The author uses a rubric to evaluate mathematics literature and discusses topics such as, "the benefits of using literature in mathematics instruction," "existing tools for the evaluation of quality," and "assessing the texts and interpreting the scores."

6. George R. Taylor, *Informal Classroom Assessment Strategies for Teachers.* Lanham, MD: Scarecrow, 2003. The text includes informal assessment strategies for teachers and observational techniques.

REFERENCES

Arenson, Karen W. (March 18, 2006). "Testing Errors Prompt Calls for Oversight." *New York Times,* pp. A1–12.

Boyd-Batstone, Paul. (November 2004). "Focused Anecdotal Records Assessment: A Tool for Standards-

Based Authentic Assessment." *The Reading Teacher,* 58, 230–239.

Bear, Donald R., Invernizzi, Marcia, Templeton, Shane, & Johnston, Francine. (2000). *Words Their Way: Word Study for Phonics, Vocabulary, and Spelling*

Instruction, 2nd ed. Upper Saddle River, NJ: Pearson, Merrill, Prentice Hall.

Clay, Marie. (1989). "Concepts about Print." *The Reading Teacher, 42,* 268–277.

Cunningham, Patricia, & Allington, Richard. (2003). *Classrooms That Work: They Can All Read And Write.* Boston: Allyn & Bacon.

Denton, Carolyn A., Dennis, J. & Fletcher, Jack M. (January/February/March 2006). "Validity, Reliabililty, and Utility of the Observation Survey of Early Literacy Achievement." *Reading Research Quarterly, 41,* 8-34.

Dillon, Sam. (26 November 2005). "Students Ace Tests, but Earn D's from U.S." *New York Times,* pp. A1, A10.

Earl, Lorna M. (2003). *Assessment as Learning: Using Classroom Assessment to Maximize Student Learning.* Thousand Oaks, CA: Corwin.

Farr, Robert, & Beck, Michael D. (2003). "Evaluating Language Development." In James Flood, Diane Lapp, James R. Squire, & Julie M. Jensen (Eds.), *Handbook of Research on Teaching the English Language Arts,* 2nd ed. Mahwah, NJ: Lawrence Erlbaum, pp. 590–599.

Goodman, Kenneth. (1967) "Reading a Psycholinguist Guessing Game." *Journal of Reading Specialists, 4,* 126–135.

Goodman, Yetta. (October 1972). "Reading Diagnosis— Qualitative or Quantitative?" *The Reading Teacher,* 32–37.

Goodman, Yetta. (2003). "Informal Methods of Evaluation." In James Flood, Diane Lapp, James R. Squire, & Julie M. Jensen (Eds.), *Handbook of Research on Teaching the English Language Arts,* 2nd ed. Mahwah, NJ: Lawrence Erlbaum, pp. 600–607.

Hamilton, Laura S., & Koretz, Daniel M. (2002). "Tests and Their Use in Test-Based Accountability Systems." In Laura S. Hamilton, Brian M. Stecher, & Stephen P. Klein (Eds.), *Making Sense of Test-Based Accountability in Education.* Santa Monica, CA: Rand, pp. 13–49.

Harris, Peggy. (March 2006). "NCTE Members Seek to Influence NCLB Reauthorization." *The Council Chronicle, 15,* 1, 4-5.

International Baccalaureate Organization. (2003). *Primary Years Programme: Language Scope and Sequence.* Grand-Sacpmmex, Geneva, Switzerland.

Jones, M. Gail, Jones, Brett D., & Hargrove, Tracy Y. (2003). *The Unintended Consequences of High-Stakes Testing.* Lanham, MD: Rowman & Littlefield.

Kohn, Alfie (2000). *The Case Against Standardized Testing: Raising the Scores, Ruining the Schools.* Portsmouth, NH: Heinemann.

McDevott, Teresa M., & Ormrod, Jeanne Ellis. (2004). *Child Development: Educating and Working with Children and Adolescents,* 2nd ed. Upper Saddle River, NJ: Pearson, Merrill, Prentice Hall.

National Assessment Governing Board. (2004). *Reading Frame-Work for the 2009 National Assessment of Educational Progress.* Washington, DC: American Institutes for Research.

No Child Left Behind. (2002). Legislative Summary. Washington, DC. U.S. Government.

Norton, Donna E. (1992). *The Impact of Literature-Based Reading.* New York: Merrill, Macmillan.

Peregoy, Suzann F., & Boyle, Owen F. (2001). *Reading, Writing, and Learning in ESL.* New York: Addison Wesley Longman.

Raphael, Taffy E., & Au, Kathryn H. (November 2005). "QAR: Enhancing Comprehension and Test Taking Across Grades and Content Areas." *The Reading Teacher, 59,* 206–221.

Ruddell, Robert B. (2002). *Teaching Children to Read and Write: Becoming an Effective Literacy Teacher,* 3rd ed. Boston: Allyn & Bacon.

Ryan, Katherine. (Winter 2003). "Shaping Educational Accountability Systems." *American Journal of Evaluation, 23,* 452–68.

Shanker, James L., & Ekwall, Eldon E. (2000). *Ekwall/Shanker Reading Inventory,* fourth edition. Boston: Allyn & Bacon.

Torgesen, J. K., & Bryant, B. R. (1994). *Test of Phonological Awareness.* Austin, TX: Pro Ed.

Woods, Mary Lynn, & Moe, Alden J. (1995). *Analytical Reading Inventory,* 5th ed. Englewood Cliffs, NJ. Lawrence Earlbaum.

Children's Literature References

Burton, Virginia Lee. (1942). *The Little House.* Houghton Mifflin.

Fleischman, Paul. (2004). *Sidewalk Circus.* Illustrated by Kevin Hawkes, Candlewick.

Gerstein, Mordicai. (2003). *The Man Who Walked between the Towers.* Roaring Book Press.

Lehman, Barbara. (2004). *The Red Book.* Houghton Mifflin.

Phonics and Phonemic Awareness

CHAPTER OUTLINE

The Importance of Phonemic Awareness
What Is Phonemic Awareness?
Building Foundations for Reading through Phonemic Awareness
Phonics Instruction
Phonics and Stages of Word Knowledge Development
Phonics Instruction for Stages of Word Knowledge Development
Integrating Phonics Skills in a Whole Language Classroom
Phonics and Spelling Connections
Using Students' Papers to Assess Phonics Skills and Spelling Errors
Choosing Spelling Words
Word Analysis Extended to Upper Grades (4–8)

After reading this chapter you will be able to answer the following questions:

1. Why are phonemic awareness and phonics important elements for reading?
2. What does research indicate about phonemic awareness?
3. How can teachers build foundations for reading through phonemic awareness, including auditory awareness and auditory discrimination?
4. What is phonics and what are some approaches to phonics instruction?
5. What is the connection between spelling and phonics instruction?
6. How can student papers be used to assess phonics skills?
7. What are the issues in selecting words in the reading and spelling programs?

Read All About It!

"Spelling-Bee Protesters 'Thru with Through' "

Seattle Times News Service, June 3, 2004

Protesters delivered a message yesterday to the national spelling bee: Enuf is enuf!

Members of the American Literacy Society picketed the 77th annual spelling bee, which is sponsored every year by Cincinnati-based Scripps Howard.

The protesters' complaints: English spelling is illogical, and the national spelling bee only reinforces the crazy spellings that they say contribute to dyslexia, high illiteracy and harder lives for immigrants.

"We advocate the modernization of English spelling," said Pete Boardman, 58, of Groton, N.Y. The Cornell University bus driver admitted to being a terrible speller.

Protester Elizabeth Kuizenga, 56, is such a good speller that she teaches English as a second language in San Francisco. She said she got involved in the protest after seeing how much time was wasted teaching spelling in her class.

Bee spokesman Mark Kroeger said good spelling comes from knowing the story behind a word—what language it comes from, what it means.

"For these kids who understand the root words, who understand the etymology, it's totally logical," he said.

The protesters contend that the illogical spelling of English words makes dyslexia more difficult to overcome and helps explain studies that suggest one in five Americans are functionally illiterate.

"If these people were able to read and write with a simplified spelling system, they would be able to fill out a job application, stay employed and stay out of prison," said Sanford Silverman, 86. The retired accountant was handing out copies of his book, "Spelling for the 21st Century: The Case for Spelling Reform."

Carrying signs reading "I'm thru with through," "Spelling shuud be lojical," and "Spell different difrent," the protesters drew chuckles from bee contestants.

"I can't believe people are picketing against something this ridiculous," said contestant Steven Maheshwary, 14, of Houston.

By day's end yesterday, 46 of the original 265 spellers remained for today's championship. The participants are competing for a top package of $17,000 in cash and other prizes.

Some of the stumpers yesterday were "phyllotaxy," "tribo-

luminescence," "ziphioid" and "dacquoise."

The National Spelling Bee is the nation's largest and longest-running educational contest. The two-day competition held in Washington, D.C., debuted in 1925. In 2004, 10 million grade school students participated in Bee competitions beginning at the local level and culminating with 265 spellers in the finals. For additional information refer to the official website of the Scripps National Spelling Bee: http://www.spellingbee.com.

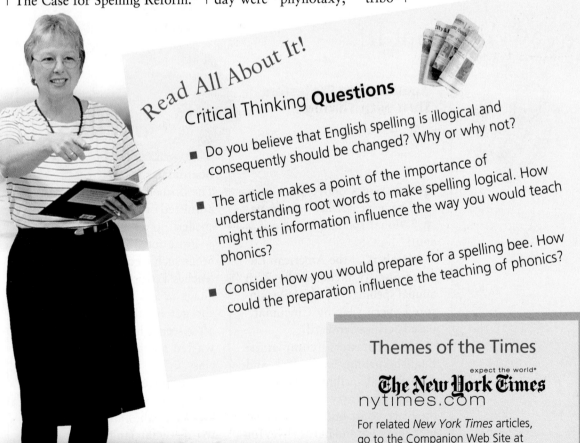

Read All About It!

Critical Thinking Questions

- Do you believe that English spelling is illogical and consequently should be changed? Why or why not?

- The article makes a point of the importance of understanding root words to make spelling logical. How might this information influence the way you would teach phonics?

- Consider how you would prepare for a spelling bee. How could the preparation influence the teaching of phonics?

As introduced in Chapter 1, most initial phonics instruction is based on a bottom-up model of the reading process in which reading instruction proceeds from sounds, to the understanding that words are made up of sounds and syllables, to the blending of sounds into words, and then to comprehension of meaning. Chapter 1 also introduced the integrated model of the reading process associated with a balanced reading approach. Most researchers agree that a balanced reading approach is the best approach for teaching phonics. This approach teaches phonics skills but emphasizes the application of those skills while students read whole, meaningful texts, rather than learning only sound-symbol relationships and practicing decoding words in isolation.

Chapter 3 presented different assessment procedures that are related to assessing phonemic awareness and phonics such as the *Ekwell/Shanker Reading Inventory,* which includes tests of phonemic awareness including rhyming words and initial sound recognition; phonics tests or inventories, which measure a student's application of phonics skills in context; sound-symbol relationships, blends, and vowels; and tests of structural analysis, which assess a student's understanding of prefixes, suffixes, compound words, syllables, and contractions.

Before progressing with this chapter, note that it is difficult to assign ages and grade levels indicating precisely when children develop phonemic awareness and when teachers should provide phonics instruction in the reading program. Some students gain these skills during pre-kindergarten experiences, while other students may not gain these skills until the first, second, or even third grades. Researchers have identified some general age guidelines related to both phonemic awareness and phonics instruction. As you read the following age-related characteristics, remember that they are meant to give an example of progress and may not apply to all students (Goswami, 1999):

- By age four, many children are able to detect syllables within words.
- By age four or five, most children are aware of rhymes and parts that make up multi-syllable words.
- By age six or seven, many children can identify individual phonemes within spoken words.

This chapter progresses from developing phonemic awareness to teaching phonics skills that encourage students to develop and apply their knowledge of sound-symbol relationships and other decoding skills in the reading program.

The Importance of Phonemic Awareness

Phonemic awareness is the ability to focus on and manipulate the smallest units of sound in spoken words. The importance of developing phonemic awareness is frequently emphasized when discussing and evaluating best practices for teaching reading and spelling. According to Patricia Cunningham and Richard Allington (2003):

Students work on rhyming words to increase their phonemic awareness.

"A child's level of phonemic awareness is a very good predictor of beginning reading success" (p. 30). Furthermore, a report from the National Reading Panel, *Teaching Children to Read* (2000), states that "Correlational studies have identified phonemic awareness and letter knowledge as the two best school-entry predictors of how well children will learn to read during their first two years of school. This evidence suggests the potential instructional importance of teaching phonemic awareness to children" (p. 2.1).

What Is Phonemic Awareness?

Phonemes are the smallest units of sounds in a spoken language. English has forty-one phonemes such as *b* and *d,* and these phonemes combine to form syllables and words such as *bat.* The National Reading Panel (2000) identifies the following types of tasks that are used to assess children's phonemic awareness or to improve phonemic awareness through instruction:

1. Phoneme isolation, which requires the recognition of individual sounds in words such as the first sound in the word *paste.*

2. Phoneme identification, which requires recognizing common sounds in different words such as the *b* sound in words such as *boy, Bill, bike.*

3. Phoneme categorization, which requires recognizing the word with a different sound in a sequence of three or four words such as *bus, bun, rug (rug).*

4. Phoneme blending, which requires listening to a sequence of sounds and combining them to form a word such as *t, i, n (tin).*

5. Phoneme segmentation, which requires breaking a word into its sounds by tapping out or counting the sounds in a word such as the three sounds found in *hit.*

6. Phoneme deletion, which requires identifying the word that remains when a phoneme is removed, such as *smile* when the *s* is removed *(mile).*

Instruction in phonemic awareness is considered an effective way to teach children to attend to and to manipulate speech sounds in words. In addition, phonemic awareness instruction helps young children learn to read and older children to improve both reading and spelling. The National Reading Panel warns, however, that "acquiring phonemic awareness is a means rather than an end. Phonemic awareness is not acquired for its own sake but rather for its value in helping learners understand and use the alphabetic system to read and write" (p. 2.6). Phonemic awareness training is intended as foundational knowledge for reading because it helps children grasp the alphabetic system. As you approach reading instruction, remember that literacy acquisition is a complex process. Teaching phonemic awareness does not ensure that children will learn to read and write. They must have many opportunities to apply their phonemic awareness abilities to real reading materials that allow them to read and comprehend those materials.

Building Foundations for Reading through Phonemic Awareness

Teachers and parents of young children have many opportunities to develop phonemic awareness. Even very young children enjoy books such as Tomie dePaola's *Baa Baa Black Sheep and Other Rhymes, Board Book* (2004), which includes many beginning sounds. Listening instruction is a central aspect of teaching phonemic awareness. Listening instruction frequently emphasizes auditory receptive language through auditory perception activities. Auditory perception includes

- **Auditory awareness:** Do children recognize that different sounds have different meanings?
- **Auditory discrimination:** Are children able to distinguish one sound from another sound?
- **Auditory blending:** Are children able to blend sounds to form words?
- **Auditory sequential memory:** Are children able to hear sounds, remember the sounds, and repeat them in the same sequence in which they hear them? (Norton, 2004)

Children with auditory perception problems may have difficulty with reading or spelling approaches that rely heavily on sound and letter relationships. Many of these children need to read using approaches such as whole language approaches that are not based on reading through decoding individual words.

The sections that follow consider how to develop each type of auditory perception: auditory awareness, auditory discrimination, and auditory discrimination of beginning, ending, and middle sounds. In addition, games and other instructional activities that may be used to teach auditory discrimination are presented.

AUDITORY AWARENESS Auditory awareness allows children to discriminate among various sounds in the environment. These sounds include street sounds, country sounds, city sounds, school sounds, or any other sounds in the environment. In order to develop this skill, teachers can use a tape recorder to record different sounds associated with the environment, ask children to listen carefully, and then have children identify the sounds.

Many auditory awareness activities can also be in the form of games. To increase auditory awareness, one kindergarten teacher used concept books—books that emphasize a central image—to frame the auditory sounds to be duplicated or identified by the class. For example, Anne Rockwell's *First Comes Spring* (1985) includes ideas for creating and identifying sounds associated with each of the seasons. Spring includes such activities as walking in rubber boots, listening to birds, jumping rope, and riding bicycles. Summer sounds include swimming, mowing the lawn, and playing baseball. Autumn sounds include raking leaves, playing football, and going to

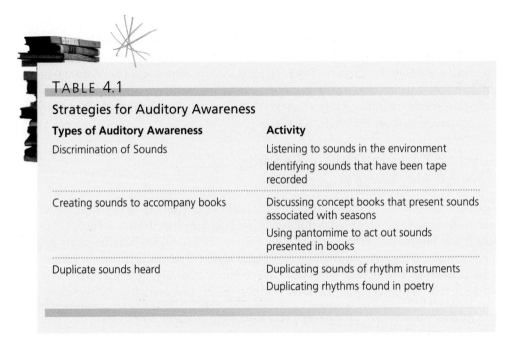

TABLE 4.1

Strategies for Auditory Awareness

Types of Auditory Awareness	Activity
Discrimination of Sounds	Listening to sounds in the environment
	Identifying sounds that have been tape recorded
Creating sounds to accompany books	Discussing concept books that present sounds associated with seasons
	Using pantomime to act out sounds presented in books
Duplicate sounds heard	Duplicating sounds of rhythm instruments
	Duplicating rhythms found in poetry

school. Winter sounds include the sounds of snowflakes falling on the ground, ice skating, and singing carols.

It is also fun for children to try to create the sounds that might accompany a book. For example, sounds that might accompany D. B. Johnson's *Henry Hikes to Fitchburg* (2000) are work sounds created by Henry's friend: filling a woodbox, sweeping the floor, the pulling weeds, painting a fence, moving a bookcase, and sitting on a train. Also, nature sounds are created by Henry: hopping across a river on rocks, carving a walking stick, climbing a tree, paddling a raft, and jumping into a pond.

Kindergarten and preschool teachers may use rhythm instruments for sound awareness activities. Children can listen carefully and duplicate rhythms by using tambourines, rhythm sticks, triangles, and blocks. Rhythmic poetry is excellent for this activity. For example, you might use the poems in the "Fun with Rhymes" section in *Sing a Song of Popcorn: Every Child's Book of Poems* (Beatrice Schenk de Regniers, et al., 1988). This section includes poems such as David McCord's "Jamboree" and "I Want You to Meet . . .", James Reeves's "A Pig Tale," and Charlotte Pomerantz's "Lulu, Lulu, I've a Lilo," and "Where Do These Words Come From?" Jane Yolen's *This* Little Piggy: Lap Songs, Finger Plays, Clapping Games, and Pantomime Rhymes (2005) includes not only instructions for using the text but also a CD of thirteen of the songs. All of the activities described in Chapter 2 under emergent literacy also increase auditory awareness and appreciation as children listen to stories and become involved in storytelling. Table 4.1 summarizes types of auditory awareness along with examples of activities that accompany them.

AUDITORY DISCRIMINATION   Auditory discrimination is the ability to hear and identify differences in letter sounds, words, and nonsense syllables. Most emergent literacy or reading readiness programs include considerable work in auditory discrimination. Providing many enjoyable activities with auditory discrimination will increase children's abilities as they listen for and identify differences in sounds and words. Albert Harris and Edward Sipay (1990) believe that auditory discrimination is a prerequisite skill for teaching phonics. They also believe that the most effective time to teach the skill is before the corresponding discrimination is to be used in printed words, such as having students repeat several rhyming words before they see them.

Studies have provided some clues about effective ways to teach auditory discrimination. For example, Lawren Leslie and Linda Allen (1999) found that teaching rhymes is one of the factors that predicts success in an early intervention program aimed at the improvement of reading with at-risk students. Donald Bear and Colleagues (2000) concur when they state that playing with sounds is one of the easiest ways to develop phonological awareness: "filling children's heads with rhyme is one of the easiest and most natural ways to focus their attention on the sounds of the English language. Books written in rhyme provide one way to do this" (p. 117). Harris and Sipey (1990) believe that as you read books with rhymes aloud, you should pause to let the children guess the rhyming word. Providing many enjoyable activities with auditory discrimination will increase children's abilities as they listen for and identify differences in sounds and words. This approach is effective using books that include rhyming elements such as those listed in Table 4.2.

To provide additional practice with auditory discrimination, poems that have a decided rhyming element can be recorded on tape. These poems can also be written on transparencies or other projection methods to be used for choral reading or visual discrimination. The following poem, "The Camel's Complaint," written by Charles

TABLE 4.2

Books with Rhyming Elements

Book:	Rhyming words:
Jane Yolen's *Off We Go!* (2000)	toe, below, go hop, slop, stop deep, sleep, creep slee, tree, me
Walt Whippo's *Little White Duck* (2000)	pad, glad bad, glad pad, sad boo, hoo, hoo
Mary Ann Hoban's *There Once Was a Man Named Michael Finnegan* (2001)	Finnegan, chin-igan-in-igan, begin-igan skin-igan pin-igan

(Continued)

TABLE 4.2

(Continued)

Book:	Rhyming words:
Jack Prelutsky's *Read-Aloud Rhymes for the Very Young* (1986)	jump, hump wiggle, jiggle hop, clop slide, glide creep, leap bounce, pounce stalk, walk frog, log tree, scree flash, splash
Bob Staake's *Hello, Robots* (2004)	meals, steels green, clean
Kevin Crossley-Holland's *Once Upon a Poem* (2004)	house, mouse care, there beds, heads cap, nap
Philemon Sturges's *She'll Be Comin' 'Round the Mountain* (2004)	honkin', hootin' shoutin', tootin' blossom, possum scamper, hamper fluffy, puffy, stuffy
Nancy Andrews-Goebel's *The Pot That Juan Built* (2002)	hot, pot head, red admire, fire black, back bone, shone
Shel Silverstein's *Runny Babbit* (2005)	swine, mine bug, mug king, sing piddle, thiddle fubby, tubby
Edward Lear's *The Quangle Wangle's Hat* (2005)	tree, see sat, hat wide, side lace, face nest, best

E. Carryl for his daughter Constance, first appeared in the children's magazine *St. Nicholas* in April 1892:

The Camel's Complaint

Canary-birds feed on sugar and seed,
Parrots have crackers to crunch;
And as for the poodles, they tell me the noodles
Have chicken and cream for their lunch.
But there's never a question
About *my* digestion—
Anything does for me.

Cats, you're aware, can repose in a chair,
Chickens can roost upon rails;
Puppies are able to sleep in a stable,
And oysters can slumber in pails.
But no one supposes
A poor camel dozes—
Any place does for me.

Lambs are enclosed where it's never exposed,
Coops are constructed for hens;
Kittens are treated to houses well heated,
And pigs are protected by pens.
But a camel comes handy
Wherever it's sandy—
Anywhere does for me.

People would laugh if you rode a giraffe,
Or mounted the back of an ox;
It's nobody's habit to ride on a rabbit,
Or try to bestraddle a fox.
But as for a camel, he's
Ridden by families—
Any load does for me.

A snake is around as a hole in the ground,
And weasels are wavy and sleek;
And no alligator could ever be straighter
Than lizards that live in a creek.
But a camel's all lumpy
And bumpy and humpy—
Any shape does for me.

Children enjoy the humorous elements of the poem. They can listen for rhyming words and then provide other words that rhyme. The rhyming words in this poem include: *crunch-lunch, question-digestion, rails-pails, supposes-dozes, hens-pens, handy-sandy, ox-fox, sleek-creek,* and *lumpy-humpy.*

To extend the rhyming dramatization and the humor of the situation in the poem, the poem could be accompanied with simple puppets, or children could act out the parts of the various animals presented in the poem.

Activities for auditory discrimination development may be very similar to games. You can clap two sound patterns and ask children if the sound patterns are alike or different. You can say two words very carefully and ask the children if you are saying the same words. For example: *sister-sled, stand-track, black-black*. This type of activity can become progressively more difficult by asking the children to listen to two words that are closer in sound. For example, *branch-ranch, dance-dance, spend-blend, shell-smell, spring-string, flock-flock, puck-stuck*.

After sharing numerous books and poems that develop rhyming elements, you can use pictures of possible rhyming words and encourage children to match pictures that rhyme from a series of cards. This type of activity might resemble Figure 4.1.

AUDITORY DISCRIMINATION OF BEGINNING, MIDDLE, AND ENDING SOUNDS

The auditory discrimination of sounds within words is harder than hearing sounds at the beginning of words. Both spelling and reading require that students hear sounds in different parts of the words. Consequently, instruction usually provides opportunities for students to listen for and identify sounds in various parts of the words. Auditory discrimination of beginning sounds is frequently developed as kindergarten and first-grade teachers associate beginning sounds with the names of students in the class or with common objects. For example, if the class is studying the beginning sound of *b*, they can identify names such as "Bernardo," "Brittany," "Bill," and "Barbara." They can develop a bulletin board with pictures and labels of items beginning with the letter. Concrete items could be placed on a table below the pictures. Placing the printed words under the pictures or the items helps students associate the sound with the visual representations. Such a display might include items such as a *book, barn, bean, bird, balloon, bench, bicycle, boat, box,* or *bear*. Table 4.3 summarizes types of auditory awareness along with examples of activities that accompany them.

After students master the beginning single consonants, they can progress to **blends** in which two letters such as *br* or *gl* form a blended sound. One enjoyable activity is to ask children to brainstorm as many words as they can think of that begin with the blend. Have the teacher or students write the words as the words are pronounced. Next, ask the students to write a story in which they use as many of the words as possible. For example, the following activity was completed by a group of second- and third-grade students using the words that begin with the *br* blend. The brainstorming resulted in the words *brag, braid, bracelet, brain, brainy, brake,*

FIGURE 4.1

Matching Written Rhyming Words

fog	can	see	slide
bell	lake	flag	dog
bake	well	tree	fan

TABLE 4.3

Strategies for Auditory Discrimination

Type of Auditory Discrimination	Activity
Discrimination of beginning sounds	Identifying beginning sounds of students' names
	Using bulletin board of pictures
	Labeling displays of pictures that begin with sounds
Blending two letters	Brainstorming words that begin with sound
	Writing (dictating) a story using the words
Discrimination of ending sounds	Identifying words that do and do not end alike
	Listening to pairs of words
Discrimination of middle sounds	Listening to pairs of words
	Brainstorming and using words in a story
Discrimination of word families	Using pantomime to act out the word that rhymes
	Playing a game of concentration

branch, brand, brat, brave, bread, break, bribe, brick, bridge, bright, bring, broke, brook, brown, and *brush*.

Next, the students reviewed the beginning sounds and the words that used the blends. The students then wrote or dictated stories using as many of the words as possible. The following is an example of one of the stories:

The *Brave* Girl and Her *Brother*

Once upon a time there was a *brave* girl. She was *brainy* and *bright*.

Her favorite object was a *brown bracelet*. She had a little *brother* who was a *brat*. He *broke* her *bracelet*. He threw it off the *bridge*. She forgave him when he went into the *brook* and found her *bracelet*.

This activity can be used as an auditory discrimination activity by having the older students read their stories to kindergarten and first-grade children. The younger children listen for the words that have the same beginning sound.

Ending single sounds are usually harder for children to discriminate than are the rhyming endings presented previously in Table 4.2. As for the beginning sounds, you can use auditory activities in which students identify whether or not two words end alike or differently. Students can listen as two pairs of words are pronounced, such as: *bat-bad, wood-sound, stream-tan, fog-flag, sing-snug,* and *grin-gum*. Picture activities similar to those activities described for beginning sounds may also be helpful.

Auditory discrimination activities that require students to discriminate between sounds in the middle of words (medial sounds) are more difficult for many students. Some reading programs require that students master this skill at the beginning of first grade, whereas other programs do not require it until the second grade.

Auditory discrimination of middle or medial sounds may follow procedures described for beginning and ending sounds. Students can listen to pairs of words such as *lamp-cat, sell-let, will-well, bump-bend, stop-rob, fun-fin, fill-swim, luck-lump,* and *dust-trot.*

Students also require opportunities to use their auditory discrimination skills in writing rather than learning skills in isolation. Second- and third-graders can brainstorm words that have the same medial sound, write and say the words, and write stories in which they use the words. This works equally as well with students who have special learning needs. Remedial reading students in third grade produced the following story. These students required considerable assistance in mastering vowel sounds, but despite their need for assistance, they were able to produce logical stories and were able to use the medial sound of short *i.*

Mister Mouse

Mister Mouse wanted to have a *picnic.*
He asked *his* friends. They *filled* a bag *with* food. They tied *it with string.*
They went to *sit* on a *hill* for the *picnic.*
They stopped for a *swim* in the *spring* by the *hill.*
Mister Mouse *hid* from *his* friends. The *picnic* was fun.

A game of pantomime may be used to reinforce the teaching of word families such as *sat, fat,* and *bat.* Word families may be written on the board. A child is chosen to be "It." The one who is "It" tells the group a word that rhymes with the word he or she has chosen. For example, if the word *bat* was chosen, the student might say *cat.* The group may be divided into teams to act out the word they think it is, or, if in a small group, each child may have an individual turn. This game is fun and it also reinforces word attack skills and comprehension of a list of words.

A game of concentration may be created by writing words on small cards. Two of each word are printed on the cards. The cards are mixed and placed word-side down on the table. The child then turns one card over and says the word, the child turns over a second card and says that word. If the words match and the child pronounces each word correctly, the child may keep the pair. When the teacher plays with the child, the child says the words that the teacher turns over. Of course, the children always win and feel very successful. The game uses good, sneaky phonics and the children are able to add these words to their sight vocabularies.

ALPHABET BOOKS AND PHONEMIC AWARENESS Books and poems that contain rhyming elements are excellent for providing foundations for phonemic awareness. Alphabet books are another form of literature that helps preschool through first-grade children make connections between letters and sounds. By using books, teachers are showing students that phonemic awareness is related to actual reading and not to isolated drills. These books have several characteristics:

1. If letter-sound identification is a major purpose for using an alphabet book, the letters and corresponding illustrations should be easily identifiable.

2. If young children use the books independently, the pages should not be cluttered with numerous objects that can confuse letter-sound identification.

Many alphabet books are also excellent for children beyond the first or second grades. Such alphabet books may be developed around specific time periods or themes that expand children's interests as well as understanding of words and concepts. See

FIGURE 4.2

Alphabet Books for Use in Language Development

Lois Ehlert's *Eating the Alphabet: Fruits and Vegetables* (1989)	develops the ABCs around food
Suse MacDonald's *Alphabetics* (1986)	presents a series of pictures that proceed from the original letter to create an object that represents the letter
Arnold Lobel's *On Market Street* (1981)	bases a trip through the market on objects from apples to zippers
Stephen T. Johnson's *Alphabet City* (1995)	presents the letters through paintings of city scenes
Bob McLeod's SuperHero ABC (2006)	alliteration emphasizes letter sounds
David Pelletier's *The Graphic Alphabet* (1996)	graphically interprets the letters

Multicultural topics can be explored through alphabet books such as

Margaret Musgrove's *Ashanti to Zulu: African Traditions* (1976)

Muriel Feelings's *Jumbo Means Hello: Swahili Alphabet Book* (1974)

Ashley Bryan's *Ashley Bryan's ABC of African American Poetry* (1997)

Cynthia Chin Lee's *A Is for Asia* (1997)

the list of books in Figure 4.2 for examples of alphabet books to use for language development. Which of the books are especially appropriate for young children? Which of the books could be used to expand vocabularies and interests of older students?

Phonics Instruction

After students have had numerous opportunities to develop their phonemic awareness, through auditory and visual discrimination activities, many are ready for more formal instruction in developing and using letter-sound relationships. This instruction of the systematic relationship between letters and sounds is usually called **phonics.**

When referring to phonics instruction, texts may use terms such as *word attack skills, word decoding techniques,* and *purposeful word study.* When using the terms word attack and purposeful word study, texts usually mean not only teaching students to use letter-sound relationships and letter patterns to decode words, but also

Reflect on Your Reading

Consider what you have read about phonemic awareness. Why do you suppose auditory awareness, auditory discrimination, and auditory discrimination of beginning, middle, and ending sounds are required for phonemic awareness?

A student reinforces her word-analysis skills as she fills in missing letters and words on a chart.

to use the context of the materials to help students identify words. Many students learn the letter-sound relationships through activities such as those described in the previous sections about developing phonemic awareness. Other students may require more direct instruction as teachers point out and reinforce knowledge about the connections.

Although the effectiveness of phonics instruction is well established, there is disagreement about how phonics should be taught:

- Should every child receive phonics instruction?
- Should phonics be taught as isolated skills?
- Should phonics only be taught within a broader, more balanced, approach to literacy?

Jean Chall (1996) suggests using decoding techniques with students who are most likely to be at risk for reading difficulties, such as students from low-income families and students with learning disabilities. Decoding techniques teach students to use the sounds of the language to identify or decode words that should be used. Chall asserts that students with special reading needs require a more systematic approach for teaching phonics. She bases her beliefs on earlier studies she cites in *Learning to Read: The Great Debate* (1967). More recent advocates for phonics instruction such as L. M. Morrow and D. H. Tracey (1997) maintain that most children need some direct systematic instruction by the teacher in order to be successful readers. Morrow and Tracy believe that students need more than natural reading activities in order for reading skills to emerge. In fact, they believe that reading skills will only emerge with direct instruction of phonics. Direct phonics instruction is often developed through isolated worksheets in which students are asked to match sounds with pictures of objects that begin with the sound or by using flash cards in which students call out the sounds.

Opponents to this type of direct phonics instruction argue that phonics should not be taught in isolation, but within reading and writing activities. In support of this

Up for Discussion

How should words be selected for instruction in the spelling program? This question has provided considerable controversy in the past. If the spelling words selected are closely related to phonological awareness, the words could be chosen because they fit specific patterns that are also taught in the phonics portion of the reading program. This approach is recommended by Johnston (1999).

Should the words be selected because they have consistent spelling patterns? Should they be selected because they have a high frequency of use in children's own reading and writing? Should the words be selected because of meanings related to word origins, structural patterns, and root words?

This student's paper shows an example of invented spelling.

approach, studies emphasizing isolated phonics instruction show that around third and fourth grade, students are able to pronounce long, multi-syllable words but are not able to comprehend or interpret what they are reading. Children whose reading instruction focuses on drills, such as worksheets and flash cards, are learning to read but have no desire to read.

Two additional terms are frequently used when providing instruction in phonics: a *synthetic approach* to phonics instruction and an *analytic approach.* In the synthetic approach, the teacher teaches sound-symbol relationships through repeated drilling of consonant sounds, followed by the blending of the sounds into words. A synthetic approach sometimes asks students to pronounce nonsense words that allow them to apply the sound-symbol generalization. Reading in context is not usually taught until students have mastered the consonant sounds such as *b, c, d, f,* and so on; the initial blends such as *cr, gl, tr,* and so on; ending consonant sounds, and vowel sounds.

An analytic phonics approach usually begins with teaching students a few sight words and then teaching the sounds represented by the sight words. For example, if the students have learned *big, boy, Bill, be, by, but, been* as sight words, the teacher would write them on the board, ask the students to listen to the words as he or she pronounces the words, and to identify if the words begin with the same sound and if they do, to name the sound. Next, the teacher would ask the students to look at the way the words are printed on the board. They should notice that the words all begin with the letter *b.* Next, the students would identify additional words that begin with the sound of *b* and the written symbol showing *b.* The teacher writes these new words as they are pronounced by the students. If using an analytic approach, subsequent lessons would teach the consonants.

Phonics and Stages of Word Knowledge Development

Research in the stages of word recognition identify the levels of word knowledge development that reflect students' understanding of how sound, pattern, and meaning are represented in English spelling. Donald R. Bear and Colleagues (2000) identify these stages as emergent reader, beginning reader (letter name–alphabetic), transitional reader (within word pattern), intermediate reader (syllables and affixes) and advanced reader (derivational relations).

Each of these stages of word knowledge include specific reader behaviors and suggest types of phonics instruction that may be appropriate. As Bear and colleagues (2000) observe,

> Children move hierarchically from easier one-to-one correspondences between letters and sounds, to more difficult, abstract relationships between letter patterns and sound, to even more sophisticated relationships between meaning units as they relate to sound and pattern. Stages are marked by broad, qualitative shifts in the types of spelling errors children commit as well as behavioral changes in their reading and writing. (p. 8)

EMERGENT READERS   During this stage children frequently write with scribbles or random letters that lack any phonetic relationship to the letters they believe they are writing. They do not systematically use the letter-sound cueing system of the language. This stage is called emergent because children's understanding of the alphabetic principle is beginning to emerge. The activities described earlier in this chapter under "Building Foundations for Reading through Phonemic Awareness" are especially important during this stage.

BEGINNING READERS   These students are beginning to understand letter-sound relationships. They start to identify words through phonetic cues. For example, they frequently make errors when reading, for example, *The bag was on the bed* rather than *The bat was on the bed*. When spelling they may spell *bat* with *bt*. Here they focus on beginning consonant sounds. As they advance in the beginning reading stage they frequently make errors in the middle vowel position as they misread or misspell *bed* for *bat*. Now they are focusing on the beginning and ending consonants, while ignoring the sounds of the vowels.

Students who are reading at this level of word knowledge need many opportunities to read phonetically regular words and to develop a sight vocabulary. They need to read and reread predictable books. They need to engage in activities such as studying beginning sounds, studying word families, and working with blends and digraphs. (Digraphs are two letters expressing one sound, such as *ea* in *bread* or *th* in *that*.)

TRANSITIONAL READERS   Children who demonstrate an awareness of the patterns that exist within words have mastered initial consonants, consonant blends, and consonant digraphs (*th* in *that*). Now children focus on the vowel. Short vowel rhymes are learned along with consonant blends such as *fl* in *fl-at* or *tr* in *tr-ap*. Most of these readers are now able to read fluently at their instructional level because they have a large sight vocabulary and are able to use context clues in the reading and their knowledge of phonics to help them decode unknown words. These readers need many opportunities to practice reading independently. They need lessons on vowel patterns such as the long vowels. Activities where students sort words according to long and short vowel patterns are beneficial.

INTERMEDIATE READERS   These readers often have difficulties with syllables and affixes. This stage of word knowledge usually occurs at the intermediate middle grades. Students at this level are experiencing polysyllabic words in their content areas. Consequently, they benefit from lessons that teach them aloud syllables, affixes, and the effects of affixes on base words. This type of activity is associated with both vocabulary development, spelling instruction, and using context clues to analyze the meanings of unfamiliar words.

ADVANCED READERS   These students are mature readers who understand that the way words are spelled provide clues to their meanings. Activities such as teaching the connections between spelling and meanings such as in *critic/criticize* are beneficial. Greek and Latin elements in words, definitions of root words, and semantic webs that trace the roots of a word are all beneficial. Students can expand this study and relate it to literature by searching for words in Greek and Roman myths.

Phonics Instruction for Stages of Word Knowledge Development

Each of the previously defined levels of word knowledge suggest both characteristics of students who are at that stage and instructional activities that are appropriate so that students progress to the next stage of word knowledge.

PHONICS FOR EMERGENT READERS   Characteristics of these students show that the emergent reader does not understand letter-sound relationships or may not understand the concept of a word. The student may not be able to recognize common sounds in different words. The activities already discussed under auditory perception including auditory awareness, auditory discrimination, auditory blending, and auditory sequential memory are essential for emergent readers. Reading to students and encouraging oral language activities such as playing with language is beneficial. Students can practice their emerging writing skills by using invented spelling.

PHONICS FOR BEGINNING READERS   These readers who are able to identify the names of letters (alphabetic level) have beginning concepts of words, are able to focus on beginning consonants when they read, and usually read one word at a time. When reading orally to students, teachers can point to the words, phrases, and sentences to reinforce the concept that words combine to make sentences, and those sentences have meaning.

Phonics teaching at this beginning level usually starts with students learning the names and sounds of the letters. As they learn the names and sounds of the letters, students usually focus on the beginning and ending consonants. Instructional activities that teach and reinforce beginning sounds include sorting pictures and words according to beginning sounds. For example, students can search through pictures and sort out all of the pictures of items beginning with *b*. These pictures might include a *book,* a *bike,* a *box,* and a *bird,* along with pictures that begin with other consonant sounds. Now students select the pictures that begin with *b,* place them in a line, and then repeat the names of the items that begin with *b.* Some teachers use magnetic boards and students sort the pictures and place them on the boards.

Word banks—words placed on individual cards—usually follow activities that have involved sorting pictures for beginning consonants. Words are placed in word banks as soon as they become part of the students' sight vocabularies. These words provide sources for students to group according to beginning consonants. For example, *but, be, big,* and *boy* may all be in the word bank of sight words. Now students sort out all of the words that begin with the sound of *b* as in *boy*. As children review the words in their word banks, they are reinforcing both their growing understanding of letter-sound relationships and their knowledge of sight words. Teachers usually continue a study of initial consonants until students recognize most of these letters and sounds.

A study of initial consonant blend and digraphs is a logical sequence to begin a study of initial consonants. Consonant blends include blends that combine *l* with another letter such as *bl, cl,* and *sl* or blends that combine *r* with another letter such as *br, gr,* and *tr*. There are also blends that begin with the same initial consonant such as *sm, st,* and *sk*. Both picture and word sorts may be used to introduce blends. Pictures for the *bl* blend, for example, might include *blanket, block,* and *blouse*. This activity expands to include the remaining blends and expands to digraphs such as *ch* and *sh*. Again, activities that involve sorting pictures and words are useful as are auditory discrimination activities such as those presented under phonemic awareness.

PHONICS FOR TRANSITIONAL READERS   Transitional readers are ready to focus on instruction that emphasizes short and long vowel word families. A study of word families is the easiest way to introduce the short vowel sounds. For example, word family groupings of short *a* sounds may be placed on a chart, on the board, or on worksheets and transparencies. The word families can also be recorded into a tape recorder so students can listen to the pronunciations as they read. The rhyming element makes this approach easier for many struggling readers. If the words are on transparencies, they are ready for group review. If the words are placed on a chart, children can read or review them individually and listen to the tape recording to check their pronunciations. Word families for the short *a* include:

and	*at*	*an*	*ack*	*ap*	*ad*
band	bat	pan	sack	cap	bad
sand	cat	ran	pack	map	sad
hand	fat	man	Jack	rap	fad
land	hat	fan	rack	clap	had
grand	mat	can	tack	slap	lad
bland	rat	tan	black	trap	mad
stand	pat	van	track	strap	pad
brand	sat	plan	snack	snap	glad

As the words in the word families are introduced ask students to use the words in a sentence. These sentences can be written on the board or on a chart. By using the words in sentences teachers are making sure that students understand the meanings of the words. As the students read the words from the short *a* word families teachers need to make sure students understand the sound of short *a* in the middle position of a word. Reinforce the short *a* sound by placing a series of *a* family words on the board. These words may be from their sight vocabulary such as: *cat, pan, sat, cap, hat, had,* and *bat*. The teacher should place his or her hand under each word as the word is pronounced. The students then pronounce the word. At this time, the teacher and the students identify the sound of *a* when it is between two consonants. Pictures and objects can be added to the family groupings of the short *a* words.

The students can reinforce the rhyming words with an activity that asks them to fill in the blank using appropriate words from the short *a* list. For example,

1. We have two _____ (hands).
2. The _____ (bat) goes with the ball.
3. The food is in a _____ (pan).
4. The apples are in a _____ (sack).
5. Put on the red _____ (cap).

The rhyming words are placed on small individual cards. The student finds the words that belong to each blank space and places them next to each sentence. After the short *a* sound has been generalized, ask students to write a story using as many short *a* words as possible. The stories can be written by the students or dictated to the teacher by the student. The following story was written by a second-grade student. This story was dictated, printed on the chalkboard, and reread by the students who then underlined the words with short *a* sounds:

Tramp and Little Scamp

Tramp and scamp like to play ball. Scamp ran back and forth on the grass. Scamp was mad when the ball landed on a branch. The cat was on the branch. He batted it back to Scamp. Now Tramp and Little Scamp are happy.

A study of word families should continue. For example, the following words can be used to study the short *e* word families:

ell	*et*	*est*	*ed*	*end*	*en*
bell	bet	nest	bed	send	ten
tell	get	rest	fed	lend	pen
sell	wet	test	led	mend	men
well	set	best	red	bend	hen
fell	let	vest	sled	blend	den
yell	met	West	shed	spend	Ben
smell	pet	Crest	Ned		Ken
spell	jet				
swell					
shell					

The following words can be used to study the short *i* word families:

ill	*ick*	*ig*	*in*	*ing*	*it*	*id*
will	pick	big	tin	sing	sit	did
fill	kick	dig	fin	ring	hit	lid
hill	sick	pig	pin	king	bit	hid
mill	brick	wig	win	wing	wit	kid
kill	thick	fig	skin	spring	fit	rid
pill				bring	kit	bid
till				swing		
still				string		

The following words can be used to study the short *o* word families:

ot	*op*	*ock*	*ob*
not	hop	sock	job
got	mop	lock	rob
hot	pop	flock	rob
dot	top	rock	sob
cot	crop	cock	cob
lot	drop	block	mob
pot	flop	shock	snob
spot	shop		
shot			
trot			
blot			
slot			

The following words can be used to study the short *u* word families:

un	*unk*	*ug*	*ump*	*uck*	*ust*
run	bunk	bug	bump	buck	rust
gun	dunk	dug	hump	duck	must
fun	junk	hug	jump	luck	trust
sun	sunk	jug	dump	tuck	dust
bun	drunk	mug	lump	suck	
	flunk	rug	pump	pluck	
	spunk	chug	slump	stuck	
	trunk	drug	stump	struck	
		plug	thump	truck	
		snug			

A study of short vowel word families can lead to a study of long vowel word families. To illustrate to the students what happens to the short vowel sound when a second vowel is placed at the end of the word, place two columns of words on the board. One column includes short *a* words and the opposite column includes the same words, but with the final *e* added:

can	can<u>e</u>
hat	hat<u>e</u>
cap	cap<u>e</u>
fat	fat<u>e</u>
tap	tap<u>e</u>
pan	pan<u>e</u>
mad	mad<u>e</u>

Read the words aloud with students and discuss the differences in pronunciation of the *a* sound when the final silent *e* is added. This process continues with other words used in the short vowel word families such as:

rip	rip<u>e</u>
hid	hid<u>e</u>
shin	shin<u>e</u>
pin	pin<u>e</u>
fin	fin<u>e</u>
kit	kit<u>e</u>
hop	hop<u>e</u>
rob	rob<u>e</u>
mop	mop<u>e</u>
rod	rod<u>e</u>
not	not<u>e</u>

The word family approach is also useful for teaching long vowel sounds such as word families with silent *e* and *ai:*

<u>*ake*</u>	<u>*ame*</u>	<u>*ain*</u>
cake	came	rain
make	fame	gain
lake	dame	main
take	same	pain
bake	game	brain
fake	lame	drain
rake	name	grain
wake	tame	plain
flake	blame	train
snake	frame	stain
brake	flame	

Students can be told that two vowels in a word make the first vowel long. This two-vowel rule can also be presented with the *ai* family— *rain, pain, grain, gain, brain, plain, main, drain, train.* After introducing students to the two-vowel rule, the teacher can extend the lesson by reading a story aloud, such as "The Hare and the Tortoise." As a group the students can talk about the story, then dictate the story back to the teacher using as many long *a* words as possible. For example, this is a story that was dictated back to me by a class of second-grade students.

The *Hare* and the Tortoise

The *hare* wanted to run a *race*. The *hare* and the tortoise ran down the *trail* to the *lake*. The *hare made* a fast start. The tortoise went like a *snail*. The *hare* could not *fail* to win. He would *take* a nap. When he did *awake*, it was too *late*. The slow tortoise had won the *race*.

As part of the exercise, students underlined the long *a* words, reread the story, and illustrated it.

The word family approach is also useful for teaching long vowel sounds such as word families with *ee:*

<u>*eet*</u>	<u>*een*</u>	<u>*eep*</u>	<u>*eed*</u>	<u>*eel*</u>	<u>*ee*</u>
meet	green	keep	feed	feel	see
street	screen	sleep	seed	wheel	three
sheet	queen	sheep	need	steel	bee

word families with long *i* and silent *e:*

<u>*ine*</u>	<u>*ide*</u>
fine	side
pine	tide
mine	ride
nine	hide
wine	wide
swine	glide
spine	stride

word families with long *o*, silent *e* and *oa:*

<u>*oke*</u>	<u>*one*</u>	<u>*oat*</u>	<u>*oad*</u>	<u>*oast*</u>
joke	cone	boat	load	coast
woke	bone	coat	road	toast
poke	stone	goat	toad	roast
smoke				
broke				
spoke				

word families with long *u* and silent *e:*

<u>*une*</u>	<u>*ute*</u>	<u>*ue*</u>
tune	cute	blue
June	flute	true
Prune	brute	Sue

Notice that many of the words in these word families include consonant blends. Consonant blends and word families are also found in books children read independently. Both blends and word families can be pointed out to students as they read or listen to Deborah Chandra's *A Is for Amos* (1999). The author uses blends and word families in words such as *clap, clop, thump,* and *stream.*

Before proceeding to phonics instruction for intermediate readers and advanced readers (see the section on Word Analysis Extended to Upper Grades (four through eight) later in this chapter) we will discuss how phonics instruction might be taught in a whole language classroom.

Integrating Phonics Skills in a Whole Language Classroom

Whole language is an approach that maintains that a child's language is the basis for all reading instruction and that literacy learning activities should be authentic and meaningful. Proponents of whole language, such as B. Moss and H. Noden (1994), argue that phonics should be taught as students are reading authentic reading materials such a newspapers and literature. B. J. Bruneau (1979) developed a model for teaching reading that follows the whole language philosophy as shown in Figure 4.3 and integrates the development of phonics skills as the final tip of the pyramid.

Notice that many of the activities developed under phonemic awareness and in emergent literacy are found in the pyramid. Reading aloud is at the base because it demonstrates teacher involvement in literature, motivates children to read, develops a sense of story, and promotes awareness of different literacy styles. Shared reading and writing help extend involvement with literacy through active participation. Big books and predictable books are often used with young students as teachers model and direct attention to letters and word patterns in the printing. Shared writing is a collaborative experience as students write charts, stories, and poems. Guided read-

FIGURE 4.3
Literacy Pyramid for Whole Language

Source: Bruneau, B. J. (1997).

ing and writing encourage students to work together in small groups to think and talk about what is read. Teachers use lessons to help students develop reading strategies and to work on particular skills.

During readers' and writers' workshops, students read and write as the teacher uses minilessons and modeling strategies for skills needed by the students. The students then read and write for a period of time. Finally, students share their work with their classmates and the teacher relates the sharing back to the objectives of the minilesson. At the top of the pyramid are the teaching of skills and strategies such as phonics, spelling, and mechanics of writing. These lessons are connected to the reading event and not taught in isolation.

Terms such as *centering literacy instruction, combination approach,* and *balanced approach* are used for programs in which teachers integrate the best strategies from both whole language and structured phonics approaches. L. M. Morrow and D. H. Tracey (1997) describe a classroom that uses a combination approach for teaching phonics in a kindergarten classroom:

> Mrs. S's class was learning about animals. She planned to focus on the consonant *"p"* during the unit since the letter appeared frequently in texts and discussions about animals. She read the book *The Pet Show* (Keats, 1972), and children noticed the letter *p* in the book title as well as in *Peter Rabbit* (Potter, 1903) and *Petunia* (Duvoisin, 1950). (p. 647)

The class activities with *p* continued as children identified the names of animals that began with the letter and placed them on a chart entitled, "Animal Names Beginning with *P*." She followed this activity with a workshop in which children wrote the letter in the appropriate place. Notice in this example how the teacher used both literature to develop an auditory skill and introduce the sounds, and a more explicit activity related to teaching the letter-sound relationships for the letter.

Phonics and Spelling Connections

There is a close relationship between phonics, reading, and spelling. Margaret Hughes and Dennis Searle (2000) note that "through frequent reading of varied texts, a reader is exposed to an extensive vocabulary, to how sound is represented in print, to the orthographic patterns" (p. 203). Donald Bear and Shane Templeton (1998) maintain that "To read and write words appropriately and fluently and to appreciate fully how words work in context, instruction must balance authentic reading and writing with purposeful word study. Word study instruction integrates spelling, phonics, and vocabulary instruction" (p. 223).

Researchers who investigate characteristics of good spellers report the importance of developing students' awareness of words because good spellers seem to depend on a sensitivity to patterns of letters within words. M. J. Adams (1990) concludes that difficulty with either phonemic analysis or knowledge of spelling patterns interferes with good spelling.

Adams expresses the importance of helping students look for and listen for patterns in words because "Successful spelling improvement depends on getting children to attend to unfamiliar patterns. . . . Research indicates that the experience of seeing a word in print is not only superior to hearing it spelled but, further, is an extremely powerful and effective means of acquiring its spelling" (p. 102). Adams quotes research that indicates that seeing a word's spelling helps even first-graders remember its pronunciation. Teachers should encourage students to look at the spellings of words by writing the words on the board, pointing to them on the page, and writing using the new words.

Other researchers point out the importance of teaching word families in both spelling and reading. Francine R. Johnston (1999) uses a developmental approach to the study of word families in which she teaches one word family at a time, such as the "at" family or the "an" family. She then recommends comparing word families that contain different short vowels such as found in *cat, but,* and *sit.* The study continues with common or familiar words that include blends and digraphs. Blends and digraphs may be added to the one-family words as students go from *pack, rack,* and *sack* to *black, track,* and *snack.*

Johnston recommends that when silent vowels begin to appear in children's **invented spellings** (children make up their own spellings for words), the children are ready to study the patterns that spell the other vowel sounds of English, such as found in *bail, jail,* and *mail.* Johnston believes that "teachers should use children's invented spellings to determine what they know and what they are ready to learn" (p. 74).

INVENTED SPELLING AND PHONICS   Teachers who encourage young children to use invented spellings frequently discover that the children write longer stories than if they are allowed to use only correct spellings. In invented spellings children are encouraged to say the words and write down the letters that they hear. You can model this approach with young children by showing them how to write a sentence under a picture by sounding out the words and then writing down the letters as they are heard. Explain to the children that invented spellings are used in their early writings, but correct spellings will come later as they learn more about words and sounds. Correct spellings are also essential as they edit their writings and produce final drafts of their work. Teachers can show students the correct spellings of words after they experiment with invented spellings.

Understanding and analyzing the stages that children use in their invented spellings helps teachers identify the developmental stages of their students and to develop appropriate instruction. Researchers such as Edmund Henderson (1985) and Henderson and Templeton (1986) have identified stages in developmental spelling by analyzing changes in children's invented spellings. They use the following stages to identify the specific stage of a child and to provide suggestions for appropriate instruction:

Stage I: Young children use symbols to represent words but they do not understand letter-sound correspondences.

Stage II: At approximately first grade, children begin to spell alphabetically by matching sounds and letters. They write words such as *TAK* for *take.*

Stage III: At about third through fourth grade, they begin to assimilate word knowledge and conventional sound patterns. Errors may include *SPEKE* for *speak.*

Stage IV: During fourth grade children increase their understanding of word patterns. They make more mature errors such as *INOCENT* for *innocent.*

Stage V: At about sixth grade many students begin to understand that spellings of words are related to meanings. They use the correct spellings of words in context and expand their knowledge of English orthography (word spelling).

Henderson and Templeton give suggestions for using these stages to provide phonics and spelling instruction. For example, they recommend that children at Stage II examine groups of words that are organized around common features such as word patterns.

Using Students' Papers to Assess Phonics Skills and Spelling Errors

The various written papers and tests produced by students at any grade level provide excellent sources for the informal assessment of phonics abilities and spelling. By analyzing a student's writings, you can identify whether or not the student accurately relates letter and sound symbols. Does the student understand word families? Does the child use appropriate consonants? Does the child omit letters? Are there errors at the beginning, the middle, or ends of words?

"Spache's Spelling Errors Test" (Norton, 2004) is one tool to analyze students' papers and assess the types of spelling errors found. The test consists of the following items to be checked:

1. A silent letter is omitted, such as in *take-tak*.
2. A sounded letter is omitted, such as in *stand-san*.
3. A double letter is omitted, such as in *letter-leter*.
4. A single letter is added, such as in *park-parck*.
5. Letters are transposed or reversed, such as *angel-angle*.
6. There is a phonetic substitution for the consonant, such as *bush-buch*.
7. There is a phonetic substitution for the vowel, such as *green-grean*.
8. There is a phonetic substitution for the syllable, such as *flies-flys*.
9. There is a phonetic substitution for the word, such as *hare-hear*.
10. There is a nonphonetic substitution for the vowel, such as *bats-bots*.
11. There is a nonphonetic substitution for a consonant, such as *camper-canper*.

As you analyze this informal spelling word test, why do you believe that Spache, an authority in reading research, included each of these items? By using the test, what information would you receive about a child's phonemic awareness? How would you provide instruction if a child consistently makes errors in one of these areas?

Choosing Spelling Words

A second recommendation for selecting spelling words is called the *frequency-of-use approach*. This approach is the one recommended by Ernest Horn, whose writings on the subject span from 1919 through 1963. In 1919 Horn recommended that if rules are used to select spelling words, the rules can be easily taught, remembered, and actually used in spelling. By 1963, Horn believed that some emphasis on phonics should be included in the spelling program. He cautioned, however, that instruction in phonics should be regarded as an aid to spelling rather than a substitute for the systematic study of words in the spelling list.

Horn maintained that the spelling words should be taken from those words that are most frequently used, with the easiest words taught in the beginning grades and the harder words taught in the upper grades. He maintained that the words most frequently used by children in their writing should be taught first. The first ten words on Horn's list include *I, the, and, to, a, you, of, in, we,* and *for.* His research indicated that the first hundred words in the high frequency list account for 65 percent of the words written by both children and adults. Consequently, Horn maintained that these words should be taught in such a way that children automatically spell them correctly.

Lists of high-frequency words such as those identified by Edward Fry (1980) are often used for this approach. According to Fry, the first hundred words on his list make up half of all written material. Why would it be important to teach both the spelling and the reading of these high-frequency words? Why do authors of "Easy-to-Read" books for beginning readers use this list? The list shown in Table 4.4 includes Fry's most common words.

A second approach to selecting spelling words is based on work by Carol Chomsky (1970), who maintained that words that have the same meaning tend to look alike, even if they have different pronunciations. Consequently, words like *nation* and *national* have similar spellings, and the meanings are consistent, even though the phonetic pronunciations are different. In this viewpoint, certain spelling patterns are considered consistent because they indicate a similar meaning or a specific part of speech.

Word Analysis Extended to Upper Grades (4–8)

Phonics instruction for the middle and upper grades falls under Bear and colleagues' (2000) classification of intermediate readers with a focus on syllables and affixes and advanced readers who study word derivations. By the time readers reach the intermediate level, phonics instruction focuses on prefixes, suffixes, and multisyllabic words. Most students read with considerable fluency, read silently faster than orally, and have rapidly expanding vocabularies. By the time readers are classified as advanced readers, instruction may focus on ways to comprehend the meanings of multisyllabic words by studying how the words are derived from Latin and Greek. A study of word derivations may be combined with the content areas of literature and science.

The word recognition skills taught in the middle and upper elementary grades are closely related to comprehension of new words. Many of these word recognition skills are called *structural analysis skills* because they help students understand word meanings. As we have seen from Henderson and Templeton's (1986) stages in invented spellings and in their recommendations for instruction in various word analysis skills, by Stage V students require the more demanding areas required to understand prefixes and suffixes.

TEACHING PREFIXES **Prefixes** are placed at the beginning of a word to modify the meaning of the word or to form a new word. Consequently, a prefix such as *un-* placed

TABLE 4.4

Fry's List of High-Frequency Written Words

First 25 words	Second 25 Words	Third 25 Words	Fourth 25 Words
the	or	will	number
of	one	up	no
and	had	other	way
a	by	about	could
to	word	out	people
in	but	many	my
is	not	then	than
you	what	them	first
that	all	these	water
it	were	so	been
he	we	some	call
was	when	her	who
for	your	would	oil
on	can	make	now
are	said	like	find
as	there	him	long
with	use	into	down
his	an	time	day
they	each	has	did
I	which	took	get
at	the	two	come
be	do	more	made
this	how	write	may
have	their	go	part
from	if	see	over

Common suffixes: -s, -ing, -ed

before *able* changes the word to *unable* and also changes the meaning of the word to "not able." Likewise, if *un-* is placed before *happy* the new word is *unhappy,* and the new meaning is "not happy." Prefixes are usually considered easier for most students than suffixes and root words because the prefixes have fairly consistent meanings.

According to a study by White, Sowell, and Yanagihara (1989), the prefixes listed in Table 4.5 are the most frequently found in English. By using a form such as that shown in Table 4.5, students can identify the meanings of the prefixes and provide examples of words using the prefixes. Allowing students to search for and use the prefixes helps them develop their understandings.

Prefixes such as *un-, under-, in-,* and *pre-* are considered easier, and are frequently taught in the second through fourth grades.

To help students understand prefixes, teachers can model how prefixes change meanings by writing a word such as *happy* on the board and discussing the meaning

TABLE 4.5

Frequently Used Prefixes

un-	re-	in-	im-	il-	dis-
en-	em-	non-	in-	im-	over-
mis-	sub-	pre-	inter-	fore-	de-
trans-	super-	semi-	anti-	under-	

of the word. Then they can place the prefix *un-* before the word and ask the students to identify what happens to the meaning of the word when it becomes *unhappy* rather than *happy*. Teachers should ensure that students understand that the new word means "not happy."

Another strategy for presenting prefixes is for teachers to lead a brainstorming activity in which students list additional words that use the prefix *un-* such as those found in Table 4.6.

Teachers can then lead a discussion about the meanings of the root words for each of the words that the students identify. Students should also search through texts and identify when authors use prefixes and how the prefixes change the meanings of words. As part of the application for teaching prefixes, students should have opportunities to use the various prefixes in their own writing.

The concept of prefixes should be reviewed regularly during both reading and spelling lessons. When prefixes are found in either reading or spelling, they should be identified by the teacher and the students.

TEACHING SUFFIXES   A **suffix** is a syllable placed at the end of the word to change its meaning, to give it a grammatical function, or to form a new word. Consequently, when *less* is added to *fear,* the word changes to mean without fear. When *al* is added to *music* to become *musical,* the word becomes an adjective.

Inflectional suffixes change the endings of words, such as the plural *s* in *girls.* White, Sowell, and Yanagihara (1989) identify the suffixes in Table 4.7 as those that appear most frequently.

TABLE 4.6

Words That Use the *un-* Prefix

unable	unaffected	unbeaten	unbelievable,
unbroken	uncomfortable	unconscious	uncover
undo	undress	unfriendly	unhealthy
unknown	untie		

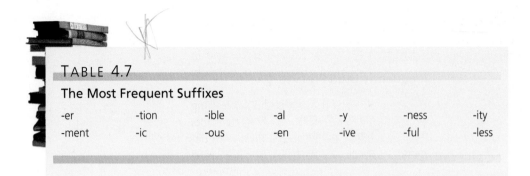

TABLE 4.7

The Most Frequent Suffixes

-er	-tion	-ible	-al	-y	-ness	-ity
-ment	-ic	-ous	-en	-ive	-ful	-less

FIGURE **4.4**

Roots and Branches for *spectus/spectare*

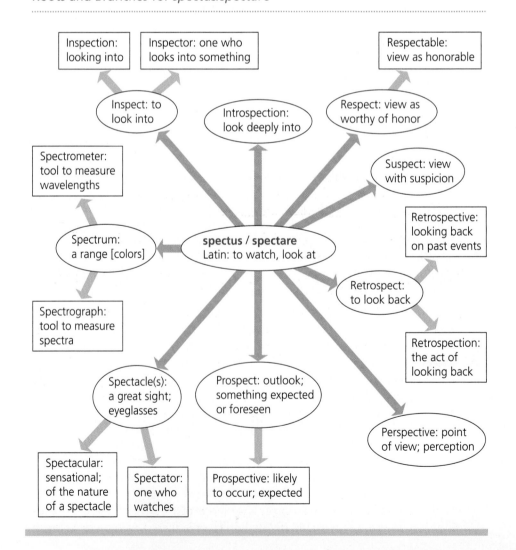

TEACHING ROOTS AND BRANCHES By the time students become advanced readers and writers, they discover words that are related in meaning may also be related in spelling. For example, *prohibit* and *prohibition* are closely related in meaning and spelling. Understanding the meaning of *prohibit* helps students understand both the meaning and spelling of *prohibition*. Likewise, the study of the roots of words shows that the meanings of many words are derived from Latin and Greek roots—for example, learning the Greek number prefix for three (*tri*) is used in many words to designate three parts such as *tricycle, tripod,* and *triad.*

Reflect on Your Reading

What approach do you think would be the most beneficial for teaching phonics in an upper elementary class? Consider how you might use your students' papers to assess phonics skills.

Janet W. Bloodgood and Linda C. Pacifici (2004) use a method for word study in which the teacher places the root word in the center of a web. Students in groups of three to five record the derived words extending from the web in one color of a marker. The students then use a dictionary to locate word meanings. The word meanings are recorded in a different color. Figure 4.4 is an example of their web using the word *spectus/spectare.*

DIFFERENTIATING INSTRUCTION

ELL Students

Oral language acquisition is especially important for children's success in learning to read and write. Betty E. Roush (2005) maintains that oral language acquisition is especially important for ELL kindergarten students:

> Phonological awareness is a powerful predictor of whether students will be successful in reading. . . . Research indicates that activities that guide children's attention to the sounds within spoken words and to the relationship between print and speech can facilitate learning to read. (p. 584)

Roush has found that dramatizing nursery rhymes such as "Hickory, Dickory Dock" and "Little Boy Blue" are especially effective. To develop the dramatization, she examines each line to determine which words can be dramatized, use pictures to help students understand the words or the concepts, explores students' prior knowledge about the content of the rhyme, reads the rhyme to the students as she points to the words, adds dramatization by modeling how to use her voice and actions to depict the rhyme, and finally asks the students to participate in the dramatizations. After completing the dramatizations, she reviews the rhyming words.

Struggling Readers and Writers

How phonics should be taught to struggling readers is often debated. Should decoding skills be taught through repeated isolated drills, or is there an alternative way to

A teacher uses a webbing approach to illustrate the different words that can be made using rhyming elements.

teach phonics? Melinda Smith and Colleagues (2004) believe "Second-grade struggling readers need more than a specific program designed to directly teach phonics. They need instruction that focuses on their constructing meaning while learning word-identification strategies" (p. 302).

These educators designed and implemented a phonics and comprehension program that begins with a whole story, moves to individual words and the sounds and patterns found within the words, and focuses on context and meaning. The lessons surround individual predictable books and are taught in the following three-day instructional sequence:

1. The teacher reads orally and the class discusses a book that has rhyming and predictable elements such as a book by Jane Yolen or Dr. Seuss. This first reading is followed by a second and third reading during which the students join in the reading. This shared reading encourages students to understand the story while learning the words in context.

2. Following the shared readings, the students identify the rhyming words, which are printed on a chart. The teacher draws attention to common spelling patterns and focuses on the sounds in the words.

3. The students are taught to focus on word families within the rhyming and predictable books. For each book, the teacher targets word families that will be taught within the context of the story. The students write the target words on individual note cards. The note cards are organized by vowel sounds and word families and placed in individual word banks.

4. After students write the words on cards, they take part in another shared reading. Now, the students hold up the card from their word banks when the word is read in the story.

5. The students create new sentences in which they use the rhyming book pattern. The teacher first models the rewriting during a whole group activity where students provide the rhyming words. Next, the students write and illustrate their own sentences.

6. Following the completion of these sentences, the students share their own interpretations. This writing is placed in the classroom library for all to read.

Gifted and Accelerated Readers and Writers

Janet W. Bloodgood and Linda C. Pacifici (2004) recommend an extension activity that follows the "Roots and Branches" web shown in Figure 4.4. This extension activity is especially beneficial for gifted and accelerated students. After students develop webs of Latin and Greek root words, they can explore Greek mythology by finding words derived from the names of Greek and Roman gods and goddesses such as *hydrant* and *hydroponics* from *Hydra*. Students can also use science sources and search for words with Greek roots and develop Greek derivation notebooks. For example, they can search for scientific vocabulary that includes some of the following Greek roots:

derm meaning *skin* as found in *epidermis* and *dermatology;*
hydr meaning water as found in *hydrant, hydrology,* and *hydroplane;*
meter meaning *measure* as found in *metric, barometer, diameter* and *perimeter;*
phil meaning *love* as in *philanthropy, philosophy,* and *Philadelphia* (brotherly love);
therm meaning *heat* as in *thermometer, thermostat,* and *thermal.*

Summary

This chapter focuses on the importance of phonemic awareness and phonics for reading instruction. Children's phonemic awareness includes auditory perception, auditory awareness, and auditory discrimination. Auditory discrimination includes discrimination of beginning, ending and middle sounds. This chapter presents many strategies for building foundations for reading through phonemic awareness, such as alphabet books.

Teachers need to understand the connections between phonics instruction and spelling instruction, including invented spelling and phonemic awareness, and the developmental stages in invented spelling. Students' papers can be used to assess phonics skills and spelling errors.

Selecting words for spelling instruction is an important current issue related to phonics. Three approaches are used, including the selection of words because of consistent spelling patterns, the selection of words for the *frequency-of-use approach,* and the selection of words that relate spellings to meaning.

Reflect on Your Reading

Many struggling readers have considerable difficulty mastering letter-sound relationships. How do the differentiated instruction suggestions provide reinforcement for phonics skills? Why might they be more motivating than worksheets that often test phonics generalizations through the memorization of rules or teaching phonics through using words in isolation?

A balanced approach to the teaching of phonics is considered preferable by many reading experts. This approach uses the best of both phonics instruction and using literature in the classroom.

Key Terms

phonemic awareness, p. 139

phonemes, p. 140

auditory awareness, p. 141

auditory discrimination, p. 141

auditory blending, p. 141

auditory sequential memory, p. 141

blends, p. 146

phonics, p. 149

invented spelling, p. 161

prefix, p. 163

suffix, p. 165

For video clips of authentic classroom instruction on **Phonics**, go to Allyn & Bacon's MyLabSchool.com. In MLS courses, click on Reading Methods, go to MLS Video Lab, and select **Module 2**.

Extend Your Reading

1. Analyze the suggestions for teaching phonics in several published basal reading series. What approach does the series recommend for the teaching of phonics?

2. Analyze the suggestions for teaching phonics in several supplementary phonics materials such as those found in basal reading programs for teaching phonics. What approach is recommended in the supplementary materials?

3. Schools frequently use published phonics games as part of their program. What are the characteristics of these games? If possible, use these games with students in the grade for which the games are published. What is the reaction of the students to these games? What phonics skills are taught through the use of games?

4. Read the reviews of several alphabet books in publisher's catalogues. Often, these can be supplied by your local booksellers or they can be requested from publishers. Then read and analyze the books. Do you agree with the reviews?

5. After reviewing published phonics games, create your own game to help students reinforce a phonics concept. If possible, try the game with a group of students. Elementary students may choose to create their own games.

6. Interview a kindergarten teacher and a lower elementary teacher. What techniques do they use in the classroom to teach phonemic awareness? Observe a kindergarten and a lower elementary classroom. What evidence do you see related to how the teacher is developing phonemic awareness?

7. Using Henderson and Templeton's (1986) suggestions for instruction that were presented in this chapter, consider how you would provide phonics and spelling instruction for students who are at a specific developmental stage. For example, Henderson and Templeton recommend that children at Stage II examine groups of words that are organized around common features such as word patterns. At Stage III, instruction would review vowel patterns, introduce digraphs and common inflections, such as *-ed, -ing, -ly*. At Stage IV, there would be a continued study of common and uncommon vowel patterns, syllables, and the study of meanings in prefixes and suffixes. At Stage V, there would be an emphasis on silent and sounded consonant patterns and an examination of the influence of Greek and Latin to English spelling and meaning.

For Further Reading

1. Adel G. Aiken, and Lisa Bayer, (2002), "They Love Words," in *The Reading Teacher,* 56, 68–74.

2. Kathleen F. Clark, (2004), "What Can I Say Besides 'Sound It Out'? Coaching Word Recognition in Beginning Reading," in *The Reading Teacher,* 57, 440–449.

3. Karin L. Dahl, et al. (2004), "Connecting Developmental Word Study with Classroom Writing: Children's Descriptions of Spelling Strategies," in *The Reading Teacher,* 57, 310–319.

4. Lori A. Helman, (2004), "Building on the Sound System of Spanish: Insights from the Alphabetic Spellings of English-Language Learners," in *The Reading Teacher,* 57, 452–460.

5. S. A. Stahl, (2002), "Saying the "p" word: Nine Guidelines for Exemplary Phonics Instruction," in International Reading Association's: *Evidence-Based Reading Instruction: Putting the National Reading Panel Report into Practice,* pp. 61–68. Newark, DE: International Reading Association.

6. Examples of Web sites for authors of children's literature cited in this chapter:

   Tomie dePaola: www.tomie.com

   Bob Staake: www.bobstaake.com

   Audrey Wood: www.audreywood.com

   Jane Yolen: www.janeyolen.com

REFERENCES

Adams, M. J. (1990). *Beginning to Read: Thinking and Learning about Print.* Urbana-Champaign: University of Illinois Center for the Study of Reading.

Bear, Donald, Invernizzi, Marcia, Templeton, Shane, & Johnston, Francine, eds. (2000). *Words Their Way: Word Study for Phonics, Vocabulary, and Spelling Instruction,* 2nd ed. Upper Saddle River, NJ: Merrill/Prentice Hall.

Bear, Donald, & Templeton, Shane. (1998). "Explorations in Developmental Spelling: Foundations for Learning and Teaching Phonics, Spelling, and Vocabulary." *The Reading Teacher,* 52, 222–243.

Bloodgood, Janet W., & Pacifici, Linda C. (November 2004). "Bringing Word Study to Intermediate Classrooms." *The Reading Teacher,* 58, 250–263.

Bruneau, B. J. (1997). "The Literacy Pyramid Organization of Reading/Writing Activities in a Whole Language Classroom." *The Reading Teacher,* 51, 158–160.

Chall, Jean. (1967). *Learning to Read: The Great Debate.* New York: McGraw-Hill.

Chall, Jean. (1996). *Stages of Reading Development,* 2nd ed. Ft. Worth, TX: Harcourt Brace.

Chomsky, Carol. (1970). "Reading, Writing, and Phonology." *Harvard Educational Review,* 40: 287–309.

Cunningham, Patricia M., & Allington, Richard L. (2003). *Classrooms That Work: They Can Read and Write.* Boston: Allyn & Bacon.

Fry, Edward. (1980). "The New Instant Word List." *The Reading Teacher,* 34, 284–290.

Goswami, U. (1999). "The Relationship between Phonological Awareness and Orthographic Representation in Different Orthographies." In M. Harris & G. Hatano (Eds.), *Learning to Read and Write: A Cross-Linguistic Perspective.* Cambridge, UK: Cambridge University Press.

Gunning, Thomas G. (2003). *Creating Literacy Instruction for All Children,* 4th ed. Boston: Allyn & Bacon.

Harris, Albert, & Sipay, Edward. (1990). *How to Increase Reading Ability,* 9th ed. New York: Longman.

Henderson, Edmund. (1985). *Teaching Spelling.* New York: Houghton Mifflin.

Henderson, Edmund, & Templeton, Shane. (1986). "A Developmental Perspective of Formal Spelling through Alphabet, Pattern, and Meaning." *Elementary School Journal,* 86, 305–16.

Horn, Ernest. (1919). "Principles of Methods in Teaching Spelling as Derived from Scientific Investigation." In *18th Yearbook of the National Society for the Study of Education,* Part II. Bloomington, Ill: Public School Publishing Co., pp. 52–77.

Horn, Ernest. (1954). "Phonics and Spelling." *Journal of Education,* 136, 233–35.

Horn, Ernest. (1957). "Phonetics and Spelling." *Elementary School Journal,* 57, 424–32.

Horn, Ernest. *Teaching Spelling* (1963). American Educational Research Association, Department of Classroom Teachers Research Pamphlet. Washington, D.C.: National Education Association.

Hughes, Margaret, & Searle, Dennis. (2000). "Spelling and 'the Second R.' " *Language Arts,* 77, 203–208.

Johnston, Francine R. (1999). "The Timing and Teaching of Word Families." *The Reading Teacher,* 53, 64–75.

Leslie, Lawren, & Allen, Linda. (1999). "Factors That Predict Success in an Early Literacy Intervention Project." *Reading Research Quarterly,* 34, 404–24.

Morrow, L. M., & Tracey, D. H. (1997). "Strategies Used for Phonics Instruction in Early Childhood Classrooms." *The Reading Teacher,* 50, 644–651.

Moss, B., & Noden, H. (1994). "Pointers for Putting Whole Language Into Practice." *The Reading Teacher,* 47, 342–344.

National Reading Panel. (2000). *Report of the National Reading Panel.* Washington, D.C., National Institute of Child Health and Human Development.

Norton, Donna E. (2004). *The Effective Teaching of Language Arts,* 6th ed. Upper Saddle River, NJ: Merrill/Prentice Hall.

Roush, Betty E. (March 2005). "Drama Rhymes: An Instructional Strategy." *The Reading Teacher,* 58, 584–587.

Smith, Melinda, Walker, Barbara J., & Yellin, David. (November 2004). "From Phonological Awareness to Fluency in Each Lesson." *The Reading Teacher,* 58, 302–307.

"Spelling-Bee Protesters 'Thru with Through.' " (3, June 2004). *Seattle Times News Service.*

Spiegel, Dixie Lee. (1998). "Silver Bullets, Babies, and Bath Water: Literature Response Groups in a Balanced Literacy Program." *The Reading Teacher,* 52, 114–124.

Children's Literature References

Andrews-Goebel, Nancy. (2002). *The Pot That Juan Built.* Illustrated by David Diaz. Lee & Low.

Bryan, Ashley. (1997). *Ashley Bryan's ABC of African American Poetry.* Simon & Schuster.

Carryl, Charles E. (April 1892). "The Camel's Complaint." *St. Nicholas.*

Chandra, Deborah. (1999). *A Is for Amos.* Illustrated by Keiko Narahashi. Farrar Straus Giroux.

Chin-Lee, Cynthia. (1997). *A Is for Asia.* Illustrated by Yumi Heo. Orchard.

Crossley-Holland, Kevin, ed. (2004). *Once Upon a Poem: Favorite Poems That Tell Stories.* Chicken House.

DePaola, Tomie. (2004). *Baa Baa Black Sheep and Other Rhymes,* Board Book. G. P. Putnam's Sons.

Ehlert, Lois. (1989). *Eating the Alphabet: Fruits and Vegetables from A to Z.* Harcourt Brace Jovanovich.

Feelings, Muriel. (1974). *Jumbo Means Hello: Swahili Alphabet Book.* Dial Press.

Hoberman, Mary Ann. (2001). *There Once Was a Man Named Michael Finnegan.* Illustrated by Nadine Bernard Westcott. Little, Brown.

Johnson, D. B. (2000). *Henry Hikes to Fitchburg.* Houghton Mifflin.

Johnson, Stephen T. (1995). *Alphabet City.* Viking.

Johnson, Stephen T. (2005). *The Quangle Wangle's Hat.* Illustrated by Louise Voce. Candlewick.

Lobel, Arnold. (1981). *On Market Street.* Illustrated by Anita Lobel. Greenwillow.

MacDonald, Suse. (1986). *Alphabetics.* Bradbury.

McLeod, Bob. (2006). *Super Hero ABC.* HarperCollins.

Musgrove, Margaret. (1976). *Ashanti to Zulu: African Traditions.* Illustrated by Leo and Diane Dillon. Dial.

Pelletier, David. (1996). *The Graphic Alphabet.* Orchard.

Prelutsky, Jack. (1986). *Read-Aloud Rhymes for the Very Young.* Illustrated by Marc Brown. Knopf.

Rockwell, Anne. (1985). *First Comes Spring.* Crowell.

Silverstein, Shel. (2005) *Runny Babbit.* HarperCollins.

Sing a Song of Popcorn: Every Child's Book of Poems. (1988) Selected by Beatrice Schenk de Regnier and others. Scholastic.

Staake, Bob. (2004). *Hello, Robots.* Viking.

Sturges, Philemon, (2004). *She'll Be Comin' 'Round the Mountain.* Little, Brown.

Whippo, Walt. (2000). *Little White Duck.* Little, Brown.

Wood, Audrey. (2003). *Alphabet Adventure.* Illustrated by Bruce Wood. Blue Sky.

Wood, Audrey. (2003). *Alphabet Mystery.* Illustrated by Bruce Wood. Blue Sky.

Yolen, Jane. (2000). *Off We Go.* Illustrated by Laurel Molk. Little, Brown.

Yolen, Jane. (2005). *This Little Piggy: Lap Songs, Finger Plays, Clapping Games, and Pantomime Rhymes.* Illustrated by Will Hillenbrand. Candlewick.

CHAPTER **5**

Vocabulary Development

CHAPTER **OUTLINE**

Guidelines for Vocabulary Development

Vocabulary Development in the Pre-K through Fourth Grades
Instructional Strategies and Activities That Relate Vocabulary to Personal Experience
Developing Word Walls
Expanding Vocabulary Knowledge by Oral Reading
Identifying Vocabulary Words for Comprehension
Using Webbing for Vocabulary Development
Developing Individualized Dictionaries and Vocabulary Notebooks

Vocabulary Development in the Fourth through Eighth Grades
Webbing and Plot Structures for Vocabulary Development (Grades 4–8)
Vocabulary in the Content Areas
Using Precise Vocabulary to Enhance Cognitive Development
Vocabulary Development for Underachieving Urban Students

Teaching Contextual Analysis
Definition and Illustration
Comparison
Author Summary
Familiar Expressions
Experience
Synonym
Building Student Responsibility for Vocabulary Development

Vocabulary Development in the Content Areas
Semantic Feature Analysis

After reading this chapter you will be able to answer the following questions:

1. Why is a strong vocabulary important for reading?
2. What are the general guidelines for vocabulary development?
3. What are effective strategies for vocabulary development in the pre-K through fourth grades?
4. What are effective strategies for vocabulary development in the fourth through eighth grades?
5. How is vocabulary developed in the content fields?
6. How is vocabulary improved through context clues?

Read All About It!

"RUOK? A Tutorial for Parents on Keeping in Touch"

by David Pogue, *New York Times,* August 19, 2004

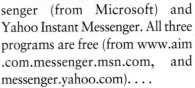

Dear Mom and Dad. . . . I may keep in touch with occasional cellphone calls and e-mail messages like this one. But hey, it's not 1998 anymore. Mostly, people my age would rather IM, Skype or text each other. . . . You probably don't have any idea what these things are so here's a little guide, a cheat sheet for communication in the modern era.

First of all, let's talk about instant-messaging software, or IM. The big three are AOL Instant Messenger (AIM), MSN Messenger (from Microsoft) and Yahoo Instant Messenger. All three programs are free (from www.aim .com.messenger.msn.com, and messenger.yahoo.com). . . .

If I'm not at my computer when you need to reach me, you can always text me. Yes, "text" is a verb these days: "He texts, she texts, whatever the pretext."

Texting is shooting out very short typed messages from cellphone to cellphone. It's really great in movies, in class, in restaurants, at loud concerts and anywhere else you can't really talk on a phone. It's probably like passing notes was in your day, except that now you can pass them to anyone on the planet and you're much less likely to get caught. . . .

We use shorthand constantly. BCNU means "Be seeing you," PCM means "please call me," L8R is "later," 2MORO is "tomorrow," WAN2 is "want to," and so on. Most of it you can figure out just by saying the letters and numbers out loud, like these: NE1, RUOK, B4, OIC.

People use these codes in IM chats and even e-mail, too, just to save time. . . . If you guys want to catch up on what's new with me, Skype, (another free chat program) is a perfect way to do it without worrying about the phone bill. The downside, of course, is that you and I both have to be at our PC's to make the call. . . .

So that's your lesson in how to keep in touch. If you have any questions, IM or text me. Ms U, lov U, alwzthinkNof U. Cu L8R!

Read All About It!
Critical Thinking Questions

- Identify the vocabulary that is related to technology. How is vocabulary changing due to technology?

- How does this vocabulary change the way people of all ages may communicate?

- How might this vocabulary influence teaching?

- What would your reaction be if this were a note you received from a student?

- Consider how you might create your own languages for communication with other teachers, your family members, or your students.

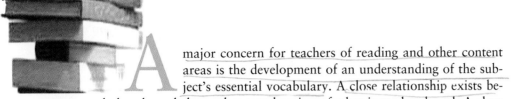

A major concern for teachers of reading and other content areas is the development of an understanding of the subject's essential vocabulary. A close relationship exists between vocabulary knowledge and comprehension of what is read or heard. A close relationship also exists between an extensive, useful vocabulary and writing. Mastering these relationships requires considerable instruction by the teacher and extensive use of vocabulary by the students.

Although there is a close relationship between vocabulary knowledge and success in reading, listening, speaking, and writing, there are also differences in the vocabulary requirements to succeed in each of these areas of literacy. Textbooks and articles on vocabulary development frequently differentiate between vocabularies used for speaking and writing and vocabularies required for reading and listening. The vocabulary needed for speaking and writing is called an **expressive vocabulary**. The vocabulary and meanings of the words used in speaking and writing are usually well established in the children's memories so that the words and their accompanying meanings are used with confidence. These words are rarely unknown to the students. In contrast, the vocabulary used in reading and listening is called a **receptive vocabulary**. To gain understandings of the meanings of unknown words when reading or listening, students may use the context of the surrounding words to discover the meaning of the unknown words. Consequently, to increase the receptive vocabulary, students need instruction in strategies that help them develop, extend, and apply their vocabularies.

How should vocabulary be taught? Should vocabulary words be taught in isolation, or should they be taught in meaningful context? How much of the vocabulary should be taught through direct instruction, and how much will be gained through incidental learning as students read a variety of materials? How important are context clues as students strive to understand the meanings of the vocabulary terms especially in the content areas? These are just a few of the questions this chapter addresses as it approaches vocabulary acquisition and understanding.

Research studies support the value of rich vocabulary as it provides a foundation for reading and relates to children's reading success. For example, the National Institute of Child Health and Human Development Early Child Care Research Network (2005) reports that vocabulary knowledge is an important component of oral language and oral language correlates with reading success. In a ten-year study that followed students from first grade to eleventh grade, Anne E. Cunningham and Keith E. Stanovich (2003) searched for early reading variables that predict reading achievement in eleventh grade. They found that a fast start in reading in first grade as measured by decoding, word recognition, and comprehension related to reading success in high school students. They identified several educational practices related to reading success and vocabulary growth. They found, for example, that extensive exposure to print is essential for vocabulary growth; that students need a combination of classroom-based vocabulary instruction and exposure to print during out-of-school reading; that verbal skills and reading efficiency are fostered by extensive amounts of reading; and that even children with limited reading and comprehension skills build vocabularies through immersion in literacy activities.

This vocabulary development is enhanced through reading books and other materials that expose children to the meanings of unknown words. Cunningham and

Stanovich report that children's books have 50 percent more "rare" or sophisticated words than found in adult prime-time television. It is these more varied words that help expand children's vocabularies by building their knowledge of word meanings. These educators also emphasize the importance of independent out-of-school reading as a way to increase vocabulary acquisition. The impact of this independent reading is shown when differences in the amount of reading are compared between children at the ninetieth percentile in reading and children at the tenth percentile. The average child at the ninetieth percentile in reading read 2.5 million words per year outside of school, while the average child at the tenth percentile read 51,000 words per year outside of school. The researchers conclude, "These are the differences that combined with the richness of print, act to create large vocabulary differences among children" (p. 669). They maintain, "the push to immerse children in literature and to increase their amount of free reading is an educational practice that is supported by evidence" (p. 672).

In addition to immersing children in literature and emphasizing free reading, Molly Fuller Collins (2005) found that vocabulary development and reading comprehension increase when teachers read picture books orally and explain the new or unusual vocabulary as they read the books. This explanation includes pointing to illustrations that help clarify vocabulary meanings, providing definitions of the words, using synonyms when possible, and using the word in a sentence that is different from that used by the author of the book. This chapter suggests how teachers can explain the vocabulary while sharing the book with students. Chapter 10 provides a lesson plan for focusing on the vocabulary with books designed for teaching ESL students.

As you proceed through this chapter, you will find teaching strategies that both increase students' understanding of vocabulary and activities that enhance their vocabulary application and expansion through reading. Children cannot gain positive lifelong reading habits without these important learning experiences.

Guidelines for Vocabulary Development

As explained in Chapter 2 in the discussion of language acquisition, preschool children experience a rapid growth in their use of and understanding for words. This growth is even faster if young children have numerous pleasant experiences with language, especially during storytelling and story reading. These experiences provide background knowledge for vocabulary development and show the meanings of the words in different contexts.

Several important principles for vocabulary instruction are meaningful for any grade level and are supported by reading research (Ruddell, 2002). For example, teachers should use a variety of approaches for teaching vocabulary, including direct instruction about word meanings, use of context clues to determine meanings, and reading a wide range of children's literature and content materials. Vocabulary instruction should encourage children's active learning as they are taught to reason out the meanings of words. New words should be related to similar words that are already known.

Ruddell emphasizes that vocabulary to be taught should be selected because it is important to the story or to the content material. This vocabulary can be taught before, during, or after reading. The choice for when to provide instruction depends on the objectives of the instruction.

Another set of research-based general guidelines that are useful at all grade levels includes three objectives for vocabulary instruction and some of the activities that may be used to meet those objectives.

First Objective: Teach students to learn words independently.

1. Read stories, books, plays, songs, poetry, fiction, and nonfiction to the class. Expose students orally to vocabulary.

2. Promote a wide variety of independent reading at home and at school. Make independent reading a regular and significant part of the curriculum.

3. Have students express themselves in writing and in speech daily.

4. Teach students to use vocabulary learning strategies that can be transferred and generalized such as contextual analysis.

5. Teach students to use dictionaries and the thesaurus.

6. Provide activities that allow students to explore the richness of word meanings and opportunities to make choices about which vocabulary words they will learn.

Second Objective: Teach students the meanings of specific words.

1. Teach synonyms or definitions of specific words.

2. Provide definition strategies or knowledge of unknown words prior to reading or listening.

3. Pre-teach critical vocabulary necessary for comprehension in reading materials and in the content areas.

Third Objective: Help students develop an appreciation for words and to experience enjoyment and satisfaction in their use.

1. Set a positive model for learning words.

2. Have fun with words by playing word games and linking content topics that are shared for entertainment and enjoyment.

3. Promote the use of vocabulary learned in school to nonschool contexts. (Baumann et al., 2003)

> **Reflect on Your Reading**
>
> Consider some of the vocabulary strategies you were taught in lower elementary and upper elementary grades. Which of these vocabulary activities were most beneficial to you? Which of these strategies helped you develop your own vocabulary?

Vocabulary Development in the Pre-K through Fourth Grades

Many of the activities and strategies for language and cognitive development and for emergent literacy are prerequisites for vocabulary development. For example, teachers who provide many opportunities for children to listen to and discuss concepts and related vocabularies in stories are encouraging students to expand their vocabularies through incidental learning. Teachers who introduce new vocabulary before children read or listen to a selection are providing direct instruction. Research supports both incidental learning through reading varied materials and direct instruction provided by the teacher. Both types of vocabulary instruction build readers' schemata, or background knowledge, for the concepts related to the words. This background knowledge is also essential for comprehension.

Instructional Strategies and Activities That Relate Vocabulary to Personal Experience

Teachers have many opportunities to help children relate vocabularies to personal experiences or to introduce or expand vocabularies that are part of the children's future experiences. First-hand experiences are especially meaningful for vocabulary development; demonstrations provide many opportunities. A first- or second-grade teacher might demonstrate the steps required and the materials necessary for an art project such as making a paper-bag puppet. This demonstration includes a list of materials and equipment such as scissors, paper bags, crayons, glue, yarn, and buttons. This list is printed on tagboard that shows examples of the materials required, such as an actual scissors, paper bags, buttons, colored paper, crayons, a glue stick, and yarn. Concrete examples of each of the materials are shown and discussed along with the printed vocabulary words. As the materials are shown and discussed, the teacher explains how each of the materials will be used when making a paper-bag puppet. Next, the teacher demonstrates how the puppet will be constructed. For example, a clown paper-bag puppet begins with a bag, and then features of the clown's face can be cut out of colored paper and glued onto the bag. Hair can be added by using yarn. Other features such as a nose, a bow tie and buttons may be added to complete the puppet. The teacher explains each step of the process by showing concrete examples and modeling how to complete the project. Students then create their own puppets as they use the vocabulary learned as part of the demonstration. This type of activity has added benefits. After finishing their puppets, students expand their oral language vocabularies by telling stories using their puppets.

There are many other experiences that relate vocabulary to children's experiences—for example, going to school for the first time and becoming familiar with the names of classmates, activities, and classroom objects is an exciting motivator for young children. Vocabularies associated with the school environment and school activities such as field trips provide opportunities for concrete examples of vocabulary associated with school experiences.

Numerous books can also be used to motivate an interest in school-related vocabularies. For example, Beth Norling's *Little School* (2003) illustrates school-related vocabulary and provides a model for children to develop their own illustrated books related to school vocabulary. The highly illustrated book follows a group of children as they prepare to go to school. The first double page identifies children by name and shows how they get ready for school. The next page labels different ways children travel to school. When the children enter the classroom an illustrated dictionary identifies some of the objects in the classroom such as *chairs, easel,* and *bookshelf.* The remainder of the book illustrates and labels art activities, games, playtime objects, outdoor play objects, and going-home activities.

This book can be used by kindergarten teachers as a model for students to create their own labeled depictions of school-related vocabularies. The students can also compare their own school activities with the ones illustrated in *Little School*. The book covers enough vocabulary and illustrations to require several days of involvement. Parents may also use the book to help their children prepare for that first day of school. The illustrations suggest that going to school is fun.

The activities for enhancing oral language development and cognitive development described in Chapter 2, "Emergent Literacy," are also excellent for vocabulary development. The labeling activities developed in Chapter 9, "The Reading and Writing Connection," provide extensive vocabulary development.

Developing Word Walls

Word walls in the classroom may be used to show various types of vocabulary relationships and connections. They are especially good for developing concepts related to categorization. These word walls, created on bulletin boards, are frequently associated with the vocabulary found in a unit of study. The word wall allows students and teachers to select meaningful words from the study, define the words, add words or phrases that connect to the concepts, and review the words and concepts. The words on the word wall become interactive as students arrange the words to form groups and add new words as they study the unit (Bear et al., 2000). The complexity of the word walls changes as the reading levels of the students advance.

Words for the word wall may be selected from key terms to be studied in a unit, words identified in a textbook, or familiar topics such as animals, communities, and transportation. For example, a word wall for first grade might begin with the study of familiar terms such as fruits. Students can add vocabulary cards showing an illustration of and written form of fruits such as *apple, orange, plum,* and *peach*. They can discuss each of the fruits and try to identify a category for the fruits. They can search for pictures showing the fruits before they are picked and sent to a grocery

A word wall may be developed around words that have common beginning sounds.

store. After this search they might decide on a category such as "Fruits That Grow on Trees." They can add illustrated word cards for additional fruits such as blueberries, strawberries, and blackberries. Now they can discuss these fruits, search for pictures showing how the fruits are grown, and consider if the fruits belong to the same category as apples and plums. They may identify a new category for the fruits such as "Fruits That Grow on Shrubs." The word wall for fruits can be expanded and rearranged to show uses for each fruit: an *apple* may become *applesauce, cider,* and *pie. Apple* on the word wall might expand to show different varieties of apples such as *Delicious, Macintosh,* and *Honey Crisp.* The varieties of apples might include the geographical locations where they are raised.

As seen from this example of fruit, the word wall may include many different topics. Other topics that are popular with lower elementary students include animals: farm animals, pets, jungle animals; transportation: cars, buses, planes, trains; sports: football, baseball, tennis, ice skating, volleyball. Any of the units studied in social studies or science provides vocabulary for the development of word walls. Word walls may be related to different types of artistic media used to illustrate books and the artists who use the media. When developing the word wall for artistic media, a table may be placed below the word wall that includes illustrated books that represent the media. Now this becomes a motivational activity as students read the books and look at the illustrations to discover more information about the media. For older students, the art and illustration books might include informational books about the media.

Expanding Vocabulary Knowledge by Oral Reading

As introduced earlier under the importance of vocabulary acquisition, Molly Fuller Collins (2005) reported significant gains in reading for students when teachers read picture books orally and explained the new or unusual vocabulary as they read the books. There are numerous highly illustrated books that teachers can read orally and follow Collins's recommendations. When reading the 2005 Caldecott Award winner, Kevin Henkes's *Kitten's First Full Moon* (2004), teachers can point to the illustrations to clarify vocabulary, provide definitions for the words, use synonyms when possible, and use the focus words in different sentences. The second page of text uses action words, for example, as kitten "closed her eyes and stretched her neck and opened her mouth and licked." The illustration shows a kitten with closed eyes, a stretched neck, and a mouth with her licking tongue protruding. As teachers point to the meanings of the words in the illustration they can define the words and provide synonyms. For example, when pointing to the kitten's stretched neck, teachers can show how the kitten's neck is reaching up toward the moon and that *stretched* means a body action in which you lengthen a part of your body to try to reach something. This discussion might continue to suggest that kitten is stretching to reach something that she wants just as "We stretch our arms to get a book on the higher shelves." *Kitten's First Full Moon* includes numerous action words that are shown in the illustrations, including *wiggled, sprang, tumbled, chased, climbed, raced,* and *leaped.* Words from *Kitten's First Full Moon* can be developed into a word wall that includes definitions, synonyms, and additional sentences using the words.

Many illustrated books lend themselves to this type of oral reading and vocabulary development, including Jennifer Belle's *Animal Stackers* (2005) Uri Shulevitz's *Snow* (1998), and the 2006 Caldecott Award winner, Norton Juster's *The Hello, Goodbye Window* (2005). Belle's book illustrates many unusual vocabulary words such as *extremely, empties, nervously, exit, growling,* and *ravenous.* Shulevitz's book illustrates vocabulary such as *umbrella, circling, swirling, twirling* and *floating.* Juster's book uses vocabulary such as *harmonica, reflections, specialty,* and *extinct.* Nonfiction books such as Catherine Brighton's *The Fossil Girl: Mary Anning's Dinosaur Discovery* (1999) include vocabularies associated with science. Brighton's book introduces a scientist who searches for new *curiosities* and *creatures,* and discovers *fossilized, fossil* and *Ichthyosaur.* This is another book that would make an interesting word wall in which the vocabulary increases to include a study of either fossils or dinosaurs.

Identifying Vocabulary Words for Comprehension

Relating important vocabulary words to plot diagrams is one way to identify vocabulary that may need to be taught before reading a text or highlighted as the text is read. (See diagramming story structures in Chapter 7). Before teaching a lesson, the teacher places the words on a plot diagram. If the words are important as part of the plot diagram, then they are important for comprehending the story. In preparing to read Jan Brett's *Goldilocks and the Three Bears* (1987) to students in the first or second grades, for example, the teacher could develop the plot diagram shown in Figure 5.1 and include the important words from the story.

FIGURE 5.1

Plot Diagram Identifying Vocabulary in *Goldilocks and The Three Bears*

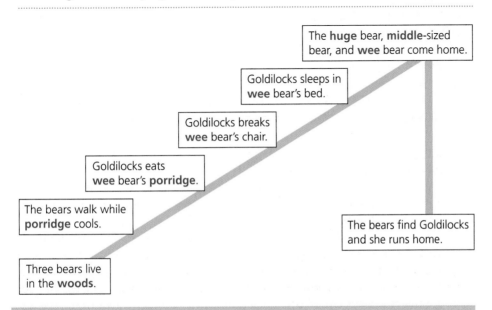

The **huge** bear, **middle**-sized bear, and **wee** bear come home.

Goldilocks sleeps in **wee** bear's bed.

Goldilocks breaks **wee** bear's chair.

Goldilocks eats **wee** bear's **porridge**.

The bears walk while **porridge** cools.

The bears find Goldilocks and she runs home.

Three bears live in the **woods**.

FIGURE 5.2

Plot Diagram Identifying Vocabulary in *Where the Wild Things Are*

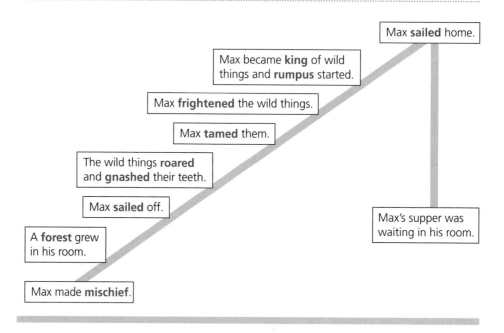

The plot diagram may also be used with students as they draw the plot structure for a story and identify and underline the vocabulary words that are important for the plot of the story. Students can be taught to develop this strategy on their own.

The second example of identifying vocabulary words through a plot diagram, as shown on Figure 5.2, was developed and taught to third-grade students by Jennifer Ferguson (2003). This example uses Maurice Sendak's *Where the Wild Things Are* (1963). (Jennifer previously taught the students how to plot story structures on a plot diagram as described in Chapter 7 in this text.)

This approach may be used at any grade level. In the section on vocabulary development with students in the upper grades, we will discuss how the approach may be used with Tomie De Paola's *The Legend of the Bluebonnet* (1983) and Selina Hasting's *Sir Gawain and the Loathly Lady* (1985). (See Figures 5.5, 5.6, and 5.7.)

Using Webbing for Vocabulary Development

Webbing, also known as semantic mapping, is an excellent way to visually show relationships between ideas and concepts. It is also a technique for expanding students' understandings of the multiple meanings of words. Webbing can be used to show the vocabulary in a single book, or it can suggest related words. A web can be drawn as a prereading vocabulary activity, or it can be a follow-up approach. Students can identify prior knowledge of vocabulary words on the web before they read a text and then add to or change the vocabulary words on the web after they have read a book. The vocabulary identified on the plot diagram may be a source for words on the web.

FIGURE 5.3

visualize connections

Vocabulary Web to Accompany *Goldilocks and the Three Bears*

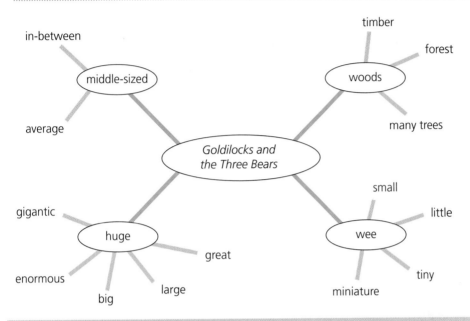

Semantic web

To create a web, place the title of the book in the center of the chalkboard, page, or transparency and have the students identify the meanings of the words as shown in Figure 5.3. A vocabulary web was developed using the words on the plot diagram for *Goldilocks and the Three Bears*. The web was completed with first- and second-grade students, who focused on the words *wee, middle-sized, woods,* and *porridge.* After placing the words on the web, the students discussed the important instances in the story, as shown in Figure 5.1. The students then discussed the relationship between the words on the web and the plot diagram. This is another approach for vocabulary development that can be used at any grade level. As in the vocabulary related to the plot diagram, students can do this as an independent activity and as a group or class activity. The words should be discussed as they are being placed on the web.

Figure 5.4 shows how a third-grade teacher extended the meanings of the words identified on the plot structure for *Where the Wild Things Are.* Notice how students expanded the vocabulary words *mischief, forest, roared, gnashed, tamed, frightened, king,* and *rumpus.* Also, notice that many of the words identified by the students are at a higher reading level than are the original words in the text.

Developing Individualized Dictionaries and Vocabulary Notebooks

Individualized dictionaries that are modeled after published dictionaries and **vocabulary notebooks** that include words and associations that are interesting to stu-

FIGURE **5.4**

Vocabulary Web to Accompany *Where the Wild Things Are*

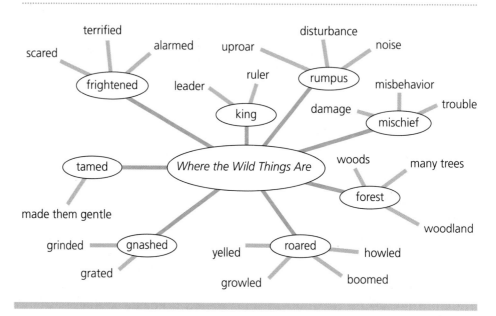

dents can accompany teacher-directed instruction, content-reading activities, extended reading activities such as those found during the study of units, or recreational reading activities. Students can choose their own approaches for highlighting interesting words to add to their vocabularies. Features that can be part of dictionaries include:

- illustrations
- personal responses to words
- synonyms
- antonyms
- phrases
- sentences that show interesting or unusual ways to use the words

The dictionaries are very useful when students are creating their own writing activities. This approach is useful for students in all grade levels.

Students in the lower elementary grades gain considerable vocabulary knowledge from picture books; consequently, they enjoy adding illustrations to their own dictionaries. Even children in pre-kindergarten and kindergarten can create vocabulary dictionaries associated with colors and shapes. Texts such as Eric Carle's *My Very First Book of Colors* (1974) and *My Very First Book of Shapes* (1974) and Tana Hoban's *Shapes, Shapes, Shapes* (1986) and *So Many Circles, So Many Squares* (1998) can be used to motivate students to create their own color and shape dictionaries. One kindergarten teacher extended this activity to include children's own experiences by asking them to draw pictures in their dictionaries that showed something that they liked about that color. For example, one student drew a red ball, while another drew a blue wagon. The teacher helped the students label their pictures to include lines such as "I play with my *red* ball." and "I ride in my *blue* wagon."

Individualized vocabulary dictionaries are easily applied to activities such as illustrating and labeling opposites. Tana Hoban's *Push-Pull, Empty-Full: A Book of Opposites* (1972) and Steve Jenkins's *Big and Little* (1996) provide models for illustrations showing opposites.

Vocabulary notebooks for students who are expanding their reading and writing abilities may include interesting new words and phrases that the students select for themselves. For example, a group of fourth-grade students developed vocabulary notebooks in which they found vivid first lines or introductory paragraphs that enticed them. They quoted these lines in their notebooks and then wrote responses that described why they liked the wording. They also searched for descriptive verbs in literature and tried to use these descriptive verbs in their own writing. This activity helped students appreciate linguistic style developed by the authors. Another group of fourth-grade students investigated the techniques authors use to develop humor in picture storybooks. They found examples of various types of humor and then wrote stories in which they modeled their writing after the humor in picture storybooks such as in Doreen Cronin's *Click, Clack, Moo: Cows That Type* (2000).

> **Reflect on Your Reading**
>
> Consider the different strategies for vocabulary development. Which of these vocabulary strategies would be most effective for students in kindergarten? Which ones do you think would be most effective to use with third- and fourth-grade students?

Vocabulary Development in the Fourth through Eighth Grades

As students progress into the upper elementary grades, both their vocabulary knowledge and vocabulary needs increase dramatically. The number of words known and the language development as reflected in the average number of words used in sentences increases for most children. While the average oral sentence length in six- to seven-year-olds is about 7.5 words, the average oral sentence length for ten- to twelve-year-olds is about 9.5 words. In addition, the older students use more sophisticated sentence structures. For example, older children "use complex sentences with subordinate clauses of concession introduced by 'nevertheless' and 'in spite of.' The auxiliary verbs 'might,' 'could,' and 'should' appear frequently. Some children have difficulties distinguishing among past, past perfect, and perfect tenses" (Norton, 2004, p. 42).

Webbing and Plot Structures for Vocabulary Development (Grades 4–8)

Webbing, a method for visually displaying relationships among ideas and concepts, is an excellent technique for expanding students' understandings of the multiple meanings of words. Webbing can accompany the vocabulary in a single book or can suggest related words in a unit or theme approach. A web can be drawn as a pre-reading vocabulary activity or it can be a follow-up approach. Students can identify prior knowledge on the web before they read and then add to and even change the web after they have read a book. Vocabulary words can be placed on a plot diagram to help them understand the relationships among vocabulary and action. (See Chapter 7 for plot diagramming of a story structure.) Diagramming the plot structure helps students relate comprehension and vocabulary.

If a web accompanies a single book such as Tomi DePaola's *The Legend of the Bluebonnet* (1983), the teacher can place the title of the book in the center of the web and the vocabulary words extend from the center. This example uses the vocabulary words *drought, famine, selfish, healing, plentiful, restored, valued,* and *sacrifice.* If the web is introduced as a prereading activity, students can identify definitions or synonyms as they read the text and explore the context clues. If the web is a follow-up activity, the students can identify definitions and synonyms after the story is read. Figure 5.5 is an example of a vocabulary web developed by fifth-grade students.

The vocabulary words emphasized on the web can be placed on a plot diagram. Students then identify the sequence of actions developed in the story by using as many of the vocabulary words as possible. This reinforces the importance of the vocabulary within the story. If the vocabulary words cannot be associated with the most important incidents in the story, the words might not be crucial to the story. The plot diagram for *The Legend of the Bluebonnet* (Figure 5.6) was developed with the same group of children as the web. To reinforce the vocabulary, the students wrote their own stories in which they used as many of the vocabulary words as possible.

Figures 5.7 and 5.8 are examples of a vocabulary web and plot diagram developed by seventh-grade students using Selina Hastings's *Sir Gawain and the Loathly Lady* (1985). Notice that the vocabulary and the concepts are more advanced. This

FIGURE 5.5

Vocabulary Web to Accompany *The Legend of the Bluebonnet*

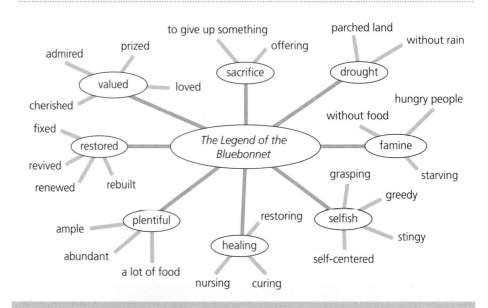

FIGURE 5.6

Plot Diagram Identifying Vocabulary in *The Legend of the Bluebonnet*

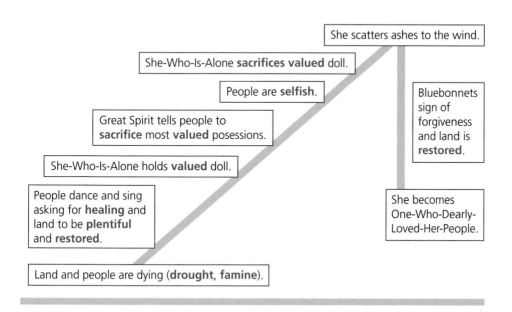

FIGURE 5.7

Vocabulary Web to Accompany *Sir Gawain and the Loathly Lady*

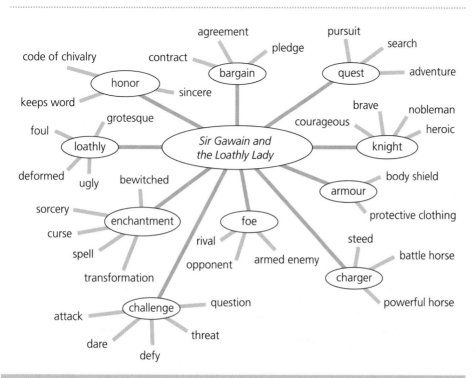

FIGURE 5.8

Plot Diagram Identifying Vocabulary in *Sir Gawain and the Loathly Lady*

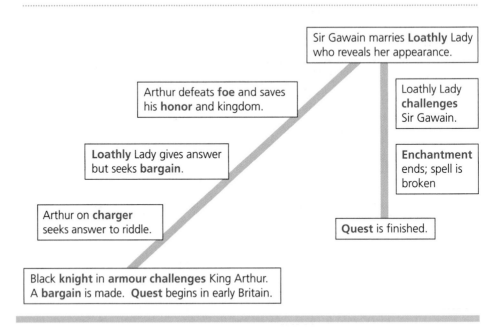

example uses the vocabulary words *loathly, bargain, quest, knight, armour, charger, challenge, foe,* and *enchantment. The Legend of the Bluebonnet* and *Sir Gawain and the Loathly Lady* are examples of folklore frequently taught in the fourth through eighth grades. In the next section, we will consider the vocabulary in specific content areas.

Vocabulary in the Content Areas

The various content areas such as social studies, history, art, science, music, language arts and literature all have specific vocabulary associated with that subject. Many of these vocabulary terms should be identified and defined, and examples given so students understand the vocabulary terms when they read in the content areas.

Table 5.1, for example, provides a useful way to help students define terms and provide examples in literature, art, and music. The table includes terms that are common for teaching reading in the content areas in the upper elementary grades. Teachers can place tables like this in the room, where students can fill in examples of the terms as they locate them in their reading. This type of activity allows students to share their knowledge with the class. This may be especially important as students expand their knowledge in art and music because these topics may be dropped from the school curriculum as schools face budget shortages or eliminate topics that are not tested.

TABLE 5.1

Vocabulary in Content Areas

Term	Meaning	Examples
Literature		
Plot	The order of events in a story	
Conflict	Characters experience a struggle in a story	
Characterization	Developing characteristics of characters in a story	
Setting	Location of story in time and place	
Theme	Underlying idea that ties the plot, characters, and setting together	
Art		
Line	Artists use of line to suggest direction, motion, energy, and mood	
Color	Variations in light and dark that give warm and cool moods	
Shape	The surface appearance of an object	
Texture	The degree of roughness or smoothness	
Music		
Beat	A unit of musical time	
Chord	Two or more notes played simultaneously	
Concert	A group of musicians playing together	
Music	Organized sound, writing down the sounds	
Opera	A musical drama that is sung	
Time Periods: Literature, History, Art, Music		
Medieval (Middle Ages)	500–1450	
Renaissance	1450–1600	
Baroque	1600–1750	
Classical	1750–1820	
Romantic	1820–1900	
Twentieth Century	1900–2000	

Using Precise Vocabulary to Enhance Cognitive Development

How important do you believe a precise vocabulary is when developing thinking skills in the content areas? According to Arthur L. Costa and Robert J. Marzano, if we are to teach students to think we must teach them by using the language associated with thinking because precise language enhances cognitive development. They maintain that to teach thinking, we must use specific cognitive terms that show students how to perform the skills we are asking of them. Instead of guiding students with phrases such as, "Let us look at these two pictures," for example, we should use specific vocabulary that asks them to do something with the pictures, such as, "Let us compare these two pictures." After asking the questions using the precise vocabularies, teachers should demonstrate how to make comparisons and do the other tasks listed on Table 5.2.

Table 5.2 shows the differences in nonprecise and precise vocabulary identified by Costa and Marzano. They believe that teachers should not use the nonprecise vocabulary and use and demonstrate precise vocabulary.

When using these precise terms, teachers instruct students in the thinking process associated with each term. For example, when making comparisons students should be encouraged to describe the thought processes they are using, the data they need, and the plans they are formulating to reach their conclusions. This is called the "Think Aloud Process." It is beneficial because it encourages students to describe their thought processes and become aware of them. This is also called *metacognition*.

Costa and Marzano (2001) describe the benefits of this process. As teachers require students to describe what is going on inside their heads,

> students become aware of their thinking processes. Similarly, they listen to their classmates describing their metacognitive processes. They develop flexibility of thought and an appreciation for the variety of ways to solve the same problem. Teachers, too, may share their thinking by making their inner dialogue external. Verbalizing questions they are asking themselves about ways to solve problems and sharing how they check their own accuracy are ways teachers can model their metacognitive processes to students. (p. 382)

As you compare the nonprecise and the precise vocabularies, think about how often teachers may replace the nonprecise vocabulary with a more precise vocabulary. What content areas do you believe would benefit from using terms such as *compare*, *predict*, and *classify*?

TABLE 5.2

Differences between Nonprecise and Precise Vocabulary

Nonprecise	Precise
Look at	*Compare* these
What will happen . . . ?	*Predict* what will happen
Place into groups . . .	*Classify* . . .
Work this problem.	*Analyze* this problem.
What do you think . . . ?	What *conclusions* can you give . . . ?
How do you explain . . . ?	What *hypothesis* might explain?
How do you know _____ is true?	What *evidence* do you have?
How else can you use . . . ?	How can you *apply* . . . ?

Vocabulary Development for Underachieving Urban Students

Fluency in oral language is a very strong predictor of reading achievement. In our discussion of emergent literacy in Chapter 2 we also emphasized the importance of reading aloud to students and providing an environment that allows students to respond to and read a variety of texts. Unfortunately, some children may have fewer experiences with books and other written materials.

Instructional approaches recommended for underachieving urban students suggest the importance of recognizing the students' culture through books they read and creating connections between the cultural experiences and theme-related vocabulary books. One of the ways to help students identify vocabulary related to their cultural experiences and to create bridges between cultural experiences and themes is to have students brainstorm lists of words and phrases they already know about a topic and then have them add new ones they think of as they read. For example, if students are reading and discussing African American literature such as Christopher Paul Curtis's *The Watsons Go to Birmingham—1963* (a 1996 Newbery Honor Book) or Curtis's *Bud, Not Buddy* (winner of the 2000 Newbery Award and the Coretta Scott King Award), they could brainstorm vocabulary related to what they already know about subjects, such as typical family experiences, differences between a northern and a southern city in the 1960s, or the detrimental impact of prejudice. For the second book, set in the Great Depression of the 1930s, students could brainstorm what they know about jazz musicians. When using *Bud, Not Buddy,* consider using Bud's "Rules and Things for Having a Funnier Life." Ask students to create their own rules and then compare them with Bud's rules.

Numerous books have themes related to "inner-city reality." Students can read these books, compare settings and themes, and identify vocabulary that relates to believable experiences. For example:

- Virginia Hamilton's *The Planet of Junior Brown* (1971)—New York City
- Walter Dean Myers's *Scorpions* (1988)
- Paula Fox's *Monkey Island* (1991)
- Theresa Nelson's *The Beggar's Ride* (1992)—Atlantic City
- Ineke Holtwijk's *Asphalt Angels* (1999)—Rio de Janeiro (for older students)

Many of the books discussed in Chapter 8, "Reading, Writing, and Literature in the Content Areas: Fourth Through Eighth Grades," have themes that are related to reality in suburban and rural settings. Books such as Katherine Hannigan's *Ida B . . . and Her Plans to Maximize Fun, Avoid Danger, and (Possibly) Save the World* (2004) have a rural setting, and books such as Carl Hiaasen's *Hoot* (2002) have a small-town setting.

Reflect on Your Reading

Consider the changing vocabulary needs of students as they mature. What are the differences between vocabulary teaching strategies used for students in Pre-K through fourth grade and for students in fourth through eighth grade?

Teaching Contextual Analysis

Contextual analysis is one of the strongest ways that readers identify the meanings of unknown words by using the context of the words around the unknown word, improving comprehension of what is read. According to Baumann, Kame'enui, and Ash (2003), "Contextual analysis is a strategy readers or listeners use to infer or predict the meaning of a word by scrutinizing the semantic and syntactic cues present in the preceding and following words, phrases, and sentences" (p. 770).

Richard and Jo Anne Vacca (1999) feel strongly about the need to teach context clues:

> Constructing meaning from context is one of the most useful strategies at the command of proficient readers. Showing readers who struggle how to make use of context builds confidence and competence and teaches the inquiry process necessary to unlock the meaning of troublesome technical and general vocabulary encountered during reading. Using context involves using information surrounding a difficult word to help reveal its meaning. (p. 70)

Contextual analysis is performed by identifying **context clues** to ascertain the meanings of unfamiliar words. There are two types of context clues. The first type is a typographical or format clue. This type of clue uses footnotes, italics, boldfaced print, parenthetical definitions, pictures, and graphs to provide immediate information about the meaning of the words. These clues may be the easiest for readers because there is a clear definition and a direct reference to the unknown word. To help students use these clues, teachers need to point out their usefulness and how the clue may give immediate meaning to a word. Typographic clues also should inform the student about important vocabulary words that may be essential to understanding (Vacca & Vacca, 1999).

Students use contextual analysis to help them identify words in an information book.

The second type of context clue is more difficult because it requires students to make inferences about the meaning of what is read. Later in this chapter, a lesson plan shows how to help students use context clues that require inferences when reading a book.

Most of the identifications of and definitions for context clues have not changed over the previous decades. McCullough's (1944) research identified the following types of context clues found in texts:

1. *Definition:* The word is defined within the content of the book.

2. *Comparison:* Contrasting words help the reader identify unfamiliar words.

3. *Summary:* The unfamiliar word is a summary of the ideas that precede the word.

4. *Familiar expression:* Knowledge of a familiar expression helps the reader identify the unknown word.

5. *Experience:* The reader's background aids in identifying an unknown word.

6. *Synonym:* A known synonym can help the reader identify an unknown word.

All of these clues are found within the books used in elementary classrooms. This is true whether the books are literature selections or content area textbooks; consequently it is important for the teacher to model how to use the context clue and to encourage students to use context clues during their independent reading.

These context clues are also extremely useful when teaching writing to students. For example, Diane Kern and Colleagues (2003) describe how they teach the principles for writing instruction by first identifying model literature that uses a type of structure such as cause and effect or summary, reading and discussing the literature, having students write similar structures, and using the lesson and the students' structures as a springboard to writing independent stories.

Teachers frequently ask for assistance in helping them locate books that are good sources for modeling context clues. Consequently, a number of sources are discussed next that may be used to model the context clues and to allow students to use their developing ability to interpret context clues and to use illustrations to help them understand meanings.

Definition and Illustration

Nonfiction texts are especially good for showing students how authors develop meanings of words through definitions. Some authors italicize important words that are defined within the context. Authors may also boldface words in the text and define them in the glossary. These techniques help students explore meanings and verify their meanings within that context. In addition, technical terms in books often are reinforced through labeled illustrations that define and clarify concepts. These illustrations help students verify unfamiliar meanings.

A good example of an author who uses definition clues to clarify the vocabulary is Catherine Paladino in *One Good Apple: Growing Our Food for the Sake of the Earth* (1999). Notice in the following example how Paladino defines the word *pesticides:*

These poisons are pesticides, man-made chemicals in the form of powders, sprays, or gases, that are used to kill insects, weeds, fungi (mold), and other living things that might damage crops. Farmers also use pesticides to make fruits and vegetables look as attractive as possible. (p. 6)

In this definition the author uses the word to show the close relationship between pesticides, poisons, and man-made chemicals. Examples are given as she refers to powders and sprays and their uses to kill insects. An illustration also shows the dangers of pesticides with the words: "Warning Pesticides: Fire will cause toxic flames" (p. 7).

Susan Campbell Bartoletti's *Hitler Youth: Growing Up In Hitler's Shadow* (2005) won both the 2006 Sibert Information Book Honor Award and the 2006 Newbery Honor Award. Notice how the author defines words that are uncommon to the readers: "Herbert belonged to the Hitlerjugend, or Hitler Youth, an organization of teenagers dedicated to Adolf Hitler. Hitler was the leader of the rising National Socialist Party, known as the Nationalsozialistische Deutsche Arbeiterpartei, or Nazis for short" (pp. 9–10).

Because this book won two prestigious awards, it provides an interesting example for analysis. Students may analyze the book to discover what techniques the author uses to encourage readers to understand this time period and to comprehend vocabulary that may not be in their background knowledge.

Sy Montgomery, the author of *The Tarantula Scientist* (2004), is another author who carefully develops his vocabulary. He both defines a term and provides a pronunciation for the difficult vocabulary: "Sam is a spider scientist, or arachnologist (pronounced 'ar-rack-NAWL-o-gist') (p. 7).

Carol Donoughue's *The Mystery of the Hieroglyphs: The Story of the Rosetta Stone and the Race to Decipher Egyptian Hieroglyphs* (1999) provides many examples of how definitions help readers understand unknown vocabulary. After a discussion of hieroglyphic script, for example, the text states: "Hieroglyph means 'sacred carving.' It is how the Greeks described the writing used by the Ancient Egyptian priests" (p. 6). The text includes examples of hieroglyphs painted on an Egyptian coffin. The author continues this technique by explaining the role of a scribe.

Comparison

Authors use relationships to help readers understand meanings. Authors might compare unknown objects with known objects or use contrasting words such as opposites to encourage readers to discover relationships. Again, illustrations can help readers understand these associations and comparisons.

Authors of science texts often use comparisons with known objects or illustrations that depict size by comparing an animal to scales in inches. In *Poison Dart Frogs* (1998), for example, Jennifer Owings Dewey compares several dart frogs to known objects: "One of the tiniest is nicknamed 'Buzzer.' It is the size of a cricket and makes a sound just like one. Another is called the strawberry poison dart frog because of its bright red skin. It is only three-quarters of an inch long" (p. unnumbered). Each of the dart frogs is shown above a ruler that encourages students to relate the size to a scale in inches.

In the 2006 Sibert Information Book Award *Secrets of a Civil War Submarine: Solving the Mysteries of the H. L. Hunley* (2005), author Sally M. Walker compares the power of a torpedo used during the Civil War with a torpedo used in modern-day warfare. Notice in the following quote how she compares the effectiveness of the two examples: "Civil War torpedoes had enough power to blow up a ship, but this success was far from guaranteed. A modern torpedo contains a propeller that pushes it through the water toward an enemy target. During the Civil War, torpedoes lacked this technology. Some didn't move at all; they were anchored to the bottom in harbors and river channels" (p. 7). In this text she describes how a man on land triggered the explosion instead of the torpedo being controlled from a submarine.

Author Summary

Authors of nonfiction books frequently use summaries to develop related ideas. Students can discuss these summaries and describe what they know about the unknown words. For example, notice how Downs Matthews in *Polar Bear Cubs* (1989) introduces the Arctic and the North Pole with the following summary:

> Picture a place so cold that oceans freeze . . . where tall trees can't grow . . . a place where the sun never shines in winter nor sets in summer. There is such a place. It is called the Arctic. It is the world of snow and ice at the North Pole. Polar bears live there. (p. 1 unnumbered)

Authors of fictional works use summaries to periodically review what has happened in the story. Students should be made aware of these summaries because the summaries help readers comprehend the text by allowing them to think about what has happened thus far in the story. In the following example, notice how Beverley Naidoo uses a summary in *The Other Side of Truth* (2000):

> There was so much to tell Papa. Too much Desertion at Victoria Station. The shock of Uncle Dele missing. Darth Vader of the alley grabbing her bag. Video Man accusing them and calling the police. Mrs. Graham taking them in, Kevin complaining. The awful Asylum Screening Unit. (p. 170)

Author summaries are an excellent way to help students understand what has happened in the story, to reinforce new vocabulary, and even to make predictions about what may happen next.

Familiar Expressions

Familiar expressions are another type of context clue that helps students understand new words. In *The Other Side of Truth,* the author uses a familiar expression in "Darth Vader of the alley grabbing their bag." In *Spiders and Their Web Sites* (2001), Margery Facklam uses the familiar concept of computer web sites to introduce spider-webs:

> People who create computer Web sites to attract attention or catch new customers are borrowing an idea millions of years old. Even before there were dinosaurs, spiders were luring insects to their web sites. (p. 4)

This is another example in which the author's use of a familiar object such as a Web site may motivate readers to make discoveries about spiders or the topic of the reading.

Experience

Using prior knowledge (schema) is one of the strongest comprehension devices to help readers comprehend new materials. Authors of nonfiction books frequently help readers understand new concepts and technical terms by relating the unknown terms to information the reader knows. This technique should be pointed out to readers so that they will try to visualize the new terms in relationship with knowledge from their previous experiences.

In *Storms* (1989), Seymour Simon encourages readers to use their knowledge of jet planes and vacuum cleaners to understand a tornado and to clarify the actions of a tornado:

> Sometimes a thunderstorm gives birth to a tornado. The wind blows hard and trees bend. Heavy rains or hailstones fall. Lightning and thunder rip the dark sky, and a howling roar like hundreds of jet planes fills the air. (p. 20)
>
> . . .
>
> Like the hose of an enormous vacuum cleaner, the tornado picks up loose materials and whirls them aloft. In less than fifteen minutes, the funnel cloud becomes clogged with dirt and air and can no longer suck up any more. (p. 22)

The experiences in this quote related to jet planes and vacuum cleaners encourage readers to not only visualize the tornado, but also to hear the accompanying sounds.

Synonym

Authors often repeat a term or idea by referring to a synonym. Sometimes the first word is known and the synonym is unknown, although authors may change this order. Molly McLaughlin uses numerous synonyms in *Dragonflies* (1989). For example, "This larva, or nymph, is quite different from its colorful flying parents" (p. 16). Teachers should point out this technique to help students understand the meanings of the new words.

LESSON PLAN:
Searching for and Teaching Context Clues

The previous examples of authors who use context clues and the lists of various types of context clues show how important it is to teach students how to use context clues to improve their comprehension of vocabulary and the text. The following example was completed with fifth- through eighth-grade readers as part of a three-year research grant (Norton, 1992) designed to improve reading ability. Part of the focus of the grant was to teach students how to use context clues to improve their comprehension.

By modeling how to use context clues, using guided practice, and applying skills to reading numerous books, students learned these important elements in the process of using context clues. For example, the previously discussed *The Legend of the Bluebonnet,* used for identifying vocabulary through plot structures and webbing, was also an excellent source for teaching context clues through both text and illustrations. Because the students in these classes were considered remedial readers and were several years below reading grade-level, there was extensive teacher-directed teaching of vocabulary, especially modeling the process that allowed students to see how context clues and illustrations relate to vocabulary.

OBJECTIVES
- To develop an understanding of context clues
- To apply the use of context clues to reading material
- To teach students how to use context clues to improve their comprehension

MATERIALS

Reading materials that contain context clues such as

Tomie DePaola's *The Legend of the Bluebonnet*

GRADE LEVELS Fifth through eighth grades

PROCEDURES

1. When teaching the context clues within *The Legend of the Bluebonnet,* write excerpts from the text on the chalkboard or on transparencies or PowerPoint slides or other presentation software. For example, the first paragraph is written with the vocabulary word <u>drought</u> underlined:

   "Great Spirit, the land is dying. Your People are dying, too," the line of dancers sang. "Tell us what we have done to anger you. End the <u>drought</u>. Save your people. Tell us what we must do so you will send the rain that will bring back life."
   (p. 1 unnumbered)

2. After reading the paragraph, the students identify, circle, and discuss the words that mean *drought:* "The land is dying." Next, they identify, circle, and discuss the words that indicate why the drought must end and words that show the dangerous consequences of the drought: "Save your people," "bring back life." The students then explore the consequences of drought and think about how terrible drought must be if the most powerful being for the tribe is asked to intervene.

3. Next, the students discuss the importance of picture clues that show the hot, yellow sun and the brown, dry earth. They consider the question, "What do the pictures add to the meaning of drought?" To understand the opposite concept, they identify, circle, and discuss the words that mean the opposite of drought: "The rain will come and the earth will be green and alive."

4. As students read the story, extend the meaning of the word drought as students identify other comparisons related to drought. These comparisons include additional cause-and-effect relationships such as:

   drought ⟶ famine, starving

   And opposite meanings:

   drought ⟶ rain, earth will be green and alive, buffalo will be plentiful

   These meanings are printed on the board, and the supporting illustrations are discussed.

5. Continue by printing additional paragraphs and context clues and using illustrations to identify and explore the meanings for *plentiful, selfish, healing, famine, valued, sacrifice,* and *restored.*

6. Finally, identify additional cause-and-effect relationships such as:

   rain ⟶ grass, plenty
   healing ⟶ rains came, brought back life
   plentiful ⟶ people will be rich again
   famine ⟶ very young and very old died
   sacrifice ⟶ offering a most valued possession

7. Identify additional opposite meanings, print them on the board, and discuss them. These cause-and-effect relationships can be extended to the descriptions of the characters and the settings.

8. With a group of your peers, locate additional books that could be used to model context clues. Try to locate books in which the illustrations also provide clues for meaning.

LESSON PLAN:
Understanding Context Clues

OBJECTIVES
1. To develop an understanding of the importance of context clues.
2. To identify the different types of context clues developed by authors.
3. To model the use of context clues so that students understand the thought processes that occur while considering the meanings.
4. To apply the use of context clues in independent reading.
5. To develop higher thought processes.
6. To apply the use of context clues in students' own writing.

MATERIALS   Choose reading materials that contain context clues such as the texts previously identified:

One Good Apple: Growing Our Food for the Sake of the Earth (1999); *The Mystery of the Hieroglyphs: The Story of the Rosetta Stone and the Race to Decipher Egyptian Hieroglyphs* (1999); *Poison Dart Frogs* (1998); *Polar Bear Cubs* (1989); *The Other Side of Truth* (2000); *Spiders and Their Web Sites* (2001); *Storms* (1989); and *Dragonflies* (1989).

Select various materials used in the content areas. Newspapers and magazines may also be used as part of this activity.

GRADE LEVELS   Fourth through eighth grades depending on the reading difficulty of the materials chosen

PROCEDURES   1. This lesson plan requires several days because you may choose to teach only one type of context clue each period. Prepare for the lesson by placing an example of a particular type of context clue on an overhead transparency or other form of classroom projection.

2. Remind students that authors use clues found within the text to help readers understand the meanings of unknown vocabulary. Explain to students that contextual analysis is a strategy that readers or listeners use to infer or predict the meaning of a word. This strategy helps them use the surrounding information to help them understand the meaning. Context clues may include illustrations, graphs, and charts. Some authors also use clues such as footnotes, italics, and boldfaced print to identify important vocabulary words.

3. Explain to the students that over the next few lessons, they will be discovering how they may use the following types of context clues to improve their understanding of the vocabulary in their books: definition, comparison, summary, familiar expressions, their own experiences, and synonyms. Discuss the importance of context clues with students. Make sure that they understand how their understanding of context clues will benefit them.

4. Choose one of the examples to model. *The Mystery of the Hieroglyphs: The Story of the Rosetta Stone and the Race to Decipher Egyptian Hieroglyphs* (1999) provides an interesting modeling choice because the text uses a number of context clues including boldface type and definition clues that are highlighted through both the text and illustrations. The subject is also one that may require considerable use of context clues unless the students are familiar with the subject and the time period.

5. Show the text you have chosen and model how you use context clues to help you understand the meanings of the words. If using *The Mystery of the Hieroglyphs,* for example, point out that in the beginning of the book the author states, "If a word is printed in bold type you can

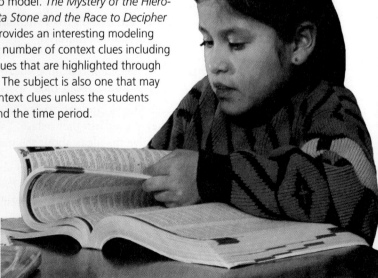

look up what it means in the Glossary on pages 46–47" (p. 3). Students should understand that you would use this information to help you understand the text.

6. Continue reading the text and model how the author uses boxed definitions including illustrations to define an unknown word.

7. After students understand definition clues, they may continue searching for similar types of definition clues in the remainder of the text.

8. Continue the lesson on definition clues by asking students to search for examples of definition clues in other materials that they read.

9. Ask students to explain their own thought processes as they develop the meanings of definition clues.

10. To provide additional application for definition context clues, ask students to use these clues in their own writing.

11. Continue the study of context clues by developing lesson plans for additional types of context clues. Include an annotated bibliography of examples of materials that develop specific types of context clues.

Reflect on Your Reading

Consider the different types of content clues defined in this chapter. Which of these context clues help you comprehend material when you are reading?

Building Student Responsibility for Vocabulary Development

Helping students activate prior knowledge, use context clues, and become involved in strategies that help them verify meanings is important. Researchers in vocabulary development stress that students should be encouraged to use a variety of strategies and to verify when meanings are making sense within a specific context. Blachowicz (1986) identifies a five-step strategy that helps students activate prior knowledge and become involved in their own vocabulary development. This strategy can be used with any type of reading material.

- First, when approaching vocabulary, have students ask themselves, "What do I already know about these words?"

- Second, ask students to preview the text and predict the meanings of the words. They should ask themselves, "What clues do I see when previewing the text that will give me ideas about the meanings of the words? What is my best guess?"

- Third, have students read the text and consider the context of the words.

- Fourth, ask students to use the initial clues and the clues from the selection to confirm and clarify their preliminary decisions about meanings. At this point they should understand that they can predict meanings of words and then read to confirm or clarify the accuracy of their predictions.

- Fifth, ask students to use the words in their own writing and to search for the words in additional readings.

How Should Vocabulary Be Taught?

Strategies related to vocabulary instruction differ depending on whether the reference is to research that suggests the best strategies for teaching vocabulary or to strategies that are often used in classrooms. Mason and colleagues (2003) contrast how vocabulary should be taught through both incidental learning by reading and listening to numerous sources and practicing the strategies that are taught with how vocabulary is frequently taught. They suggest that effective strategies encourage students to actively process new word meanings, use discussions to actively teach word meanings, and learn from meaningful contexts.

They conclude, however, that many vocabulary activities used in schools are not effective strategies:

> By contrast, consider the common types of school activities that are meant to teach vocabulary: words and meanings to match on workbook pages, packaged programs that drill on lists of unrelated words, guessing a word meaning by reading a sentence or two, looking up lists of words in the dictionary, and brief introductions of words before students read. If the words are already known, these activities are no help; they are busy work. If the words are not known, much more support for learning is needed. None of the activities listed above produces the kind of vocabulary knowledge that affects overall comprehension. (p. 924)

In your reading methods class, debate the strategies used for teaching vocabulary. Which approaches do you believe are the most effective? Why do you believe they are the most effective? From your observations of elementary classrooms, are Mason and colleagues correct in their descriptions of how vocabulary is taught? How will you teach vocabulary?

The teacher points out the meaning of a word within the context of a sentence.

Vocabulary Development in the Content Areas

The various content areas provide many opportunities for teaching vocabulary development. The in-depth study of subjects in the middle elementary and middle school years created through the use of units in social studies, history, geography, and science are excellent ways to help students build on prior knowledge and discover new meanings for words. As students conduct research and write research papers, they develop higher thought processes as they question, think about, and interact with a problem to be solved. For example, one of the goals for social studies education is to engage students in inquiry and problem solving about significant human issues. Another goal is to help them participate in interactive and cooperative classroom study that brings together students from all ability levels.

Consider how geography educators recommend that vocabulary be taught and expanded. For example, James M. Goodman, Jeanie Sisson, and Connie Jones in *The GEO Reader II* (1992) provide ideas for ways to incorporate geography into the curriculum. Many of the ideas are related to the development of vocabulary required for the understanding of geography. As you read the following suggestions, imagine what vocabulary words you would include and how you would teach the concepts related to the geography curriculum in the upper elementary grades:

Discovering Our Continent: Native Americans

The topic of studying early Native American cultures is found in many curriculum guides for social studies and geography for the upper elementary grades and for middle school.

1. Create a list of Native American words found in books. Compile the words into a picture glossary of Native American terms. Be careful to avoid stereotypical words.

2. Find descriptive Native American geographic names such as Talking Rock or Rising Fawn. Why should these names be chosen? Write an imaginary story about how a particular location got its name.

3. Draw an outline of a Native American shelter used during an earlier time period. Within the outline write a poem describing life in the home and the appropriate tribe.

Our Land and Its Resources

1. Create a bulletin board that includes famous natural features.

   Ask students to identify and label the features.

2. Compile an alphabet book with the title "North American National Parks" or "State Parks in _____." Use glossaries to help identify terms.

3. Create a pictorial glossary of water terms including *river, lake, bay, gulf,* and *isthmus.* Find examples of each term on a map.

4. Chart the ways that deserts and mountains are alike and different. Illustrate the definitions.

5. In a writer's log or journal keep a list of interesting geographic names. Use the "World Almanac" to locate the meanings of these words.

Discovering Changing Landscapes and Changing Cultures

1. For a comparison and contrast activity, compare maps of the same area from different time periods. Try to determine which map was earlier. What are the clues to when each map was published?

2. For a classifying activity for vocabulary, classify terms related to landscapes and cultures according to those made by people and those made by nature.

Semantic Feature Analysis

Semantic feature analysis is a method for associating vocabulary development and text comprehension. Semantic feature analysis is closely related to developing background information (schema theory) because the procedure helps students activate prior knowledge by encouraging them to associate personal experiences with concepts discussed. This approach helps students understand the semantic relationships or hierarchical organization of words so that readers can create bridges between

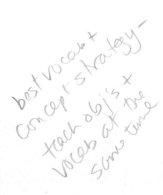

ideas and acquire deeper understandings of what is read. It is also beneficial for teaching relationships between vocabulary and a content area such as science.

According to Anders and Bos (1986), "When semantic feature analysis is used before, during, and after reading, it encourages students to predict relationships, read for confirmation, and integrate new and old learning" (p. 611). This approach can be used with a full book, a unit, or a chapter. The steps in this approach are:

- Teachers first read the material to determine the major ideas that will be gained from that reading.

- Teachers list words and phrases related to those ideas.

- They examine the list and determine which words or phrases represent the most important ideas and concepts.

- They identify words and phrases that represent details (the vocabulary words) that are related to the ideas and concepts.

- Ideas and concepts and important vocabulary are then placed on a chart with the important ideas across the top and the related vocabulary listed down the side.

The chart in Table 5.3 was developed with sixth-grade students who were reading Patricia Lauber's *Volcano: The Eruption and Healing of Mount St. Helens* (1986).

The chart should be duplicated so that each student can complete the chart, add to it, and refer to it during reading and discussion. It is helpful if the teacher displays a model chart to introduce the procedure, the topic, and the vocabulary and ideas that will be studied. Students are encouraged to add their personal experiences or understandings during the discussion.

Students then use the chart to determine the relationships between each of the important ideas and the important vocabulary. If the relationship is positive, the students place a (+) sign in the square. If the relationship is negative, they place a (−) sign in the square. A zero (0) represents no relationship and a question mark (?) shows that an answer cannot be reached without more information.

During class, the teacher leads a discussion in which students chart the relationships and justify their choice of markings. Anders and Bos observe that

> Student involvement during the discussion is critical to the success of the semantic feature analysis strategy. One key to a successful discussion is to ask students why they reach a certain relationship rating. This seems to encourage them to use their prior knowledge regarding the topic. (p. 614)

In this example notice how closely the semantic feature analysis can be related to content areas and comprehension of key ideas and vocabulary within the content areas.

Reflect on Your Reading

Choose another content area such as science, and identify the vocabulary ideas that you would use to teach that vocabulary.

Handwritten margin notes:
- Can be used
- prereading strategy
- words w/some exp
- during strategy
  (To find connections)
- summarize

TABLE 5.3

Semantic Feature Analysis of a Science, Nonfiction Book

Important Ideas

	Signs of waking volcano	Mount St. Helens is an old volcano	Molten rock turns to lava	Volcanoes have bowl-shaped craters at the top	The Cascade Range is a chain of volcanoes	Volcanoes are to be feared	There is a need to predict volcanic eruptions
Related vocabulary							
Earthquake							
Eruptions							
Magma							
Pumice							
Gas and steam							
Explosions							
Swelling and cracking							
Geologists							
Measuring the bulge							
Instrument recording							
Avalanche							
Seismometer							
Pressure							
Mudflows							

DIFFERENTIATING INSTRUCTION

ELL Students

Developing oral proficiency through vocabulary development is crucial for reading success of ELL students (Droop and Verhoeven, 2003). These educators found that extensive vocabulary training is essential through multiple exposure to words by familiarizing students with various genres and subject areas. Vocabulary activities in which ELL students discuss the illustrations in a story before reading the story and predict what the story will be about and the meanings of vocabulary likely to be found in the book helps expand understanding of vocabulary. Predictable texts such as those found in many cumulative books help students predict the vocabulary that follows. Highlighting the vocabulary in books to be read helps students focus on the essential vocabulary in the story.

The plot diagramming used to reinforce vocabulary and the vocabulary webs to accompany a story developed in this chapter are especially beneficial. ELL students should keep folders of these vocabulary diagrams and webs. The words can be used as sources for vocabulary during writing activities.

Struggling Readers and Writers

Making connections between the vocabulary in a book and personal experiences with those words is essential if struggling readers are to comprehend the meanings of the words. Ann Ketch (2005) describes how several teachers used a "think/pair/share" activity to engage students in the thinking process and expand their understanding of vocabulary.

In a first-grade classroom, the teacher read a book aloud and asked students to think about a character in the book. She asked students to share with a peer words that might describe the character. The students talked about how the character was similar to a sibling or friends. Then, the students shared the words they believed described the character. The teacher then wrote words such as *spoiled, self-centered,* and *conceited* as descriptive words and character traits.

The teacher and students then used this list of vocabulary words in a writing activity. Ketch points out that the teacher "could have easily written the list of character traits without engaging students in a think/pair/share activity, but the students would not have gone through the thinking process. Students need to experience the process in order to become thinkers" (p. 12).

Gifted and Accelerated Readers and Writers

Students enjoy reading and evaluating books that have been chosen as "Children's Choices" by their peers. "Children's Choices for 2005" is published in *The Reading Teacher* (October 2005). The choices are the result of ten thousand school children who read and vote on newly published books. The 2005 list includes seventeen

■ ELL students use the illustrations in a book to help them predict the vocabulary in the text.

books chosen by "Advanced Readers." Several of these books also provide sources for advancing vocabulary skills. For example, Paul B. Janecko's *Top Secret: A Handbook of Codes, Ciphers, and Secret Writing* (2004) includes directions for and vocabulary associated with creating codes, ciphers, and other methods of concealment. An answer key is included that allows readers to practice and then check their answers.

In *Faraway Worlds* (2004), Paul Halpern asks readers to think about the existence of other planets outside the solar system and to consider what life might be like on those planets. In *Show; Don't Tell! Secrets of Writing* (2004) Josephine Nobisso gives readers suggestions for writing in different genres of literature. Books that motivate students to create their own writings are among the best ways to help students expand their own vocabularies.

Summary

This chapter provides general guidelines for vocabulary development including both direct instruction in teaching vocabulary and indirect approaches that emphasize the extensive reading of a broad range of literature and content materials. Research-based vocabulary instruction emphasizes teaching students to learn words independently, teaching students the meanings of specific words by emphasizing synonyms or definitions, pre-teaching critical vocabulary, and helping students develop an appreciation for words by experiencing enjoyment in their use.

Vocabulary development in the pre-kindergarten through fourth grades includes instructional strategies and activities that encourage students to relate vocabulary to personal experience. In addition, strategies such as identifying crucial vocabulary words on plot diagrams and using webbing to visually display relationships among vocabulary words and extended meanings are crucial.

Vocabulary development in the fourth through eighth grades extends vocabulary knowledge, as older students require a broader understanding of vocabulary and how the vocabulary supports comprehension in the content areas. Webbing and plot structures using vocabulary words is a major strategy to help students relate vocabulary to comprehension. Teaching students to use context clues is important especially in the content areas in the upper grades.

Reflect on Your Reading

Why is enhancing vocabulary development essential for reading instruction for all students? Why are approaches such as discussing illustrations, engaging students in the thinking process, and using a wide range of literature important when developing an understanding of vocabulary?

Key Terms

expressive vocabulary, p. 177

receptive vocabulary, p. 177

word walls, p. 181

webbing, p. 184

vocabulary notebooks, p. 185

contextual analysis, p. 194

context clues, p. 194

semantic feature analysis, p. 204

For video clips of authentic classroom instruction on **Vocabulary**, go to Allyn & Bacon's MyLabSchool.com. In MLS courses, click on Reading Methods, go to MLS Video Lab, and select **Module 3**.

Extend Your Reading

1. With a group of your classmates, discuss how you would teach the importance of vocabulary to either lower or upper elementary students. What are the most important concepts and how would you introduce them? Choose a book appropriate for students in Pre-K through fourth grade and another book appropriate for students in fourth through eighth grade. Develop a vocabulary web and a plot diagram that reinforces the important vocabulary in each book. Discuss how you would teach an understanding of the vocabulary.

2. Visit an elementary school classroom. What type of vocabulary activities do you observe? How much emphasis is being placed on vocabulary development? In what ways does vocabulary development change with the content that is being taught? How are strategies for developing independent knowledge of vocabulary being reinforced throughout the school day? Are you able to identify examples of direct and indirect teaching of vocabulary? If you are, what are the strategies? When students do not understand the meanings of words, how do teachers help students develop an understanding of the vocabulary?

3. Developing an appreciation for and a love of words and language is one of the goals of vocabulary development. With a group of your peers, suggest ways that you will help students develop this appreciation and love. What techniques allowed you to develop an appreciation for vocabulary and language? Describe a memory in which a teacher, a librarian, or a parent helped you develop your love for language? Share this memory with your group. How will you use similar motivation in your own class?

4. Setting a positive model for learning words is one of the ways to develop an appreciation for words. What does a positive model for developing an appreciation for words mean to you? Describe how your classroom and your teaching will create this positive model.

5. Select books that you would like to use with a group of students in Pre-K through fourth grade or with a group of students in fourth through eighth grade. Develop plot diagrams that identify the words that are important for comprehending the story. As you develop the plot diagrams with the vocabulary, note any relationships between words that could be used to extend understandings of the vocabulary to personal experiences. How would you teach this important vocabulary? Share the plot diagrams with your class.

6. Choose one of the ideas listed under "Discovering Our Continent: Native Americans," "Our Land and Its Resources," or "Discovering Changing Landscapes and Changing Cultures." Develop the teaching strategy for vocabulary that you would use.

7. Create a semantic feature analysis for a book related to the content areas. Some interesting choices might include:

Karen Alonso's (1999) *Schenck v. United States: Restrictions on Free Speech.*

Linda Jacobs Altman's (1999) *Slavery and Abolition in American History.*

Jennifer Armstrong's (2005) *Photo by Brady: A Picture of the Civil War.*

Susan D. Bachrach's (2000) *The Nazi Olympics: Berlin 1936*

Natalie Bober's (2001) *Countdown to Independence: A Revolution of Ideas in England and Her American Colonies: 1760–1776.*

Brian Floca's (2000) *Dinosaurs at the Ends of the Earth: The Story of the Central Asiatic Expeditions.*

James Cross Giblin's (2000) *The Century That Was: Reflections on the Last One Hundred Years.*

Jane Goodall's (2001) *The Chimpanzees: I Love Saving Their World and Ours.*

Philip Hoose's (2001) *We Were There, Too!: Young People in U.S. History.*

Philip Hoose's (2004) *The Race to Save the Lord God Bird.*

Diane McWhorter's (2004) *A Dream of Freedom: The Civil Rights Movement From 1854 to 1968.*

Sy Montgomery's (2004) *Search for the Golden Moon Bear: Science and Adventure in the Asian Tropics* and

Sy Montgomery's (2004) *The Tarantula Scientist.*

Toni Morrison's (2004) *Remember: The Journey to School Integration.*

For Further Reading

1. As students advance in the grades, they are also required to develop vocabulary related to technical skills and to a wider range of content. Read Walter Minkel's "The Next Big Thing: Why 21st-Century Skills Are a Librarian's New Best Friend," *School Library Journal,* May 2003, p. 41. What vocabulary skills are necessary for the 21st Century?

2. To gain a better understanding of technological literacy and the requirements for vocabulary and understanding, read Louanne Smolin and

Kimberly Lawless's "Becoming Literate in the Technological Age: New Responsibilities and Tools for Teachers," in *The Reading Teacher,* March 2003. What new insights into techno-logical vocabulary do you gain from this article?

3. To discover how a second-grade teacher uses Web logs, or blogs, to increase students' learning and to increase technology links between home and school, read Jeffrey Selingo's "In the Classroom, Web Logs Are the New Bulletin Boards," *New York Times,* Thursday, August 19, 2004, p. E7.

4. Several authors discussed in this chapter have Web sites, including

Jan Brett: www.janbrett.com
Eric Carle: www.eric-carle.com
Tomie dePaola: www.tomie.com

REFERENCES

Anders, Patricia, & Bos, C. (1986). "Semantic Feature Analysis: An Interactive Strategy for Vocabulary Development and Text Comprehension." *Journal of Reading, 29,* 610–616.

Baumann, James F., Kame'enui, Edward J., & Ash, Gwynne E. (2003). "Research on Vocabulary Instruction: Voltaire Redux." In James Flood, Diane Lapp, James R. Squire, & Julie M. Jensen (Eds.). *Handbook of Research on Teaching the English Language Arts,* 2nd ed., Mahwah, NJ: Lawrence Erlbaum, pp. 752–785.

Bear, Donald R., Invernizzi, Marcia, Templeton, Shane, & Johnston, Francine. (2000). *Words Their Way: Word Study for Phonics, Vocabulary, and Spelling Instruction,* 2nd ed. Upper Saddle River, NJ: Merrill/Prentice Hall.

Blachowicz, C. (1986). "Making Connections: Alternatives to the Vocabulary Notebook." *Journal of Reading, 29,* 643–649.

Children's Book Council (October 2005). "Children's Choices for 2005." *The Reading Teacher, 59,* 157–172.

Collins, Molly Fuller (October-December 2005). "ESL Preschoolers' English Vocabulary Acquisition of Storybook Reading." *Reading Research Quarterly, 40,* 406–408.

Costa, Arthur L., & Marzano, Robert J. (2001). "Teaching the Language of Thinking." In Arthur L. Costa (Ed.). *Developing Minds: A Resource Book for Teaching Thinking,* 3rd ed. Alexandria, VA, pp. 379–383.

Cunningham, Anne E., & Stanovich, Keith E. (2003). "Reading Matters: How Reading Engagement Influences Cognition." In James Flood, Diane Lapp, James R. Squire, & Julie M. Jensen (Eds.). *Handbook of Research on Teaching the English Language Arts,* 2nd ed. Mahwah, NJ: Lawrence Erlbaum, pp. 666–675.

Droop, M., & Verhoeven, L. (2003). "Language Proficiency and Reading Ability in First- and Second-Language Learners." *Reading Research Quarterly, 38,* 78–103.

Ferguson, Jennifer. (2003). "Literary Elements Project." College Station: Texas A&M University.

Goodman, James M., Sisson, Jeanie, & Jones, Connie. (1992). *The GEO Reader II.* Wichita, KS: National Reading Incentive Program.

Kern, Diane, Andre, Wendy, Schilke, Rebecca, Barton, James, & McGuire, Margaret Conn. (May 2003). "Less Is More: Preparing Students for State Writing Assessments." *The Reading Teacher, 56,* 816–826.

Ketch, Ann. (September 2005). "Conversation: The Comprehension Connection." *The Reading Teacher, 59,* 8–13.

Mason, Jana M., Stahl, Steven A., Au, Kathryn H., & Herman, Patricia A. (2003). "Reading: Children's Developing Knowledge of Words. In James Flood, Diane Lapp, James R. Squire, & Julie M. Jensen (Eds.). *Handbook of Research on Teaching the English Language Arts,* 2nd ed. Mahwah, NJ: Lawrence Erlbaum, pp. 914–930.

McCullough, Constance. (1944). "Recognition of Context Clues in Reading." *Elementary English Review, 22,* 1–5.

Minkel, Walter. (May 2003). "The Next Big Thing: Why 21st-Century Skills Are a Librarian's New Best Friend." *School Library Journal, 49,* 41.

National Institute of Child Health and Human Development Early Child Care Research Network. (2005). "Pathways to Reading: The Role of Oral Language in the Transition to Reading." *Developmental Psychology, 41,* 428–442.

Norton, Donna E. (2004). *The Effective Teaching of Language Arts,* 6th ed. Upper Saddle River, NJ: Merrill/Prentice Hall.

Norton, Donna E. (1992). *The Impact of Literature-Based Reading.* New York: Merrill/Macmillan.

Pogue, David. (19 August 2004). "RUOK? A Tutorial for Parents." *New York Times,* p. E1, 6.

Ruddell, Robert B. (2002). *Teaching Children to Read and Write: Becoming an Effective Literacy Teacher,* 3rd ed. Boston: Allyn & Bacon.

Selingo, Jeffrey. (19 August 2004). "In the Classroom, Web Logs Are the New Bulletin Boards." *New York Times,* p. E7.

Smolin, Louanne, & Lawless, Kimberly A. (March 2003). "Becoming Literate in the Technological Age: New Responsibilities and Tools for Teachers." *The Reading Teacher,* 56, 570.

Vacca, Richard T., & Vacca, JoAnne L (1999*). Content Area Reading: Literacy and Learning across the Curriculum,* 6th ed. New York: Longman.

Children's Literature References

Alonso, Karen. (1999). *Schenck v. United States: Restrictions of Free Speech.* Enslow.

Altman, Linda Jacobs. (1999). *Slavery and Abolition in American History.* Enslow.

Armstrong, Jennifer. (2005). *Photo by Brady: A Picture of the Civil War.* Atheneum.

Bachrach, Susan D. (2000). *The Nazi Olympics: Berlin 1936.* Little, Brown.

Bartoletti, Susan Campbell. (2005). *Hitler Youth: Growing Up in Hitler's Shadow.* Scholastic.

Belle, Jennifer. (2005). *Animal Stackers.* Illustrated by David McPhail. Hyperion.

Bober, Natalie. (2001). *Countdown to Independence: A Revolution of Ideas in England and Her American Colonies: 1760–1776.* Simon & Schuster.

Brett, Jan. (1987). *Goldilocks and the Three Bears.* Dodd, Mead.

Brighton, Catherine. (1999). *The Fossil Girl: Mary Anning's Dinosaur Discovery.* Millbrook.

Carle, Eric. (1974). *My Very First Book of Colors.* Crowell.

Carle, Eric. (1974). *My Very First Book of Shapes.* Crowell.

Cronin, Doreen. (2000). *Click, Clack, Moo: Cows That Type.* Simon & Schuster.

Curtis, Christopher Paul. (1999). *Bud, Not Buddy.* Delacorte.

Curtis, Christopher Paul. (1995). *The Watsons Go to Birmingham—1963.* Delacorte.

DePaola, Tomie. (1983). *The Legend of the Bluebonnet.* Putnam.

Dewey, Jennifer Owings. (1998). *Poison Dart Frogs.* Boyds Mill.

Donoughue, Carol. (1999). *The Mystery of the Hieroglyphs: The Story of the Rosetta Stone and the Race to Decipher Egyptian Hieroglyphs.* Oxford University.

Facklam, Margery. (2001). *Spiders and Their Web Sites.* Illustrated by Alan Male. Little, Brown.

Floca, Brian. (2000). *Dinosaurs at the Ends of the Earth: The Story of the Central Asiatic Expeditions.* Dorling Kindersley.

Fox, Paula. (1991). *Monkey Island.* Orchard.

Giblin, James Cross, ed. (2000). *The Century That Was: Reflections on the Last One Hundred Years.* Atheneum.

Goodall, Jane. (2001). *The Chimpanzees: I Love Saving Their World and Ours.* Scholastic.

Halpern, Paul. (2004). *Faraway Worlds.* Illustrated by Lynette R. Cook. Charlesbridge.

Hamilton, Virginia. (1971). *The Planet of Junior Brown.* Macmillan.

Hannigan, Katherine. (2004). *Ida B . . . and Her Plans to Maximize Fun, Avoid Danger, and (Possibly) Save the World.* Greenwillow.

Hastings, Selina. (1985). *Sir Gawain and the Loathly Lady.* Illustrated by Juan Wijngard. Lothrop, Lee & Shepard.

Hiaasen, Carl. (2002). *Hoot.* Knopf.

Henkes, Kevin. (2004). *Kitten's First Full Moon.* Greenwillow.

Hoban, Tana. (1972). *Push-Pull, Empty-Full: A Book of Opposites.* Macmillan.

Hoban, Tana. (1986). *Shapes, Shapes, Shapes.* Greenwillow.

Hoban, Tana. (1998). *So Many Circles, So Many Squares.* Greenwillow.

Holtwijk, Ineke. (1999). *Asphalt Angels.* Front Street.

Hoose, Philip. (2004). *The Race to Save the Lord God Bird.* Farrar, Straus & Giroux.

Hoose, Philip. (2001). *We Were There, Too! Young People in U.S. History.* Farrar, Straus & Giroux.

Janeczko, Paul B. (2004). *Top Secret: A Handbook of Codes, Ciphers, and Secret Writing.* Illustrated by Jenna LaReau. Candlewick.

Jenkins, Steve. (1996). *Big and Little.* Houghton Mifflin.

Juster, Norton. (2005). *The Hello, Goodbye Window.* Illustrated by Chris Raschka. Hyperion.

Lauber, Patricia. (1986). *Volcano: The Eruption and Healing of Mount St. Helens*. Bradbury.

Matthews, Downs. (1989). *Polar Bear Cubs*. Photographs by Dan Guravich. Simon & Schuster.

McLaughlin, Molly. (1989). *Dragonflies*. Walker.

McWhorter, Diane. (2004). *A Dream of Freedom: The Civil Rights Movement from 1854 to 1968*. Scholastic.

Montgomery, Sy. (2004). *Search for the Golden Moon Bear: Science and Adventure in the Asian Tropics*. Houghton Mifflin.

Montgomery, Sy. (2004). *The Tarantula Scientist*. Photographs by Nic Bishop. Houghton Mifflin.

Morrison, Toni. (2004). *Remember: The Journey to School Integration*. Houghton Mifflin.

Myers, Walter Dean. (1988). *Scorpions*. Harper & Row.

Naidoo, Beverley. (2000). *The Other Side of Truth*. HarperCollins.

Nelson, Theresa. (1992). *The Beggar's Ride*. Orchard.

Nobisso, Josephine. (2004). *Show; Don't Tell! Secrets of Writing*. Illustrated by Eva Montanari. Gingerbread House.

Norling, Beth. (2003). *Little School*. Kane/Miller.

Paladino, Catherine. (1999). *One Good Apple: Growing Our Food for the Sake of the Earth*. Houghton Mifflin.

Sendak, Maurice. (1963). *Where the Wild Things Are*. Harper & Row.

Shulevitz, Uri. (1998). *Snow*. Farrar, Straus & Giroux.

Simon, Seymour. (1989). *Storms*. William Morrow.

Walker, Sally M. (2005). *Secrets of a Civil War Submarine: Solving the Mysteries of the H. L. Hunley*. Carolrhoda.

CHAPTER 6

Developing Approaches for Fluency and Comprehension

CHAPTER **OUTLINE**

Schema Theory
Mental Imagery
Graphic Organizers
   Semantic Maps
   Improving Comprehension through Time Lines
Using Modeling Techniques
Using Questioning Strategies
   Literal Recognition
   Inference
   Evaluation
   Appreciation
   Questioning Strategies to Use While Reading
Predicting Outcomes to Improve Comprehension
Developing Fluency in Reading
   Guided Repeated Oral Reading
   Independent Silent Reading

After reading this chapter you will be able to answer the following questions:

1. What is schema theory and how is it related to reading instruction?
2. What is mental imagery and how is it related to reading instruction?
3. What are graphic organizers and how are they related to improving comprehension?
4. How can modeling techniques improve comprehension?
5. How are questioning strategies related to comprehension?
6. How are predicting outcomes related to comprehension?

Read All About It!

Two articles appearing in the "Science News" section of *New York Times* (July 27, 2004) illustrate the importance of teaching students to read articles that use visual representations such as maps and time lines to enhance the comprehension of information.

A Far-Reaching Fire Makes a Point about Pollution

by Andrew C. Revkin

In 1859, the American oceanographer Matthew Fontain Maury, one of the first scientists to describe Earth's seas and skies as integrated systems, wrote, "It is only the girdling encircling air, that flows above and around all that makes the whole world kin."

Last week, a pair of globe-scanning NASA satellites, *Terra* and *Aqua,* reinforced that notion as they tracked the sooty remains of fire-swept Alaskan black spruce forests wafting high over coastal Louisiana and beyond.

Such measurements have increasingly been showing how pollution that was once perceived as local is, at least in part, global. By 2010, for example, scientists project that a third of the smog-forming ozone in California air will originate in the booming economies of Asia.

In this case, the link between the Far North and the Deep South started with fire-friendly conditions in Alaska. This has been one of the worst fire seasons in the state since 1950, when officials first started keeping records, with nearly four million acres turned in 492 fires so far—more than half started by people and the rest by lightning.

The moist air that usually starts sweeping in from the Bering Sea by mid-July is absent, officials said, keeping forests vulnerable. And there has been ample lightning, with some 8,000 ground strikes estimated in a two-day stretch last week.

The emissions from all that combustion took an unusual path. A week ago, the atmosphere over North America was in a pattern more typical of winter, with high pressure sitting over the West and low pressure running from Hudson Bay nearly to the Gulf of Mexico.

This sent the jet stream, essentially a speeding river of high-altitude air, veering far south of the normal Canada-spanning path, and the Alaskan smoke went along for the ride, at 100 miles an hour.

The illustration that accompanies the article shows a map with the caption: Smoke from fires in Alaska has traveled south. At right, a satellite image shows it hanging over Louisiana, bottom center, and other Southern states on July 19 (p. D1).

In the second article, "African Pastoral: Archaeologists Rewrite History of Farming," Brenda Fowler uses a timeline titled "Stones Into Plowshares" to show the "Earliest dates cereals were grown as crops, as generally agreed by archaeologists. Estimates of even earlier dates for some crops are disputed." The time line in the article shows from 11,000 B.C. to today.

Read All About It!

Critical Thinking **Questions**

- What is the impact of graphic aids when reporting scientific information?

- How did the graphic aids improve comprehension of the articles?

- Why do you believe that newspapers use graphic aids to support news articles?

- In addition to these articles, search newspapers to locate any visual aids that add to the comprehension of the stories. As a teacher, how might you use these visual aids in your classroom?

Themes of the Times

expect the world®

The New York Times

nytimes.com

For related *New York Times* articles, go to the Companion Web Site at www.ablongman.com/norton1e and click on *Themes of the Times.*

Comprehension, the act of understanding what is read, heard, or seen, is considered one of the ultimate goals of reading instruction. Comprehension instruction is the focus of several recent reports that provide many guidelines for teachers, such as "Effective Practices for Developing Reading Comprehension" (Duke & Pearson, 2002), whose authors explain, "To borrow a term from the decoding debate, comprehension instruction should be balanced. By this we mean that good comprehension instruction includes both explicit instruction in specific comprehension strategies and a great deal of time and opportunity for actual reading, writing, and discussion of text" (p. 207).

Before we proceed, let us review balance for comprehension that is found in the interactive model of the reading process discussed in Chapter 1. This model stresses the importance of using balanced reading approaches. It is also the model frequently discussed in relation to effective approaches for teaching reading. The interactive model of the reading process is a combination of the bottom-up (text-based) and top-down (reader-based) models. In this interactive model, reading comprehension is seen as an interactive process in which both text and reader's knowledge play key roles. It is called an interactive model because the reader begins by looking at the print and decoding words and sentences and then uses prior knowledge to predict what will happen in the story and comprehend the text.

By reviewing this definition of the interactive model, we also discover the importance of reading strategies presented in the previous chapters. These chapters present the foundations for reading comprehension. Chapter 2 focuses on the development of language and cognitive skills that are essential for acquiring reading ability. Chapter 4 focuses on developing word recognition skills that allow students to decode the words they are reading. Chapter 5 focuses on developing the meanings of the words that are read. In this chapter we will also strive for a balanced reading approach that includes explicit instruction in specific comprehension strategies and opportunities for students to read and discuss actual texts.

Paul Neufeld (2005/2006) identifies reading behaviors of expert readers when reading in the content areas. He specifies before reading and during reading strategies that should be taught as part of the reading curriculum because the strategies improve comprehension. For example, before reading a text, students should identify their purpose for reading such as to prepare for a class discussion, to write a report, to review for a test, or to read for enjoyment. They should understand that their purpose may affect the way they read. During this before reading stage they need to do an overview of the text in which they identify major topics covered in the text and notice how the text is organized. Before reading they should activate their prior knowledge by identifying what they know about the topic and predicting what they believe the text is about.

Neufeld identifies the strategies students should be taught to use while they are reading. These comprehension strategies should encourage students to pay attention to the key words used in the text and note the way the text is organized, to stop while reading and summarize the main ideas, and to create a visual organizer (such as a semantic map) that captures the main points and ideas of the text. While reading they should be taught that it may be necessary to reread parts of the text in order to clarify their understandings, to seek help from an adult, or to search for additional resources such as books or web sites that help clarify a topic.

In *Best Practice: New Standards for Teaching and Learning in America's Schools* (Zemelman, Daniels, & Hyde, 1998), the authors summarize effective strategies for developing reading comprehension, such as activating prior knowledge (schema theory), helping students make and test predictions, providing structural help during reading, teaching comprehension skills in the context of meaningful literature, and providing after-reading applications. In this section we will discuss some of these comprehension strategies and present applications for using the strategies with children in the lower and upper elementary grades.

Schema Theory

Schema theory emphasizes the importance of activating relevant prior knowledge before students read a selection and helping them fill in the gaps that might hinder comprehension. According to schema theory, the basis for comprehension of what is read is the reader's *schema*, or organized knowledge about the subject. In this theory, a reader uses prior knowledge when developing understanding of specific types of texts, events that are described in a text, and clues in a text that help readers create meaning from the text. The National Reading Panel (2000) found that activating relevant prior knowledge helps children understand and remember what they read. The panel concludes: "Prior knowledge studies indicate that prior learning or learning that precedes reading enhances comprehension of what is read. In this sense, reading about a subject after learning about it in other ways would be part of a program of instruction in a content area" (p. 4, 108).

Some authors of books realize the importance of either identifying possible prior knowledge or presenting background knowledge that is important for understanding. Tina Packer uses such a technique when she introduces each selection in *Tales from Shakespeare* (2004). In this book for middle to upper elementary students, Packer first presents background information about William Shakespeare and the time period in which Shakespeare lived and wrote (England, during the Renaissance [or rebirth] 1564–1616). Next, she introduces each of the twelve plays with an introduction that both motivates interest and provides a framework for reading the play. The following example shows how she introduces *Macbeth*:

> What happens when ambition turns evil? What happens when a man betrays his king, his friend . . . his own soul? Those questions are at the heart of Macbeth. "Fair is foul, and foul is fair" when the warrior-hero Macbeth and his wife aspire to become king and queen of Scotland. They think their only way to the throne is by the sword. But evil deeds have a way of revealing themselves. (p. 67)

Next, Packer presents the cast of players with their names and identification. In this introduction she also gives the time and place for *Macbeth*: eleventh-century, Scotland.

Finally, she presents a retelling of the play that corresponds with the introduction. Notice how she sets the stage for the upcoming drama in the first two lines of the play: "Thunder crashed and rumbled across the barren Scottish heath. A lightning bolt silhouetted two men on horseback before the gloom swallowed them up" (p. 69).

Information about the author, Tina Packer, also highlights her credibility as a reteller of Shakespeare's plays. She is the president and artistic director of Shakespeare and Company, and she has directed all of the plays included in the book.

When we consider the total reading curricula, we realize that prior knowledge is crucial and also varies considerably among students when comprehending different forms of reading. Joan Peskin (1998), for instance, found considerable differences between the responses from students that she calls expert and novice readers of poetry. The expert readers used their prior knowledge of poetry to interpret the poetry by using structure, rhythm, word play, and rhyme scheme as clues. Expert readers also knew how to scan a poem to search for meaning and to make use of visual representations to highlight structural elements. In contrast, the novice readers of poetry did not use any of these clues to help them comprehend the poem. Peskin concluded that the experts had separate schemata for particular genres, in this case poetry. Having a schema for poetry increases both understanding and enjoyment.

Strategies that help students of all grade levels to activate prior knowledge and fill in the gaps include prereading discussions that review and identify prior knowledge, providing information to help students use their prior knowledge, and identifying any gaps in that knowledge. To accomplish this it is important that teachers and students make use of maps, films, pictures, and historical time lines before students approach a reading assignment. The following lesson plan is an example of a strategy used with students in the upper elementary and middle school grades to develop prior knowledge and fill in the gaps before students read Avi's *Crispin: The Cross of Lead* (2002), winner of the 2003 Newbery Award.

> **Reflect on Your Reading**
>
> What types of prior knowledge are crucial to develop comprehension of a book set in an earlier historical period, or a text about space exploration, or a poem? What gaps might need to be filled in order for students to develop comprehension of any of these subjects?

Visual aids in newspapers help readers gain understanding of the subject.

LESSON PLAN:

Developing Schema for Crispin: The Cross of Lead

OBJECTIVES	1. To review or introduce knowledge needed to comprehend the reading of historical fiction
	2. To review knowledge of or introduce new understandings about Medieval England in A.D. 1377
	3. To discuss picture books that illustrate settings typically found in Medieval England
	4. To conduct prereading research into topics related to Medieval England
	5. To summarize what has been learned about Medieval England and to make conclusions about the benefits of developing prior understandings before reading a book
MATERIALS	Avi's *Crispin: The Cross of Lead* (2002) and David Macaulay's *Castle* (1977) and *Cathedral: The Story of Its Construction* (1973), as well as various maps of England
GRADE LEVELS	Upper elementary and middle school (Grades 4–8)
BOOK SUMMARIES	*Crispin: The Cross of Lead*

BOOK SUMMARIES

Crispin: The Cross of Lead

- The 2003 Newbery Award winner, is set in fourteenth-century Medieval England.
- Crispin, the thirteen-year-old protagonist, is a poor orphan who must flee for his life after his mother dies and he is accused of a crime that he did not commit.
- An encounter with a juggler saves Crispin's life and makes it possible for Crispin to make discoveries about his own heritage and to make a life for himself.

Cathedral: The Story of Its Construction

- a 1972 Caldecott Honor Award
- presents detailed drawings that illustrate a medieval town, the workmen who are the builders, and the construction of the cathedral

Castle

- a 1978 Caldecott Honor Award
- presents detailed drawings of the construction of a castle and the surrounding town, complete with walls built for security

PROCEDURES	1. Introduce *Crispin* so that students understand the requirements for reading and understanding historical fiction. Ask the students

questions such as, "What is historical fiction?" And, "How is the word *historical* related to fiction?" Make sure students understand that the historical part of this genre means the setting is accurate for the time period and the characters' experiences, conflicts, and resolutions of the conflicts reflect what is known about the time period. Students should understand that although all of these elements need to be accurate for the time period, the word fiction means the details of the story did not actually happen even though it seems very believable. Ask the students to share examples of historical fiction they have read. Ask them to discuss what makes these books historical fiction. Make a list of their responses.

2. Introduce the setting of *Crispin* by showing and discussing a map of England. If you are using a current map, make sure students understand that the cities and towns shown on the map may not have been on a map of Medieval England.

3. To provide background information about Medieval England, ask students to investigate and share with the class some of the characteristics of this age. Examples might include: the work of peasants, the impact of the plague (also known as the Black Death), the social structure, the role of lords and rulers, the influence of the church, the levels of education and types of transportation, descriptions of jobs, and descriptions of villages and larger towns.

4. To provide background visualization for some of the buildings and jobs from this time period, show and discuss *Castle and Cathedral: The Story of Its Construction*. These books have detailed drawings showing various occupations, step-by-step processes of building, and floor plans.

5. Ask students to summarize what they know about Medieval England before they read *Crispin*.

6. As they read *Crispin*, ask students to verify the importance of developing prior knowledge before they read the book. Ask, "What prior knowledge helped you understand the book and the time period? Are there still gaps in your knowledge about Medieval England that would help you fully comprehend *Crispin*?"

7. This lesson plan can easily be the forerunner for a total unit on Medieval England. If this becomes a unit, students may use their answers to "Are there still subjects that you need to understand before fully comprehending *Crispin*?" to help develop the unit.

Mental Imagery

Having students visualize a setting, situation, or character is known as **mental imagery**. Mental imagery, also known as visualization or mental rehearsal, may be used to identify and clarify students' prior knowledge of a subject before they begin a study of the topic, to set the mood or to change the mood for a literature selection being read to the students, and to describe a setting or details related to a content area. Let us first consider how we could use mental imagery to identify and clarify prior knowledge about a category of literature. Try this experiment: close your eyes and imagine a scene as you say, "Once upon a time in a land far away." What do you visualize? Most of you will probably see a castle or dense woods. This visualization both places you in the land of folktales and helps you understand that you know both the time and place of a typical "once upon a time" setting in a folktale.

The National Reading Panel (2000) found that using mental imagery or visualizing a setting, situation, or character to develop understanding improved both students' memory and comprehension for what is read.

If you were doing this activity with younger students, you would know by their answers if the students have the prior knowledge about the setting and time of folktales. If they do not describe the possible settings for a folktale, then show and discuss illustrated versions of folktales. For example, there are numerous illustrated folktales, such as those adapted from the Brothers Grimm and Charles Perrault. It is easy to locate picture books that show settings such as castles, deep forests, and cottages in the woods.

When reading aloud to students, you can stop periodically and ask them to visualize a setting and a mood. Books that do not have illustrations encourage listeners to use their imaginations to visualize the details and the mood of a setting. For example, when reading Armstrong Sperry's *Call It Courage* (1940) to students in the middle grades, stop at places that show different moods, such as the description of the storm and Mafatu's reactions to the storm in Chapter Two: "All around him now was a world of tumbling water, gray in the hollow, greenish on the slopes. The wind tore off the combing crests and flung the spray at the sky. . . . So busy was Mafatu with the paddle that there was no time for thought" (p. 21).

Stop periodically and have students visualize and describe different settings and the moods created by the author, such as descriptions of the island and Mafatu's reactions (p. 54) and of course the final passage when Mafatu comes home and is greeted by his father (p. 115).

You may ask students how the use of mental imagery helped them to visualize both the settings and the moods developed by the author. How did this approach also help them understand the conflicts experienced by Mafatu and Mafatu's character?

Mental or visual imagery can be used with any age group and subject areas. Mental imagery also helps students comprehend and remember the details associated with various content fields. In geography, for example, students can use mental imagery to visualize various landforms such as canyons, mountains, prairies, and river valleys. In social studies, students might visualize the details associated with types of transportation found in various time periods. A timeline of cars from the earliest Model Ts to the most advanced racing cars produces interesting visual images. Art teachers frequently have students use mental imagery before they draw or paint a picture. Teachers of writing may use the technique to help students provide details for their writings or to expand their imaginations.

Reflect on Your Reading

As you read various literature selections or texts for content areas, try to identify ways that mental imagery could help you visualize the texts. How does this type of imagery increase your understanding and enjoyment of a subject? How does mental imagery increase comprehension?

Graphic Organizers

Graphic organizers include visual displays of information. **Graphic organizers** such as those found in semantic maps or webs, flowcharts, and time lines, are a means in which various terms and concepts are arranged to show their relationships to one another. The articles in the "Read All About It" section at the beginning of the chapter used graphic organizers to help readers comprehend the information in the science articles. The report of the National Reading Panel (2000) concludes that the use of visual or semantic organizers benefits the student in terms of better memory for what is read. Duke and Pearson (2002) report: "a visual display helps readers understand, organize, and remember . . . The text is verbal, abstract, and eminently forgettable; by contrast, the flowchart is visual, concrete, and arguably more memorable" (p. 218). The graphic organizers they recommend include semantic maps and flow charts. In addition, graphic organizers may be used with either narrative or expository text.

Semantic Maps

Semantic maps, also known as webbing, are the visual display of related concepts or vocabulary. These are among the most useful of the graphic organizers. They may be used to visually display concepts and vocabulary related to the concepts. They are equally effective when providing an outline for units or mapping the literary elements found in a book. Semantic maps are also useful for improving comprehension because they can be related to schema theory. While filling out the maps or webs, students are exploring their prior knowledge and, through discussions, filling in gaps in that knowledge.

DISPLAYING CONCEPTS THROUGH SEMANTIC MAPS   Creating semantic maps is easily related to concepts appropriate for lower elementary or upper elementary students. The activity can be used before reading about a subject in order to identify prior knowledge or it can be used to summarize information learned after reading an article or a book. The technique has the added advantage of being useful as a class or group activity, or as an individual assignment or strategy.

Figure 6.1 presents a semantic map or web for lower elementary grades that presents concepts associated with pets. To develop this semantic map related to pets, the teacher places the word *pets* in the center of the map or web. In this example, the students identified several examples of pets that are familiar to them. In this map, lower elementary students identified cats, dogs, and rabbits. Next, they brainstormed to list words and phrases that could describe the pets. Figure 6.1 shows a completed semantic map of concepts for lower elementary grades.

Semantic maps are excellent for developing concepts related to the science curriculum. A map may be developed to accompany a study of weather in the upper elementary grades. For example, the teacher can draw the map or web with storms in the center. Next, the words *thunderstorms, hail storms, lightning, tornado, hurricanes,* and *storm tracking* may be placed on the map. As a prereading activity to discover students' prior knowledge, the students could fill in as much information as they know about storms. After learning about storms during science class, the students could finish the map by adding any new information.

FIGURE 6.1

Semantic Map of Pets

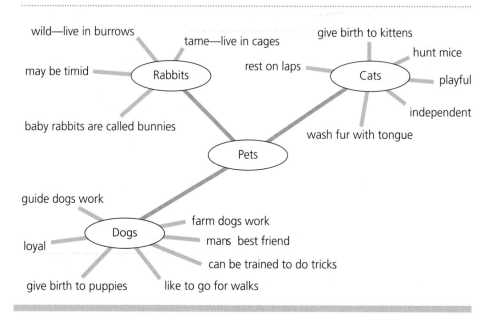

SEMANTIC MAPS RELATED TO DEVELOPING INTEREST IN A UNIT　Semantic mapping may be used with students in any grade level. It is an excellent way to brainstorm with students to allow them to identify areas of interest. As they identify a specific area of interest and read or listen to stories around that area, students can add information to the semantic map or show the information using other forms of graphic organizers.

The following unit (a unit extends over a longer period of time than an individual lesson plan), shows how this approach can be used with students in the lower elementary grades who are interested in reading and comparing "Little Red Riding Hood" variants from different cultures. This type of unit is popular with university students who are either planning to teach or who are teaching in the second through fourth grades. Notice that it uses both semantic mapping and charting.

FOCUS UNIT:
Comparing Variants of the "Little Red Riding Hood" Tale

OBJECTIVES　　1. To expand understanding of cultural contexts in folklore variants
　　　　　　　　2. To use a semantic map to foster interest in the unit

3. To use a chart to compare the elements in the "Little Red Riding Hood" tale found in the versions of Perrault and Lang (French), Grimm (German), and Chang and Young (Chinese)
4. To analyze the appropriateness of the illustrations for different versions of "Little Red Riding Hood"

MATERIALS	Locate as many variants of the "Little Red Riding Hood" tale as are available.
	The French versions are found in *Perrault's Complete Fairy Tales* (1961, 1982) and Andrew Lang's *The Red Fairy Book* (1960). A German version is Trina Schart Hyman's retelling of the Brothers Grimm's *Little Red Riding Hood* (1983). A Chinese version is Ed Young's *Lon Po Po: A Red-Riding Hood Story from China* (1989).

GRADE LEVELS	Second through fourth grades

PROCEDURES	1. Introduce this unit by explaining that students will be reading several different versions of a folktale. These versions are from different cultures and have different plots. Explain to the students that as they read or listen to these stories, they will be comparing the different versions of the tales according to specific events in the story. Place a semantic map on the board and encourage students to fill in the map with the questions they would like to investigate. Figure 6.2 is an example of what this map might contain; it was completed with the assistance of a group of third- and fourth-grade students.
	2. After students have brainstormed the information that they wish to investigate, place the major categories for comparison on a chart similar to the one in Table 6.1. Read each of the stories and ask students to discuss and then place the appropriate information from each story on the chart. Continue this activity until all the variants have been read and discussed. Table 6.1 illustrates some of the major similarities and differences and also includes some additional information discovered by the students.
	3. Discuss the similarities and differences found in the tales. Ask the students to look carefully at the illustrations in Trina Schart Hyman's and Ed Young's versions. Ask them to compare the moods of the stories and to suggest how these stories may reflect the content of the tales and the cultures from which they are told.

INDEPENDENT PROJECTS AND OTHER ACTIVITIES WITH THE UNIT	1. For creative drama (skits or plays) divide the class into smaller groups and have each group prepare one of the tales to share with the class.
	2. For a written personal response, ask the students to choose one of the variants of the folktales and describe their personal responses to the tale. Some students might choose to respond to the roles of the female characters in the different variants.

3. To respond to the folktales through music, encourage students to identify music that seems appropriate for the different moods created by the text and illustrations in the illustrated versions from Germany, France, and China. Ask groups of students to prepare dramatic readings in which they show the illustrations and accompany the reading with music.
4. This unit could be extended to additional comparisons of folktales such as "Cinderella."

FIGURE 6.2
Semantic Map of Questions to Investigate in "Little Red Riding Hood" Variants

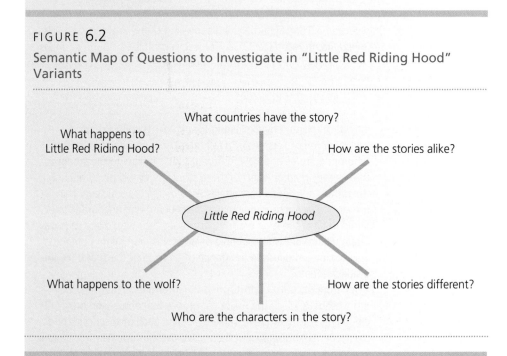

USING SEMANTIC MAPS TO PROVIDE INTEREST IN A UNIT IN THE UPPER GRADES A considerable amount of instructional time in grades four through eight, especially in social studies and history, includes developing studies of various cultures. These cultural studies frequently begin with semantic mapping of information known about a culture and extend to information that students want to investigate. One of the activities that has proven successful with these older students is to have them investigate the cultural values of a group as represented by the literature of the group, including folktales, myths, legends, poetry, and biographies and other nonfiction sources. Students then investigate the authenticity of these cultural values, identify stories that support those cultural values, and discuss how the cultural values are supported in the stories. The frameworks for the following semantic maps were developed with fifth- through eighth-grade students (Norton, 2005). The students used numerous examples of literature from the various cultures to complete the semantic maps.

TABLE 6.1

Chart Comparing Variants of "Little Red Riding Hood"

Variants	French (Perrault)	German (Grimm)	Chinese (Young)
What is taken to Grandmother?	Cake and pot of butter	Loaf of bread, butter, wine	(not told)
Where does Grandmother live?	"yonder by the mill"	In the woods by the big oak trees, near blackberry hedge	In the country
Who discovers Wolf's deception?	No one	Huntsman	Shang, the eldest Daughter
What happens to Little Red Riding Hood?	Wolf gobbled her up	Eaten and then jumps out of wolf when huntsman cuts wolf open	The three girls outwit the wolf
What happens to the wolf?	Eats Grandmother and Little Red Riding and escapes	He is killed by the huntsman who skins him and nails him to the door	Girls kill him
Moral stated	"From this story one learns that children, especially young lasses, pretty, courteous and well-bred, do very wrong to listen to strangers"	"I will never wander off the forest path again, as long as I live. I should have kept my promise to my mother"	None stated

An example of a semantic map that may be used to begin the research and the unit is shown in Figure 6.3. The group of students who developed the map began by studying Native American traditional values and used examples of authentic folktales, myths, and legends from the Blackfoot people. For this visual display they placed the culture to be studied in the center of the map. They identified information they wanted to investigate—in this case, values of the people, admired qualities respected by the people, qualities not respected by the culture, beliefs of the people, and history of the people as reflected in traditional tales.

Next, they identified the location of the Blackfoot people on a map. Michael J. Cadato and Joseph Bruchac's *Keepers of the Animals: Native American Stories and Wildlife Activities for Children* (1991) includes a map of the cultural areas and tribal locations of native North Americans. They chose the Blackfoot people because there is considerable literature written about the people and the group wanted to know more about Native Americans who lived on the Great Plains.

Next, they searched the library for sources of folktales, myths, and legends written about or by Native Americans. The following titles were of special interest in a search for Native American traditional cultural values sources (Blackfoot–Great Plains):

Olaf Baker's *Where the Buffaloes Begin* (1981)

Paul Goble's *Beyond the Ridge* (1989), *Buffalo Woman* (1984), *The Dream Wolf* (1990), *The Girl Who Loved Wild Horses* (1978), *The Gift of the Sacred*

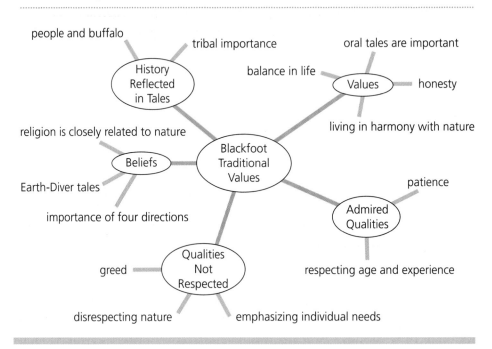

FIGURE 6.3

Semantic Map of Native American Traditional Values

Dog (1980), *Iktomi and the Boulder: A Plains Indian Story* (1988), *Iktomi and the Berries* (1989)

Jennifer Berry Jones's *Heetunka's Harvest: A Tale of the Plains Indians* (1994)

As the students read the books, they completed the semantic map by filling in the various categories. They supported their placements by placing titles of stories that reflected the various values on the semantic map. After reading one of the books together and discussing the values reflected in the books, students read additional books either in smaller groups or individually. Again, they discussed their findings and placed them on the semantic map. One of the activities that heightened comprehension was the need for students to support each of their findings through oral presentation.

The students extended this unit about Native American Traditional Values by reading biographies, autobiographies, and other nonfiction sources to discover if the traditional Native American values were also found in other types of literature. Students discovered that many of the traditional values were still respected by the people.

This approach may be used with the search for traditional cultural values with other groups. The following books were valuable in the search for African traditional values:

Verna Aardema's *Anansi Does the Impossible: An Ashanti Tale* (1997), *Bringing the Rain to Kapiti Plain: A Nandi Tale* (1981), *Misoso: Once Upon a Time Tales from Africa* (1994), *This for That: A Tonga Tale* (1997)

Brent Ashabranner and Russell Davis's *The Lion's Whiskers and Other Ethiopian Tales* (1996)

Ashley Bryan's *Beat the Story-Drum, Pum—Pum* (1980)

T. Obinkaram Echewa's *The Magic Tree: A Folktale from Nigeria* (1999)

Tony Fairman's *Bury My Bones But Keep My Words: African Tales for Retelling* (1993)

The following books were valuable when developing a unit on Mayan traditional cultural values:

Rudolfo Anaya's *Maya's Children: The Story of La Llorano* (1997)

John Bierhorst's *The Monkey's Haircut and Other Stories Told by the Maya* (1986)

Jane Anne Volkmer's *Song of Chirimia—A Guatemalan Folktale* (1990)

You can extend these cultural values to webs that include Aztec, Mexican, and South American cultural values.

Improving Comprehension through Time Lines

The newspaper article at the beginning of this chapter used time lines to effectively show changes in history. Authors who write about improving comprehension in the content areas frequently emphasize these visual adaptations. For example, Zemelman, Daniels, and Hyde (1998) identify techniques for improving reading comprehension such as providing students with structural help while they read and teaching reading comprehension as a thinking process. One way to teach students to respond to the structure of a text is to have them develop time lines that help them visualize a person's life. Most biographies use a structure that follows the life of the biographical character. This chronological order provides a perfect source for developing time lines that emphasize important dates in a character's life. For this type of activity to be used with students in grades four through eight, choose carefully written biographies such as Russell Freedman's: *Franklin Delano Roosevelt* (1990), *Eleanor Roosevelt: A Life of Discovery* (1993), *Lincoln: A Photobiography* (1987), *Out of Darkness: The Story of Louis Braille* (1997), and *The Wright Brothers: How They Invented the Airplane* (1992). Other excellent biographies may be chosen from works by Jean Fritz: *Bully for You, Teddy Roosevelt!* (1991), *The Great Little Madison* (1989), and *Make Way for Sam Houston* (1986); Albert Marrin's *Old Hickory: Andrew Jackson and the American People* (2004), or Marilyn Nelson's *A Wreath for Emmett Till* (2005). For younger students in grades two and up, you could create time lines for *Franklin and Eleanor* (2004) by Cheryl Harness, *Rosa* (2005), by Nikk Giovanni, *Young Thomas Edison* (2006), by Michael Dooling, and *Theodore* (2006) by Frank Keating.

Reflect on Your Reading

Consider the graphic organizers discussed in this section: semantic maps and time lines. How might these graphic organizers help you comprehend information presented in your own course work? What could you include on a semantic map that would help you remember the content presented in this chapter? How could you use time lines to help you comprehend information you read about in a history text? How might you use a time line to show important dates in your life?

LESSON PLAN:

Developing a Time Line from Russell Freedman's Franklin Delano Roosevelt

OBJECTIVES	1. To develop an understanding that biographies frequently follow the life of a real person through a chronological order of the person's life
	2. To develop a graphic depiction through a timeline of Roosevelt's life
	3. To discuss the importance of the events in the timeline and to consider how these events might have influenced Roosevelt's actions when he was president of the United States
	4. To compare a time line of Franklin Roosevelt with one drawn after reading Freedman's *Eleanor Roosevelt: The Life of Discovery*
MATERIALS	Russell Freedman's *Franklin Delano Roosevelt* (1990) and *Eleanor Roosevelt: A Life of Discovery* (1993)
BOOK SUMMARIES	*Franklin Delano Roosevelt*
	■ a biography of the man who was president of the United States from 1933 to 1945
	■ proceeds from his birth in 1882 to his death in 1945
	Eleanor Roosevelt: A Life of Discovery
	■ a biography of the wife of the president
	■ includes many of her own accomplishments, such as becoming an American delegate to the United Nations
PROCEDURES	1. To apply the information gained from schema theory, it is important to review prior knowledge or present new information about how to identify and evaluate a biography such as the following criteria for evaluation: the author develops the life of a real person; the details including dates, places, and names of other people should be accurate; the settings must be actual places and accurate for the time period; the characters should reflect several sides of the person; the plot and conflict must actually have happened; and the author should list the primary sources used to obtain the information.
	2. To apply the information gained from schema theory, it is important to review prior knowledge or introduce new information about the time period for Franklin Delano Roosevelt, 1882–1945, and the historical significance of his life as president during the Depression and World War II. Ask the students, "Why is it necessary that the setting and conflict for this book include historically accurate information? What might happen to the biography if setting and conflict are not accurate? What are some ways that we

can authenticate the accuracy of the details in the biography?" Students frequently suggest that a biography contains numerous dates and occurrences that can be verified through library research. Students might suggest that drawing a time line that includes specific dates and events would help them identify the important historical happenings in a person's life.

3. Ask the students to look briefly at the text and the photographs in *Franklin Delano Roosevelt*. Ask questions such as, "Do you notice dates, happenings, and locations that can be verified? And, do you think the book would be an easy book to verify? Why or why not?" Make sure the students understand that the historical background for this book covers two of the most dynamic occurrences in American life: the Great Depression and World War II. They also should understand that information about these time periods and Roosevelt's actions during those periods are found in numerous nonfiction sources.

4. As students read this book, have them individually or in groups develop time lines of the most important occurrences in Roosevelt's life. Have each group draw time lines for the whole book or ask students to draw time lines for specific chapters. The time line in Figure 6.4 was drawn by a group of seventh-grade students.

FIGURE 6.4

A Time Line of Roosevelt's Life

1882 ● Born, Hyde Park, New York

1900 ● Majored in history and government at Harvard

1905 ● Entered Columbia Law School
Married Eleanor Roosevelt

1910 ● New York State Senate

1913 ● Assistant Secretary of Navy, W.W.II

1921 ● Victim of polio

1929 ● Governor of New York during stock market crash and Depression

1933 ● Took office as President of the United States

1933 ● First radio report to American people—Fireside Chat

1940 ● First peace-time draft

1941 ● Declaration of War with Japan after Pearl Harbor. War declared with Germany

1945 ● Died, Warm Springs, Georgia

5. After the students draw the time lines, have them share these important historical happenings with the class. Ask them to state why they chose certain times and occurrences. Have the students compare their time lines.

6. Ask students to verify the accuracy of these dates and occurrences through library research. They may use sources such as history books, other biographies about Roosevelt, and newspaper and magazine stories about the time period. They might find it valuable to interview people who lived during this time period or read interviews about people who lived during the time period.

7. Have students consider how the various experiences in Roosevelt's life would have influenced him as president of the United States.

8. After students have completed this analysis using a timeline, ask them to evaluate Russell Freedman's ability to create an accurate biography that includes authentic historical and geographical settings as well as personal occurrences in Roosevelt's life.

9. An interesting comparative activity may be developed by reading about and creating a time line of Eleanor Roosevelt's life. What are the similarities in the time lines? How did Freedman develop a biography to show that Eleanor Roosevelt was a person of substance in her own right and not just the wife of the president?

10. Ask students to evaluate the effectiveness of using time lines to help them understand and comprehend a biography. What are the advantages in developing a time line? What are the limitations or difficulties?

Using Modeling Techniques

Modeling, a technique in which an adult describes his or her thought processes when reading a text, is one of the most effective ways to improve students' comprehension. Laura Roehler and Gerald Duffy (1984) have developed modeling approaches that place an adult in an active role with students and that show the adult's thought processing to the students. Dole, Duffy, Roehler, and Pearson (1991) found that modeling is one of the most effective ways to improve comprehension. This approach has been used to help students understand such literary elements as characterization, author's style, and theme (Norton 1992, 2003). This approach has been demonstrated with students ranging from kindergarten through college and graduate school.

In this section we will show how modeling can be used to improve comprehension of author's style to students in the lower elementary grades. A second example will demonstrate teaching comprehension of characterization to students in the upper grades. The basic concepts of this modeling approach are:

1. When planning the lesson, the teacher must determine: What are the requirements for effective reasoning so students will understand the story or the use of the literary element? Using schema theory, what prior knowledge will need to be reviewed or what knowledge gaps will need to be filled? This prior knowledge may refer to both literary elements such as characterization, setting, conflict, and theme,

and to an understanding of genres of literature such as historical fiction, biography, and poetry. Effective reasoning may require that students understand the time and place for a story or the characteristics of a genre.

2. Provide an introduction to inferencing, which means going beyond information the author provides and hypothesizing about main ideas, so that students understand that they will be using clues stated in the story to answer questions that are not stated in the story but are only implied by the author. Ask students to explain why it is important for comprehension to be able to make inferences about what they read. Explain to students that they will be involved in an approach that proceeds from a text example read orally to them, to a question that results from the text example, to an answer to the question, to an exploration about the evidence that produced the answer, and finally to the thought processes that they used to reach the answer. Explain to the students that you will model this procedure with text, question, answer, evidence, and reasoning until you are sure that they understand the process. At that point the students will enter into the process by answering questions, providing evidence, and expressing their reasoning.

3. Develop an introduction to the story or to the genre of literature. This introduction may focus on the type of literature, such as poetry or biography; the literary element, such as simile or characterization; or the setting for the story, such as 1700s America.

4. Develop the series of text, questions, answers, evidence, and reasoning. (Five examples will ensure that all students understand the process.)

5. Develop a conclusion that allows students to state what they have learned and to consider what they would still like to learn about the topic.

Reflect on Your Reading

Think about a book that you would like to use in a classroom with children. What aspect of the book would you need to model? How would your modeling help a child's comprehension of the book and, specifically, of the various literary elements of the story?

LESSON PLAN:
Modeling Similes
with Lower Elementary Students

OBJECTIVES
1. To be involved in a modeling activity designed to show students how to analyze evidence from the text and to speculate about the meanings of similes
2. To understand the requirements for effective reasoning when thinking about similes
3. To appreciate and understand the author's use of similes
4. To identify and illustrate similes that have meaning in the students' lives

---

GRADE LEVELS   Early elementary: Kindergarten through third grade

MATERIALS	Leo Lionni's *Swimmy* (1963) and Hugh Lewin's *Jafta* (1983)
BOOK SUMMARIES	*Swimmy* is a picture story book about a group of fish and how they are saved from a predator by the intelligent actions of Swimmy. *Jafta* is a picture story book in which the illustrator develops comparisons between Jafta's actions and those of the animals in South Africa.

PROCEDURES	1. This lesson on similes follows the instructional sequences in a modeling lesson:
	  a. the teacher identifies the requirements for effective reasoning
	  b. the teacher develops an introduction to similes
	  c. the teacher identifies the importance of similes to the students
	  d. the teacher introduces the story
	  e. the teacher proceeds with the modeling examples and brings the students into the thought processes and discussions.
	
	2. Identify the requirements for effective reasoning so that the lesson helps students understand those requirements. For example, effective understanding of similes requires students to
	  a. go beyond information authors provide in the text
	  b. know that similes are comparisons that authors make between something in the text and something that is not in the text
	  c. know that similes are introduced with the clue words *like* and *as,*
	  d. know that authors use similes to develop more vivid descriptions and characterizations
	  e. think about how one object is like another object.
	
	3. Develop an introduction to similes that either reviews previous knowledge or fills in the gaps for students who do not understand similes. For example, tell students
	
	    some authors use a special kind of writing called figurative language. This kind of language allows authors to use fewer words but to write more vividly. Similes are a kind of figurative language in which an author compares one thing to another thing. Today we will be listening for ways that authors use similes to make us see pictures in our minds.
	
	  You may use *Jafta* as an illustrated example of similes. Encourage students to provide their own examples of similes.
	4. Explain to the students that in this modeling activity they will listen as you read portions of a story, ask a question about a simile, answer the question, provide evidence or clues from the story that tell why you gave that answer, share how you thought about the story and the simile to reach the answer. As part of the introduction, discuss the meanings of evidence and reasoning.

5. Develop an introduction to the story that places students in a setting for a little fish who lives at the bottom of the sea. You might use the comprehension technique of imagery by asking students to close their eyes and imagine that they are a small fish swimming around in a large ocean.

6. Provide the first modeling example. For this lesson do not show the illustrations before you read the book. You want students to use the similes, not the illustrations, to work through the process. Read orally through page 1. Ask students, "What does Swimmy look like?" Answer the question: "Swimmy is shiny and deep black." Provide the evidence: "The author used the simile clue *as*. The author says that only one of the fish is "as black as a mussel shell." Provide your reasoning to reach the answer. You could say, for example,

> I know that the author is telling me to think about more infor-mation because I saw a simile. I know the comparison is be-tween Swimmy's color and a black mussel shell. I know from my own experience that there are many shades of black. Also, I know from seeing a mussel shell in water at the beach that it is dark black and shiny. If I close my eyes I can see a small, black, shiny fish swimming among many other fish who are black.

Now share the picture and compare the students' visualizations with the actual illustrations.

7. Provide the second modeling example, but first make sure the students understand the procedure. If they do not, model another example completely. If students understand the process, let them join the discussion by providing an answer, the evidence, and the reasoning. Read pages 4 through 10. Stop after "a lobster, who walked about like a water-moving machine." Ask students, "How does the lobster move?" Ask students to provide answers, evi-dence, and reasoning to reach the answer.

8. Continue this process. Examples of questions and text include:

> Pages 11 through 17: "What do the sea anemones look like?"

> Page 18: "What does Swimmy see? Why is this important to the story? How is this school different from Swimmy's school?"

> Read through the end of the text. Ask, "What was Swimmy's plan? What messages is the author telling us?"

> Even the youngest students understand that the messages are: "it is important to work together, it is important to have a plan, and being different is not bad."

> Finally, reread the story and let students enjoy the similes and their new comprehension of the story.

9. Conclude the lesson by having students discuss what they have learned about similes. They can also create their own similes.

LESSON PLAN:
Modeling Inferencing Characterization with Students in the Upper Grades

Before beginning the lesson, review the general guidelines for modeling described in the previous modeling lesson.

OBJECTIVES

1. To develop an understanding of the requirements for effective reasoning
2. To be involved in a modeling activity designed to show students how to analyze evidence from the text and to speculate about characters
3. To appreciate and understand an author's use of inferences when developing characterization

GRADE LEVELS Middle through upper elementary and middle school (Grades 4–8)

MATERIALS Jean Fritz's *The Great Little Madison* (1989) and Alice Provensen's *The Buck Stops Here: The Presidents of the United States* (1990)

BOOK SUMMARIES

The Great Little Madison

■ a biography of the fourth president of the United States
■ lived from 1751–1836
■ played a major role in the Continental Congress

The Buck Stops Here: The Presidents of the United States

■ a highly illustrated informational book
■ shows the contributions of the various presidents including James Madison

PROCEDURES

1. Review the requirements for effective reasoning especially for inferring characterization. Develop an introduction to characterization that encourages students to review what they know about how authors develop characterization: narrative, thoughts of others about the character, thoughts of the character, character's actions, and dialogue. Ask students to share examples of how authors develop three-dimensional, believable characters. They can share their favorite characters and describe how the authors created memorable characters.

2. Develop an introduction to the biography, *The Great Little Madison.* Students should understand that a biography is written about a person who actually lived and the story should be authentic for time, place, and characters. Provide some background information about Madison's time period, 1751–1836, and the role he played in both the Continental Congress and as the fourth president of

the United States. Share maps with the students to show them the locations of the original Colonies. Also share illustrations that depict the historical setting of the United States during Madison's lifetime. The highly illustrated *The Buck Stops Here: The Presidents of the United States* can be used to introduce students to the accomplishments of the previous presidents and to the contributions of the fourth president, James Madison.

3. You may also share Fritz's philosophy about writing a biography found in her article, "Biography: Readability Plus Responsibility" (1988). Ask students to hypothesize about how her philosophy will influence her writing.

4. Review the modeling process that you will use that begins with an excerpt from the text, a question, an answer to the question, the evidence for the answer, and the reasoning used to answer the question. Explain to the students that this modeling activity will focus on the first two chapters of *The Great Little Madison*.

5. Provide the first modeling example. Read from the beginning of the book on page 7–8. Ask, "What does Fritz tell us about Madison's character from the references to his father's library and the listing of some of these books?" Provide the answer, your evidence, and your thought processes to reason out the answer.

6. Provide the second modeling example. At this point, verify that the students understand the procedure. If they do not, model another example completely. When the students understand the process, let them join the discussion by providing an answer, the evidence, and the reasoning. It is advisable to ask the students to jot down brief answers to the questions, evidence, and reasoning. These notes will increase the quality of the discussion that follows each question.

7. Logical places for questions and discussions: Read to end of next paragraph on page 9. Ask, "What can we infer about James Madison from the courses and subjects that he studied in school? What do we know about Madison's attitude toward his education?" Allow students to answer and provide evidence and their reasoning.

8. Continue reading chapters 1 and 2 and ask questions about implied characterization: For example, pages 10 and 11 describe Madison's reactions to Princeton, the types of learning and even the pranks that excited him, and the affairs of the country that interested him.

9. Ask students to summarize what they have learned from reading and analyzing characterization in chapters 1 and 2. Students can search for additional evidence of Madison's characterization as they complete the book. They can trace the development of characterization through various incidents that happen to him throughout his life. Students can consider, "How does Madison change as he grows older and acquires additional experiences and obligations? Are any actions and beliefs consistent throughout his life? If so, what are they?"

Using Questioning Strategies

Questioning strategies are well-known techniques within reading programs. Critics of comprehension instruction believe that questions on tests, especially, and in daily lessons too often encourage students to respond at the lowest levels of the thought process. A taxonomy of comprehension can be used to develop or to evaluate questions that can accompany any part of the curriculum. Reading methods students divided into groups and used Barrett's Taxonomy of Comprehension (1972) to write questions that could accompany Beverly Cleary's *Dear Mr. Henshaw* (1983). The purpose of the task was to not only understand the various comprehension questions, but also to develop an understanding about how the questions could be used with a selection of literature that was being read by elementary students.

The following series of questions illustrate how questioning strategies can be developed around Barrett's four levels of reading comprehension: literal recognition of recall, inference, evaluation, and appreciation. The questions listed exemplify each level on the taxonomy. Depending on the book and the instructional purpose, you might want to develop more or fewer questions. The college students provided numerous questions because they were exploring the various types of questions they could develop. (It is not necessary to use all of these questions when discussing a book.)

Literal Recognition   *recall*

Literal recognition requires students to identify information provided in the literature. Teachers can require students to recall the information from memory after reading or listening to a story, or to locate the information while reading a selection. Literal-level questions such as the following often include the words *who, what, when, where,* and *why:*

1. Recall of details: How old was Leigh Botts when he first wrote to Mr. Henshaw? What is the name of Leigh's dog? What is Leigh's father's occupation? Where does the story *Dear Mr. Henshaw* take place?

2. Recall of sequence of events: What was the sequence of events that caused Leigh to place an alarm on his lunch box? What was the sequence of events that caused Leigh to write to Mr. Henshaw and to write in his diary?

3. Recall of comparisons: Compare the way that Leigh thought of his mother and the way he thought of his father.

4. Recall of character traits: Describe Leigh's response to Mr. Henshaw when Mr. Henshaw asks Leigh to answer 10 questions about himself.

Inference

When students infer an answer to a question, they go beyond the information the author provides and hypothesize about such things as details, main ideas, sequence of events that might have led to an occurrence, and cause-and-effect relationships.

Inference is usually considered a higher-level thought process; the answers are not specifically stated within the text. Examples of inferential questions include the following:

1. Inferring supporting details: At the end of the book, Leigh says that he "felt sad and a whole lot better at the same time." What do you think he meant by this statement?

2. Inferring main idea: What do you believe is the theme of the book? What message do you think the author is trying to express to the reader?

3. Inferring comparisons: Think about the two most important characters in Leigh's life—his mother and his father. How are they are alike and how are they different? Compare Leigh at the beginning of the book when he is writing to Mr. Henshaw with Leigh at the end of the book when he is writing in his diary and writing true stories for school.

4. Inferring cause-and-effect relationships: If you identify any changes in Leigh, what do you believe might have caused those changes?

5. Inferring character traits: On page 73 Leigh decides that he cannot hate his father anymore. What does this tell us about Leigh and about his father? Why do you think Leigh's father sent him twenty dollars?

6. Inferring outcomes: At one point in the story, Leigh wishes that his mother and father would get back together. What do you think would have happened to the story if they had? How would Leigh's life have changed? How would his mother's life have changed? What might have been the outcome of the writing contest at school if Leigh had not had the advantages of his advice from Mr. Henshaw?

Evaluation

Evaluation questions require students to make judgments about the content of the selection by comparing it with *external criteria*, such as what authorities say about a subject or *internal criteria*, such as the reader's own experience or knowledge. The following are examples of evaluative questions:

1. Judgment of adequacy or validity: Do you believe that an author would take time to write to a child and take such an interest in him? Why or why not?

2. Judgment of appropriateness: Do you believe that Leigh's story, "A Day on Dad's Rig" was a good story for the Young Writers' Yearbook? Why or why not?

3. Judgment of worth, desirability, or acceptability: Do you believe that Leigh had the right to feel the way he did toward his father? Why or why not? Do you believe that Leigh was right in his judgment that his father did not spend enough time with him? Why or why not? Was Leigh's mother's judgment correct at the end of the book? What would you have done?

Appreciation

Appreciation of literature requires a heightening of sensitivity to the techniques the authors use to evoke an emotional response from their readers. Questions can encourage students to respond emotionally to the plot, identify with the characters, react to the author's use of language, and react to an author's ability to create a visual image through the choice of words in the text. The following are examples of questions that stimulate appreciation:

1. Emotional response to plot or theme: How did you respond to the plot of *Dear Mr. Henshaw?* Did the author hold your attention? If so, how? Do you believe the theme of the story was worthwhile? Why or why not? Pretend you are either recommending this book to someone else or recommending that this book not be read; what would you tell that person?

2. Identification with characters and incidents: Have you ever felt or known anyone who felt like Leigh? What caused you or the person to feel that way? How would you have reacted to the theft of an excellent lunch?

3. Imagery: How did the author encourage you to see Leigh's home, his neighborhood, and his school? Close your eyes and try to describe your neighborhood or town. How would you describe it so that someone else could "see" it?

Questioning Strategies to Use While Reading

Educators emphasize the importance of teaching students to use specific strategies before, during, and after they read. For example, Jay McTighe and Frank T. Lyman Jr. (2001) state that good readers "concentrate on their purpose for reading, monitor their comprehension, and adjust their approach when necessary. Poor readers, on the other hand, are less mindful of such effective strategies. In fact, they tend to perceive reading as 'decoding' rather than as the construction of meaning" (p. 386). Consequently, while they are in the process of reading, good readers

- tell themselves what the author is saying
- ask themselves if what they are reading makes sense
- picture what the author describes
- identify the main ideas
- predict what will happen next

If they do not comprehend the material, good readers

- try to identify the problem
- remind themselves what it is they want to find out
- look back and ahead in the material
- slow down
- ask for help

After they read, good readers

- retell what they have read using their own words
- summarize the most important details and ideas

TABLE 6.2

Possible Activities in a Scaffolded Reading Experience

Prereading	During Reading	Postreading
Relating the reading to students' lives	Silent reading	Questioning
Motivating	Reading to students	Discussion
Activating and building background knowledge	Supported Reading	Writing
Pre-teaching vocabulary	Oral reading by students	Drama
Pre-teaching concepts	Modifying the text	Artistic and nonverbal activities
Pre-questioning, predicting, and direction setting		Application and outreach activities
Suggesting strategies		Building connections
		Re-teaching

Source: From Clark, Kathleen F., & Graves, Michael F. (2005, March). Scaffolding students' comprehension of text. *The Reading Teacher, 58*(6), 570–580.

- ask themselves questions and answer their own questions
- picture in their minds what the author has described
- decide what in the material was especially interesting or was enjoyable

As you can see from these reading strategies, good readers use many of the strategies we have discussed. They visualize, they ask questions, they summarize their reading, and when necessary they ask for help. Many students, however, will not use these effective strategies unless they have many opportunities to discover that the strategies do, indeed, help them comprehend the materials.

Kathleen F. Clark and Michael F. Graves (2005) expand on the previous list of what good readers do by describing some of the activities that teachers can use to help students comprehend their materials. They discuss the importance of scaffolding, using strategies that research studies support so that they can accomplish the reading requirements. *Scaffolding* for comprehension includes activities such as modeling, guided practice, and application of the comprehension strategies. As shown in Table 6.2, they divide their activities among "Pre-reading, During Reading, and Post-reading." Also, notice the importance they place on developing background knowledge and using questioning strategies.

Figure 6.5 illustrates how Clark and Graves (2005) use these scaffolded reading activities when teaching comprehension skills with a selection of literature, *The Story of Ruby Bridges* (Cole, 1995).

Reflect on Your Reading

Read and evaluate the questioning strategies listed in the previous sections. How would the use of these questions develop a more in-depth discussion of the book?

FIGURE 6.5

Scaffolded Reading Experience Activities for *The Story of Ruby Bridges* (Coles, 1995)

Activities in regular type are for students who will find the book relatively easy; those in **bold italic** are additional or alternative activities for students who will find the book more of a challenge.

Prereading	Motivating
	Building background knowledge
	Building text-specific knowledge
	Direction setting
During reading	***Reading to students***
	Silent reading
Postreading	Questioning and small-group discussion
	Writing
	Working with art

Prereading

- Motivate students by encouraging them to talk about problems they have encountered and how they solved them. They might also talk about some of the obstacles they encountered and what kept them going.
- Build relevant background knowledge by asking students to think about books they have read in which the characters faced a challenge they thought was difficult or impossible but were able to triumph in the end. Then, have students talk about the problems the characters encountered and how they overcame them. If necessary, you can share a few books that exemplify this theme.
- ***Build text-specific knowledge*** for students who need more assistance by previewing the biography. Begin by explaining what a bibliography is, emphasizing that this is a true story about something that happened to a real person. Introduce the setting, the main characters, and enough of the story line to whet students' appetite for the biography.
- ***Direction setting*** for stronger readers might consist of simply telling students to look for the challenges Ruby faces and how she handles them. ***Direction setting*** for less skilled readers might consist of asking them to look for one problem Ruby faces and her solution to that problem.

During reading

- ***Reading some of the story aloud*** can get less skilled readers off to a good start and leave them with a manageable amount of reading to do.
- Silent reading is appropriate for students who can successfully read the book on their own.

Postreading

- Answering questions that get at the essence of the biography in small groups will give all students an opportunity to review the book's important events and issues.
- Writing gives students an opportunity to solidify their understanding of the biography or to respond to it. You will probably want to suggest some topics—tell about the most challenging problem Ruby faced, tell what you admire most about Ruby, or tell how you would have reacted in Ruby's place.
- ***Working with art*** gives students who struggle with writing another way to solidify their understanding of the story or respond to it. Students might draw pictures illustrating significant events in the biography or make collages suggesting their responses to significant events. Of course, artistic activities are often appropriate alternatives for good writers, too.

Source: Figure from Clark, Kathleen F., & Graves, Michael F. (2005, March). Scaffolding students' comprehension of text. *The Reading Teacher,* 58(6), 570–580.

Predicting Outcomes to Improve Comprehension

Good readers use cues in the text and their own prior knowledge to make predictions. Appropriate texts for this type of approach can be in the form of predictable books in which story structures, repetitive phrases, language style, various literary devices, and illustrations encourage students to predict what will happen next. Stories such as "The Three Billy Goats Gruff" have predictable story structures and plot developments that encourage students to predict what will happen next and therefore improve comprehension of the text.

Books that use repetitive language help younger children predict the story and encourage them to join in the story. Michael Rosen's *We're Going on a Bear Hunt* (1989) includes considerable repetitive language that encourages students to predict the next lines. Some books require prior knowledge of the alphabet to predict what happens next. Books such as Chris Van Allsburg's *The Z Was Zapped* (1987) encourage students to predict the line that will follow each illustration.

Some texts are written in the form of questions or are presented in such a way that teachers can stop and ask students to predict what might happen. Jonathan Shipton's *What If?* (1999), for example, begins with the question, "What if it stopped raining and you went outside, and down at the end of the garden you found . . ." (p. 1, unnumbered). Both the text and the illustrations continue with this "What if?" motif.

Many books written for older students lend themselves to predictions. These books may also motivate writing as students respond to the challenge of predicting what might happen next. For example, Louis Sachar's *Holes* (1998, 1999 Newbery Award) is a very popular book. Before students read the book, they can listen to or read Chapter 1, in which Sachar briefly describes the setting for Camp Green Lake, and the very brief Chapter 2, in which Stanley Yelnats is given a choice: "The judge said, 'You may go to jail, or you may go to Camp Green Lake.'" Students can make predictions about Camp Green Lake and what could happen to Stanley while he is there. When using the technique of predicting outcomes, ask students to write down their predictions and then compare their predictions with what happens in the book or story.

Some authors write their books in such a way that the writing style encourages making predictions. Students can be taught to look for writing styles that encourage them to stop and predict what will happen next. Lloyd Alexander concludes each chapter in *The Remarkable Journey of Prince Jen* (1991), for example, with comments and questions that ask readers to predict what will happen next. Students may also make up their own questions they would like to ask at the end of selections. When they read, they can decide if their questions were answered.

Other books lend themselves to predicting what will happen next in a character's life. For these, students can write a sequel experience to that presented in the book. After reading Karen Cushman's *The Midwife's Apprentice* (1995, 1996 Newbery Award), for example, they may predict what happens to the poor girl in the story after they read this quote at the end of the book:

> Jane Sharp! It is I, Alyce, your apprentice. I have come back. And if you do
> not let me in, I will try again and again. I can do what you tell me and take

what you give me, and I know how to try and risk and fail and try again and not give up. I will not go away!' The door opened. Alyce went in. And the cat went with her. (p. 116)

Writing a sequel is especially good for writing and predicting because the students need to use the knowledge they gained from reading the book before they can respond in a meaningful way. They need to make use of information about setting, especially time period, characterizations, and conflicts that will probably influence a sequel to the book.

Newspaper articles are also good choices for teaching older students reading, research, and predicting skills. The consequences of global warming, for example, are reported and debated in many newspaper articles. Students who are interested in science most likely already have an understanding of global warming and may have background knowledge related to the possible consequences of global warming. They can read these articles, use the data provided, and predict what they believe will happen in the future. Will environmentalists or industrialists win the battle? Why? For example, one newspaper headline reads: "As Polar Ice Turns to Water, Dreams of Treasure Abound" (Krauss, et al., 10 October, 2005). This is the type of article that combines map reading and reading to analyze the political, environmental, and scientific consequences of changes in the environment. The article discusses the impact of melting ice on shortening ocean transportation because of newly opened sea

Up for Discussion

What are the most important components for developing a fluent reader? Can a student become a fluent reader without enjoying reading? Or, are fluency and a love of reading interchangeable? If a child successfully passes reading tests, but does not read for enjoyment or to gain information, is he or she a fluent reader? If a child does not continue to read as an adult, will the adult remain a fluent reader?

Advocates of the various models of the reading process and approaches to reading instruction discussed in Chapter 1 disagree about what is fluency and how it should be developed. Some educators believe it is more important to sound out words, while others believe that understanding word meaning is the primary purpose of fluency. Most educators, however, agree that all students acquire fluency as a result of extensive reading.

Independent, silent reading improves fluency and enjoyment of reading in all ages.

A study reported in *Reading Today* (August–September 2005) reveals that the "Harry Potter" series has had a major impact on literacy and reading habits in Great Britain. The study shows that 84 percent of teachers reported that the Harry Potter books helped improve students' literacy and 67 percent of teachers reported that the series turned nonreaders into readers. Why did the series have such a strong impact on students? How does this relate to students' fluency?

Source: "It's Official: Potter Helps." (August-September 2005). *Reading Today*, 23, 26.

routes between cities such as Tokyo and London from 15,000 miles to 8,500 miles, the exploration for oil and gas in territories that may be uncovered, and the resulting conflicts between the countries that are now interested in the newly exposed territory. By reading the article and exploring the visuals students can make predictions about the consequences for the earth. They can consider questions such as: What is the impact for transportation costs and for world trade if transportation time can be cut in half? What will happen if the United States, Russia, Canada, and Finland all seek ownership of the emerging land and want to develop the oil and gas fields? And, they can make predictions about what they believe will happen and then follow the news to discover how closely their predictions come true. They can also search for other articles on similar topics such as Andrew C. Revkin's "Climate Data Hint at Irreversible Rise in Seas" (24 March, 2006). Now they can compare the articles and decide if their predictions are supported by the information in and the conclusions reached by the findings expressed in this article.

> **Reflect on Your Reading**
>
> Think of a book that you have read recently. Were there clues that made the next chapter, a character, a conflict, the resolution of a conflict, the book's ending, or the book as a whole predictable?

Developing Fluency in Reading

The goal of reading instruction is to develop the ability to read fluently with rapid word recognition and comprehension. Richard Venezky (2003) states that fluency requires automatic word attack and understanding of meaning. This word recognition needs to be completed rapidly if the reader is to achieve higher levels of comprehen-

A teacher uses a story web to help students comprehend the literary elements in a story.

sion. Venezky believes that educators should not debate the teaching of word attack skills but should teach students how to build up rapid word recognition that is automatic.

S. Jay Samuels (1994) emphasizes that fluent readers have mastered each of the sub-skills of reading so that reading is automatic. Samuels identifies several principles that help students automatically make connections between sound-symbol relationships and meaning:

1. Practice in reading leads to automaticity and fluency.

2. This practice includes recognizing the sounds of the letters and spelling patterns.

3. Repetition of words leads to automaticity and fluency.

4. Organizing words into phrases helps students break word-by-word reading.

5. When encouraging grouping of words and phrases, we may need to place less emphasis on a child's oral reading that demands total accuracy.

6. Practice results in higher fluency when the material to be read is meaningful to the students.

7. Fluent readers do not separate reading into skills but perceive the reading process more wholistically.

Two types of reading are frequently mentioned when improving students' fluency in reading: guided repeated oral reading and independent silent reading.

Guided Repeated Oral Reading

Repeated reading requires children to read passages from books with some teacher assistance. This assistance is especially important in interpreting the oral passages. One of the more interesting repeated oral reading strategies is the use of choral reading. Choral reading is the interpretation of a selection by two or more voices speaking as one. Children discover that speaking voices can be combined in a way that is similar to singing voices combined in a choir. This approach encourages students to interpret what they read through oral presentations and increases comprehension of what is read. J. L. Eldredge (1990) found, for example, that using choral reading in which the teacher emphasizes correct phrasing, intonation, and pitch improves both comprehension and vocabulary.

When doing choral reading with young children have them explore the rhythm of the poetry or other rhymes by having them clap the rhythm as they repeat the rhyme. Mother Goose rhymes provide excellent sources for repeated choral reading. Older students can learn to use inflection, pitch, and intensity of voice as they interpret orally a poem or other work during choral reading. Mary Howitt's *The Spider and the Fly,* illustrated by Tony DiTerlizzi (2002) provides a source for experimenting with various voices during repeated choral readings. A. A. Milne's (2002) *There's Always Pooh and Me* includes poems that may be divided in numerous ways. Poems such as "Buckingham Palace" allow six different student groups to each present a choral arrangement of their own verse. Many of the poems are written in different formats that suggest how the poems might be read. "Journey's End," for example, has lines going up a hill as Christopher Robin climbs to the top of the hill and lines going down as he goes back to the bottom of the hill. Students can use clues from the way the text is printed to aid them in reading with inflections, pitch, and intensity.

When teaching rhyming schemes in words, use the choral reading of poems such as Edward Lear's *The Owl and the Pussycat* (1991). Beginning sounds, rhythm, and rhyming words are developed in David McCord's "The Pickety Fence" found in *Far and Few: Rhymes of the Never Was and Always Is* (1974). Poetry is excellent for choral reading and practicing reading until the use of language becomes fluent.

Each year the International Reading Association asks young readers to select their favorite books and identifies the winners as "Children's Choices." They also issue tips for parents, primary caregivers, and educators to use when reading the books with children. They recommend that children at the beginning reading levels be encouraged to browse through books as they pretend to read the story. Children may tell the story to themselves or attempt to read highlighted words. The following reading recommendations identified for sharing books with children include many guided and interactive recommendations ("Books Children Love, Chosen by Children," 2005):

Reflect on Your Reading

Think about your own experiences with reading. What teacher, reading experiences, or reading approaches inspired you and made you want to read more?

1. As the story is read, have children point to the pictures on each page.
2. Let children pretend to read the story as an adult points to the pictures.
3. Read alternate pages with the children, ask each other questions, and discuss the story
4. Use computer programs to expand children's interests in the topics
5. Compare and contrast various video adaptations of the books.

An annotated list of the 2005 "Children's Choices" appears in the October 2005 issue of *The Reading Teacher*.

Independent Silent Reading

Practice in reading leads to automaticity and fluency. Consequently, the activities introduced in Chapter 1, such as uninterrupted sustained silent reading, recreational reading groups, and literature circles, provide opportunities for students to practice their word recognition, comprehension, and fluency. The most important advice for teachers is to encourage students to read as much as possible in and outside the classroom. Asking students questions such as, "What books are you reading at home?" creating a classroom environment that encourages reading by providing a specific class time or lunchtime each week where students are able to share books they are reading or hope to read with their classmates, creating a classroom book of "Book Reviews" where students write their recommendations of books they finish at home, encouraging students to read when they would normally watch television, and encouraging students to keep a reading log, are all things teachers can do to encourage students to read outside the classroom.

DIFFERENTIATING INSTRUCTION

This chapter presented several successful strategies for improving comprehension including using mental imagery, graphic organizers, modeling, questioning strategies, predicting outcomes, and guided repeated oral reading. These strategies are equally important when considering differentiated instruction that meets the reading needs of all students in the class. Modifications in materials, instructional strategies, or types of follow-up assignments may be required. Let us consider how we might modify instruction to meet the needs of each of our focus groups.

ELL Students

When teaching reading comprehension to ELL students, successful instructional practices suggest the need for both modifying the reading materials to be used and the instructional strategies. For example, Kimberly Lenters (2004/2005) recommends using reading materials that keep pace with the oral vocabulary development of the students and that provide authentic experiences for the students so that they have the background knowledge needed for them to make personal connections with the text. To provide meaningful reading materials use a language experience approach (see Chapter 10). When possible, Lenters recommends translations alongside the English texts to enhance comprehension and to support the first-language reading skills.

Drama has been identified as a technique to help students in multilingual classrooms generate knowledge and increase comprehension. Carmen L. Medina and Gerald Campano (2006) describe a literacy activity with fifth-grade Latino students in which the students read a book and then expand on their understanding of the characters in the book by role playing various aspects of the book. For example, the students explored the inner feelings that might be felt by one of the characters, speculated about what might happen in the character's future, and interviewed the characters in the book. The students assumed the roles of the various characters or asked questions of the characters. The teacher expanded the activity by having the students complete a writing-in-role activity in which they wrote diary entries in either English or Spanish. Medina and Campano conclude that creative drama helps "students explore characters' fictional lives but also their own actual lives and identities in schools" (p. 339).

Struggling Readers and Writers

Successful reading programs designed to prevent reading and writing problems use a combination of meaningful strategies that teach and reinforce students' developing comprehension capabilities. For example, Pamela A. Miles and colleagues (2004/2005) describe a successful instructional plan for students who begin school at low literacy levels. As a result of the program, 75 percent of these first-grade students are fluent readers by the end of the year.

This plan, a modification of Reading Recovery (Clay, 1993), is based on a five-day plan that follows an introduction of a new book and activities to use with the same book. The next week follows a similar five-day plan, but with a new book and appropriate reading strategies. The five-day plan includes the following reading-comprehension strategies:

Day 1: Introduce the new book, activate students' prior knowledge about the content of the book, discuss any new concepts and language, encourage them to make predictions, and teach them a particular reading strategy that will be used as they read the book. The teacher distributes a copy of the book to each child in a small-group setting. Each student softly reads the book orally while the teacher checks students' reading. After completing the reading, the teacher and students discuss the reading and how the students used various strategies to comprehend the story.

Day 2: Using the same book read on day 1, the students discuss or retell the story discussing elements such as character, plot, and setting. The teacher may use graphic organizers or questioning strategies to build comprehension. The teacher provides a language minilesson that helps students comprehend the text. This might focus on the interpretation of punctuation marks. The students reread the new book. The teacher administers a weekly running record of individual student reading of the book. This activity allows teachers to monitor progress, observe strengths and weaknesses, and make decisions about grouping. Students also have opportunities to read individually other familiar books.

Day 3: The focus is on working with words. The teacher instructs students on strategies they can use to identify and construct meaning from words such as using letter-sound relationships or visual patterns that help construct meaning. Lessons may include activities such as extending word walls or working with rhymes.

Day 4: The focus is on student writing. The teacher models a minilesson on a writing skill. A print-rich environment includes word walls and posters illustrating color and number words. The students are encouraged to write about their own experiences, to pay attention to letter details, phonemes, and sequences of letters. They are taught to use familiar words they have learned, but to use invented spellings for new words. The teacher acts as a facilitator during this writing process. When completed, the students share their writing within their small group.

Day 5: The focus is on teacher evaluation about what has happened during the previous four days. At this time, decisions are made about appropriate reading activities for the next week such as texts and reading comprehension strategies to be taught, and minilessons planned.

Gifted and Accelerated Readers and Writers

This chapter discusses how various graphic organizers can be used to enhance comprehension. Mary C. McMackin and Nancy L. Witherell (2005) describe how they teach students to draw conclusions as part of their comprehension instruction. For gifted readers, these educators advocate an approach in which teachers first think

[Handwritten margin notes:]
① pre-reading
motivation
read
discuss

② re-read for
specific purpose
– elements
– punctuation

③ vocab
meaning

④ writing

⑤ evaluation

Houghton Mifflin
Open Court

FIGURE 6.6

Challenging-level Graphic Organizer Considering Conclusions

Name _____ Date _____

I read

page _____

paragraph(s) _____

Think about the passage you just read and list what you know for sure.

Stop, think about this information, and relate it to your experiences.

What else were you able to figure out from the passage you read?

While figuring this out, what connections did you make to your own experiences or to something you've read?

Source: Figure from McMackin, Mary, & Witherell, Nancy L. (2005, November). Different routes to the same destinations: Drawing conclusions with tiered graphic organizers. *The Reading Teacher,* 59(3), 242–252.

about the students who will easily achieve the desired outcome and then create a graphic organizer that challenges the students to use complex thinking about the concept, strategy, or skill.

McMackin and Witherell recommend, for example, the challenging-level graphic organizer found in Figure 6.6 to aid accelerated readers with drawing conclusions. Notice in this graphic organizer that students read until they identify a place where they can draw conclusions independently.

ELL students use "buddy reading" to improve their fluency in English.

Summary

Developing approaches and strategies allow teachers to improve comprehension of students. Schema theory emphasizes the necessity of activating prior knowledge or filling in the information gaps before students read a selection.

Mental imagery is a way to improve memory for and comprehension of what is read. Graphic organizers are another useful tool for comprehension and include semantic maps or webs. Semantic maps are tools for developing concepts and interest in a unit. Comprehension can also be improved through the use of time lines and flow charts.

Modeling is considered one of the most important techniques for improving comprehension of what is read. Two modeling lessons are developed in the chapter.

Methods for developing different levels of questioning strategies are another technique to improve comprehension. This section describes a taxonomy of comprehension and provides examples of questions that include literal recognition and recall, inference, evaluation, and appreciation. Students can also improve comprehension by predicting outcomes.

Reflect on Your Reading

Comprehension of what is read is the ultimate goal for all students. What characteristics of Reading Recovery make it effective with struggling readers? Why do you think that McMackin and Witherell advocate graphic organizers that challenge gifted and accelerated readers and writers? How might the graphic organizer in Figure 6.6 be modified to meet the needs of ELL students or struggling readers and writers?

Key Terms

comprehension, p. 217

schema theory, p. 218

mental imagery, p. 221

graphic organizers, p. 223

semantic maps, p. 223

modeling, p. 232

literal recognition, p. 238

inference, p. 239

evaluation, p. 239

appreciation, p. 240

For video clips of authentic classroom instruction on **Comprehension**, go to Allyn & Bacon's MyLabSchool.com. In MLS courses, click on Reading Methods, go to MLS Video Lab, and select **Module 5**.

Extend Your Reading

1. Develop a lesson plan in which you highlight the use of one of the graphic organizers discussed in this section: semantic maps or timelines. Include in your lesson plan an annotated bibliography of materials, especially books, that you could use for semantic maps or time lines. For example, you might include Jean Fritz's *The Lost Colony of Roanoke* (2004) for third- and fourth-graders. Hudson Talbott's illustrations include maps that depict the possible routes for the 115 colonists (1584–1590) who sailed to America only to disappear without a trace. Another book for third grade and up that develops content area concepts is Meredith Hooper's *The Island That Moved: How Shifting Forces Shaped Our Earth* (2004). A time line could be created for the book that shows how the island traveled through the ages to finally stop near the Antarctic peninsula. The author and illustrator traveled with scientists when researching the book. Share your lesson plan with your class.

2. Develop a lesson plan in which you model a literary element for young children. If you are teaching, present the model to a group of lower elementary students. What were their reactions to the story? How did the use of the modeling technique increase the oral discussions and comprehension among your students?

3. Develop a modeling lesson in which you teach inferencing of characterization to students in the upper grades. Share the modeling lesson with your reading methods class or with a group of school children. Make any changes in the modeling lesson after you evaluate the effectiveness of the lesson.

4. With a group of your peers, select a text you would like to use. Create a series of comprehension questions that include literal, inference, evaluation, and appreciation levels of comprehension. (This taxonomy is appropriate for any grade level. The questions depend on the reading level of the book chosen and the developmental level of the students.)

5. Read books that use a questioning format such as Joan Holub's *Why Do Birds Sing?* (2004) and *Why Do Snakes Hiss? And Other Questions about Snakes, Lizards, and Turtles* (2004). These books, recommended for first grade and up, include photographs and drawings to support the answers. How effective are the questioning strategies? Are the questions answered to the satisfaction of your readers? For a question and answer book designed for even younger children you could analyze the questions in John Butler's *Whose Nose and Toes?* (2004), a board book written for preschool children, or analyze the question and answer format in Dori Chaconas's *Momma, Will You?* (2004).

6. Look through books and newspaper articles with the intention of finding materials that have predictable elements, such as how an author's style or use of language can be predictable. Create an annotated bibliography of the materials you have chosen. Include several sentences describing what elements make each book or article predictable. Share these with your classmates.

7. Consider the development of reading fluency. How would advocates for each of the following models of the reading process define a fluent reader: the bottom-up model, the top-down model, and the interactive model? How would advocates for each of the following approaches to reading instruction define fluency: phonics approaches, sub-skills approaches, whole language approaches, literature-based approaches, and balanced-reading approaches?

For Further Reading

1. Analyze the texts that are recommended in this chapter for a specific grade level. What prior knowledge is needed before students will succeed reading these texts? Look at a scope and sequence for teaching reading or social studies in a specified grade level. Does the curriculum develop the necessary prior knowledge before students go to the next level?

2. Analyze a book written for the upper elementary or middle school grades. Identify the prior knowledge that would be necessary for producing success at that level. Identify how you would develop this prior knowledge.

3. With a group of your peers, develop an annotated bibliography of books and other references, including Web sites, that could be used to develop background knowledge for a unit that is normally taught at a specific grade level.

4. If possible, observe a teacher and use a taxonomy of comprehension to identify the levels of questions that are asked by the teacher. Document the levels of comprehension that are asked. Is there a higher frequency of one level of comprehension? If there is a higher frequency for one type of question, what does this infer for the teaching of comprehension?

5. Interview a teacher about his or her philosophy about the teaching of comprehension? How does the teacher believe that comprehension should be taught? What techniques and strategies does the teacher use? How does the teacher rate the ability of her students to comprehend the materials that they read?

6. Many of the authors of books listed in this chapter have Web sites. Read about the following authors on their Web sites:

   Hudson Talbott: www.hudsontalbott.com
   Cheryl Harness: www.cherylharness.com
   Joan Holub: www.joanholub.com

REFERENCES

Barrett, Thomas (1972). "Taxonomy of Reading Comprehension." In *Reading 360 Monograph*. Lexington, MA: Ginn.

Clark, Kathleen F., & Graves, Michael F. (March 2005). "Scaffolding Students' Comprehension of Text." *The Reading Teacher*, 58, 570–580.

Clay, Maria. (1993). *Reading Recovery: A Guidebook for Teachers in Training*. Portsmouth, NH: Heinemann.

Dole, J., Duffy, G., Roehler, L., & Pearson, P. D. (1991). "Moving from the Old to the New: Research on Reading Comprehension Instruction." *Review of Educational Research*, 61, pp. 239–264.

Duke, Nell K., & Pearson, P. David (2002). "Effective Practices for Developing Reading Comprehension." In Alan E. Farstrup & S. J. Samuels (Eds.), *What Research Has to Say about Reading Instruction*, 3rd

ed. Newark, DE: International Reading Association, pp. 205–242.

Eldredge, J. L. (1990). "Increasing the Performance of Poor Readers in Third Grade with a Group-Assisted Strategy." *Journal of Educational Research,* 84, 69–77.

Fowler, Brenda. (27 July, 2004). "African Pastoral: Archaeologists Rewrite History of Farming." *The New York Times,* p. D2.

"It's Official: Potter Helps." (August-September 2005). *Reading Today,* 23, 26.

Krauss, Clifford, Myers, Steven Lee, Revkin, Andrew C., & Romero, Simon. (October 2005). "As Polar Ice Turns to Water, Dreams of Treasure Abound." *New York Times,* pp. A1, 11–12.

Lenters, Kimberly. (December 2004-January 2005). "No Half Measures: Reading Instruction for Young Second-Language Learners." *The Reading Teacher,* 58, 328–336.

McMackin, Mary C., & Witherell, Nancy L. (November 2005). "Different Routes to the Same Destination: Drawing Conclusions with Tiered Graphic Organizers." *The Reading Teacher,* 59, 242–252.

McTighe, Jay, & Lyman, Frank T. Jr. (2001). "Clueing Thinking in the Classroom: The Promise of Theory-Embedded Tools." In Arthur L. Costa (Ed.), *Developing Minds: A Resource Book for Teaching Thinking,* 3rd ed. Alexandria, VA: Association for Supervision and Curriculum Development.

Medina, Carmen L., & Campano, Gerald. (March 2006). "Performing Identities through Drama and Teatro Practices in Multilingual Classrooms." *Language Arts* 83, 332–341.

Miles, Pamela A., Stegle, Kathy W., Hubbs, Karen G., Henk, William A., & Mallette, Marla H. (December 2004/January 2005). "A Whole-Class Support Model for Early Literacy: The Anna Plan." *The Reading Teacher,* 58, 318–327.

National Reading Panel (2000). *Report of the National Reading Panel.* Washington, DC: National Institute of Child Health and Human Development.

Neufeld, Paul. (December 2005/January 2006). "Comprehension Instruction in Content Area Classes." *The Reading Teacher,* 59, 302–312.

Norton, Donna E. (1992). *The Impact of Literature-Based Reading.* Upper Saddle River, NJ: Merrill/Prentice Hall.

Norton, Donna E. (2005). *Multicultural Children's Literature: Through the Eyes of Many Children.* Upper Saddle River, NJ: Merrill/Prentice Hall.

Norton, Donna E. (2007). *Through the Eyes of a Child: An Introduction to Children's Literature,* 7th ed. Upper Saddle River, NJ: Merrill/Prentice Hall.

Ogle, Donna (1989). "Study Techniques that Ensure Content Area Reading Success." In D. Lapp, J. Flood, & N. Farnman (Eds.), *Content Area Reading and Learning: Instructional Strategies.* Englewood Cliffs, NJ: Prentice Hall. pp. 225–234.

Peskin, Joan. (1998). "Constructing Meaning When Reading Poetry: An Expert-Novice Study." *Cognition and Instruction,* 16, 235–263.

Revkin, Andrew C. (27 July, 2004). "A Far-Reaching Fire Makes a Point about Pollution." *New York Times,* p. D1.

Revkin, Andrew C. (24 March, 2006). "Climate Data Hint at Irreversible Rise in Seas." *The New York Times,* A12.

Roehler, L. R., & Duffy, G. (1989). "The Content Area Teacher's Instructional Role: A Cognitive Mediational View." In Diane Lapp, James Flood, & N. Farnam (Eds.), *Content Area Reading and Learning: Instructional Strategies.* Englewood Cliffs NJ: Prentice Hall, pp. 115–122.

Samuels, S. Jay. (1994). "Toward a Theory of Automatic Information Processing in Reading, Revisited." In R. Ruddell, M. Ruddell, & H. Singer (Eds.), *Theoretical Models of Processes of Reading,* 4th ed. Newark, DE: International Reading Association, pp. 816–837.

Venezky, Richard. (2003). "Literacy Learning after High School." In James Flood, Diane Lapp, James R. Squire, & Julie M. Jensen (Eds.), *Handbook of Research on Teaching the English Language Arts,* 2nd ed. Mahwah, NJ: Lawrence Erlbaum, pp. 405–412.

Zemelman, S., Daniels, H., & Hyde, A. (1998). *Best Practice: New Standards for Teaching and Learning in America's Schools,* 2nd ed. Portsmouth, NH: Heinemann.

Children's Literature References

Aardema, Verna. (1981). *Bringing the Rain to Kapiti Plain: A Nandi Tale.* Illustrated by Beatriz Vidal. Dial Press.

Aardema, Verna. (1994). *Misoso: Once Upon a Time Tales from Africa.* Illustrated by Reynold Ruffins. Knopf.

Aardema, Verna. (1997). *This for That: A Tongo Tale.* Illustrated by Victoria Chess. Dial Press.

Aardema, Verna. (1997). *Anansi Does the Impossible:*

An Ashanti Tale. Illustrated by Lisa Desimini. Simon & Schuster.

Alexander, Lloyd. (1991). *The Remarkable Journey of Prince Jen.* G.P. Dutton.

Anaya, Rudolfo. (1997). *Maya's Children: The Story of La Llorona.* Illustrated by Maria Baca. Hyperion.

Ashabranner, Brent, & Davis, Russel. (1996). *The Lion's Whiskers: And Other Ethiopian Tales.* Illustrated by Helen Siegh. Linnet.

Avi. (2002). *Crispin: The Cross of Lead.* Hyperion.

Baker, Olaf. (1981). *Where the Buffaloes Begin.* Illustrated by Stephen Gammell. Warne.

Bierhorst, John. (1986). *The Monkey's Haircut and Other Stories Told by the Maya.* Illustrated by Robert Andrew Parker. William Morrow.

Bryan, Ashley. (1993). *Beat the Story-Drum, Pum-Pum.* Atheneum.

Butler, John. (2004). *Whose Nose and Toes?* Viking.

Caduto, Michael J., & Joseph Bruchac. (1991). *Keepers of the Animals: Native American Stories and Wildlife Activities for Children.* Illustrated by John Kahionhes Fadden. Fulcrum.

Chaconas, Dori.(2004). *Momma, Will You?* Illustrated by Steve Johnson and Lou Fancher. Viking.

Cleary, Beverly. (1983). *Dear Mr. Henshaw.* Illustrated by Paul O. Zelinsky. William Morrow.

Coles, Robert. (1995). *The Story of Ruby Bridges.* Scholastic.

Cushman, Karen. (1995). *The Midwife's Apprentice.* Clarion.

Dooling, Michael. (2006). *Young Thomas Edison.* Holiday House.

Echewa, T. Obinkaram. (1999). *The Magic Tree: A Folktale from Nigeria.* Illustrated by E. B. Lewis. William Morrow.

Fairman, Tony. (1993). *Bury My Bones but Keep My Words: African Tales for Retelling.* Illustrated by Meshack Asare. Henry Holt.

Freedman, Russell. (1987). *Lincoln: A Photobiography.* Clarion.

Freedman, Russell. (1990). *Franklin Delano Roosevelt.* Clarion.

Freedman, Russell. (1991). *The Wright Brothers: How They Invented the Airplane.* Holiday.

Freedman, Russell. (1993). *Eleanor Roosevelt: A Life of Discovery.* Clarion.

Freedman, Russell. (1997). *Out of Darkness: The Story of Louis Braille.* Illustrated by Kate Kiesler. Clarion.

Fritz, Jean. (1986). *Make Way for Sam Houston.* Illustrated by Elise Primavera. G.P. Putnam's Sons.

Fritz, Jean. (1989). *The Great Little Madison.* G.P. Putnam's Sons.

Fritz, Jean. (1991). *Bully for You, Teddy Roosevelt.* Illustrated by Mike Wimmer. G.P. Putnam's Sons.

Fritz, Jean. (2004). *The Lost Colony of Roanoke.* Illustrated by Hudson Talbott. G.P. Putnam's Sons.

Giovanni, Nikki. (2005). *Rosa.* Illustrated by Bryan Collier. Henry Holt.

Goble, Paul. (1978). *The Girl Who Loved Wild Horses.* Bradbury.

Goble, Paul. (1980). *The Gift of the Sacred Dog.* Bradbury.

Goble, Paul. (1984). *Buffalo Woman.* Bradbury.

Goble, Paul. (1988). *Iktomi and the Boulder: A Plains Indian Story.* Orchard.

Goble, Paul. (1989). *Beyond the Ridge.* Bradbury.

Goble, Paul. (1989). *Iktomi and the Berries.* Watts.

Goble, Paul. (1990). *The Dream Wolf.* Bradbury.

Grimm, Brothers. (1983). *Little Red Riding Hood.* Retold and illustrated by Trina Schart Hyman. Holiday.

Harness, Cheryl. (2004). *Franklin and Eleanor.* Dutton.

Holub, Joan. (2004). *Why Do Birds Sing?* Illustrated by Anna DiVito. Dial Press.

Holub, Joan. (2004). *Why Do Snakes Hiss? And Other Questions about Snakes, Lizards, and Turtles.* Illustrated by Anna DiVito. Dial Press.

Hooper, Meredith. (2004). *The Island That Moved: How Shifting Forces Shape Our Earth.* Illustrated by Lucia de Leiris. Viking.

Howitt, Mary. (2002). *The Spider and the Fly.* Illustrated by Tony DiTerlizzi. Simon & Schuster.

Jones, Jennifer. (1994). *Heetunka's Harvest: A Tale of the Plains Indians.* Illustrated by Shannon Keegan. Rinehart.

Keating, Frank. (2006). *Theodore.* Illustrated by Mike Wimmer. Simon & Schuster.

Lang, Andrew. (1960). *The Red Fairy Book.* Random House.

Lear, Edward. (1991). *The Owl and the Pussycat.* Illustrated by Jan Brett. G.P. Putnam's Sons.

Lewin, Hugh. (1983). *Jafta.* Illustrated by Lisa Kooper. Carolrhoda.

Lionni, Leo. (1963) *Swimmy.* Knopf.

Lowry, Lois. (1989). *Number the Stars.* Houghton Mifflin.

Macaulay, David. (1973). *Cathedral: The Story of Its Construction.* Houghton Mifflin.

Macaulay, David. (1977). *Castle.* Houghton Mifflin.

Marrin, Albert. (2004). *Old Hickory: Andrew Jackson and the American People.* Dutton.

McCord, David. (1974). *Far and Few. Rhymes of the Never Was and Always Is.* Little, Brown.

Milne, A. A. (2003). *There's Always Pooh and Me: A Collection of Poems.* Illustrated by Ernest H. Shepard. Dutton.

Nelson, Marilyn. (2005). *A Wreath for Emmett Till.* Illustrated by Philippe Lardy. Houghton Mifflin.

Packer, Tina, retold by. (2004). *Tales from Shakespeare.* Scholastic.

Perrault, Charles. (1961, 1982). *Perrault's Complete Fairy Tales.* Illustrated by W. Heath Robinson. Dodd, Mead.

Provensen, Alice. (1990). *The Buck Stops Here: The Presidents of the United States.* HarperCollins.

Rosen, Michael. (1989). *We're Going on a Bear Hunt.* Illustrated by Helen Oxenbury. Macmillan.

Sachar, Louis. (1998). *Holes.* Farrar, Straus & Giroux.

Shipton, Jonathan. (1999). *What If?* Illustrated by Barbara Nascimbeni. Dial Press.

Sperry, Armstrong. (1940). *Call It Courage.* Macmillan.

Van Allsburg, Chris. (1987). *The Z Was Zapped.* Houghton Mifflin.

Volkmer, Jane Ann. (1990). *Song of Chirimia—A Guatemalan Folktale.* Carolrhoda.

Young, Ed. (1989). *Lon Po Po: A Red-Riding Hood Story from China.* Philomel.

CHAPTER

7

Reading, Writing, and Literature in the Content Areas
Kindergarten through Fourth Grades

CHAPTER **OUTLINE**

Reading and Literature in English/Language Arts
  Teaching the Literature Content for English/Language Arts
  Developing Knowledge of Literary Genres

Reading and Literature in Social Studies
  Using Different Parts of a Book
  Differences between Fiction and Nonfiction
  Similarities and Differences between Versions of a Folktale

Reading and Literature in Science
  Connections between Science Centers and Literature
  Analyzing Organization of Science Literature

Reading and Art
  Illustrations That Depict the Literary Elements
  Reinforcing Emergent Literacy by Examining Illustrations in Alphabet Books
  Comparing Illustrators' Interpretations of the Same Story
  Using Art to Develop Book Reports
  Using Art Books to Teach Following Directions
  Art Lessons Using Caldecott Books

After reading this chapter you will be able to answer the following questions:

1. What content might be found in a scope and sequence chart for reading in the content areas in the lower elementary grades?
2. What are effective strategies for teaching reading of literature in English/language arts?
3. What research skills are needed for kindergarten through fourth-grade content areas?
4. What are effective strategies for teaching reading in social studies?
5. What are effective strategies for teaching reading in science?
6. What are effective strategies for teaching reading in art?

Read All About It!

"Suutarila Journal; Educators Flocking to Finland, Land of Literate Children"

by Lizette Alvarez, *New York Times,* April 9, 2004

SUUTARILA, Finland—Imagine an educational system where children do not start school until they are seven, where spending is a paltry $5,000 a year per student, where there are no gifted programs and class sizes often approach 30. A prescription for failure, no doubt, in the eyes of many experts, but in this case a description of Finnish schools, which were recently ranked the world's best.

Finland topped a respected international survey last year, coming in first in literacy and placing in the top five in math and science. Ever since, educators from all over the world have thronged to this self-restrained country to deconstruct its school system— "educational pilgrims," the locals call them—and, with luck, take home a sliver of wisdom.

"We are a little bit embarrassed about our success," said Simo Juva, a special government adviser to the Ministry of Education, summing up the typical reaction in Finland, where boasting over accomplishments does not come easily. "Perhaps next year," he said, wistfully, "Finland will place second or third."

The question on people's minds is obvious; how did Finland, which was hobbled by a deep recession in the 1990s, manage to outscore 31 other countries, including the United States, in the review by the Organization of Economic Cooperation and Development [OECD] last September? The rankings were based on reading, math, and science tests given to a sample of 15-year-olds attending both public and private schools. United States students placed in the middle of the pack.

Finland's recipe is both complex and unabashedly basic. It is also similar to that in other Nordic countries. Some of the ingredients can be exported (its flexibility in the classroom, for example) and some cannot (the nation's small, homogenous population and the relative prosperity of most Finns, to name two).

If one trait sets Finland apart from many other countries it is

the quality and social standing of its teachers, said Barry MacGraw, the director for education at the OECD. All teachers in Finland must have at least a master's degree, and while they are no better paid than teachers in other countries, the profession is highly respected. Many more people want to become teachers after graduating from

> **"Reading to children, telling folk tales and going to the library are activities cherished in Finland."**

upper schools than universities can actually handle, so the vast majority are turned down. "Teaching is the No. 1," Outi Pihlman, the English teacher at Suutarila Lower Comprehensive School, said about a recent survey asking teenagers to name their favorite profession. "At that age, you would think they would want anything but to go back to school. . . ."

Children here start school late on the theory that they will learn to love learning through play. Preschool for six-year-olds is optional, although most attend. And since most women work outside the home in Finland, children usually go to day care after they turn one.

At first, the seven-year-olds lag behind their peers in other countries in reading, but they catch up almost immediately and then excel. Experts cite several reasons: reading to children, telling folk tales and going to the library are activities cherished in Finland. Lastly, children grow up watching television shows and movies (many in English) with subtitles. So they read while they watch TV.

As long as schools stick to the core national curriculum, which lays out goals and subject areas, they are free to teach the way they want. They can choose their textbooks or ditch them altogether, teach indoors or outdoors, cluster children in small or large groups.

While there are no programs for gifted children, teachers are free to devise ways to challenge their smartest students. The smarter students help teach the average students. "Sometimes you learn better that way," said Pirjo Kanno, the principal in Suutarila.

Students must learn two foreign languages—Swedish is required by law, and most also take English. Art, music, physical education, woodwork and textiles (which is mostly sewing and knitting) are obligatory for girls and boys. Hot and healthy school lunches are free. There are also 90 computers scattered about the school, and students are free to attend homework clubs staffed by assistants after school.

Despite the accolades, Finnish officials say they are far from perfect. Boys, for example, perform much worse than girls in reading, and with so many wanting to become teachers, too few are willing to leap outside the social service sphere.

Read All About It!

Critical Thinking Questions

- What elements of Finnish education do you believe are important for high reading achievement?

- What elements of this education would you like to include in your own classroom?

- If you could visit the schools, what "sliver of wisdom" would you take home?

Themes of the Times

The New York Times
expect the world®
nytimes.com

For related *New York Times* articles, go to the Companion Web Site at www.ablongman.com/norton1e and click on *Themes of the Times*.

The "Read All About It" feature at the beginning of this chapter provides both a challenge to reading educators and several guidelines for teaching reading and literature in the kindergarten through fourth-grade curriculum. Why does Finland have the highest literacy rate in the world? According to Finnish educators, there are three characteristics found in all schools:

1. Teachers read orally to children.

2. Teachers teach the folktales that reflect the culture.

3. All students spend considerable time in the library where they read all types of literature and conduct research using literature.

In addition, students study foreign languages, art, and music. There is considerable research that reinforces the use of languages, art, and music to improve comprehension.

At a recent international conference of reading teachers, the teachers were asked what experiences they had in elementary school that developed their own love for reading:

1. They read many different genres of literature.

2. They had class discussions in which they responded to the literature and other types of reading materials.

3. They completed enjoyable independent activities that allowed them to complete in-depth reading and analysis of the materials.

4. They took part in units and other activities that stressed higher thought processes and connected reading and writing.

Notice how their responses are similar to those of the Finnish educators.

Useful guidelines and suggestions for reading in the content areas are found in documents published by organizations such as the International Reading Association (IRA) and in publications developed by schools and school districts. For example, the IRA ("Examining Evidence," 2002) reviewed best practices and developed a position statement that includes the following practices related to reading and literature in the content areas:

1. Teach reading for authentic meaning-making literacy experiences for pleasure, to be informed, and to perform a task.

2. Use high-quality literature.

3. Use multiple texts that link and expand concepts.

4. Balance teacher- and student-led discussions.

5. Build a whole-class community that emphasizes important concepts and builds background knowledge.

6. Give students plenty of time to read in class.

7. Give students direct instruction in comprehension strategies that promote independent reading. Balance direct instruction, guided instruction, and independent learning.

This position statement provides general guidelines that should be used by reading teachers. This chapter will develop strategies that focus on many of these best practices. For more detailed descriptions of what might be included at each grade level, teachers can use scope and sequences developed to guide and evaluate specific reading programs. For example, the **language scope and sequence** for the International Baccalaureate Organization" (2003) includes all of the previous guidelines, but develops more detailed expectations for student learning in kindergarten through fourth grade.

The following examples represent a few of the expectations for ages five to seven:

1. Recall the plot and characters in a story.

2. Understand and respond to the ideas and feelings expressed in reading materials.

3. Recognize and use different parts of a book (title page, contents page, page numbers, index).

4. Know the difference between fiction and nonfiction.

5. Begin to use reference books, dictionaries, and computers with confidence.

6. In art, compare differences between real and animated objects or images and use critical and analytical skills to respond to familiar media.

Children ages seven to nine are expected to:

1. Read and sort a variety of texts connected with the current unit of inquiry.

2. Recognize and appreciate different literary styles and genres.

3. Identify and detail the main elements in a story including setting, characters, plot, and theme. Highlight similarities and differences between versions of the same story such as found in folktales.

4. Perform dramatic readings chosen from literature and their own creative writing.

5. In art, study and interpret what is seen in a picture and describe the elements in the picture.

This chapter develops strategies that allow students to gain understandings within these areas of reading. The following chapter extends this scope and sequence into the fourth through eighth grades.

Reading and Literature in English/Language Arts

The teacher in lower elementary grades spends a major part of each day teaching reading. Some of this time is spent teaching word attack skills through phonemic awareness and phonics as described in Chapter 2 (Emergent Literacy) and Chapter 4 (Phonics). Some of the time is spent developing specific vocabulary skills as described in Chapter 5 and comprehension skills as described in Chapter 6.

Many of the guidelines for best practices identified by the position statement of the IRA fall under the realm of a broader content such as that found in English/

language arts. This is the area for studying high-quality literature, taking part in literacy experiences for various reasons, using multiple texts to expand concepts, building background knowledge, and balancing direct instruction with reading that promotes independent reading.

Most of the areas identified in the scope and sequence are developed through reading, listening to, and discussing literature and other forms of written materials. Many of the approaches to teaching reading identified in Chapter 1 require an understanding of literary elements. If the class is using a literature-based approach or a whole language approach, the abilities needed to recognize and discuss literary elements such as plot and characters in a story, respond to feelings developed during the reading, and qualify differences between literary genres are very important. These abilities are also important in a balanced reading approach in which students apply skills learned in reading to the reading of authentic literature. Many basal-reading approaches suggest extending the skills developed through the lessons to the independent reading of recommended literature. When using a unit approach in any of the content areas, students need to select appropriate sources, read and analyze the materials, draw conclusions about the content of the material, and understand how the materials relate to the objectives or themes of the unit.

There are proven strategies and techniques that enhance both understanding and pleasure of reading in all of the content areas. There are strategies and techniques for teaching the content and also for providing the practice. In the English/Language Arts curriculum, daily oral reading to the students and storytelling by students and teachers models reading and language fluency, introduces students to a variety of genres in literature, provides background knowledge about literature and content needed for understanding of genres such as folktales, and increases comprehension of those genres. Teachers in Finland identified reading orally to children as extremely important.

Reading aloud to children is a major focus of Chapter 2, "Emergent Literacy." Chapter 2 presented the research supporting reading aloud, selecting the materials, and guidelines for developing the reading aloud experience. This chapter extends the values of reading orally to students by suggesting various groupings that motivate students to read and discuss texts.

The English/language arts curriculum also has content requirements as detailed in the previously discussed scope and sequence. Within the content are such expectations for students in grades K–4 as understanding the settings, plot, characters, and theme of a story; knowing differences between fiction and nonfiction; and recognizing and appreciating different genres of literature. This section begins with strategies for teaching the content and then develops ways for providing the practice.

Teaching the Literature Content for English/Language Arts

Chapter 6 stressed reading skills related to schema theory and developing understanding through such techniques as mental imagery, graphic organizers, modeling, questioning strategies, and predicting outcomes. All of these reading strategies are also related to the effective reading of materials in the English/language arts curriculum. Many of the examples in the previous chapter showed how to use literature when teaching the techniques. This chapter focuses on specific content that is required to understand literature such as the literary elements found in stories (plot, conflict, characterization, setting, theme, style, point of view); and characteristics of different genres (folktales, fantasy, poetry, realistic fiction, historical fiction, biography, and nonfiction).

DEVELOPING KNOWLEDGE OF LITERARY ELEMENTS   Reading and discussing the facts found in literature are easier than identifying and analyzing the literary aspects. A good literature program enables students to go beyond the factual level. Reading and discussing good children's literature increases students' awareness, enables them to discover the techniques an author uses to create a believable plot or memorable characterizations, and provides standards for comparison. To read, respond to, and discuss the literature students need to have understandings of the following (Norton, 2007):

1. **Plot**: the plan of action or sequence of events in the story. A good plot has the following characteristics:

   - The plot has a beginning, a middle, and an end.
   - The plot allows students to become involved in the action, to feel the conflict developing, to recognize the climax, and to respond to a satisfactory ending.
   - Plots for younger readers usually follow a chronological order.
   - Cumulative action as found in "The House That Jack Built" allows younger readers to follow the action.

     Examples of literature with plots that are easy for students to identify include Verna Aardema's cumulative tale, *Why Mosquitoes Buzz in People's Ears* (1975), Jim Aylesworth's *The Gingerbread Man* (1998), and Steven Kellogg's *The Three Little Pigs* (1997).

2. **Conflict**: the struggle and action as characters face problems and overcome difficulties. Understandings include:

   - Conflicts in books written for younger readers usually have one character, human or animal, in conflict with another character. (Person versus person.)
   - Nature may also cause the conflict when a character overcomes problems related to the setting of the book. (Person versus nature.)
   - Person versus self and person versus society conflicts are common in books for older readers.
   - The conflict must be believable for the age of the readers.

     Examples of books with easily understood conflicts include Jan Brett's *Goldilocks and the Three Bears* (1987) (girl versus the bears); Steven Kellogg's *Jack and the Beanstalk* (1991) (Jack versus the giant); Beatrix Potter's *The Tale of Peter Rabbit* (1902, 1986), Peter versus Mr. McGregor; Jean Van Leewen's *Benny & Beautiful Baby Delilah* (2006) (Benny versus his new sister).

3. **Characterization**: the development of a character in a book so that readers understand the strengths, weakness, past, hopes, and fears of the character:

   - Illustrations in books may help develop memorable characters.

- Authors may describe the character's thoughts.
- Authors may develop the actions of the character.
- Dialogue often reveals information about characters.

   Examples of literature with easily understood characterizations: Maurice Sendak's *Where the Wild Things Are* (1963), E. B. White's *Charlotte's Web* (1952), and Ed Young's *My Mei Mei* (2006).

4. **Setting:** *where* the story takes place as well as the *time*—whether it is past, present, or future:

- Setting may be developed through illustrations.
- Details of setting in historical fiction and nonfiction must be true to the time period and location.
- The author must provide enough details so that readers can visualize the setting.
- If the setting causes a person versus nature conflict, the setting needs to be described or illustrated so that readers understand the danger.

   Examples of literature that have settings that are easily described include Michael Garland's *My Cousin Katie* (1989) (life on a farm); Jean Craighead George's *Everglades* (1995) (geography of the Florida Everglades); George Ella Lyon's *One Lucky Girl* (2000) (destruction associated with a tornado).

5. **Theme:** the central idea that ties the plot, characterizations, and setting together into a meaningful whole.

- The theme may be the author's purpose for writing the story or the message.
- Authors of books for younger readers frequently state the theme.
- Authors of books for older students usually imply the theme through characterizations and conflict resolutions.
- Memorable themes usually relate to the reader's needs and age levels.

   Examples of literature which have easily identifiable themes include Lauren Child's *The Princess and the Pea* (2006), Michael Hague's *Aesop's Fables* (1985) and Patricia Polacco's *Appelemando's Dream* (1991).

6. **Style:** the way the author chooses to arrange the words to create the story.

- Sounds may appeal to the senses.
- Word choices and sentence lengths may create a leisurely or frightening mood.
- Figurative language may allow readers to visualize concepts in new ways.

   Examples of literature with especially appealing styles include Monica Brown's *My Name Is Gabriela: The Life of Gabriela Mistral* (2005), Helen Cooper's *Pumpkin Soup* (1999), and Lloyd Moss's *Zin! Zin! Zin! A Violin* (1995).

7. **Point of view:** the angle of vision from which the story is told.

- Readers need to identify who tells the story, and how much information about the characters and incidents this person can reveal.

- Description of an incident differs depending on the feelings, viewpoints, motives, and beliefs of the person telling the story.

- The choice of point of view can affect how much children of different ages believe and enjoy a story.

Examples of literature that have easily identifiable points of view include Dorothea P. Seeber's *A Pup Just for Me: A Boy Just for Me* (2000), where two points of view are developed, and Jane Yolen's *Owl Moon* (1987).

DEVELOPING UNDERSTANDING OF LITERARY ELEMENTS   Students need many opportunities to read and discuss books that invite them to discover how authors and illustrators develop these literary elements. What are some of the instructional strategies that teachers can use to develop understanding of plot, conflict, characterization, setting, theme, and point of view? Fortunately, there are many highly illustrated books that encourage students in Kindergarten through fourth grades to read for both enjoyment and understanding. There are also a variety of approaches including plot structures, semantic mapping, drama, and children's drawings that enhance the instruction of each of the following:

1. **Plot structures:** There is a close relationship between students' understanding of the organizational structure of a book and comprehension of the text (McMackin, 1998).

   - Use the following activities: Use picture books to build an understanding of text structure. For example, ask students to tell the plot of Barry Moser's *The Three Little Pigs* (2001) by following the illustrations.

   - To further an understanding of plot structures, after reading the story ask students to act out the tale. They can be the first little pig and build a house from straw and as the wolf they can huff and puff and blow the house in. As the second pig they can build a house from sticks and as the wolf they can huff and puff and blow the house in. Finally, as the third pig they can build a house of bricks and as the wolf try unsuccessfully to blow the house down. As they act out this story, they also discover that the structure of the story not only has a beginning, a middle, and an end, but it is also developed on building materials that become stronger and stronger.

   - Finally, they can place the story on a plot structure such as the one shown in Figure 7.1.

   As the plot diagram is drawn, review with students the terminology on the diagram. Ask them to identify the incidents from their drama that correspond to each part of the diagram. Be sure students understand that the problem and story develops because the pigs and the wolf have different motives for their actions. (Two plot diagrams that combine knowledge of plot and related vocabulary are developed in Chapter 5.)

2. **Conflict:** The story of *The Three Little Pigs* includes both plot structure and conflict. Through the acting out of the story and drawing the plot diagram, students respond to this person versus person conflict and develop an understanding that stories have a beginning in which the conflict, or problem and characters, are introduced, a middle that moves the action toward a climax, and an ending that

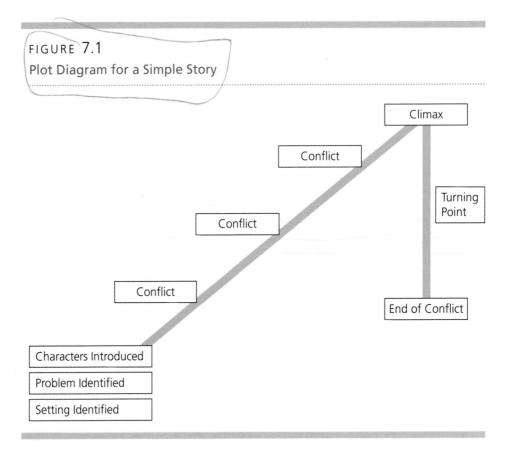

FIGURE 7.1
Plot Diagram for a Simple Story

offers a resolution to the conflict. Through both drama and plot structures they learn that stories must have a logical sequence that gradually builds until the conflict is resolved.

3. **Characterization:** Students need many opportunities to respond to the characters in a story and to discover ways that authors develop believable characters through descriptions, actions, thoughts of the character, and dialogue.

■ Help students gain clues about characterization through studying illustrations. For example, "What do the illustrations in Karen Ackerman's *Song and Dance Man* (1988) tell us about character?" Now read the text, "Is our information correct? What additional information do we have about this character?"

■ Use books that help students predict how a story may end or a sequence to a story because of characters' actions. For example, after reading Chris Van Allsburg's *Jumanji* (1981) ask, "What will happen when Danny and Walter, who never read instructions, try to play with the puzzle?"

4. **Setting:** Picture storybooks with their vivid illustrations, are among the best sources for developing observational and writing skills related to setting. The following activities are especially appropriate for developing understandings of setting:

Parents who read to their children increase children's literacy development.

- Share books with familiar settings. Read the stories while encouraging students to look carefully at the settings, and then describe these settings in detail. The discussion can emphasize students' reactions to the settings as well as descriptive words and phrases they think describe the settings. Ask students to write or dictate their own descriptions of the settings that include the points made during the discussions. Books such as Mitra Modarressi's *Yard Sale!* (2000) have familiar settings as well as an ending that is full of surprises.

- Share and discuss books that show both nature as a peaceful setting and nature as a threatening, antagonistic setting. Discuss the differences in both illustrations and text. For example, Robert McCloskey's *Time of Wonder* (1957, 1985), begins with a peaceful setting in Maine with all the fun experienced by a family. The setting changes as a storm approaches, the hurricane rushes in, and trees are uprooted. The text ends as the setting is again peaceful, and becomes a time of wonder.

5. **Theme:** Give students an understanding of theme by asking students "What's the author's message?" (Beck et al., 1996). Read and discuss books that show how an author develops themes such as the following:

- Begin with books in which the theme is clearly stated, such as is found in Arnold Lobel's *Fables* (1980). Each of the fables includes a message, a moral that the teller believes should make a difference in our lives. Although moral and theme are not exactly alike, students can readily identify the author's message in a fable. Consequently, fables provide an easy introduction to theme and provide a bridge between the moral in the fable and the theme in longer, more complex literature.

- Expand the understanding of theme into folktales such as Trina Schart Hyman's retelling of Grimm's *Little Red Riding Hood* (1983). Ask students to support the message they think is important, such as, "It is important to mind your mother," or, "Do not talk to strangers." The illustrations, character's actions, character's thought, and the way the story ends supports the themes.

6. **Style:** Students should read books in which they develop an understanding that many of the previous literary elements are enhanced through authors' style. The following examples are effective with Kindergarten through fourth-grade students:

   ■ Many books written for younger students use personification, giving human characteristics to objects and animals. Read books such as Virginia Lee Burton's *The Little House* (1942) and discuss the illustrations in a wordless book such as Emily Arnold McCully's *Picnic* (1984); ask students to identify the human characteristics—feelings, actions, and life styles—that the authors give to their characters. Explain that this is called personification.

   ■ One of the best ways to increase students' appreciation of style is to ask them to read and dramatize books such as Lloyd Moss's *Zin! Zin! Zin! A Violin* (1995).

7. **Point of View:** To understand point of view students need to think about the literature from the author's perspective:

   ■ Beck and colleagues (1996) found that students can understand point of view if they begin with theme and are asked questions such as, "What's the author's message?" Then proceed to "Why do you think the author wants us to know about this?" This type of understanding is developed through group discussions.

   ■ Students can rewrite familiar stories but change the point of view of the characters. For example, how would Beatrix Potter's *The Tale of Peter Rabbit* (1902, 1986) change if it were told through the point of view of Mr. McGregor who is trying to keep rabbits out of his garden. Who would now be the antagonist(s) in the story? How would they create sympathy for the gardener?

USING SEMANTIC MAPPING OR WEBBING TO SUMMARIZE LITERARY ELEMENTS
Semantic mapping is a technique that students use to visually show the relationships among ideas. It has been used in numerous studies to increase reading comprehension (Lapp, Flood, & Hoffman, 1996). The technique is especially effective for helping students identify the literary elements in a story and then fill in the supporting information for each of the literary elements.

To develop the semantic map, first place the title of the book in the center of the map or web. Next, draw the literary elements on a diagram as shown in Figure 7.2.

Review each of the terms with students to make sure that students can identify the meanings of each of the literary elements. Next, have students read or listen to the book identified in the center of the web. The information on the web may be completed after the book is read or the book may be reread to help students identify the supporting information. The semantic map shown in Figure 7.3, completed by second-grade students, illustrates the technique used with *The Tale of Peter Rabbit*.

This approach may be used as a group activity after students have listened to or read a book, or it may be used as an individual activity after students have read a book. The first time the activity is used, the teacher should model it. The strategy is an excellent way for students to develop book reports and to prepare for oral discussions.

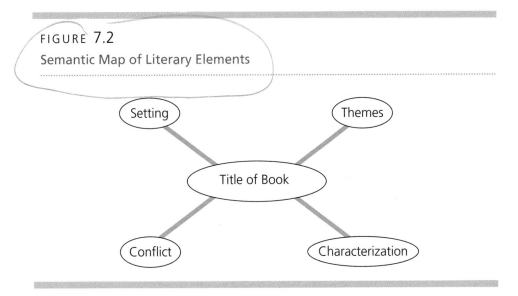

FIGURE 7.2

Semantic Map of Literary Elements

Developing Knowledge of Literary Genres

The scope and sequence included at the beginning of this chapter emphasized that students ages five to seven should know the difference between fiction and nonfiction and students ages seven to nine should recognize and appreciate different literary genres. When teachers use a variety of literatures in the reading curriculum, students will read folktales, historical fiction, poetry, contemporary realistic fiction, biography, and informational materials. One of the best ways to increase understanding of these specific genres is to develop genre-based units that allow students

1. to read and identify characteristics of the specific genre;
2. to develop a series of questions that help them decide whether a selection meets the genre criteria;
3. to test the criteria on new selections;
4. to use those characteristics to write original stories that meet the characteristics of the genre;
5. to compare the characteristics of that genre with other genres according to such literary elements as setting, characterization, and plot development.

A unit using a study of various "Cinderella" variants is developed later in this chapter in "Reading and Literature in Social Studies."

This section on developing knowledge of literary genres defines characteristics of various genres and provides examples of genre-literature that is appropriate for students in K through fourth grades. Teachers may use these definitions and examples to help students develop their own definitions for each genre and provide suggestions for how that genre should be read. For example, are there different requirements for writing and reading genres that are fiction, such as fantasy, and nonfiction, such as biography or information books? Are there different purposes

FIGURE 7.3

Completed Semantic Map of *The Tale of Peter Rabbit*

for reading and writing each of these genres? This section includes picture books because they are the most common literature read to and by younger children.

Picture Books   Picture books include a sequence of illustrations that complements text or even takes the place of words, as in wordless books. The illustrations in a picture book are an integral part of the action in the book where the characters, settings, and actions are shown through the illustrations. There is complete integration when the words emphasize a detail, clarify an action, or link pictures together. In Maurice Sendak's *Where the Wild Things Are* (1963), for example, the rhythmic sounds of the words augment the illustrations. The descriptions of gnashing teeth and rolling

When a teacher instructs students in the characteristics of a literary genre, the students increase both their comprehension of and their enjoyment for reading that genre.

eyes also provide information that cannot be fully shown in the illustrations. Examples of picture books that may be read and discussed to help students clarify the definition of picture books include:

- Emily Arnold McCully's *Picnic* (1984), which develops both plot and characterization through illustrations in a wordless book.

- Helen Cooper's *A Pipkin of Pepper* (2005), an illustrated book in which the illustrations depict the setting and considerable conflict, but the text also adds to the understanding by varying the size of the print. "NO!" is written in large uppercase letters, and the illustrations show the animals reacting violently to the taste of soup without "a speckle of salt." This is also an excellent book to model the influence of printed clues when reading a book aloud.

- John J. Muth's *Zen Shorts* (2005) is an example of an illustrated book in which the illustrator uses colored illustrations to tell a contemporary story and black-and-white illustrations to accompany the classic Zen stories.

- Arthur Yorinks's *Hey Al* (1986), where the text and the illustrations play more equal roles. The developing conflict is enhanced as illustrations increase in size as the setting becomes fanciful and the plot nears the climax.

Discussion topics and questions to help students decide if a book is a picture book:

1. Describe the picture sequence in the book. Does the book contain a picture sequence that complements the words or even takes the place of the words?

2. Use the illustrations to describe the setting and the characterizations. Are the illustrations an integral part of the settings, the actions, and the characterizations?

3. Describe the importance of the illustrations and the text. Are the illustrations of at least equal importance when compared to the written text?

4. Describe how you respond to the illustrations. Do the illustrations encourage interpretation, reflection, and viewers' response?

Folktales   Folktales are part of traditional literature that were handed down from generation to generation through word of mouth. Traditional literature includes folktales, myths, and legends. (We will emphasize folktales because they are commonly read in lower elementary grades.) Folktales are considered fiction; they are set in any time and any place ("Once upon a time in a great forest . . ."). The human characters range from poor peasants who search for riches to princes who quest for thrones or objects of power. The nonhuman characters may be supernatural adversaries such as ogres and witches who entice human characters into dangerous circumstances. Animals in folktales may be adversaries such as the cunning wolf or they may be loyal companions. Magical objects, spells, and transformations frequently assist or hinder the characters as they complete their tasks.

Examples of folktales that may be shared and discussed include:

■ Verna Aardema's *Who's in Rabbit's House?* illustrated by Leo and Diane Dillon (1977), a Masai folktale from Africa.

■ Charles Perrault's *Cinderella,* retold and illustrated by Barbara McClintock (2005), a folktale from France.

■ Ed Young's *I, Doko: The Tale of a Basket* (2004), a tale from Nepal.

Discussion topics and questions to help students decide if a book is a folktale:

1. What is the original cultural source for the tale? Is the tale part of a body of literature that was originally passed down through the oral tradition?

2. Does the adapter or translator identify the original cultural source for the tale?

3. How does the tale meet the characteristics of a folktale? Is it fictitious, set in any time and any place, and includes human or nonhuman characters?

Modern Fantasy   Unlike folktales that have no original author, modern fantasy has an original author, even though some of the stories sound like folktales. Modern fantasy is fiction in which the author takes the reader into a time and a setting where the impossible becomes convincingly possible. To create a fantasy experience authors alter or manipulate one or more of the literary elements from what is expected in the real world. The elements that are most apt to be changed are setting, characters, and time. Not all of these elements need to be manipulated in any one book.

Examples of modern fantasy that may be shared and discussed include:

■ A. A. Milne's *Winnie-the-Pooh* (1926, 1954), the adventures of a toy and his friends.

■ E. B. White's *Charlotte's Web* (1952), with farm animals that talk.

■ Margery Williams's *The Velveteen Rabbit,* with various illustrators of the original text first published in 1958, a story in which a toy rabbit becomes real because of love.

Discussion topics and questions to help students decide if a selection is modern fantasy:

1. How has the author manipulated or altered the literary elements so that the story takes place in a world other than the real world of today?

2. What is the evidence that the setting has been altered?

3. What is the evidence that the characters are different from characters living in the real world?

4. How did the author make readers believe that the story could be real?

Contemporary Realistic Fiction   Settings and stories in contemporary realistic fiction must be in the contemporary world as we know it. The characters act like real people. If the characters are animals, they must behave like animals, not personified versions of people. The conflicts and the ways that characters overcome their conflicts must revolve around problems that are possible in today's world. The problems must also be resolved in ways that are possible in this world. To develop believable stories, authors rely on relevant subjects, everyday occurrences, and realism.

Examples of contemporary realistic fiction that may be read and discussed:

■ Diane Gonzales Bertrand's *Uncle Chente's Picnic* (2001), written in English and Spanish, follows a Latino family as they prepare for a Fourth of July picnic.

■ Beverly Cleary's *Ramona Quimby, Age 8* (1981) is a story about a spunky, humorous girl.

■ Kelly Cunnane's *For You Are a Kenyan Child* (2006) highlights the Kenyan countryside and culture as well as family responsibility.

■ Karen English's *Hot Day on Abbott Avenue* (2004) is a story about two friends who have a fight and then eventually make up.

Discussion topics and questions related to contemporary realistic fiction:

1. Describe the setting. Is everything in the setting possible in the contemporary world as we know it?

2. Describe the characters. Do all the characters act like real people or real animals?

3. Describe the conflict and the plot development. Do the problems seem real in the contemporary world? Do the characters solve their problems in ways that could actually happen?

Historical Fiction   Historical fiction is a story written about an earlier time. Even though the story is fiction, the setting needs to be accurate for the time period. Even though the characters are fictional, they need to have actions, beliefs, and values that are realistic for the historical setting. The conflicts must reflect the historical time period.

Examples of historical fiction that can be read and discussed:

■ Patricia MacLachlan's *Sarah, Plain and Tall* (1985) is set in one of the prairie states in the 1800s.

- Margaree King Mitchell's *Uncle Jed's Barbershop* (1993) is set in the segregated south of the 1920s when an African American finally attains his dream.

- Patricia Polacco's *The Butterfly* (2000) is set in Nazi-occupied France during World War II.

Discussion topics and questions related to historical fiction:

1. What is the time period developed in the book? Are both the time and place described so that they seem real for that time period? If there are illustrations, are they accurate for the time and place?

2. How do the fictional characters appear and behave? Is their appearance accurate for the time period? Do they dress and act as if they belonged to the time period?

3. What are the problems that the characters must overcome? Are these problems that actually occurred during the time period?

4. How does the author make readers believe that the story seems real for the time period?

Biography—Nonfiction   Biographies are books written about real people, living or dead. A biography must be a true story (nonfiction) about the main character and all of the other people in the story. The people must be real, and their actions, the settings, and the conflicts must have happened. Readers need to know, however, that understanding the point of view of the author is very important when reading biographies. Authors can change how a biographical character appears by what they decide to reveal about the character and how they interpret the happenings in the person's life.

Examples of biographies to read and discuss include:

- Laurence Anholt's *Stone Girl, Bone Girl: The Story of Mary Anning* (1999).

- Kathleen Krull's *Wilma Unlimited: How Wilma Rudolph Became the World's Fastest Woman* (1996).

- Peter Sis's *Follow the Dream: The Story of Christopher Columbus* (1991).

Discussion topics and questions related to biography:

1. Who is the biographical subject? Did that person really exist?

2. What is the plot and conflict in the story? Did this conflict really happen?

3. How does the author make you believe that the story is about a real person?

4. How does the author let the reader know that the person and the incidents really happened? Are there author's notes that tell readers how the author conducted research into the life of the person?

5. If photographs are used, how do they add to the information about the person?

Informational Books—Nonfiction   These nonfiction texts are used to supplement or to teach many of the content areas. The subjects range from history and culture to nature and science. There are also informational books that provide directions for activities from drama to cooking or photography. Accuracy in the content is very important; consequently, students need to be taught to evaluate the information in the books (McMackin, 1998).

Examples of nonfiction informational books that may be used for reading and discussion include:

- Deborah Dunleavy's *The Jumbo Book of Drama* (2004), part of the "Kids Can Press Jumbo Book Series."
- Dorothy Hinshaw Patent's *The Right Dog for the Job: Ira's Path from Service Dog to Guide Dog* (2004).
- Paul Showers's *A Drop of Blood* (2004), part of the "Let's-Read-and-Find-Out Science Series."

Discussion topics and questions that may be used to increase understanding include:

1. What is the subject of the book? Do the facts appear to be accurate?

2. Who is the author of the book? Does the author have the qualifications to write a book on the subject? How can you tell?

3. How do the illustrations help readers understand the subject?

4. How does the book encourage readers to explore the subject?

5. How does the organization of the book help readers understand the subject?

PROVIDING THE PRACTICE As supported by schema theory, students who read widely and frequently develop sets of knowledge about the world and about literature that improve their comprehension skills and their ability to appreciate new experience with literature. Teachers may use several different types of groupings to increase reading. Some of these groupings provide opportunities for students to discuss books that they have read, while the focus for other groupings is to provide opportunities for students to use dramatic presentations to interpret the readings.

Literacy Circles Literacy circles, often called literature circles, are formed as small groups of students meet to discuss books they have read or even listened to during oral reading by an adult. To develop the circles, teachers may identify the books that will be discussed, place the books in an attractive area of the classroom, prepare a brief introduction to the books or to the topic, allow students to preview the books, and ask the students to identify the books that they will read and discuss.

Next, students read their chosen book or listen to the book being read. During this reading they consider information about the setting, plot, and characters that they want to discuss. After reading their chosen book, they meet in their group to talk about and respond to their reading. Students may begin or lead the discussion. Or, the teacher may take on the role of discussion leader.

While literacy circles may focus on any topic, an interesting subject for the beginning of school is reading and responding to books about going back to school. Many of these books discuss the anxiety felt by children when they return to school. But the books also show how book characters anticipate going to school and gain self confidence as part of the experience. Interesting responses occur when students read and discuss these books and then compare the way the book characters may handle the beginning of school with the students' own reactions. For this topic, stu-

Partner reading provides practice in literacy.

dents could select, read, and discuss any of the following books (grade levels are included):

- Maya Ajmera and John D. Ivanko's *Back to School* (2001): photographs of students going to school in Bangladesh, Niger, Saudi Arabia, and Rwanda (1–5).

- Margery Cuyler's *100th Day Worries* (2000): a first-grader is concerned about what to take to school to illustrate the 100th day of attendance (K–2).

- Julie Danneberg's *First Day Jitters* (2000): a girl is very nervous about her first day of school until the principal takes her into the classroom to meet her class. (K–3).

- Lee Bennett Hopkins's *School Supplies: A Book of Poems* (1996): the poems focus on topics related to back to school (K–4).

- Ellen Jackson's *It's Back to School We Go! First Day Stories from around the World* (2003): eleven students tell about schooling in their countries (K–5).

- Soyung Pak's *Sumi's First Day of School Ever* (2003): a Korean girl is concerned about starting school in the United States (K–3).

Specialists in child development, such as Teresa M. McDevitt and Jeanne Ellis Ormrod (2004), believe that students benefit from discussing the emotions experienced by characters they study in literature and history. They explain that "stories provide many opportunities to talk about emotional states. . . . Children in the elementary grades are able to make sensible guesses about how characters' emotional states lead them to particular courses of action" (p. 386). All of the books listed about back-to-school experiences encourage students to empathize with another character, discuss a topic that is of real interest to them, realize that many children have similar feelings and emotions, discover cultural similarities and differences related to going to school, and recognize ways to develop self-confidence and replace feelings of anxiety with feelings of anticipation.

Focused Recreational Reading Groups   Students read more and remember more of the content when they are interested in what they are reading (Guthrie et al., 1998). Selecting specific types of reading that interests students, may be a focus for recreational reading groups. Two of the position statements from the International Reading Association (IRA, 2002) provide rationales for using focused recreational reading groups. The IRA recommends balancing direct instruction, guided instruction, and independent learning and teacher- and student-led discussions. To meet these recommendations, focused recreational reading groups can follow teachers' direct instructions about a form of literature, a characteristic of a literary genre, or a literary element. For example, following a series of lessons that use direct instruction to teach students how to search for theme in a book, students can read a wide variety of high-quality literature (another IRA position statement) and use the strategies taught by the teacher during independent learning. Focused recreational reading groups give students the opportunity to choose and read literature selections that deal with a specific subject taught in the class or theme or topic and to respond verbally to features of literature.

To balance discussions led by teachers and students, the focused recreational reading groups can use both types of discussions. When beginning the groupings, teachers lead the discussions in one large group of readers. To act as role models for independent reading behaviors, teachers begin the sharing by telling something interesting about the book they are reading. After this initial experience, teachers structure the groupings by dividing the class into approximately three groups. Students bring their books to one of the three circles, read independently for about thirty minutes, and then share orally something interesting about their reading. Teachers maintain an active involvement in each group's sharing experience.

Recreational reading groups can easily focus on genres of literature or specific literary elements. Consequently, they provide opportunities to practice reading and sharing many more selections than would be possible within the reading curriculum. For example, after students have read folktales in class and discussed their characteristics, they are ready to develop broader understandings of folktales from a specific country. After the class reads and discusses a folktale from Africa, for instance, a recreational reading group could focus on additional African folktales such as those found in the following list. (A readability level is included for each book.)

- Verna Aardema's *Anansi Does the Impossible: An Ashanti Tale* (1997) R:4.
- Verna Aardema's *Who's in Rabbit's House?* (1977) R:3.
- Ashley Bryan's *The Story of Lightning and Thunder* (1993) R:5.

After the class reads and discusses an African American folktale they could read:

- Virginia Hamilton's *Bruh Rabbit and the Tar Baby Girl.* (2003) R:4.
- Joel Chandler Harris's *Jump! The Adventures of Brer Rabbit,* Adapted by Van Dyke Parks (1986) R:4.
- Joel Chandler Harris's *The Tales of Uncle Remus: The Adventures of Brer Rabbit,* retold by Julius Lester (1987) R:4.

Similar recreational reading groups can focus on any of the genres of literature and the literary elements that make the literature interesting to the students. They might share beginning paragraphs or authors' styles that are appealing. This sharing allows the students to read orally to the group a selection that they choose. Poetry in particular is conducive to this more relaxed environment, which encourages students to read for personal enjoyment and to share passages that are particularly illuminating and exciting. The oral sharing could emphasize the elements particular to narrative poetry, such as plot and characterization, and also the elements common to all types of poetry, such as rhythm. Narrative poetry that might be read and discussed include

- Kathi Appelt's *Oh My Baby, Little One* (2000)
- Julie Fields's *The Green Lion of Zion Street* (1988)
- Edward Lear's *The Owl and the Pussycat,* illustrated by Jan Brett (1991)
- Nancy Willard's *The Tale I Told Sasha* (1999)

When students share books they enjoy they are also motivating other students to read the same literature. A classmate provides a powerful critic.

Partner Reading   Peer-assisted reading is another grouping and learning strategy that improves comprehension of what is read and provides additional practice with reading (Fuchs et al., 1997). This approach matches a stronger reader and one that is weaker in reading ability. Each pair of students reads the materials and then follows the reading with any of the following three ways for structuring the partner reading:

1. *Partner reading and retelling:* In this example, the stronger reader reads a selection aloud for five minutes. The weaker reader then reads aloud the same passage. Following this reading, the weaker reader describes the material that is read.

2. *Paragraph summary:* Both of the readers read a passage one paragraph at a time. The stronger reader then helps the weaker reader identify the subject and the main idea of each paragraph.

3. *Prediction relay:* Both students read a page. The weaker reader summarizes the text and also makes a prediction about what the next page will include. The students then read the following page, and the weaker reader confirms or rejects the prediction. This process continues as the students read the page, summarize the content, and make predictions about the following page.

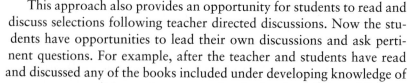

This approach also provides an opportunity for students to read and discuss selections following teacher directed discussions. Now the students have opportunities to lead their own discussions and ask pertinent questions. For example, after the teacher and students have read and discussed any of the books included under developing knowledge of literary elements or developing knowledge of literary genres, the partner reading approach could focus on a literary element found in the literature or on the characteristics of a selection that cause the selection to be labeled one of the genres. Can students read a new selection and predict what genre of literature it is? Or, can they identify a particular pleasing example of author's style?

Readers' Theater   **Readers' theater** is an oral interpretation of literature in which the students read the script aloud instead of memorizing the parts as in other types of theater presentations (Norton, 2004). Children's literature provides many excellent examples of texts that have sufficient dialogue or passages that can be changed into dialogue and read by students as if they are performing in a play. Materials that are good for readers' theater include these characteristics:

- The story includes a well-designed plot.
- The action is easy to follow.
- The ending is clear and satisfying.
- The characters are understandable through the dialogue.
- There is sufficient dialogue or these are passages that can be changed into dialogue.
- Repetitive words and phrases enhance the experience if they encourage audience participation.

Teachers of students in K through fourth-grade classrooms can develop a simplified readers' theater that includes the following steps:

1. After selecting a story that meets the above characteristics, have the students read the selection silently and discuss the characteristics of the story that make it good for readers' theater.
2. Read the story orally as a group. Let the students choose parts, or designate which part each student will read.
3. During a third reading, have each student read his or her part but also act it out.
4. A director, who may be the teacher, reads the title, the cast of characters, and a description of the setting or actions.
5. During a fourth reading, the story and cast of characters are introduced and the players walk through the action as they read their parts.

The following selections provide effective sources for readers' theater because the books include both dialogue and humorous or adventurous situations:

- Doreen Cronin's *Click, Clack, Moo: Cows That Type* (2000);
- Diana Engel's *Josephina Hates Her Name* (1989);
- Petra Mathers's *Theodor and Mr. Balbini* (1988);
- Pat Mora's *The Bakery Lady* (2001), written in both English and Spanish.

Choral Reading   **Choral reading** is a method that allows students to interpret the language through the use of two or more voices speaking as one. It is a group activity that allows children to experience, enjoy, and increase their interest in poetic elements such as rhymes, to use their voices to build up to the climax in a story, or to create the mood of a story or poem through the use of voices that range from soft to loud. During a choral reading experience, students discover that speaking voices can be combined as effectively as singing voices.

Teachers of children with special reading needs find that choral reading provides repeated reading practice and develops a realization that reading can be fun. Because choral reading is a group activity, it builds positive group attitudes and realizations that some activities are better if they are performed cooperatively. Reading performance and vocabulary knowledge for lower ability readers is improved through choral reading in which the teacher emphasizes correct phrasing, intonation, and pitch (Eldridge, 1990).

Here are some general guidelines for developing choral reading activities:

- Choose materials that interest the age level of the students. Younger children like nonsense and active words and humorous selections.

- Encourage students to select and interpret the materials. Allow them to experiment with the material, improvise the scenes of the selection, and try different arrangements for choral reading.

- Allow them to listen to each other as they try different interpretations of the reading and to discuss their responses to those interpretations.

The following lesson plan suggests ways that choral reading may be developed using nursery rhymes with children in the lower elementary grades. It uses the nursery rhymes to show students different choral arrangements.

FOCUS ACTIVITY:
Lesson Plan for Choral Reading of Nursery Rhymes

OBJECTIVES	1. To respond to poetry or other literature through an enjoyable group activity
	2. To interact with the rhythm and tempo of literature through an oral presentation
	3. To heighten an understanding of literary elements

| GRADE LEVELS | Lower elementary (K–4, depending on selections) |

PROCEDURES	1. Select poems or other literature selections appropriate for the reading ability of the students. Poems and rhymes with refrains are especially appropriate for younger students because they can participate almost immediately in the activity.
	2. Allow students to help select and interpret the materials.
	3. Encourage students to explore the rhythm in the language. For example, students can clap out fast and slow rhythms as the teacher reads poetry and nursery rhymes aloud.
	4. Develop a series of experiences in which students try out various types of choral arrangements before experimenting with their own interpretations. The following examples show five different arrangement patterns using nursery rhymes (nursery rhymes are found in numerous sources):

Refrain arrangement: The teacher or a child reads the body of a poem or rhyme and the class responds in unison during the refrain or chorus:

LEADER: A farmer went trotting upon his gray mare,

GROUP: Bumpety, bumpety, bump!

LEADER: With his daughter behind him so rosy and fair.

GROUP: Lumpety, lumpety, lump!

LEADER: A raven cried "Croak!" and they all tumbled down,

GROUP: Bumpety, bumpety, bump!

LEADER: The mare broke her knees, and the farmer his crown.

GROUP: Lumpety, lumpety, lump!

LEADER: The mischievous raven flew laughing away,

GROUP: Bumpety, bumpety, bump!

LEADER: And vowed he would serve them the same the next day,

GROUP: Lumpety, lumpety, lump!

Line-a-child or line-a-group arrangement: One child or group of children reads one line, another child or group reads the next line, a third child or group reads the third line, and so forth:

GROUP A: This little pig went to market;

GROUP B: This little pig stayed at home;

GROUP C: This little pig had roast beef;

GROUP D: And this little pig had none;

GROUP E: This little pig said, "Wee, wee, wee! I can't find my way home."

Antiphonal or dialogue arrangement: This arrangement requires alternate speaking by two groups. Boys' voices can be balanced against girls' voices, high voices against low voices:

GROUP A: Little boy blue, come blow your horn,

GROUP B: The sheep's in the meadow, the cow's in the corn;

GROUP A: Where is the boy who looks after the sheep?

GROUP B: He's under the haystack fast asleep,

GROUP A: Will you wake him? No, Not I;

GROUP B: For if I do, he'll be sure to cry.

Cumulative arrangement or crescendo arrangement is used when a poem builds to a climax. One group reads the first line, the first and second groups read the second line, and so forth, until the poem reaches its climax, at which time all the groups read together:

GROUP A: Little Miss Muffet

GROUP A AND B: Sat on a tuffet,

GROUP A, B, AND C: Eating her curds and whey;

GROUP A, B, C, AND D: Then came a great spider, And sat down beside her,

GROUP A, B, C, D, AND E: And frightened Miss Muffet away.

Unison arrangement: The entire group or class presents a whole selection together. Good choices are shorter poems and nursery rhymes:

WHOLE GROUP: Twink, twink, twink, twink.

Twinkety, twinkety, twink!

The fireflies light their lanterns,

Then put them out in a wink.

5. After students have tried various types of choral reading arrangements, allow them to experiment with different arrangements using the same poem. Present the arrangements, and discuss the effectiveness of each approach. They should consider the influence of voices and types of arrangements on the rhythm, tempo, feelings and moods expressed by the poems.

Reading and Literature in Social Studies

The content of social studies and history includes many opportunities for students and teachers to learn about the cultures of various countries, to learn about the history of their own country, and to develop units that reinforce the study of both literary elements and genres of literature found in the English/language arts curriculum. The development of units is an especially powerful way for students to be introduced to the inquiry method as they choose a topic to study, formulate questions about the topic, plan their study, gather and sort information, synthesize and organize information, and present reports. (The steps in developing the inquiry method are presented in Chapter 8.)

The scope and sequence for cognitive development in social studies discussed in Chapter 2 of this text identified the social studies skills taught in the early elementary grades including kindergarten: applying critical-thinking skills, gaining information through visual sources, sequencing and categorizing information, identifying main ideas and expressing ideas orally. Grade two: creating written and visual materials, using problem-solving processes, and decision-making skills to gather information and predict consequences. Grade four: applying critical thinking skills and using problem-solving and decision-making skills when conducting research. At each of these grade levels literature selections help students develop an understanding of history, geography, and citizenship.

Several of the competencies identified in the scope and sequence at the beginning of this chapter are essential if students are to locate information and conduct research in

Reflect on Your Reading

The previously described strategies under "Providing the Practice" encourage students to read widely and apply the strategies they learn about reading literature in the English/language arts curriculum. Consider both the motivational quality of the strategies and the potential for enhancing the lessons taught about literature through more direct instruction. Which strategies have the greatest motivational impact? Which strategies reinforce learning by extending independent discovery? What additions would you add to each strategy to increase both the motivational and the learning potentials?

the social studies. For example, recognizing and using different parts of a book, knowing the difference between fiction and nonfiction; and reading and sorting a variety of texts connected with the current unit of inquiry such as discovering similarities and differences found in folktales.

Using Different Parts of a Book

Teaching students to use the parts of a book such as the table of contents, index, glossary, and further readings is important if students are to become independent learners. As part of this learning experience they need to understand the importance of each of these parts of a book.

Teachers can model with students how they use each of these parts of a book during their own selections of materials and inquiry. Select a book that includes important reading aids that you might use when choosing materials to share with students during social studies. Introduce and describe each of the aids found in the book. Discuss the purpose for the aids and how they help you find information. For example, *Sing a Song of Popcorn: Every Child's Book of Poems,* selected by Beatrice Schenk de Regniers (1988), includes poems that you might read as part of various content areas.

The table of contents in the book divides the poems according to "Fun with Rhymes," "Mostly Weather," "Spooky Poems," "Story Poems," "Mostly Animals," "Mostly People," "Mostly Nonsense," "Seeing, Feeling, Thinking," and "In a Few Words." Note that each of the poems under these categories includes the page number within the text. Be sure that students understand the convenience of locating the poems through the table of contents and the accompanying page numbers, rather than searching through the whole book to find a category of poem you want to share. Also share and discuss the importance of the other aids in the book including an "Index of Titles," an "Index of First Lines," an "Index of Authors," and "About the Artists." Students can use these aids to locate a specific poem in the text.

Although many of the books written for students in the lower elementary grades do not include page numbers or aids such as a table of contents, there are anthologies that may be used by students to locate information for a unit of study. If students are studying Native American cultures and literature from the Southwest, for example, they could discover the advantages of a table of contents, an index, notes about the contributors to the text, and a bibliography of additional materials in Nancy Wood's *The Serpent's Tongue: Prose, Poetry, and Art of the New Mexico Pueblos* (1997).

When learning about various occupations they can use Pat Cummings and Linda Cummings's *Talking with Adventurers* (1998) to investigate the use of a table of contents, a map showing the location of the fieldwork sites for each adventurer, and an extensive glossary of terms. If studying the history of the United States government or the presidents of the United States, they can use Katherine Leiner's *First Children: Growing Up in the White House* (1996) to discover the importance of a table of contents, an afterword that includes additional information about each president, a family tree showing each president's children, a selected bibliography of additional sources, and a list of credits for the photographs and engravings used in the book. This book also makes an interesting project for students. It ends with Chelsea Clinton. Students can extend the book to include the latest children of the current president.

Differences between Fiction and Nonfiction

When students conduct research as part of a unit of study, they need to understand the differences between fiction and nonfiction or fact (International Baccalaureate Organization, 2003). While some lessons or units such as a study of the poetic elements or locating plot development and conflict usually use fictional sources, other units and lesson plans such as discovering the origins of symbols associated with holidays require nonfiction.

Begin by discussing with students their understandings of the meaning of fact, as used in nonfiction materials, and fiction. When is each of these terms used? Students can use their classroom dictionaries and thesaurus to look up the terms. They can find and discuss definitions such as "Fact is something that has happened or is true." They can also locate and discuss synonyms such as truth, reality, certainty, and accuracy. For fiction they can find and discuss definitions such as, "something that has been made up, something that did not happen." They can locate and discuss synonyms such as story, tale, yarn, fantasy and falsehood.

Collect several books and ask students to read or listen to the books and categorize the books according to fiction and nonfiction. After reading the books, ask students to divide them into categories of fiction and nonfiction and to provide reasons for their categorizations. You may use many of the books previously discussed under literary elements and genres. Students might develop a chart such as the one found in Table 7.1.

Similarities and Differences between Versions of a Folktale

Studying variants of the same folktale found in different countries and cultures encourages students to develop understandings of cultural diffusion and common needs

TABLE 7.1

Differences between Fiction and Nonfiction

Fiction	Why Is It Fiction?	Nonfiction	Why Is It Nonfiction?
Van Allsburg's *The Polar Express* (1985)		Peter Sis's *Follow The Dream* (1991)	
E. B. White's *Charlotte's Web* (1952)		Margery Facklam's *Spiders and Their Web Sites* (2001)	
Jim Aylesworth's *Goldilocks and the Three Bears* (2003)		Kathleen Krull's *Wilma Unlimited* (1996)	

and problems (International Baccalaureate Organization, 2003). Variations of "Cinderella," for example, are found in cultures throughout the world. Such a unit also helps students understand that folktales change across time. The following unit is appropriate for students in grades two through four.

FOCUS UNIT:
Comparing Different Versions of "Cinderella"

OBJECTIVES

1. To read and enjoy variations of the same folktale
2. To identify common elements within the folktales and discover how the culture is reflected in the tales
3. To discover that folktales are excellent sources of information about a culture
4. To become aware of cultural diffusion

audience
— more than just grade level

GRADE LEVELS Second through fourth

MATERIALS A selection of tales that reflect the "Cinderella" motif found in various cultures. Examples of literature include:

(French) Charles Perrault's *Cinderella,* illustrated by Marcia Brown (1954) or *Cinderella* (2005) illustrated by Barbara McClintock

(German) Brothers Grimm's "Cinderella" in *Household Tales* (1973)

(English) Charlotte Huck's retelling of *Princess Furball* (1989)

(North Carolinian) William Hooks's *Moss Gown* (1987)

(Native American–Zuni) Penny Pollock's *The Turkey Girl* (1996)

(Native American–woodlands Indians) "The Indian Cinderella" in Virginia Haviland's *North American Legends* (1979)

(African) John Steptoe's *Muffaro's Beautiful Daughters* (1987)

(Vietnamese) Lynette Dyer Vuong's *The Brocaded Slipper* (1982)

(Chinese) At-Lang Louie's *Yeh Shen: A Cinderella Story from China* (1982)

(Jewish) Josepha Sherman's "Cinderella" in *Rachel the Clever and Other Jewish Folktales* (1993)

PROCEDURES

1. Explain to the students that some folktales have common story types found in cultures throughout the world. These folktales are called variants because they have basic elements in common, but they differ in such areas as settings, names of characters, magical objects, tasks to be completed, and obstacles to be overcome.
2. After students have read or listened to several "Cinderella" stories, ask them to identify the common elements in different versions,

such as those retold by Grimm and Perrault. Remind the students that the common elements should be general, such as "the heroine has a lowly position in the family." A list from Grimm and Perrault might include:

- The heroine has a lowly position in the family.
- The heroine is treated badly by stepsisters.
- The heroine accomplishes difficult tasks.
- The heroine meets a person who is important in the culture.
- The heroine is kept from meeting the person because she lacks clothing to attend a function.
- The heroine is helped by a supernatural being.
- The heroine is warned to return by a certain time.
- The person of great worth is attracted to the heroine.
- There is a test for the rightful heroine.
- The heroine passes the test and marries the person of great worth.

3. Ask the students to identify how each of these common elements are developed in the German and French tales, but also discuss some specific differences. For example, the girl in the German version receives her wishes from a bird on the tree on her mother's grave and the girl in the French version receives wishes from a fairy godmother. The endings are also different: The German version ends unhappily for the stepmother and stepsisters while the French version ends in forgiveness of the stepsisters and their marriage to noblemen.

4. After students have identified common elements and discussed specific examples across the German and French "Cinderella" tales, ask them to read or listen to variants from other cultures. During this activity they identify the elements that are similar and those that are different. Why do the elements in the stories change? How are these changes related to the cultures in which the tales were originally told? They should also analyze the illustrations for cultural information—the illustrations in the Chinese "Cinderellas," for example, illustrate considerable cultural background through the illustrations.

5. The Native American "Cinderella" variants are especially rich with cultural and setting information that is important in the social studies curriculum. When reading or listening to "The Indian Cinderella," for example, the students can identify the elements in the story that are common to the previously listed elements. Then they can identify the elements that reflect the Native American setting (woodlands) or the Native American culture. A list of Native American setting and cultural elements from "The Indian Cinderella" includes the following points:

- The setting is on the Atlantic coast.
- The person of great worth is Strong Wind, a great Indian warrior.
- Strong Wind lives in a tent near the sea.
- The heroine is one of three daughters of a great chief.
- The test is to describe the invisible Strong Wind and the sled that he pulls across the sky.

- The heroine patches her clothes with bits of birch bark.
- The heroine passes the test and describes Strong Wind as pulling his sled with the rainbow and holding a bow string that is the Milky Way.
- The heroine's raven hair is restored.
- The heroine marries Strong Wind and helps him do great deeds.
- The elder sisters are changed into aspen trees as punishment for their lies and cruelty.

6. As part of social studies, students should understand that the story has many of the "Cinderella" elements but is also set firmly in the culture of the woodlands Indians. As do many Native American tales, the story has a close relationship with nature and the tale concludes with an answer to why something occurs in nature: The elder sisters who were changed into aspen trees still tremble when Strong Wind approaches because they fear his anger.

7. This unit can be expanded to include art activities as students draw the various settings. They may place the stories on a map of the world. They may also prepare their favorite stories for an oral story-telling concert in which they also share cultural knowledge gained from the folktales.

After students complete a unit such as this "Cinderella" unit, teachers learn a great deal by listening to and reading their responses to the literature. The responses are significant because they let teachers discover how much information about the plot, conflict, and theme of the story the students understand. The following is an example of a response to questions given by a third-grade student. Students in the class were introduced to this "Cinderella" unit (Garcia, 2003). They read and discussed the literature, drew plot structures, developed literary webs using the books, and shared their plot diagrams and webs with their classes. The students read *Yen-Shen: A Cinderella Story from China* (1982). The spellings are in the student's original writing.

QUESTION: What emotions did you feel as you read the literature?

STUDENT: "I felt very sad because she was a slave and because it wasn't fair."

QUESTION: What is your first response or reaction to the literature?

STUDENT: "My first reaction was why were they jelous of her if she was not rich and my first response was she was sufering."

QUESTION: What in the text or in the reading of the literature caused you the most trouble?

STUDENT: "When they did not let her go to the ball."

QUESTION: If you were to write about your reading, upon what would you focus?

STUDENT: "I will focus on why they were jealus of the sister."

QUESTION: Do you think this is a good piece of literature? Why? Why not?

STUDENT: I think this is very good literature to read because it shows you how to apreciate and care about your family members."

QUESTION:	What sort of person do you think the author is?
STUDENT:	"I think that he is very good on writing stories on China because he wants to create stories to tell kids about China and to show them how to care for each other."
QUESTION:	Does the story remind you of any other literature or personal experiences you have had?
STUDENT:	"It reminds me of the Little Red Hen because the hen stays with the cake and the girl with the guy." (Personal experiences:) "Yes, my friend has a step mother and she is not like this one, she is nice."

Reading and Literature in Science

According to the definition of social studies developed by the National Council for the Social Studies (1992), there is a relationship between social studies and science. According to the National Council, students should study advances in science and discover how these advances affect the development of society. As part of this study, students understand changes in ways people live, learn, and work—past, present, and future—through analyzing the relationships among science, technology, society, and the environment. As part of this study, students begin to use a scientific method to locate and analyze information, and to solve problems and make decisions.

There is also a close relationship between science and literature. In science students use both hands-on experiences and literature selections, for example. The classroom for early elementary students usually includes science centers or interest centers in which students are encouraged to observe and examine objects visually and through touch and hearing and to use all of their senses to describe objects. At the centers students may classify or sort objects by grouping them according to a property such as color or size. After sorting, they may describe the process they used to categorize the materials. To help the students make decisions and to expand their reading ability, the centers include highly illustrated books that focus on the content of the science center.

Connections between Science Centers and Literature

When teaching through a science center teachers introduce the center in such a way that students relate the subject matter to any past experiences and previous knowledge (Maxim, 1989). The students identify what they know and what they would like to find out about the subject. The teacher may refer to a book read on the subject and ask students to list questions that resulted from the reading. Or, teachers may introduce a film about the subject and ask

Reflect on Your **Reading**

This section on reading and literature in the English/language arts presents many of the strategies that encourage students to comprehend and enjoy the various types of texts used in the English/language arts curriculum. These strategies also provide opportunities to balance the reading curriculum by extending reading beyond the teaching of word attack strategies. How important are these English/language arts strategies for developing a total reading curriculum? Which approach for teaching reading in the English/language arts were part of your elementary education?

students to describe what they observe in the film and then expand the discussion to additional questions they would like answered. For example, the science center might include animals such as turtles, gerbils, hamsters, or guinea pigs. When introducing the center, teachers ask students to share what they know about the animals. They introduce any new vocabulary related to the science center and describe a learning experience such as investigating the habits of the animal and discovering information about care and feeding. Teachers may also introduce specific literature selections that are included at the science center.

There are many nonfiction books that enhance the subject matter for science or interest centers. A brief list of some of the subjects and the literature selections that could be included in the science center follows:

Butterflies	Eve Bunting's *Butterfly House* (1999)
	Kathryn Lasky's *Monarchs* (1993)
	Laurence Pringle's *An Extraordinary: The Story of a Monarch Butterfly* (1997)
	Butterfly House is especially good for a science center because it shows how a girl and her grandfather build a house for a larva and then watch it turn into a butterfly. Bunting includes details for raising a butterfly including finding a larva, preparing the jar, building the butterfly house, feeding the butterfly and releasing it back into nature.
Insects	Melvin Berger's *Spinning Spiders* (2003).
	Sandra Markle's *Creepy, Crawly Baby Bugs* (1996)
Potatoes	John Coy's *Two Old Potatoes and Me* (2003) presents steps in growing potatoes from cutting sprouts to planting pieces.
Frogs	Joy Cowley's *Red-Eyed Tree Frog* (1999)
	Vivian French's *Growing Frogs* (2000)
	Growing Frogs is another excellent text because it provides directions for collecting frog eggs, placing them in a fish tank, watching the eggs hatch into tadpoles, and observing various stages as the tadpoles grow into frogs. The book concludes with the need to return the frogs to the pond from which the eggs were collected.

Analyzing Organization of Science Literature

Teachers can help students read for understanding by analyzing the organization patterns in science literature (Norton & Norton, 2003). For example, many of the literature selections use organizational formats that help students comprehend the materials. Students can identify the advantages for using the format in informational literature and describe how an understanding of the format will improve their comprehension. After students identify and discuss the various formats, they can use the different formats in their own writing about science. The following examples illustrate question-answer and chronological-order formats found in science-related literature.

QUESTION-AND-ANSWER FORMATS   Seymour Simon's *New Questions and Answers about Dinosaurs* (1990) and Sylvia Funston's *The Dinosaur: Question and Answer Book* (1992) are both written in this format. Teachers may show students how this format works by sharing examples from the text, for example,

QUESTION: "Which was the largest meat-eater?"

ANSWER: "Tyrannosaurus, the 'tyrant lizard,' was the biggest meat-eating dinosaur" (p. 26). (The text provides additional information.)

QUESTION: "Which was the smallest dinosaur?"

ANSWER: "The smallest adult dinosaur whose bones have been found is named Compsognathus . . . It was about the size of a chicken (p. 29).

The Dinosaur: Question and Answer Book begins with test questions such as "What is a dinosaur?" and "Where did dinosaurs come from?" For each question, students choose from a series of three answers. They score their tests and are rated, from "room for improvement," to "you're on the right track," to "Dino-Buff." The text then continues with questions such as, "Where do you know where to look for dinosaurs?" answers to the questions, and illustrations that help develop understanding.

CHRONOLOGICAL ORDER   This format is a favorite for authors who write science materials. Books such as Thomas Locker's *Sky Tree: Seeing Science through Art* (1995) follow the same tree through the seasons of the year. The chronological order begins with the summer tree, and continues to the autumn tree, the winter tree, and the spring tree. In addition to illustrations that show the chronological order, the text concludes with a question-and-answer format, for example, following Autumn Tree: "What does the painting show us about autumn colors?" The text provides answers about autumn colors.

William T. George uses a chronological order that follows a turtle from sunrise to sunset in *Box Turtle at Long Pond* (1989). The heavily illustrated text begins, "It is dawn at Long Pond" and continues throughout the day until "The sun is dropping in the sky" to the final page when "The sun sets on the far side of Long Pond. The evening air grows colder. . . . It has been a long day" (unnumbered pages).

Joannne Cole follows the growth of a puppy in *My Puppy Is Born* (1991). Photographs and text follow the puppy from the time of birth through the first eight weeks. Through this chronological order readers follow the growth of the puppy during the first eight weeks, as the puppy is unable to see or hear, as the puppy nurses, and then as its eyes open and it takes a first step.

Students can find additional literature that uses a chronological format and discuss why the format is good in many of the science books. They can answer, "What subjects should be written in chronological order? How does chronological order in these subjects help readers understand the science concepts? How do the illustrations in the books help with the order of events?"

Finally, ask students to write their own illustrated books that use either a question-and-answer format or a chronological-order format. These books can be placed in the classroom library or in the science center and should be shared with an audience.

> **Reflect on Your Reading**
>
> How important is it to develop an understanding of reading through science? Consider newspapers and popular magazines. How are scientific articles written to help readers grasp the significance of the topic? How can literature be used to improve scientific understandings?

Up for Discussion

Declining Reading Habits

This chapter focuses on using literature in the content fields. Most of the strategies discussed are designed to develop both a love for literature and an understanding of literature, whether it is in the English/language arts, social studies, science, or art curricula. To develop exciting curricula requires students to read, discuss, and share findings using the literature. They need to become excited by the inquiry method and how they can use literature to make discoveries. This means that students need to become life-long readers and learners.

Within the last 20 years, however, something has happened to the reading habits of Americans. The National Endowment for the Arts reported a "bleak assessment" of the state of reading in America. "According to the endowment's survey, compiled from 2002 Census Bureau data, reading in general has gone down over the last 20 years, and reading of literature in particular. For the first time in our history, less than half the adult population reads fiction, poetry or plays" (McGrath, 2004).

Parents become involved in the excitement of reading and developing literacy for life when they help students pick out their books.

What has happened in the past 20 years that caused this to happen? How have your own reading habits changed? Do you read fiction and poetry? Why or why not? If you read fiction and poetry what motivates you to read? Can you identify a teacher, a librarian, or another adult who motivated you to read and acted as your role model? Can you identify some ways that you could make a difference and bring a love for reading into the lives of students?

When discussing this topic you may want to consider how Shelley Worman, winner of the 2004 Giant Step Award, changed not only the reading habits of students in a North Carolina school but also advanced the reading levels of the students. The school, with culturally diverse students from 18 countries and who speak seven languages, progressed from a failing level to one where more than 86 percent of the students perform at or above grade level in reading and math (Whelan, 2004). You may consider the impact of the following characteristics of the school:

- The library has an open door policy allowing students to come to the library every day. The library's yearly circulation went from 28,800 to 105,000.
- There is a close relationship between the library and the classroom. For example, a second-grade class uses the library to research how environmental changes affect pond life, another class is doing an author study of Marc Brown, and the librarian is making connections with the local American Kennel Club to create a reading program on pet care. The librarian helps teachers find materials that can be used in their units.
- Third through fifth grade ESL (English as a Second Language) students learn about each other's countries in a cultural awareness project that helps improve reading, writing, vocabulary, and research skills. The students published a 52-page guidebook arranged alphabetically by country.
- What made a difference in this school? How might this approach increase lifelong reading among the students? Why do you believe that the approach also increased reading and math scores?

Reading and Art

A study of art in grades K–4 is one of the best ways to relate literature and the content areas of English/language arts, social studies, and science. Through art, students in English/language arts can follow the literary elements of plot, conflict, characterization, and theme in the drawings found in books. They can reinforce emergent literacy skills related to the alphabet and phonemic awareness by investigating a range of alphabet books and comparing the images found in the books. In social studies, they can make discoveries about the home, school, and community and learn about the diverse nature of their world. Illustrated texts are especially meaningful as students take part in units about various cultures. Through the pictures, both photographs and paintings, they learn about habitats and other characteristics of the people's lives. In science, the illustrations in books help them visualize the power of nature and the characteristics of animals. In the art curriculum they learn about the elements of art such as line and color and the artistic media such as watercolors and oils. Just as in author studies, in art they can study the artists who created the works. They can enrich their vocabularies by learning the terminology associated with these artistic elements and the artists who created the pictures.

Fortunately, teachers and students have access to all of the beautifully illustrated books that have won Caldecott Medal and Honor Awards. These books are usually purchased by both school and public libraries. In addition, the books stay in print longer than many other books. Consequently, they are easily located.

Illustrations That Depict the Literary Elements

This study of illustrations may be part of an analysis of the literary characteristics of plot, conflict, characterization, and theme developed earlier in this chapter. Now students first use the illustrations to follow and identify the literary elements, decide on the effectiveness of the illustrations when developing each of the literary elements, and discuss the impact of the illustrations, which frequently, add to the development of the literary elements. Then they compare the effectiveness of the illustrations and the text. Books that have won the Caldecott Medal and Honor Awards for illustration are especially good for this analysis.

Plot Development and Conflict	Maurice Sendak's *Where the Wild Things Are* (1963, 1964 Caldecott)—The illustrations become larger on the page as the conflict develops. At the point of the greatest conflict, the illustrations take up double-page spreads without any words on the page.
Conflict	Eve Bunting's *Smoky Night* (1994, 1995 Caldecott)—The artist's collage illustrations depict the conflict associated with the Los Angeles riots. The objects chosen for the collages (such as dry cereal) effectively depict the setting and the magnitude of the destruction. The expressions on the faces reinforce this conflict. Students may also discover that this type of conflict is called "person against society."

Characterization	Bill Peet's *Bill Peet: An Autobiography* (1989, 1990 Caldecott Honor)—The illustrations, drawn in his characteristic cartoon style, depict Peet's life and his experiences as an artist for Walt Disney films such as "The Sword in the Stone." Peet wrote and illustrated 35 books for children. Consequently, his illustrated books would make a good artist's study and an investigation of cartoon-style-drawings.
Theme	Eric Rohmann's *My Friend Rabbit* (2002, 2003 Caldecott)—The illustrations depict the theme that friendship is important. But, they also show that trouble follows when these friends get together. The illustrations show the power of movement and line to advance the plot of the story.
	Toni DeTerlizzi's *The Spider and the Fly* (2002, 2003 Caldecott Honor). This cautionary tale is good for theme as the fly is captured when she listens to the flattering words of the spider. The black and white illustrations depict the spooky setting for the old house and the story that begins, " 'Will you walk into my parlor?' said the Spider to the Fly." Students can respond to the impact of line and color in the illustrations.

Some teachers collect all of the Caldecott Medal and Honor books, using them for discussions of both artistic elements and literary elements, as well as for artist studies.

Reinforcing Emergent Literacy by Examining Illustrations in Alphabet Books

There are literally dozens of alphabet books that may be used for this purpose. Depending on the ages of the students, some of the alphabet books illustrated for younger children are intended to teach the alphabet by presenting a letter and an object that begins with the letter. Alphabet books illustrated for students in second through fourth grades are usually more complex and may have themes that make them appropriate for unit studies. For this type of activity, share the various purposes for alphabet books with students and collect a variety of books. Ask students to examine the illustrations in the books, compare the layouts of the texts, respond to the effectiveness of the illustrations, and discuss the images created by the artists. The following alphabet books are categorized by subject:

AWARD-WINNING ALPHABET BOOKS   Three alphabet books have won the Caldecott Honor award and provide interesting discussions about and comparisons of artistic elements:

Stephen T. Johnson's *Alphabet City* (1995, 1996 Caldecott Honor)

The paintings show how the artist was inspired to relate the alphabet to objects that he saw along a city street. The letter *A*, for example, is a construction sawhorse. The book is also excellent for developing students' observational skills as they look for and draw alphabet-related objects in their own environments.

Suse MacDonald's *Alphabatics* (1986, 1987 Caldecott Honor)

Line and movement are very strong in the illustrations as the artist begins with a letter and turns the letter until it illustrates an object beginning with the letter. For example, the letter *Aa* begins with a block showing *A;* the next illustration tilts the *A* on its side and places it on waves; the third illustration places the *A* upside down on the waves; the forth illustration adds details to turn the *a* into an *ark.* The final full-page illustration shows an ark on the ocean with animals in the boat.

David Pelletier's *The Graphic Alphabet* (1996, 1997 Caldecott Honor)

In this alphabet book written for older students, the artist uses various shapes to portray the meanings of the letters. For example, a letter *A* is shown with pieces cut out of the top of the letter. The pieces are depicted falling down the letter to show the word *Avalanche.*

ALPHABET BOOKS WITH SPECIFIC THEMES   When responding to and discussing the illustrations in these alphabet books, students can also evaluate the categorizations of objects chosen to illustrate the themes:

Chris L. Demarest's *Firefighters A to Z* (2000)

Henry Horenstein. *A is for . . . ?: A Photographer's Alphabet of Animals* (1999)

Kathleen Krull's *M Is for Music* (2003)

Bob McLeod's *Super Hero ABC* (2006)

Jill Thornhill's *The Wildlife ABC: A Nature Alphabet Book* (1990)

After students have responded to the illustrations in many different alphabet books, they can create a class alphabet book with matching images. Alphabet books provide many models for the students because they can illustrate books with paintings, photographs, and even objects that might be found in a collage.

Comparing Illustrators' Interpretations of the Same Story

Since different artists have illustrated many well-known folktales, older poems, and fantasies, students can analyze the different interpretations and discuss the effectiveness of the art when presenting the same story (International Baccalaureate Organization, 2003). Students can also compare the artwork over different time periods.

Margery Williams's *The Velveteen Rabbit* has been illustrated by William Nicholson (1958); Allen Atkinson, (1984); Michael Hague, (1983); Ilise Plume, (1982); Michael Green, (1982); Tien, (1983). Students may also wish to consider what it is about the story that makes it so appealing to many artists.

Folktales such as "Snow White and the Seven Dwarfs," "Cinderella," "Three Billy Goats Gruff," and "The Three Little Pigs" have been illustrated by numerous artists. Collect as many different artistic interpretations as possible and ask

An art project is an excellent way to develop a book report.

students to compare the illustrations and discuss their responses to the illustrations. Which illustrations do they believe are the most effective? Why are they the most effective?

Use the illustrated versions of the various "Cinderella" tales listed in the Focus Unit: "Comparing Different Versions of Cinderella" developed earlier in this chapter. Ask students to compare the illustrations from the various cultures and to describe how the artists depict the cultures through the illustrations.

Using Art to Develop Book Reports

Art provides an interesting alternative to written book reports. To interpret a book through art, students need to understand not only the impact of various artistic elements, but also the genre of literature and the major literary elements found in the literature. After reading a fantasy such as C. S. Lewis's *The Lion, the Witch, and the Wardrobe* (1950), for example, they can draw a map of the fictional Narnia that shows all the important details of the setting. This makes a good small-group activity. After students read the book and draw all the important points in the book, they can use the map to present an oral book report.

When students create posters to advertise a book, they choose a literary element that is important in the book. They also consider the best artistic elements, such as line, color, shape, and texture, and the best artistic media to create the poster. Smaller projects such as drawing bookmarks can also replace the written book report.

Creating book jackets provides an interesting book report. The book jacket may be for a book written by the student or one read by the student. A book jacket includes a cover that attracts the reader, a summary of the story that motivates a reader to read the book, and a blurb about the author or illustrator of the book. If the book is a nonfiction source, the book jacket may also include a note from the

Reflect on Your Reading

Many schools are cutting art programs in order to provide more instructional time for subjects that will be tested in federally mandated tests. What are the consequences for such decisions? What are the advantages or disadvantages for using class time, especially in K–4 grades, for responding to art, discussing art in books, and doing art activities with the students? What reading skills can be reinforced through the study of art in illustrated books?

author that presents some of the research used to write the story. This activity summarizes strategies learned when comprehending a story, studying the impact of various artistic elements, and researching and writing biographies about authors and artists.

Using Art Books to Teach Following Directions

Clear, detailed drawings that illustrate how to accomplish different art activities are useful when teaching students to follow directions. Cathryn Falwell's *Butterflies for Kiri* (2003), for example, provides directions for creating an origami butterfly. Peter H. Reynolds's *The Dot* (2003) is a source of motivation for students who say that they cannot draw. Jim Arnosky's *Drawing from Nature* (1982) includes directions for drawing water, landforms, plants, and animals. The step-by-step pencil sketches illustrate techniques that artists use to interpret nature. Denis Roche's *Loo-Loo, Boo, and Art You Can Do* (1996) includes step-by-step instructions for developing eleven art projects, such as making potato prints. Many of these art projects could be included in an art center.

Art Lessons Using Caldecott Books

Debi Englebaugh's *Art through Children's Literature* (1994) provides many interesting ideas for developing lessons using Caldecott Award books. The book is divided by artistic media and provides opportunities to develop students' understanding of each of these media. The book begins with a useful listing of media and examples of artists whose award-winning books depict the media of pencil, crayon, marker, colored pencil, chalk, stencils, collage, watercolor, tempera paint, color mixing, and prints. The text follows the same organization and develops lesson plans for each of the art concepts.

Teachers can collect books that exemplify the artists who use a specific medium and ask students to investigate the requirements for using the medium, compare the illustrations of artists who use the same medium, respond to the impact of the medium, and even try to use the medium in their own art work. Some of the following artists use tempera paint, for example, Lynd Ward, Barbara Cooney, Ed Emberley, Alice and Martin Provensen, Ludwig Bemelmans, Marcia Brown, Nonny Hogrogian, Maud and Miska Petersham.

DIFFERENTIATING INSTRUCTION

ELL Students

Paired reading, an approach to help children read with parents' support, is beneficial for both ELL students and struggling readers. Helaine Donovan and Marilyn Ellis (2005) describe how they use this approach with all students in the second grade, as well as students in ELL programs in grades three through five. They begin the activity by inviting parents to a workshop in which the teachers instruct parents and children in the paired reading method by modeling the approach. The modeling includes book selection, discussing illustrations, talking about characters, predicting the plot, and practicing the paired reading.

They present the following steps for the paired reading process:

1. The child chooses the book.
2. The parent and child discuss the book.
3. The parent and child read the book aloud together.
4. The child signals when he or she wants to read to the parent.
5. If the child makes an error or does not know the word, the parent says the word for the child and the child repeats the word.
6. The child reads the sentence again with the corrected word and continues reading.
7. The process is continued until the book is finished.

At this time, the student and parent sign a contract that they will read for a minimum of 10 minutes each day for the next six weeks. The teachers continue to have weekly workshops during which participants share their success stories. At each workshop teachers present various literary activities for parents and children such as using music to accompany the reading or exploring the geography in the setting for a book. For example, they may use the Internet to explore content in a book about space. At the end of the six weeks, teachers pass out parent and child questionnaires that call on the participants to express their reactions to the experience.

Donovan and Ellis have conducted paired reading programs for twelve years, during which time more than 300 students and their parents have taken part in the programs. Donovan and Ellis affirm that their work continues "to generate interest in paired reading, a community project and professional presentation, by communicating the successes of student achievements and the positive effects on parents" (p. 177).

Struggling Readers and Writers

One of the challenges for teachers in the content areas of social studies and science is to teach students how to read and comprehend the text. Research suggests that

When parents and children read together they heighten both the enjoyment of reading and the attainment of literacy skills.

strategies such as activating prior knowledge, questioning while reading, constructing mental images of ideas expressed in the text, summarizing ideas, and identifying important information increases comprehension (Pressley, 2000).

Sherry Kragler and colleagues (2005) analyzed primary level science and social studies textbooks to identify the effectiveness of comprehension instruction provided in the teachers' manuals that accompanied the texts. They found, for example, that in the science texts the manuals did not include modeling of "strategic reading behaviors the students can use while reading" (p. 256). These educators recommend that when teachers use published science and social studies texts with struggling readers the teachers

> need to preview the lessons to determine which strategies fit, as well as when to embed modeling in the lesson. For example, a teacher may decide to help students summarize a chapter. The teacher can synthesize the information in his or her own words for the students as they read the text. This models for students how to use their own language to summarize rather than copy from a textbook. Once a strategy is modeled, then the teacher needs to provide guided practice while the students use the strategy with their content materials. (pp. 258–259)

To benefit from reading content area books in the primary grades, struggling readers need extra support. Teachers need to demonstrate how to effectively accomplish the skills taught in the series. Modeling how to discover such topics as identifying the main idea, cause and effect relationships, and comparing and contrasting will benefit the struggling reader and provide strategies that he or she may use throughout the grades.

Gifted and Accelerated Readers and Writers

Gifted and accelerated readers read many books independently, both during and out of school. These students frequently select reading as their favorite pastime. They know that reading gives them enjoyment, but reading also is a way for them to gain information about subjects that interest them. Because of their varied interests and extensive reading, accelerated students also have background knowledge that helps them comprehend more difficult books.

Helping students choose books for independent reading is a major obligation of teachers in the lower elementary grades. Jessica Ann Wutz and Linda Wedwick

FIGURE 7.4
Bookmatch Classroom Poster

 ### Book length
- Is this a good length for me?
- Is it too little, just right, or too much?
- Do I feel like committing to this book?

 ### Ordinary language
- Turn to any page and read aloud.
- Does it sound natural?
- Does it flow? Does it make sense?

 ### Organization
- How is the book constructed?
- Am I comfortable with the print size and number of words on a page?
- Are chapters short or long?

 ### Knowledge prior to book
- Read the title, view the cover page, or read the summary on the back of the book.
- What do I already know about this topic, author, or illustrator?

 ### Manageable text
- Begin reading the book.
- Are the words in the book easy, just right, or hard?
- Do I understand what I read?

 ### Appeal to genre
- What is the genre?
- Have I read this genre before?
- Do I like or expect to like this genre?

 ### Topic appropriateness
- Am I comfortable with the topic of this book?
- Do I feel like I am ready to read about this topic?

 ### Connection
- Can I relate to this book?
- Does this book remind me of anything or anyone?

 ### High interest
- Am I interested in this book?
- Am I interested in this author/illustrator?
- Do others recommend this book?

Source: Figure from Wutz, Jessica Ann, & Wedwick, Linda. (2005, September). BOOKMATCH: Scaffolding book selection for independent reading. *The Reading Teacher*, 59(1), 16–32.

(2005) use a *Bookmatch* approach, as found in Figure 7.4, that helps students decide if a book is appropriate for their independent reading.

To use the *Bookmatch* approach, teachers model how they would use the questions on the list to select a book to read to the class or to select a book that they are interested in reading. Students can use the questions on the list when they are writing book reports about their independent reading. They can also use the list when evaluating books or when recommending or not recommending the books for others to read. Student recommendations are strong motivators. Other students frequently read books chosen by others. They also enjoy discussing books with other students who have read the same book.

Summary

A scope and sequence and guidelines from the International Reading Association help teachers make connections between the content and effective strategies for teaching reading from kindergarten through fourth grades. The teacher in lower elementary grades spends a major part of each day teaching reading and some of this time is spent teaching reading through the content areas. The English/language arts curriculum includes developing knowledge of literary elements and literary genres. Techniques such as semantic mapping and plot structures help students understand literary elements. Literary circles, focused recreational reading groups, partner reading, readers' theater, and choral reading all provide necessary practice in reading skills. In the social studies curriculum students learn important reading skills such as using different parts of a book, understanding differences between fiction and nonfiction, and investigating similarities and differences between versions of a folktale. The science and reading curricula are enhanced through science centers and literature and analyzing the organization of science literature. Through the study of art, students can follow literary elements, reinforce emergent literacy skills, make discoveries about the diverse nature of their world and learn about the elements of art such as line and color and artistic media, develop comparative skills, and practice following directions.

Reflect on Your Reading

How would you model this *Bookmatch* approach with a group of gifted and accelerated students? How might this model change if you were using it with ELL students or with struggling readers and writers?

Key Terms

language scope and sequence, p. 261

plot, p. 263

conflict, p. 263

characterization, p. 263

setting, p. 264

theme, p. 264

style, p. 264

point of view, p. 264

literacy circles, p. 275

readers' theater, p. 279

choral reading, p. 279

For video clips of authentic classroom instruction on **Reading and Literature in the Content Areas**, go to Allyn & Bacon's MyLabSchool.com. In MLS courses, click on Reading Methods, go to MLS Video Lab, and select **Module 6**. And remember: there is also an entire MLS course for **Content Area Reading**, containing six additional video clips.

Extend Your Reading

1. Visit an elementary school classroom. How does the teacher incorporate literature, reading strategies, and content knowledge in the classroom?

2. Imagine how you would use the IRA guidelines for best practices and the scope and sequence to develop instructional activities that instill a love for and an understanding of reading among kindergarten through fourth-grade students. Visualize your reading classes and the content areas of English/language arts, social studies, science, and art. What reading materials and strategies will you use that prepare younger children to develop knowledge in areas such as identifying and detailing the main elements in a story, recognizing the characteristics of different genres, performing dramatic readings, and studying pictures in art? Consider the IRA guidelines, the International Baccalaureate Scope and Sequence and the characteristics identified by Finnish educators. What similarities can you identify?

3. The "Up for Discussion" feature emphasizes the importance of a school librarian in the development of the reading and content area curricula. Interview a librarian. How does the librarian work with both teachers and students? Does the librarian believe it is important to have a close relationship with teachers?

4. Visit a kindergarten or early childhood classroom where the teacher uses science centers, interest centers, or art centers? If possible, watch the children as they use the centers. How do the students make discoveries about the content?

5. Start a list of Web sites that may be used by students as they investigate a subject in the content areas.

6. Look at the science section in a newspaper. What scientific subjects are found in the newspaper? How are the scientific articles written to help readers grasp the significance of the topic? For example, the "Science Times" section in the *New York Times* (Revkin, Sept. 14, 2004) includes an article on Hurricane Ivan as it approaches the southern coast of the United States. The article begins with a question, "But Where Is It Going?" and includes a map showing the current path of the hurricane force winds. Why is this subject of considerable importance to people living in the path of the hurricane? How could teachers use students' interest in this subject as they develop units on hurricanes? What literature would help students realize the impact of hurricanes? How might you use other types of

literature, such as Armstrong Sperry's *Call It Courage* (1940, 1971), to help students understand the force of a hurricane?

7. Choose one artistic medium and identify artists whose work reflects that medium. What can you learn about the medium and why the artist uses that medium. You might consider why some artists change their media to represent the books they illustrate. For example, Marcia Brown used very different artistic media for Blaise Cendrars's *Shadow* (1982) and for Perrault's *Cinderella* (1954). *Shadow* uses collage and contrasting black and white shapes to create a frightening mood. In contrast, *Cinderella* uses fine lines and pastel colors to create a fairytale setting. Why do you believe that Marcia Brown changed her media and artistic elements so dramatically? What would have been the results if she had used the same approach for both books?

8. Consider the following definition of social studies developed by the National Council for the Social Studies (1992):

> Social studies is the integrated study of the social sciences and humanities to promote civic competencies. . . . The primary purpose of social studies is to help young people develop the ability to make informed and reasoned decisions for the public good as citizens of a culturally diverse, democratic society in an interdependent world." (p. 1)

With a group of your peers, think about how you would develop this integrated approach and teach students to make informed and reasoned decisions. Because one of the social studies goals is cultural diversity, you might consider how you could extend the unit on Cinderella to a major study of a culture. How could you use the appropriate "Cinderella" story to begin an inquiry into that culture? Are there questions about the culture that would result from reading the "Cinderella" stories? What would you want students to know about the culture? How would they compare the "Cinderella" story with other stories or information about the culture? How could students determine whether or not the cultural information found in the "Cinderella" story is accurate for the culture? What sources might you use to help students expand their cultural studies?

For Further Reading

1. Cathy Collins Block, and Susan E. Israel (September 2004), "The ABC's of Performing Highly Effective Think-Alouds," in *The Reading Teacher*, 58, 154–167.

2. Patricia L. Bloem, and Anthony L. Manna, (May 1999), "A Chorus of Questions: Readers Respond to Patricia Polacco," in *The Reading Teacher*, 52, 802–808. The authors describe an author study with students in second and fourth grades.

3. Lynell Burmark, (2002), *Visual Literacy: Learn to See, See to Learn.* Alexandria, VA: Association for Supervision and Curriculum Development. The text provides guidance in producing various types of visual messages and communications.

4. Douglas, Fisher, James, Flood, Diane, Lapp, and Nancy Frey, (September 2004), "Interactive Read-Alouds: Is There a Common Set of Implementation Practices?" in *The Reading Teacher,* 58, 8–17. The authors examine the read-aloud practices of 25 expert teachers to identify common practices.

5. School Library Journal (April 2004), "Curriculum Connections: Kindergarten–Grade 3, Books, Multimedia, and Web Sites," in *School Library Journal,* 50, 17–29. The article recommends curriculum connections for classes in K–3 grade for literature selections that focus on American history, world history and geography, social studies, multicultural titles, philosophy and myths, science and math, health and safety, family and guidance, sports and crafts, the arts, folktales, poetry, picture books, beginning readers, and first chapter books.

6. School Library Journal (Fall 2004), "Curriculum Connections," in *A Supplement to School Library Journal.* The curriculum connections for K–3 include topics such as American history, social studies, current events, multicultural titles, the arts, language & literature, and poetry.

7. Many of the authors discussed in this chapter have Web sites:

Laurence Anholt: www.anholt.co.uk
Jim Arnosky: www.jimarnosky.com
Jan Brett: www.janbrett.com
Jean Craighead George: www.jeancraigheadgeorge.com
Steven Kellogg: www.stevenkellogg.com
Patricia Polacco: www.patriciapolaco.com
Jane Yolen: www.janeyolen.com

REFERENCES

Beck, I. L., McKeown, M. G., Worthy, J., Sandora, C. A., & Kucan, L. (1996). "Questioning the Author: A Yearlong Classroom Implementation to Engage Students With Text." *The Elementary School Journal,* 96, 385–414.

Block, Cathy Collins, & Israel, Susan E. (September, 2004). "The ABC's of Performing Highly Effective Think-Alouds." *The Reading Teacher,* 58, 154–167.

Bloem, Patricia L., & Manna, Anthony L. (1999). "A Chorus of Questions: Readers Respond to Patricia Polacco." *The Reading Teacher,* 52, 802–808.

Burmark, Lynell. (2002). *Visual Literacy: Learn to See, See to Learn.* Alexandria, VA.

Donovan, Helaine, & Ellis, Marilyn. (October, 2005). "Paired Reading—More Than an Evening of Entertainment." *The Reading Teacher,* 59, 174–177.

Eldridge, J. L. (1990). "Increasing the Performance of Poor Readers in Third Grade with a Group-Assisted Strategy." *Journal of Educational Research,* 84, 69–77.

Englebaugh, Debi. (1994). *Art through Children's Literature: Creative Art Lessons for Caldecott Books.* Westport, CT: Teacher Ideas Press.

Fisher, Douglas, Flood, James, Lapp, Diane, & Frey, Nancy (September 2004). "Interactive Read-Alouds: Is There a Common Set of Implementation Practices?" *The Reading Teacher,* 58, 8–17.

Fuchs, D., Fuchs, L. S., Mathes, P. G, & Simmons, D. C. (1997). "Peer-Assisted Learning Strategies: Making Classrooms More Responsive to Diversity." *American Educational Research Journal,* 34, 174–206.

Garcia, Norma. (2003). "Students' Responses to a Cinderella Unit." College Station: Texas A&M University.

Guthrie, J. T., Cox, K. E., Anderson, E., Harris, K., Mazzoni, S., & Rach L. (1998). "Principles of Integrated Instruction for Engagement in Reading." *Educational Psychology Review,* 10, 177–199.

Hertz, M., & Swanson, K. L. (1999). "We Love to Read—A Collaborative Endeavor to Build the Foundation for Lifelong Readers." *Reading Horizons,* 39, 209–229.

International Baccalaureate Organization. (2003). *Primary Years Programme: Language Scope and*

Sequence. Geneva, Switzerland: International Baccalaureate Organization.

International Reading Association. (August-September, 2002). "Examining Evidence: New IRA Position Statement on Evidence-Based Reading Instruction." *Reading Today,* 20, 1, 4.

Kragler, Sherry, Walker, Carolyn A., & Martin, Linda E. (November 2005). "Strategy Instruction in Primary Content Textbooks." *The Reading Teacher,* 59, 254–261.

Lapp, Diane, Flood, James, & Hoffman, R. P. (1996). "Using Concept Mapping as an Effective Strategy in Content Area Instruction." In D. Lapp, J. Flood, & N. Farnan (Eds.), *Content Area Reading and Instruction: Instructional Strategies,* pp. 291–305. Boston: Allyn & Bacon.

Maxim, George W. (1989). *The Very Young,* 3rd ed. Upper Saddle River, NJ: Pearson/Merrill/Prentice Hall.

McDevitt, Teressa M., & Ormrod, Jeanne Ellis. (2004). *Child Development: Educating and Working with Children and Adolescents,* 2nd ed. Upper Saddle River, NJ: Pearson/Merrill/Prentice Hall.

McMackin, M. C. (1998). "Using Narrative Picture Books to Build Awareness of Expository Text Structure." *Reading Horizons,* 39, 7–20.

McGrath, Charles. (July 11, 2004). "What Johnny Won't Read." *New York Times,* p. 3.

National Council for the Social Studies. (1992). *A Vision of Powerful Teaching and Learning in the Social Studies: Building Social Understanding and Civic Efficacy.* Washington, DC: Position Statement of the Task Force on Standards for Teachers and Learning in Social Studies.

Norton, Donna E. (2004). *The Effective Teaching of Language Arts,* 6th ed. Upper Saddle River, NJ: Pearson/Merrill/Prentice Hall.

Norton, Donna E. (2007). *Through the Eyes of a Child: An Introduction to Children's Literature,* 6th ed. Upper Saddle River, NJ: Pearson/Merrill/Prentice Hall.

Norton, Donna E., & Norton, Saundra E. (2003). *Language Arts Activities for Children,* 5th ed. Upper Saddle River, NJ: Pearson/Merrill/Prentice Hall.

Pressley, M. (2000). "What Should Comprehension Instruction Be the Instruction Of?" In M. L. Kamil, P. B. Mosenthal, P. D. Pearson, & R. Barr (Eds.), *Handbook of Reading Research.* Mahwah, NJ: Erlbaum, pp. 545–561.

A Supplement to School Library Journal (April 2004). "Curriculum Connections: Kindergarten–Grade 3, Books, Multimedia, and Web Sites." *School Library Journal,* 50, 17–29.

Revkin, Andrew C. (14 September 2004). "But Where Is It Going?" *New York Times,* p. D1.

Whelan, Debra Lou. (June 2004). "Shaking Things Up." *School Library Journal,* 50, 44–46.

Wutz, Jessica Ann, & Wedwick, Linda. (September 2005). "Bookmatch: Scaffolding Book Selection for Independent Reading." *The Reading Teacher,* 58, 17.

Children's Literature References

Aardema, Verna. (1975). *Why Mosquitoes Buzz in People's Ears.* Illustrated by Leo and Diane Dillon. Dial Press.

Aardema, Verna. (1977). *Who's in Rabbit's House?* Illustrated by Leo and Diane Dillon. Dial Press.

Aardema, Verna. (1997). *Anansi Does the Impossible: An Ashanti Tale.* Illustrated by Lisa Desimini. Simon & Schuster.

Ackerman, Karen. (1988). *Song and Dance Man.* Illustrated by Stephen Gammell. Knopf.

Ajmera, Maya, & Ivanko, John D. (2001). *Back to School.* Charlesbridge.

Anholt, Laurence. (1999). *Stone Girl, Bone Girl: The Story of Mary Anning.* Illustrated by Sheila Moxley. Orchard.

Appelt, Kathi. (2000). *Oh My Baby, Little One.* HarperCollins.

Arnosky, Jim. (1982). *Drawing from Nature.* Lothrop, Lee & Shepard.

Aylesworth, Jim, retold by. (1998). *The Gingerbread Man.* Illustrated by Barbara McClintock. Scholastic.

Aylesworth, Jim, retold by. (2003). *Goldilocks and the Three Bears.* Illustrated by Barbara McClintock. Scholastic.

Berger, Melvin. (2003). *Spinning Spiders.* Illustrated by S. D. Schindler. HarperCollins.

Bertrand, Diane Gonzales. (2001). *Uncle Chente's Picnic.* Illustrated by Paula Rodriguez Howard. Art Publico.

Brett, Jan. (1987). *Goldilocks and the Three Bears.* Dodd, Mead.

Brown, Monica. (2005). *My Name Is Gabriela/Me Ilamo Gabriela: The Life of Gabriela Mistral/la vida de Gabriela.* Illustrated by John Parra. Luna Rising.

Bryan, Ashley. (1993). *The Story of Lightning and Thunder.* Atheneum.

Bunting, Eve. (1994). *Smoky Night.* Illustrated by David Diaz. Harcourt Brace.

Bunting, Eve. (1999). *Butterfly House.* Illustrated by Greg Shedi. Scholastic.

Burton, Virginia Lee. (1942). *The Little House.* Houghton Mifflin.

Cendrars, Blaise. (1982). *Shadow.* Illustrated by Marcia Brown. Scribners.

Child, Lawren, adapted by. (2006). *The Princess and the pea.* Photographs by Polly Borland. Hyperian.

Cleary, Beverly. (1981). *Ramona Quimbly, Age 8.* Dell.

Cole, Joanne. (1991). *My Puppy Is Born.* Photographs by Jerome Wexler. William Morrow.

Cooper, Helen. (2005). *A Pipkin of Pepper.* Farrar, Straus, & Giroux.

Cooper, Helen. (1999). *Pumpkin Soup.* Farrar, Straus, & Giroux.

Cowley, Joy. (1999). *Red-Eyed Tree Frog.* Photographs by Nic Bishop. Scholastic.

Coy, John. (2003). *Two Old Potatoes and Me.* Knopf.

Cronin, Doreen. (2000). *Click, Clack, Moo: Cows That Type.* Illustrated by Betsy Lewin. Simon & Schuster.

Cummings, Pat, & Cummings, Linda, compiled by. (1998). *Talking with Adventurers.* National Geographic.

Cuyler, Margery. (2000). *100th Day Worries.* Illustrated by Arthur Howard. Simon & Schuster.

Danneberg, Julie. (2000). *First Day Jitters.* Illustrated by Judy Love. Charlesbridge.

Demarest, Chris L. (2000). *Firefighters A to Z.* Simon & Schuster.

de Regniers, Beatrice Schenk, selected by. (1988). *Sing a Song of Popcorn: Every Child's Book of Poems.* Scholastic.

DiTerlizzi, Tony. (2002). *The Spider and the Fly.* Simon & Schuster.

Dunleavy, Deborah. (2004). *The Jumbo Book of Drama.* Illustrated by Jane Kurisa.

Engel, Diana. (1989). *Josephina Hates Her Name.* William Morrow, 1989.

English, Karen. (2004). *Hot Day on Abbott Avenue.* Illustrated by Javaka Steptoe. Clarion.

Facklam, Margery. (2001). *Spiders and Their Web Sites.* Illustrated by Alan Male. Little, Brown.

Falwell, Cathryn. (2003). *Butterflies for Kiri.* Lee & Low.

Fields, Julie. (1988). *The Green Lion of Zion Street.* Illustrated by Jerry Pinkney. Macmillan.

French, Vivian. (2000). *Growing Frogs.* Illustrated by Alison Bartlett. Candlewick.

Funston, Sylvia. (1992). *The Dinosaur Question and Answer Book.* Little, Brown.

Garland, Michael. (1989). *My Cousin Katie.* Crowell.

George, Jean Craighead. (1995). *Everglades.* Illustrated by Wendell Minor. HarperCollins.

George, William T. (1989). *Box Turtle at Long Pond.* Illustrated by Lindsay Barrett George. Greenwillow.

Grimm, Brothers. (1979). *Household Tales.* Illustrated by Mervyn Peake. Schoken.

Grimm, Brothers. (1983). *Little Red Riding Hood,* retold and illustrated by Trina Schart Hyman. Holiday.

Hague, Michael, selected by. (1985). *Aesop's Fables.* Holt.

Hamilton, Virginia. (2003). *Bruh Rabbit and the Tar Baby Girl.* Illustrated by James E. Ransome. Scholastic.

Harris, Joel Chandler. (1986). *Jump! The Adventures of Brer Rabbit.* Adapted by Van Dyke Parks. Illustrated by Barry Moser. Harcourt.

Harris, Joel Chandler. (1987). *The Tales of Uncle Remus: The Adventures of Brer Rabbit.* Retold by Julius Lester. Illustrated by Jerry Pinkney. Dial Press.

Haviland, Virginia. (1979). *North American Legends.* Illustrated by Ann Strugnell. Philomel.

Hooks, William. (1987). *Moss Gown.* Illustrated by Donald Carrick. Clarion.

Hopkins, Lee Bennett. (1996). *School Supplies: A Book of Poems.* Illustrated by Renee Flower. Simon & Schuster.

Horenstein, Henry. (1999). *A is for . . . ?: A Photographers Alphabet of Animals.* Harcourt Brace.

Huck, Charlotte, retold by. (1989). *Princess Furball.* Illustrated by Anita Lobel. Greenwillow.

Jackson, Ellen. (2003). *It's Back to School We Go! First Day Stories from around the World.* Illustrated by Jan Davey Ellis. Millbrook.

Johnson, Stephen T. (1995). *Alphabet City.* Viking.

Kellogg, Steven. (1991). *Jack and the Beanstalk.* William Morrow.

Kellogg, Steven. (1997). *The Three Little Pigs.* William Morrow.

Krull, Kathleen. (2003). *M Is for Music.* Illustrated by Stacy Innerst. Harcourt.

———. (1996). *Wilma Unlimited: How Wilma Rudolph Became the World's Fastest Woman.* Illustrated by David Diaz. Harcourt Brace.

Lasky, Kathryn. (1993). *Monarchs*. Photographs by Christopher Knight. Harcourt Brace.

Lear, Edward. (1991). *The Owl and the Pussycat*. Illustrated by Jan Brett. Putnam's Sons.

Leiner, Katherine. (1996). *First Children: Growing Up in the White House*. Illustrated by Katie Keller. Tambourine.

Lewis, C. S. (1950). *The Lion, the Witch, and the Wardrobe*. Macmillan.

Lobel, Arnold. (1980). *Fables*. Harper & Row.

Locker, Thomas. (1995). *Sky Tree: Seeing Science through Art*. HarperCollins.

Louie, At-Lang. (1982). *Yeh Shen: A Cinderella Story from China*. Illustrated by Ed Young. Philomel.

Lyon, George Ella. (2000). *One Lucky Girl*. Dorling Kindersley.

MacDonald, Suse. (1986). *Alphabatics*. Bradbury.

MacLachlan, Patricia. (1985). *Sarah, Plain and Tall*. Harper & Row.

Markle, Sandra. (1996). *Creepy, Crawly Baby Bugs*. Walker.

Mathers, Petra. (1988). *Theodor and Mr. Balbini*. Harper & Row.

McClintock, Barbara, retold by. (2005). *Cinderella*. Scholastic.

McCloskey, Robert. (1956, 1985). *Time of Wonder*. Viking.

McCully, Emily Arnold. (1984). *Picnic*. Harper & Row.

McLeod, Bob. (2006). *Super Hero ABC*. HarperCollins.

Milne, A. A. (1926, 1954). *Winnie-the-Pooh*. Illustrated by Ernest H. Shepard. Dutton.

Mitchell, Margaree King. (1993). *Uncle Jed's Barbershop*. Illustrated by James Ransome. Simon & Schuster.

Modarressi, Mitra. (2000). *Yard Sale!* Dorling Kindersley.

Mora, Pat. (2001). *The Bakery Lady*. Pinat Books.

Moser, Barry, retold by. (2001). *The Three Little Pigs*. Little, Brown.

Moss, Lloyd. (1995). *Zin! Zin! Zin! A Violin*. Illustrated by Marjorie Priceman. Simon & Schuster.

Muth, Jon J. (2005). *Zen Sharts*. Scholastic.

Pak, Soyung. (2003). *Sumi's First Day of School Ever*. Illustrated by Joung Un Kim. Viking.

Patent, Dorothy Hinshaw. (2004). *The Right Dog for the Job: Ira's Path from Service Dog to Guide Dog*. Photographs by William Munoz. Walker.

Peet, Bill. (1989). *Bill Peet: An Autobiography*. Houghton Mifflin.

Pelletier, David. (1996). *The Graphic Alphabet*. Orchard.

Perrault, Charles. (1954). *Cinderella*. Illustrated by Marcia Brown. Scribner's.

Polacco, Patricia. (1991). *Applemando's Dreams*. Philomel.

Polacco, Patricia. (2000). *The Butterfly*. Philomel.

Pollock, Penny, retold by. (1996). *Turkey Girl: A Zuni Cinderella Story*. Illustrated by Ed Young. Little, Brown.

Potter, Beatrix. (1902). *The Tale of Peter Rabbit*. Warner.

Pringle, Laurence. (1997). *An Extraordinary: The Story of a Monarch Butterfly*. Illustrated by Bob Marstall. Orchard.

Reynolds, Peter H. (2003). *The Dot*. Candlewick.

Roche, Denis. (1996). *Loo-Loo, Boo, and Art You Can Do*. Houghton Mifflin.

Rohmann, Eric. (2002). *My Friend Rabbit*. Roaring Book Press.

Seeber, Dorothea P. (2000). *A Pup Just for Me; A Boy Just for Me*. Illustrated by Ed Young. Philomel.

Sendak, Maurice. (1963). *Where the Wild Things Are*. Harper & Row.

Sherman, Josepha. (1993). *Rachel the Clever and Other Jewish Folktales*. August House.

Showers, Paul. (2004). *A Drop of Blood*. Illustrated by Edward Miller. HarperCollins.

Simon, Seymour. (1990). *New Questions and Answers About Dinosaurs*. Illustrated by Jennifer Dewey. William Morrow.

Sis, Peter. (1991). *Follow the Dream: The Story of Christopher Columbus*. Knopf.

Sperry, Armstrong. (1940). *Call It Courage*. Macmillan.

Steptoe, John. (1987). *Muffaro's Beautiful Daughters*. Lothrop, Lee & Shepard.

Thornhill, Jill. (1990). *The Wildlife ABC: A Nature Alphabet*. Simon & Schuster.

Van Allsburg, Chris. (1981). *Jumanji*. Houghton Mifflin.

Van Allsburg, Chris. (1985). *The Polar Express*. Boston: Houghton Mifflin.

Van Leewen, Jean. (2006). *Benny & Beautiful Baby Delilah*. Illustrated by LeVyen Pham. Dial Press.

White, E. B. (1952). *Charlotte's Web*. Illustrated by Garth Williams. Harper & Row.

Williams, Margery. (1958). *The Velveteen Rabbit*. Illustrated by William Nicholson. Doubleday.

Williams, Margery. (1982). *The Velveteen Rabbit*. Illustrated by Ilise Plume, Godine.

Williams, Margery. (1982). *The Velveteen Rabbit*. Illustrated by Michael Green. Running Press.

Williams, Margery. (1983). *The Velveteen Rabbit*. Illustrated by Michael Hague. Holt, Rinehart, and Winston.

Williams, Margery. (1983). *The Velveteen Rabbit*. Illustrated by Allen Atkinson. Knopf.

Williams, Margery. (1983). *The Velveteen Rabbit*. Illustrated by Tien. Simon & Schuster.

Willard, Nancy. (1999). *The Tale I Told Sasha*. Illustrated by David Christiana. Little, Brown.

Wood, Nancy, ed. (1997). *The Serpent's Tongue: Prose, Poetry, and Art of the New Mexico Pueblos*. Dutton.

Yolen, Jane. (1987). *Owl Moon*. Illustrated by John Schoenherr. Philomel.

Yorinks, Arthur. (1986). *Hey Al*. Illustrated by Richard Egielski. Farrar, Straus & Giroux.

Young, Ed. (2004). *I, Doko: The Tale of a Basket*. Philomel.

Young, Ed. (2006). *My Mei Mei*. Philomel.

CHAPTER 8

Reading, Writing, and Literature in the Content Areas
Fourth through Eighth Grades

CHAPTER **OUTLINE**

Reading and Literature in English/Language Arts
  Applying Analytical Reading Skills to a Book
  Teaching Authentication of Setting in English/Language Arts
Developing Research Skills for Reading in Content Areas
  Choose a Topic and Formulate Questions
  Plan
  Gather
  Sort
  Synthesize and Organize
  Evaluate
  Present/Report
Developing Reading Skills in the Content Areas
  Reading in Social Studies and History
  Reading and Science
  Reading and Art
  Reading and Writing Connections in the Content Areas

After reading this chapter you will be able to answer the following questions:

1. What content might be included in a scope and sequence for reading in the content area?
2. What are some strategies that are effective for teaching reading in English/language arts?
3. What are effective strategies for teaching reading in social studies and history?
4. What inquiry processes could be useful for improving research skills when teaching reading in science?
5. What are some strategies for teaching reading in science?
6. What are effective strategies for teaching reading in art?
7. What are some reading and writing connections in the content areas?

Read All About It!

"Summer Reading List Blues"

by Barbara Feinberg, *New York Times,* July 18, 2004

I don't remember exactly what books were on the summer reading list handed out on the last day of school when I was 10—more than 30 years ago—but I do recall that they were merely "suggested reading." I can remember scraps of stories: children making kooky inventions; a lonely girl making a Japanese doll house out of bright fabric; something about a fat little witch afraid of Halloween.

But mostly it's the easy feeling I remember when I picture reading that summer. I imagine myself sitting under a broad, shady tree, surrounded by distant hills, turning pages of a crinkly covered library book. There is a breeze high in the branches. I might never have actually sat under such a tree then; we lived in the city, and it's unlikely we went away that summer. I've come to think it's just as likely I am remembering an expansive landscape conjured by the books themselves. In any case, it is a shady place I recall, one that let my mind rest, and roam.

. . .

(Feinberg continues her article by questioning the realistic content of the required summer reading lists that are handed out to students today in many elementary grades. She cites one example that is accompanied by "In September you will be given a computer-generated test on your summer reading. This will count as 20 percent of your grade, or two quiz scores." She questions this practice and continues her article.)

. . .

But what makes a book useful to a child? . . . The kind of realistic fiction that seems more "useful" according to my observation of my children and their friends, affords its young heroes and heroines a certain measure of emotional protection. These novels manage to relay rich material, but don't need to tell all, and instead are quirkily selective, in a way that feels consistent with how an authentic child might filter experience. *The*

Devil's Arithmetic, by Jane Yolen, about the Holocaust, and

> " But what remains most loved, and most useful in helping children "face adversity," is the realm of fantasy, or the realm of the slightly less real world—like Louis Sachar's *Holes,* for example. "

The Watsons Go to Birmingham—1963, by Christopher Paul Curtis, about the racist

South, are books my 16-year-old son and 12-year-old daughter loved when they were 10. . . .

But what remains most loved, and most useful in helping children "face adversity," is the realm of fantasy, or the realm of the slightly less real world—like Louis Sachar's *Holes,* for example. A universe where scary things are blunted—that is, by a blanket of fantasy—is easier to enter; it's helpful too for the main character to have access to a tiny bit of magical power. One need only to remember Harry Potter, after all, has had to deal with the murder of his parents and an abusive foster family. His magic accompanies him; he is looked out for at every turn. Rather than confronting evil in the form of a violent realistic father, say, it is vastly less stressful for some children to con-

template evil in the form of "he who must not be named" . . .

We seem to have lost sight of what children can actually process, and more important, of their own innate capacities. Instead of our children being free to roam and dream and invent on their own timetable, and to read about children doing such things, we increasingly ask our children to be sober and hard-working at every turn, to take detailed notes on their required texts with Talmudic attention, to endure computer-generated tests. And the texts we require them to pore over have become all too often about guarded, world-weary, overburdened children, who are spending their childhoods trying to cope with the mess their parents left behind.

Read All About It!
Critical Thinking **Questions**

- What is your response to the content of books recommended for summer reading?

- Do you agree with Feinberg's concerns that too many books force characters to face adversity?

- What books do you remember reading with pleasure during the summer?

- What are the advantages or disadvantages of asking children to read books from a specific reading list?

- What are the advantages or disadvantages of having children take computer-generated tests about the books they read?

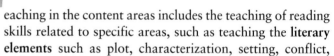

eaching in the content areas includes the teaching of reading skills related to specific areas, such as teaching the **literary elements** such as plot, characterization, setting, conflict, point of view, and theme that are important for reading and writing in English/language arts. It also includes teaching the contextual skills to improve understanding of social studies and science. Teaching reading in these areas requires the mastery of comprehension related to the content areas. For example, in the fourth through eighth grades students in history and social studies need to develop such understandings as the reasons for the conflict between the American Colonies and Great Britain that led to the Revolutionary War. In the upper elementary grades, writing and research skills become an increasingly large part of the curriculum. Students need to be able to apply critical-thinking skills in their assignments and use problem-solving and decision-making skills.

Reading and Literature in English/Language Arts

The English teacher has a formidable task. Students are expected to read a wide range of books and to gain understanding and knowledge from books, newspapers, and magazines. The previous chapters have discussed teaching reading in the lower elementary grades, which takes students from beginning understandings of literacy as they acquire initial reading skills. At this lower level, teachers provide instruction in various word attack and comprehension skills so that students understand the meanings of words, the structure of books, and how to gain knowledge from reading.

The International Baccalaureate Organization (IBO), founded in the 1960s, grew out of international school efforts to establish a common curricular framework for children whose families live a mobile lifestyle, such as children of diplomats. These schools are found throughout the world and include more than two hundred schools within the United States. The guidelines for these schools include many opportunities to awaken the natural intelligence of all students and to teach students to recognize the relationships between the subjects they study in school and the world in which they live.

The Language Scope and Sequence for the International Baccalaureate Organization (2003) provides detailed expectations about what students should learn in the fourth through eighth grades that relate to reading in the English/language arts curriculum. For example, students will be able to:

- Read widely across genres and show interest in a variety of reading
- Identify genres of literature such as science fiction, poetry, biography, and historical fiction
- Categorize literature according to fable, myth, biography, novel, and essay
- Identify different types of conflict in literature
- Make informed judgments about an author's purpose
- Locate, access, organize, and synthesize information from a variety of sources

■ Use specific vocabulary to respond to and analyze poetry (line, stanza, rhyme scheme, etc.)

Some of these expectations were presented in the previous chapter on teaching content subjects in the lower grades. Other areas will be developed through activities within this chapter.

As shown by this scope and sequence, students need to be introduced to more in-depth reading and analysis of books as they progress into the upper grades. Mortimer J. Adler and Charles Van Doren's best-selling classic, *How to Read a Book: The Classic Guide to Intelligent Reading* (1972), includes stages and rules that readers can use when outlining a book and later when applying informed criticism of the book. It is very helpful for teaching students in the middle and upper elementary grades, and it has been used in university classes. The following series of lessons uses Adler and Van Doren's stages in analytical reading and then applies these stages to the reading of a book that won the 2004 Newbery Medal, Kate DiCamillo's *The Tale of Despereaux* (2003). As you read and analyze each of the stages, identify how the technique increases both analytical and critical reading abilities. Notice how the approach increases and improves student involvement in discussion and writing about a book. Also notice how many of the areas listed in the previous scope and sequence are covered in this approach.

Applying Analytical Reading Skills to a Book

Analytical reading is an in-depth strategy that applies informed criticism to a book. Adler and Van Doren (1972) identify the following stages in analytical reading:

First Stage: Rules for Finding What a Book Is About:
1. Classify the book according to kind and subject matter. For example, what is the genre of the literature and what are the characteristics of that genre?
2. Briefly state what the book is about.
3. List and outline the major parts of the book.
4. Define the problem or problems the author has tried to solve.

Second Stage: Rules for Interpreting a Book's Content
5. Identify and interpret the author's key words.
6. Understand the author's leading propositions by identifying and discussing the author's most important sentences.
7. Know the author's arguments by identifying them in the text.
8. Determine which of the problems the author has solved and which have not been solved. Find out the author's solutions.

Third Stage: Rules for Criticizing a Book as a Communication of Knowledge
9. Do not begin criticizing the book until you have completed your interpretation. Suspend judgment until you can say, "I understand."
10. When you disagree, do so reasonably.
11. Respect the differences between knowledge and personal opinion by giving reasons for critical judgments.

Share each of these stages with upper elementary students. Why are these stages critical? What do you discover about the book by analyzing the book according to each of these stages? Why is the approach identified as an approach for fostering and improving analytical reading? Why is analytical reading important? Why is analytical reading especially important in the English/language arts curriculum?

APPLYING THE STAGES TO *THE TALE OF DESPEREAUX* (2003)

1. Ask students to identify and discuss the kind and subject matter in *The Tale of Despereaux*. For example, this book is modern fantasy. Writers of fantasy develop plots by changing one or more of the story elements in such a way that readers believe that the story is possible (suspending disbelief) even though readers know that in our world it is impossible. Readers must decide whether or not DiCamillo created believable plot, characters, setting, and theme.

2. Ask students to briefly describe the book. For example: this story tells how a small but intelligent mouse saves a human princess from a vicious and determined rat that tries to take his revenge on the princess. (The author is especially effective when developing conflict, theme, and an interesting style.)

3. List the major parts of the book in order of their happenings. A listing of major incidents in the development of plot and conflict might include the following points:

- Despereaux lives in a castle and has unusual abilities because he can read.
- Large, mean rats live in the dungeon beneath the castle.
- The Mouse Council punishes Despereaux because he interacts with the humans.
- As punishment, Despereaux is sent to the dungeon.
- Despereaux hears the rats' plans to capture the princess and bring her into the darkness of the dungeon.
- Despereaux is in the dungeon with only a sewing needle to use to defend him and save the princess.
- The power of love makes it possible for Despereaux to save the princess.

4. Define the problem. As seen from the outline of conflict and plot, the author develops a story in which a small hero uses his intelligence and bravery to rescue a human princess from the evil powers of the rats who live in the dark dungeon.

5. Identify and discuss the meanings for key words and phrases in the story. Some of the words include *dungeon, consorts,* and *light versus dark, power of light, power of music, symbol,* and *fate.*

6. Identify and discuss the important sentences in the text. This book has several important literary elements that could be the focus for discussion, including important sentences related to conflict, author's style, and theme. If theme is chosen, for example, ask students to identify and discuss sentences that show the importance of

- the power of love
- the power of stories
- the power of light
- every action having a consequence

- the power of hope
- the importance of free choice

7. Know the author's arguments by finding them and constructing their sequence. One of the best ways to discover DiCamillo's arguments is to identify and discuss the themes, as listed above, in the book.

8. Determine which of the problems the author has solved. For example, the author solves the problem of the kidnapped princess by allowing Despereaux to use his intelligence and beliefs to rescue her. The author uses a series of incidents to help readers understand the importance of the various powers that make it possible for the hero, Despereaux, to overcome the darkness and realize the importance of free choice.

9–11. Criticism: Before students develop critical judgments of this book, they should conduct their own research into questions such as

- How did the author develop a story that causes readers to believe that this fantasy could happen? (Suspending disbelief)

- How did the author develop conflict, especially of person versus society? Is this conflict important in this story and also in your life?

- What influence did the author's style have on your responses to the reading? (The author talks directly to the reader.)

- Why do you think the author develops themes such as "Forgiveness is a powerful ability" and "Free choice is essential in life?" Are these themes also important in your life?

To add to the discussion of the book, students may read and respond to an interview with author Kate DiCamillo (Horning, 2004). They may also try the same approach using DiCamillo's *The Miraculous Journey of Edward Tulane* (2006).

Teaching Authentication of Setting in English/Language Arts

One of the purposes for the setting in a story is to provide accurate descriptions of the location for the story. If the setting is imaginary, the author must bring the setting to life. Whether the setting is a real or an imaginary place, a believable setting helps readers share what the characters see, smell, hear, and touch. When a story is set in an identifiable geographical location, details should be accurate. Ask students to explain why an accurate setting is important in a book. Explain to students that the class will discover how to critically evaluate a book in order to answer the questions: Are the settings in this book accurate? Can we find nonfiction information books or information on the Internet that prove that the settings as described in the fictional book are accurate?

APPLYING AUTHENTICATION OF SETTING TO *THE THIEF LORD* (2002) *The Thief Lord*, Cornelia Funke's 2003 Mildred L. Batchelor Award–winning text, is set in Venice, Italy. The author identifies and describes numerous locations such as bridges, palaces, and statues that may be authenticated by making comparisons with other books and articles about Venice.

You may introduce this activity by sharing the beliefs of Bo and Prosper, the two main characters in *The Thief Lord*. They consider Venice to be a magical place because of the way it was described by their mother:

And everything is exactly like she said it would be. When we got off the train at the station—Bo and me—we were so scared that it wasn't going to be true—the houses on stilts, the roads made of water, the lions with wings. But it's all true! The world is full of wonders—that's what she always told. (p. 132)

For this activity, explain to the students that they will verify whether or not the author of *The Thief Lord* and Bo and Prosper are correct when they say that everything is exactly like she said it would be. Ask students to read Funke's book and identify and describe as many settings as they can find in *The Thief Lord*. This list might include, for example, a map of Venice, canals used for transportation, the Rialto Bridge, the Doge's Palace, gondolas, the Grand Canal, vaporetto and vaporetto stops, St. Mark's Square, Palazzo Contarini, Basilica San Marco, the lion fountain at the side entrance of the Basilica, Sacca della Misericordia (a small bay to the north of the city), Dorsoduro (the southernmost quarter of Venice), Santa Maria di Valverde, and islands in the lagoon.

Vendela in Venice (1999), the nonfiction book by Christina Bjork with illustrations by Inga-Karin Erikson, is one source that may be used for comparisons and authentication of settings described in *The Thief Lord*. One of the first sources for authentication is a map of Venice. Both books open with maps on which various locations are identified. Many of the same settings are described and illustrated in *Vendela in Venice*. Ask students to identify descriptions of settings that are important in *The Thief Lord*, such as a ride on the vaporetto, the Doge's Palace, the Bridge of Sighs, St. Mark's Square, the gondolas, the islands, the statues, and various shops. Now have them identify the same settings in *Vendela in Venice*, many of which are shown through photographs. Which settings are similar? Are there any settings that do not seem as authentic? Which ones, and why do they not seem to be authentic? Which seem to be the most authentic, and why?

Ask students to compare Bo's and Prosper's remembrances of Venice with Vendela's descriptions of her last visit to Venice. How are these descriptions the same and how are they different? As Vendela describes her last visit to Venice,

We took the vaporetto on a farewell trip along the Grand Canal, said goodbye to all the palaces and one or two little svassi. Just before the Rialto Bridge, I saw a big rat running up a molding outside a house right above the water. We went under the bridge, past the market stalls, past the church where St. Lucia is buried, and past the dreary railway station to the terminus at Piazzale Roma, where we got off. (p. 86)

Ask students to summarize their findings. Is the setting in *The Thief Lord* authentic? Which of the descriptions seemed the most authentic? What made these settings seem authentic? How do authentic settings help bring books to life? Additional books that are excellent for authentication include:

Reflect on Your Reading

Think about the Language Scope and Sequence identified by the International Baccalaureate Organization (2003) listed earlier in this chapter. Which of the activities covered thus far would develop this scope and sequence? How would you predict that additional categories in the scope and sequence would be developed through the content areas of social studies, science, art, and writing?

Susan Campbell Bartoletti's *Hitler Youth: Growing Up in Hitler's Shadow* (2005). This 2006 Sibert Information Book Honor Award and 2006 Newbery Honor Award is set in Germany during World War II.

Josef Holub's *An Innocent Soldier* (2005). This 2006 Batchelder Award for Foreign Language Translation is set in 1811 during Napoleon's march across Europe in hopes of conquering Russia.

Diane McWorter's *A Dream of Freedom: The Civil Rights Movement from 1954 to 1968* (2004). This nonfiction text is written by a Pulitzer Prize-winning author.

Developing Research Skills for Reading in Content Areas

It is through the content areas of literature, including social studies and history, science, art, and writing, that teachers have opportunities to help students discover and use a research process that allows them to pick topics, ask questions about the topics, plan their investigations, gather and sort information, synthesize and organize the information, evaluate what they have collected, and report their findings, either orally or in writing. This is a research method known as an inquiry method that will be useful throughout life. Each of these steps in the inquiry method needs to be taught and students need numerous opportunities to develop and apply these important skills.

Choose a Topic and Formulate Questions

This is the beginning of the research cycle where students consider a topic and think about what they already know about a topic and what they would like to know about the topic. In addition to what they already know and what they want to discover, they should learn to narrow the question to one that is neither too broad nor too narrow. They may be led through a series of smaller questions that help them find the answers to the bigger question that requires problem solving.

For example, with a focus unit on World War II developed later in this chapter, let us consider how we might use this inquiry/research method. Within the unit are five topic areas that could be investigated. Teachers may divide these topics within the class or choose to focus on one of them. A table such as the one shown in Table 8.1 is helpful.

If the topic is World War II students can identify which location or subtopic for the war they want to study, such as England and Europe at War, the Holocaust, the Resistance, War and North America, or War in the Pacific. Brainstorming information for the table will help students formulate relevant questions and lead them to broader understandings about the topic.

Plan

After they have formulated their questions, students will need help identifying the resources they will need to investigate their questions. They should consider where they

TABLE 8.1

Discover Questions to Investigate

Topic to Be Covered	What We Know about the Topic	Questions We Want to Investigate

would find the resources, among literature (biographies, information books, and historical fiction), encyclopedias, newspaper files, interviews with WWII veterans, and information on the Internet. If the students are planning with a team, they should identify each team member's responsibilities.

Gather

Students now locate and collect the resources identified during planning. They record information by taking notes that relate to the questions. They need to understand the importance of using a variety of sources, particularly primary sources when available, and recording notes from references. As part of the gathering phase, teachers help students summarize main ideas, organize and sort information, and efficiently use the sources including printed materials, the Internet, and interviews.

Sort

Students go through their information and decide which information helps them answer the main questions. They decide whether or not they have enough information, or if they require additional information.

Synthesize and Organize

Students organize their information to create an answer and become prepared for a final oral or written report. In a group, they can organize information and consider what will be in the final presentation. If the final presentation is to be a written report, they can write a first draft, revise the draft, organize the information into a logical sequence, and plan the layout for the final written report.

Evaluate

Now students ask the important questions: Did we answer our main questions? Are we ready to present a report? How will we present the report so it makes sense to the class? Are there areas that need to be improved? As part of the evaluation, students can consider how well the group worked together during the research process, and also evaluate the quality of the sources and the importance of their original questions.

Present/Report

Students are now ready to present the final report. They may present the report orally, using illustrations, posters, or other visuals. Or, they may present written reports. Oral reports frequently accompany written reports so students share their findings in a variety of ways. Older students can include a bibliography of sources used to conduct the research.

Reflect on Your Reading

Think about an oral presentation that you gave when you were in elementary school. What made the research interesting for you and your audience? As you were listening to reports given by other students, what elements made the presentations interesting and worthwhile to you?

Developing Reading Skills in the Content Areas

In this section we will discuss specific strategies for teaching reading in the content areas of social studies and history, science, art, and writing.

Reading in Social Studies and History

This part of the curriculum is closely related to reading instruction. In the upper elementary and middle grades, one teacher frequently teaches both reading and social studies. Reading a book about history with comprehension and developing an understanding of the sweep of history and how historical occurrences influence current

Recreational reading allows students to practice their skills and to discover the pleasure associated with reading.

actions are among the highest goals of the social studies and history curriculum. Being able to identify and argue for or against a point of view is also essential.

Teachers of reading and social studies frequently combine the two subjects through the use of units in which students use numerous sources to explore issues related to a time period and to conduct research about the various characters who made a difference during the time period. Three of the units that have been the most successful with my students include "The American Revolution and Writing the Constitution," "The Civil War," and "World War II." All three of these time periods are included in the Social Studies Knowledge and Skills section referred to in Chapter 2. In this chapter, we will develop a unit around the third subject, "World War II."

AUTHENTICATING LITERATURE IN SOCIAL STUDIES AND HISTORY   **Authenticating literature** is an exciting way to enhance inquiry. It allows students to conduct research into a topic and make decisions about the accuracy of a text. Students often have moments of discovery when they conduct research and write historical essays or biographies using some of the same strategies as historians.

When introducing nonfiction books about World War II it is important to discuss the need for accuracy in the literature. Have students consider what would happen if the information presented in books is incorrect.

To authenticate a book about Europe during the war, students can create a time line and identify specific dates and important locations such as the invasion of Normandy. They can verify these dates and locations with other nonfiction sources. Students may locate newspaper articles printed at the time from online and library microfiche sources. They can read biographies about military figures, nurses, and journalists. They can also interview people who lived through the time period: for example, I have had students who interviewed a German immigrant who was a child during the war and whose family escaped to America in search of a better life, an American soldier who was stationed in England during the war, and a nurse who took care of the war wounded in a hospital in New York.

Students frequently become excited when they conduct this type of research because it is like playing detective. One fifth-grade student shared this excitement when he discovered that three different biographies gave three different dates for an historical figure's birth date. This student then conducted his own research to find out which date was correct. After he discovered the biography that was correct, he wrote letters to the publishers of the other two biographies to tell them about the error. This student was rewarded with letters from the two biographers, who thanked him for taking the time to write and let him know the date would be corrected in future editions.

This experience verifies that students are able to conduct their own research and to use this research to evaluate what they read. This process empowers students in their abilities to read and investigate as they discover that their own research can be as good or sometimes better than research introduced in the text. Through this research, they also discover the need for research and accuracy in their own writing. This authentication activity is a logical introduction to the study of a specific historical time period, such as the following focus unit on World War II.

FOCUS UNIT:
A Study of World War II

The theme for this unit on history that includes a major war is based on words by Thomas Paine during the Revolutionary War: "These are the times that try men's souls." This quote is certainly appropriate for an introduction of the subjects that can be studied around the issues and happenings of World War II. Articles and editorials that focus on war frequently mention that today's students need to be able to understand history and to use history to grope for solutions. In a 2003 editorial in the *New York Times* (February 7, 2003, p. A29), Adlai Stevenson III compares the views of his father, Adlai Stevenson, who argued about Cuban missiles in 1962, with those of Colin Powell, who argued for the necessity of war with Iraq. Stevenson III titles his article "Different Man, Different Moment." Articles such as these point out the necessity for teachers to encourage students to apply ideas from history, to debate the issues, and to try to find solutions for current difficulties.

OBJECTIVES

1. To identify the genres of literature used in the unit and to discuss the characteristics of the genres that make them valuable for the unit
2. To understand the sweep of history and how World War II influenced so many people
3. To identify themes in historical fiction and biography depicted in the literature and to develop an understanding that certain themes are found in times of war

4. To understand the qualities in characters that allow them to overcome obstacles
5. To authenticate historical fiction through nonfiction sources
6. To understand that heroes in history are not just the "great" people; that ordinary people also can become heroes
7. To identify and debate issues that have perplexed people across time
8. To relate art and music to World War II

MATERIALS

The books and other materials chosen for this unit focus on five major settings and conflicts found in World War II literature: England and Europe at War, the Holocaust, the Resistance, War and North America, and War in the Pacific and the Internment of Japanese Americans.

GRADE LEVEL

Upper elementary and middle school, although some of the picture books are appropriate for younger grades

BOOK SUMMARIES

Each of these summaries are divided according to the major settings and conflicts:

England and Europe at War

The following books develop this setting and time period:

- Ronald J. Drez's *Remember D-Day: The Plan, The Invasion, Survivor Stories* (2004) chronicles the progress of the war in Europe and the actual day of the invasion.
- Michael Foreman's *War Boy: A Country Childhood* (1990) and *After the War Was Over* (1996) are autobiographies that describe the author's experiences growing up in England during the 1940s.
- Michelle Magorian's *Good Night, Mr. Tom* (1983), historical fiction, develops a story about a boy who is evacuated from London to the English countryside.
- Peter Hartlin's *Crutches* (1988) develops themes associated with the terrible consequences of war and the struggle for freedom in a historical fiction text.

The Holocaust

Themes in the literature include the consequences of hatred and prejudice, the search for religious and personal freedom, the role of conscience, and obligations that must be met toward others. The following books develop this setting and time period:

- Chana Byers Abells's *The Children We Remember* (1986) includes photographs from the Yad Vashem Archives in Jerusalem. The photographs contrast early lives of real people with later experiences.
- Michael Leapman's *Witnesses in War: Eight True-Life Stories of Nazi Persecution* (1998) is based on remembrances of Holocaust survivors.
- Barbara Rogasky's *Smoke and Ashes: The Story of the Holocaust* (1988) begins with the history of anti-Semitism and proceeds to

the experiences between 1933 and 1945. Photographs showing life in the camps add to the sense of tragedy.

- William Kaplan and S. Tanaka's *One Family's Escape from War-Torn Europe* (1998) follows the members of the Kaplan family as they escape from Europe and eventually reach Canada. The authors develop the theme that many people risked their lives and helped the Jewish people.
- Uri Orlev's *The Island on Bird Street* (1984) is a historical novel set in the Jewish ghetto of Warsaw, Poland.
- Anne Frank's *Anne Frank: The Diary of a Young Girl: The Definitive Edition* (1995) is among the most widely read and discussed autobiographies of the Holocaust. It provides an intimate view of family life during the Holocaust.
- Anita Lobel's *No Pretty Pictures: A Child of War* (1989) is an autobiography centered on the author's experiences during her years in Krakow, while in hiding in the countryside, while living in the Warsaw Ghetto, and during internment in various concentration camps.
- The art and poetry associated with the Jewish experience are revealed in Sharon Keller's *The Jews: A Treasury of Art and Literature* (1992), Ellen Frankel's *The Jewish Spirit: A celebration in Stories and Art* (1996), and Hana Volavkova's . . . *I Never Saw Another Butterfly . . . Children's Drawings and Poems from Terezin Concentration Camp, 1942–1944* (1993).

The Resistance

The following books develop the importance of the resistance movement:

- Louis Lowry's *Number the Stars* (1989), set in Copenhagen during the 1940s, develops a fictional story around the actions of the Danish Resistance.
- Milton Meltzer's *Rescue: The Story of How Gentiles Saved Jews in the Holocaust* (1988) is an informational book that shows that many people risked their lives to help the Jewish people. This kind of informational book is very useful in helping readers authenticate historical fiction books such as *Number the Stars*.

War and North America

Historical fiction may emphasize North America as a sanctuary for people escaping war in Europe. Biographies of political leaders frequently emphasize the decisions they must make because of the war. The following books provide sources for this subject:

- Kit Pearson's *The Sky Is Falling* (1989) begins with the dangers of war in England, continues with a description of the voyage to Canada, and concludes with the often traumatic experiences faced by two children as they adjust to living in a new country.
- Mary Downing Hahn's *Stepping on the Cracks* (1991) explores moral dilemmas associated with war. The author develops both

person-versus-society and person-versus-self conflicts as children living in College Park, Maryland, discover a deserter from the army.

■ Miriam Bat-Ami's *Two Suns in the Sky* (1999), a winner of the Scott O'Dell Award for Historical Fiction, chronicles both the problems of Jewish refugees in America during the war and the responses to the refugees by Americans living near the refugee shelters.

The following biographies encourage readers to explore the roles of political leaders in times of war:

■ Russell Freedman's *Franklin Delano Roosevelt* (1990) includes many photographs and lists additional books about Roosevelt.

■ Freedman's *Eleanor Roosevelt: A Life of Discovery* (1993) realistically portrays Eleanor Roosevelt by drawing on her memoirs.

■ Katherine Leiner's *First Children: Growing Up in the White House* (1996) includes an interesting sidelight related to the Roosevelts.

War in the Pacific and the Internment of Japanese Americans

The following books develop this experience:

■ Yoshiko Uchida's *Journey to Topaz* (1971) and *Journey Home* (1978) tell about a Japanese American family's experiences after the bombing of Pearl Harbor.

■ Graham Salisbury's *Under the Blood Red Sun* (1994) develops the historical time period associated with the Japanese bombing of Pearl Harbor on December 7, 1941.

■ Lawrence Yep's *Hiroshima* (1995) is set in 1945 Japan during the time of the nuclear bombing. Yep includes both the crewmen on the Enola Gay and the children in a Hiroshima classroom.

■ Tatsuharu Kodama's *Shin's Tricycle* (1995) is a true experience of a Japanese teacher who survived the bombing, but saw his child die. The boy's tricycle has been recovered and is located in the Peace Museum in Hiroshima.

■ Ken Mochizuki's *Passage to Freedom: The Sugihara Story* (1997) is a highly acclaimed biography of the Japanese consul to Lithuania who helped many Jewish refugees escape from the Holocaust even though the Japanese government denied Sugihara's request to issue visas.

■ David Patneaude's *Thin Wood Walls* (2004) is set in the Tule Lake Relocation Camp in California during the time of the internment of Japanese Americans.

PROCEDURES AND ACTIVITIES

1. Begin the unit by exploring with students how much they know about World War II. On a world map identify areas that were affected by the war. Explain to the students that they will be reading about the war under the five topics: England and Europe at War, the Holocaust, the Resistance, War and North America, and War in the Pacific and the Internment of Japanese Americans. Point out each of these locations and lead a discussion with the students that allows them to identify what they know about each topic and to list questions that they would like to have answered. A table such as Table 8.2 could be used.

TABLE 8.2

Background Knowledge for World War II

Topic to Be Covered	What We Know	Questions We Want to Investigate
England and Europe at War		
The Holocaust		
The Resistance		
War and North America		
War in the Pacific and the Internment of Japanese Americans		

Explain to the students that they will be reading numerous books and other materials associated with the five topics around World War II. As they read various books they will be identifying the locations featured in the books and placing the locations on the maps. During this activity and discussion make sure that the students understand the sweep of history, why the war was called "World War II," and how World War II influenced so many people.

2. Review the genres of literature that will be read in this unit. Ask students to provide and discuss the characteristics of historical fiction (fictional literature written about a specific earlier time period in which the settings, conflicts, characters, and themes reflect what is really known about the time period); biography (the life of a real person in which the author develops information that is factually accurate); autobiography (the story about a person's life told by the person who actually lived it); and informational books (books about specific subjects in which the facts should be accurate).

3. The approach for conducting research and inquiry described earlier in this chapter is excellent for this unit. Students can follow this approach by choosing topics related to the subject, asking questions about the topic, planning their investigations, gathering and sorting information, synthesizing and organizing information, evaluating what is collected, and reporting their findings.

4. As they conduct their research, ask students to search for conflicts and issues, identify and consider the importance of themes developed during each topic, identify characteristics of people who overcome obstacles, and identify the historical events taking place. They may try to find the following themes identified by Norton (2002) for World War II literature:

   ■ People will seek freedom from religious and political persecution.
   ■ Prejudice and hatred are destructive forces.
   ■ Moral obligations and personal conscience are strong forces.

Students involved in a focus unit investigate a topic and enhance their reading and research skills.

- Freedom is worth fighting for.
- Family love and loyalty help people endure catastrophic experiences.

Ask students to consider if these themes are still important today.

5. Additional activities that may be conducted as part of the unit:
   - Authenticate an historical fiction selection.
   - Through creative writing ask students to respond to a biographical character.
   - Interview people who lived during World War II.
   - Create a museum that reflects the student's town during World War II.
   - Debate an issue identified in the unit.

6. To conclude the unit, ask students if they have investigated and answered all the questions they originally asked. Also, ask them to summarize what they have learned about World War II.

Social Studies and Point of View

The content areas of English, social studies, history, and science require that students be able to understand and respond to point of view. For example, the authors of many of the materials about World War II in the previous unit have definite viewpoints. Writers have several options when they tell their stories. Who tells the story? How much information about the characters and the incidents is this person allowed to know? Consequently, the description of an incident can differ depending on the feelings, viewpoints, motives, and beliefs of the person telling about the incident. The **point of view** is the perspective from which the story is told. Think of a book that you know well and try to determine the point of view. For example, who tells the story in Beatrix Potter's classic tale, *Peter Rabbit?* Is the storyteller sympathetic to the rabbit family or to Mr. McGregor? How do you know that the storyteller is sympathetic to the rabbit family? How would the story change if it were told from the gardener's point of view? We might be more likely to empathize with Mr. McGregor's need to safeguard his garden. We might even sympathize with Mr. McGregor as he tries to catch the rabbit.

Authors have four options when developing point of view. Let us look at each of these options and use examples of the various viewpoints by quoting excerpts from the books in the previously developed unit on World War II.

1. *First-person point of view:* The narrator uses "I" to tell the story. Autobiographies such as *Anne Frank: The Diary of a Young Girl: The Definitive Edition* (1995) provide many examples:

   > My father, the most adorable father I've ever seen, didn't marry my mother until he was thirty-six and she was twenty-five. My sister Margot was born in Frankfurt am Main in Germany in 1926. I was born on June 12, 1929. I lived in Frankfurt until I was four. Because we're Jewish, my father immigrated to Holland in 1933. (p. 7)

2. *Omniscient point of view:* The author tells the story in the third person, with the author referring to *they, he,* or *she.* The author is not restricted to the knowledge, experience, and feelings of one person. An omniscient point of view is considered the most flexible because the knowledge is unlimited. The author can interpret all behaviors, understand all motives, and even look into numerous characters' thoughts. An example of literature that may be used to model the omniscient point of view is Katherine Leiner's *First Children: Growing Up in the White House* (1996). One passage states:

   > From what Sistie had overheard, her mother had caused an awful scandal by divorcing her father and bringing her and Buzzie to live in the White House. But Sistie enjoyed seeing her aunts, uncles, and cousins as they came and went to and from the Mansion. Her youngest uncles, Franklin and John, drifted in and out, bringing friends home from college for lively parties in the East Room. They told her tales of life with their father, her grandfather. (p. 87)

3. *Limited omniscient point of view:* The author concentrates on the experiences of one character, but can be all-knowing about other characters. A book that uses this point of view is Pearson's *The Sky Is Falling In* (1989):

   > The eight children under the charge of Miss Nott were crammed into one compartment. Derek was the eldest and Gavin the youngest. Two of the children across from Norah

were boys about Lucy's age . . . She tried to talk to them, but Dulcie was too shy to answer and Norah didn't feel like being friendly. (p. 41)

4. *Objective point of view:* The author reports what the characters do or say or reports incidents, but does not explain why characters act in certain ways. This is the point of view chosen by many authors of informational texts and newspaper articles. To model this point of view, read a straight news story out of a newspaper. You could compare this news story with an editorial and show students how the two types of writing differ.

Discuss with students examples of these various points of view and ask them to consider the advantages and disadvantages of each one. You might refer to the literature that was chosen for the unit on World War II and ask students to reflect on why authors would choose these different points of view. You can also ask students to write about an incident using the four different points of view. Ask them to consider how their writing changed depending upon the point of view.

FOCUS ACTIVITY:
Teaching Point of View in Social Studies and History

Books that are written to show the points of view of different characters or the different points of view of society are excellent for expanding understanding and comprehension of point of view and for showing readers how an author can develop different or even opposite points of view. Miriam Bat-Ami's *Two Suns in the Sky* (1999), winner of the Scott O'Dell Award for Historical Fiction, is written using first-person point of view. One voice is that of Adam, a Jewish refugee who now lives in a shelter near Oswego, New York. The other voice is that of Chris, an American girl who lives near the camp. The author alternates the text using the different voices. In addition, the text is filled with societal attitudes toward Jewish refugees and Jewish attitudes toward the American society.

For this activity, consider how to identify two contrasting points of view: one of advocacy toward the Jewish refugees and one of attack toward the refugees. Introduce advocacy and point of view by asking students what each term means. For example, they may identify terms associated with advocacy such as *support, defend, endorse,* and *protect.* Terms related to attack might include *assault, criticize,* and *denounce.* Discuss each of these terms and their meanings.

Next, ask students to list some of the things that they or an author might wish to support. Now ask them to tell you some of the words they would use in their effort to support this point of view. Brainstorm a list with the students that might include positive terms or phrases such as *best school, smartest student, working for freedom, believing in the American way,* and *honest mayor* or *school board.*

Now, ask students to list some of the things that an author might choose to attack and terms that the author might use. If the students have completed the unit about World War II, presented earlier in the chapter, they can list some of the words they found in the literature about the five topics around the subject: England and Europe at War, the Holocaust, the Resistance, War and North America, and War in the Pacific and the Internment of Japanese Americans.

Introduce *Two Suns In the Sky* and tell the students that they will be searching for the points of view found in the literature by citing examples of the values expressed by the characters and the words they use to express those values. For example, read Adam's reaction to being free: "That was the fourth day of June 1944. Rome was liberated, and I continued to ask myself what it would look like, this picture of a boy who was free: Yes, we are free!" (p. 20). Ask students to identify the words that Adam uses to express his point of view about freedom. Read another example such as Chris's response to the July 4th: "We had the best holiday picnic on the lake. I love Lake Ontario. It stretches on so far you think you are looking forever" (p. 28). Discuss with the students how they visualize the two responses. Do words like *free, best holiday* and *I love* influence their identification of positive or negative points of view?

Ask students to read the book and search for examples of advocacy and to describe what the characters are advocating. A few of the examples are found on the following pages: (The page numbers are from the hardcover edition.)

- Chris advocates the setting for a happy Independence Day by describing picnics along the lake (p. 29).
- Adam advocates his positive view point of Chris and freedom by describing her eyes that knew nothing of hiding (p. 53).
- Adam advocates peace and freedom as he describes America as a beautiful land with peaceful sounds in the place of war sounds (p. 77).
- Chris advocates intelligence as she describes Adam as a boy who is not afraid to show how smart he is (p. 128).
- Adam voices his love for America, its people, and its customs (p. 165).

Ask students to summarize what they find in the book that develops support for a point of view or for a person. How does this point of view help them understand the characters in the book?

As they read the book ask them to search for the examples of attack such as the following:

- Adam attacks the years they lived without ration cards and had to live on turnips (p. 18).

- The townspeople predict disaster because the refugees will be eating their food, walking their streets, and wearing funning clothes (p. 46).
- Adam attacks the use of gas to kill people (p. 50).
- Chris expresses her father's belief that the only problem with Roosevelt is that he is not Irish Catholic (p. 135).
- Chris's father has a negative attitude toward his daughter's friendship with Adam (p. 143).

Ask students to summarize what they have discovered about how authors develop negative points of view toward characters by attacking people or groups. Ask them how they could use this information to evaluate an author's point of view. Using newspaper and magazine articles or television and radio broadcasts, ask students to identify points of view about current topics. Ask them to find examples of both advocacy and attack, and to consider why this information might be valuable to them.

To extend the understanding of point of view to poetry, ask students to read and respond to some of the poems in Hana Volavkovd's *. . . I Never Saw Another Butterfly . . . Children's Drawings and Poems from Terezin Concentration Camp, 1942–1944* (1993). Ask students to read, respond to, and discuss the points of view expressed in the poems and even in the artwork. As they read the poems, they will discover that most of the poems are expressing a point of view of attack against the imprisonment of the people in the concentration camp. They will find words such as *fear, dirty, flies that carry disease, streets of death, deserted, pain,* and *toughened.*

A focus unit in science frequently extends to the outside environment.

Reading and Science

A brief review of the science and technology lists of knowledge and skills identified in Chapter 2 indicates that by fifth grade, students should understand the impact of science and technology on life in the United States and by sixth grade they should understand the relationships among science and technology and political, economic, and social events. These knowledge and skills extend into the middle grades through the science curriculum. The implications for teaching these relationships among science and technology, and political, economic, and social events include reading and discussing current conservation programs designed to preserve endangered animals. This is a topic of great interest to many students and the materials for reading and discussing this topic are readily available.

In this section we focus on developing a unit around conservation programs designed to preserve endangered animals and the environment. The unit encourages students to conduct research using both printed texts and newspaper and other informational sources. There are also opportunities for them to take part in debates and interviews. One of the strongest motivators for this unit is a realization that students can actually make a difference.

FOCUS UNIT:
Developing a Unit around Conservation Programs

OBJECTIVES
1. To identify issues related to conservation programs designed to preserve endangered species and the environment
2. To identify and discuss the science and technology, and the political, economic, and social events related to the preservation of endangered species and the environment
3. To conduct research using the Internet and newspapers to identify the issues and the solutions that groups have used to protect endangered species and the environment
4. To identify conflicting points of view in relation with endangered species and the environment and to discuss the motivation for conflicting points of view
5. To interview various individuals in the community about issues related to endangered species and the protection of the environment especially global warming
6. To conduct a debate that reflects these various points of view
7. To develop a proposal or a plan of action that suggests a solution for the issues being studied

MATERIALS
Books that focus on the issues of endangered species or the protection of the environment, such as Carl Hiaasen's *Hoot* (2002, 2003 Newbery Honor) and Catherine Paladino's *One Good Apple: Growing Our Food for the Sake of the Earth* (1999). Newspaper articles such as

Walecia Konrad's "Finally, Kiawah Becomes Trendy (But Don't Touch Those Trees)" *New York Times* (7 February 2003, p. D1). Magazine articles such as Jeffrey Kluger's "By Any Measure, Earth Is at . . . the Tipping Point" in *Time* magazine's Special Report: Global Warming (April 3, 2006). Newspaper and magazine articles should be searched for current content. Web sites that include information on endangered species and the environment. Poems that reflect a concern for the environment such as Shonto Begay's *Navajo: Visions and Voices across the Mesa* (1995).

GRADE LEVEL	Upper elementary, middle school
BOOK SUMMARIES	<ul><li>*Hoot* is a fictional story that focuses on environmental protection and saving the burrowing owls in Florida.</li><li>*One Good Apple: Growing Our Food for the Sake of the Earth* is an informational book that explores the destructiveness of certain pesticides and fertilizers.</li><li>*Navajo: Visions and Voices across the Mesa* is a collection of poems written by a Navajo poet and artist. The poems reflect Begay's respectful attitude about the earth.</li></ul>
MAGAZINE SUMMARIES	The article "By Any Measure, Earth Is at . . . the Tipping Point" is part of a special *Time* report on global warming. The cover of the magazine reads: "Be Worried. Be Very Worried." It clarifies the issue by listing a series of concerns including: "Climate change isn't some vague future problem—it's already damaging the planet at an alarming pace. Here's how it affects you, your kids and their kids as well." The inside articles include Kluger's feature article as well as articles that focus on how global warming threatens your health, how China and India can either help save the world or destroy it, and discussions of people who the magazine identifies as climate crusaders. Photographs show the influence of global warming that cause the ice caps to melt, the consequences of devastating drought, rising waters that are drowning low-lying communities, and animals that may become extinct because of global warming.
MOTIVATION AND INTRODUCTION FOR THE UNIT	Students can brainstorm their ideas about the importance of (or the nonimportance if that is their belief) of protecting endangered species and the environment. *One Good Apple* includes a number of statistics and pictures that could be shared by students.
PROCEDURES	1. Discuss and list any of the issues that students identify. 2. Ask the students to search the newspapers, the Internet, and radio and television for any information related to endangered species or preserving the environment, especially related to land development and global warming.

3. Ask the students to identify any issues and any conflicting points of view that might be involved in land development.

4. Introduce *Hoot* by Carl Hiaasen and explain to the students that in the book a group of middle-school students discover that an endangered bird, the burrowing owl, will loose its home and potential life of its babies if a developer is allowed to bulldoze a lot and put up a pancake restaurant. Discuss possible issues and points of view.

5. Read the book and ask the students to identify the two conflicting points of view: "A pancake house will bring in money to the community and the lives of the burrowing owls are not important" versus "The burrowing owls are on the endangered species list and the construction company lied about conducting an Environmental Impact Study on the building site."

6. Ask the students to respond especially to chapters 20 and 21 and the Epilogue. These chapters describe how some of the middle-school students and their parents developed a peaceful protest that eventually saved the owls. These chapters also highlight how the media may be used to influence public opinion.

7. Students may read *One Good Apple* and identify problems and possible solutions related to protecting the environment. The articles in *Time* magazine provide many points for protecting the environment from global warming.

8. Ask students to interview other students and people in the neighborhood about their ideas about problems and possible solutions related to preserving endangered species and protecting the environment.

9. Ask students to respond to author and poet Shonto Begay and his belief about protecting the earth. Ask the students to read orally poems that reflect Begay's beliefs.

10. Students can develop a plan of action that addresses a problem related to endangered species, protecting the environment or global warming. They should remember that the characters in *Hoot* made a difference in their community.

11. Students may take part in a debate that allows them to argue the two sides of the issue.

Reading and Art

The language of art provides another challenge for students as they try to interpret and understand either artworks themselves or books about art. But, thankfully, art provides an enjoyable way for even lower ability readers to gain aesthetic literacy. **Aesthetic literacy** is the ability to read or interpret images in order to enjoy, appreciate, and understand them. Jack A. Hobbs and Jean C. Rush (1997) point out the complex role of aesthetic literacy:

Creating a work of art (as an artist does), or estimating its significance (as an art critic does), or verifying the authenticity of a work made in the past (as an art historian does), or discussing the nature of art (as an aesthetician does) are all inventive activities. . . . Aesthetic literacy can benefit all children, whether or not they grow up to be artists, art critics, art historians, or aestheticians. (p. 13)

This chapter's purpose is not to produce art; instead, its purpose is to help students to become art critics and to read illustrations. In this role, according to Hobbs and Rush, students analyze the elements of art such as line, color, mood, and symbolism created by the artist. As we proceed we will discover that the elements of art as shown through book illustrations and paintings are closely related to the literary elements, especially setting, conflict, characterization, and theme.

The search for artistic elements that emphasize content such as line and color is called **aesthetic scanning**. Lyn Ellen Lacy (1986) refers to the reading of art as visual literacy during which viewers analyze illustrations according to the artistic elements of line, color, value, shape, space, and texture. Lacy does an in-depth analysis of these visual elements by analyzing how artists use these elements in Caldecott Award books. You can read her book to discover how each artistic element is used by illustrators.

A brief summary of these artistic elements shows that lines help artists show direction, develop motion, and enhance energy and mood. Horizontal and vertical lines suggest lack of movement, triangular lines suggest safety, diagonal lines show loss of balance, jagged lines portray danger, and circular lines show change. Color is another strong artistic element that suggests mood. For example, strong blacks and reds create quite different moods than do pastel colors. Sometimes artists use contrasts in colors such as values of light and dark to develop conflict or even to show characterization. Differences in shapes vary from strong geometric shapes to irregular shapes that may only suggest a setting. The artist may use space on a page to show conflict. If a character is isolated from others with space in between, what does this suggest? Texture may be the most important element when an artist creates a setting in nature. Now texture may make viewers believe that they can almost touch the feathers on an owl, the bark on a tree, or the smoothness and fragility of a butterfly's wings.

ART CRITICISM   Students in the elementary grades have many opportunities to respond to, interpret, and evaluate works of art through the beautiful illustrations found in Caldecott Award books (award given for the quality of illustrations) and heavily illustrated books that develop the lives of famous artists. Art historian Donna K. Reid (2004) provides criteria for evaluating a work of art, useful for both reading and art teachers:

- Does the art attract the viewer's attention? If so, how?
- What type of emotional response is caused by the art?
- Is the art original and creative?
- What medium does the artist use? (Watercolors, oils, woodcuts, collage, etc.?)
- What visual elements does the artist use? (Line, color, shape, texture) Are they effective?
- What is the message of the painting?
- Does the painting have a memorable image?

Artists Barbara Cooney, Leo and Diane Dillon, Ezra Jack Keats, Robert Mc-Closkey, Maurice Sendak, Chris Van Allsburg, and David Wiesner have illustrated numerous works and their books are found in most libraries. The books are excellent for teaching both the reading of text and the reading of art. Students may want to evaluate how closely the art reflects the printed stories.

The following books include color reproductions of artists' works and biographical information that may also be used to apply criteria for art criticism:

- Diane Stanley's *Leonardo DaVinci* (1996)
- John Duggleby's *Artist in Overalls: The Life of Grant Wood* (1995)
- Robyn Montana Turner's *Frida Kahlo* (1993)
- Gary Schwartz's *Rembrandt* (1992)
- Richard Meryman's *Andrew Wyeth* (1991)
- Bill Peet's *Bill Peet: An Autobiography* (1989)

AN EXAMPLE OF READING ARTISTIC ELEMENTS Paul Goble's *The Girl Who Loved Wild Horses* (1978) is a Native American story in which the illustrations can be read for lines and colors that depict mood and can be compared with the figurative language that depicts mood in the story. This book may be shared with students in all elementary and middle-school grades. Most students are not aware of the artistic elements in the book. Before sharing this book remind students how lines and colors can depict mood. As part of the discussion place the semantic map shown in Figure 8.1 on the board or on a transparency.

Next, read the story orally and show the illustrations. If desired you may divide the students into groups with one group identifying how line depicts mood, a second group identifying how color depicts mood, and a third group identifying how language depicts mood. Tell the students that each group will report its findings to the

FIGURE 8.1

Semantic Map of *The Girl Who Loved Wild Horses*

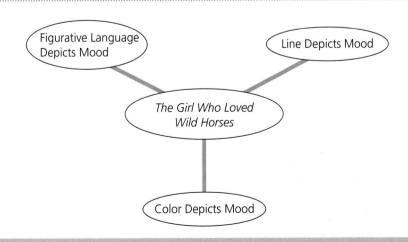

whole class and will discuss the impact of line, color, and figurative language on the mood of the story. This approach has been used with both middle and upper elementary students and with university students.

The semantic maps shown in Figures 8.2, 8.3, and 8.4 were developed with three groups of fifth-grade students:

Each group of students presented their portion of the web. They used the illustrations and textual examples to defend and describe how the illustrations created the mood and how the figurative language supported the mood. They concluded that they could read a story through the art and that it is important for the art to support the mood of the story.

You may extend this activity to include the illustrations in many other books. The Caldecott Award and Honor books are especially good for such an activity because the award is given to the illustrator. You might choose Lacy's text *Art and Design in Children's Picture Books* (1986) to provide a more in-depth look at how line, color, light and dark, shape, and space are used by artists in several Caldecott books.

ART AND SYMBOLISM **Symbolism** is something in the reading or art that represents another thing by association. Symbolism in art is another area of art criticism identified by Hobbs and Rush (1997). The illustrations in Paul Goble's *The Girl*

FIGURE 8.2

Semantic Map of "Line Depicts Mood"

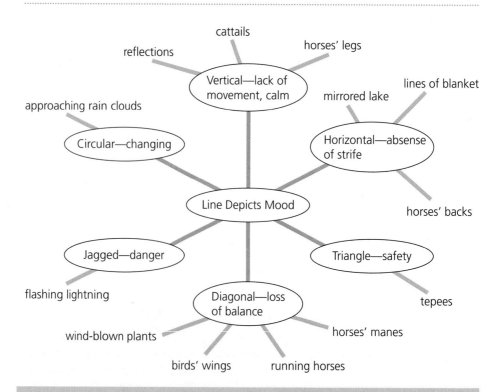

FIGURE 8.3

Semantic Map of "Color Depicts Mood"

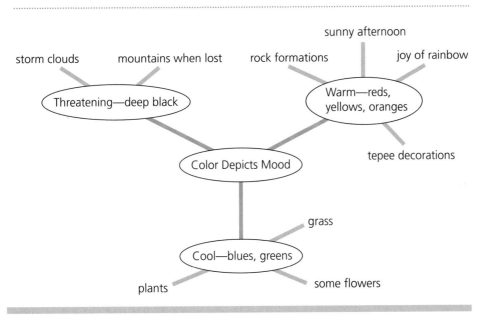

FIGURE 8.4

Semantic Map of "Figurative Language Depicts Mood"

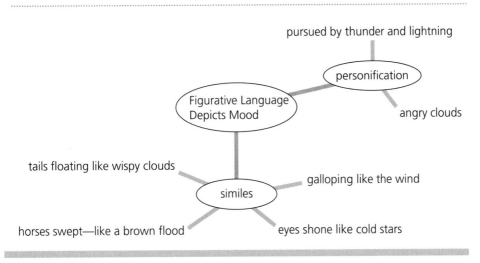

Who Loved Wild Horses that we used for showing the relationships between mood through line, color, and figurative language may also be used to identify symbols in Native American art and literature (Norton & Norton, 2003). For example, ask students to locate the following symbols found in the illustrations for *The Girl Who*

TABLE 8.3

Meaning of Symbols in *The Girl Who Loved Wild Horses*

Symbols	Meanings	Story Interpretation
braids	experience	
butterfly	life, child's toy	
circle	wholeness	
evening	rest, dreams	
hawk	one who has no enemies	
lake	mirror or wholeness	
rainbow	myths, strengths, connection of spiritual and physical	
river	spirit of life	
stone	power	
thunderbird	thunder and lightning, part of creation story	
touching ground	contact with nature, laws of Mother earth	
turtle	traditions, old symbol	

Loved Wild Horses and to discuss how they can interpret the art and the story through the symbols in Table 8.3. They can fill in the story interpretation.

Ask the students to search for these symbols in the art and discuss how the symbols relate to the meaning of the story. You may extend this activity by analyzing additional books written and illustrated by Paul Goble, including: *Beyond the Ridge* (1989), *Buffalo Woman* (1984), *The Dream Wolf* (1990), *The Gift of the Sacred Dog* (1980), *Iktomi and the Berries* (1989), and *Iktomi and the Boulder* (1988). This type of activity also helps develop multicultural understanding among students.

Shen Fu and Stephen Allee (1990) identify the symbols shown in Table 8.4 in Chinese art. Collect examples of Chinese art in paintings or in illustrated books and ask students to locate the symbols.

You may collect a variety of Chinese art books and ask students to search for any of the symbols in the art. These symbols are also found in Chinese folklore and poetry. They can be used when researching the accuracy of Chinese folklore and poetry.

ART HISTORY   This is another topic of importance related to comprehension of art identified by Hobbs and Rush (1997). Art that was painted during specific time periods and locations provides excellent sources for developing understanding of the historic, geographic, and cultural content of books. During a recent class, university students were able to find art that was painted during the time periods of the historical fiction and biographies that they were reading and sharing with public school students. They found H. W. Janson and Anthony F. Janson's *History of Art* (1997)

TABLE 8.4

Chinese Symbols in Art and Literature

Symbol	Meaning	Story Interpretation
dragon and phoenix	supernatural attributes	
tiger and eagle	strength and bravery	
wild geese	spirit of freedom	
hawk	heroic image of man	
rooster	independent spirit	
flowering plum	hardiness, Spring	
orchid	fragrance, Summer	
chrysanthemum	recluse, Autumn	
evergreen bamboo	resilience, Winter	

and Marily Stokstad's *Art History* (2005) to include many paintings that could be used to evaluate and identify the four purposes for settings also found in texts: historical background, mood, symbolism, and antagonist.

Paintings such as Jan Steen's "The Feast of St. Nicholas," for example, reveal extensive information about the clothing, food, and lifestyles of people living in Europe in the 1600s. There are numerous paintings that show setting as mood, such as Claude Lorraine's "A Pastoral Landscape," painted in 1650, Theodore Rousseau's "A Meadow Bordered by Trees" (c. 1840–45), Claude Monet's "Water Lilies" (1907), or Vincent Van Gogh's "Wheat Fields and Cypress Trees" (1889). Setting as symbolism is found in John Constable's "Salisbury Cathedral from the Meadows," painted (1829–34). Setting as antagonist is found in Casper David Friedrich's "The Polar Sea" (1824).

Encourage students to search for the various purposes for setting that may be found in artworks. They can use the artworks that develop a specific geographical or historical background to describe the background and then compare the backgrounds to those described in books. This is an excellent way to improve comprehension.

Reading and Writing Connections in the Content Areas

By the time most children reach the upper elementary and middle school years, they have the readiness skills required for writing. They can form letters, they know how to punctuate and spell, and they can construct at least simple sentences and paragraphs. Some of these processes become automatic while others take time, attention, and skill development even for experienced adults.

The focus of this chapter is on the writing requirements and instruction in the content areas as students are required to search for information pertaining to a topic,

Journal writing is part of an effective program in reading in the content areas.

gather the information, and organize and write the information into a meaningful whole. Many of the writing activities recommended in this chapter were developed and tested with teachers and their students as part of a three-year study reported by Sadoski, Wilson, and Norton (1997).

Writing in the content areas takes on several roles that are often categorized as expressive writing, imaginative writing, and expository writing. The units and lesson plans described in this chapter encourage all three types of writing.

EXPRESSIVE WRITING IN THE CONTENT AREAS   Expressive writing encourages students to explore their reactions to and express their feelings and opinions about a topic. This form of personal expression may be in the form of journals, learning logs, and reflective letters.

Journals   Journals are less formal in nature than other types of writing. Journals, however, provide opportunities for students to think about what they already know or feel about a subject or to respond to a new topic. When writing journals in English class, students may identify characters in books and explain why they think the characters are memorable. These characters may be protagonists or antagonists. The activity around Kate DiCamillo's *The Tale of Despereaux* (2003) could motivate numerous journal entries as students respond to either the heroic or less heroic characters. Or, they may respond to the characters in Cornelia Funke's *The Thief Lord* (2002).

Two additional Newbery Honor Awards for 2003 provide strong emotional reactions in some readers and are excellent sources for journal responses. Patricia Reilly Giff's *Pictures of Hollis Woods* (2002) is about an unhappy orphan girl who has lived in many foster homes until she is finally sent to live with an elderly artist who needs her and is eventually adopted by a caring family. The sequence of plot in the book follows memories that are reinforced through pictures drawn by the main character. Students may either write responses to what happens to Hollis or they may use her technique to create journals of their own lives. What pictures would they draw to illustrate different times and experiences in their lives?

Ann M. Martin's *A Corner of the Universe* (2002) deals with mental disabilities and a suicide. Students may respond to the friendship between a 12-year-old girl and an uncle who has been hidden in a home for disabled persons by the family. There are numerous person-versus-self and person-versus-society conflicts that may cause emotional responses. Interestingly, Martin also uses pictures to develop portions of the conflict as the girl searches old photograph albums trying to find pictures of her uncle.

Learning Logs When writing learning logs, students respond to and reflect on what they have learned in a lesson, project, or unit of study. They can explain why they think the lesson is important, how they will use the information in the future, and what more they would like to know about a topic.

P. Q. MacVaugh (1990) found that learning logs helped students retain information and develop understanding. The logs may also generate ideas for writing projects and further research into a topic.

Reflective Letters Writing reflective letters encourages expressive writing, improvement of writing skills, and the development of papers and projects in content areas. Dawn Swartzendruber-Putnam (2000) has students write reflective letters at the end of each unit of study. This letter accompanies any written piece and focuses on the writing and research process. She points out that before she accepts this written product, "It must be accompanied by a reflective letter. . . . Students may write about favorite parts of the piece, any weaknesses they see in this particular piece, what new techniques they tried that differed from their regular process. . . . The letters are more polished and thoughtful than the logs" (p. 90).

IMAGINATIVE WRITING IN THE CONTENT AREAS *Creative writing* and *poetic writing* are terms frequently used when describing imaginative writing. This type of writing includes imaginative and experimental thinking. The activities described in previous chapters such as diagramming and identifying components of plot structures; using think-aloud techniques to help students write plot structures, conflicts, and settings; and analyzing poetic structures and writing original poetry using those structures are all ways to develop and expand imaginative writing.

EXPOSITORY WRITING IN THE CONTENT AREAS Expository writing requires students to inform, record, report, and explain ideas. It is the writing that is frequently developed in informational or nonfiction texts. A considerable portion of the writing related to social studies, history, and science is considered nonfiction, as students need to investigate and report findings related to the topics. Advice from editor and author Jean E. Karl (1994) provides guidelines for authors of nonfiction literature that may be shared with school-age students. Karl presents steps in the writing process that include

- Making a list of topics that he or she would like to write about
- Narrowing the topic to a subject that can be covered
- Checking the library and other sources to discover what has been written about the topic
- Deciding if the student cares enough about the topic to conduct further research and write about the topic

Karl's advice is important to students before they write on a topic and certainly relates to reading in the content areas: "Read as much as you can, talk with experts if you can, absorb as much information as is possible. Make notes to yourself so you will not forget salient points—either on cards that may be filed by topic or in a notebook. Jot down names of especially helpful books so that you can come back to them as needed" (p. 80).

Improving the quality of both writing and discussions in the content areas is certainly a major goal for instruction. Kim O'Day (1994) describes a writing technique that she uses in middle-school social studies classes. To improve discussions and independent thinking and to increase the number of participants in the discussions, she asks students to list their ideas in their notebooks before the discussion. She classifies this type of writing as prewriting. She observes, "In my classes, more passive students who rarely entered discussions in the past usually now, through a pre-write, have the time and ability to carefully think out a concept or question" (p. 39).

This prewriting or pre-thinking activity is easily adapted to the techniques, lessons, and units already described in this chapter. For example, students could enumerate what they already know and questions they would like to research before taking part in the unit about World War II. They could write about their prior knowledge in relation to endangered species and the environment before beginning the unit on conservation programs. These prereading and writing strategies also help motivate interest in the topic.

USING NONFICTION LITERATURE TO MOTIVATE WRITING IN THE CONTENT AREAS   The nonfiction literature that is frequently used in social studies, history, and science provides another resource for writing activities. Students can investigate the writing techniques, research required, and types of information found in the texts they read in the content areas. The following activity using Russell Freedman's *Lincoln: A Photobiography* (1987) shows how this approach was used with a group of fifth-grade students.

FOCUS ACTIVITY:
Understanding the Writing Techniques of an Award-Winning Biographer

The 1988 Newbery Award winner, Russell Freedman's *Lincoln: A Photobiography* (1987), provides an excellent source for analyzing various writing techniques used by authors. The American Library Association selected this book as the most distinguished contribution to children's literature for 1987. A group of fifth-grade students chose the following techniques in this book as among their favorite writing techniques:

1. Freedman uses examples from Lincoln's own speeches to introduce each chapter. This gains the reader's attention and makes Lincoln seem like a believable person. A good example of this technique is the introduction to "Dreadful War":

When I think of the sacrifice yet to be offered and the hearts and homes yet to be made desolate before this dreadful war is over, my heart is like lead within me, and I feel at times like hiding in a deep darkness. (p. 93)

2. Freedman separates fact from fiction by letting readers know when information cannot be proven. A good example of this technique is Freedman's discussion of Lincoln and Ann Rutledge:

He also fell in love—apparently for the first time in his life. Legend tells us that Lincoln once had a tragic love affair with Ann Rutledge, daughter of the New Salem tavern owner, who died at the age of twenty-two. While this story has become part of American folklore, there isn't a thread of evidence that Lincoln ever had a romantic attachment with Ann. Historians believe that they were just good friends. (p. 28)

3. Freedman uses chronological order to develop the story of Lincoln's life. First, Lincoln is described as a poor, backwoods farm boy. Next, his life in law and politics is explored. Then Freedman discusses Lincoln's life as president in Washington, D.C.

4. Freedman increases interest in Lincoln's life by including photographs of Lincoln's own writings. For example, there is a photograph of a page from Lincoln's copybook and one of Lincoln's handwritten Gettysburg Address. This brings readers closer to Lincoln and also shows them that Freedman did a lot of research.

5. Freedman presents and discusses photographs of newspaper drawings and posters from Lincoln's time period. Included in these photographs are a cartoon ridiculing Lincoln's secret arrival in Washington; a cartoon showing Lincoln, General McClellan, and Jefferson Davis fighting over the Union; a poster about *Uncle Tom's Cabin;* and a poster offering a $100,000 reward for the murderer of Lincoln.

6. Freedom includes many photographs of places, people, and battles. This helps readers understand the events that took place. Freedman lists where he obtained the photographs at the back of the book. This also suggests careful research.

To extend this activity, students may investigate Freedman's writing techniques in additional biographies. The focus unit on World War II includes two additional biographies by Freedman: *Eleanor Roosevelt: Life of Discovery* (1993) and *Franklin Delano Roosevelt* (1990). What techniques does Freedman use in these books to create believable and authentic biographies? Are the techniques similar to those he used in *Lincoln: A Photobiography?*

Students may apply these techniques in their own writings. Have them use Freedman's techniques to research and write short biographies about people who they would like to know more about or people who are associated with units of study in the content areas.

USING NEWSPAPERS TO MOTIVATE WRITING IN THE CONTENT AREAS

Newspapers are an important reading source in the content areas. Newspapers also provide interesting sources for motivation of writing. Jack Heffron (2000), an editor for *Writer's Digest*, recommends that prospective authors read everything in a newspaper, from the front-page news to the comics. He states: "Make a list of the stories you find interesting and amusing. Also list any ideas for your writing that you find. Do this for a week. Begin a folder in which you place articles that interest you. Keep this folder active and current" (p. 123). These articles are then used to inspire different types of writing.

Try this approach in your college reading class. Bring copies of your local paper and national papers to class. What news articles could you use to expand interest in writing in any of the content areas? Develop a file of ideas and share them with your class.

Up for Discussion

Censorship

The changing content and subject matter of books that are read in the upper elementary and middle school grades and the types of activities that surround the books may result in conflicting differences of opinion about the materials. On one hand, some books more closely reflect the conflicts and life choices facing many young adults living in the twenty-first century. There are stories about substance abuse, street crimes, and different life styles. Students are also encouraged to read and to respond to a wide variety of literatures and to express their own responses toward various themes and values found in the literature.

In earlier centuries, students read highly controlled texts published for literature, reading, social studies, and history courses. Through the process of censorship dictated by publishing companies, many concerns of reviewers over controversial content were excluded from the texts. In contrast, many teachers now use a variety of materials as they develop units and other individualized reading assignments. These current reading materials may cover subjects that were not found in earlier textbooks.

As a result of the reduced control of classroom reading selections, pressure groups challenge books that they believe are offensive. According to John S. Simmons (2000), the number of book challenges in school libraries in grades five through nine have increased dramatically. The most cited reasons for these complaints according to Simmons are offensive language, sexual descriptions, incidents of violence, and treatment of Satanism and the occult. Popular books that are often challenged include Katherine Paterson's *A Bridge to Terabithia* (1977), Lois Lowry's *The Giver* (1993), Madeleine L'Engle's *A Wrinkle in Time* (1962), Judy Blume's *Blubber* (1974), and the various "Harry Potter" books.

An example of the reasons for protesting and challenging the "Harry Potter" books are explored in Kimbra Wilder Gish's "Hunting Down Harry Potter: An Exploration of Religious Concerns about Children's Literature" (2000). Gish uses Biblical quotes to reinforce her negative reactions to certain content in the Harry Potter books, such as presentation of witches, divination, wizards, and portrayal of "Muggles"—nonmagical people.

USING BOOKS TO MOTIVATE WRITING IN THE CONTENT AREAS   In *The Child That Books Built: A Life of Reading* by Francis Spufford (2002), a British journalist and literary critic discusses how books he read in childhood influenced his life. The book's inside cover description begins, "In this extended love letter to children's books and the wonders they perform, Francis Spufford makes a confession: books were his mother, his father, and his school. Reading made him who he is." In the book he discusses how different books influenced him at various stages in his life. These books were so important, he writes, that "They freed us from the limitations of having just one life with one point of view; they let us see beyond the horizon of our circumstances" (p. 10).

Using a process similar to Spufford's, teachers can ask students to identify books that have influenced them during different stages of their lives. Spufford begins by de-

An opposing viewpoint about the Harry Potter books is expressed by Nicholas Tucker (1999), who explores the popularity of the books and concludes,

It is always cheering for children's literature critics when young readers show that they can still become totally hooked on fiction. Descriptions of children utterly absorbed in a Potter book are very heartening at a time when the joys of reading are so often challenged by other juvenile habits and activities. . . . Seeing the Potter stories at the top of various newspaper best-seller lists means that there are now more adults taking an interest in what their children read even to the extent of enjoying some of the same books for themselves. (p. 233)

As you read the various Harry Potter books and other books that are on the lists of the most censored books, develop your own responses to the books. Discuss your responses with your reading methods class.

To extend your understanding of censorship challenges, you can use the format described by Jean E. Brown (2000) to create a censorship simulation. Brown recommends the following steps:

1. Create a setting in which you describe the demographics of the hypothetical community or school where the challenge will take place.
2. Select the book that will be challenged.
3. Identify student roles such as teacher, administrator, community members, librarian, supporter of the complaint, and those who oppose the complaint.
4. Create the initial complaint that shows the cause for the challenge.
5. Develop a plan for action such as reading, discussing, and writing about the literature and reading articles that reflect various views.
6. Role-play the experience.
7. Ask students to assess and reflect upon what they have learned about censorship and how they might handle challenges to the materials read in their classes.

This gifted reader reads books to enhance her knowledge of a topic.

Reflect on Your *Reading*

Which of these content areas is most appealing to you as a teacher? Consider your own background knowledge and experiences. How would your knowledge and experiences enrich your students' learning in the content areas of social studies, science, art, and writing?

scribing the importance of fairy tales when he was first beginning to read and progresses to the impact of *The Hobbit* and *Middle Earth* (Tolkien) and books from the Narnia Series such as *The Lion, the Witch and the Wardrobe* (C. S. Lewis). He then proceeds to the importance of the Laura Ingalls Wilder books such as *Little Town on the Prairie*. Finally he discusses books he read while in high school such as F. Scott Fitzgerald's *The Great Gatsby*, war novels, science fiction, and poetry of Wordsworth.

Teachers can develop this same activity with their students. Young readers can identify Mother Goose rhymes or fairytales that have influenced them and why. Older students can be asked questions such as, What books have made an impact on your life? Are there certain books you read over and over again? Which characters have you most identified with?

DIFFERENTIATING INSTRUCTION

ELL Students and Struggling Readers and Writers

Using visual clues is an effective way to help students understand concepts in content areas. Pamela J. Farris and Portia M. Downey (2005) call this approach *concept muraling*. It is a direct instructional approach that visually represents the material to be taught by using visual clues to present an overview of the concepts in a text. They conclude that the approach is especially beneficial for English language learners and struggling readers and writers.

To develop a concept mural, scan the content of the material to be read and identify six to eight major points that can be shown with simple visual representations or illustrations taken from a text. One of Farris and Downey's examples introduces a text about Abraham Lincoln. For the concepts in the text, they use a drawing of a picture book to represent Lincoln's limited formal schooling, but his desire to learn, a split-rail fence to represent his rural background, a desk depicting his law career, a picture of a slave, illustrations of soldiers during the Civil War, a picture of Lincoln as president, and a sign for Ford's Theater.

The teacher points to each illustration drawn on a transparency, poster board, or chart paper. He or she presents several points about each illustration. Then the teacher asks students to review information about each of the pictures. After this introduction to the topic, each student creates his or her concept mural in a notebook, labels each illustration with appropriate vocabulary words, and writes a brief phrase about the concept depicted in the illustration.

Teachers and librarians help each other as they choose materials to be used in the classroom.

Following this visual experience, the students read the assigned text and discuss the content. As a unit of study progresses, students add any additional information or illustrations. Farris and Downey find that this type of visual instruction enables both ELL students and struggling readers to engage in class discussions.

Gifted and Accelerated Readers and Writers

Many gifted and accelerated readers have highly developed interests in a topic. For example, a first-grade student may have read all of the dinosaur books in the school library, or a fifth-grade student may be so interested in photography that he or she has immersed himself or herself in the subject, including the history of the subject and the pioneers who developed various photographic techniques. To read these books requires advanced literacy skills.

Barbara Moss (2005) believes that if today's students are to acquire the literacy skills that are required for success in the 21st century,

> they need to be able to not just read informational texts, but read them critically, evaluating their "true value" and relevance. Furthermore, they need to be able to compare and contrast information across a variety of sources, see the relationships among the information they find, and synthesize those findings. (p. 52)

Moss suggests that idea circles are excellent vehicles for creating these types of learning experiences. Idea circles are a form of grouping in which students are involved in small-group peer-led discussions about concepts involving information texts. This concept learning involves facts gained from the texts, relationships between these facts, and explanations about why these relationships exist.

The idea circles may begin with questions that the students wish to explore such as questions about World War II that might introduce the unit developed in this chapter. Students would use a variety of literature selections, textbooks, maps, and the Internet to answer the focus questions and to form concepts related to the topic, explain the relationships, and synthesize their findings.

Summary

This chapter focuses on reading in the content in the middle and upper elementary grades (grades four through eight). There is special emphasis on using literature in these content areas. Reading and literature in English/language arts is enhanced by reading widely across genres and taking part in analytical reading and authenticating the various literary elements in the books read. An approach to developing research skills in the content areas follows a sequence that identifies topics, asks questions about the topic, plans investigations, gathers and sorts information, synthesizes and organizes information, evaluates what is collected, and reports the findings. Units help students apply these research and inquiry skills to the content areas. Being able to analyze point of view is very important when reading content area materials. The content area of art allows students to comprehend both the text and the illustrations in a book. The illustrations often extend an understanding of such content as mood, setting, and conflict. Writing is an important connection that helps students comprehend information and respond to materials in the content areas.

Reflect on Your Reading

Barbara Moss (2005) presents some of the literacy skills that will be required for success in the 21st century. She emphasizes the importance of comparing and contrasting information across a variety of disciplines. What literacy skills do you believe will be essential for success in the 21st century? How will you foster the development of these skills?

Key Terms

literary elements, p. 312

analytical reading, p. 313

authenticating literature, p. 320

point of view, p. 327

aesthetic literacy, p. 333

aesthetic scanning, p. 334

symbolism, p. 336

Where the classroom comes to life!

> For video clips of authentic classroom instruction on **Reading and Literature in the Content Areas**, go to Allyn & Bacon's MyLabSchool.com. In MLS courses, click on Reading Methods, go to MLS Video Lab, and select **Module 6**. And remember: there is also an entire MLS course for **Content Area Reading**, containing six additional video clips.

Extend Your Reading

1. Observe several classes in which teachers provide instruction in the content areas. Make notes on the teaching strategies that you believe are the most effective. Share your observations with your class.

2. Choose either "The American Revolution and Writing the Constitution" or "The Civil War." With a group of your peers, follow the model for the focus unit on World War II presented in this chapter and develop a unit on one of these topics. Include the objectives for the unit, the materials you will use, the grade level or levels for the unit, book summaries, and procedures and activities around the unit.

3. Interview a teacher about how he or she teaches in the content areas.

4. Develop a file of ideas for teaching writing in the content areas. If you are teaching, collect samples of students' responses to different types of writing prompts.

5. Begin a file of copies of artworks that could be used for aesthetic interpretations.

6. Choose one of the content areas and begin an annotated bibliography of different types of literature that could be used with that content area.

7. Begin a folder of newspaper and magazine articles that add understanding to a content area.

8. Start a list of Web sites that may be used by students when they conduct research in one of the content areas.

9. *Aesthetic literacy* refers to the ability to "read" or interpret images in order to enjoy, appreciate, and understand them. With a group of your peers, respond to Alberto Manguel's (2000) statement that aesthetic responses to art go back to the sixteenth century, where

   > a painting, whether a portrait or a scene, whether religious or allegorical, historical or private, was meant to be read. This was an inherent and essential feature of the aesthetic act: the possibility, through a shared vocabulary, of communication between the viewpoint of the artist and the viewpoint of the audience. (p. 121)

Present your responses to the class. You may choose to identify art that represents different time periods and respond to the possible aesthetic act between artist and audience of different time periods. Remember that many of the beautiful stained glass windows in cathedrals told stories to a congregation that was mostly illiterate. This audience received the stories through the art. What kind of stories do you receive by "reading" the art?

10. To increase your understanding of aesthetic literacy and the importance of "reading" or interpreting images, choose a painting and write a story to accompany that painting. Share your story with the class. Are they able to identify the painting that motivated your story?

11. Create a list of books that have been influential in your life based on *The Child That Books Built: A Life of Reading,* by Francis Spufford (2002). You may use and discuss any genre of literature and any content that might have influenced your life.

For Further Reading

1. Donna K. Reid, (2004), *Thinking and Writing about Art History,* 3rd ed. Upper Saddle River, NJ: Pearson. The text includes ideas for "Researching and Writing about Art History" and "Sample Student Essays."

2. Young Adult Library Services Association (April 2004), "YALSA's 2004 selected Videos/DVDs & Audiobooks for Young Adults." *School Library Journal.*

3. Arthur L. Costa, ed. (2001), *Developing Minds: A Resource Book for Teaching Thinking.* Alexandra, VA: Association for Supervision and Curriculum Development. Section VII includes "Thinking in School Subjects."

4. Many of the authors whose books are discussed in this chapter have Web sites, for example, Judy Blume: www.judyblume.com and Katherine Paterson: www.terabitha.com.

REFERENCES

Adler, Mortimer, & Van Doren, Charles. (1972). *How to Read A Book: The Classic Guide to Intelligent Reading.* New York: Simon & Schuster.

Brown, Jean E. (Spring-Summer 2000). "Creating a Censorship Simulation." *The ALAN Review,* 27, pp. 27–30.

Farris, Pamela J., & Downey, Portia M. (December 2004/January 2005). "Concept Muraling: Dropping Visual Crumbs along the Instructional Trail." *The Reading Teacher,* 58, 376–380.

Frankel, Ellen. (1997). *The Jewish Spirit: A Celebration in Stories and Art.* New York: Stewart, Tabori & Chang.

Fu, Shen, & Allee, Stephen. (1990). *Contemporary Calligraphy and Painting from the Republic of China.* Arlington, VA: International Council on Education for Teaching.

Gish, Kimbra Wilder. (May-June 2000). "Hunting Down Harry Potter: An Exploration of Religious Concerns about Children's Literature." *The Horn Book,* 76, pp. 262–271.

Heffron, Jack. (2000). *The Writer's Idea Book.* Cincinnati, OH: Writer's Digest.

Hobbs, Jack A., & Rush, Jean C. (1997). *Teaching Children Art.* Upper Saddle River, NJ: Prentice Hall.

Horning, Kathleen T. (April 2004). "The Tale of DiCamillo." *School Library Journal,* 50, 44–47.

Janson, H. W., & Janson, Anthony F. (1997). *History of Art,* 5th ed, revised. New York: Abrams.

Karl, Jean E. (1994). *How to Write and Sell Children's Picture Books.* Cincinnati, OH: Writer's Digest.

Keller, Sharon. (1992). *The Jews: A Treasury of Art and Literature.* New York: Hugh Lauter Levin.

Kluger, Jeffrey. (3 April 2006). "By Any Measures, Earth Is at . . . the Tipping Point." *Time,* 167, 34–42.

Konrad, Walecia. (7 February 2003). "Finally, Kiawah Becomes Trendy (But Don't Touch Those Trees)." *New York Times,* p. D1.

Lacy, Lyn Ellen. (1986). *Art and Design in Children's Picture Books.* Chicago: American Library Association.

MacVaugh, P. Q. (1990). "Writing to Learn: A Phenomenological Study of the Use of Journals to Facilitate Learning in the Content Areas." *Dissertation Abstracts International,* 51:04A (University Microfilms No. 90–24, 465).

Manguel, Alberto. (2000). *Reading Pictures.* New York: Random House.

Moss, Barbara. (September 2005). "Making a Case and a Place for Effective Content Area Literacy Instruction in the Elementary Grades." *The Reading Teacher,* 59, 46–55.

Norton, Donna E. (2002). "Developing the World War II Collection." *Encyclopedia of Library and Information Science,* Vol. 72, 99–113.

Norton, Donna E. (2007). *Through the Eyes of a Child: An Introduction to Children's Literature,* 7th ed. Upper Saddle River, NJ: Pearson/Merrill/Prentice Hall.

Norton, Donna E., & Norton, Saundra E. (2003). *Language Arts Activities for Children,* 5th ed. Upper Saddle River, NJ: Pearson/Merrill/Prentice Hall.

O'Day, Kim. (January 1994). "Using Formal and Informal Writing in Middle School Social Studies." *Social Education,* 58, 39–40.

Reid, Donna K. (2004). *Thinking and Writing about Art History,* 3rd ed. Upper Saddle River, NJ: Pearson/Prentice Hall.

Sadoski, Mark, Wilson, Victor L., & Norton, Donna E. (1997). "The Relative Contributions of Research-Based Activities to Writing Improvement in Lower and Middle Grades." *Research in the Teaching of English,* 31: 120–150.

Simmons, John S. (Spring-Summer 2000). "Middle Schoolers and the Right to Read." *The ALAN Review,* 27, pp. 45–49.

Spufford, Francis. (2002). *The Child That Books Built: A Life in Reading.* New York: Henry Holt.

Stevenson, Adlai, III. (7 February 2003). "Different Man, Different Moment." *New York Times,* p. A29.

Stokstad, Marilyn. (2005). *Art History,* 2nd ed. Upper Saddle River, NJ: Pearson, Prentice Hall.

Swartzendruber-Putnam, Dawn. (September 2000). "Written Reflection: Creating Better Thinkers, Better Writers." *English Journal,* 90: 88–93.

Tucker, Nicholas. (1999). "The Rise and Rise of Harry Potter." *Children's Literature in Education,* 30, pp. 221–234.

Children's Literature References

Abells, Chana Byers. (1986). *The Children We Remember.* Greenwillow.

Bartoletti, Susan Campbell. (2005). *Hitler Youth: Growing Up in Hitler's Shadow.* Scholastic.

Bat-Ami, Miriam. (1999). *Two Suns in the Sky.* Front Street.

Begay, Shonto. (1995). *Navajo: Visions and Voices across the Mesa.* Scholastic.

Bjork, Christina. (1999). *Vendela in Venice.* Illustrated by Inga-Karin Erikson, Translated by Patricia Crampton. Raben & Sjogren.

Blume, Judy. (1974). *Blubber.* Bradbury.

DiCamillo, Kate. (2003). *The Tale of Despereaux*. Illustrated by Timothy Basil Ering. Candlewick.

DiCamillo, Kate. (2006). *The Miraculous Journey of Edward Tulane*. Illustrated by Begram Ibatoulline. Candlewick.

Drez, Ronald J. (2004). *Remember D-Day: The Plan, The Invasion, Survivor Stories*. National Geographic.

Duggleby, John. (1995). *Artist in Overalls: The Life of Grant Wood*. Chronicle.

Fitzgerald, F. Scott. (1925, 1996). *The Great Gatsby*. Scribner's Sons.

Foreman, Michael. (1990). *After the War Was Over*. Arcade.

Foreman, Michael. (1990). *War Boy: A Country Childhood*. Arcade.

Frank, Anne. (1995). *Anne Frank: The Diary of a Young Girl: The Definitive Edition*. O. H. Frank & M. Pressler (Eds.), translated by S. Massotty. Doubleday.

Freedman, Russell. (1987). *Lincoln: A Photobiography*. Clarion.

Freedman, Russell. (1990). *Franklin Delano Roosevelt*. Clarion.

Freedman, Russell. (1993). *Eleanor Roosevelt: Life of Discovery*. Clarion.

Funke, Cornelia. (2002). *The Thief Lord*. Translated by Oliver Latsch. Scholastic.

Giff, Patricia Reilly. (2002). *Pictures of Hollis Woods*. Random House.

Goble, Paul. (1978). *The Girl Who Loved Wild Horses*. Bradbury.

Goble, Paul. (1980). *The Gift of the Sacred Dog*. Bradbury.

Goble, Paul. (1984). *Buffalo Woman*. Bradbury.

Goble, Paul. (1988). *Iktomi and the Boulder*. Orchard.

Goble, Paul. (1989). *Beyond the Ridge*. Bradbury.

Goble, Paul. (1989). *Iktomi and the Berries*. Watts.

Goble, Paul. (1990). *The Dream Wolf*. Bradbury.

Hahn, Mary Downing. (1991). *Stepping on the Cracks*. Clarion.

Hartlin, Peter. (1998). *Crutches*. Translated by E. D. Crawford. Lothrop, Lee & Shepard.

Hiaasen, Carl. (2002). *Hoot*. Knopf.

Holub, Josef. (2005). *An Innocent Soldier*. Translated by Michael Hofmann. Scholastic.

Kaplan, William, & Tanaka, S. (1998). *One Family's Escape from War-Torn Europe*. Groundwood.

Kodama, Tatsuharu. (1995). *Shin's Tricycle*. Walker.

Leapman, Michael. (1998). *Witnesses In War: Eight True-Life Stories of Nazi Persecution*. Viking.

Leiner, Katherine. (1996). *First Children: Growing Up in the White House*. Tambourine.

L'Engle, Madeleine. (1962). *A Wrinkle in Time*. Farrar, Straus & Giroux.

Lewis, C. S. (1950, 2004). *The Lion, the Witch and the Wardrobe*. Illustrated by Pauline Baynes. HarperCollins.

Lobel, Anita. (1998). *No Pretty Pictures: A Child of War*. Greenwillow.

Lowry, Lois. (1989). *Number the Stars*. Houghton Mifflin.

Lowry, Lois. (1993). *The Giver*. Houghton Mifflin.

Magorian, Michelle. (1983). *Good Night, Mr. Tom*. Penguin.

Martin, Ann M. (2002). *A Corner of the Universe*. Scholastic.

McWhorter, Diane. (2004). *A Dream of Freedom: The Civil Rights Movement from 1954 to 1968*. Scholastic.

Meltzer, Milton. (1988). *Rescue: The Story of How Gentiles Saved Jews in the Holocaust*. Harper & Row, 1988.

Meryman, Richard. (1991). *Andrew Wyeth*. Abrams.

Mochizuki, Ken. (1997). *Passage to Freedom: The Sugihara Story*. Lee & Low.

Orlev, Uri. (1984). *The Island on Bird Street*. Translated by H. Halkin. Houghton Mifflin.

Paladino, Catherine. (1999). *One Good Apple: Growing Our Food for the Sake of the Earth*. Houghton Mifflin.

Paterson, Katherine. (1977). *A Bridge to Terabithia*. Illustrated by Donna Diamond. Crowell.

Patneaude, David. (2004). *Thin Wood Walls*. Houghton Mifflin.

Pearson, Kit. (1989). *The Sky Is Falling*. Viking.

Peet, Bill. (1989). *Bill Peet: An Autobiography*. Houghton Mifflin.

Potter, Beatrix. (1902). *The Tale of Peter Rabbit*. Warne.

Rogasky, Barbara. (1988). *Smoke and Ashes: The Story of the Holocaust*. Holiday.

Rowling, J. K. (1998). *Harry Potter and the Sorcerer's Stone*. Illustrated by Mary Grandpre. Scholastic.

Sachar, Louis. (1998). *Holes*. Farrar, Straus & Giroux

Salisbury, Graham. (1994). *Under the Blood Red Sky*. Doubleday.

Schwartz, Gary. (1992). *Rembrandt*. Abrams.

Stanley, Diane. (1996). *Leonardo DaVinci*. William Morrow.

Tolkien, J. R. R. (1938). *The Hobbit*. Houghton Mifflin.

Turner, Robyn Montana. (1993). *Frida Kahlo*. Little, Brown.

Uchida, Yoshiko. (1971). *Journey to Topaz*. Scribner's Sons.

Uchida, Yoshiko. (1978). *Journey Home.* Athenaeum.

Volavkova, Hana. (1993). . . . *I Never Saw Another Butterfly . . . Children's Drawings and Poems from Terezin Concentration Camp, 1942–1944.* Schocken.

Wilder, Laura Ingalls. (1941, 1953). *Little Town on the Prairie.* Illustrated by Garth Williams. Harper-Collins.

Yep, Lawrence. (1995). *Hiroshima.* Scholastic.

Yolen, Jane. (1988). *The Devil's Arithmetic.* Viking.

CHAPTER 9

The Reading and Writing Connection

CHAPTER **OUTLINE**

Current Attitudes toward Writing Instruction Related to Reading
How Should Writing Be Taught?
Three Types of Writing That Relate to Reading
  Expressive Writing
  Imaginative Writing
  Expository Writing
Expressive Writing and Emergent Literacy
  Labels in the Classroom
  Charts Listing Daily Activities
  The Writing Center
  Language Experience Activities
Imaginative Writing
  Imaginative Writing for Emergent Literacy
  Imaginative Writing through Poetry Appreciation and Writing Workshops
Expository Writing
  Expository Writing in Emergent Literacy
  Teaching Reading and Writing through Expository Writing Workshops
  Reading and Writing an Opinion Article
  Understanding Viewpoints through Expository Writing

After reading this chapter you will be able to answer the following questions:

1. Why is writing a critical value for developing reading understanding?
2. What are the current attitudes toward writing and reading instruction?
3. What is the writing process as it relates to reading?
4. How are reading and writing taught through expressive writing?
5. How are reading and writing taught through imaginative writing?
6. How are reading and writing taught through expository writing?

Read All About It!

"In the Classroom, Web Logs Are the New Bulletin Boards"

by Jeffrey Selingo, *New York Times*, August 19, 2004

Last spring, when Marisa L. Dudiak's second-grade class in Frederick County, Md., returned from a field trip to a Native American farm, all the students wanted to do was talk about what they saw. But instead of leading a discussion about the trip, Mrs. Dudiak had the students sign on to their classroom Web log.

There they wrote about learning to use a bow and arrow, sitting inside a teepee and petting a buffalo. The short entries were typical of second-grade writing, with misspelled words and simple sentences. Still, for Mrs. Dudiak, the exercise proved more fruitful than a group discussion or a hand-written entry in a personal journal.

"It allowed them to interact with their peers more quickly than a journal," she said, "and it evened the playing field." Mrs. Dudiak said she found that those who were quiet in class usually came alive online.

Classroom Web logs, or blogs, many of which got their start in the last school year, are becoming increasingly popular with teachers like Mrs. Dudiak as a forum for expression for students as young as the second-grade level, and in almost any subject. In the blogs, students write about how they attacked a tough math problem, post observations about their science experiments or display their latest art projects.

For teachers, blogs are attractive because they require little effort to maintain, unlike more elaborate classroom Web sites, which were once heralded as a boon for teaching. Helped by templates found at sites like tblog.com and movabletype .org, teachers can build a blog or start a new topic in an existing blog by simply typing text into a box and clicking a button . . .

Teachers say that the interactivity of blogs allowed them to give students feedback much more quickly than before.

> "Teachers who use blogs say that students put a lot more thought and effort into their blog writing, knowing that parents and others may read their work on the Web."

"I used to have this stack of hard-copy journals on my desk waiting to be read," said Catherine Poling, an assistant principal at Kemptown Elementary School, also in Frederick County, Md., who ran a blog last year when she taught third grade at a nearby school. "Now I can react to what they say immediately, and students can respond to each other."

In one blog entry, for instance, Ms. Poling asked her students what qualities they looked for when rating books for a statewide award. When several students responded that a book has to be creative and grab their attention, she posted a follow-up question asking them if they used the same criteria for both fiction and nonfiction books.

While such a question could have just as easily been posed during a classroom conversation, teachers who use blogs say that students put a lot more thought and effort into their blog writing, knowing that parents and others may read their work on the Web.

. . . Sometimes, the long reach of the Web has turned bloggers into modern-day pen pals, allowing students to collaborate easily with their peers in other classes or even other countries. Some social studies classes at Hunterdon Central Regional High School in Flemington, NJ, for instance, are using a blog to study the Holocaust with high school students in Krakow, Poland.

One of the goals of classroom blogs, advocates say, is to get students to write more often. Even so, few entries seem to come after school hours and during the summer. . . . This has led some teachers who are critical of blogs to question whether

the technology has actually done anything to interest students in writing. Critics also worry that the casual nature of writing on the Web may encourage bad habits that are hard to break, like e-mail-style abbreviations, bad grammar and poor spelling. . . .

Debbie Contner, an assistant principal at one of the district's six schools, Hamilton-Mainevill Elementary (Cincinnati), who used a blog when she taught fourth grade at the school last year, said that teachers become receptive to blogs once they see how easy it is to set one up.

"If it gets kids excited about learning," Mrs. Contner said, "we might as well try it."

Read All About It!
Critical Thinking Questions

- What new techniques and strategies are elementary teachers using to motivate their students to write about their reading and other school projects?

- How do teachers evaluate these newer approaches to writing?

- What are the advantages or disadvantages of using this technology?

- How might it increase reading and writing?

- What questions could the reading teacher use about books in addition to asking students to evaluate the quality of the books that should get awards?

Reading and writing are natural connections because reading a wide variety of materials improves writing by presenting students with models for writing, and writing in response to reading enhances students' abilities to respond emotionally and to critically evaluate what they read. Consequently, interactions between reading and writing enhance both reading and writing. This chapter focuses on the importance of writing and reading interactions and how teachers may improve both writing and reading through these interactions.

Writing encourages students to apply skills that they learn in reading, for example, when writing students use the vocabulary, apply their knowledge of story structures and literary characteristics gained in reading, and use the various types of context clues studied in reading in their own writing. In reading they learn how authors develop point of view and themes; while writing they apply this critical knowledge to their own papers and projects.

Several researchers emphasize how writing influences reading. Hansen (1987) for example, concludes, "Writing is the foundation of reading . . . When our students write, they learn how reading is put together because they do it. They learn the essence of print" (pp. 178–179). Farnan and Dahl (2003) emphasize this importance when they conclude, "Readers notice the ways words are spelled, the way authors use a phrase or sentence to create an image, how a certain word conveys the right connotation, and how a writer leads readers through a clear explanation of a complex process" (p. 994).

A classroom study with second-grade students (Lancia, 1997) provides strong reasons for the positive influence of using reading and writing together. Lancia describes using read-alouds, independent reading, guided reading, shared reading, teacher-student conferencing, and writing workshops. He found that students' writings reflect the use of literary devices modeled during the reading of literature such as plot ideas and devices for creating plot, characterizations, conflicts, and genre characteristics. He concludes that borrowing from literature shows the positive interaction between reading and writing. In addition, he believes that children make natural connections between reading and writing through their daily interactions with books. This chapter makes many connections between reading and writing in both direct instruction and independent reading and writing activities.

Current Attitudes toward Writing Instruction Related to Reading

There is no one favored approach to teaching writing. Some educators recommend approaches that emphasize the process of writing, whereas others recommend those that emphasize the goals of writing. Many teachers consider both the process and the resulting products of writing.

In the *New York Times* (May 28, 2003), Michael Winerip describes the experiences of an accomplished kindergarten teacher, Ms. MacLeish, who fears that the kindergarten world she knows and has raised to a fine art is being destroyed because "A single high-stakes test score is now measuring Florida's children, leaving little time to devote to their character or potential or talents or depth of knowledge. Kindergarten teachers throughout the state have replaced valued learning centers (home center, art center, blocks, dramatic play), with paper and pencil tasks, dittos, coloring sheets, scripted lessons, workbook pages" (p. 20). Instead of ditto sheets, Ms. MacLeish's room is filled with baskets of books by her favorite authors, author studies, writing examples, drama, and singing.

Winerip's article reflects two very diverse ways of teaching reading and writing. Should worksheets and workbooks replace the drama used in Ms. MacLeish's kindergarten? Studies reported by Betty Jane Wagner (2003) show that imaginative expression through drama is an effective way to promote literacy because drama produces maturity in student writing; drama is correlated with word-writing fluency; both drama and drawing produce second- and third-grade writers whose writing shows better organization, ideas, context, and style; and role-playing improves persuasive writing of fourth- and fifth-grade students.

Wagner concludes that the studies show "dramatic play in kindergarten correlates with word-writing fluency, and educational drama under a teacher's guidance is effective in improving subsequent writing in studies at second-, third-, fourth-, fifth-, eighth- and ninth-grade levels and at remedial college freshman levels" (p. 1014). Wagner cites other studies that highlight the power of the performing arts to improve reading and writing through choral reading of poetry, storytelling, and story dramatization.

Diane Kern and colleagues (2003) are very critical about the way writing is currently being taught in this time of standard-based assessments. They worry that 'teaching to the test' will not teach students to write to inform, to persuade, or to retell a story. This is an issue that is currently being debated as schools are concerned about meeting federally and state-mandated performance goals. Betty Sternberg (Winerip, 2006), Connecticut's education commissioner, is concerned about the move to test writing through multiple-choice tests rather than written examples. In response to a suggestion that Connecticut switch to multiple-choice tests and eliminate writing tests to cut costs, Sternberg's response shows the importance of testing writing through actual writing examples: "Writing is an essential skill that every youngster needs to succeed. Eliminating it is not an option" (p. A21). There are, however, guidelines reported by both research studies and professional organizations that help clarify how the interaction between reading and writing should be developed.

The following five guiding principles should prevail when organizing a writing curriculum and working with student writers:

Principle 1	Writing helps students develop an individual voice by linking writing activities to real life issues.
Principle 2	Students need to be active participants in writing through choosing writing topics, selecting audiences, brainstorming ideas, revising work in progress, and reflecting on finished writing.
Principle 3	Writing requires both variety and direct instruction through practicing various kinds of writing for different purposes. Teachers need to provide direct instruction in the organization and technical composition related to different writing styles.
Principle 4	Literature provides writing models and authentic purposes for writing because writing is best learned during meaningful reading and writing activities.

[handwritten margin notes:] What evidence seen addressed in school are we doing this? how to enhance? Time for kids Weekly Readers journal writing

[handwritten note:] — expository text best for primary grades

Principle 5   The teacher should write along with the students in order to model the value and importance of writing (Kern, et al., 2003).

The reading and writing standards identified by the National Council of Teachers of English (NCTE) and the International Reading Association (IRA, 1996) reinforce the importance of connecting reading and writing. They include:

1. Students should read a wide range of print and nonprint texts including fiction and nonfiction and classic and contemporary works to build an understanding of texts and cultures, to acquire new information, and to gain personal fulfillment.

2. Students should read a wide range of literature from many genres and periods of time to build an understanding of the human experience.

3. Students should apply a wide range of strategies in order to comprehend, interpret, evaluate, and appreciate texts.

4. Students should use a wide range of strategies as they write and they should use different writing elements to communicate with different audiences for different purposes.

5. Students should participate as knowledgeable, reflective, creative, and critical members of literacy communities.

6. Students should use spoken, written, and visual language for learning, enjoying, persuading, and exchanging ideas.

Reflect on Your Reading

Consider Ms. MacLeish's situation as a kindergarten teacher. Which side would you be on? Would you use worksheets and workbooks to teach reading and writing, or would you use learning centers and numerous literature selections to motivate students to read and write? How would you support your position?

As we proceed through this chapter on reading and writing we will try to include all of these suggestions and requirements. We will also discover that writing and teaching writing are both exciting and complex. Consequently, to be effective, most of the writing and reading suggestions require that teachers also do the activities. Writing requires practice and participation not only reading about the topic.

How Should Writing Be Taught?

Studies investigating the teaching of writing indicate considerable changes over the past two decades. Anne Haas Dyson and Sarah Warshauer Freedman (2003) report that studies of writing have shifted from studies that analyzed pieces of writing to studies about the writers' actual composing processes as they write. Newer studies of writing investigate the decisions that writers make as they plan, revise, and edit their work.

George Hillocks's (1986) review of research on composition is one of the most frequently cited studies about effective writing approaches and implications for teaching activities related to writing. Hillocks's findings illustrate the importance of many of the writing activities and principles discussed in this chapter.

Hillocks summarizes research on written composition by identifying characteristics of the most effective mode of instruction and identifying characteristics of skilled and unskilled writers during the **writing process**. Analyze the following characteristics of the most effective mode of instruction and consider how you would include those characteristics in your writing and reading lessons:

1. Writing instruction emphasizes processes such as prewriting, composing, and revising.

2. Prewriting activities help develop the skills to be applied during the writing.

3. Lessons include specific objectives for learning.

4. Writing activities help students learn the procedures for using those forms during the writing process.

5. Include interaction with peers and feedback during the total writing process rather than primarily at the end of a composing activity.

Now consider the following differences between skilled and unskilled writers and think about how you would use this information to assess students during the writing and reading process.

1. During the writing process students should explore the subject by thinking about the topic, reviewing what is known, collecting information, considering characteristics of the audience, and reflect about approaches that will be used:

> Skilled writers: take time to explore the topic and use many strategies.

> Unskilled writers: do little exploring of the topic and do not consider exploring to be important or useful.

2. During the writing process students should include planning, during which time they make choices about content and organization:

> Skilled writers: take time to plan and use a variety of techniques such as listing, sketching, and diagramming.

> Unskilled writers: do little planning before or during writing.

3. During the drafting portion of the writing process students should choose their words carefully and craft their sentences:

> Skilled writers: write in ways that are less like speech and show sensitivity to the readers.

> Unskilled writers: imitate speech and are preoccupied with spelling and punctuation.

4. During the revising portion of the writing process students should evaluate what they write and make changes in form and content:

> Skilled writers: either revise very little or revise extensively. Extensive revisions examine larger issues such as content and reader appeal.

> Unskilled writers: approach revising as error-hunting spelling or grammatical errors and copying over in ink.

According to Hillocks, the most effective instruction is characterized by specific objectives aimed to increase the use of figurative language in writing, to select materials and problems that engage the students in the processes that are essential for the specific writing activities, and to include small-group problem-centered discussions. In effective

instruction, teachers frequently give brief introductory lessons about the principles to be studied and applied during small-group activities and then during the independent work. It is worthwhile to note Hillocks's assumptions about the most effective composition approaches:

1. Teachers actively seek to develop identifiable writing skills in students.
2. Students develop skills by using them orally before using them in writing.
3. The major function of prewriting activities is to develop writing skills.
4. The use of skills such as generating criteria to define a concept is complex, and therefore may require collaboration with and feedback from others.

Jackie Proett and Kent Gill (1986) identify activities that make up the writing process before students write, while students write, and after students write. Before students write they:

- build ideas for the content of writing by brainstorming, semantic mapping, researching, outlining, and watching films and other media.
- develop and order their writing by developing details and examples, developing chronological order, classifying ideas, or structuring by cause and effect.

While students write they:

- consider their own background for writing a piece, identify their audience, think about their purpose for writing and the likely result of the writing, and identify the form for the writing.
- make decisions about word choices, language, sentence structures, and syntax.

After students write they:

- revise their work by getting responses through editing groups, reading their writing aloud, expanding and clarifying ideas, and proofreading and polishing the work.
- make decisions about sharing the work through various ways of sharing and publishing the work.

In addition to the steps in the writing process, Proett and Gill identify six principles that they believe should be used to guide the selection of activities included in the process approach:

1. Students require frequent guided writing experiences.
2. Students need to produce more writing than a teacher can evaluate carefully; consequently not all papers should be selected for careful evaluation.
3. Students can practice the steps in the writing process such as brainstorming, focused timed writing, sentence combining, and small-group editing one at a time, but they need to experience the entire process on a single writing project in order to develop a sense of working from start to finish on a paper.
4. All elements of the writing process should be undertaken at some time during class so teachers can coach and monitor progress. Real teaching must continue after the assignment is given, through all stages of the process. This may not be possible if writing is always a homework activity.

5. Writing is a complex activity. It involves the simultaneous application of a series of intellectual and physical activities. In the classroom, teachers must break activities into manageable segments to give learners a chance to handle them successfully.

6. There has been no clearly accepted linear sequence for writing skill development. Consequently, students need many opportunities to apply their emerging skills to the writing process.

> **Reflect on Your Reading**
>
> Consider the similarities and differences found in the models for the writing process discussed. How would you make connections with reading while students are writing? How would you help students after they have finished the initial writing phase?

Cunningham and Allington (2003) are critical of the way writing is taught in schools. They believe that instruction focuses on editing skills *not any more!* such as penmanship, spelling, mechanics of writing, and grammar, rather than giving students an opportunity to think, compose, and write. Instead, they spend most of their time concentrating on the skills. These authors ask: Are children being taught the wide range of writing that is necessary in and out of school? Are children being taught to search out, gather, and organize information? Are they being taught to revise? Are they also learning how to spell?

The connections between reading and writing and the steps in the writing process are very strong in Cunningham and Allington's concerns; they are also apparent in the guidelines for writing recommended by Jean E. Karl (1994), an editor and an author of children's nonfiction books.

Karl presents steps in the writing process that begin with the writer choosing a subject by listing the topics that he or she would like to write about, narrowing the topic to a subject that can be covered, checking the library to discover what else has been written on the topic, and deciding if the potential author cares enough about the topic to conduct further research. Karl stresses that prior to writing an author needs to "read as much as you can, talk with experts, if you can, absorb as much information as is possible. Make notes to yourself so you will not forget salient points—either on cards that may be filed by topic or in a notebook. Jot down names of especially helpful books so that you can come back to them as needed. Keep track of where you found pictures and charts that might be of help to an illustrator" (p. 30).

After completing the initial research, the writer decides what goes into the text. Now the writer asks: What is the most important point that I want to make? What information do I need to include that will help the reader understand my subject? After writing a final outline, the author is ready to write a first draft that makes every word count.

After the first draft, the writer is ready to revise, if necessary. Now the writer asks Does the beginning set the tone, and does the tone continue throughout the paper? Do ideas follow each other in logical order? Are the transitions logical? Does the summary convey the material covered? This is the time to read the writing aloud and let others read the writing and comment on the meaning.

Three Types of Writing That Relate to Reading

There are three types of writing that are closely related to the reading curriculum (Norton, 2004): expressive writing, imaginative writing, and expository writing.

An appreciation for writing is one of the goals for literacy for life.

Expressive writing activities encourage writers to explore their reactions and to express their moods, feelings, and opinions. They may provide personal responses to the books they read. This is an important activity in reader response approaches. Imaginative writing includes original writing, experimental thinking, and writing to entertain. This is found in reading as students read poetry and other works of fiction. Expository writing informs, reports, and explains. This is found in reading as students read nonfiction materials such as biographies and trade books that develop science and history subjects.

Expressive Writing

Expressive writing relates to personal expression of feelings about one's reading or other experiences. It may take many forms, such as a diary, journal, or letter. Expressive writing may encourage children to write personal narratives about their own lives or to respond to the experiences of characters they read about in books. Teachers use journal writing to encourage students to express ideas and to react in personal ways. Journals or diaries may be used to encourage students to write about what they think about a piece of reading.

Writers' logs and writers' journals are other forms of expressive writing. In writers' logs students respond to and reflect on what they have learned from their reading and writing. Writers' journals may be closely related to the reading of literature. They are natural bridges between expressive and imaginative writing. In the writers' journal students include information about story ideas, characterizations, language choices, and sensory experiences that they would like to develop into more expanded writings. They may express feelings about new experiences, extend their experiences through newspaper articles, collect interesting expressions and quotes, describe real or imaginary places or people, relive memories of pleasant and unpleasant experiences, and consider questions that fascinate them.

Young children frequently write narratives about their own personal experiences. These stories may be in the form of autobiographical experiences or stories about people who are close to the child.

Imaginative Writing

Imaginative writing is also frequently called poetic writing or creative writing. This writing includes original writing created by the students that uses both imaginative and experimental thinking. The child who creates an original work rather than copying the piece from a published source, poem, fairy tale, story, or puppetry script is engaged in this type of imaginative writing. Writing poetry and drama allows experimentation with the sounds and impact of well-chosen words. Writing their own story helps students understand the development of plot, characterization, and theme. This type of writing requires numerous experiences with reading and listening to and discussing stories before students understand the structures required for writing.

Expository Writing   *to inform* *reports*

Expository writing is probably the most common writing developed in school. It may be called explanatory writing because it presents facts, ideas, or opinions usually about nonfiction subjects. This type of writing, found in most content areas, may require researching and writing comparisons, organizing formats that develop cause and effect relationships or logical sequences of events, authenticating a biography or an informational book, using technology to research information, and writing a finished essay or composition.

In this next section we consider more in-depth activities to develop the writing process and to help students relate reading and writing, especially those developed through writing workshops.

Reflect on Your Reading

How important are expressive, imaginative, and expository reading and writing in your own life? When do you use each type of reading and writing? Is one type of reading and writing more useful in your daily life? If so, which one?

Expressive Writing and Emergent Literacy

Preschool children and those in kindergarten and lower elementary grades need many opportunities to see teachers writing and to develop the understanding that spoken words can be written down and reread. They need daily opportunities to read different forms of writing, to understand that writing has different purposes, and to express themselves through writing. This expression may be in the first stages of scribbling or in a mature form in which the letters form recognizable words. These daily opportunities may result from labels in the classroom, charts that list daily activities, working in the writing center, or taking part in language experience activities that result in class, small group, or individual chart stories.

Labels in the Classroom

One of the most meaningful labels in the classroom is a child's own name. When children first come to school, they should be given their own nametags. These labels may be used to introduce each child to the rest of the class. Some teachers take each child's picture using an instant camera and place the children's pictures along with their nametags on a bulletin board. Nametags may also be placed on each child's locker or coat hook. Now children can match their nametags with the name on their locker or other storage facility.

Labels can be placed on various items in the classroom. To allow children to make the connections between the printed word and the object, children can first identify an item such as *desk* and then watch as the teacher prints the word on a card, rereads the word, asks the children to read the word, and places the word on the corresponding object. Several labels may be printed and discussed each day. Labeling may be expanded as students learn descriptive words such as a *red telephone* or a *hamster cage.*

Students may be introduced to the purposes for labels in their daily lives—for example, the label *crayon* on their boxes of crayons or labels on cereal boxes that tell them what type of cereal they are eating. Cereal boxes show that both words and illustrations may be used as informative labels. Again, these labels may be used to expand written language as children add action words to the labels—for example, "I eat Cornflakes."

Charts Listing Daily Activities

Children like to know the activities that occur throughout the day. These lists of activities may be printed on charts or on chalkboards. As the teacher prints the activities, students should have opportunities to watch the writing and to read the words. Activities include such experiences as "story time," "learning centers," "reading class," "science projects," and "play time."

Children's responsibilities provide another opportunity for expansion of early writing literacy. Now teachers list the daily or weekly responsibilities with the student's name next to each of the chores; for example:

Daily Chores

Jane:	Feed the hamster
Rodney:	Water the plants
Chris:	Turn off the lights
Carmen:	Straighten the library books
Beth:	Wash the art tables

The Writing Center

A writing center needs a table with chairs as well as tools such as crayons, pencils, magic markers, felt-tipped pens, paper, and sometimes computers. The center usually includes various types of materials that may be used to motivate specific types of writing. Greeting cards, for example, along with blank folded paper, may stimulate children to create their own holiday or birthday cards. Wordless books may provide the structure for a story. Highly illustrated magazines or photographs may suggest a story. Teachers frequently include vocabulary charts that list the words studied in reading or in spelling. Easy to use picture dictionaries are beneficial. Writing centers usually provide space for children to post their writing and for other children to respond to the writing.

Language Experience Activities

Using a language experience approach means that children dictate their ideas about their experiences to a teacher who writes them down, usually on a chart, for children to see and to read. The language experience approach stimulates oral language, writing, and reading. As students express their ideas orally, they see their oral ideas transformed into writing, and they read back the story that results from their own experiences. The language experience approach is closely related to schema theory because children use their own experiences and background knowledge to create the written product.

Consequently, reading and comprehension are strengthened because students have considerable knowledge about the story before they are expected to read or answer questions. The language experience approach is also a major teaching approach that is associated with the top-down model of reading. In the top-down model reading begins with meaning before students are expected to decode words.

Reflect on Your Reading

Writers' journals are natural bridges between expressive and imaginative writing. Have you had experiences writing in a journal? Were you encouraged to keep a reading journal by a teacher? In what ways would writing in a journal aid in the development of your personal expression?

To conduct a language experience activity for emergent literacy, first provide an interesting experience that children may experience, discuss, and then create a chart story about. The interesting experience might be a field trip, for example, a movie, a puppet show, a science experiment, or a guest speaker. Second, lead a discussion that allows students to talk about their experience, expand their ideas, and share their observations. Finally, select a large tagboard chart on which to write the children's observations. A chart on which the teacher writes the words with a marking pen is preferable to writing the story on the chalkboard because the charts may be retained so that students may read them in the future.

The teacher usually begins the writing experience by asking students to provide a sentence that introduces the story or a sequence of experiences. As the first sentence is stated by a child, the teacher asks the children to watch as the words are written beginning at the top left side of the chart. The teacher points out that the sentence begins with a capital letter and proceeds from left to right. The teacher pronounces each word as it is written. After the chart story is completed, the teacher reads the whole story while placing a hand under the appropriate words. Children are usually asked to reread the chart after the teacher. Teachers may identify a sentence contributed by a specific child by placing the child's name on the chart next to the sentence. The teacher may ask that student to read his or her sentence. Comprehension questions may follow the reading of the chart. Students may illustrate the chart story and older students may write, illustrate, and read their individual language experience stories.

Imaginative Writing

Terms such as *poetic writing, creative writing,* and *imaginative writing* are used to describe fictional prose, poetry, or drama. The purpose of this writing is frequently defined as being to inform and delight. Poetic writing uses both imaginative and experimental thinking. To elicit this type of creative expression from children, teachers must provide a great deal of nurturing, exploration of language, and experiences that foster creativity.

Imaginative Writing for Emergent Literacy

Developing creative and imaginative writers during emergent literacy requires a rich environment that fosters imaginative and experimental thinking. The environment needs to develop children's awareness and sensitivity through activities in which they experience visual stimulation, sounds, smell, tastes, and feelings. This environment should allow children to make discoveries, ask questions, and find answers.

Becoming a successful adult requires numerous experiences with writing including writing using technology.

The environment should encourage children to create meaning with words and to explore different types of reading and writing. The environment should provide many opportunities to test the effectiveness of their communications by sharing their ideas and their writings with an audience.

Marian Diamond (1998) emphasizes the need for an enriched environment that nurtures intelligence and creativity. She describes this environment as one that overflows with posters, writings, art, books, science corners, listening stations, music, art centers, writing centers, and clicking keyboards.

Within this enriched environment, teachers need to foster a style of thinking that fosters creative and imaginative thinking if imaginative writing is to flourish. Robert J. Sternberg (2001) identifies the legislative style of thinking that helps children do creative and independent projects and to express their own creative thoughts and points of view. Sternberg suggests that teachers frame instruction to emphasize creative performances by using terms such as: "Create . . . , Invent . . . , If you . . . , Imagine . . . , Design . . . , How would you . . . ?, Suppose . . . , and Ideally . . ." (p. 199).

These types of discussions and writing activities suggest to students that in imaginative writing, writers use language as an art medium to simultaneously inform and entertain. Let us consider how we might use these types of framing instructions for students in the kindergarten and lower elementary grades. We will include selections of literature that might be used as a motivator:

"CREATE . . ."   After reading "The Polliwogs" (p. 24) in Douglas Florian's *Omnibeasts* (2004), review and act out the movements of the polliwog as he wriggles, quivers, shivers, jiggles, and jogs. Ask the students to think of another animal and create a list of words that describe the movements of the animal. This can be a real or an imaginary animal. Young children can create a chart story while older students create their own imaginative list of words and use the words to create a longer story.

"INVENT . . ."   After reading Helen Cooper's *A Pipkin of Pepper for the Pumpkin Soup* (2005) invent soup that you would create or a spice that you would add to a soup. A story might include: "Where would you go to get the ingredients? How would you make the soup? How would your friends react to the soup?"

"IF YOU . . ."   After reading Catharina Valcky's *Lizette's Green Sock* (2005) ask the students to think about what they would do if they were in Lizette's place and had only one sock? How would they use the sock? They might also think about friendship, and why it was important for Lizette to have a friend like Bert. Ask the students to create their own "If You . . ." story that describes something they might find and what they would do with the object.

"IMAGINE . . ."   After reading Doreen Cronin's *Duck for President* (2004) imagine that an animal that you know, maybe a pet, decides to run for president. You might ask students to consider: "What would the animal want if elected? How would the animal conduct the campaign? What would happen when the animal is in charge of the country?"

"DESIGN . . ."   After reading Kevin Henkes's *So Happy* (2005), design a way that you would cross a stream or think about what you would do if you were bored like the boy. Students could write or dictate a story about something that would make their lives better.

"HOW WOULD YOU . . . ?"   After reading April Pulley Sayre's *Stars Beneath Your Bed: The Surprising Story of Dust* (2005), ask students how they would look for dust in their environment? They might consider: "What does dust do for you? What would happen if there was no dust in the environment?" They can write a story about their own imaginary experiences in either a world of dust or a world without dust.

"SUPPOSE . . ."   After reading Chih-Yuan Chen's *Guji Guji* (2004) ask the students to suppose that they found a very unusual egg: "What animal might hatch out of the egg? How would the other animals react to the egg? Would you want the animal to go to live with its own kind of animal? Why or why not?"

"IDEALLY . . . ?"   After reading one of the chapters from Rosemary Wells's *Yoko's World of Kindness: Golden Rules for a Happy Classroom* (2005), ask students to think about how they would write a story that expresses their own golden rules for living. For example, the first story, "Mamma, Don't Go!" develops the golden rule, "It is not easy to say good-bye. But, the one who loves us always comes back" (p. 1). The story is about a young kitten who goes to school for the first time but does not want her mother to leave the classroom after taking her to school. By the sixth chapter, "Make New Friends," Yoko is happy because she has made new friends. Now the golden rule is, "Some people shine like a star in the first moment. Others keep their light hidden until they are ready to show us" (p. 129). These stories have numerous creative writing possibilities because they reflect children's own concerns as they begin school.

Imaginative Writing through Poetry Appreciation and Writing Workshops

For this development of imaginative writing for all age students, we will first focus on creative writing through poetry and then discuss other activities that enhance imaginative writing. Why should we use poetry to nurture creativity? Poet Naomi Shihab Nye (2002) says that poetry is the most intimate literary genre because, "Poetry slows us down, cherishes small details. . . . We need poetry for nourishment and for noticing, for the way language and imagery reach comfortably into experience" (p. xvi).

Poetry, whether read or written, encourages students to contemplate a carefully chosen word or to vicariously taste and visualize the effect of language. Educator and literary critic Harold Bloom (2001) emphasizes the importance of poetry for him: "When I was a child, each time I fell in love with a poem, I read it again and again until I had it by heart. Then I would go off by myself, whether indoor or outdoor, in order to have the pleasure of chanting it endlessly to myself" (p. 19). He identifies the poetry of Rudyard Kipling, Lewis Carroll, and Edward Lear as especially meaningful for him when he was a child.

Caroline Kennedy (2005), in her introduction to *A Family of Poems: My Favorite Poetry for Children,* says it best for teachers of young children: "Writing a poem forces us to think about what we really want to say, and helps us understand ourselves and shape our lives. If you start when you are young, you will see that words and ideas have the power to change the world" (p. 10). These beliefs expressed by both poets and lovers of poetry provide us with the reasons for using poetry in imaginative writing.

Sharing and discussing the works of established writers as well as writing and sharing original poems in groups allows students to experiment with the sounds of language and to explore the moods and feelings developed in a carefully crafted piece of poetry. For students to enjoy writing and reading poetry, however, they may require numerous experiences with all types of poetry.

One of the best ways teachers can create a nurturing environment that fosters creative expression is through the use of writing workshops in the classroom. **Writing workshops,** which have been the core coursework of undergraduate and graduate creative writing programs throughout the country, can effectively be used in elementary and middle school classrooms. Writing workshops build a collaborative classroom environment that encourages children to view each other as valuable resources. Workshops increase students' abilities to communicate orally and through writing. They enhance children's knowledge of writing and give children opportunities to apply that knowledge to discussions of literature.

Developing poetry workshops is one of the most appealing portions of writing workshops because they allow children to develop a greater awareness of language and word use. When children develop this awareness by concentrating on the building blocks of language found in poetry, they are able to apply this awareness to all of their writing. Many teachers and undergraduate students admit that they do not like poetry reading or poetry writing because of the way it was taught to them in elementary, middle school and in high school. They often describe memories in which poetry was associated with teacher questioning that required them to interpret a poem the way it would be accepted by the teacher rather than allowing students to discuss various responses to a poem.

This section identifies poems to share and discuss with children to help them develop an appreciation of poetic elements and the different forms of poetry. It introduces poets who write certain forms of poetry. It suggests ways to use poetry in dramatizations and presents ideas for the writing of poetry. Several lesson plans illustrate how students can develop an understanding for and an appreciation of poetry as well as writing poetry.

PROGRESSION OF POEMS IN POETRY WORKSHOPS FROM EASY TO COMPLEX

Recommendations for poems that range from the easy to complex allow teachers to select poetry appropriate for younger students or for students in upper grades who have little knowledge about poetry. Workshop materials include poems that can be used to accompany various content fields, to develop appreciation of poetic elements, to introduce forms of poetry, to investigate the poets who write certain types of poetry, and to select poems that help students during their own writing processes.

The poetry shown in Table 9.1 progresses from easy to complex and includes poetry to accompany a study of a culture or a content area. It is the poetry that can be read orally and on a daily basis, not only when a unit is taught. This poetry helps students develop an appreciation of different styles of poetry before they are asked to do more analytical activities such as identifying various poetic elements and forms of poetry.

POETIC ELEMENTS   Poets use language in different ways to encourage readers to hear, feel, and see the subjects of their poems. Let us first define the various poetic elements and then identify poems in which the poets use those poetic elements. All of the poetic elements discussed in this section are found in poems collected in *Knock at a Star: A Child's Introduction to Poetry* (Kennedy & Kennedy, 1999). They are also found in many additional anthologies of poetry. Michael Driscoll's *A Child's Introduction to Poetry* (2003) includes a CD recording of the poems read by professional actors.

Rhythm   Rhythm, the movement of words in a poem, is one of the first elements that attracts listeners and readers to poetry. It is the quality of a poem that encourages young children to accompany a poem with skipping or with rhythm instruments. Rhythm encourages children to join in orally, experiment with language, and move to the rhythms. An example of rhythm can be found in Eve Merriam's "Windshield Wiper." As students listen to this poem they can easily experiment with the rhythm of the wiper.

Rhyme   Rhyme, word patterns that end alike such as the *at* in *cat* and *bat,* is one of the poetic elements found in many poems for young children. In fact, many younger children will define poetry as literature that rhymes. If you read the poems in any collection of nursery rhymes, you will discover many rhyming elements. Rhyming words may occur at the ends of lines or within the lines in poems. For example, in "The Eagle," by Alfred Lord Tennyson, the poet rhymes *hands, lands, stands* and *crawls, walls, falls.*

TABLE 9.1

Progression for Poetry Study

Level	Example
A. Very Young Children: Nursery Rhymes with Strong Rhythms	Tomie dePaola's *Tomie dePaola's Mother Goose* (1985) Jane Yolen's *This Little Piggy: Lap Songs, Finger Plays, Clapping Games, and Pantomime Rymes* (2005)
B. Narrative Poems in Which Illustrations Tell the Story	
1. Easier Poems	Kathi Appelt's *Oh My Baby, Little One* (2000)
2. Harder Poems	Roy Gerrard's *Wagon's West!* (1996)
3. Hardest Poems	Alfred Noyes's *The Highwayman* (1981)
C. Narrative Poems Found in Longer Stories	Randall Jarrell's *The Bat-Poet* (1963)
D. Sequence of Poems by One Poet with a Study of Biographical Information	
1. Easier	poems by Jack Prelutsky and Shel Silverstein
2. Harder	poems by Gwendolyn Brooks, Emily Dickinson, Robert Frost, Langston Hughes, Robert Louis Stevenson
E. Poetry That Accompanies a Study of a Culture	
1. Native American	Nancy Wood's *The Serpent's Tongue* (1997)
2. African American	Walter Dean Myers's *Harlem* (1997) Marilyn Nelson's *A Wreath for Emmett Till* (2005)
3. Latino	Francisco Alarcon's *Laughing Tomatoes* (1997)
4. Asian	Demi's *Dragon Kites and Dragonflies* (1986) Nikki Grimes's *Tai Chi Morning* (2004)
5. Jewish	Hana Volavkova's *. . . I Never Saw Another Butterfly . . .* (1993)
6. Middle Eastern	Naomi Shihab Nye's *The Space Between Our Footsteps* (1998)
F. Poetry to Accompany Content	
1. Science/Nature	Paul Fleischman's *Joyful Noise: Poems for Two Voices* (1988) Jon Scieszka and Lane Smith's *Science Verse* (2004)
2. History	Henry Wadsworth Longfellow's *The Midnight Ride of Paul Revere* (2001)
3. Geography	Diane Siebert's *Heartland* (1989) James Berry's *Around the World in Eighty Poems* (2002)

Alliteration   Alliteration is the repetition of initial consonants or groups of consonants to create sound patterns. In Morris Bishop's "Song of the Pop-bottlers" the initial sound of *p* is used so many times that the poem becomes a tongue-twister. "Sing
Me a Song of Teapots and Trumpets," by N. M. Bodecker, uses words beginning
with *t* in one verse, words beginning with *sn* in another verse, and words beginning
with *p* in another verse. Kennedy and Kennedy classify these poems in a section titled "Word Play," where "the results can surprise poet and reader. At its best, such

word play can be as exciting as a fast game of street hockey, as suspenseful as the next move in a game of chess" (p. 101).

Assonance   Assonance is the repetition of vowel sounds in words. Poems such as Eve Merriam's "Notice to Myself" use numerous repetition of vowel sounds such as in *idling-sidling, ambling-rambling,* and *doodling-noodling.*

Repetition   Repetition allows poets to emphasize words, phrases, lines, and even whole verses. For example, in "While I Slept," Robert Francis repeats the phrase "while I slept" six times. Repetition in poetry encourages listeners to join in when the poem is read orally.

Imagery   Imagery encourages readers or listeners to see, hear, taste, smell, and touch words created by the poet. Several types of imagery or figurative language are found in poetry, including similes, metaphors, and personification.

- Similes are direct comparisons between things that have something in common but are essentially different. When poets use similes they use words such as like or as. For example, in Dudley Randall's "Blackberry Sweet," the poet compares lips that are as "curved as cherries" and as "sweet as blackberries."

- Metaphors are implied comparisons between things that have something in common but are essentially different. For example, in "September," John Updike describes breezes that taste of apple peel and plates that are polished with the morning haze.

- Personification means giving human emotions and characteristics to inanimate objects, abstract ideas, and nonhuman living things. In "The Wind," for example, James Stephens describes a wind that is able to shout, stand up, whistle, kick, and thump branches with its hand.

FORMS OF POETRY   When poets refer to forms of poetry they mean the poetic forms found in lyric, narrative, ballads, limericks, concrete, and haiku poems. Each of these poems follows a specific format that allows students to categorize them and to write poems that follow that form.

Lyric Poems   Lyric poems are brief poems that never tell a complete story but have a lyrical, or songlike, quality. These poems are frequently sung or are accompanied by music. *In Knock at a Star,* Kennedy and Kennedy place lyric poems in a section titled "Songs," remarking, "Back whenever poetry began, it was probably sung. In ancient Greece, poems were sung to the strumming of a lyre, a stringed instrument. . . . In the middle ages, kings and other lords kept minstrels—poets and musicians— to play and sing for them" (p. 124). Several lyric poems are also accompanied by music, including "Riddle Song," "I Had a Little Nut Tree," and "On Top of Old Smoky."

Narrative Poems   Narrative poems tell stories. With rapid action and typically chronological order, story poems have long been favorites of children. In "Mummy Slept Late and Daddy Fixed Breakfast," poet John Ciardi tells a humorous story about Daddy's experiences making waffles that look like gravel pudding, look like a manhole cover, and need a hack-saw to cut. In "John Henry" the anonymous poet tells the story about the steel-driving man. The narrative poems listed in Table 9.1, such as Roy Gerrard's *Wagon's West!* (1996) and Alfred Noyes's *The Highwayman* (1981), are excellent sources of narrative poems that are book-length examples. Shorter narrative poems are found in *Once Upon a Time: Favorite Poems That Tell Stories* (2004).

Limericks   Limericks are short, witty poems that have five lines; the first, second, and fifth lines rhyme and have three pronounced beats each, and the third and fourth lines rhyme. Edward Lear, who wrote poems in the nineteenth century, is one of the most popular poets who used the limerick form. Another example is William Jay Smith's "There Was a Young Lady Named Rose." Susan Pearson's *Grimericks* (2005) is a collection of poems in limerick form.

Concrete Poems   Concrete poems are poems that seem to be physically real, they can be seen or touched; for example, a concrete poem about a vase would be written in the form of a vase. In a concrete poem, the poet may use the shape of the poem to emphasize its meaning. Douglas Florian's "Seashells" is written in a form that might duplicate the view of seashells scattered on the shore. Norma Farber's "For a Quick Exit" includes words written that seem to move like an escalator.

Haiku   Haiku is an ancient form of Japanese poetry. (A word of caution: some people believe that the haiku has lost its meaning through translations into other languages.) Haiku has a very strict format. It has three lines; the first has five syllables, the second line has seven, and the final line has five syllables. Haiku poets frequently write about nature and the cycle of the seasons. Examples appropriate for students include "Ancient pool. Sound" by Basho, translated by Olivia Gray, "A Bantam Rooster" by Kikaku, translated by Harry Behn, "Now the swing is still" by Nicholas Virgillio, and "Out after dark . . ." and "Midnight sirens—" by Penny Harter. Jack Prelutsky's *If Not for the Cat* (2004) is a collection of 17 haiku poems about animals.

POETS WHO WRITE CERTAIN TYPES OF POETRY   Some teachers develop lessons around poets who use specific forms or address certain topics in their work. For example, nonsense and humor poetry is very popular with teachers and students in the lower elementary grades. Poets who write nonsense and humor include Edward Lear, Shel Silverstein, and Jack Prelutsky.

Nature poems allow poets and readers to observe nature with a different vision. Teachers may also choose nature poems to accompany science topics. Poets who write about nature include Robert Frost, Aileen Fisher, and Paul Fleishman.

Poets who choose to write about characters, situations, and locations include Myra Cohn Livingston and David McCord. Byrd Baylor writes poetry about the Southwest and the Native American people who live there.

Most poems develop moods and feelings. Poems written by minority poets may be especially revealing. Poems such as Arnold Adoff's *All the Colors of the Race* (1982) reflect the thoughts and feelings of a girl of biracial heritage. Langston Hughes's poems such as "Dreams" and "Merry-Go-Round" were written during an earlier time period in African American history and depict the feelings and struggles of African American people who are trying to live in equality. *Hispanic, Female and*

Young: An Anthology (1994), edited by Phyllis Tashilk, includes poetry and other writing by young Latina students in New York City's El Barrio neighborhood.

USING POETRY IN DRAMATIZATIONS   Performing poetry is an excellent way to improve understanding of poetry and also provide a means for sharing children's poetry with an audience. In the lower to middle elementary grades, poems such as Clement C. Moore's "A Visit From St. Nicholas" provide excellent sources for acting out. In the middle to upper elementary grades poems such as Henry Wadsworth Longfellow's "A Midnight Ride of Paul Revere" and John Greenleaf Whittier's "Barbara Frietchie" offer opportunities to act out a poem that also relates to history.

Providing background information will enhance comprehension of the poems. For example, to add to an understanding of "Barbara Frietchie," have students conduct research about the setting in Frederick, Maryland, 1862, the Union and Confederate armies, the Confederate and Union states, the Battle of Antietam at Sharpsburg, and background information about the poet, John Greenleaf Whittier.

As part of their background information about "Barbara Frietchie" they can use the following quote by Whittier included in an illustrated version of the poem by Nancy Winslow Parker (1992): "The poem of Barbara Frietchie was written in good faith. The story was no invention of mine. It came to me from sources which I regard as entirely reliable; it had been published in newspapers, and had gained public credence in Washington and Maryland before my poem was written. . . . John G. Whittier, Amesbury, 6 Mo. 10, 1886" (p. 31).

"Barbara Frietchie" has numerous lines that lend themselves to dramatic interpretations such as "'Shoot, if you must, this old gray head, But spare your country's flag, she said." Before performing the poems, ask students to decide how they would interpret various scenes and discuss the techniques that the poets used to enhance such dramatic times in history. They may also consider what made poets focus on these historical times.

This dramatization activity should progress into a poetry writing and reading activity in which students read history books, newspapers from both earlier and contemporary times, and other sources such as interviews with people who might have had personal connections with the historical time period, such as ancestors, history professors, or museum curators.

The goal of this type of activity is to search for other stirring experiences that might be turned into narrative poems. Students will discover that poets, including themselves, who write about historic time periods, must conduct considerable research to make sure their poems are historically accurate.

WRITING POETRY WITH STUDENTS   If you have shared these poetry activities with children, you have encouraged them to read and critically respond to poetry. The next part of the poetry writing workshop is to write. For many K through eighth-grade students and teachers, poetry writing is a natural extension of the previous activities. We have included important activities that are identified in the writing process such as sharing poetry through oral reading, experiencing poetry several times of the day, discussing how poets effectively use poetic elements, dramatizing poetry to encourage understanding of moods and feelings, and discovering how and why various poets choose their subjects.

Web Sites to Motivate Poetry Writing   Technology can provide a powerful source for motivating children to read and write poetry. The following Web sites may be helpful when motivating students to write:

Favorite Poem Project: www.favoritepoem.org/. Boston University, the Poetry Society of America and the Library of Congress. Includes video clips and ideas for developing a "Favorite Poems Community Reading." Grades seven and up.

Fern's Poetry Club: pbskids.org/arthur/games/poetry/. Public Broadcasting Corporation. Students are encouraged to write and submit poems. Explains different forms of poetry. Grades 2–5.

Giggle Poetry: www.gigglepoetry.com. Meadowbrook Press. Includes numerous humorous poems as well as contests that children may enter. Instructional ideas are found on a "Poetry Teachers" link. Grades K–6.

Listen and Write: www. Bbc.co.uk/education/listenandwrite/home.htm. British Broadcasting Corporation. Includes a library of audio clips, motivations for writing, poetry, and lesson plans. Grades 4–8.

FEATURE FOCUS UNIT

As part of a poetry workshop, Jana Wright Prewitt (2001) developed and taught a poetry writing activity for her fourth-grade students that related poetry, poetry writing, and content areas. For this writing activity, she discovered that providing some suggestions for formats helps her students. In science class she had students write a "Science is . . ." poem in which they use their five senses and their emotions to describe science. She asked them "What kinds of things around you every day have to do with science? What do you think of when you think of science? One of the poems they created follows:

Science Is . . .

Science is experimenting with things that bubble and make me laugh.
    Science is baby birds hatching in a nest.
Science is baking a chocolate cake for my eleventh birthday.
    Science is cleaning my cut after I fell from my bicycle.
Science is going to sleep and dreaming of cotton candy and a roller coaster.
    Science is picking flowers and planting tomatoes.
        Science is finding a cure for cancer.

Prewitt recommends that this poetry writing activity be conducted at the beginning of the year and then again at the end. She uses this activity to discover how the attitudes and ideas related to science change over the year.

In language arts, Jana uses the diamante form of poetry to have students learn about antonyms. She first reviews with students the form she wants them to use:

Line 1:   Antonym 1 (i.e., Happy)
Line 2:   Two adjectives describing line 1
Line 3:   Three participles (-ing)
Line 4:   Four nouns or a phrase
Line 5:   Three participles indicating change
Line 6:   Two adjectives describing line 7
Line 7:   Antonym 2 (i.e., Sad)

The following diamante poem resulted from this lesson:

Stop

Halt, Freeze

Breaking, Pausing, Ending

The light is green.

Proceeding, Moving, Traveling

Start, Continue

Go

For a geometry unit, Jana had her students write shape poems such as the following:

Triangle

A triangle is pleased with herself.

A triangle is friendly and fun-loving.

It smells like pine needles and Christmas trees.

Sometimes, a triangle tastes like Doritos on a picnic.

Triangles look in all directions to see what goes on.

For poetry writing as part of a study of Native American tribes in social studies, Jana asked her students to write cinquains that described one of the tribes. She introduced the cinquain as a five-line poem that had these characteristics:

Title

Two words describing title

Three action words (-ing)

Four-word phrase about the title

Title or synonym for title

The following poem resulted from this lesson:

Caddos

Mound Builders

Farming, Hunting, Gathering

The largest Texas tribe

Caddos.

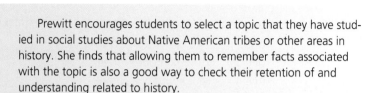

Prewitt encourages students to select a topic that they have studied in social studies about Native American tribes or other areas in history. She finds that allowing them to remember facts associated with the topic is also a good way to check their retention of and understanding related to history.

This teacher's use of poems that follow a pattern is supported by findings reported by Margaret A. Moore-Hart (2006) who found that patterned writing of poetry "helps struggling writers feel more comfortable with their writing and promises positive experiences with writing for all students" (p. 330).

REVISION OF POETRY   Revision of poetry frequently occurs during initial read-alouds of the poetry in which the teacher or a peer writing group asks the writer to clarify a topic or to expand on an idea. Perhaps there is a word or phrase that would improve the clarity or mood of the poem. This may be especially important when students are writing historical narrative poems about a specific time or person in history. When encouraging students to revise their poetry, it is important to identify parts of the poem that you believe are especially effective.

SHARING STUDENTS' POETRY   Sharing poetry written by the students is essential if students are to gain confidence in their writing or to understand that their writing is important. Sharing poetry does not always require elaborate formats. One possibility is to have students publish their finished poems in a class journal. This publishing encourages students to revise their works and provides an audience for the poetry. These journals are frequently shared with other grades and with parents or other appreciative adults. Reading the poetry aloud to classmates, posting the poems on bulletin boards, sending the poems to a friend or relative through e-mail are all ways that poetry may be shared with an audience. Remember, however, that all poetry does not need to be shared with an audience. Many children gain pleasure from keeping their own individual journals and reviewing how their poetry has changed over time.

ADDITIONAL IDEAS FOR DEVELOPING READING OF AND WRITING IMAGINATIVE WRITING   This section includes additional ideas for developing reading and writing of imaginative texts. Some of the activities identify and use the language in award-winning books as models for reading and writing. Other ideas focus on the ability of teachers to improve their students' linguistic styles through model texts, to use the story structures in wordless books to formulate written stories, and to use easy-to-read books to increase sentence sophistication through sentence combining. All the activities should follow the writing process that uses prewriting activities that motivate writing, the actual writing related to the subject, revision, and sharing the results of the activity with an audience.

Identifying and Modeling Opening Lines and Paragraphs That Hook the Reader   This is an excellent way to combine reading and writing. Students will discover how authors entice their readers into the text either in a book or in a magazine or newspaper article. What techniques do they use to encourage readers to stay involved with a text? One of the favorite activities designed to answer this question is to ask students to search through award-winning and other age-appropriate books and interesting articles to discover how authors use opening lines, quotations, or questions to provide this interest. This activity is closely related to developing reading comprehension and appreciation because the students need to read various sources and search for examples of a writing style that actually interest them. Choosing these opening lines also provides opportunities for students to read the lines orally and to discuss the impact of the lines.

This is an easy activity to conduct with a class. Collect award-winning books, books written for specific age levels, and interesting articles and ask students to search for opening lines and paragraphs that catch their interest. The writing styles created by the authors of these books and articles become the models for the students. Students listen to or read the material, discuss the techniques that the author uses to gain their interest, and identify how they might use these models in their own writing. They should have opportunities to apply these writing skills.

This type of activity may be used with any grade level. For example, kindergarten and first grade children might listen to the following opening lines in Ho Baek Lee's *While We Were Out* (2003): "The apartment is quiet. They've all gone to Grandma's house. There is somebody on the balcony though. Who forgot to lock the door? A little push, and . . ." (unnumbered). After listening to or reading this opening, students can hypothesize about what will happen when the rabbit who is on the balcony opens the door and goes into the house. Now they can use their own imaginations to write or dictate a story about what might happen. The concluding sentence may also be shared and students could fill in the missing story: "She's had a wonderful adventure, and the family will never know. Or will they?" (unnumbered). Students enjoy sharing their own writing. They may enjoy the stories created by their classmates as much as the story created by the author.

You do not even need to use a specific book to develop this "what if" type of motivation for imaginative writing. You can present your own introduction and ask students to fill in the possible story in such a way that they would be interested in learning more about the incident or the character. Students can also brainstorm "what if" incidents that would make interesting plots for stories.

During brainstorming, a group of first-grade students identified some of the following situations that could be used in imaginative writing:

What If . . .

What if the swings on the playground kept going up, up in the air?
What if my dog started to talk?
What if I found myself in the land of wild things in *Where the Wild Things Are* (Maurice Sendak, 1963)?
What if I could become an arrow and visit the sun like in *Arrow to the Sun* (Gerald McDermott, 1974)?

As you may notice, some of these situations are taken from children's own possible experiences and others reflect the books that they have been reading and discussing in their classroom.

Linguistic Style Comprehending figurative language and other descriptive words in reading and using them in writing is a difficult area for many students. Modeling how to interpret and comprehend figurative language is important for developing comprehension in reading and later for use in writing. A favorite book to use as a model with lower elementary students, for example, is Eve Bunting's *The Man Who Could Call Down Owls* (1984). Bunting uses descriptive language in comparisons, like a boy moving "quietly as an owl in flight," a smile of an evil man that is "cold as death," and chirping that fills "the night with love" (unnumbered pages). She describes the setting in such a way that readers believe if they go out in the woods at night they just might find the man who loves owls.

When using this book, a third-grade teacher read and discussed the book and then shared with her students a nature story in which she used Bunting's writing style as a model to show her students how they could use figurative language. She then asked the students to use figurative language in their own writing.

Another good example of effective figurative language is found in Jane Yolen's *Owl Moon* (1987), in which the author uses personification and similes such as "The trees stood still as giant statues" and the train whistle that blows "like a sad, sad song" (unnumbered pages). It is interesting to compare the linguistic style of Bunting and Yolen as they both describe a night that is complete with owls.

Helping students strengthen their writing through the use of effective and pleasing linguistic styles is often accomplished during the revision stage of the writing process. By sharing these examples with students, you can show them how they could use such elements as similes, metaphors, and personification to increase the interest in their own writing.

Discovering and Using Story Structures in Wordless Books   Wordless books may be the ideal writing format model for many students. The settings, the characters, and the plot are all presented through illustrations. Students write the story that could accompany the illustrations. There are even wordless books that could accompany a content area such as science or history. Wordless books may be used as either a group writing activity or an individual writing response. To use a wordless book in writing:

1. Ask the students to observe each of the illustrations and to notice the details and the plot development.

   - Who are the characters in the book?
   - Where is the setting for the book and how do the illustrations develop the setting?
   - What is the plot of the story?
   - How do the illustrations depict and support the developing conflict?

2. Ask students to think about the style they would use to accompany the book.

   - What style of writing would you use?
   - What is a good way to write beginning lines that attract attention and interest?

Some wordless books are ideal for younger children in the first and second grades, such as Emily Arnold McCully's *Picnic* (1984) and *School* (1987), which follows a mouse family as they do activities familiar to most children. Mercer Mayer's wordless books about the experiences of frog in *A Boy, a Dog, a Frog, and a Friend*

(1971) are also simple enough for children in the lower elementary grades. David Wiesner's *Free Fall* (1988) depicts what happens on Tuesday night when frogs float through the air.

Teachers in the lower elementary grades frequently use the wordless-book format as the structure for a language-experience approach in which students increase their reading ability by dictating their own story and then practicing their reading through this story. All of these easier wordless books provide excellent sources for plot formats.

Wordless books may also be used with older students, in the fourth or fifth grades where their writing may relate to the content areas. For example,

- John S. Goodall's *Paddy Under Water* (1984) may be used in a science class in which the students use their knowledge about the sea to write the story.

- Peter Sis's *Dinosaur!* (2000) includes a listing of dinosaur names and a dedication, "For the dinosaurs at the American Museum of Natural History, New York City."

- Eric Rohmann's *Time Flies* (1994) also includes dinosaurs. Students who write accompanying stories for the dinosaur wordless books could try to write stories that are scientifically accurate.

- John S. Goodall's *The Story of a Main Street* (1987) traces the same street from medieval through contemporary times.

- David Wiesner's *Free Fall* (1988) provides an opportunity for students to use their imaginations.

A sixth-grade teacher and her students used *Free Fall* to write a story in poetic form. Here is the beginning of the poem they wrote:

There once was a boy who was reading a book
after falling asleep this is the journey he took.
He dreamed of a far away land and here begins
the story of kings, knights, and all their glory.

Notice how the teacher and her students used both their knowledge of poetry and of story structure to create an interesting text for a wordless book. The illustrations, by an award-winning artist, provided the structure for the narrative poem.

Web Sites to Motivate Imaginative Writing   The following Web sites include motivation for and suggested ideas designed to enhance imaginative writing:

Myths, Folktales, and Fairy Tales: teacherscholastic.com/writewit/mff/index.htm. Scholastic. Authors and storytellers guide students to write their own tales. Jane Yolen's section helps students write myths. Grades 2–8.

Silly Sentence Machine: pbskids.org/readingrainbow/bookem/silly-sentence.html. PBS Kids. Viewers select a word or picture from each of five columns. The words are then strung together to create sentences.

Reflect on Your Reading

Literature provides a motivational source for imaginative writing. Think about various literature selections that you have read that may have motivated you to write when you were in elementary school. Also, try to answer the question that the teacher posed in the "Read All About It!" feature. What criteria would you use for books that win awards and could motivate imaginative writing?

Story Starter.: www.thestorystarter.com. Joel Heffner. Includes words and phrases designed to motivate students to write their own stories. Grades 4–8.

Wacky Web Tales: www.eduplace.com/tales. Houghton Mifflin. Includes fill-in-the-blank stories in which students complete sentences with nouns, verbs, adjectives, and adverbs. A "Parts of Speech Help" defines the terms. Grades 3–6.

Expository Writing

Expository writing is very common in classrooms. It is writing in which the author presents facts, ideas, or opinions such as in the nonfiction writing found in history, biographies, and autobiographies. In his discussion of thinking styles, Robert J. Sternberg (2001) identifies two types of thinking styles that may be used to enhance expository writing. The executive instructional style, for example, emphasizes responses where students respond with factual statements such as: "Who said . . . ?, Summarize . . . , Who did . . . ?, When did . . . ?, What did . . . ?, How did . . . ?, Repeat back . . . , and Describe . . ." (p. 199). The judicial instructional style emphasizes analytical activities that involve statements such as: "Compare and contrast . . . , Analyze . . . , Evaluate . . . , In your judgment . . . , Why did . . . ?, What caused . . . ? What is assumed by . . . ?, and Critique . . ." (p. 199).

Expository Writing in Emergent Literacy

One of the easiest types of expository writing for young children is biographical or autobiographical writing. This type of writing reflects something that is very close to the children. They also understand that this writing uses factual information. Sternberg's factual response framework is easily included in this writing and drawing; for example, children can create a book titled, "Myself and My Family." Before asking children to do this activity, teachers can model the activity by creating their own book in which they tell and illustrate something about themselves. Information might include brothers and sisters, place of birth, extended family members, favorite activities including books or sports, favorite foods, and living with pets. This book could be illustrated with drawings or photographs.

After showing and discussing the book, ask the students to suggest subjects they would like to include in their own books. This writing/illustrating activity may take several days. Students may choose to illustrate a page for each family member or other topic and then write or dictate a few lines or even a story about the person or topic. Asking students to illustrate each page provides teachers with time to individually help each student with the writing or dictating. When the books are completed, allow children to share their family books with the class.

Expository writing in the lower elementary grades may be related to the social studies or science curriculum. For example, following a study of community helpers, students can summarize what they have learned about people such as firemen or policemen. This could be in the form of a chart story in which children have the opportunity to review and read back factual information. During a study of bugs in the science curriculum, they can draw illustrations of the bugs and write factual information next to the drawings. Philemon Sturges's *I Love Bugs!* (2005) provides a model for this type of nonfiction reading and expository writing.

If the students are focusing on shapes, colors, numbers, letters, or opposites, teachers can use Saxton Freymann's *Food for Thought: The Complete Book of Concepts for Growing Minds* (2005) as a model of and motivator for writing and illustrating. Students can take part in analytical activities such as Sternberg's judicial instruction that involves comparing and contrasting. They can observe and describe the shapes: circle, oval, triangle, square, and rectangle. They can identify and list additional objects that have the same shapes. They can write or dictate descriptions of the objects. They can compare and contrast shapes that are somewhat alike, such as circles and ovals or squares and rectangles.

The section of the book on opposites provides another good source for comparing and contrasting. Students can describe and contrast differences in *up-down, big-little, happy-sad, hot-cold, near-far, come-go, give-receive, whisper-shout,* and *awake-asleep.* This activity may take several days as teachers focus on the meanings of each of the opposites and students provide additional examples of these opposites. This type of activity is good for cognitive development as students write or dictate factual information that describes characteristics of opposites. Math can be added to these descriptions by asking students to measure objects and use the measurements to provide factual data for their writing.

Teaching Reading and Writing through Expository Writing Workshops

Expository writing workshops allow teachers and students to practice with various formats of informational literature. This is the place to apply through writing many of the suggestions about vocabulary development and comprehension in Chapters 5 and 6. This is also the place to teach students to use and to apply research skills such as:

- using the library as a source
- locating Web sites that extend knowledge and writing compositions that use these sources
- responding to, writing reactions to, and creating various types of articles found in newspapers
- responding to an opinion page that includes editorials on subjects that are of world or local interest and writing their own opinion articles
- responding to and creating their own literature, museum, music, television, and movie reviews
- applying some of the reading skills required to become a critic.

This section focuses on two types of reading and writing connections for expository writing: the researching and writing required to write a paper that evaluates the accuracy or authenticity of a book, and the researching and writing required to write a newspaper opinion article or a critical evaluation.

EXPOSITORY WRITING WORKSHOP DESIGNED TO WRITE EVALUATIONS OF A BOOK The following workshop is designed for fourth- through eighth-grade teachers and for students who are preparing to teach those grades. A survey of upper elementary teachers found the following needs that could be met through a workshop:

1. University students are not being taught to conduct research and to write compositions that reflect sound research; consequently they cannot teach these skills to public school students.

2. Both university and public school students have few opportunities to write compositions that require critical and reflective thinking.

3. Both university and public school students are not receiving enough instruction in the reading and evaluating of multicultural literature, especially Hispanic and African American.

4. Both university and public school students need assistance in evaluating materials to be used in all of the content fields. This is especially true with materials that are chosen to accompany history and social studies subjects.

STEPS IN DEVELOPING THE WORKSHOP

1. Evaluate prior knowledge and present any unknown information before the students conduct their own research and write their critical evaluations. You may use several class periods to review the research terminology. For example, students may discuss the meanings of each of these terms and how authors develop them: geographical and social settings, values and beliefs expressed by the characters, political ideologies reflected in the literature, major events that make up the plot of the material, major themes that are important in the story, and the type of conflicts and how the conflicts are developed. All suggestions, good or not, should be discussed.

2. Next, the students take part in a library experience in which a librarian shows them how to verify the reliability of each of the elements to evaluate. The librarians can also discuss how to use various Web sites to conduct research, in addition to the journals and books.

3. Introduce and discuss the total authentication project. Ask students to select a biography, an autobiography, or an historical fiction text to evaluate according to the following areas:

- Author's source notes and any other references provided:

   What is the quality of the source notes? What is the information provided that would help in an authentication project? Does the source note provide information about such areas as the setting for the text, the conflict that is being developed, the sources used by the author, and the qualifications of the author to write this text? If the source note is not adequate, what information should be in the source note? (After reading and evaluating source notes, some students may choose to write their own source notes. Some students may change their chosen text because there is not enough information in the source note.)

- The geographical and social settings depicted by the author:

   Use several nonfiction sources to evaluate this area. Maps and photographs of areas are especially good for identifying and describing geographical locations.

- The values and beliefs stressed by the major characters in the text:

   Compare these values and beliefs with other sources. This area is especially important when dealing with books about other cultures or subjects such as the Jewish people during the Holocaust or African Americans during times of slavery.

- Any political ideologies evident in the book:

  Is there hidden bias? If so, what is the bias? This is especially necessary when dealing with controversial subjects that might have several interpretations.

- The major events that make up the plot of the story:

  Draw time lines of major events and use nonfiction sources to evaluate the historical accuracy of the text. State how the author makes the book believable, if the story is accurate. Identify and prove any inaccuracies found in the book.

- The major themes in the book:

  Are these themes found in other writings about the time period or the personages?

- The conflicts in the book:

  Do the conflicts reflect actual conflicts of the time period? Use reliable adult nonfiction sources.

4. Synthesize the authenticity of the book and make recommendations for classroom use. In what areas was the text authentic? In what areas was the text not authentic? How would you use this text and this approach in the fourth- through eighth-grade classrooms?

EXAMPLE FROM *THE WATSONS GO TO BIRMINGHAM–1963:* Katie Fletcher (2003) first authenticated Christopher Paul Curtis's *The Watsons Go to Birmingham—1963* (1995) for her own information and then taught the authentication process to a group of sixth-grade students. She describes how she taught this process and some of the related activities she developed with her students:

> I used supplemental reading materials that encouraged children to evaluate the incidents in the novel. We found material that discussed the events that led up to the church bombing in Birmingham, as well as more detailed events of the aftermath. I had children take part in small group discussions during which I led them to compare and contrast life in the 1960s versus modern days. This was an appropriate time to talk about all of the people who made the Civil Rights struggle a reality including Martin Luther King, Jr., Rosa Parks, and the many people who went to jail for this cause.
>
>   My students created a time line of events that made it more possible for all Americans to share the same rights. I had my students write journal entries about prejudice and racism. They wrote about experiences at school or home that are similar to Kenny's experiences.
>
>   I used *The Watsons Go to Birmingham—1963* to teach students about United States geography by following the Watson's trip from Flint, Michigan, to Birmingham, Alabama.

We discussed the politics of segregation how political agendas have changed over the years.

We picked out events from the story that tell us about the characters and illustrated these characterizations through a mural of the Watson family and their lives.

Katie concluded her description of her classroom activities with a statement of why she taught this book: "I believe it is vital that children have a thorough understanding of our history, both good and bad. Gaining knowledge of the history of Civil Rights at an early age makes children more likely to grow up desiring justice and equality for all people, thus helping to promote values with each new generation."

Web Sites Used to Authenticate
The Watsons Go to Birmingham—1963

Bron Daniels. "Spirituality Helps Some Blacks Cope with Stress." *The Michigan Daily* (18 September 2003). michiganandaily.com/vnews/display.v/ART/2003/09/18/3f693a5ele55d

"Map." Michigan and Alabama: Yahoo, 2003. travel.yahoo.com/p-travelguide

Cathy Smith. Climatology Chart: Birmingham and Flint: *Climate Diagnostics Center* Oct. 2003. www.cdc.noaa.gov/cgi-bin/Usclimate/city.pl?

Dave Weich. "Christopher Paul Curtis Goes to Powells—2000." Interview. Powells.com (5 April 2000). www.powells.com/authors/curtis.html

EXPOSITORY WRITING WORKSHOP DESIGNED TO WRITE A CRITICAL EVALUATION OR AN OPINION ARTICLE   Writing critical evaluation or opinion articles require numerous cognitive strategies. According to Michael Pressley and Karen R. Harris (2001), good readers reflect on the reading, decide which parts are worth remembering, and think about how they might use ideas from the text. Likewise, good writers draw upon a rich store of strategies for planning, writing/drafting, and revising. They draw upon past knowledge, consider their audience, are knowledgeable about the problem, and conduct research when required.

WRITING A CRITICAL EVALUATION OF AN AWARD-WINNING BOOK   This reading and writing activity requires both in-depth reading of a text and writing that evaluates literary elements such as style, characterization, and theme. It also requires students to make judgments about the audience appeal of the book. This activity may also place readers in a situation to agree or disagree with a published evaluation. To make these criticisms they must be able to support their positions.

Reading and writing critical reviews of award-winning books provide two types of reading. Students must read and evaluate a book, and read and evaluate a critical review of the book. They need to be able to agree or disagree with the review and defend their positions. Before selecting award-winning books, students need to understand why the awards, especially the Caldecott and Newbery Awards, are so important. Eden Ross Lipson (2004) maintains, "The children's book awards, decided by large committees of librarians, are important to parents and publishers, who value the gold and silver stickers as symbols of quality and buy accordingly. Libraries and bookstores immediately order hardcover copies of winning titles, and the books remain in print for years" (p. B6).

This information may be used to motivate students to conduct their own critical evaluations and write their own critiques of the books. For example, the Caldecott and Newbery Medal winners, or award-winning books from any time period, provide opportunities for this type of evaluation and writing activity. In *New York Times* (January 13, 2004), Lipson provides information that could be used by students to write a critical review of the 1994 Caldecott winner, Mordicai Gerstein's *The Man Who Walked between the Towers* (2003). Says Lipson, "The Caldecott Medal has occasionally been given to books that deal with nonfiction subjects. Few children's books have addressed the 9/11 attacks, but 'The Man Who Walked Between the Towers' concludes: 'Now the towers are gone. But in memory, as if imprinted on the sky, the towers are still there. And part of that memory is the joyful morning, August 7, 1974, when Philippe Petit walked between them in the air' " (p. B1).

Lipson's article provides additional information that could be used in a critical review of the book. He writes, "Mr. Gerstein, in a telephone interview from his studio in Massachusetts, said he started the book immediately after the attacks of September 11, 2001. 'I had lived in New York,' he said, 'and the towers were part of my furniture. I had a 1987 *New Yorker* profile of Philippe on my shelf. I went right to it, reread the profile and wrote the book.' 'It was a difficult book to sell,' he said, 'so immediate and so raw. Some publishers thought it had negative connotations' " (p. B6).

Students may consider two evaluative criteria when writing their own reviews. Books may be placed under two categories: illustrations in picture books and nonfiction books. The author/illustrator needs to meet the criteria for evaluating each type of book. Before students write their own evaluations, they may consider the following criteria (Norton, 2007):

Criteria for evaluating illustrations:

1. The illustrator's use of line, color, shape, and texture should complement or extend the plot, characterization, setting, and theme in the text.
2. The illustrations should stimulate aesthetic appreciation.
3. The artistic style should enhance the author's style.
4. The illustrations should help readers anticipate the story's action and its climax.
5. The illustrations should develop the characters.
6. The illustrations should be historically, culturally, and geographically accurate.

Criteria for evaluating informational books:

1. All facts should be accurate.
2. Stereotypes should be eliminated.
3. Illustrations should clarify the text.
4. Analytical thinking should be encouraged.
5. The organization should aid understanding.
6. The style should stimulate interest.

To write a critique of a book, students should first read the book carefully. If the book wins an award for illustrations, they can consider the above criteria. They can also respond to their personal feelings about the book. Students could also read and write criticisms of books selected from the "Best Illustrated Books" identified in *New York Times*. Now they have books they can use for comparisons. The 10 books identified in the listing include:

1. *Brundibar* (2003), retold by Tony Kusher and illustrated by Maurice Sendak. (Refer to Gregory Maguire's review of this book in *New York Times,* November 16, 2003, p. 22.)

2. *The Man Who Walked between the Towers* (2003), written and illustrated by Mordicai Gerstein (the Caldecott Medal winner).

3. *While We Were Out* (2003), written and illustrated by Ho Baek Lee. (This book is from South Korea.)

4. *Charming Opal* (2003), written and illustrated by Holly Hobbie.

5. *The Wolves in the Walls* (2003), Written by Neil Gaiman and illustrated by Dave McKean.

6. *Otto's Trunk* (2003), written and illustrated by Sandy Turner.

7. *The Tree of Life* (2003), written and illustrated by Peter Sis. (This is an informational book related to science.)

8. *Alice's Adventures in Wonderland* (2003), adaptation of Lewis Carroll's original tale, illustrated by Robert Sabuda. (Refer to Steven Heller's review in *New York Times Book Review,* November 16, 2003, p. 26.)

9. *Beegu* (2003), written and illustrated by Alexis Deacon.

10. *When Everybody Wore a Hat* (2003), written and illustrated by William Steig.

Because the Caldecott Award–winning book is included in this list, students could pretend that these are the books that will be considered for the Caldecott award. They can role-play their possible discussions as if they are part of the American Library Association's committee for selecting the Caldecott Award winner. They can also write critical reviews of the books that they chose. They may develop their own exhibit by placing the books in the library along with their reviews of the books.

FEATURE UNIT:
Critical Evaluation
of African American Literature

As an introduction to this reading and writing activity, ask students to discuss why it is important to read excellent books about many cultures and groups of people. Ask students to identify the types of books they would like to read. Also ask them to consider how they would evaluate the books about African Americans. Students may discuss why it is important to develop criteria for selecting and evaluating African American or other types of multicultural literature. They may develop their own criteria or discuss the following criteria:

1. The illustrations should be authentic for the time period and the geographical locations.
2. The characters should appear natural without perpetuating stereotypes.
3. Social issues and problems should be depicted frankly and accurately.
4. The historical details should be accurate. (Norton, 2005).

A study of African American music could accompany this activity. Students usually enjoy responding to the music and relating their feelings about the music to their feelings about the books. Use books such as those found in Table 9.2. Did the books develop the same emotional appeal as the music? Why or why not?

A study of African Americans who are or were prominent in the arts, politics, and sports could also accompany this activity. Examples of books that could be used for this activity are included in Table 9.3. The critical responses through writing could be added to the suggestions for a library exhibit that focused on music. When students display their responses to these books, they usually encourage other students to read the books and create their own responses.

TABLE 9.2
Books Related to African American Music

Russell Freedman	*The Voice That Challenged a Nation: Marian Anderson and the Struggle for Equal Rights* (2004)
Ntozake Shange	*Ellington Was Not a Street* (2004)
Jerry Pinkney	*God Bless the Child* (2004)
Chris Raschka	*Charlie Parker Played Be-Bop* (2004)

TABLE 9.3

Books Related to Prominent Individuals Who Are African American

Tonya Bolden	*The Champ: The Story of Muhammad Ali* (2004)
Tonya Bolden	*Portraits of African American Heroes* (2004)
Tonya Bolden	*Wake Up Our Souls: A Celebration of African American Artists* (2004)
Louise Borden and Mary Kay Kroger	*Fly High! The Story of Bessie Coleman* (2004)
Lesa Cline-Ransome and James E. Ransome	*Major Taylor Champion Cyclist* (2004)
Laura Driscoll	*Smart about Scientists: George Washington Carver: The Peanut Wizard* (2004)
Nikki Giovanni	*Rosa* (2005)
Jan Greenberg	*Romare Bearden: Collage of Memories* (2004)
Joe Harper	*Wilma Rudolph, Olympic Runner* (2004)
Johanna Johnston	*They Led the Way: 14 American Women* (2004)
Deloris Jordan and Roslyn Jordan	*Salt in His Shoes: Michael Jordan in Pursuit of a Dream* (2004)
Walter Dean Myers	*I've Seen the Promised Land: The Life of Dr. Martin Luther King, Jr.* (2004)
Denise Patrick	*A Lesson for Martin Luther King, Jr.* (2004)
Sharon Robinson	*Promises to Keep: How Jackie Robinson Changed America* (2004)

Reading and Writing an Opinion Article

Newspapers and magazines are filled with opinion articles, and television and radio news shows frequently include experts who speak on two sides of a controversial subject. This type of writing appeals to many students because it provides them with opportunities to expand on their own viewpoints related to current issues. To read or write opinion articles, however, requires knowledge about the various viewpoints. Students need to distinguish between fact and opinion. They must also be able to cite evidence that supports their opinion.

In the workshop approach for writing an opinion article, the students, usually in grades three through eight, first define fact versus opinion. They look up the terms in several different sources, such as the *Oxford Universal Dictionary, Webster's Dictionary of the English Language,* and *Roget's 21st Century Thesaurus.* They then develop a table that contrasts the information. Such a table might be similar to Table 9.4.

Students discuss the meaning of each of the terms and then locate examples of newspaper articles and opinion columns that exemplify fact or opinion writing. They also identify fact and opinion items on the television and radio. For example, the CNN program "American Morning" is mostly factual reporting, while the CNN program "Crossfire" reflects two diverse opinions.

TABLE 9.4

Fact Versus Opinion

Fact:	Something that really occurred
	Truth, reality, accomplishment
	Deed, evidence, specific statistic
Examples from news articles:	
Opinion:	A belief or conviction based on what seems probable or true but not on demonstrable fact
	What one thinks about a particular thing, subject, or point
	A judgment resting on belief of an expert, considered advice
	Belief, assumption, attitude, feeling, hypothesis, judgment, point of view, persuasion, slant, viewpoint
Examples from opinion articles:	

Students then read the articles, listen to broadcasts, and discuss what aspects of the articles or broadcasts make them fact or opinion. This type of activity works well in any region of the country. It allows students to gain understanding of local, national, and international issues.

One of the issues written about during a 2004 workshop was terrorism. Questions asked included: "Are we overcoming the threat of terrorism?" "Is terrorism still happening throughout the world?" "How could we make the world safer from terrorists?" "Who has ideas that will make the world safer?" "Why is there an increase in terrorism?" This subject held a personal interest for everyone.

Students should read a variety of opinion columns and listen to news broadcasts and take careful note about how writers present their attitudes, beliefs, and points of

Up for Discussion

Read, read, read is a guiding principle for improving reading comprehension for elementary students. We know that teachers who love to read are able to share their enthusiasm with students. We also know that students need many opportunities to write, write, write if they are to develop their abilities. We know that students need to write for different purposes and for different audiences. As in reading, is it equally important for teachers to write for different purposes and to show students their own writing processes?

During a recent writing workshop with teachers, the teachers were asked, "How many of you give in-class writing assignments to your students?" (All raised their hands.) "How many of you enjoy giving in-class writing assignments to your students? (All enthusiastically raised their hands.) "How many of you do these in-class writing assignments along with your students?" (A few embarrassed looks, downward eyes, and no hands raised.) When asked why they did not personally write along with their students, they had various responses such as: "I'm not a writer," "I'm too embarrassed to share my own work with older students," "I'm too self-conscious to share my writing." These responses to writing are all similar to those expressed by many children.

After the teachers participated in several writing exercises in the workshop, they said they learned a great deal about their own writing process and realized the impact of the writing assignments on their students. Put yourself in the place of these elementary school teachers and discuss the following questions:

When teachers conduct writing workshops they provide feedback to students throughout the writing process.

1. How important do you believe personal writing is for the teacher of reading and writing?
2. What types of writing should the teacher be able to model?
3. What are the characteristics of teachers who are themselves reluctant writers versus teachers who are positive about their own writing?
4. Why do you believe that it is important for teachers to take part during in-class writing?

view. What words do opinion writers use? What are the qualifications of people who write opinion pieces? How do opinion writers support their viewpoints?

Some additional issues students might focus on could include the questions:

1. Should the United States send a manned mission to Mars? The students may use both news articles and opinion pieces to write their own opinion articles. Many of them may consider the pros and cons of spending billions of dollars. Others may consider any scientific advancement gained from previous space exploration.

2. Should states and schools reduce their budget problems by eliminating art and music?

3. What should be the qualifications for a teacher in the public schools? Should the qualifications be different for elementary, middle school, or high school teachers? What courses should a teacher take to be qualified to teach different subjects? What knowledge should a teacher have to teach a specific content area? Who should certify that teachers are qualified? This is an issue that is important to both public and private school students.

Reading and writing opinion articles may also be extended to oral debates as students develop their positions and then debate the issues. Many students discover that they need to have more information to defend a position if the position takes the form of an oral debate. For example, students may consider the pros and cons of technology through e-mail after reading Rachel Donadio's (2005) essay "Literary Letters, Lost in Cyberspace," which asks the question, "In an age of e-mail and instant messages, will biographers and historians have access to authors' correspondence anymore?" (pp. 14–15). To debate the positive and negative consequences for future historians who conduct research about historical characters, students need to research the sources used by historians when they write about the backgrounds of a person. Students need to consider the types of letters and other documents that are now available to researchers. They need to consider the advantages and disadvantages to both the original personage and the historian if letters are sent and replies received through e-mail. Will or should the e-mail documents be available to historians? How could the documents be made available?

Understanding Viewpoints through Expository Writing

Several teachers of seventh- and eighth-grade students have used selected chapters from Auriana Ojeda's *Teens at Risk: Opposing Viewpoints* (2003) to introduce writing and debating activities that require students to take positions on a topic, conduct research, and write their own position statements. The following writing topics have been popular with older students:

Pro	*Con*
1. More teenage criminals should be tried as adults.	1. Teenage criminals should not be tried as adults.
2. Curfew laws can reduce teenage crime and violence.	2. Curfew laws do not reduce crime and violence.
3. Age restrictions on alcohol reduce teen drinking.	3. Age restrictions on alcohol do not reduce teen drinking.
4. Drug education programs reduce teen drug use.	4. Drug education programs do not reduce teen drug use.

The science curriculum provides numerous topics that lend themselves to reading, expository writing, and debating activities. The results of and the possible causes of the devastating hurricanes were the subjects of many magazine and newspaper articles in 2005. For example, the feature stories and the front-page illustration for *Time* (October 3, 2005) are titled, "Are We Making Hurricanes Worse? The Impact of Global Warming, The Cost of Coastal Development, Plus: Charting the Gulf Coast Destruction" (Front page). The articles that address the subject are written in forms that lend themselves to debate and research, for example, Jeffrey Kruger's (2005) "Global Warming: The Culprit? Evidence mounts that human activity is helping fuel these monster hurricanes" (pp. 42–46). Students can read articles like these, conduct research on the subject of global warming, and find advocates who provide facts related to global warming and those who challenge the concept. By reading articles such as Oliver Morton's "Mars: Planet of Ice" in

Reflect on Your *Reading*

How important is expository writing in both the elementary school and in your own experiences? Why is it important to teach students to be critical readers, to evaluate what they read and hear, and to identify differences between facts and opinions? What would be the consequences if students do not have these abilities?

National Geographic and Andrew C. Revkin's "In a Melting Trend, Less Arctic Ice to Go Around" in the *New York Times,* students discover that writers of expository articles frequently use the latest statistics to develop their arguments. Revkin, for example, quotes research from the National Snow and Ice Data Center in Boulder, Colorado and he includes the center's Web site (*www.nsidc.org*) to support his facts and the position developed in his article. Before students write expository articles they can read reputable articles to discover how professional writers use factual data to support their positions.

DIFFERENTIATING INSTRUCTION

ELL Students

The writings of ELL children who write and speak in two languages may be an excellent source for information about children's literacy development and their writing process. Renée Rubin and Verónica Galván Carlan (2005) analyzed the writing samples of 100 children ages 3 to 10 who wrote in both Spanish and English. They make several helpful suggestions to teachers of ELL students:

1. Ask children to write in both languages to obtain a broader picture of their literacy; they may have greater writing development in one language than the other.
2. Children should be encouraged to value writing as a way to express ideas and not just view it as an exercise in spelling correctly or copying words.
3. Children should be encouraged to talk about their writing and the writing process.
4. ELL children should read orally what they have written in both English and their native language.
5. Teachers should value the students' writing even if there are errors.
6. Teachers should encourage students to write about topics that are familiar to them from their own culture.
7. Teaching spelling patterns should be emphasized rather than memorization or words. Teachers of Spanish-speaking children should help them see similarities and differences between Spanish and English spelling patterns.
8. The writing samples should be used to informally assess children's strengths and weaknesses and to design instruction.

Rubin and Carlan conclude: "Teachers of bilingual children should provide their children with many opportunities for writing and encourage them to view their bilingualism as a strength" (p. 738).

Melisa Cahnmann (2006) believes that reading and writing poetry is especially important for ELL students if they are to become lifelong readers and writers. She states: "Reading, living, and writing bilingual poetry can elucidate the goal of bilingual education—to provide an educational environment where students' home languages and cul-

A teacher makes discoveries about a student's literacy development by analyzing the student's writing.

tures are visible and valued as resources in the classroom. Through reading, living, and writing bilingual poetry any teacher can foster multiliteracy in the classroom without being a speaker of those languages" (p. 351). Cahnmann recommends using poetry books such as Lori Carlston's (1994) *Cool Salsa: Bilingual Poems on Growing Up Hispanic in the United States* as sources for poetry and models for writing.

Joel E. Dworin (2006) describes a writing project with fourth-grade Latino students in which the students gather stories from family members. Many of these stories are told in Spanish and translated by the students into English. Dworin emphasizes that the students are encouraged to use "two languages for thinking, communicating, and writing in the classroom" (p. 510). He believes that the children's intellectual development is enhanced through this process.

Struggling Readers and Writers

Many struggling readers and writers have difficulty generating content, setting goals, organizing their writing, and evaluating and revising their writing. M. Marchisan and S. R. Alber (2001) conclude, "Resistant writers can be taught to write using the writing process approach paired with the tools of technology, direct instruction, and a committed, well-trained teacher" (p. 161). They identify the following strategies that are effective when teaching struggling writers using the writing process:

- **Prewriting stage:** Ask students to think about topics that are of interest to them; have them use visual imagery to visualize the details about the topic; model prewriting procedures they can use such as story webs.

- **Writing stage:** Use their word banks to help identify and use vocabulary; cowrite a story with the students; help the students use word-processing programs in their writing.

- **Revision stage:** Use minilessons to provide direct instruction for writing errors; provide a self-evaluation checklist; conference with students to provide guidance for revising a draft; teach students to use the computer for editing; keep writing portfolios.

- **Publishing and sharing stage:** Use an author's chair in which students can read their works; display writing in the room; create class newsletters or newspapers that include students' writings.

Notice that these stages of the writing process are similar to the stages used with all students. Each of the stages, however, requires extra modeling by the teacher and other supports that help students develop the higher cognitive processes that are needed to be successful writers.

Gifted and Accelerated Readers and Writers

To encourage students to develop and share their creative writings and to respond to the writings of others are two objectives that allow gifted and accelerated students to explore and expand their creative writing abilities. For example, gifted and accelerated students can use Internet sites that allow them to electronically publish their short stories, poems, and essays. Examples of these locations include:

Kids Bookshelf (www.kidsbookshelf.com)
Cyberkids (www.cyberkids.com)
Kids' Space Connection (www.KS-connection.org)
KidPub (www.kidpub.org/kidpub)

Encourage students to regularly post essays about writing, reviews about favorite books, their creative short stories, and their original poetry. Electronic publishing encourages feedback from a distant audience of peers. Explain to students that they can submit writing in progress and, ideally, receive constructive criticism for their writing. If a link is provided to a writer's e-mail address, readers are able to respond immediately to a work they like and ask the writer questions. Students should also be encouraged to read and respond to the writings of other students.

Summary

Five guiding principles for teaching writing include linking writing activities to real life issues, becoming active participants in writing, using a variety of direct and indirect instruction, using literature to provide writing models, and modeling writing through teacher participation. The stages in the writing process are: 1) prewriting activities that motivate the writing through activities such as brainstorming, identifying the audience, and gathering material; 2) the actual writing activity during which students organize material and write a first draft; and 3) the revising portion of writing, which includes rereading, revision of content, preparing the final copy, and proofreading.

Three types of writing relate to reading: expressive writing, imaginative writing, and expository writing. Workshops can be useful to teach imaginative writing and expository writing.

Reflect on Your Reading

How would a teacher of ELL students use the modifications of the writing process recommended for struggling readers and writers? The prewriting stage asks students to think about and to visualize details about the topic. Consider why it is effective for teachers of ELL students to encourage students to write about topics that are familiar to them and from their own culture. What are some topics that ELL students might choose?

Key Terms

writing process, p. 361

expressive writing, p. 364

imaginative writing, p. 364

expository writing, p. 365

writing workshops, p. 370

For video clips of authentic classroom instruction on **The Reading and Writing Connection**, go to Allyn & Bacon's MyLabSchool.com. In MLS courses, click on Reading Methods, go to MLS Video Lab, and select **Module 4**. Videos on this topic can also be found in the MLS Video Lab for the **Language Arts** course.

Extend Your Reading

1. Locate a news article that discusses writing. What issues are presented? How does the author depict writing in schools? If there is an issue with students' achievement in writing, what solutions are discussed? Do you agree or disagree with the solutions? Why or why not?

2. With a group of your peers, read and discuss some of the poems recommended in the Table 9.1. How would you use these poems to help elementary students develop an appreciation for poetry? How would your own appreciation for poetry be extended through reading or listening to these poems? You can add additional poems that you believe should be included under each of the categories.

3. As part of a lesson or a unit, share and discuss the different forms of poetry with students. What are the characteristics of each form of poetry? How important is an understanding of the poetic elements for the comprehension of and writing related to poetry?

4. Choose one of the poets discussed in this chapter. Conduct research that allows you to identify the poems written by the poet that fall under the specific category. As part of your research, find information that indicates why the poet writes that type of poetry. Why, for example, do Jack Prelutsky and Shel Silverstein write humorous poems? What type of humor is found in their poems? Why do elementary students like this type of humor?

5. Choose one of the areas described in the section on writing poetry with students. Identify a grade level and develop a lesson plan that allows you to teach children in that age group to appreciate, to read with understanding, and to write poetry. Remember to include the various stages in the writing process in

your lesson plan. How will you introduce and interest students in listening to and reading poetry? How will you involve the students in the actual writing of poetry and the revision of the poetry? How will you provide an audience that allows the students to share their writing or to encourage other students to read the writing?

6. Many of the classics in children's literature provide interesting opening lines for students in the second through fourth grades. Reading and sharing the opening lines in the classics may help students understand why they are considered favorites of both elementary students and their parents. With a group of your peers, collect award-winning books or other written materials. (These are usually easy to find because most school and public libraries order Newbery Medal and Honor books.) The following books are good for this activity:

> For younger readers: E. B. White's *Charlotte's Web* (1952) and A. A. Milne's *The House at Pooh Corner* (1928)

> For older readers: Stephanie S. Tolan's *Surviving the Applewhites* (2002), Karen Cushman's *The Midwife's Apprentice* (1995), James Cross Giblin's *The Life and Death of Adolf Hitler* (2002)

As you read the beginning paragraphs, identify the techniques the authors use to attract your interest. You might compare the writing styles in excellent materials with the writing styles in materials that are not so well written. If you are teaching, do this activity with your students. Compile a collection of opening lines that attract the students and reasons that these opening lines appeal to the students.

7. Visit a school or interview a teacher. What evidence do you find that teaching includes the writing process? What part of the writing process is most visible? What part of the writing process does the teacher believe is the most important?

8. Visit several classrooms. How are the teachers using drama? Interview the teachers to discover their attitudes toward drama.

9. Survey several teachers about the NCTE and IRA guiding principles shown in this text. What are their reactions to these guiding principles? Which ones guide their own teaching? Why are these guiding principles considered important?

10. With a group of your peers, identify how reading and writing were connected in your elementary education. What were the most successful experiences? What experiences led to a positive attitude about writing? What experiences led to a less than positive attitude about writing?

11. To heighten your understanding of expressive writing, keep a journal of your own reactions to materials you read. What types of literature and writing create the most responses for your journal?

12. With a group of your peers, develop a workshop that provides instruction on one type of writing. What literature or other reading materials should you add to your workshop? Include the steps in the writing process in your workshop.

13. Begin a collection of articles and other reading materials that provides a focus for an expository writing activity pertaining to a specific subject. If the expository writing activity is a critical evaluation, include examples of critical evaluations from more than one side of an argument or issue.

14. Help upper elementary or middle school students develop a showcase for their own writing. This showcase might be in the form of a book showing students' poetry or other writings, a display of critical pieces such as authentication of literature, or a writers' festival in which students share their own writing with an audience.

15. With a group of your peers, develop a list of ways in which you, as teachers, can use your own writing to motivate students to write. How will you show them that you value writing and use writing in your own life?

For Further Reading

1. Stephanie Dix. (March 2006). "I'll Do It My Way: Three Writers and Their Revision Practices," in *The Reading Teacher,* 59, 556–573.

2. Audrey A. Friedman, & Christina A. Cataldo, (October 2003), "Characters at Crossroads: Reflective Decision Makers in Contemporary Newbery Books," in *The Reading Teacher,* 56, 102–112.

3. Kathy Ganske, Joanne K. Monroe, & Dorothy S. Strickland, (October 2003), "Questions Teachers Ask about Struggling Readers and Writers," in *The Reading Teacher,* 57, 118–128.

4. William A. Henk, Barbara A. Marinak, Jesse C. Moore, & Marla H. Mallette, (January 2004), "The Writing Observation Framework: A Guide for Refining and Validating Writing Instruction," in *The Reading Teacher,* 57, 322–333.

5. Dorothy J. Leal, (September 2003), "Digging up the Past, Building the Future: Using Book Authoring to Discover and Showcase a Community's History," in *The Reading Teacher,* 57, 56–60.

6. Dorothy J. Leal. (December 2005/January 2006). "The Word Writing Café: Assessing Student Writing for Complexity, Accuracy, and Fluency," in *The Reading Teacher,* 59, 340–350.

7. Author Web sites that are useful for books in this chapter include:

   Tonya Bolden: www.tonyabolden.com

   Nikki Grimes: www.nikkigrimes.com

   Gerald McDermott: www.geraldmcdermott.com

REFERENCES

Bloom, Harold. (2001). *Stories and Poems for Extremely Intelligent Children of All Ages.* New York: Scribners.

Cahnmann, Melisa. (March 2006). "Reading, Living, and Writing Bilingual Poetry as Scholartistry in the Language Arts Classroom." *Language Arts,* 83, 342–352.

Carter, Carrie. (2003). "Authentication of *Brundibar.*" Paper presented at College Station, Texas: Texas A&M University.

Cunningham, Patricia M., & Allington, Richard L. (2003). *Classrooms That Work: They Can All Read and Write,* 3rd ed. Boston: Allyn & Bacon.

Diamond, Marian. (1998). *Magical Trees of the Mind: How to Nurture Your Child's Intelligence, Creativity and Healthy Emotions from Birth through Adolescence.* New York: Putnam.

Donadio, Rachel. (4 September 2005). "Literary Letters, Lost in Cyberspace." *The New York Times Book Review,* pp. 14–15.

Dworin, Joel E. (March 2006). "The Family Stories Project: Using Funds of Knowledge for Writing." *The Reading Teacher,* 59, 510–520.

Dyson, Anne Haas, & Freedman, Sarah Warshauer. (2003). "Writing." In James Flood, Diane Lapp, James R. Squire, & Julie M. Jensen (Eds.), *Handbook of Research on Teaching the English Language Arts,* 2nd ed. Mahwah, NJ: Lawrence Erlbaum, pp. 967–992.

Farnan, Nancy, & Dahl, Karin. (2003). "Children's Writing: Research and Practice." In James Flood, Diane Lapp, James R. Squire, & Julie M. Jensen (Eds.), *Handbook of Research on Teaching the English Language Arts,* 2nd ed. Mahwah, NJ: Lawrence Erlbaum, pp. 993–1007.

Fletcher, Katie. (2003). "Authenticating *The Watsons Go to Birmingham—1963*" Paper presented at College Station, Texas: Texas A&M University.

Freyman, Saxton. (2005). *Food for Thought: The Complete Book of Concepts for Growing Minds.* New York: Scholastic.

Heller, Steve. (16 November 2004). "Alice's Adventures." *The New York Times Book Review,* p. 26.

Hansen, J. (1987). *When Writers Read.* Portsmouth, NH: Heinemann.

Hillocks, George. (1986). *Research on Written Composition: New Directions for Teaching.* Urbana, IL: National Conference on Research in English.

Karl, Jean E. (1994). *How to Write and Sell Children's Picture Books.* Cincinnati: Writer's Digest.

Kern, Diane, Andre, Wendy, Schilke, Rebecca, Barton, James, & McGuire, Margaret. (May 2003). "Less Is More: Preparing Students for State Writing Assessments." *The Reading Teacher,* 56, 816–826.

Kruger, Jeffrey. (October 2005) "Global Warming" The Culprit?" *Time,* 166, 42–46.

Lancia, P. (1997). "Literary Borrowing: The Effects of Literature on Children's Writing." *The Reading Teacher,* 50, 470–475.

Lipson, Eden Ross. (13 January 2004). "Award for a Tale of a Daring Walk between Towers." *New York Times,* pp. B1, B6.

Lodge, Sally. (8 December 2003). "African-American Children's Books." *Publishers Weekly,* 250, 39–42.

Maguire, Gregory. (16 November 2003). "Brundibar" *The New York Times Book Review,* p. 22.

Marchisan, M., & Alber, S. R. (2001). "The Write Way: Tips for Teaching the Writing Process to Resistant Writers." *Intervention in School and Clinic,* 36, 154–162.

Mies, K. Elaine. (1997). "Poetry Reading and Writing Unit for Eighth Grade Students." College Station, Texas: Texas A&M University.

Moore-Hart, Margaret A. (December 2005/January 2006). "A Writer's Camp in Action: A Community of Readers and Writers." *The Reading Teacher,* 59, 326–338.

Morton, Oliver. (2004). "Mars: Planet of Ice." *National Geographic* 203, 2–30.

National Council of Teachers of English and International Reading Association (1996). *Standards for the English Language Arts.* Urbana, IL and Newark, DE: Author.

Norton, Donna E. (2004). *The Effective Teaching of Language Arts,* 6th ed. Upper Saddle River, NJ: Merrill/Prentice Hall.

Norton, Donna E. (2005). *Multicultural Children's Literature,* 2nd ed. Upper Saddle River, NJ: Merrill/Prentice Hall.

Norton, Donna E. (2007). *Through the Eyes of a Child: An Introduction to Children's Literature,* 6th ed. Upper Saddle River, NJ: Merrill/Prentice Hall.

Pressley, Michael, & Harris, Karen (2001). "Teaching Cognitive Strategies for Reading, Writing, and Problem Solving." In Arthur L. Costa (Ed.), *Developing Minds,* 3rd ed. Alexandra, VA: Association for Supervision and Curriculum Development, pp. 466–470.

Prewitt, Jana Wright. (2001). "A Poetry Collection for Reading and Writing." College Station, TX: Texas A&M University.

Proett, Jackie, & Gill, Kent. (1986). *The Writing Process in Action: A Handbook for Teachers.* Urbana, IL: National Council of Teachers of English.

Revkin, Andrew C. (29 September 2005). *New York Times,* pp. A1, A8.

Rubin, Renée, & Carlan, Verónica Galván. (May 2005). "Using Writing to Understand Bilingual Children's Literacy Development." *The Reading Teacher,* 58, 728–739.

Selingo, Jeffrey. (19 August 2004). "In the Classroom, Web Logs Are the New Bulletin Boards." *New York Times,* p. E7.

Sternberg, Robert J. (2001). "Thinking Styles." In Arthur L. Costa (Ed.). *Developing Minds*, 3rd ed. Alexandra, VA: Association for Supervision and Curriculum Development, 197–201.

Sturges, Philemon. (2005). *I Love Bugs!* Illustrated by Shari Halpern. New York: HarperCollins.

"Talkin' About Black Books" (8 December 2003). *Publishers Weekly*, 250, 24–38.

Wagner, Betty Jane. (2003). "Imaginative Expression." In James Flood, Diane Lapp, James R. Squire, & Julie M. Jensen (Eds.), *Handbook of Research on Teaching the English Language Arts*, 2nd ed. Mahwah, NJ: Lawrence Erlbaum, pp. 1008–1025.

Winerip, Michael. (28 May 2003). "The Changes Unwelcome, A Model Teacher Moves On." *New York Times*, p. A20.

Winerip, Michael. (22 March 2006). "Do Standardized Tests Hurt Standards?" *New York Times*, p. A21.

Children's Literature References

Adoff, Arnold. (1982). *All the Colors of the Race*. Illustrated by John Steptoe. Lothrop, Lee & Shepard.

Alarcon, Francisco. (1997). *Laughing Tomatoes*. Illustrated by Maya Christina Gonzalez. Children's.

Appelt, Kathi. (2000). *Oh My Baby, Little One*. Illustrated by Jane Dyer. Harcourt.

Berry, James. (2002). *Around the World in Eighty Poems*. Illustrated by Katherine Lucas. Chronicle Books.

Bolden, Tonya. (2004). *Portraits of African-American Heroes*. Dutton.

Bolden, Tonya. (2004). *The Champ: The Story of Muhammad Ali*. Illustrated by R. Gregory Christie. Knopf.

Bolden, Tonya. (2004). *Wake Up Our Souls: A Celebration of African American Artists*. Smithsonian Museum.

Borden, Louise, & Kroger, Mary Kay. (2004). *Fly High! The Story of Bessie Coleman*. Illustrated by Teresa Flavin. Aladdin.

Bunting, Eve. (1984). *The Man Who Could Call Down Owls*. Illustrated by Charles Mikolaycak. Macmillan.

Carlson, Lori. (1994). *Cool Salsa: Bilingual Poems on Growing up Latino in the United States*. Holt.

Carroll, Lewis. (2003). *Alice's Adventures In Wonderland*. Illustrated by Robert Sabuda. Simon & Schuster.

Chen, Chih-Yuan. (2004). *Guji Guji*. LaJolla, CA: Miller.

Cline-Ransome, Lesa, & Ransome, James E. (2004). *Major Taylor Champion Cyclist*. Atheneum.

Cooper, Helen. (2005). *A Pipkin of Pepper for the Pumpkin Soup*. Simon & Schuster.

Cronin, Doreen. (2004). *Duck for President*. Illustrated by Betsy Lewin. Simon & Schuster.

Curtis, Christopher Paul. (1995). *The Watsons Go to Birmingham—1963*. Delacorte.

Cushman, Karen. (1995). *The Midwife's Apprentice*. Clarion.

Deacon, Alexis. (2003). *Beegu*. Farrar, Straus & Giroux.

Demi. (1986). *Dragon Kites and Dragonflies*. Harcourt Brace Jovanovich.

dePaola, Tomie. (1985). *Tomie dePaola's Mother Goose*. Putnam.

Driscoll, Laura. (2004). *Smart about Scientists: George Washington Carver: The Peanut Wizard*. Grosset & Dunlap.

Driscoll, Michael. (2003). *A Child's Introduction to Poetry*. Illustrated by Meredith Hamilton. Black Dog.

Fleischman, Paul. (1988). *Joyful Noise: Poems for Two Voices*. Illustrated by Eric Beddows. Harper & Row.

Florian, Douglas. (2004). *Omnibeasts*. Harcourt.

Freedman, Russell. (2004). *The Voice That Challenged a Nation: Marian Anderson and the Struggle for Equal Rights*. Clarion.

Gaiman, Neil. (2003). *The Wolves in the Walls*. Illustrated by Dave McKean. HarperCollins.

Gerrard, Roy. (1996). *Wagon's West!* Farrar, Straus, & Giroux.

Gerstein, Mordicai. (2003). *The Man Who Walked between the Towers*.? Roaring Brook Press.

Giblin, James Cross. (2002). *The Life and Death of Adolf Hitler.* Clarion.

Giovanni, Nikki. (2005). *Rosa.* Illustrated by Bryon Collier. Henry Holt.

Goodall, John S. (1984). *Paddy Under Water.* Atheneum.

Goodall John S. (1987). *The Story of a Main Street.* Macmillan.

Greenberg, Jan. (2004). *Romare Bearden: Collage of Memories.* Smithsonian Institution.

Grimes, Nikki. (2004). *Tai Chi Morning.* Illustrated by Ed Young. Cricket Books.

Harper, Joe. (2004). *Wilma Rudolph, Olympic Runner.* Illustrated by Meryl Henderson, Aladdin.

Henkes, Kevin. (2005). *So Happy!* Illustrated by Anita Lobel. Greenwillow.

Hobbie, Holly. (2003). *Charming Opal.* Little, Brown.

Jarrell, Randall. (1963). *The Bat-Poet.* Illustrated by Maurice Sendak. Macmillan.

Johnston, Johanna. (2004). *They Led the Way: 14 American Women.* Puffin.

Jordan, Deloris, & Jordan, Roslyn. (2004). *Salt in His Shoes: Michael Jordan in Pursuit of a Dream.* Illustrated by Nadir Nelson. Aladdin.

Kennedy, Caroline. (2005). *A Family of Poems: My Favorite Poetry for Children.* Illustrated by Jon Muth. Hyperion.

Kennedy, X. J., & Kennedy, Dorothy, eds. (1999). *Knock on a Star: A Child's Introduction to Poetry.* Illustrated by Karen Lee Baker. Little, Brown.

Kushner, Tony, retold by. (2003). *Brundibar.* Illustrated by Maurice Sendak. Hyperion.

Lee, Ho Back. (2003). *While We Were Out.* Kane/Miller.

Longfellow, Henry Wadsworth. (2001). *The Midnight Ride of Paul Revere.* Illustrated by Christopher Bing. Handprint.

Mayer, Mercer. (1971). *A Boy, a Dog, a Frog, and a Friend.* Dial Press.

McCully, Arnold. (1984). *Picnic.* New York: Harper & Row.

McCully, Arnold. (1987). *School.* Harper & Row.

McDermott, Gerald. (1974). *Arrow to the Sun.* Viking.

Milne, A. A. (1928). *The House at Pooh Corner.* Illustrated by Ernest Shepard. Dutton.

Myers, Walter Dean. (1997). *Harlem.* Illustrated by Christopher Myers. Scholastic.

Myers, Walter Dean. (2004). *I've Seen the Promised Land: The Life of Dr. Martin Luther King Jr.* Illustrated by Leonard Jenkins. HarperCollins.

Nelson, Marilyn. (2005). *A Wreath for Emmett Till.* Illustrated by Philippe Lardy. Houghton Mifflin.

Noyes, Alfred. (1981). *The Highwayman.* Illustrated by Charles Keeping. Oxford.

Nye, Naomi Shihab. (2002). *19 Varieties of Gazelle: Poems of the Middle East.* HarperCollins.

Nye, Naomi Shihab, ed. (1998). *The Space between Our Footsteps: Poems and Paintings from the Middle East.* Simon & Schuster.

Ojeda, Auriana, ed. (2003). *Teens at Risk: Opposing Viewpoints.* Greenhaven Press.

Once Upon a Time: Favorite Poems that Tell stories. (2004). Foreword by Kevin Crossley-Holland. Chicken House/Scholastic.

Patrick, Denise. (2004). *A Lesson for Martin Luther King, Jr.* Illustrated by Rodney Pate. Aladdin.

Pearson, Susan. (2005). *Grimericks.* Illustrated by Gris Grimly. Marshall Cavendish.

Pinkney, Jerry. (2004). *God Bless the Child.* HarperCollins.

Prelutsky, Jack. (2004). *If Not for the Cat.* Illustrated by Ted Rand. Greenwillow.

Raschka, Chris. (2004). *Charlie Parker Played Be-Bop.* Orchard.

Robinson, Sharon. (2004). *Promises to Keep: How Jackie Robinson Changed America.* Scholastic.

Rohmann, Eric. (1994). *Time Flies.* Crown.

Sayre, April Pulley. (2005). *Stars beneath Your Bed: The Surprising Story of Dust.* Greenwillow.

Scieszka, John, & Smith, Lane. (2004). *Science Verse.* Viking.

Sendak, Maurice. (1963). *Where the Wild Things Are.* Harper & Row.

Shange, Ntozake. (2004). *Ellington Was Not a Street.* Simon & Schuster.

Siebert, Diane. (1989). *Heartland.* Illustrated by Wendell Minor. Crowell.

Sis, Peter. (2000). *Dinosaur!* Greenwillow.

Sis, Peter. (2003). *The Tree of Life.* Farrar, Straus & Giroux.

Steig, William. (2003). *When Everybody Wore a Hat.* HarperCollins.

Tolan, Stephanie S. (2002). *Surviving the Applewhites.* HarperCollins.

Turner, Sandy. (2003). *Otto's Trunk.* HarperCollins.

Valcky, Catharina. (2005). *Lizette's Green Sock.* Clarion.

Volavkova, Hana. (1993). *. . . I Never Saw Another Butterfly . . .* Schocken.

Wells, Rosemary. (2005). *Yoko's World of Kindness: Golden Rules for a Happy Classroom.* Illustrated by John Nez and Judy Wheeler. New York: Hyperion.

White, E. B. (1952). *Charlotte's Web.* Illustrated by Garth Williams. Harper & Row.

Wiesner, David. (1988). *Free Fall.* Lothrop, Lee & Shepard.

Wood, Nancy, ed. (1997). *The Serpent's Tongue: Prose, Poetry, and Art of the New Mexico Pueblo.* Dutton.

Yolen, Jane. (1987). *Owl Moon.* Illustrated by John Schoenherr. Philomel.

Yolen, Jane, ed. (2005). *This Little Piggy: Lap Songs, Finger Plays, Clapping Games, and Pantomime Rhymes.* Illustrated by will Hillenbrand. Candlewick.

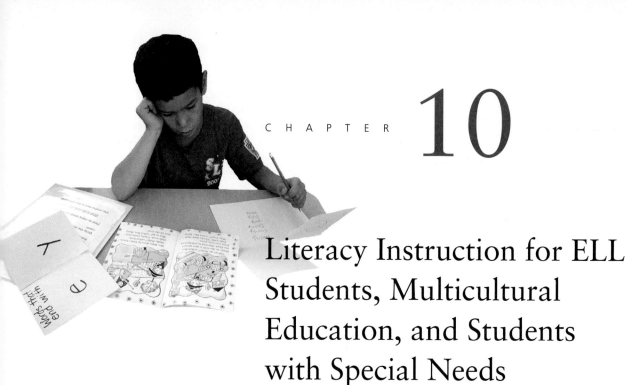

Literacy Instruction for ELL Students, Multicultural Education, and Students with Special Needs

CHAPTER **OUTLINE**

Programs for Students Whose First Language Is Not English
ESL Programs
Bilingual Programs
Issues in the Selection of Programs

The Most Effective Programs for Teaching ELL Students
Oral Language and Vocabulary Development
Reading Materials and Approaches for Comprehension
Developing Family Support with ELL Students
Extending Phonemic Awareness

Multicultural Education through Multicultural Literature
Examples of Literature for Native American Study Presented by Phases
Examples of Literature for African American Study Presented by Phases
Examples of Literature for Latino Study Presented by Phases
Examples of Literature for Asian American Study Presented by Phases
Instructional Strategies Used with Multicultural Literature
Using Technology to Learn about the Latino Culture

Students with Special Needs in Reading
Characteristics of Students with Special Needs in Reading and Approaches for Intervention
Intervention Strategies for Specific Special Needs

After reading this chapter you will be able to answer the following questions:

1. How does diversity effect the American classroom?
2. What programs are available for students whose first language is not English?
3. What are the most effective instructional practices for teaching linguistically and culturally diverse students?
4. What is multicultural education and why is it so important?
5. What are some characteristics of students with special needs in reading?
6. What are effective intervention strategies for students with specific needs in reading?

Read All About It!

"The Lessons of Classroom 506: Is There a Place in Class for Thomas?"

by Lisa Belkin, *New York Times,* September 12, 2004

It was the first day of school last year, Sept. 8, 2003. The kindergartners were arriving in batches at Classroom 506 at the Manhattan School for Children, on 93rd Street between Amsterdam and Columbus Avenues. . . . The parents noticed that while the class list, posted by the cubbies, had barely a dozen names, a small army of teachers—including an occupational therapist, a speech therapist, an "augmentative communication" expert and several other aides—had greeted them at the door. Even those who were arriving as kindergarten parents for the first time could sense that the class was different.

"Inclusion" said Suzanne Blank, the head teacher in Classroom 506. "Inclusion" is the latest in a series of evolving strategies for special-needs education. Though the definition of the word varies, inclusion, as used by educators, generally means making a child with a disability a full part of the class. Instead of merely placing that child in a standard classroom for part or even most of the day and expecting him to keep up (a strategy often known as "mainstreaming"), inclusion involves rearranging the class—both the physical space and the curriculum—to include him. Ideally, once an inclusive classroom is rethought and reconfigured, it will serve clusters of children with special needs, not just one, so that impaired and non-impaired children can come to see one another as peers. Proponents of inclusion say that it is the best way to prepare all children for the real world; skeptics contend that it too often gives teachers responsibility for impaired students without giving them sufficient training and resources, resulting in children with special needs getting improper attention and children without special needs not getting enough attention—a poor-quality education for everyone in the class.

. . .

[Belkin continues the article by describing the physical environment. Of special interest to reading teachers is her description of story time.]

. . .

It was story time in Classroom 506. Suzanne Blank gath-

> **"Inclusion, as used by educators, generally means making a child with a disability a full part of the class."**

ered the students on the rug and placed the storybook on an easel up front. This book was not like

any she used to teach kindergarten in the same classroom the year before. It was oversize—each page was two feet wide and two feet high. And the pages were laminated, with two Velcro strips along the bottom. On the top row of Velcro, words were attached forming the text of the story: "Who will help me plant this wheat?" asked the little red hen. "Not I!" said the duck. "Not I!" said the cat. "Not I!" said the dog. On the lower row was a series of pictures that corresponded to the words above. The word "duck" was represented by an image of a duck; a hand putting a small plant into the ground represented the verb "plant."

Children who cannot hear learn sign language. Children who cannot see learn Braille. Children who can hear but cannot speak, like Thomas, learn their own lan-

guage too. The symbols used in Classroom 506 are known as Mayer-Johnson symbols—thousands of little pictures that represent words and actions and thoughts. Long before nonverbal children can write or read, they can recognize symbols that mean "I want" and "milk" and point to them to make themselves understood. Thomas had been immersed in these symbols since he was a 1-year-old child. His wheelchair tray was filled with dozens of them—ways of saying yes, no, happy, mad, wash, play, eat, and drink. His teachers were now using that foundation to teach him to read.

Read All About It!
Critical Thinking **Questions**

- What is your response to the issues about inclusion versus mainstreaming?

- Why do you think this approach to the education of a child with special needs is working so well with Thomas?

- If you visited the classroom, how would it be different from other kindergarten classes?

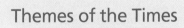

The content of this chapter covers three very important subjects for the reading teacher. First is the challenge of working with students whose first language is not English. Teachers are challenged with providing the most effective instructional programs and learning strategies for these students so that they will succeed in reading, writing, and speaking English. Second is the multicultural nature of most of our classrooms. Teachers need to enhance cross-cultural understanding and encourage students to understand and respect each other's cultural values and beliefs. Teaching through multicultural literature is especially meaningful for students who are reading authentic literature about their own cultures.

Multicultural literature and activities are also necessary for all students because of the need to expand multicultural understanding in our culturally diverse world. Third is the **at-risk** student or struggling reader who is falling behind in reading. Teachers must select intervention programs or corrective reading instruction that matches the academic needs of these students.

The number of foreign-born students in the United States is increasing rapidly. Diversity has always been a strength of the American culture. The locations from which the immigrants come to the United States has changed considerably in the past decade. Between 1890 and 1920 most immigrants came from European countries such as Germany, Poland, Ireland, Hungary, and Russia. The immigration pattern has now changed. According to a 1998 *Washington Post* article, "The overwhelming majority of immigrants come from Asia and Latin America—Mexico, the Central American countries, the Philippines, Korea, and Southeast Asia" (Booth, March 1998 p. 7).

Reading educators such as Hoffman and Pearson (2000) observe that. "It is projected that between 2000 and 2020 there will be 47 percent more [Latino] children aged five to thirteen in the United States than are there today" (p. 28). These educators conclude that teachers must have knowledge about the culture and linguistic diversity found in schools. A study reported in the *NCELA Newsline Bulletin* (2002) found that out of approximately three million public school teachers surveyed, 41 percent reported teaching students with limited English proficiency. Unfortunately, only 12.5 percent of the teachers had received eight or more hours in training that focused on this population. With that many students with limited English proficiency in our schools, the questions occur: What programs are available for students whose first language is not English? And, what instructional practices are available to the teacher who has the students in his or her classroom?

Programs for Students Whose First Language Is Not English

Before discussing the programs, the issues related to the programs, and strategies related to instruction of students whose first language is not English, we need to identify the terms used to describe the students. These terms will be found in the literature and may be used by teachers and researchers who are describing their programs and the students who are in the programs. For example, **English as a Second Language** speakers are usually abbreviated as (ESL). Other terms used in the literature include *Limited English Proficient* (LEP), **English Language Learners** (ELL), *Potentially English Proficient* (PEP), *Readers and Writers of English as an Additional Language* (REAL), *English as a New Language* (ENL), and *English Speakers of Other Languages* (ESOL) The two major programs discussed in the literature about reading instruction for ELL students are ESL (English as a Second Language) and Bilingual Education.

ESL Programs *English as Second Language*

Advocates for ESL approaches to education emphasize that the language of instruction whether it is reading or another content area should all be done in English. ESL is an immersion in English language approach. The belief behind the program is that total immersion including speaking, listening, and reading, in the second language helps students become proficient in the second language more rapidly than other approaches. Child development experts Teresa McDevitt and Jeanne Ormrod (2004) maintain that immersion works better for some students than for other students because the effectiveness of the program depends on the students' proficiency in their native language before they begin their second-language instruction; it also depends on whether students have ongoing opportunities to continue developing their first language while they study the second language. McDevitt and Ormrod point out, "If instruction in a second language somehow undermines children's development in the first language, it is likely to have deleterious effects on their cognitive development. Immersion programs are typically effective only when children already have a solid foundation in their first language and have regular opportunities to use and enhance their skills in that language; in such circumstances, learning a second language doesn't interfere with cognitive development." (p. 312)

Bilingual Programs

In bilingual programs students are instructed in academic subject areas in their native language while also being taught to speak and write in the second language. Ideally, students in bilingual programs move from being taught in their native language to all English education classes. The belief behind bilingual programs is that students, especially those who have recently moved to the United States, will gain in overall academic achievement when they are taught in their native language. Bilingual programs require that all students in the class speak the same native language. Many bilingual programs are found in the primary grades (K–3); the belief is that early instruction allows children to gain English skills more rapidly than if instruction started at a later time. As students progress through bilingual programs they may be placed in transitional programs that are designed to help students make the transition between the native language and classes taught in English.

Claude Goldenberg (2005), executive director of the Center for Language Minority Education and Research at California State University, Long Beach, advocates **bilingual education** because "knowing two languages or more could help make us a linguistically more rich, diverse society. Knowing two or more languages confers intellectual, cultural, economic, and other benefits to individuals and societies" (p. 8). Goldenberg admits, however, that research studies have not shown the best way to help students transfer knowledge and skills learned from the first language to English. Even though the research is not conclusive, Goldenberg believes that all students benefit from clear instruction, well-designed tasks, guidance and feedback from an adult, and opportunities to practice their new skills.

Teachers in either the bilingual or transitional programs should be able to speak both the children's native language and English. In addition, they need to understand and use strategies that are the most effective for teaching the content areas.

Issues in the Selection of Programs

Which approach—ESL or bilingual education—provides the fastest route to English proficiency for English language learners (ELL)? Are students more proficient when instruction is exclusively in English? Or, is the fastest way toward proficiency a combination program that uses students' native language in classroom settings for extended periods of time? Large-scale research studies that evaluate the two types of programs provide conflicting evidence. For example, Sarah Hudelson, Leslie Poynor, and Paula Wolfe (2003), authorities in bilingual and ESL education, report that one study found no significant differences between children in bilingual education and in ESL classes. Another study found that time spent in the native language as in bilingual programs might contribute to later achievement in English. These researchers conclude that the most important concern for educating students with limited English is a well-implemented program.

> **Reflect on Your Reading**
>
> Place yourself in the role of a student who enters American schools without being able to speak or read English. What obstacles would you face? What strengths would you bring to your education? Now place yourself in the role of the teacher. How will you prepare yourself to meet the needs of ELL students?

The Most Effective Programs for Teaching ELL Students

What are the characteristics of effective programs for linguistically and culturally diverse students? Researchers and educators working with ELL students have reported both general guidelines for working with the students and more specific instructional strategies that are helpful to teachers of reading. For example, the National Center for Research on Cultural Diversity and Second Language Learning (Garcia, 1991) presents the following general practices for teaching ELL students:

1. Instruction in basic skills and academic content is organized around thematic units; learners often contribute to the selection of the units.

2. Students work together in small groups and teachers interact with students, resulting in high levels of communication.

3. Collaborative learning takes place in which students ask questions and seek assistance from each other.

4. Latino students are encouraged to use their native language.

5. Educators have high levels of commitment to the students and their families.

Notice how similar these effective instructional strategies are to those identified by Tharp (1997) who searched the research to identify generic principles of instruction that contribute to high levels of academic achievement for language minority learners:

1. Learning takes place through joint activity among teachers and students.
2. Competency in language and literacy is developed through all instructional activities, especially purposeful conversation, not through drills and rules.
3. Teachers form bridges between school and instruction by including family and community life.
4. Teachers challenge students with complex, intellectually challenging learning.
5. Teachers engage students through questioning and sharing ideas and knowledge.

As you can see, these guidelines emphasize effective teaching strategies and approaches that are used throughout the curriculum. Many of these guidelines are similar to those presented earlier, but they provide specific instructional strategies for teaching of reading to ELL students. Kimberly Lenters (2005) searched the research for reading instruction and developed guidelines in five areas of reading instruction that focus on oral language development, reading materials, phonemic awareness, comprehension, and first-language reading support. Table 10.1 presents Lenters's guidelines.

The next section describes some of the instructional practices that contribute to high levels of academic achievement among students with limited English proficiency. Many of the instructional practices developed are strategies that are useful for all classroom teachers, not only students classified as ELL students. Many of these suggested strategies for teaching ELL students have been developed previously in this book. This is fortunate because classroom teachers can use these strategies for both regular students and those who need extra instruction because of limited English proficiency. Reading strategies such as previewing the text, choral reading, shared reading, paired reading, books on tape, multicultural literature, interactive writing, and reading aloud are excellent for ELL students. We have discussed all of these strategies earlier in this book, but there are, however, extra details that make the strategies even more effective with ELL students.

Oral Language and Vocabulary Development

Building an oral vocabulary is extremely important for the success of ELL students. Kimberly Lenders (2005) reviewed the research associated with reading instruction for young second-language learners and concluded: "Because it takes young second-language learners between seven and ten years to reach the academic proficiency of their first-language peers, explicit attention must be given to building vocabulary throughout the primary and intermediate years of education" (p. 331). Vocabulary must be fostered through multiple exposure to words in a variety of genres, subject areas, and context.

Many of the activities for language development and emergent literacy discussed in Chapter 2 are extremely important when working with ELL students. Reading aloud to students and focusing on the new vocabulary while reading is very impor-

TABLE 10.1

Guidelines for Reading Instruction for ELL Students

Oral language

- Develop the child's oral vocabulary to the point of basic communicative competence before attempting reading instruction.
- Continue to work on vocabulary training with the child well beyond the point of basic communicative competence to ensure adequate vocabulary for increasingly more difficult text.
- Provide opportunity for second-language children to converse in the classroom, being careful not to place undue emphasis on accurate speech.

Reading materials

- Remember that the child must know 90% to 95% of the vocabulary in the text before that text is used for reading instructional purposes.
- Use graded readers with second-language readers to ensure that text difficulty keeps pace with vocabulary development. But be sure to supplement with authentic literature first in read-alouds, then shared reading, and finally independent reading to ensure second-language readers are exposed to text that reflects natural speech.
- Encourage and provide opportunity for rereading of text.

Phonemic awareness

- Extend phonemic awareness training to include phonics instruction, using materials that teach sound-symbol correspondences in a multisensory and systematic manner.

Comprehension

- Use a language experience approach to provide meaningful materials the child is able to read.
- Pay attention to cultural biases in text and illustrations presented to young second-language learners.
- Fill in the missing cultural information when materials must be used that are culturally unfamiliar to the learner.
- When possible, use translations alongside English texts to enhance comprehension and support first-language reading skills. Parents and older siblings may be enlisted for this process.
- Allow students to respond to text in their first language.

First-language reading support

- Form strong home-school connections with the families of second-language learners.
- Value the child's first language.
- Find any means possible to ensure that the child receives reading instruction in his or her first language.

Source: Figure from Lenters, Kimberly. (2004, December). No half measures: Reading instruction for young second-language learners. *The Reading Teacher, 58*(4), 328–336.

tant, for example, because it encourages language development, vocabulary expansion, and introduces ELL students to the sounds of the English language.

For the ultimate vocabulary experience, however, teachers need to go beyond merely reading the story aloud. Molly Fuller Collins (2005) tested an approach in which young students listened to stories while the teacher pointed to the illustrations, provided brief definitions of targeted vocabulary words, presented a synonym for the word where appropriate, and used the vocabulary within a sentence that was different from the sentence in the text. Positive benefits resulted for the children; she recommended that teachers provide detailed explanations for new vocabulary. Also notice the importance of pointing to the illustrations in highly illustrated storybooks in order to expand comprehension.

Whether the story is read aloud to the students or the students read the story individually and discuss the book, most programs for English language learners recommend providing many opportunities for listening to and reading literature and other materials. Hickman, Pollard-Durodola, and Vaughn (2004) for example, recommend a five-step approach for improving vocabulary knowledge and comprehension for students with limited English proficiency who are learning to read:

- Select a fictional or informational text, introduce the story, and introduce three or four new vocabulary words that are found in a 200–250 word passage from the text. Each vocabulary word is spoken by the teacher and repeated by the students and a definition is provided.

- Read the passage out loud; ask questions that focus on literal and inferential comprehension of the text.

- Read the passage while focusing on the vocabulary words. Guide the students in creating original sentences using the vocabulary words.

This teacher is developing family support with the parents of an ELL student.

- Extend comprehension by asking students to discuss the story and the vocabulary words as they relate to their own ideas and experiences.
- Summarize what was learned, the main events and ideas from the passage, and understandings of the new vocabulary words.

This approach is continued daily until the reading of the chosen text is completed. Now the teacher reviews the challenging words and involves the students in an activity such as creating a short story in their own words.

Many of the suggestions for vocabulary development presented in Chapter 5, "Vocabulary Development," help extend knowledge of the targeted vocabulary. As students begin to read the words, word walls may be developed. Vocabulary webs help expand the meanings of the words. Children can develop picture dictionaries that further enhance their understandings of the targeted vocabulary. The targeted words may be used to write simple stories that students share orally with their classmates.

Later in this chapter, we present illustrated picture books that allow students to talk about their own cultures and compare their cultural experiences with those illustrated in the picture books. The section on multicultural literature also discusses books for older readers that accurately depict a culture. This type of activity both encourages comprehension of the story and allows students to share their own background experiences and cultural knowledge.

Reading Materials and Approaches for Comprehension

Prereading activities are especially important, no matter what reading materials are used with ELL students. Schema theory emphasizes the importance of building background knowledge prior to reading. One of the best approaches to use with reading materials for ELL students is to use modeling as presented in Chapter 6, "Developing Approaches for Fluency and Comprehension." Modeling allows the teacher to introduce unusual vocabulary, assess students' background knowledge, and allow students to understand the thought processes that the teacher uses to arrive at appropriate answers. Modeling encourages ELL students to explore their reasoning and share their ideas orally.

There are also an increasing number of books published in two languages, especially in Spanish and English. Students can use a shared-reading activity in which the non-English speaker reads the text in his or her native language and an English speaker reads the text in English. After each student reads the text, they can share their understandings. Reading materials may also be tape-recorded and placed in a listening center. Now the ELL students can listen repeatedly to the story. Some teachers highlight the vocabulary that is found on the recording.

Two approaches with reading materials are especially beneficial for ELL students. One is the use of literature circles to encourage students to read and share their responses to the texts. Another highly recommended approach is the language experience approach. As you read about these approaches consider why they would be recommended for ELL students.

USING LITERATURE CIRCLES When using literature circles with first-grade bilingual students, Carmen M. Martinez-Roldan and Julia M. Lopez-Robertson (2000) found that the students paid close attention to the illustrations to help them get meaning from the text. The students also focused on social, cultural, and political issues when discussing a book. When discussing Pat Mora's *Thomas and the Library Lady* (1997), for example, a story about the son of a migrant worker, they emphasized the importance of reading for Thomas and agreed that reading might help make him smart. These first-grade students also connected with issues such as unfair treatment of others.

Remember that one of the effective instructional strategies identified earlier in this chapter is to encourage Latino students to use their native language. If students cannot read the texts, teachers might ask children to help them pronounce the Spanish words. The following picture storybooks are written in both English and Spanish:

- Diane Gonzales Bertrand's *Uncle Chente's Picnic* (2001)
- Samuel Caraballo's *Estrellita Says Good-Bye to Her Island* (2002)
- Diana Cohn's *Yes, We Can!* (2002)
- Pat Mora's *The Bakery Lady* (2001)

Poetry is another genre of literature that can be used in literature circles or with whole class discussions. Poetry, according to Melisa Cahnmann (2006), is a very important genre of literature to use for reading and writing activities. The poetry is short and provides powerful ways to focus on the impact of vocabulary and word phrases. Students can read orally their favorite poems or share vivid vocabulary or lines that appeal to them. Choral arrangements in which students join in during repeated lines are especially good for students who are learning English. (There is a lesson plan for developing choral arrangements with nursery rhymes in Chapter 7). The following books of poetry include poems from different cultural groups:

- Francisco X. Alarcon's *Laughing Tomatoes and Other Spring Poems* (1997)— The poems are written in both English and Spanish.

- Demi's *In the Eyes of the Cat: Japanese Poetry for All Seasons* (1992)

- Mary Ann Hoberman's *My Song Is Beautiful: Poems and Pictures in Many Voices* (1994)

- Issa's *Cool Melons—Turn to Frogs!: The Life and Poems of Issa* (1998)—Japanese haiku.

- Naomi Shihab Nye's *This Same Sky: A Collection of Poems from around the World* (1992)

THE LANGUAGE EXPERIENCE APPROACH   The language experience approach is a highly recommended strategy for teaching reading to ELL students. The approach is especially worthwhile because it allows students to see the connections between oral and written language. According to Susanne F. Peregoy and Owen F. Boyle (2001) the language experience approach is recommended for ELL students because the students provide the text, through dictation, that becomes the source for reading instruction. Consequently, the resulting material is tailored to the students' language proficiency, background knowledge, interests, and cultural strengths.

The philosophy of the language experience approach emphasizes that children's ideas are worth expressing, writing down, and reading. The language experience is motivated by activities such as art, literature, and classroom experiences that stimulate oral expression. Following the motivating activity, the children dictate a story about this experience. Finally, the students read their own dictated stories.

A language experience story may be a group or an individual activity. Many teachers introduce the language experience approach as a group activity in which the story is dictated on a chart as a group chart story. Now the motivational activity involves the group and encourages oral language and a cooperative activity. For example, a first and second grade teacher of ELL students who were mostly Latino introduced a series of photographs that showed people celebrating the "Day of the Dead". The students talked about their own experiences associated with the celebration. Next, the teacher asked the children to think about a story that they would like to tell about the celebration. Now each child in the group had an opportunity to tell something that would be written on the chart. The teacher listened as each child provided a sentence for the story. The sentence was printed on the chart using the exact language dictated by the child. As the child dictated the sentence, the teacher asked the children to watch carefully as the teacher printed the words. The child then read the sentence as the teacher placed her hand under each word as it was read. Then the whole group read the sentence as the teacher continued to focus attention on each word. The language experience continued as additional children added to the dictated story, read their individual sentences, and then joined the whole group in the reading. If desired, the name of the child contributing the sentence may be placed next to the sentence on the chart story.

After completing the chart story, the group read the whole story and talked about how they responded to the experience. The teacher pointed out how the words were written from left to right on the chart and how the sentences were written from top to bottom. This was especially important for many of the first-grade children who were just beginning to learn to read. The teacher asked them to think about a title for their story and printed their suggestion at the top of the chart. The second-grade children copied the chart story as part of a writing exercise and then illustrated their own story. The students continued to use both the chart story written by the teacher and their own written examples as reading materials. They took their own stories home and shared them with their parents. New vocabulary words from the chart story were discussed and added to the word wall.

The teacher continued to use numerous motivational activities associated with the Latino culture. The children listened to music and then dictated a story about how the music made them feel, and they listened to Latino folktales and wrote their own versions of the tales. The language experience approach may be motivated by many class-related activities. Motivation might result in a dictated chart story about a science experiment, a story about the actions of an animal brought to the class, or a story following a field trip.

The language experience approach may also be used to develop individual materials in which each student dictates and reads a story to the teacher. This activity may follow an art project in which each child draws a picture and then dictates and reads his or her own individual story. One teacher of ELL students produced successful individual language experience stories by having students dictate and illustrate stories about their family members. These are effective reading materials because the students dictate stories about experiences and people who are important to them. Teachers of older students may read stories about their culture and then have students choose a literary element and dictate stories about one of the characters, the setting, or the conflict. These reading materials may be placed in the library and become sources for all of the students to read.

Language experience stories may be used to help students expand their sight vocabularies and comprehend written language. For example, to check if the words are part of the child's sight vocabulary, the teacher isolates the words and asks the child to identify individual words. If the child knows the words, the words are printed on a small card and placed into the child's file box labeled with the child's name. If the child has difficulty with the words, the teacher shows the total sentence within the story and helps the child use the context clues to identify the word.

Language experience stories may also be used to reinforce comprehension and story structure. For example, cut the language experience stories into sentence strips, mix up the strips, and ask the students to place the strips in order to develop an understandable story. This is an excellent way to reinforce chronological order following the dictation of a chart story about the steps in a science experiment or the sequence of actions in a plot development.

The language experience approach is also a favorite instructional approach for students with special needs. As long as the dictated stories relate to the students' backgrounds or experiences they provide meaningful instructional reading materials and provide the critical background that allows the students to comprehend what they read.

HELPING LEARNERS CONSTRUCT KNOWLEDGE   Building background knowledge is especially important for increasing comprehension for what is read. Dawnene D. Hammerberg (2004) believes that helping students draw on prior knowledge and use their own cultural backgrounds is an important strategy to help students understand themselves and others. This happens, according to Hammerberg, when students draw upon their cultural identities to help them understand.

Learning also occurs when students take part in interactive learning where they make connections between a text and their lives. The following lesson plan was used with a third-grade class of students that included several Hmong children in the classroom. It demonstrates how a teacher may use the background of the students to help classmates develop comprehension for a story. It also shows how the approach develops self-esteem among members of the minority group.

LESSON PLAN:
Developing Background Knowledge and Respect for Cultural Identity

OBJECTIVES	1. To provide background knowledge before reading a book about the Hmong people.
	2. To develop a collaborative learning experience where students learn from each other.
	3. To develop respect for another culture and use experiences of family members.
GRADE LEVELS	Grades three and four (This lesson was taught to third-grade students.)
MATERIALS	Dia Cha's *Dia's Story Cloth: The Hmong People's Journey of Freedom* (1996). Maps showing the route of the Hmong people from China, to Laos, to Thailand, and to the United States. (This approach may be used with literature that focuses on the cultural identity of any students that are members of the class.)
PROCEDURES	1. Read and discuss the following introduction to the book: "This story cloth shows the journey of my people. We are called Hmong, which means 'free people.' Our journey begins long ago in China, and continues to Laos and then the refugee camps in Thailand. For

over 125,000 Hmong people, the journey ends in the United States" (unnumbered).

2. Ask the students to relate their own family experiences in coming to America and compare those experiences with Cha's experiences. If possible, invite older family members to come to class and share experiences.

3. On the maps, show and discuss the people's journey from China to the United States.

4. To increase collaborative learning, encourage class members to ask questions.

5. Share information about why the story is told through needlework rather than painting or photographs. Share and discuss, "Hmong people living here today continue the tradition of needlework. The stitches in a Hmong story cloth make pictures of life. The story cloth will tell you about our life" (unnumbered).

6. Read the story, asking the Hmong students to interact and comment about the content as the story is read.

7. Expand the idea of a story cloth to other cultures. Encourage students to draw their own histories in pictures and share the pictures with the class. Encourage students to ask questions about the story cloths

Developing Family Support with ELL Students

Studies on reading improvement with Latino students show the value of parents reading aloud to and with their children. Robert W. Ortiz and Rosario Ordonez-Jasis (2005) found that Latino parents choose materials to share with their children if they find the materials interesting, helpful, and important to them. Consequently, they recommend "including multicultural literature that reflects the rich and diverse realities and interests of Latino families" (p. 116). They recommend that teachers choose books that preserve the Latino tradition, celebrate the richness of the culture, tell personal stories about people who share similar experiences and values, and address social issues and concerns. Allowing students to share and discuss their readings with their families encourages strong home and school connections. If the children share their parents' responses to the readings, children and parents discover that the teacher respects their culture and background.

Programs that model instructional strategies that ELL parents can use with their own children are very helpful. I will never forget my own experiences while providing such instruction to parents of Latino and Russian immigrant families in a Chicago suburban school. I modeled some of the instructional strategies that their teachers were using to develop comprehension of reading materials and showed them how they could reinforce those same strategies at home. The interest among the parents was so high that we had to move the evening sessions to larger rooms and extend the sessions to include more strategies that parents could use at home. Many of the parents brought their children with them and we worked on the strategies together. Many of the books that we used are discussed in the multicultural section of this chapter.

Reflect on Your Reading

Consider the effective instructional practices for teaching students who are English language learners (ELL) with limited English proficiency. Why is it so important to help students identify prior knowledge and use their cultural backgrounds when comprehending a text? Think about your own elementary education. Can you identify an experience when teachers used cultural information from students in the class? Why is it important to encourage students to share their cultural experiences?

Extending Phonemic Awareness

The guidelines for successful reading instruction presented earlier in this chapter (Table 10.1), emphasize extending phonemic awareness to include phonics instruction that teaches sound-symbol correspondences in a multisensory and systematic manner. Kimberly Lenders (2005) concludes: "For young children, explicit, systematic instruction in second-language sounds and symbols does appear to address perceived auditory weaknesses, just as it does for first-language children with poorly developed phonemic awareness" (p. 333). This conclusion suggests that ELL students need many of the activities suggested for emergent literacy, phonemic awareness, and phonics instruction discussed in Chapter 4, "Phonics and Phonemic Awareness." Activities that stress auditory discrimination and phoneme blending are especially important.

Multicultural Education through Multicultural Literature

Native American author Michael Dorris (1979) found that the best way to study Native American literature and culture was to begin with a study of broad oral traditions, narrow to specific tribal experiences, continue with a study of biography and autobiography of the culture, and conclude with a story of contemporary Native American writing. Joseph Campbell, in *The Power of the Myth* (1988), maintains that to understand a culture, students should begin with the folklore of the people.

The sequence of study I have developed modifies the Dorris model and emphasizes literature written for children and adolescents including genres such as historical fiction and poetry that are important in children's literature and in the elementary school curriculum. This sequence of study also expands the cultural group from a study of Native American cultures to a study of Latino, African American, Asian, and Middle Eastern literature. This five-phase model for studying multicultural literature first appeared in *The Reading Teacher* (September 1990).

This sequence for multicultural literature study is the model used in this chapter:

Phase I   Traditional literature (Generalizations and broad views from a cultural group)

     a. Identify distinctions among folktale, fable, myth, and legend.

     b. Identify ancient stories that have commonalties and are found in many regions.

     c. Summarize the nature of oral language, role of traditional literature, role of audience, and literary style.

Phase II   Traditional tales from one area (Narrower view such as Native American folklore from the Great Plains, Latino folktales and legends from Mexico and the southwestern United States)

a. Analyze traditional myths and other story types and compare with Phase I findings.

b. Analyze and identify values, beliefs, and themes in the traditional tales of one region.

Phase III   Autobiographies, biographies, and historical nonfiction that reflects an earlier time in history

a. Analyze values, beliefs, and themes identified in traditional literature.

b. Compare the information in historical nonfiction with autobiographies and biographies.

Phase IV   Historical fiction

a. Evaluate according to authenticity of setting, conflicts, characterization, theme, language, and traditional beliefs and values.

b. Search for role of traditional literature.

c. Compare with nonfiction autobiographies, biographies, and historical information.

Phase V   Contemporary fiction, biography, and poetry

a. Analyze the inclusion of any beliefs and values identified in traditional literature and biographical literature.

b. Analyze characterization and conflicts.

c. Analyze themes and look for threads across the literature.

Phase 5 concludes with the contemporary realistic fiction, poetry, and biography written for children by authors whose work represents that cultural group. It searches for values and beliefs that are still important to the culture.

As can be seen from this model, the sequence includes many areas previously discussed in this text. Students develop an understanding of characteristics of literary genres such as folktales as they analyze the values and beliefs in the tales. They discover the power of literary elements as they search for themes and compare characteristics of settings and conflicts in the literature. Students improve their comprehension of text as they use the information found in traditional literature to authenticate the values and beliefs expressed by figures in historical fiction or compare the information found in nonfiction with that developed by authors or historical fiction or contemporary stories. They discover the power of an inquiry approach as they use the five phases to make connections across literary and cultural time periods and to compare and evaluate the literature.

The study of **multicultural literature** is a powerful means for teachers to help students develop an appreciation and understanding of both literary and cultural heritage. Because there are literature selections ranging from picture storybooks for younger children to more complex novels written for older students, the approach can be modified for use at any grade level.

Multicultural education considers the values, beliefs, and perceptions of various cultural groups. It is designed to enhance cross-cultural understanding as students discover the contributions of various groups within our society. Denise Ann Finazzo

(1997) defines multiculturalism as a child-centered approach to learning: "It begins with the child's understanding of self and the building of self-esteem, moves to an understanding and acceptance of others, and finally expands to a development of concern for larger problems and issues outside the child's immediate environment" (p. 101).

Multicultural study should be used with all students in a classroom because it allows students of diverse backgrounds to learn about each other. Rena Lewis and Donald Doorlag (1995) give the following reasons for developing multicultural education:

1. Commonalties among people cannot be recognized unless differences are acknowledged.

2. A society that interweaves the best of all of its cultures reflects a truly mosaic image.

3. Multicultural education can restore cultural rights by emphasizing cultural equality and respect.

4. Students can learn basic skills while also learning to respect cultures; multicultural education need not detract from basic education.

5. Multicultural education enhances the self-concepts of all students because it provides a more balanced view of the American society.

6. Students must learn to respect others.

Alora Valdez (1999) maintains that

> All children need multicultural education in order to learn to challenge and reject racism and other forms of discrimination; to accept and affirm pluralism; and to advance the democratic principles of social justice . . .
> Young people are acquiring knowledge or beliefs that are sometimes invalid . . . It is essential that all the members of our society develop multicultural literacy—a solidly based understanding of racial, ethnic, and cultural groups and their significance in U.S. society. (p. 3)

Multicultural education is an exciting subject for reading classes and content areas such as English, social studies, history, and art. Excellent multicultural literature teachers can develop instructional programs that meet all of the characteristics of effective programs for linguistically and culturally diverse students discussed earlier. The academic content can be organized around thematic units, students can work together in smaller or larger groups and students and teachers can take part in collaborative learning. Several units and lesson plans that either include or focus on multicultural literature have already been developed in this text. The focus unit in Chapter 6, for example, "Comparing Variants of 'Little Red Riding Hood,'" used versions from China, France, and Germany. The focus unit in Chapter 7, "Comparing Different Versions of 'Cinderella,'" included variants of the folktale that reflect the values of different cultures. Within the section about art education, Chapter 7 included an analysis of the illustrations in Native American literature including semantic maps and meanings of Native American symbols. Chapter 7 also included meanings of symbols in Chinese art and literature.

In this chapter we focus on African American, Native American, Latino, and Chinese American cultures. The multicultural literature study is organized according to the five-phase approach already outlined in this chapter. We begin with examples using Native American literature that reflects the five phases. Next, the chapter includes lists of African American, Latino, and Asian literature that may be used in a similar study. Finally, the chapter presents instructional strategies that may be used with the various five phases.

Examples of Literature for Native American Study Presented by Phases

Before beginning this study of Native American culture, discuss the importance of the oral tradition in transmitting the values and beliefs of the people. Students should understand that the oral tales were handed down for many generations before they were transcribed into written form. Show a map of North America so that students understand the diversity of locations that could be selected for a study of Native American folklore. Michael J. Caduto and Joseph Bruchac's *Keepers of the Earth: Native American Stories and Environmental Activities for Children* (1989) includes a map of tribal locations as they appeared around 1600.

PHASE I: TRADITIONAL LITERATURE   Collect as many examples of stories that meet Bierhorst's (1978) story types found in Native American folklore: 1) creation myths that show how physical or social order was brought to the tribal world; 2) tales that deal with family and tribal drama, needs, and conflicts; 3) trickster tales that represent fair and foul actions; and 4) crossing-the-threshold tales that reflect major changes such as going in and out of the animal world and leaving childhood for adulthood. The trickster tales are especially good for younger students. The following examples are found in children's literature collections and individual stories. (An interest level (I) by age of students is included following each entry.)

1. Creation myths or setting-the-world-in-order tales that focus on creating the earth and earth's various animal and plant life:

   ■ "Turtle Dives to the Bottom of the Sea: Earth Starter the Creator," a Maidu tale from California, and "The Woman Who Fell from the Sky: Divine Woman the Creator," a Huron myth from northeastern United States found in Virginia Hamilton's *In the Beginning: Creation Stories from Around the World* (1988). I: all

   ■ "The Earth on Turtle's Back," an Onondaga tale from the northeastern woodlands, and "Four Winds: The Diné Story of Creation" found in Michael J. Caduto and Joseph Bruchac's *Keepers of the Earth: Native American Stories and Environmental Activities for Children* (1989). I: all.

   ■ "The Great Flood" found in Nancy Wood's *The Serpent's Tongue: Prose, Poetry, and Art of the New Mexico Pueblos* (1997). I: 8+.

   ■ Barbara Juster Esbensen's *The Star Maiden* (1988). I: all.

Multicultural literature provides background knowledge for a study of Martin Luther King, Jr.

2. Family drama tales that focus on family needs and conflicts such as learning from elders, providing protection, and obtaining food:

■ Lois Duncan's *The Magic of Spider Woman* (1996) tells about the importance of having a balanced life. I: all.

■ Lois Ehlert's *Mole's Hill: A Woodland Tale* (1994) is a Seneca tale that stresses the need to use one's wit to overcome problems. I: 5–8.

3. Trickster tales that reveal both good and bad conduct are found throughout North America:

■ Gerald McDermott's *Raven: A Trickster Tale from the Pacific Northwest* (1993), and *Coyote: A Trickster Tale from the American Southwest* (1994). I: all.

■ Paul Goble's *Iktomi and the Boulder: A Plains Indian Story* (1988), and *Iktomi and the Berries* (1989). I: 4–10.

4. Crossing threshold tales that depict transformations as characters go into and out of the animal world are especially popular in stories retold for children:

■ Paul Goble's *Buffalo Woman* (1984) shows the bond between animals and humans and *Beyond the Ridge* (1989) follows an elderly Plains Indian as she goes from life to death. I: all.

■ Laura Simms's *The Bone Man: A Native American Modoc Tale* (1997) is the story of a boy who goes from frightened child to a warrior whose strength comes from courage and compassion. I: 6–8.

As students read the literature in Phase I they should summarize the generalizations that they have made about Native American folklore. (Strategies for using the literature are developed later in this chapter.)

PHASE II: TRADITIONAL LITERATURE FROM ONE OR TWO NATIVE AMERICAN PEOPLES (Let the students decide which group they would like to study. There are numerous collections of folklore from the Great Plains, for example, written in illustrated picture books.) During Phase II, students should read multiple tales from a specific region and identify the dominant values, beliefs, and themes found in that literature. The following examples are from Native American peoples living on the Great Plains:

- Tomi dePaola's *The Legend of the Bluebonnet* (1983) values living in harmony with nature. I: all.

- Olaf Baker's *Where the Buffaloes Begin* (1981) values the interactions between the buffalo and the Great Plains Indians. I: all.

- Paul Goble's *Star Boy* (1983) values bravery and obedience. I: 6–10.

PHASE III: NONFICTION LITERATURE THAT REFLECTS THE HISTORICAL PER-SPECTIVE   This literature includes historical informational books, biographies, and autobiographies about the tribal culture selected during Phase II. As students read this literature they use knowledge gained from phases I and II to evaluate the inclusion of accurate values, beliefs, and philosophies. They should read a number of sources, evaluate the authenticity of historical information, and identify the historical happenings that influenced the culture.

Helping students evaluate children's biographies about earlier Native American characters is especially critical. Students should ask: Are the values and beliefs expressed by the biographical characters authentic? Do they correspond with the values and beliefs identified in the traditional literature? Are the historical settings and happenings authentic for the time period? All of the biographies about this earlier period should be read with caution and even some skepticism. Many of the books written for children do not reflect the actual conflicts related to land and religion experienced by the Native peoples. Older students enjoy using this topic for inquiry to discover the accuracy of the literature.

The following texts are useful during Phase III study:

- Dorothy Morrison's *Chief Sarah: Sarah Winnemucca's Fight for Indian Rights* (1980). I: 10+.

- Dorothy M. Johnson's *Warrior for a Lost Nation: A Biography of Sitting Bull* (1969). I: 10+.

- Paul Goble's *Death of the Iron Horse* (1987). I: 8+.

- Russell Freedman's *Buffalo Hunt* (1988) and *An Indian Winter* (1992). I: 8+.

- Tim Tingle's *Walking the Choctaw Road* (2003). I: 10+.

PHASE IV: HISTORICAL FICTION   Students read, analyze, and evaluate historical fiction according to authenticity of setting, credibility of conflict, believability of characterization, authenticity of traditional beliefs expressed by the characters, and appropriateness of themes and authors' styles. There is excellent historical fiction including:

- Jan Hudson's *Sweetgrass* (1989), about a Blackfoot girl who grows up during the winter of a smallpox epidemic in 1837 (Canadian award-winner). I: 10+.

- Louise Erdrich's *The Birchbark House* (1999), the story of an Ojibwa girl in 1847. (A National Book Award finalist, written by a member of the Ojibwa tribal group.) I: 8+.

- Farley Mowat's *Lost in the Barrens* (1996, 1984), the story of a Cree Indian and his friend lost in Canada (Canadian award-winner). I: 9+.

PHASE V: CONTEMPORARY LITERATURE   During the final phase students read, analyze, and evaluate contemporary poetry, fiction, and biography. They search for evidence of continuity within the literature, examples of images, themes, values, and sources of conflict. Comparisons may be made between literature written by members of the cultural group and nonmembers. Examples of literature include:

■ Chief Jake Swamp's *Giving Thanks: A Native American Good Morning Message* (1995) is a message of peace and appreciation for Mother Earth in picture book format. I: 5–8.

■ George Littlechild"s *This Land Is My Land* (1993) by Cree author and illustrator presents the importance of nature and the ancestors in picture book format. I: 8+.

■ Virginia Driving Hawk Sneve's *Dancing Teepees: Poems of American Indian Youth* (1989) includes both ancient and contemporary poems from various locations. I: all.

■ White Deer of Autumn's *Ceremony—In the Circle of Life* (1983) provides an excellent text for showing the comparisons in values between folklore and realistic fiction. I: all.

■ Older students may read and analyze Jamake Highwater's Ghost Horse cycle, which traces three generations of a Great Plains family in *Legend Days* (1984), *The Ceremony of Innocence* (1985), and *I Wear the Morning Star* (1986). I: 12+.

Students may conclude their study of Native American literature by tracing the threads that emerged across the various genres of literature. They should consider what they have discovered about a people and the literature that formulate their foundations.

Examples of Literature for African American Study Presented by Phases

The same approach is used for the study of African and African American literature. Examples of the literature for each phase include the following:

PHASE I: AFRICAN ROOTS THROUGH TRADITIONAL LITERATURE   Nelson Mandela's *Nelson Mandela's Favorite African Folktales* (2002) retells 32 folktales from various African countries. The text includes a map that shows the location of each tale.

■ Verna Aardema's *Who's in Rabbit's House?* (1977) and *Anansi Does the Impossible: An Ashanti Tale* (1997) are trickster tales that show how the smallest beings can outwit those that are much larger. I: 4–8.

■ Verna Aardema's *How the Ostrich Got Its Long Neck* (1995) is a pourquoi tale that explains why an animal has certain characteristics. I: 4–8.

■ Ashley Bryan's *Beat the Story-Drum, PumPum* (1980) is a collection of stories several of which explain animal characteristics. I: all.

■ Ann Griffalconi's *The Village of Round and Square Houses* (1986) reveals how a social custom began in which women and children live in the round house and men live in the square house. I: 4–9.

- Gerald McDermott's *Zomo the Rabbit: A Trickster Tale from West Africa* (1992). I: 4–9.
- Aaron Shepard's *Master Man: A Tall Tale of Nigeria* (2001). I: all.

PHASE II: EXTENSION OF TALES INTO FOLKLORE OF THE AMERICAN SOUTH

- Virginia Hamilton's *The People Could Fly: American Black Folktales* (1985). I: 9+.
- Joel Chandler Harris's *Jump! The Adventures of Brer Rabbit*, adapted by Van Dyke Parks (1986) and *Jump Again! More Adventures of Brer Rabbit* (1986); *The Tales of Uncle Remus: The Adventures of Brer Rabbit*, retold by Julius Lester (1987) and *More Tales of Uncle Remus: Further Adventures of Brer Rabbit* (1988). I: all.
- Robert D. San Souci's *The Talking Eggs: A Folktale from the American South* (1989) and *The Faithful Friend* (1995). I: all.
- Steven Sanfield's *The Adventures of High John the Conqueror* (1989). I: 8+.

PHASE III: HISTORICAL BIOGRAPHIES AND NONFICTION

- David A. Adler's *A Picture Book of George Washington Carver* (1999). I: 7–9.
- Raymond Bial's *The Underground Railroad* (1995) includes first-person accounts. I: 9+.
- Tonya Bolden's *Maritcha: A Nineteenth-Century Girl* (2005). I: 9+.
- Jeri Ferris's *Go Free or Die: A Story about Harriet Tubman* (1988). I: 7–9.
- Jean Fritz's *Harriet Beecher Stowe and the Beecher Preachers* (1994). I: 8–12.
- Virginia Hamilton's *Anthony Burns: The Defeat and Triumph of a Fugitive Slave* (1988) and *Many Thousand Gone: African Americans from Slavery to Freedom* (1993). I: 8–12.
- Milton Meltzer's *The Black Americans: A History in Their Own Words, 1619–1983* (1984). I: 10+.
- Marilyn Nelson's *Carver: A Life in Poems* (2001). I: 10+.
- Marilyn Nelson's *A Wreath for Emmett Till* (2005). I: 10+.

PHASE IV: HISTORICAL FICTION

- Monjo's *The Drinking Gourd* (1970) is a story about the Underground Railroad written for younger students. I: 7–9.
- Gary Paulsen's *Nightjohn* (1993), set in the time of slavery; a slave teaches children to read. I: 10+.
- Mildred Taylor's *Roll of Thunder, Hear My Cry* (1976) and *Let the Circle Be Unbroken* (1981) are set in Mississippi during Segregation. I: 10+.

PHASE V: CONTEMPORARY POETRY, BIOGRAPHY, NONFICTION, AND FICTION

- Choose poetry selections by Langston Hughes, Gwendolyn Brooks, Tom Feelings, and Eloise Greenfield

- There are numerous biographies of Martin Luther King. Also biographies of Barbara Jordan, Malcolm X, and Langston Hughes
- Lynne Barasch's *Knockin' On Wood: Starring Peg Leg Bates* (2004). I: 6–9.
- Tonya Bolden's *Wake Up Our Souls: A Celebration of Black American Artists* (2004). I: 10+.
- John Duggleby's *Story Painter: The Life of Jacob Lawrence* (1998). I: all.
- Carol Fenner's *Yolanda's Genius* (1995). I: 10+.
- Russell Freedman's *The Voice That Changed a Nation: Marian Anderson and the Struggle for Equal Rights* (2004). I: 10+.
- Niikki Giovanni's *Rosa* (2005) I: all. (The 2006 Caldecott Honor).
- Laban Carrick Hill's *Harlem Stomp! A Cultural History of the Harlem Renaissance* (2003). I: 10+.
- Diane McWhorter's *A Dream of Freedom: The Civil Rights Movement from 1954 to 1968* (2004). I: 10+.
- Tony Morrison's *Remember: The Journey to School Integration* (2004). I: all.

Examples of Literature for Latino Study Presented by Phases

The study of literature from Hispanic areas is more complex than a study of Native American or African American cultures. The literature may be from South America, Cuba, Puerto Rico, Mexico, or the U.S. Southwest. We will begin with the ancient folklore from Aztec and Mayan cultures and then proceed to the newer folktales and tales that reflect interactions with other cultures.

PHASE I: ANCIENT AZTEC AND MAYAN FOLKLORE

- John Bierhorst's *The Monkey's Haircut and Other Stories Told by the Maya* (1986) I: 8+.
- Vivien Blackmore's *Why Corn Is Golden: Stories about Plants* (1984). I: all.
- Shana Greger's *The Fifth and Final Sun: An Ancient Aztec Myth of the Sun's Origin* (1994). I: 8–10.
- "Four Creations to Make Man: Maker and Feathered Serpent the Creators," in Virginia Hamilton's *In the Beginning: Creation Stories from around the World* (1988). I: all.
- Deborah Lattimore's *The Flame of Peace: A Tale of the Aztecs* (1987). I: all.
- Gerald McDermott's *Musicians of the Sun* (1997). I: all.

PHASE II: NARROWING THE SELECTIONS TO NEWER LATINO FOLKTALES AND TALES THAT REFLECT INTERACTIONS WITH OTHER CULTURES

- Verna Aardema's *The Riddle of the Drum: A Tale from Tizapan, Mexico* (1979). I: 6–10.
- John Bierhorst's *Doctor Coyote: A Native American Aesop's Fables* (1987) is translated from an Aztec manuscript, and *Spirit Child: A Story of the Nativity* (1984). I: all.

- Tomie dePaola's *The Lady of Guadalupe* (1980). This is one of the most popular books with Mexican American students. I: all.

- Joe Hayes's *El Cucuy: A Bogeyman Cuento in English and Spanish* (2001); *Pajaro Verde: The Green Bird* (2002); and *Tell Me A Cuento: Four Stories in English and Spanish* (1998). I: all.

- Harriet Rohmer, Octavio Chow, and Morris Vidaure's *The Invisible Hunters* (1987) reflects the impact of the first European traders. Told in both English and Spanish. I: all.

- Harriet Rohmer and Dorminster Wilson's *Mother Scorpion Country* (1987) is written in both English and Spanish. I: all.

PHASE III: NONFICTION LITERATURE FROM HISTORICAL PERSPECTIVES

- Milton Meltzer's *The Hispanic Americans* (1982). I: 9–12.

- Carolyn Meyer and Charles Gallenkamp's *The Mystery of the Ancient Maya* (1985). I: 10+.

- Johan Reinhard's *Discovering the Inca Ice Maiden: My Adventures on Ampato* (1998). I: 8+.

PHASE IV: HISTORICAL FICTION

- Sid Fleischman's *Bandit's Moon* (1998) is set during the California Gold Rush. I: 8+.

- Scott O'Dell's *The Captive* (1979), *The Feathered Serpent* (1981), and *The Amethyst Ring* (1983) are set during the Spanish conquest of Mexico in the early 1500s. I: 10+.

- Scott O'Dell's *The King's Fifth* (1966) tells the story of Coronado and the conquistadors as they search for the cities of gold in the American Southwest. I: 10+.

PHASE V: CONTEMPORARY LATINO LITERATURE

Picture Storybooks:

- Diane Gonzales Bertrand's *Uncle Chente's Picnic* (2001) is written in English and Spanish. I: 6–10.

- Monica Brown's *My Name Is Gabriela: The Life of Gabriela Mistral* (2005) is written in English and Spanish. I: 4–8.

- Rebecca Emberley's *Let's Go: A Book in Two Languages* (1993) and *My Day: A Book in Two Languages* (1993) are written for beginning readers and emerging literacy. I: 4–8.

- Richard Garcia's *My Aunt Otilia's Spirits* (1987). I: 5–8.

- Pat Mora's *The Bakery Lady* (2001) is written in English and Spanish, and *Thomas and the Library Lady* 1997). I: 7–10.

- Leo Politi's *Song of the Swallows* (1949). I: 5–8.

Middle and Upper Elementary:

- Sandra Cisneros's *The House on Mango Street* (1983). I: 12+.

- Joseph Krumgold's *. . . And Now Miguel* (1953) is the story of a ranching family in New Mexico. I: 10+.

- Nicholasa Mohr's *Felita* (1979) set in a Puerto Rican neighborhood in New York and *Going Home* (1986) when she returns to Puerto Rico. I: 9+.

- Gary Paulsen's *The Crossing* (1987). I: 12+.

- Pam Muñoz Ryan's *Becoming Naomi León* (2004) is about a girl who discovers her Mexican heritage when she visits Mexico.

- Gary Soto's *Baseball in April and Other Stories* (1990), *Big Bushy Mustache* (1998), *Chato and the Party Animals* (2000), Taking *Sides* (1991), and *Pacific Crossing* (1992). Gary Soto is one of the most popular authors with older readers. I: 8+.

Examples of Literature for Asian American Study Presented by Phases

There are several Asian cultures that may be studied. The literatures that include the most examples are Chinese, Japanese, and stories from India. There is considerable folklore published in highly illustrated texts from each of these cultures. There are also examples that include collections of tales told by Chinese Americans.

PHASE I: FOLKLORE FROM ASIA

- Marilee Heyer's *The Weaving of a Dream: A Chinese Folktale* (1986). I: 8+.

- Eric Kimmel's *Ten Suns: A Chinese Legend* (1998). I: 6–10.

- Margaret Mahy's *The Seven Chinese Brothers* (1990). I: 5–8.

- Neil Philip's *The Spring of Butterflies and Other Chinese Folktales* (1986). I: 9+.

- Katherine Paterson's *The Tale of the Mandarin Ducks* (1990), a Japanese tale. I: 5–10.

- Anne Laurin's *The Perfect Crane* (1981), a Japanese tale. I: 5–9.

- Robert D. San Souci's *The Samurai's Daughter: A Japanese Legend* (1992) I: 5–8.

- Ed Young's *The Lost Horse* (1998) and *Lon Po Po: A Red-Riding Hood Story from China* (1989). I: all.

PHASE II: ASIAN AMERICAN FOLKLORE

- Paul Yee's *Tales from Gold Mountain: Stories of the Chinese in the New World* (1990). I: 10+.

- Laurence Yep's *The Rainbow People* (1989), a collection of twenty tales collected from Chinese Americans. I: 9+.

PHASE III: HISTORICAL NONFICTION

- Rhoda Blumberg's *Commodore Perry in the Land of the Shogun* (1985) follows Perry's attempts to open Japan to U.S. trade. I: 8+.

- Russell Freedman's *Confucius: The Golden Rule* (2002), a biography. I: all.
- Paul Strathern's *Exploration by Land: The Silk and Spice Routes* (1994) presents information about the ancient routes linking China with the West. I: 9+.

PHASE IV: HISTORICAL FICTION

- Erik Christian Haugaard's *The Boy and the Samurai* (1991), set in Japan during the 1400s and 1500s. I: 10+.
- Adeline Yen Mah's *Chinese Cinderella and the Secret Dragon Society* (2005) is set in China, 1937–1945. I: 10+.
- Jean Merrill's *The Girl Who Loved Caterpillars* (1992) is a picture book set in twelfth-century Japan. I: 5–8.
- Linda Sue Park's *A Single Shard* (2001), set in 12th-century Korea.
- Allen Say's *Grandfather's Journey* (1993) is a picture storybook set during the time of early immigration. I: all.
- Jeff Stone's *Tiger: The Five Ancestors* (2005) is set in time of warrior monks. I: 10+.
- Laurence Yep's *Dragon's Gate* (1993), set in the Sierra Nevada mountains in 1867 during the time of building the transcontinental railroad, and *Dragon's Wings* (1973), set in 1903 San Francisco. I: 10+.

PHASE V: CONTEMPORARY ASIAN AND ASIAN AMERICAN LITERATURE

- Sherry Garland's *The Lotus Seed* (1993). A Vietnamese family resettles in the United States. I: 5–8.
- Cynthia Kadohata's *Kira-Kira* (2004) is a Japanese American story about friendship. I: 10+.
- Tatsuharu Kodama's *Shin's Tricycle* (1995) relates a true experience during World War II. I: all.
- Lensey Namioka's *Yang the Youngest and His Terrible Ear* (1995). I: 8–12.
- Pegi Deitz Shea's *Tangled Threads: A Hmong Girls Story*. (2003). I: 10+.
- Jerry Stanley's *I Am an American: A True Story of Japanese Internment* (1994). I: 10+.
- Ian Wallace's *Chin Chiang and the Dragon's Dance* (1984). I: 5–8.
- Kate Waters and Madeline Slovenz-Low's *Lion Dancer: Ernie Wan's Chinese New Year* (1990) is set in Vancouver. I: 5–8.
- Gloria Whelan's *Homeless Bird* (2000), set in modern India. I: 10+.
- Laurence Yep's *The Amah* (1999), *Child of the Owl* (1975), *Later, Gater* (1995), *Star Fisher* (1991), and *Thief of Hearts* (1995). I: 10+.

Instructional Strategies Used with Multicultural Literature

When using the multicultural literature listed under the five phases, teachers may develop inquiry units around specific themes that allow students to conduct in-depth studies of a culture, or they may choose to study a portion of the literature and focus on shorter lesson plans and strategies that take less time to complete. We begin with a focus unit and then include additional activities that may be used with each phase. Remember that the general practices identified for the effective instruction of ELL students (Garcia, 1991; Thorp, 1997) emphasized instruction in basic skills and academic content organized around thematic units, instruction that is intellectually challenging, and teachers engage students through questioning and sharing ideas and knowledge. These instructional goals are developed through units that study various cultural groups.

DEVELOPING UNITS STUDYING ONE OF THE CULTURAL GROUPS   The multicultural literature listed earlier in this chapter provides an excellent source for developing units of study. Units are also one of the effective strategies for providing instruction for ELL students, bilingual, and ESL students.

FOCUS UNIT:
A Multicultural Literature Study

OBJECTIVES	1. To develop an understanding of one of the cultural groups (African American, Native American, Latino, or Asian American 2. To identify values and beliefs first developed through the oral tradition and identify cultural threads that are also found in contemporary works 3. To increase self-understanding of members of a cultural group 4. To increase respect among and between cultural groups 5. To increase comprehension abilities and reading skills through an inquiry activity
GRADE LEVELS	Grades two through eight. (The grade level depends on the interest levels of the materials selected for study.)
MATERIALS	Choose materials appropriate for the cultural group identified by the students and teacher. The list of sources under "Multicultural Literature" provides many examples.
PROCEDURES	1. The research method or inquiry approach discussed in Chapter 8 in "Developing Research Skills for Reading in Content Areas" may be used in this unit. (Before developing the unit review this inquiry approach that progresses from choosing a topic and formulating questions, to planning the investigation, to gathering and locating the resources, to sorting the information and deciding which information helps answer the main questions, to synthesizing and organizing the information needed to answer questions, to evaluating the study, and finally to presenting the final report.) 2. Begin the unit by involving students in the selection of the cultural group to be studied. Develop a chart that includes "topic to be

covered," "what we know about the topic," and "questions we want to investigate." Brainstorm with the students to fill in the chart. This chart expands as students begin their study and identify further questions to investigate.

3. If following the five-phase study of a culture, begin Phase I by collecting as many traditional tales as you can find (folktales, myths, and legends.) Make sure that students understand that these traditional tales were handed down by word of mouth through storytellers. Also, these early stories were told to the people as a way to pass on their values and beliefs. Locate the sources of the traditional tales on a map.

4. As students read the traditional tales they search for the traditional values and beliefs reflected in the tales. Share with them information that the rewards and punishments developed in folklore usually reflect what behaviors are valued and what behaviors the people reject. One way to make comparisons is to have the students fill in a chart such as the one in Table 10.2.

5. Students can summarize information about values and beliefs discovered by reading numerous tales. Which values and beliefs are found in several literature selections? Why do the students believe that the values and beliefs would be important to the people? What do these values and beliefs reveal about the people?

6. An oral storytelling activity may be part of phase one. Students select literature and prepare it for an oral presentation that might be similar to one found in the early culture. They should prepare the story, develop an introduction to the story, and share the story orally.

7. Now students focus on a narrower selection of folklore. If they started with African folklore, have them expand to African American folklore, or Native American folklore from a specific region, or

TABLE 10.2

Comparing Values and Beliefs in Folklore from _____ People

Title of Tale:	Questions:	Answers:
	1. What is the major problem?	1.
	2. What reward is desired by the _____ people?	2.
	3. What actions are rewarded or admired by the people?	3.
	4. What rewards are given to the heroes, heroines, or great people?	4.
	5. What are the personal characteristics of the heroes, heroines, or great people?	5.

Latino folklore from the Southwest, or Chinese American tales. They can expand their charts for values and beliefs and compare the stories in the Phase I with stories in Phase II. What are the similarities and differences? Why would there be similarities? Why might there be differences?

8. For Phase III have students search for evidence that the values and beliefs depicted in the folklore are also depicted in biographies and autobiographies. Do the values, beliefs, and philosophies appear to be authentic? Have students use nonfiction information texts to evaluate the authenticity of biographies. If possible, they may compare biographies and autobiographies written about the same person. Are the settings, dates, conflicts, characterizations similar in several sources?

9. For Phase IV have students read, analyze, and evaluate historical fiction according to authenticity of setting, credibility of conflict, believability of characterization, authenticity of traditional beliefs expressed by the characters, and appropriateness of themes and author's style.

10. For Phase V have students read, analyze, and evaluate contemporary poetry, fiction, and biography. Ask them to search for evidence of continuity within the literature, examples of images, themes, values, and sources of conflict. Comparisons may be made between literature written by members of the cultural group and nonmembers.

11. Ask students to summarize their findings about the cultural group. If they are working in groups, each group can review whatever questions they answered. Are there questions that still need to be investigated? How would they investigate those questions?

ADDITIONAL ACTIVITIES TO BE USED WITH VARIOUS PHASES This type of study and unit lends itself to numerous activities.

To reinforce learnings from Phase I:

1. Select one of the folktales and prepare it as a play.
2. Draw a semantic map of the cultural information discovered.
3. Collect as many trickster tales as possible, and compare the tales according to Native American tribe or cultural group.
4. Investigate the illustrations in a heavily illustrated book. How is the culture reflected in the illustrations?

To reinforce learnings from Phase II:

1. Create a museum that shows important artifacts from the cultural groups that influenced the folklore.
2. Select music that reflects the culture and play the music to accompany a reading of a folktale from the culture.
3. Choose a folktale that is not illustrated and draw the illustrations that might accompany the folktale.

4. If studying Native American cultures, compare the tales from the Northwest and the Southwest. What are the similarities and differences among the tales? Have students investigate how the geography of the regions might influence the tales.

To reinforce learnings from Phase III:

1. Interview several families who are members of the culture. Develop a history of the people that reflects the earlier experiences of family members.

2. Compare biographies written for students in the first and second grades with biographies written for students in the upper elementary and middle school. What are the differences in the biographies? What accounts for those differences?

3. Develop a time line of famous personages from the culture.

4. Create a collage depicting the history of the culture.

To reinforce learnings from Phase IV:

1. Write a sequel to an historical fiction text.

2. As a creative writing and art activity, choose a character who might have lived during the period and develop a story about his or her life. Illustrate the story with historically appropriate drawings.

3. Investigate the life and writings of one of the award-winning authors of historical fiction. Why did the author choose the subject? What research did the author conduct to develop authentic settings and conflicts?

4. Conduct a television or radio interview in which the students go back in time and interview one of the characters in historical fiction. What questions would they ask the characters? What answers might the characters give?

To reinforce learnings from Phase V:

1. After reading a biography about an athlete, a scientist, or an author who is a member of the culture, conduct a library search to discover records set by the athlete, discoveries made by the scientist, or literature written by the author.

2. Choose a book written about a contemporary member of the cultural group and ask students to compare their own lives with the lives of the person profiled in the book.

3. Several books about contemporary cultures develop family pictures. Develop a class scrapbook showing family pictures and have each child tell a story about growing up in his or her own family.

4. Write a poem that reflects what students have learned about a culture.

These activities may become part of a unit on the culture. Consequently, units provide many opportunities for students to reinforce literacy skills as well as

make discoveries about other cultures. Activities such as writing critical reviews of the literature found in any of the phases encourage students to make comparisons of the literature and to develop higher levels of comprehension and study skills required to write the critical reviews. Ideally, students will develop understandings of other cultures or of their own culture.

Using Technology to Learn about the Latino Culture

Web sites provide additional sources for conducting research about a culture. The following Web sites provide information for researching the ancient and contemporary Latino cultures:

Ancient Observations:

- Chichen Itza: www.exploratorium.edu/ancientobs/chichen/index.html. Exploratorium. The site includes a tour of Mayan ruins and history of the ancient Maya, as well as maps and mythology. Grades 5 and up.

- ArchaeOlog: www.olog.amnh.org/archaeology/index.html. American Museum of Natural History. The site takes viewers on an "Inca Investigation" and they may use an interactive map of Peru's Huanuco Pampa. Grades 3–8.

Hispanic Heritage:

- Celebrate Hispanic Heritage: www.teacher.scholastic.com/activities/hispanicindex.htm. Scholastic. The site includes Hispanic history in the Americas through biographies, interactive maps, and time lines. Grades 2–8.

- Celebrate Hispanic Heritage Month with the National Register of Historic Places: www.cr.nps.gov/nr/feature/hispanic. National Park Service. Includes parks, monuments, and trails as well as social studies lesson plans. Grades 6 and up.

- Cinco De Mayo: A Celebration of Mexican Heritage: www2.worldbook.com/we/features/cinco/html/cinco.htm. World Book. The site includes facts for students who are conducting research in areas such as "History of Mexico" and "Hispanic Americans." Grades 4 and up.

- Hispanic Reading Room: www.loc.gov/rr/hispanic. The Library of Congress site presents primary-source materials such as manuscripts and photographs related to the Hispanic culture. Grades 8 and up.

- Learn About Flamenco!: www.si.umich.edu/CHICO/flamenco. Culural Heritage Initiative Community Outreach. The site includes audio components and graphics that encourage interaction with the rhythms. Grades 3 and up.

These Web sites provide additional sources of materials for studying the Latino culture. They may also provide materials that may be used to authenticate specific pieces of literature.

Reflect on Your Reading

Why is it important to select multicultural literature that is authentic for the culture? What is the message given to students if the literature is not authentic? When selecting activities to accompany the literature, is it important to develop activities that enhance students' abilities to make discoveries about the culture? How does an inquiry method add to the multicultural understandings and comprehension skills of the students?

Up for Discussion

Issues Related to Multicultural Literature

Have multicultural literature books changed in the last twenty years? What would be the impact of a shortage of multicultural books for elementary students? What would be the impact of a shortage of books about a culture for ELL students? What would be the impact of the books if they were filled with negative stereotypes of the cultures? These are questions that educators have discussed and debated during the past twenty years. The availability of multicultural literature has changed dramatically since Nancy Larrick's, "The All-White World of Children's Books" (1965) in which she found a shortage of books that reflected other cultures. She reported a lack of books about minorities and that the few available books were filled with stereotypes. How do you think this shortage of books would affect teaching cultural diversity or ESL or bilingual students?

Students use both newspapers and computers to gain background knowledge

Several educators conducted studies in the 1970s and 1980s and found not only a shortage of books, but negative stereotypes in much of the available literature. For example, Dorothy May Broderick (1971) analyzed books published before the late 1960s and found the following stereotypes of African Americans:

1. The people are not physically attractive.
2. The people are musical.
3. The people combine religious fervor and superstitious beliefs.
4. The people are required to select goals that benefit African American people.
5. The people are dependent on white people for whatever good things they acquire.

If all the literature you read about African Americans contained these stereotypes, what would your attitude be toward African American people? If you are an African American student and this is the only literature you read about your own people, what would be your level of self-esteem?

Locate books in the library that were written before the 1970s and compare the books with the newer ones among the multicultural literature lists found in this chapter. Are the same stereotypes found in the newer books? Why do you believe that the stereotypes are no longer found in most of the newer books? What was the influence of authors such as Nancy Larrick? Can you locate this influence in the numbers of multicultural literature books with later publication dates?

Students with Special Needs in Reading

When elementary programs are evaluated, reading achievement, either excellent or below normal, is almost always cited. Success in learning to read is usually associated with school achievement. The majority of referrals for learning difficulties in elementary grades result from problems learning to read.

The terms used for students with special needs in reading and the programs identified to correct those needs also change over time. The "Read All About It!" feature at the beginning of this chapter discussed both inclusion and mainstreaming.

One way to identify current terms is to search through reading journals to locate terms that are used by writers of articles published in the journals. By looking at articles in *The Reading Teacher* published between 2001 and 2004, for example, we discover these terms used to describe students with special needs in reading: students at risk, struggling readers, students with learning disabilities or learning difficulties, students with cognitive difficulties, remedial readers, students with memory deficiencies, and students who lack linguistic sophistication. The programs that are recommended for the students include terms such as intervention programs, focusing on student learning outcomes, corrective reading instruction, remedial reading instruction, instruction matched to academic needs, and programs that enrich the environments of at-risk students.

Whatever terminology is used the articles usually include two types of information: characteristics of students that affect reading development and instructional approaches that are effective for overcoming the reading difficulties of students who have those characteristics. Notice how the following review of research associated with students with reading difficulties identified by Chall and Curtis (2003) includes both the characteristics of and the approaches for overcoming reading difficulties:

> What we need to remember is that the vast majority of children who lag behind in reading can be helped, whether they are behind because of a less academically stimulating home or school environment or because of a learning difficulty that may or may not be neurologically based. The research on both groups of children points to the benefits of instruction that is designed to raise their level of reading development . . . For children who are at risk of reading failure, a more formal, direct kind of instruction—aimed at building on their strengths while addressing their needs—has been shown to be the most beneficial (p. 418).

This chapter covers both some of the characteristics of students that have special needs and suggestions for helping students with those characteristics overcome their reading difficulties.

Characteristics of Students with Special Needs in Reading and Approaches for Intervention

Overcoming reading problems is a complex task. If it were not there would be no outcry when schools do not reach specified achievement levels in reading. Unfortunately, there is not a "one size fits all" approach to helping students with special needs in reading. Instead, instruction needs to match children's academic needs. For example, if students show deficiencies in comprehension, they may need instruction that helps them comprehend text structures and word meanings or provides extensive background knowledge before they read. If they have weak decoding abilities they may need specific techniques to improve their word-attack skills.

Table 10.3 outlines characteristics of students and identifies some of the teaching strategies and techniques that have been used effectively to overcome the difficulties. Remember that all students with reading difficulties do not have all of these characteristics. It is important for teachers to identify the types of reading difficulties and then provide instruction that allows students to overcome the problems. As you read through the

TABLE 10.3

Characteristics of Students with Reading Difficulties and Intervention Strategies

Characteristics of Students	Intervention Strategies
1. Phonemic discrimination problems may be reflected in spelling difficulties (Joseph, 1999; Zutell, 1998).	Use word boxes to help children match sounds to print (Joseph, 1999). Use word sorting techniques (Zutell, 1998).
2. Weakness in recognizing high-frequency words (Cunningham & Allington, 2003)	Use "Word Walls" to improve reading and writing of high-frequency words (Cunningham & Allington, 2003).
3. Weakness in comprehension of text (Lubliner, 2004). Inability to make inferences (Dewitz & Dewitz, 2003)	Teach students to generate main-idea questions (Lubliner, 2004). Model strategy instruction (Dewitz & Dewitz, 2003).
4. Weakness in word meanings and background knowledge (Curtis, 1996)	In high-poverty schools, focus on student learning outcomes and reading success (Adler & Fisher, 2001).
5. Difficulty with reading fluency and automatic word recognition (Stahl & Kuhn, 2002)	Encourage reading aloud from a variety of familiar materials, stress comprehension in the content areas, use assisted reading and modeling (Stahl & Kuhn, 2002).
6. Problems comprehending narrative themes and figurative language (Schmidt et al., 2002)	Use inquiry learning to assist in developing literacy (Schmidt, et al., 2002). Use picture books and mental imagery (Hibbing & Rankin-Erickson 2003).
7. Lack of linguistic sophistication as shown in short, simple sentences (Lerner, 2000)	Use sentence expansion techniques, oral language activities such as role playing, storytelling, and puppetry (Lerner, 2000).
8. Deficiencies in memory (Lerner, 2000)	Help students organize materials in logical order, relate new material to what students know, use mnemonic strategies and flannel boards. Teach rhymes and finger plays that encourage auditory memory (Lerner, 2000).

characteristics, notice that students' reading difficulties may be due to a number of different problems. Some relate to difficulties with phonemic awareness, while other problems relate to broader areas of comprehension. All of the studies that identify student characteristics and develop instructional strategies emphasize the importance of identifying student needs and matching the needs to appropriate instruction. In the next section, we will discuss some of the strategies that have been the most successful.

Intervention Strategies for Specific Special Needs

Successful **intervention** strategies have carefully developed instructional objectives that help the students develop their skills and relate the new skills to previous knowledge. Many of these instructional strategies use more direct and explicit instruction than might be needed for students who are not considered at risk. There are also numerous opportunities for students to apply their developing skills through a variety of experiences. Some intervention strategies emphasize the development of a literacy environment that helps students develop important background knowledge and prepares them for reading through the types of activities discussed in Chapter 2, "Emergent Literacy." The following section is structured according to the characteristics of students and intervention strategies identified in Table 10.3.

PHONEMIC DISCRIMINATION PROBLEMS   Discrimination problems associated with the sounds of letters and words may be caused by difficulties in hearing fine differences of sounds. These difficulties may also cause problems in spelling. Auditory discrimination training may help through the use of rhyming words and other activities suggested under emergent literacy in this text. Laurice Joseph (1999) recommends using word boxes with children who have difficulty hearing the order of sounds in words. This approach is based on one used in the Reading Recovery program as it helps children attend to orthographic features as they write the letters of a word in their proper sequence. The approach develops phonemic awareness, word identification, and spelling skills.

To develop a word box:

- Draw a rectangle and divide it into sections corresponding to the sounds heard in the word.

- Place a picture of the word at the top of the rectangle.

- Place counters below the divided sections on the rectangle.

- Have the child say the word slowly as he or she places the counters in their appropriate sections.

- Magnetic letters then replace the counters, and the child places the letters onto the appropriate spaces in the word boxes.

- Have the child spell the word by writing the letters in the respective spaces on the word box.

The use of magnetic letters and writing letters in the boxes helps students process the visual patterns in words. Figure 10.1 shows a word box that might accompany the word *cat*.

Joseph recommends extending the use of word boxes through the use of a "Word Wall" of words that share similar spelling patterns and drawing boxes around each letter or letter combinations that represent the sound pattern. For example, a word wall for *cat* could include the *at* family of rhyming words. To create a word wall for *cat* use a large sheet of paper and write the words that have the *at* spelling pattern under the word *cat*. Directions for developing a word wall follow in the next section.

WEAKNESS IN RECOGNIZING HIGH-FREQUENCY WORDS   High-frequency words are those words found many times in most beginning basal readers and other reading materials. Cunningham and Allington (2003) observe that many struggling readers have difficulty recognizing high-frequency words such as *was, the,* and *what* because the words are not logically spelled. They recommend "doing" a word wall versus "having" a word wall with struggling readers because having a word wall frequently means that the words are listed but not used by the students. For Cunningham and Allington, "doing a word wall" means

FIGURE 10.1

A Word Box for *Cat*

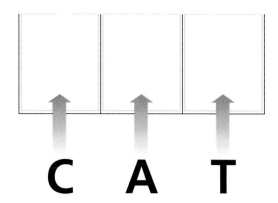

- Limiting the words to those most commonly needed by students in their reading and writing.

- Adding words gradually—about five a week.

- Making the words very accessible and writing them in big letters.

- Using a variety of colors so that words such as *that, them,* and *this* are not confused.

- Practicing the words by chanting and writing the words because struggling readers are not good visual learners and cannot just look at and remember words.

- Doing a variety of review activities to provide practice so that words are read and spelled instantly and automatically.

- Making sure that word-wall words are spelled correctly by the students when they do writing activities.

The selection of the words for the word wall may be chosen from the high-frequency words taught in a basal reader or from literature selections that children are reading. Words are placed on the wall alphabetically under the appropriate letter of the alphabet. When confusing words are added, they should be written on different colored paper. Cunningham and Allington suggest that "most teachers add five new words each week and do at least one daily activity in which the children find, write, and chant the spelling of the words. The activity takes longer on the day that words are added because you will want to take time to make sure that students associate meanings with the words" (p. 41).

To clap, chant, and write words, students number a sheet of paper from 1 to 5. The teacher calls out five words from the word wall, says a sentence for each word, asks a child to find and point to the word on the word wall, and asks all the children to clap and chant the spelling. Then the five words are written on the paper after which a child spells the words as the students check their own spellings and correct any misspellings.

Other activities to use with the word wall include asking students to locate words that rhyme with _____, using sentences with missing words that are completed with words from the word wall, thinking of a word and providing clues to the word's identity, and developing writing activities that require students to use the word wall. The word wall in this case becomes a dictionary.

WEAKNESS IN COMPREHENSION OF TEXT   Struggling readers may be able to read the words but not understand or comprehend what they read. Problems in reading comprehension have been noted by many teachers and researchers. The inability to make inferences is frequently noted in students with comprehension problems and intervention programs may be developed to try to overcome that problem.

Peter and Pamela Dewitz (2003) found that a modeling strategy helped students make inferences. For struggling readers, they recommend a direct explanation and modeling of the inferential process by the teacher. As teachers read, they show where they made specific connections to help them understand the text. Where important details are linked to main ideas, where connections are made to prior knowledge, or where any other connections help them construct meaning from the text. Teachers think aloud and describe their own thinking process behind their reading. They state, "Talking about text characteristics is essential because teachers and students need to know when to make a specific type of connection. (See a modeling of inferential comprehension developed in Chapter 6, "Developing Approaches for Fluency and Comprehension." The chapter includes a modeling lesson using similes for lower elementary students and a modeling lesson for inferencing characterization with students in the upper grades.)

WEAKNESS IN WORD MEANINGS AND BACKGROUND KNOWLEDGE   Struggling readers may have difficulty because they lack background knowledge. Students in high-poverty schools and neighborhoods may not have the literacy experiences that foster reading achievement (Curtis, 1996). Data from the National Assessment of Educational Progress (1999) shows large differences in reading performance related to students' poverty levels. Fortunately, all schools with students below the poverty level are not failing in reading. Reading researchers are looking closely at high-poverty schools where students succeed and drawing conclusions about what makes the schools successful.

For example, Martha Adler and Charles Fisher (2001) asked the questions, "What do early reading programs look like in high-poverty, high-performing schools? How have these schools allocated resources to develop, implement, and sustain their early reading programs?" (p. 617). They report several key features in a program with both high poverty levels and high-performing schools:

1. There is a strong focus on student learning outcomes. The school climate is learning-oriented. In the early reading program, the teachers expect that students will learn to read.

2. There are multiple reading programs in every classroom. Teachers use such varied approaches as direct instruction of phonics, phonemic awareness, vocabulary development, and guided reading and writing. "They do not allow themselves to become locked into a "one size fits all" solution." (p. 617)

3. There is a shared responsibility for student success where teachers meet with parents to discuss student progress and share information about student learning outcomes.

4. There is strong leadership through both the principal and classroom teachers.

5. The staff constantly seeks solutions to reading problems. More experienced teachers mentor new teachers.

DIFFICULTY WITH READING FLUENCY AND AUTOMATIC WORD RECOGNITION

Why is fluency and automatic word recognition so important? How do students make the transition from decoding to fluent reading? Reading researchers Steven Stahl and Melanie Kuhn (2002) investigated reading fluency and concluded:

> We know what does not work. The "round robin" reading of our childhood, in which children take turns reading in a group, leads to a great deal of wasted classroom time, because children who are not reading look ahead, daydream, or engage in otherwise nonprint-related activities. Inviting children to read on their own also does not work, because children tend to be on task less and read less challenging materials. To develop fluency, we need teacher-directed lessons in which children spend the maximum amount of time engaged in reading-connected text. (p. 582)

Struggling readers benefit from assisted reading in which they read aloud from a variety of familiar materials. They need opportunities to read with partners to increase the time spent reading in school. Teachers stress comprehension in the content areas and use modeling to demonstrate fluency in reading.

LACK OF LINGUISTIC SOPHISTICATION   When students' own writing is characterized by short, simple sentences, they may have difficulty either comprehending longer sentences or developing their own writing that uses complex sentences (Lerner, 2000). Oral language activities such as role-playing, storytelling, and puppetry help students expand their own language. Sentence expansion techniques help them develop more sophisticated sentences (Lerner, 2000).

To develop sentence expansion activities with lower elementary students start with simple sentences such as "Carolyn rode her bicycle." Then ask the students specific questions that could be used to expand information in the sentence such as, "How did Carolyn ride her bicycle?" If students say slowly or rapidly add the words to the sentence. Now the sentence becomes, "Carolyn rode her bicycle rapidly." Next they might want to consider, "Where did Carolyn ride her bicycle?" If they say, "To the store," this can be added to the sentence so it reads, "Carolyn rode her bicycle rapidly to the store." Finally, they might consider, "Why did she want to go to the store?" If the answer is to buy a loaf of bread, the expanded sentence becomes "Carolyn rode her bicycle rapidly to the store to buy a loaf of bread." This technique can be used as students add information to a simple sentence that includes information about *who, what, when, where, how,* and *why.*

Reflect on Your Reading

Why is it so important that the educators realize that "one size fits all" is not appropriate when teaching reading to students with special needs? Why might an approach that focuses on letter-sound relationships not be the best reading approach for a students whose main difficulty is with comprehension? In contrast, why might an approach that emphasizes only comprehension not be appropriate for a student who is having difficulty decoding words? When you are teaching, how will you provide instruction for students who have reading difficulties?

DEFICIENCIES IN MEMORY CAUSE DIFFICULTIES IN ORGANIZING MATERIALS
Lerner (2000) found that deficiencies in memory cause difficulty when students try to organize materials in logical order. To help students organize materials Lerner recommends teaching students to look for clues in writing such as first, second, and third to help them comprehend organization. Strategies such as using flannel boards to retell stories and plot structures help students organize and remember what is read. Teaching rhymes and finger plays also encourages auditory memory as well as developing emergent literacy. The pictures in wordless books are especially good for helping students organize a story in a logical sequence.

DIFFERENTIATING INSTRUCTION

ELL Students

This chapter has discussed the most effective programs for teaching students whose first language is not English. In addition to using strategies such as the language experience approach, shared readings, and numerous oral language activities that expand vocabularies, ELL students benefit from being involved in reading and oral language activities that focus on their culture and allow them to share their backgrounds with other students.

Some of my university students who are preparing to teach have developed a storytelling activity with elementary students around an experience in Pat Mora's *Tomas and the Library Lady* (1997). In this Latino picture book, Papa Grande tells traditional stories to his grandson, Tomas. He tells Tomas that there are many other stories in the library and that Tomas should read the stories and then tell the stories to his family.

This source provides a motivational activity for creating a storytelling incident as well as locating additional stories. Several students who speak Spanish also interviewed older members of the Latino community. The students collected the stories and retold them as part of a storytelling concert. Other students read and retold stories found in the library.

Marilyn Carpenter (2006) recommends using poetry written in two languages for ELL students or poems about bilingual experiences. You may use her recommendations for poems that include bilingual poems written in English and Spanish and poems that focus on Korean and Chinese heritage.

Struggling Readers and Writers

Combining literature, drama, and history is a strategy that connects students' comprehension of a text to their own understandings of reading, culture, and history. John Kornfeld and Georgia Leyden (2005) describe how they used a successful five-month-long unit to increase first-grade students' involvement with texts and understanding of history. These educators read and discussed picture books according to three categories:

1. Life and culture in Africa through folktales, history, and geography
2. Slave life in America through picture books that focus on plantation life, slave rebellion, and the Underground Railroad
3. The U.S. civil rights movement

A teacher uses an interest in foods to develop vocabulary comprehension.

through picture-book biographies of Rosa Parks and Martin Luther King Jr.

After reading and discussing the picture books, the class chose several books to perform as plays. They also added backdrops. For example, they retold Aardema's *Who's in Rabbit's House?* In addition to developing the play they created masks that were similar to those worn by the actors in the book. To accompany a play of *I Am Rosa Parks* by Parks and Haskins, students role-played the bus scene from the book.

To develop plays, the teachers assigned parts according to students' requests. They asked questions such as, "What do you think the character would say or do at this point?" (p. 231). Each time they practiced the play, they added new dialogue and actions. The students brainstormed to determine such areas as what props and costumes they needed or what music would help the production. Kornfeld and Leyden identify the reading competencies developed by students as part of the unit:

> Student research was an integral component of all of these endeavors. Students consulted reference books to determine the flora and fauna for the *Who's in Rabbit's House?* backdrop; they searched out further information on the Birmingham, Alabama, bus boycott after reading *I Am Rosa Parks.* . . . Students frequently returned to the texts and pictures of the stories themselves, while listening to and examining other related works of fiction and nonfiction. In their zeal to create the most historically accurate renditions of these stories, the students became fully immersed in all aspects of the productions. (p. 233)

As part of the unit, the teachers included guided reading and writing lessons. Students retold stories, practiced reading the scripts orally, wrote about African American history in their journals, studied logical sequence of cause

and effect in actual historical events, and read and shared numerous books related to the unit.

Does a unit such as this allow teachers to develop the reading standards identified for a specific grade level? Kornfeld and Layden conclude:

> Because they were engaged in authentic tasks that required them to develop and use many literacy skills, students met at least 41 of the 57 English language arts standards of the California State Board of Education for their grade level, as well as many content standards in other subjects read—and with far more zeal than if they had instead been given worksheets to complete. (p. 237)

Gifted and Accelerated Readers and Writers

Many ELL students are also gifted students. They may learn rapidly and enjoy reading more complex books in their native language or they may have special talents in art, music, drama, or creative writing. For example, one group of very gifted Latino students used their knowledge of their culture to create a museum that shows important artifacts from the cultural groups that influence Latino literature. They chose Mayan and Aztec cultures and included drawing of art, clothing, and architecture. They developed an introduction to their museum and created a multicultural festival that included storytelling, music, masks, pottery, and posters depicting cultural history (Norton, 2005).

This type of presentation may accompany the study of any culture. It is especially meaningful if there are students from the culture in the class. Gifted and accelerated students also enjoy reading and discussing books that have hidden symbols related to the culture or themes that are authentic for the culture. One student said, "I enjoy books where the author develops the themes through the actions of the characters. I like to see if the character really knows what it means to be Latino and to live in the culture." The multicultural books identified in this chapter provide many opportunities for students to trace the development of important themes that are meaningful to a culture.

Summary

The number of foreign-born students in schools in America is increasing rapidly. It is projected that there will be an increase of 47 percent in Latino children by 2020. Students whose first language is not English take part in ESL programs or in bilingual programs. Studies provide mixed reviews of which of the programs are the most effective. However, the most effective instructional practices have been identified by the

National Center for Research on Cultural Diversity and Second Language Learning. Helping learners build background knowledge is one of the most important ways for increasing comprehension for what is read. When students draw upon their cultural identities and take part in interactive learning they begin to make connections.

A five-phase study for using multicultural literature focuses on beginning with a study of broad oral traditions, narrows to specific tribal or cultural experiences, continues with a study of biography and autobiography of the culture, extends to historical fiction, and concludes with contemporary writings. Examples of literature that develop each of the five phases include African/African American, Native American, Latino, and Asian/Asian American literature.

Articles that discuss studies of students with special needs in reading usually present characteristics of students that affect their reading development and instructional approaches that are effective for overcoming the reading difficulties of students who have those characteristics. Characteristics of students with reading difficulties include phonemic discrimination problems, weakness in recognizing high-frequency words, weakness in comprehension of text, weakness in word meanings and background knowledge, difficulty with reading fluency and automatic word recognition, problems comprehending narrative themes and figurative language, lack of linguistic sophistication, and deficiencies in memory. There are intervention strategies that help students with these specific special needs.

Reflect on Your Reading

Consider the various literacy skills discussed in this textbook and then review the activities recommended for the unit for struggling readers and writers. Kornfeld and Layden (2005) noted that this unit met at least 41 English language arts standards. What standards would be met by teaching a first-grade unit on African and African American literature and culture?

Key Terms

at-risk students, p. 408

English as a Second Language (ESL), p. 408

English Language Learners (ELL), p. 409

bilingual education, p. 409

multicultural education, p. 420

intervention, p. 439

For video clips of authentic classroom instruction on **Reading Instruction for Diverse Learners**, go to Allyn & Bacon's MyLabSchool.com. In MLS courses, click on Reading Methods, go to MLS Video Lab, and select **Module 9**. Videos on this topic can also be found in the MLS Video Lab for the **English Language Learners** course.

Extend Your Reading

1. The "Read All About It!" article discusses two types of intervention programs: "Inclusion" and "Mainstreaming." Conduct library research to find advocates for each of these programs. What are the advantages and disadvantages of each program?

2. There are issues about the effectiveness of ESL versus bilingual educational programs. Locate articles that discuss each of the programs. Locate any advantages or disadvantages associated with the programs. Try to find research that supports each of the programs. What are the statistics related to reading achievement?

3. Select one of the instructional strategies for improving reading comprehension with ELL students such as using literature circles. Develop an annotated bibliography of books that are written in both English and Spanish that could be used in literature circles.

4. Choose one of the cultural groups discussed under "Multicultural Literature." Select an author or illustrator who publishes in that area. Develop an annotated bibliography of books written or illustrated by that author or illustrator.

5. Extend the multicultural literature to multicultural art and music. What art would you include? What artists depict the culture or are members of the cultural group? What music would you include? Which musicians are members of the cultural group? You may want to start a library of recordings that could be used with students to reinforce a study of the culture.

6. Puppetry may be used to expand interest in storytelling and comprehension of the language. Use puppetry to enhance a storytelling experience such as Verna Aardema's *Who's in Rabbit's House?* (1977).

7. Choral reading is an excellent way to help students with reading difficulties practice their reading. Develop an annotated bibliography of stories and poems that could be used for choral reading arrangements. You might try some of the materials that are written in both English and Spanish. Spanish-speaking students could respond in Spanish, while English-speaking children could respond in English.

8. As a field experience, visit a school that has students who are linguistically or culturally diverse. If the students are linguistically diverse, what strategies does the school use to teach English? If the major emphasis is on the cultural diversity of the students, how does the school make use of the cultural strengths of the students to improve their literacy? What evidence do you see on bulletin boards, in interest centers, or in library centers that the school honors diversity? If possible, ask teachers how they use the cultural diversity of the parents to help develop understandings of various cultures. What evidence do you see that cultural diversity is part of the content areas such as social studies, art, and music? Share your findings with your methods class.

For Further Reading

Students with Limited English Proficiency

1. Caroline, Barratt-Pugh, & Mary, Rohl. (April 2001), "Learning in Two Languages: A Bilingual Program in Western Australia," in *The Reading Teacher,* 54, 664–676. The article analyzes a bilingual program in a primary school.

2. Lori A, Helman. (February 2004), "Building on the Sound System of Spanish: Insights from the Alphabetic Spellings of English-Language Learners," in *The Reading Teacher.* 57, 452–460.

3. Timothy O, Oyetunde. (May 2002). "Second-Language Reading: Insights from Nigerian Primary Schools," in *The Reading Teacher,* 55, 748–755. The text describes strategies used to teach reading to a nonreader of English.

4. Richard Ruiz (March 2006), "Suggestions for Further Reading on Multilingualism," *Language Arts,* 83, 353. The list of readings include "Building a Knowledge Base" and "Connecting to Practice."

Students with Special Needs in Reading

1. Kathleen S, Cooter, & Robert B. Cooter, Jr. (April 2004), "Issues in Urban Literacy: One Size Doesn't Fit All: Slow Learners in the Reading Classroom," in *The Reading Teacher,* 57, 680–684. The authors discuss topics such as "The school-to-prison pipeline," "Why shadow kids have been left behind," and "Hopeful signs on the horizon."

2. Diaane, Karther. (October 2002). "Fathers with Low Literacy and Their Young Children," in *The Reading Teacher,* 56, 184–193. The author describes a study in which fathers monitored their children's progress and participated in book reading.

3. Patricia Ruggiano, Schmidt; Sussan, Gillen; Teresa Colabufo, Zollo; & Rhaenel, Stone. (March 2002), "Literacy Learning and Scientific Inquiry: Children Respond," in *The Reading Teacher,* 55, 534–548. The authors describe how scientific inquiry may be used to help students with special needs in literacy.

4. Sheila W. Valencia, & Buly, Marsha Riddle (March 2004), "Behind Test Scores: What Struggling Readers Really Need," in *The Reading Teacher,* 57, 520–531. The authors analyze specific reading abilities of students who fail a state reading test.

5. Rehate, Valtin & Ingrid M, Naegele. (September 2001), "Correcting Reading and Spelling Difficulties: A Balanced Model for Remedial Education," in *The Reading Teacher,* 55, 36–45. Cognitive development provides the theoretical framework for this model.

6. Maryellen, Vogt & Patty, Nagano (November 2003), "Turn It on with Light Bulb Reading! Sound-Switching Strategies for Struggling Readers," *The Reading Teacher,* 57, 214–221. The article describes a strategy that includes oral reading with note taking and discussions about miscues, skills, and strategies.

7. Margo, Wood & Elizabeth Prata, Salvetti. (September 2001), "Project Story Boost: Read-Alouds for Students at Risk," in *The Reading Teacher,* 55, 76–83. The authors describe how structured read-alouds help at-risk kindergarten students develop familiarity with literacy.

REFERENCES

Adler, Martha A., & Fisher, Charles W. (March 2001). "Center for the Improvement of Early Reading Achievement: Early Reading Programs in High-Poverty Schools: A Case Study of Beating the Odds." *The Reading Teacher, 54,* 616–619.

Belkin, Lisa. (12 September 2004). "The Lessons of Classroom 506: What Happens When a Boy with Cerebral Palsy Goes to Kindergarten Like All the Other Kids." *New York Times,* pp. 40–49, 62, 104, 110.

Bierhorst, John. (1978). *The Red Swan: Myths and Tales of the American Indians.* New York: Farrar, Straus & Giroux.

Booth, William. (2 March 1998). "Diversity and Division: America's New Wave of Immigration Is Changing Its 'Melting Pot' Image." *The Washington Post National Weekly Edition,* pp. 15, 6–8.

Broderick, Dorothy May. (1971). *The Image of the Black in Popular and Recommended American Juvenile Fiction, 1827–1967.* New York: Columbia University University Microfilm No. 7104090.

Cahnmann, Melisa. (March 2006). "Reading, Living, and Writing Bilingual Poetry as Scholartistry in the Language Arts Classroom." *Language Arts, 83,* 342–352.

Campbell, Joseph. (1988). *The Power of Myth.* New York: Doubleday.

Carpenter, Marilyn. (March 2006). "Poetry About Bilingual Experiences." *Language Arts, 83,* 348.

Chall, Jeanne S., & Curtis, Mary E. (2003). "Children with Reading Difficulties." In James Flood, Diane Lapp, James R. Squire, & Julie M. Jensen (Eds.), *Handbook of Research on Teaching the English Language Arts,* 2nd ed. Mahwah, NJ: Lawrence Erlbaum, 413–420.

Collins, Molly Fuller. (October-December 2005). "ESL Preschoolers' English Vocabulary Acquisition from Storybook Reading." *Reading Research Quarterly,* 40, 406–408.

Cunningham, Patricia M., & Allington, Richard L. (2003).*Classrooms That Work: They Can All Read and Write,* 3rd ed. Boston: Allyn & Bacon.

Curtis, Mary E. (1996). "Intervention for Adolescents 'At Risk.'" In L. R. Putnam (Ed.), *How to Become a Better Reading Teacher.* Englewood Cliffs, NJ: Prentice-Hall, pp. 231–239.

Dewitz, Peter, & Dewitz, Pamela K. (February 2003). "They Can Read the Words, But They Can't Understand: Refining Comprehension Assessment." *The Reading Teacher, 56,* 422–435.

Dorris, Michael. (1979). "Native American Literature in an Ethnohistorical Context." *College English,* 41, 147–162.

Finazzo, Denise Ann. (1997). *All for the Children: Multicultural Essentials of Literature.* Albany: Delmar.

Ganske, Kathy, Monroe, Joanne K., & Strickland, Dorothy S. (October 2003). "Questions Teachers Ask About Struggling Readers and Writers." *The Reading Teacher, 57,* 118–128.

Garcia, E. (1991). *Education of Linguistically and Culturally Diverse Students: Effective Instructional Practice.* Washington DC: National Center for Research on Cultural Diversity and Second Language Learning.

Goldenberg, Claude. (August–September 2005). "An Interview with Claude Goldenberg." *Reading Today,* 23, 8–9.

Hammerberg, Dawnene D. (April 2004). "Comprehension Instruction for Socioculturally Diverse Classrooms: A Review of What We Know." *The Reading Teacher, 57,* 648–658.

Hibbing, Anne Nielsen, & Rankin-Erickson, Joan L. (May 2003). "A Picture Is Worth a Thousand Words: Using Visual Images to Improve Comprehension for Middle School Struggling Readers." *The Reading Teacher, 56,* 758–770.

Hickman, Peggy, Pollard-Durodola, Sharolyn, & Vaughn, Sharon. (May 2004). "Storybook Reading: Improving Vocabulary and Comprehension for English-Language Learners." *The Reading Teacher, 57,* 720–730.

Hoffman, James, & Pearson, P. David. (January-March 2000). "Reading Teacher Education in the Next Millennium: What Your Grandmother's Teacher Didn't Know That Your Granddaughter's Teacher Should." *Reading Research Quarterly, 35,* 28–44.

Hudelson, Sarah, Poynor, Leslie, & Wolfe, Paula. (2003). "Teaching Bilingual and ESL Children and Adolescents." In James Flood, Diane Lapp, James R. Squire, & Julie M. Jensen (Eds.), *Handbook of Research on Teaching the English Language Arts,* 2nd ed. Mahwah, NJ: Lawrence Erlbaum, 421–434.

Joseph, Laurice M. (January 1999). "Word Boxes Help Children with Learning Disabilities Identify and Spell Words." *The Reading Teacher, 52,* 348–356.

Kornfeld, John, & Leyden, Georgia. (November 2005). "Acting Out: Literature, Drama, and Connecting with History." *The Reading Teacher, 59,* 230–238.

Larrick, Nancy. (11 September, 1965). "The All-White World of Children's Books." *Saturday Review,* 48, 63.

Lerner, Janet W. (2000). *Children with Learning Disabilities,* 8th ed. Boston: Houghton Mifflin.

Lenders, Kimberly. (December 2004-January 2005). "No Half Measures: Reading Instruction for Your Second-Language Learners." *The Reading Teacher,* 58, 328–336.

Lewis, Rena, & Doorlag, Donald. (1995). *Teaching Special Students in the Mainstream,* 4th ed. Upper Saddle River, NJ: Merrill/Prentice Hall.

Lubliner, Shira. (February 2004). "Help for Struggling Upper-Grade Elementary Readers." *The Reading Teacher,* 57, 430–435.

Martinez-Roldan, Carmen M., & Lopez-Robertson, Julia M. (January 2000). "Initiating Literature Circles in a First-Grade Bilingual Classroom." *The Reading Teacher,* 53, 270–281.

McDevitt, Teresa M., & Ormrod, Jeanne Ellis. (2004). *Child Development: Educating and Working with Children and Adolescents,* 2nd ed. Upper Saddle River, NJ: Pearson/Merrill/Prentice Hall.

NCELA Newsline Bulletin. (June 11, 2002). "NCES Survey: Over 40 Percent of U.S. Teachers Teach LEPs." www.ncbe.gwe.edu/newline/soos/0611.htm.

Norton, Donna E. (2005). *Multicultural Children's Literature: Through the Eyes of Many Children,* 2nd ed. Upper Saddle River, NJ: Pearson/Merrill/Prentice Hall.

Norton, Donna E. (2005). (September 1990). "Teaching Multicultural Literature in the Reading Curriculum." *The Reading Teacher,* 44, 25–40. Also in Michael F. Opitz (Ed.), *Literacy Instruction for Culturally and Linguistically Diverse Students.* Newark, DE: International Reading Association, 1998, 213–228.

Ortiz, Robert W., & Ordonez-Jasis, Rosario. (October 2005). "Leyendo Juntos (Reading Together):New Directions for Latino Parents' Early Literacy Involvement." *The Reading Teacher,* 59, 110–121.

Peregoy, Susanne F., & Boyle, Owen F. (2001). *Reading, Writing, and Learning in ESL,* third edition. New York: Longman.

Schmidt, Patricia Ruggiano, Gillen, Susan, Zollo, Teresa Colabufo, & Stone, Rhaenel. (March 2002). "Literacy Learning and Scientific Inquiry: Children Respond." *The Reading Teacher,* 55, 534–548.

Stahl, Steven A., & Kuhn, Melanie R. (March 2002). "Center for the Improvement of Early Reading Achievement: Making It Sound Like Language: Developing Fluency." *The Reading Teacher,* 55, 582–584.

Thorp, R. (1997). *From At-Risk to Excellence: Research Theory and Principles for Practice.* Santa Cruz, CA: Center for Research on Education, Diversity and Excellence.

Valdez, Alora. (1999). *Learning in Living Color: Using Literature to Incorporate Multicultural Education into the Primary Curriculum.* Boston: Allyn & Bacon.

Zutell, Jerry (April-June 1998). "Word Sorting: A Developmental Spelling Approach to Word Study for Delayed Readers." *Reading & Writing Quarterly: Overcoming Learning Difficulties,* 14, 219–238.

Children's Literature References

Aardema. Verna. (1977). *Who's in Rabbit's House?* Illustrated by Leo and Diane Dillon. Dial Press.

Aardema. Verna. (1979). *The Riddle of the Drum: A Tale from Tizapan, Mexico.* Illustrated by Tony Chen. Four Winds.

Aardema. Verna. (1995). *How the Ostrich Got Its Long Neck.* Illustrated by Marcia Brown. Scholastic.

Aardema. Verna. (1997). *Anansi Does the Impossible: An Ashanti Tale.* Illustrated by Lisa Desimini. Simon & Schuster.

Adler, David A. (1999). *A Picture Book of George Washington Carver.* Illustrated by Dan Brown. Holiday.

Alarcon, Francisco X. (1997). *Laughing Tomatoes and Other Spring Poems.* Illustrated by Maya Christina Gonzalez. Children's Press.

Baker, Olaf. (1981). *Where the Buffaloes Begin.* Illustrated by Stephen Gammell. Warne.

Barasch, Lynne. (2004). *Knockin' On Wood: Starring Peg Leg Bates.* Lee & Law.

Bertrand, Diane Gonzales. (2001). *Uncle Chente's Picnic/El Picnic de Tio Chente.* Illustrated by Pauline Rodriguez Howard. Pinata Books.

Bial, Raymond. (1995). *The Underground Railroad.* Houghton Mifflin.

Bierhorst, John. (1987). *Doctor Coyote: A Native American Aesop's Fables.* Illustrated by Wendy Watson. Macmillan.

Bierhorst, John. (1986). *The Monkey's Haircut and Other Stories Told by the Maya.* Illustrated by Robert Andrew Parker. William Morrow.

Bierhorst, John. (1984). *Spirit Child: A Story of the Nativity.* Illustrated by Barbara Cooney. William Morrow.

Blackmore, Vivien. (1984). *Why Corn Is Golden: Stories about Plants.* Illustrated by Susana Martinez-Ostos. Little, Brown.

Blumberg, Rhoda. (1985). *Commodore Perry in the Land of the Shogun.* Lothrop, Lee & Shepard.

Bolden, Tonya. (2005). *Maritcha: A Nineteenth-Century American Girl.* Abrams.

Bolden, Tonya. (2004). *Wake Up Our Souls: A Celebration of Black American Artists.* Abrams.

Brown, Monica. (2005). *My Name Is Gabriela/Me Ilamo Gabriela: The Life of Gabriela Mistral/la vida de Gabriela.* Illustrated by John Parra. Luna Rising.

Bryan, Ashley. (1980). *Beat the Story-Drum, PumPum.* Atheneum.

Caduto, Michael J., & Bruchac, Joseph. (1989). *Keepers of the Earth: Native American Stories and Environmental Activities for Children.* Illustrated by John Kahionhes Fadden and Carol Wood. Fulcrum.

Caraballo, Samuel. (2002). *Estrellita Says Good-bye to Her Island.* Illustrated by Pablo Torrecilla. Pinata Books.

Cha, Dia. (1996). *Dia's Story Cloth: The Hmong People's Journey of Freedom.* Illustrated by Chue and Nhia Thao Cha. Lee & Low.

Cisneros, Sandra. (1983). *The House on Mango Street.* Art Publico.

Clifton, Lucille. (1983). *Everett Anderson's Good-bye.* Illustrated by Ann Grifalconi. Holt, Rinehart & Winston.

Cohn, Diana. (2002). *Yes, We Can!* Illustrated by Francisco Delado. Cinco Puntos.

Demi. (1992). *In the Eyes of the Cat: Japanese Poetry for All Seasons.* Translated by Tze-si Huang. Henry Holt.

dePaola, Tomie. (1980). *The Lady of Guadalupe.* Holiday.

dePaola, Tomie. (1983). *The Legend of the Bluebonnet.* Putnam.

Duggleby, John. (1998). *Story Painter: The Life of Jacob Lawrence.* Chronicle.

Duncan, Lois. (1996). *The Magic of Spider Woman.* Illustrated by Shonto Begay. Scholastic.

Ehlert, Lois. (1994). *Mole's Hill: A Woodland Tale.* Harcourt Brace.

Emberley, Rebecca. (1993). *Let's Go: A Book in Two Languages.* Little, Brown.

Emberley, Rebecca. (1993). *My Day: A Book in Two Languages.* Little, Brown.

Erdrich, Louise. (1999). *The Birchbark House.* Hyperion.

Esbensen, Barbara Juster. (1988). *The Star Maiden.* Illustrated by Helen K. Davis. Little, Brown.

Fenner, Carol. (1995). *Yolanda's Genius.* McEldery.

Ferris, Jeri. (1988). *Go Free or Die: A Story about Harriet Tubman.* Carolrhoda.

Fleischman, Sid. (1998). *Bandit's Moon.* Illustrated by Jos A. Smith. Greenwillow.

Freedman, Russell. (1988). *Buffalo Hunt.* New York: Holiday.

Freedman, Russell. (1992). *An Indian Winter.* Illustrated by Karl Boddmer. Holiday.

Freedman, Russell. (2002). *Confucius: The Golden Rule.* Illustrated by Frederic Clement. Scholastic.

Freedman, Russell. (2004). *The Voice That Challenged a Nation: Marian Anderson and the Struggle for Equal Rights.* Clarion.

Fritz, Jean (1994). *Harriet Beecher Stowe and the Beecher Preachers.* Putnam's Sons.

Garcia, Richard. (1987). *My Aunt Otilia's Spirits.* Illustrated by Robin Cherin and Roger Reyes. Children's Press.

Garland, Sherry. (1993). *The Lotus Seed.* Illustrated by Tatsuro Kluchi. Harcourt Brace.

Giovanni, Nikki. (2005). *Rosa.* Illustrated by Bryan Collier. Henry Holt.

Goble, Paul. (1989). *Beyond the Ridge.* Bradbury.

Goble, Paul. (1984). *Buffalo Woman.* Bradbury.

Goble, Paul. (1987). *Death of the Iron Horse.* Bradbury.

Goble, Paul. (1989). *Iktomi and the Berries.* Watts.

Goble, Paul. (1988). *Iktomi and the Boulder: A Plains Indian Story.* Orchard.

Goble, Paul. (1983). *Star Boy.* New York: Bradbury.

Greger, C. Shana. (1994). *The Fifth and Final Sun: An Ancient Aztec Myth of the Sun's Origin.* Houghton Mifflin.

Griffalconi, Ann. (1986). *The Village of Round and Square Houses.* Little, Brown.

Hamilton, Virginia. (1988). *Anthony Burns: The Defeat and Triumph of a Fugitive Slave.* Knopf.

Hamilton, Virginia. (1988). *In the Beginning: Creation*

Stories from around the World. Illustrated by Barry Moser. Harcourt Brace.

Hamilton, Virginia. (1993). *Many Thousand Gone: African Americans from Slavery to Freedom.* Illustrated by Leo and Diane Dillon. Knopf.

Hamilton, Virginia. (1985). *The People Could Fly: American Black Folktales.* Illustrated by Leo and Diane Dillon. Knopf.

Hamilton, Virginia. (1971). *The Planet of Junior Brown.* Macmillan.

Hannah, Johnny. (2005). *Hot Jazz Special.* Candlewick.

Harris, Joel Chandler. (1986). *Jump! The Adventures of Brer Rabbit.* Adapted by Van Dyke Parks. Illustrated by Barry Moser. Harcourt Brace.

Harris, Joel Chandler. (1986). *Jump Again! More Adventures of Brer Rabbit.* Adapted by Van Dyke Parks. Illustrated by Barry Moser. Harcourt Brace.

Harris, Joel Chandler. (1987). *The Tales of Uncle Remus: The Adventures of Brer Rabbit,* retold by Julius Lester. Dial Press.

Harris, Joel Chandler. (1988). *More Tales of Uncle Remus: Further Adventurers of Brer Rabbit,* retold by Julius Lester. Dial Press.

Haugaard, Erik Christian. (1991). *The Boy and the Samurai.* Houghton Mifflin.

Hayes, Joe. (2001). *El Cucuy: A Bogeyman Cuento in English and Spanish.* Illustrated by Honorio Robledo. Cinco Puntos.

Hayes, Joe. (2002). *Pajaro Verde: The Green Bird.* Illustrated by Antonio Castro L. Cinco Puntos.

Hayes, Joe. (1998). *Tell Me a Cuento: four Stories in English and Spanish.* Illustrated by Geronimo Garcia. Cinco Puntos.

Heyer, Marilee. (1986). *The Weaving of a Dream: A Chinese Folktale.* Viking.

Highwater, Jamake. (1984). *The Ceremony of Innocence.* Harper & Row.

Highwater, Jamake. (1986). *I Wear the Morning Star.* Harper & Row.

Highwater, Jamake. (1984). *Legend Days.* Harper & Row.

Hill, Laban Carrick. (2003). *Harlem Stomp! A Cultural History of the Harlem Renaissance.* Little, Brown.

Hoberman, Mary Ann, selected by. (1994). *My Song Is Beautiful: Poems and Pictures in Many Voices.* Little, Brown.

Hudson, Jan. (1989). *Sweetgrass.* Philomel.

Hopkinson, Deborah. (1999). *A Band of Angels: A Story Inspired by the Jubilee Singers.* Atheneum.

Issa. (1998). *Cool Melons—Turn to Frogs!: The Life and Poems of Issa.* Translated by Matthew Golub. Illustrated by Kazuko G. Stone. Lee & Low.

Johnson, Dorothy M. (1969). *Warrior for a Lost Nation: A Biography of Sitting Bull.* Westminster.

Kadohata, Cynthia. (2004). *Kira-Kira.* Atheneum.

Kimmel, Eric, retold by. (1998). *Ten Suns: A Chinese Legend.* Illustrated by Yongsheng Xuan. Holiday.

Kodama, Tatsuharu. (1995). *Shin's Tricycle.* Translated by Kazuko Hokumen-Jones. Illustrated by Noriyuki Ando. Walker.

Krumgold, Joseph. (1953). *. . . And Now Miguel.* Illustrated by Jean Charlot. Crowell.

Lattimore, Deborah. (1987). *The Flame of Peace: A Tale of the Aztecs.* Harper & Row.

Laurin, Anne. (1981). *The Perfect Crane.* Illustrated by Charles Mikolaycak. Harper & Row.

Littlechild, George. (1993). *This Land Is My Land.* Children's Book Press.

Mah, Adeline Yen. (2005). *Chinese Cinderella and the Secret Dragon Society.* HarperCollins.

Mahy, Margaret. (1990). *The Seven Chinese Brothers.* Illustrated by Jean and Mou-Sien Tseng. Scholastic.

Mandela, Nelson. (2002). *Nelson Mandela's Favorite, African Folktales.* W. W. Norton.

McDermott, Gerald. (1994). *Coyote: A Trickster Tale from the American Southwest.* Harcourt Brace.

McDermott, Gerald. (1997). *Musicians of the Sun.* Simon & Schuster.

McDermott, Gerald. (1993). *Raven: A Trickster Tale from the Pacific Northwest.* Harcourt Brace.

McDermott, Gerald. (1992). *Zomo the Rabbit: A Trickster Tale from West Africa.* Harcourt Brace.

McWhorter, Diane. (2004). *A Dream of Freedom: The Civil Rights Movement from 1954 to 1968.* Scholastic.

Meltzer, Milton. (1984). *The Black Americans: A History in Their Own Words, 1619–1983.* Crowell.

Meltzer, Milton. (1982). *The Hispanic Americans.* Photographs by Morrie Camhi and Catherine Noren. Crowell.

Merrill, Jean. (1992). *The Girl Who Loved Caterpillars.* Illustrated by Floyd Cooper. Putnam.

Meyer, Caroly, & Gallenkamp, Charles. (1985). *The Mystery of the Ancient Maya.* Atheneum.

Mohr, Nicholasa. (1979). *Felita.* Illustrated by Ray Cruz. Dial Press.

Mohr, Nicholasa. (1986). *Going Home.* Dial Press.

Monjo. N. (1970). *The Drinking Gourd.* Illustrated by Fred Brenner. Harper & Row.

Mora, Pat. (2001). *The Bakery Lady.* Illustrated by Pablo Torrecila. Pinata Books.

Mora, Pat. (1997). *Thomas and the Library Lady.* Illustrated by Colon. Knopf.

Morrison, Dorothy. (1980). *Chief Sarah: Sarah Winnemucca's Fight for Indian Rights.* Atheneum.

Morrison, Toni. (2004). *Remember: The Journey to School Integration*. Houghton Mifflin.

Mowat, Farley. (1996, 1984). *Lost in the Barrens*. Illustrated by Charles Geer. McClelland & Stewart.

Myers, Walter Dean. (1997). *Harlem*. Illustrated by Christopher Myers. Scholastic.

Namioka, Lensey. (1995). *Yang the Youngest and His Terrible Ear*. Illustrated by Kees de Kiefte. Little, Brown.

Nelson, Marilyn. (2001). *Carver: A Life in Poems*. Front Street.

Nelson, Marilyn. (2005). *A Wreath for Emmett Till*. Illustrated by Philippe Lardy, Houghton Mifflin.

Nye, Naomi Shihab, selected by. (1992). *This Same Sky: A Collection of Poems from around the World*. Four Winds.

O'Dell, Scott. (1983). *The Amethyst Ring*. Houghton Mifflin.

O'Dell, Scott. (1979). *The Captive*. Houghton Mifflin.

O'Dell, Scott. (1981). *The Feathered Serpent*. Houghton Mifflin.

O'Dell, Scott. (1966). *The King's Fifth*. Houghton Mifflin.

Park, Linda Sue. (2001). *A Single Shard*. Houghton Mifflin.

Paterson, Katherine. (1990). *The Tale of the Mandarin Ducks*. Illustrated by Leo and Diane Dillon. Lodestar.

Paulsen, Gary. (1987). *The Crossing*. Doubleday.

Paulsen, Gary. (1993). *Nightjohn*. Delacorte.

Petry, Ann. (1955). *Harriet Tubman: Conductor on the Underground Railroad*. Crowell.

Philip, Neil. (1986). *The Spring of Butterflies and Other Chinese Folktales*. Lothrop, Lee & Shepard.

Politi, Leo. (1949). *Song of the Swallows*. Scribner's Sons.

Reinhard, Johan. (1998). *Discovering the Inca Ice Maiden: My Adventures on Ampato*. Washington D.C.: National Geographic.

Rohmer, Harriet, Chow, Octavio, & Vidaure Morris. (1987). *The Invisible Hunters*. Illustrated by Joe Sam. Children's Book Press.

Rohmer, Harriet, Chow, Octavio, Vidaure Morris, & Wilson, Dorminster. (1987). *Mother Scorpion Country*. Illustrated by Virginia Stearns. Children's Book Press.

Ryan, Pam Muñoz. (2004). *Becoming Naomi León*. Scholastic.

Sanfield, Steven. (1989). *The Adventures of High John the Conqueror*. Illustrated by John Ward. Watts.

San Souci, Robert D. (1995). *The Faithful Friend*. Illustrated by Brian Pinkney. Simon & Schuster.

San Souci, Robert D. (1992). *The Samurai's Daughter: A Japanese Legend*. Illustrated by Stephen T. Johnson. Dial Press.

San Souci, Robert D. (1989). *The Talking Eggs: A Folktale from the American South*. Illustrated by Jerry Pinkney. Dial Press.

Say, Allen. (1993). *Grandfather's Journey*. Houghton Mifflin.

Shepard, Aaron. (2001). *Master Man: A Tall Tale of Nigeria*. Illustrated by David Wisniewski. HarperCollins.

Simms, Laura. (1997). *The Bone Man: A Native American Modoc Tale*. Illustrated by Michael McCurdy. Hyperion.

Sneve, Virginia Driving Hawk. (1989). *Dancing Teepees: Poems of American Indian Youth*. Illustrated by Stephen Gammell. Holiday.

Soto, Gary. (1990). *Baseball in April and Other Stories*. Harcourt Brace.

Soto, Gary. (1998). *Big Bush Mustache*. Illustrated by Joe Cepeda. Knopf.

Soto, Gary. (2000). *Chato and the Party Animals*. Illustrated by Susan Guevara. Putnam.

Soto, Gary. (1992).*Pacific Crossing*. Harcourt Brace.

Soto, Gary. (1991). *Taking Sides*. Harcourt Brace.

Stanley, Jerry. (1994). *I Am an American: A True Story of Japanese Internment*. Crown.

Stone, Jeff. (2005). *Tiger: The Five Ancestors*. Random House.

Strathern, Paul. (1994). *Exploration by Land: The Silk and Spice Routes*. Macmillan.

Swamp, Chief Jake. (1995). *Giving Thanks: A Native American Good Morning Message*. Illustrated by Erwin Printup Jr. Lee & Low.

Taylor, Mildred. (1981). *Let the Circle Be Unbroken*. Dial Press.

Taylor, Mildred. (1976). *Roll of Thunder, Hear My Cry*. Dial Press.

Tingle, Tim. (2003). *Walking The Choctaw Road*. Cinco Puntos Press.

Wallace, Ian. (1984). *Chin Chiang and the Dragon's Dance*. Atheneum.

Waters, Kate, & Slovenz-Low, Madeline. (1990). *Lion Dancer: Ernie Wan's Chinese New Year*. Atheneum.

Whelan. Gloria. (2000). *Homeless Bird*. HarperCollins.

White Deer of Autumn. (1983). *Ceremony—In the Circle of Life*. Illustrated by Daniel San Souci. Raintree.

Wood, Nancy, ed. (1997). *The Serpent's Tongue: Prose, Poetry, and Art of the New Mexico Pueblos*. Dutton.

Yee, Paul. (1990). *Tales from Gold Mountain: Stories of the Chinese in the New World.* Macmillan.

Yep, Laurence. (1999). *The Amah.* Putnam's Sons.

Yep, Laurence. (1975). *Child of the Owl.* Harper & Row.

Yep, Laurence. (1993). *Dragon's Gate.* HarperCollins.

Yep, Laurence. (1973). *Dragon's Wings.* Harper & Row.

Yep, Laurence. (1995). *Later, Gater.* Hyperion.

Yep, Laurence. (1989). *The Rainbow People.* Illustrated by David Wiesner. Harper & Row.

Yep, Laurence. (1991). *Star Fisher.* William Morrow.

Yep, Laurence. (1995). *Thief of Hearts.* HarperCollins.

Young, Ed. (1989). *Lon Po Po: A Red-Riding Hood Story from China.* Philomel.

Young, Ed. (1998). *The Lost Horse.* Harcourt Brace.

Computer-Assisted Instruction and Reading and Writing

CHAPTER **OUTLINE**

Taxonomy for Using Technology in the Classroom
Media for Communication
Media for Expression
Media for Inquiry
Media for Construction

Research Studies Connecting Reading and Technology

Using Technology in the Reading Curriculum
Using Technology to Enhance Word Recognition and Vocabulary
Using Technology to Enhance Reading Comprehension
Using Technology to Enhance Literary Research
Evaluating Software for Reading Comprehension

The Reading and Writing Connection and Technology
Designing Classrooms for Writing through Technology
Writing Software

Teaching Students the Meaning and Consequences of Plagiarism

After reading this chapter you will be able to answer the following questions:

1. What are the different uses for technology that are meaningful for K–8 students?
2. What do research studies reveal about reading and computer-assisted instruction?
3. What are some strategies for using technology in the reading and writing curriculum?
4. Why is it important to teach students the meaning of and consequences resulting from plagiarism?

Read All About It!

"Old Search Engine, the Library, Tries to Fit into a Google World"

by Katie Hafner, *New York Times,* June 21, 2004

For the last few years, librarians have increasingly seen people use online search sites not to supplement research libraries but to replace them. Yet only recently have librarians stopped lamenting the trend and started working to close the gap between traditional scholarly research and the incomplete, often random results of a Google search.

"We can't pretend people will go back to walking into a library and talking to a reference librarian," said Kate Wittenberg, Direc-

tor of the Electronic Publishing Initiative at Columbia University.

Ms. Wittenberg's group recently finished a three-year study of research habits, including surveys of 1,233 students across the country, that concluded that electronic resources have become the main tool for information gathering, particularly among undergraduates.

"We have to respond to these new ways and figure out how to create the content that will be available," Ms. Wittenberg said. . . .

While the accuracy of online information is notoriously uneven, the ubiquity of the Web means that a trip to the stacks is no longer the way most research begins.

"The nature of discovery is changing," said Joseph Janes, chairman of library and information science at the University of Washington. "I think the digital revolution and the use of digital resources in general is really the beginning of a change in the way humanity thinks and presents itself." . . .

The biggest problem is that search engines like Google skim only the thinnest layers of information that has been digitized. Most have no access to the so-called deep Web, where information is contained in isolated databases like on-line library catalogs. . . .

"Google searches an index at the first layers of any Web site it goes to, and as you delve beneath the surface it starts to miss stuff," said Mr. Duguid, co-author of "The Social Life of Information." "When you go deeper, the number of pages just becomes absolutely mind-boggling."

Reference librarians are trying to bring material from the deep Web to the surface. In recent months, dozens of libraries began working with Google and other search engines to help put their collections within reach of a broader public. . . .

> "The potential is there for this to be a real bonus to humanity, because we can see more and read more and do more with it."

Many experts, even those who specialize in digital material, say that losing the tactile experience of books and relying too heavily on electronic resources is certain to exact a price. How do you know it's the appropriate universe from which to draw your materials? It has huge ramifications for the nature of instruction and scholarship.

At the same time, many reference librarians say that the new reliance on electronic resources is making their role as guides to undiscovered material more important than ever.

Thomas Mann, a reference librarian in the main reading room of the Library of Congress, was reminded of this recently while helping a visitor who was researching a 1942 famine in Greece. A Google search had yielded little useful information.

"While he was looking at newspaper articles from the 1940s that we had digitized," Dr. Mann said, "I set up a search on the terminal next to him in another database of historical abstracts and history journals. In less than a minute, I pulled up citations for five articles about the famine and helped the visitor put in requests for the paper copies. We can show people things they don't ask for," Dr. Mann said.

Some library experts welcome the change with few reser-

vations. "Although it seems like an apocalyptic change now, over time we'll see that young people will grow up using many ways of finding information," said Abby Smith, director of programs at the Council on Library and Information Resources, a nonprofit group in Washington.

"We'll see the current generation we accuse of doing research in their pajamas develop highly sophisticated searching strategies to find high-quality information on the Web," Dr. Smith said.

Dr. James said that, like many others, he occasionally pined for the days spent in musty library stacks, where one could chance upon gems by browsing the shelves. "You can think of electronic research as a more impoverished experience," Dr. James said. "But in some ways it's a richer one, because you have so much more access to so much more information. The potential is there for this to be a real bonus to humanity, because we can see more and read more and do more with it. But it is going to be very different in lots of ways."

Read All About It!

Critical Thinking Questions

- What are the possible consequences for libraries as more people use Google, and other search engines, to conduct research?

- How reliable are the Internet sources? How will you teach your students to use both the librarian as a resource and the Internet?

- How important is the technology revolution in the world of traditional library sources? How important is the librarian for teachers who are teaching students to use research and library skills?

- Do you agree that the current generation of children will be able to use the Internet to find high-quality information on the Web? As a teacher, how will you make this happen?

Themes of the Times

expect the world®

The New York Times

nytimes.com

For related *New York Times* articles, go to the Companion Web Site at www.ablongman.com/norton1e and click on *Themes of the Times*.

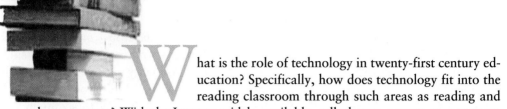

What is the role of technology in twenty-first century education? Specifically, how does technology fit into the reading classroom through such areas as reading and language arts? With the Internet widely available, cell phones, pagers, text messaging, e-mail, and wireless networks, what types of technology are worthwhile for the reading teacher? Arthur L. Costa (2001) introduces the section of his book on teaching thinking skills through technology with this quote from *The Age of the Scholar:* "We live in a time of such rapid change and growth of knowledge that only he who is in a fundamental sense a scholar—that is, a person who continues to learn and inquire—can hope to keep pace, let alone play the role of guide" (p. 471).

This chapter considers the technology revolution and how it influences the reading curriculum. Technology is changing so rapidly that information presented in printed texts quickly goes out of date. For example, Bertram Bruce and James Levine (2003) acknowledge that many of their ideas discussed in their 1991 book about technology are now irrelevant or have been superseded by new technological developments.

Taxonomy for Using Technology in the Classroom

To deal with these rapid changes in technology, Bruce and Levine say we must apply a four-part taxonomy to the uses of new media and technology in the curriculum, including media for communication, media for expression, media for inquiry, and media for construction. A brief review of each of these applications shows us the potential for using technology in the K–8 classroom.

Media for Communication

Developing communication skills through writing and speaking are major objectives of the K–8 curriculum. Computer-assisted instruction includes teaching students to use **e-mail** that allows them to read and write directly on a computer screen. This instruction may also include how to use graphics, voice, and video within their messages. It is not unusual for photographs to be sent along with e-mail messages.

Media for communication also includes document preparation as found in desktop publishing and support systems like spelling checks, grammar checks, and style aids. There are programs that assist writing through generating ideas. There are also **software programs** available that help students with document preparation. As students take their papers through the writing process, desktop publishing and support systems make it possible for students to create their own books.

Under media for communication are found technologies for teaching, such as tutoring systems, instructional simulations, and educational games. There are reading games such as those designed to reinforce phonics. This chapter includes criteria for evaluating these instructional programs.

Media for Expression

Students may also use computer-assisted technologies to expand their creative abilities. One of the criticisms of some of the programs available for instruction is that the programs do not encourage creativity and creative expression. Instruction that explores media for expression includes drawing and painting programs, interactive video, animation software, and multimedia composition. Some of the programs may be used to create personal diaries, poetry, and other media for communication.

Media for Inquiry

Databases of information help students search for information and explore new ideas. This is one of the most important areas for teachers in the content areas as information can be supplemented and authenticated. For example, research reports may be improved through the use of information found on databases. Students may also identify topics of interest for research and narrow those topics to manageable subjects.

Reflect on Your Reading

Consider Bertram Bruce and James Levine's (2003) statement that much of the technology they presented in a book published in 1991 is now irrelevant or superseded by new technological developments. What older technologies are now irrelevant? Where do you think technology will be in twenty years? How might the reading classroom change because of new technological developments? Which of the older technologies do you believe will still be important? How might these new technologies change the way reading is taught?

Media for Construction

Within this category is the possibility for constructing Web pages and creating stories for communication or expression. Students can write their stories, create their art works, and develop their research papers. By creating Web pages and posting their work on the Web, students can share their ideas with audiences around the world. The potential for this type of construction and sharing is just beginning to be found in classrooms around the country.

Research Studies Connecting Reading and Technology

The research studies highlight the expanding role of technology in the classroom, areas that need to be studied, and concerns related to technology. But the *Report of the National Reading Panel* (2000), the NRP, found few research studies that related to reading and computer technology. The panel concluded: "Computer technology is different from other areas the NRP analyzed. It cannot be studied independently of instructional content and is not an instructional method itself" (p. 17). The panel used limited findings to conclude that adding speech to computer-presented text may be a promising use of technology in reading and that using computers as word processors may be very useful given that reading instruction is most effective when combined with writing instruction.

James M. Wilson (2001) believes that technology will present new methods for learning and these methods are in the pioneering or emergent stage. He sees the greatest implications in the areas of learning, creativity, and thinking. All of these areas are certainly important for fostering reading. They are also areas that future researchers will investigate.

Studies reported by Walter Minkel (2002) state that various forms of media are influential in children's lives. Consequently, teachers should not ignore technologies like television and the Internet because most children watch television for three to five hours every day and at least 60 percent of families with children have Internet access at home. Minkel's concern is that "few young people receive training in media literacy—in how to evaluate what they are looking at for bias and accuracy" (p. 31). To overcome concerns related to the use of the Internet, Minkel maintains that students need to be taught about the meaning of intellectual property and plagiarism. Later in this chapter is a section on teaching students the meaning and consequences of plagiarism. (To overcome concerns related to evaluating accuracy of materials, Chapter 9 includes an authentication project.)

Edward Tenner (2006) reports two studies that add to Minkel's concerns. He asks: "Does Google promote information illiteracy? (p. A12). Tenner reports two studies that may support this observation. For example, a study by the National Center for Education Statistics found "The number of college graduates able to interpret complex texts proficiently has dropped since 1992 from 40 percent to 31 percent" and a report from England finds "that the ability of undergraduates to read critically and write cogently has fallen significantly since 1992. Students are not just more poorly prepared, a majority of queried faculty members believe, but less teachable" (p. A12). Various people cited by Tenner believe that students are using search engines for short cuts to locating information without being taught how to structure their searches to gain better information and to produce the literate, lifelong learners needed for the future.

Reflect on Your Reading

If you could design a research study that evaluated the use of computer-assisted instruction in the reading curriculum, what would you select to study? Using the information that you have gained from reading the previous chapters on reading instruction, what areas would you develop through technology? Why are there so few studies that relate to this new area of technology?

Using Technology in the Reading Curriculum

Even though few research studies link advances in reading with technology, numerous applications and teaching ideas are found in textbooks and in journal articles. Many of these articles provide suggestions for using technology to enhance or reinforce skills within the reading curriculum, such as word recognition and vocabulary. Other suggestions provide broader applications for reading development and practical ideas for using technology in the reading curriculum.

Using Technology to Enhance Word Recognition and Vocabulary

Barbara J. Fox and Mary Jane Mitchell (2000) provide extensive guidelines for selecting software and examples of software designed to enhance phonemic awareness,

These students have many opportunities to use computers in all areas of literacy instruction.

phonics ability, and vocabulary. For phonemic awareness they recommend programs that develop skills for detecting rhymes and alliteration and identifying sounds in words, sound blending, sound substitutions, and sound deletions.

- Software programs designed for phonemic awareness include: *Daisy's Quest* (Great Wave Software, 1992), and *Daisy's Castle* (Great Wave Software, 1993).
- Software programs designed to develop phonics abilities include tutorial software such as *SuperSonic Phonics* (Curriculum Associates, 1997), *Let's Go Read! An Island Adventure* (Edmark, 1998), and *Let's Go Read! An Ocean Adventure* (Edmark, 1998).
- Software programs designed for vocabulary development include: *Carmen Sandiego Word Detective* (The Learning Company, 1997) and *Word Munchers Deluxe* (The Learning Company, 1996).

Guidelines such as those found in Table 11.1 are useful for evaluating skill-development software.

Using Technology to Enhance Reading Comprehension

Reading comprehension may be one of the broadest and most rewarding areas for using technology in the reading curriculum. E. D. Hirsch Jr. (2004) writes that many Americans can read but do not comprehend their reading because they do not have the cultural literacy background knowledge of history, literature, art, music, science, and math, required for comprehension. Hirsch argues,

> Successful reading requires more than an ability to decode, or "sound out," words. It also requires adequate background knowledge, or "cultural literacy." Without background knowledge of history, literature, art, music,

TABLE 11.1

Guidelines for Evaluating Skill-Development Software

Does the software:

- Have a webbed design so that students do not practice skills they have already mastered?
- Use voices that are clear?
- Sequence skills from easy to difficult?
- Allow students to bypass lengthy introductions once they are familiar with the program?
- Provide for different levels of difficulty within skills?
- Use pictures that are easy to identify?
- Provide opportunities to apply skills when reading?
- Include a management system to help the teacher keep track of the skills students have practiced? Use words in students' speaking vocabularies to illustrate or explain principles?
- Provide explanations of the principles students are learning and/or practicing?
- Give students access to a dictionary to help them learn words when spelling or writing?
- Provide opportunities for students to use skills when writing?

Source: Fox & Mitchell, 2000, p. 45.

> science and math, students will read—but without comprehension. . . .
> Content-rich reading selections should be part of an integrated curriculum
> that builds up the broad knowledge and varied vocabulary required for
> true reading comprehension. (p. 13A)

As an example of his concern, Hirsch cites students who had difficulty comprehending test passages that referred to Ulysses S. Grant and Robert E. Lee because they were unfamiliar with the Civil War.

Web sites and various software programs can help students expand their knowledge about history, literature, music, and art. Similarly, many of the comprehension and writing techniques already discussed in this book require students to go beyond prior knowledge to develop background understanding. For example, developing questioning strategies that go beyond literal recognition requires students to make inferences that go beyond the information the author provides. Evaluation questions require students to make judgments about the content of the text by comparing it with external criteria, such as what authorities on a subject say. Appreciative questions require students to respond with sensitivity to the techniques that authors use in order to have emotional impacts on their readers. These questions encourage children to respond emotionally to the plot, identify with the characters, react to an author's use of language, and react to an author's ability to create a visual image through word choices in the text. The information in the text may be expanded through software programs.

Using Technology to Enhance Literary Research

Software programs and web sites may provide students with the background knowledge that allows them to comprehend at higher levels. Web sites that work like **electronic libraries and resources** such as area art museums and various Smithsonian museums are especially appealing. For example, the Smithsonian Institution (www.smithsonian.org) includes online resources such as "Art & Design," "History & Culture," and "Science & Technology."

Developing units and lesson plans that focus on literature selections may require introductions that provide information on authors' backgrounds or geographical or historical backgrounds of specific novels or time periods. Shelley B. Wepner and Lucinda C. Ray (2000) describe how the software *Reading Galaxy* (1996) is used to introduce the novels *Hatchet* and *Julie of the Wolves*. This program uses a game-show format to provide characters, settings, initial conflicts, and author backgrounds for thirty novels that are popular in middle schools.

A primary source for historical documents is the Library of Congress On-line (www.loc.gov). The special collection "American Memory" is particularly interesting because it includes documents, motion pictures, photographs, and sound recordings that trace different aspects of the American experience. One of the virtual exhibits in American Memory is called "Words and Deeds in American History: Selected Documents Celebrating the Manuscript Division's First 100 Years." This exhibit contains original works that have been copied and transferred into digitized images. This Library of Congress site is especially helpful when searching for background information for reading about various time periods in history. The site also improves students' understanding of American history.

If students are reading books with Scottish or English backgrounds they can search on the Internet for images and information about the country or the culture. To begin a search, students could use a search engine such as *yahooligans* (http://yahooligans.yahoo.com) to do a country search for Scotland, under United Kingdom. Another useful site is BBC Online where students can find information on ancient and modern Scotland (www.bbc.co.uk/history/scottishhistory). A related BBC site (www.bbc.co.uk/history/forkids) is aimed at younger students. It offers a "walk through time" with a chronological time line of Scottish history for children ages seven to nine. Castles of Britain includes a "Castle Learning Center" (www.castles-of-Britain.com/castle6.html) which presents information about everyday life in medieval Scotland including building materials, the life of a knight, a history of dungeons, and what it was like to live in a castle.

The School Library Journal provides an excellent source for identifying software and other media through their "Multimedia Review" that evaluates video and audio products and CD-ROMs. The journal frequently includes articles that highlight the best in software. For example, "Essential Software" (Buckleitner, 2004) identifies and discusses ten programs that the author believes are perfect for public libraries. Several of these recommended programs can be found in Table 11.2. According to the journal, all of the "recommended programs are not only well designed and entertaining, but they're easy to use, worth every dollar, and can survive being handled by eager young library users" (p. 56).

Electronic books are available on both CD-ROMs and Internet sites. In addition to text, electronic books may include animated graphics and sounds. Examples of CD-ROMs that include expanded features are Marc Brown's *Arthur's Teacher*

TABLE 11.2

Highly Recommended Software

Blue's Clues: Blue Takes You to School (Atari, www.atari.com) is designed for preschool through kindergarten. In this software students learn what animals eat, they learn to navigate a boat around obstacles, or listen to various rhythms to discover who is playing the right beats.

Nick Jr. Little Bill Thinks Big (Scholastic, www.scholastic.com) is designed for preschool–grade 1. This character, created by comedian Bill Cosby, reinforces skills and concepts such as numbers, counting, sorting, sequencing, and following directions.

I Spy Fantasy (Scholastic) is designed for Kindergarten–grade 4. Based on the *I Spy Fantasy Book,* the adventures take place in a castle, an undersea setting, and in outer space. The software includes games and scavenger hunts and 54 challenging riddles.

The Powerpuff Girls Learning Challenge # 2: Princess Snorebucks (Riverdeep/The Learning Company, www.learningcompany.com) is designed for grades 1–5. Students use math and reading skills, music, creativity, logic, and knowledge of basic Spanish words to help the girls gain their quest.

Liberty's Kids CD-ROM: The Real Adventures of the American Revolution (Riverdeep/The Learning Company) is designed for grades 3–6. A partnership with the PBS television series, the program takes students back to the time of the American Revolution. In the role of reporters, students interview soldiers, townspeople, statesmen and other personages to gather facts about events of the Revolution, such as the Boston Tea Party and the Declaration of Independence.

Explore the World of Thomas Day (Thomas Day Project, www.thomasday.net), designed for grades 4–9, is an interactive exploration of the life and times of a free African American who owned the largest furniture-manufacturing business in North Carolina before the Civil War. The students' mission is to free one of Day's apprentices who has been jailed. To accomplish their task, students need to locate and read replicas of more than 40 original documents. The format of the program encourages students to learn about history.

Inspiration Version 7.5 (Inspiration Software, www.inspiration.com) is designed for grades 6–12. The program allows students to brainstorm, outline, and organize construction webs to visualize relationships between different items and concepts. One example encourages them to understand a pond's ecosystem.

Ancient History: Lives and Times in Ancient Egypt, Greece, and the Roman Empire (Teaching for Thinking, www.teachingforthinking.com) is designed for grades 6–12. Nefertiti presents Egypt, Archimedes discusses Greece, and Cleopatra introduces the Roman Empire. Students can click on any one of the three characters to discover information about art, food, science, and key events.

Trouble (1996) and *Just Grandma and Me Deluxe* (1997). CD-ROMs of biographies reproduced by Troll Associates such as *Young Abraham Lincoln: Log-Cabin President* (1996) and *Young Harriet Tubman: Freedom Fighter* (1996) include both electronic and printed versions of the books.

In addition to CD-ROMs, electronic books are also available on Internet sites. Wepner and Ray (2000) warn, however, "Most of the stories are told in a linear fashion with little opportunity for the interactive play that CD-ROM electronic books afford" (p. 83).

FOCUS ACTIVITY:

⭐ Reading Strategies for Computer-Based Classrooms

Reading on the Web is different from other types of reading because it requires visual literacy skill to comprehend multimedia components. Readers must be able to evaluate text and nontext including images and other graphic materials (Sutherland-Smith, 2002). Strategies for teaching Web reading should involve:

1. Keyword searches in which teachers model explicit instructions about how to narrow the scope of a keyword search to find information.
2. Provide clear guidelines that help students identify the purpose for the search and an approximation of how many searches may be necessary.
3. Teaching students to evaluate images and graphics so that they understand that drawings and photographs can manipulate readers' responses and also be manipulated by web site producers. Teach students how to decode and authenticate the image as well as the text.
4. Teaching students that everything on the Web is not always documented and evaluated in the same way that the publishing process requires of texts in a library.

[handwritten margin notes: lesson plans must have an objective (specific) that you measure — model explicit instruction (scaffolding steps)]

[handwritten margin notes: teach them to manipulate: Scroll, advance screens]

[handwritten margin notes: wikipedia ✱ look at source Valuable?]

Evaluating Software for Reading Comprehension

In addition to teaching students reading strategies for computer-based classrooms, teachers and students need to evaluate software used to enhance reading comprehension. Wepner and Ray (2000, 91) provide the following guidelines:

1. The activities and tasks within the program are compelling enough to hold students' interest.
2. The instructions to students are clear, concise, and easy to follow without significant adult help.
3. The graphics and sound are high quality, are an integral part of the concepts and content taught, and are appropriate for the age level intended.
4. The content fits into or expands what students are supposed to be learning.
5. The program stretches students' imagination and creativity beyond ordinary means.
6. The program provides enough practice of important concepts, especially if you are looking for a program that builds skills.

Reflect on Your Reading

What technology could be the most effective for improving reading ability? What types of software programs could you use to enhance reading? Consider how you would use Hirsch's concerns about cultural literacy to provide background for students before they read about a specific topic? What topics might you teach, especially in a content area of reading that would require additional background knowledge?

7. The program fosters interaction and cooperative activities, especially if you are looking for these kinds of activities within your classroom.

8. The text is narrated so that students can read the book or passage independently, and the text is highlighted as it is read so that students can follow along.

9. The program will develop with the students over the course of the year, or accommodate differing ability or age levels.

10. Record-keeping or assessment features are built into the program, especially if this is an important issue in providing accountability for your use of technology.

11. The publisher provides a teacher's guide, with lessons, ways to introduce the program to your students, and supplementary handout materials to assist you.

12. A printed copy of a book on screen is available for students to use independently.

The Reading and Writing Connection and Technology

One way to relate writing and literature through technology is to <u>write or respond to book reviews published on a web site</u>. This activity encourages critical reading and writing skills as students first explore the components of a good review by reading various reviews. Through this activity they discover that the review summarizes the plot of the story in a few sentences by answering these questions:

■ What was the story about?

■ Who were the main characters?

■ What did the main characters do in the story?

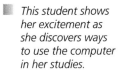
This student shows her excitement as she discovers ways to use the computer in her studies.

- Who was your favorite character and why?

  The review may relate to a personal experience by answering these questions:

- Could you relate to any of the characters?
- Have you ever done the same things or felt the same way as the characters in the book?

  The review might include your opinion about the book:

- Did you like the book? What was your favorite part?
- What was your least favorite part?
- What would you change if you could?

The review might include recommendations:

- Would you recommend this book to another person?
- Who would like this book?

Students can also read examples of reviews written by other children. Book reviews written by children and published on the Internet can be found at the following web sites:

Education Place (www.eduplace.com/kids/rdg/chall.html)

Kids Bookshelf (www.kidsbookshelf.com/review.asp)

Spaghetti Book Club (www.spaghettibookclub.org)

World of Reading (www.worldofreading.org)

They may also read reviews written by other students about the same book and respond to these reviews by agreeing or disagreeing with the reviews.

Designing Classrooms for Writing through Technology

Jean M. Casey (2000) suggests that a classroom designed for writing through technology should have

1. A computer center with at least six networked computers where budding writers are writing across the curriculum all day long.

2. A U-shaped coaching table for you to conference with children on their writings and give them feedback and suggestions.

3. An editing section, with baseball caps labeled "Editor," where lots of peer conferencing, collaboration on stories, and editing takes place.

4. A telecommunications center where at least one computer is hooked up to an online service and students communicate daily with their counterparts elsewhere in the world.

5. A presentation station where, using HyperStudio, groups of children can develop plays, stories, reports and presentations and then, using the projection monitor, share them with the entire class. (This can be the same as the teacher's station in the front of the class.)

6. An Internet station with computers that are hooked up to the Internet for global penpal communications. (Casey, 2000, pp. 79, 81)

We have already shown in Chapter 9 how technology can be used to enhance an authentication project. In that instance, students used various Web sites and other library sources to locate information that either supported or questioned the accuracy of information provided in a book. They used this information to write reports that authenticated the quality and accuracy of the author's source notes, the geographical and social settings of books, the values and beliefs reflected in the text, the political ideologies, the plot development, the conflicts, and the themes. A list of useful web sites is included in the chapter.

Reflect on Your Reading

What are the motivational advantages or disadvantages of using Internet sites to read or submit book reviews? How can writing for audiences expand the writing process?

Writing Software

Numerous software programs such as those found in Table 11.3 are designed to help students with the writing process.

TABLE 11.3

Software Programs for Writing

Inspiration Software, Education Edition [ages 9 and up] (Inspiration Software, Inc.). Helps students develop ideas and organize their thinking using webs, outlines and diagrams.

Secret Writer's Society [ages 7 to 9] (Panasonic Interactive Media) Takes students through the basic steps of writing: planning, drafting, revising, editing, and sharing. Teaches basic skills needed for good writing such as topic sentences and punctuation.

The Write Connections [ages 2 to 8] (Children's Choice) Focuses on teaching the principles of handwriting. Presents letters and numbers in a multimedia format.

Writers Studio (Computer Curriculum Corporation, 1998) Designed to help students in third grade and up through the writing processes associated with prewriting, drafting, revising, editing, and publishing.

Expression (Sunburst Communications, 1996) Helps students through graphic planning and word processing.

EasyBook Deluxe (Sunburst Communications, 1998) and *Storybook Weaver Deluxe* (The Learning Company, 1996) Help students develop stories that integrate stories with graphics.

Kid Works Deluxe (Knowledge Adventure, 1997) Includes a feature for teachers in which they can place an overlay on top of the writing so they can comment on the writing and make suggestions to the students.

The Print Shop Deluxe (The Learning Company, 1996), *Frame Maker* (Adobe Systems, 1995), and *Student Writing Center* (The Learning Company, 1993)

More complete programs that include word processors. The programs frequently include various formats for writing, spelling checks, and graphic designs.

The Current State of Technology in the Classroom

Technology results in both good and bad experiences in the classroom. On the positive side, students have access to more information that is easily located. On the negative side, students are not conducting in-depth research and are often copying sources from the Internet without giving source information. What issues surround using technology in the classroom? If technology is to add to reading and writing capabilities of students, what areas need further research? What areas seem to be the most promising for developing literacy? If you could choose an area of research in the use of technology in the classroom, what would you choose? Why do you believe that your topic is important? How might the results change the way technology is used in the classroom?

Software programs may be used to reinforce skill development

Teaching Students the Meaning and Consequences of Plagiarism

Plagiarism is the use of another person's ideas and writings without giving credit to the source of the information. This is a major issue in today's classrooms as students copy ideas, especially from Web sites, as if the ideas and writings are their own. Walter Minkel, the technology editor of *School Library Journal* (April 2002), cites an increased permissiveness among a cut-and-paste generation of students and their parents who do not understand that it is wrong to copy. To develop his points, Minkel quotes a Pew Internet & American Life Project that finds that 94 percent of students with access to the Internet use it for research and 71 percent of these students use it as their main source of information for school projects. Minkel concludes that "the Web has turned out to be a double-edged sword: while providing swift access to sought-after information, it has made cheating irresistibly easy and more pervasive" (p. 51). Numerous studies suggest that students are not averse to plagiarizing from Internet sites when they write their papers.

To overcome plagiarism, teachers need to define plagiarism for students and show them how to recognize it and how to credit words of others correctly. Students need to understand that when they plagiarize they are not learning the useful research skills that they will need throughout their education. Students must understand that plagiarism at many universities will result in expulsion. In other situations plagiarism results in lawsuits.

Reflect on Your Reading

Why is it important to teach students that plagiarism is wrong? How have Internet sites and search engines added to the pervasive problem of plagiarism?

R. W. Burniske (2000) recommends an exercise with students in which the teacher asks students to imagine that they have spent several weeks creating a Web site on which they have original pictures and essays they have written. She asks students to consider how they would feel if someone "borrowed" the pictures and essays without asking permission. How would they feel if someone used the information as if it were her or his own idea? Then she explains to students that people who borrow the material without permission are using other people's words or ideas as if they are their own, and that this is called plagiarism. Just as the students must provide document sources for printed information, they must also provide sources for information taken from the Internet.

Several Web sites help teachers combat plagiarism. For example, "The New Plagiarism: Seven Antidotes to Prevent Highway Robbery in an Electronic Age" (www.fno.org/may98/cov98may.html), created by *From Now On: The Educational Technology Journal,* provides teachers with methods to discourage plagiarism, such as encouraging students to solve problems rather than sending them on Internet "scavenger hunts." Web sites such as www.plagiarized.com have links for teachers to read including "Catching a Cheater," "Dead Giveaways," and "Prevention Guidelines."

APPLYING CHILDREN'S LITERATURE FEATURE:
Thematic Unit: Literature, Movies, and Technology

USE WEB SITES TO ENHANCE THE SETTINGS FOR THE HARRY POTTER BOOKS AND MOVIES

OBJECTIVES
1. To increase interest in a book by locating settings on web sites.
2. To increase ability to use technology.
3. To increase understandings of the importance of settings in literature and in movies.
4. To discuss and write evaluations that compare texts, movies, and recorded versions of a book.

GRADE LEVEL Fourth through eighth

MATERIALS
- Any of the Harry Potter books by J. K. Rowling:

  Harry Potter and the Sorcerer's Stone (1997)

  Harry Potter and the Chamber of Secrets (1999)

  Harry Potter and the Prisoner of Azkaban (1999)

  Harry Potter and the Goblet of Fire (2000)

Harry Potter and the Order of the Phoenix (2003)

Harry Potter and the Half-Blood Prince (2005)

- Screen versions of the books that have been turned into movies.
- Voice recorded versions of the books performed by Jim Dale. (Jim Dale's recordings of the various Harry Potter books won him a Grammy Award in 2000.)
- Listings of web sites of locations where the movies were filmed. The British Tourist authority publishes a brochure, "Harry Potter and the Philosopher's Stone: Discovering the Magic of Britain." This brochure refers to the British title of the first movie and identifies the locations of the filming and web sites that correspond to each of the locations.

PROCEDURES

1. Share with students the information that the Harry Potter movies were filmed on historic sites in England. These sites were selected because they were believed to capture the settings in the Harry Potter books.
2. Show a map of England on which students may place the locations.
3. Consider the following locations and search web sites where available to explore additional information about the settings:
   - Alnwick Castle, Alnwick, Northumberland
     The castle grounds provide the settings for some of Hogwart's exteriors. (www.alnwickcastle.com).
   - Goathland Station, Goathland, North Yorkshire
     The station is the setting for Hogsmeade Station and the arrival of students on the Hogwarts Express.
   - Gloucester Cathedral, Gloucester
     The cathedral provides the backdrop for several scenes. Students from Kings' School appeared as extras. (www.birminghamuk.com/gloucestercathedral.htm).
   - Bodleian Library, Oxford
     The library recreates some of the interiors at Hogwarts. (www.bodley.ox.ac.uk)
   - Christ Church, Oxford
     The great hall is the setting for Hogwarts school. (www.chch.ox.ac.uk)
   - London Zoo, London
     The reptile house is the setting where Harry discovers his ability to talk to snakes. (www.londonzoo.co.uk).
   - King's Cross Station, London
     The station is the location for Platform 9 3/4 from which the students board the train for Hogwarts School of Witchcraft and Wizardry.
   - Lacock Abbey, Lacock, near Chippenham, Wiltshire
     The abbey provides the settings for interior scenes of Hogwarts school. (www.nationaltrust.org.uk).
4. Ask the students to search web sites where available and evaluate the choice of each location for the Harry Potter movie. Ask them to locate passages from the books that describe these settings. Ask

them to compare the written versions of the settings with the Web sites. If desired, the students may view at least portions of the movies and add the movies to their comparisons.

5. On a map of England, identify the locations of the settings.

6. If desired, listen to the recorded versions of the text created by Jim Dale. (They may visit Jim Dale's web site at www.jim-dale.com). For this experience, they may discuss and respond to Dale's ability to create voices for each of the characters and create appropriate moods that reflect the conflict. Some classes may choose to try their own oral interpretations of the characters in one of the books. This activity highlights the ability of the voice to develop characterization and extend understanding of conflict.

7. This unit may be expanded by asking students to conduct additional research on each of the settings. They may write their reports in a form that could be placed on the Internet or shared with other students in published text. They may also write book reviews that include findings from the web sites.

DIFFERENTIATING INSTRUCTION

ELL and Struggling Readers and Writers

Some computer programs and Internet sites include features that allow students to read or listen to a story in both English and Spanish and more are expanding to include languages such as Russia, French, and Japanese. This feature helps ELL students. Other programs lend themselves to vocabulary expansion through text-to-speech functions that assist struggling readers who are not yet able to read independently.

Linda D. Labbo (2005) reviews several programs that assist in literacy development. For example, ELL students can use the software program *Little Monster at School* (Broderbund) as Little Monster learns about the ABC's, music, math, and science. This interactive text can be read in English or Spanish, so ELL students whose first language is Spanish can read or listen to the Spanish version before they approach the English text.

The software *Blue's Clues: ABC Time Activities* (Viacom & Humongous Entertainment) reinforce phonics and rhyming skills. Students play games, answer questions, and create stories using the words. An interactive activity allows students to select a missing word in order to complete a rhyme. The Web site www.literacycenter.net

An ELL class is enriched when the teacher reads books written in the students' language

includes alphabet games. This site is helpful because the name of each letter is spoken as students interact with the site.

Labbo (2006) emphasizes that "Desktop publishing programs offer opportunities for English Language Learners (ELLs) to write in supportive and purposeful ways by using the computer as a composing partner" (p. 329). For example, during the brainstorming process of writing she identifies Pics 4 Learning (www.pics4learning.com/indexphp?view=browse) as a source that inspires writing because it consists of thousands of images that help students expand their ideas for writing. While re-reading, revising, and editing drafts she recommends Author's Computer Chair (www.readingon line.org/electronic/rt4-04_column/) because the program allows students to cut, paste, and manipulate text.

Struggling readers and writers may be motivated to use their computers for writing by reading or listening to Dietlof Reiche's *Freddy in Peril* (2004). The author develops an articulate hamster who can read and write with the help of a Mac computer. Freddy uses his owner's computer to write his stories and e-mail to send messages.

Gifted and Accelerated Readers and Writers

One of the challenges facing a teacher of gifted and accelerated students is to continually help students expand their experiences and interests so they stay motivated. Many gifted and accelerated students are already involved with special projects at school or at home that are enhanced through technology. After introducing a unit on space, for example, a teacher encouraged her accelerated fifth-grade science students to identify individual projects related to space that they would like to research outside of class. She kept the requirements of their final projects open, but encouraged them to keep a daily journal tracking their individual research projects.

One student researched the qualifications for and training process of astronauts. In his journal he wrote about his research discoveries as well as a daily reflection "If I were an astronaut." At the end of the unit, in addition to his factual reporting, he produced several stories of science fiction.

During this unit, students visited planetariums, interviewed scientists, became scientific pen pals by e-mail, and watched scientific programs such as "NOVA." Students used an article by Kate Mitchoff (2005) to locate web sites recommended by *School Library Journal*. The following interactive web sites provide exciting information and challenge for accelerated students who want to learn more about space science.

Cool Cosmos: www.Coolcosmos.ipac.caltech.edu/.

Infrared Processing and Analysis Center and the SIRTF Science Center at California Institute of Technology. (Gr. 5+)

This interactive web site explores the universe through a study of infrared technology. Students can build a model cyber telescope and take part in online games with space themes.

NASAKids: kids.msfc.nasa.gov.

National Aeronautics and Space Administration (NASA) (Gr. 6+)

Students can discover cutting-edge technology as they learn about space probes. They can explore how astronauts live in space and learn more about a career with NASA.

Reflect on Your Reading

How can technology help differentiated instruction? What are the characteristics of programs that reinforce reading instruction for ELL or struggling readers and writers? What types of technology are especially effective for gifted and accelerated readers? What characteristics of web sites would challenge these readers?

RunawayUniverse: www.pbs.org/wgbh/nova/universe/.

WGBH Science Unit (Gr. 6+)

This site is developed by the television program "NOVA" in association with PBS. It includes a time line of the creation of the universe. The web site answers questions such as, "How large is the universe?"

The Space Place: spaceplace.nasa.gov/en/kids.

National Aeronautics and Space Administration (Gr. 3+)

An interactive site allows students to create a star finder and find information about the planets. They can watch interviews with NASA scientists.

When working with gifted and accelerated students, teachers need to be open-ended in their assignments in order to allow the gifted student room to explore his or her individual creativity.

Summary

This chapter focuses on the expanding use of technology in schools in the twenty-first century. Instructional technology can be organized into a four-part taxonomy: media for communication, media for expression, media for inquiry, and media for construction. Technology can be used in the reading curriculum to enhance word recognition, vocabulary, and reading comprehension. Guidelines are useful for evaluating skill development software.

Software programs can help students with various aspects of the writing process. Furthermore, in this age of the Internet, students must know the meaning and consequences of plagiarism.

Key Terms

e-mail, p. 460

software programs, p. 460

web sites, p. 464

electronic library and resources, p. 465

electronic books, p. 465

plagiarism, p. 471

mylabschool
Where the classroom comes to life!

For video clips of authentic classroom instruction on **Technology in the Classroom**, go to Allyn & Bacon's MyLabSchool.com. In MLS courses, click on Foundations/Intro to Teaching, go to MLS Video Lab, and select **Module 8**.

Extend Your Reading

1. Choose an article in a literacy journal that emphasizes either research in technology or the application of technology in education. Prepare a review of the article and either discuss it in class or use the written review as an assignment. The following articles are a few choices that you might consider:

   ■ Bette Chambers, et al. (2002), "Developing a Computer-Assisted Tutoring Program to Help Children at Risk Learn to Read," in *Educational Research and Evaluation*, 7, 223–239.

   ■ Linda D. Labbo, et al. (November 2003), "Teacher Wisdom Stories: Cautions and Recommendations for Using Computer-Related Technologies for Literacy Instruction," in *The Reading Teacher*, 57, 300–304.

   ■ Joyce F. Long, et al. (Autumn 2001), "The Effectiveness of Persuasive Messages: Comparing Traditional and Computerized Texts," in *Theory Into Practice*, 40, 266–270.

2. Read the most current *Reading Teacher* or *School Library Journal* to identify any sources that evaluate computer-assisted programs for use in the classroom. What are the latest programs being recommended?

3. With a group of your peers review and evaluate the effectiveness of software programs recommended by the *School Library Journal*. You might consider questions such as: Are the software programs easy to use, are they age appropriate? How will they interest students? Is the content accurate? How does the program reinforce learning in the reading program? How does the program expand the interests of the students?

4. Develop a unit similar to the thematic unit found in this chapter that uses both literature and web sites. Additional examples of units that use both literature and web sites are developed by Shelley B. Wepner and Lucinda C. Ray (2000), who develop lesson plans around fables, an author study, a slavery unit, and a survival unit.

5. Choose an area of literacy study and identify web sites that would provide background information for the study.

6. Choose a web site discussed in Phyllis Levy Mandell and Alex Sinclair's "Web Site Review" in *School Library Journal* (October 2004), 71–72. Evaluate how you would use one of the web sites for Black History/Civil Rights or Native Americans Today. How would the information on the web site add to the background knowledge of your students?

For Further Reading

1. Jane E. Maslin, et al. (April 2002), "Teaching Ideas," in *The Reading Teacher*, 55, 628–640.

2. Donna J. Merkley, et al. (November 2001), "Addressing the English Language Arts Technology Standard in a Secondary Reading Methodology Course," in the *Journal of Adolescent and Adult Literacy*, 45, 220–232.

3. Walter Minkel (May 2003), "Keys to the Future: When Should Students Learn Proper Keyboarding Skills?" in *School Library Journal*, 49, 34–36.

4. Charol Shakeshaft, et al. (January 2002), "Choosing the Right Technology," in *School Administrator,* 59, 34–37.

5. Pamela A. Solvie, et al. (February 2004), "The Digital Whiteboard: A Tool in Early Literacy Instruction," in *The Reading Teacher,* 57, 484–487.

6. William H. Teale, et al. (April 2002), "Exploring Literacy on the Internet," in *The Reading Teacher,* 55, 654–660.

7. Umesh Thakkar, et al. (November 2001), "Extending Literacy through Participation in New Technologies," in the *Journal of Adolescent & Adult Literacy,* 45, 212–220.

REFERENCES

Arthur's Teacher Trouble [Computer software]. (1993). Cambridge, MA: Broderbund/The Learning Company.

Bruce, Bertram, & Levin, James. (2003). "Roles for New Technologies in Language Arts: Inquiry, Communication, Construction, and Expression." In James Flood, Diane Lapp, James R. Squire, & Julie M. Jensen (Eds.) *Handbook of Research on Teaching the English Language Arts,* 2nd ed. Mahwah, NJ: Lawrence Erlbaum, pp. 649–657.

Buckleitner, Warren. (February 2004). "Essential Software." *School Library Journal,* 50, 56–58.

Burniske, R. W. (2000). *Literacy in the Cyberage.* Arlington Heights, IL: Skylight. *Carmen Sandiego Word Detective,* version 1.0 [computer software], (1997). Cambridge, MA: Broderbund/The Learning Company.

Casey, Jean M. (2000). *Creating the Early Literacy Classroom.* Englewood, CO: Libraries Unlimited.

Chambers, Bette, Abrami, Philip C., McWhaw, Katherine, & Therrien, Michel Charles (2001). "Developing a Computer-Assisted Tutoring Program to Help Children at Risk Learn to Read." *Educational Research and Evaluation,* 7, 223–239.

Costa, Arthur L., ed. (2001). *Developing Minds: A Resource Book for Teaching Thinking,* 3rd ed. Alexandria, VA: Association for Supervision and Curriculum Development.

Daisy's Castle, version 1.0 [computer software] (1993). Scotts Valley, CA: Great Wave Software.

Daisy's Quest, version 1.0 [computer software] (1992). Scotts Valley, CA: Great Wave Software.

EasyBook Deluxe [computer software] (1998). Pleasantville, NY: Sunburst Communications.

Expression [computer software] (1996), Pleasantville, NY: Sunburst Communications.

Fox, Barbara J., & Mitchell, Mary Jane. (2000). "Using Technology to Support Word Recognition, Spelling, and Vocabulary Acquisition." In Shelley B. Wepner, William J. Valmont, & Richard Thurlow (Eds.). *Linking Literacy and Technology: A Guide for K–8 Classrooms.* Newark, DE: International Reading Association, pp. 42–75.

Frame Maker [computer software]. (1995). San Jose, CA: Adobe Systems.

Hafner, Katie. (June 21, 2004). "Old Search Engine, the Library, Tries to Fit into a Google World." *The New York Times,* pp. A1, A16.

Hirsch, E. D., Jr. (February 25, 2004). "Many Americans Can Read But Can't Comprehend." *USA Today,* p. A13.

Just Grandma and Me Deluxe [computer software]. (1997). Cambridge, MA: Broderbund/The Learning Company.

Kid Works Deluxe [computer software]. (1997). Torrance, CA: Knowledge Adventure.

Labbo, Linda D. (November 2005). "Books and Computer Response Activities That Support Literacy Development." *The Reading Teacher,* 59, 288–292.

Labbo, Linda D. (March 2006). "Using the Computer as English Language Learners' Composing Partner." *Language Arts,* 83, 329.

Labbo, Linda D., Leu, Donald J. Jr., Kinzer, Charles, Cammack, Dana, Kara-Soteriou, Julia, & Sanny Ruby. (November 2003). "Teacher Wisdom Stories: Cautions and Recommendations for Using Computer-Related Technologies for Literacy Instruction." *The Reading Teacher,* 57, 300–304.

Lankshear, Colin, & Snyder, Ilana. (2000). *Teachers and Techno-Literacy: Managing Literacy, Technology and Learning in Schools.* St. Leonard, Australia: Allen & Unwin.

Let's Go Read! An Island Adventure, version 1.02 [computer software]. (1998). Redmond, WA: Edmark.

Let's Go Read! An Ocean Adventure, version 1.0 [computer software]. (1998). Redmond WA: Edmark.

Long, Joyce F., Holleran, Theresa A., & Esterly, Elizabeth. (Autumn 2001). "The Effectiveness of Persuasive Messages: Comparing Traditional and Computerized Texts." *Theory Into Practice,* 40, 266–270.

Mandell, Phyllis Levy, & Sinclair, Alex. (October 2004). "Web Site Review." *School Library Journal,* 50, 71.

Maslin, Jane E., Nelson, Matthew E., Duffelmeyer Frederick A., McVee, Mary B., & Dickson, Ben A. (April 2002). "Teaching Ideas." *The Reading Teacher,* 55, 628–640.

Merkley, Donna J., Schmidt, Denise A., & Allen, Gayle. (November 2001). "Addressing the English Language Arts Technology Standard in a Secondary Reading Methodology Course." *Journal of Adolescent & Adult Literacy, 45,* 220–232.

Minkel, Walter. (April 2002). "Media Literacy—Part of the Curriculum?" *School Library Journal, 48,* 31.

Minkel, Walter. (May 2003). "Keys to the Future: When Should Students Learn Proper Keyboarding Skills?" *School Library Journal, 49,* 34–36,

Mitchoff, Kate. (December 2005). "The Heavens Above." *School Library Journal, 51,* 69–70.

Norton, Donna E. (2004). *The Effective Teaching of Language Arts,* 6th ed. Upper Saddle River, NJ: Merrill/Prentice Hall.

Norton, Donna E., & Norton, Saundra E. (2003). *Language Arts Activities for Children,* 5th ed. Upper Saddle River, NJ: Merrill/Prentice Hall.

The Print Shop Deluxe [computer software]. (1996). Cambridge, MA: Broderbund/The Learning Company.

Reading Galaxy [computer software]. (1996). Cambridge, MA: Broderbund/The Learning Company.

Report of the National Reading Panel (2000). Washington, DC: National Institute of Child Health and Human Development.

Selingo, Jeffrey. (5 February 2004). "When a Search Engine Isn't Enough, Call a Librarian." *New York Times,* p. E7.

Shakeshaft, Charol, Mann, Dale, Becker, Jonathan, & Sweeney, Kara. (January 2002). "Choosing the Right Technology." *School Administrator, 59,* 34–37.

Solvie, Pamela A. (February 2004). "The Digital Whiteboard: A Tool in Early Literacy Instruction." *The Reading Teacher, 57,* 484–487.

Storybook Weaver Deluxe [computer software]. (1996). Cambridge, MA: The Learning Company.

Student Writing Center [computer software]. (1993). Cambridge, MA: The Learning Company.

Sullivan, Jane E., & Sharp, Jean. (2000). "Using Technology for Writing Development." In Shelley B. Wepner, William J. Valmont, & Richard Thurlow (Eds.). *Linking Literacy and Technology: A Guide for K–8 Classrooms.* Newark, DE: International Reading Association, 106–132.

Sutherland-Smith, Wendy. (April 2002). "Weaving the Literacy Web: Changes in Reading from Page to Screen." *The Reading Teacher, 55,* 662–670.

SuperSonic Phonics, version 1.0 [computer software]. (1997). North Billerica, MA: Curriculum Associates.

Teale, William H., Labbo, Linda D., Kinzer, Chuck, & Leu Jr., Donald J. (April 2002). "Exploring Literacy on the Internet." *The Reading Teacher, 55,* 654–660.

Tenner, Edward. (March 26, 2006). "Searching for Dummies." *New York Times,* p. A12.

Thakkar, Umesh, Hogan, Maureen P., Williamson, Jo, & Bruce, Bertram C. (November 2001). "Extending Literacy through Participation in New Technologies." *Journal of Adolescent and Adult Literacy, 45,* 212–220.

Wepner, Shelley B., & Ray, Lucinda C. (2000). "Using Technology for Reading Development." In Shelley B. Wepner, William J. Valmont, & Richard Thurlow (Eds.), *Linking Literacy and Technology: A Guide for K–8.* Newark, DE: International Reading Association, 76–105.

Wilson, James M. (2001). "Technology and Thinking: The Evolving Relationship." In Arthur Costa (Ed.), *Developing Minds: A Resource Book for Teaching Thinking,* 3rd ed. Alexandra, VA: Association for Supervision and Curriculum Development. 474–478.

Word Munchers Deluxe, version 1.02 [computer software]. (1996). Cambridge, MA: MECC/The Learning Company.

Writers Studio [computer software]. (1990). Sunnyvale, CA: Computer Curriculum Corporation.

Young Abraham Lincoln: Log-Cabin President [computer software]. (1996). Mahwah, NJ: Troll.

Young Harriet Tubman: Freedom Fighter [computer software]. (1996). Mahwah, NJ: Troll.

Children's Literature References

Craighead, George Jean. (1972). *Julie of the Wolves.* Illustrated by John Schoenherr. Harper & Row.

Paulsen, Gary. (1987). *Hatchet.* Bradbury.

Reiche, Dietlof. (2004). *Freddy in Peril.* Translated by John Brownjohn. Illustrated by Joe Capeda. Scholastic.

Rowling, J. K. (1997). *Harry Potter and the Sorcerer's Stone.* Scholastic.

Rowling, J. K. (1999). *Harry Potter and the Chamber of Secrets.* Scholastic.

Rowling, J. K. (1999). *Harry Potter and the Prisoner of Azkaban.* Scholastic.

Rowling, J. K. (2000). *Harry Potter and the Goblet of Fire.* Scholastic.

Rowling, J. K. (2003). *Harry Potter and the Order of the Phoenix.* Scholastic.

Rowling, J. K. (2005). *Harry Potter and the Half-Blood Prince.* Scholastic

Putting It All Together
Literacy Instruction That Works

CHAPTER **OUTLINE**

Balanced Literacy
Balance between Published Reading Programs and Trade Books
Balancing between Prescribed Instruction and Instruction Based on Individual Learners
Balance between Teacher-Guided Instruction and Independent Reading
Balance between Teacher-Directed Instruction and Center-Based Discoveries
Balance That Integrates Listening, Speaking, Reading, and Writing

Grouping Arrangements for Reading Instruction
Reading Aloud to Students
Ability Level Groupings
Reading Interest Groups
Book Clubs
Shared Reading Groups
Shared Writing Groups
Partner Reading Groups
Coaching Groups
Flexibility and Transitioning between Groups

Organizing the Classroom

After reading this chapter you will be able to answer the following questions:

1. What is a balanced literacy approach to teaching reading? What instruction should be balanced?

2. What are the uses of and advantages for various types of grouping arrangements for reading instruction?

3. How does the philosophy for reading instruction influence the organization of the classroom?

4. What is the difference between readability and leveling of instructional materials? What are the advantages and disadvantages of each approach?

Read All About It!

"Harlem Kindergartners Receive a Key to the Future"

by Elissa Gootman, *New York Times,* September 30, 2004

Tiffany Hedges, 24, arrived at the Apollo Theater yesterday morning expecting some kind of education announcement. What she learned was that her son Tyrell, 5, would be one of 400 Harlem kindergartners to receive a free college education.

Tyrell's school, Public School 161, was one of five Harlem elementary schools whose entire kindergarten classes will be the next beneficiaries of Say Yes to Education, a program aimed at helping children in poor urban neighborhoods overcome the obstacles to high school graduation and higher education.

Students at the schools—Public Schools 57, 83, 161, 180 and 182—will get extra help including tutoring and special summer school programs, throughout the next 13 years. If all goes well, they will have college fully paid for, wherever they get in.

The announcement was made by George Weiss, a Hartford money manager who has created similar, although smaller, programs in Hartford, Philadelphia and East Cambridge, Mass. Mr. Weiss has pledged $20 million toward the Harlem program, which is expected to cost $50 million, and is trying to raise the rest.

"What we're trying to do is raise the expectations of a whole school, and working together, we can level the playing field,"

Mr. Weiss told the kindergartners, parents and teachers who gathered at the Apollo after being told by their principals only that there would be an important educational announcement. . . .

Other companies have offered donations in kind—IBM offered computer labs; the law firm of Bingham McCutchen offered free legal services to the children's families for 15 years; and Harlem Hospital Center offered to provide all health care services—but so far, the money has not poured in. Mr. Weiss said he had raised about $160,000.

Each successive Say Yes to Education program has started with younger children and included more support services. In Harlem, siblings of Say Yes children will be eligible for smaller college scholarships, and their parents will be eligible for continuing education programs and scholarships. An extra reading teacher and social worker will be placed in each of the five schools.

Harlem was selected because of its high dropout rates and proximity to Teachers College at Columbia University, which is helping with the program. But the five schools were selected for their strengths. . . .

Dr. Jacqueline Ancess, a member of the selection committee, said the goal was to choose stable schools with strong, innovative principals.

"Say Yes is adding some resources to a school that already has a foundation," said Dr. Ancess, a co-director of the National Center for Restructuring Education, Schools and Teaching at Teachers College. "This is not a program that has the intention to go into a school that is in very desperate straits and turn it around."

Read All About It!
Critical Thinking Questions

- Why do you think this program for helping students get a college education begins in kindergarten?

- What are the resources that Say Yes to Education is adding to the schools that should make a difference for educating the students?

- Why do you think the program includes provisions for the total family? What are the motivational factors behind involving the total school and family?

- If you visited one of these schools, what impacts of the program might be visible?

How do contemporary teachers provide instruction in reading? A study of elementary reading instructional practices reported by teachers and administrators (Baumann, Hoffman, Duffy-Hester, & Ro 2000), found that the majority of today's teachers:

1. Teach in self-contained, heterogeneous classes.
2. Use a significant amount of instructional time for reading.
3. Provide explicit instruction in phonic analysis.
4. Administer mandated standardized tests.
5. Report that struggling or underachieving readers are their greatest challenge.
6. Use a balanced, eclectic approach to teaching reading that uses both basals and trade books.
7. Use an emergent literacy perspective rather than a reading readiness viewpoint.
8. Have access to school and classroom libraries.

This final chapter addresses the concerns of teachers teaching reading in this real world. We focus especially on developing a balanced, eclectic approach to teaching reading that uses both basals and trade books (various selections of fiction and non-fiction literature). The chapter addresses concerns of teachers who are in self-contained, heterogeneous classes as they try to manage their reading instruction through various types of groupings and discussion formats that allow for both teacher-directed and center-based discovery.

Balanced Literacy

A **balanced reading** program according to D. Ray Reutzel (1999) is not a *this* versus *that* approach, but one that offers "a comprehensive, seamless blend of factors related to reading success, coupled with a solid cadre of reading instructional approaches: reading aloud, language experience, shared reading, guided reading, interactive writing, independent writing, and independent reading" (p. 322). As teachers develop a balanced program they provide:

- balance between published reading materials such as basal series and trade books
- balance between sequenced, prescribed instruction and instruction based on individual learners
- balance between teacher guided instruction and independent reading
- balance between teacher-directed instruction and center-based discoveries
- balance that integrates all of the language arts including listening, speaking, reading, and writing

This balance of instruction is central to a presentation by the 2005 President of the International Reading Association, Richard L. Allington (June/July 2005). He argues that reading instruction needs to go beyond the "Five Pillars of Effective

A teacher uses a combination of materials to develop literacy for life.

Reading Instruction" identified by the National Reading Panel that includes phonological awareness, phonics, fluency, vocabulary, and comprehension. To these five areas for effective instruction, Allington adds five additional pillars including matching pupils and texts; providing access to an array of interesting texts, providing student choices about what to read, and encouraging collaboration with other children while reading; providing classroom organization that includes a balance of whole-group, small-group, and side-by-side lessons every day; providing instruction in the connections between writing and reading; and including access to expert tutoring.

Another argument for balanced reading instruction is advanced by the Alliance for Excellent Education reported in *Reading Today* (February-March 2005). The report, written by Gina Biancarosa and Catherine Snow for the Carnegie Corporation, states that middle school students need a "more balanced approach to literacy education that builds on what was taught in earlier grades" (p. 23). The report highlights 10 elements for effective adolescent literacy programs that are important for the reading curriculum. Notice how these elements require a balanced instructional approach: (1) direct, explicit comprehension instruction, (2) instructional principles embedded in content reading, (3) motivated and self-directed learning, (4) text-based collaborative learning, (5) tutoring, (6) diverse texts, (7) intensive writing, (8) technology instruction, (9) ongoing assessment, and (10) extended time for literacy.

Balance in middle-school reading is also highlighted in a description of two schools that won the International Reading Associations Exemplary Reading Program Awards (*Reading Today,* 2004). The article emphasizes reading through the content areas, book clubs, book talks, book buddy programs, literature circles, and oral presentations that "give students the chance to share their enthusiasm for reading" (p. 17).

This balance that includes both instruction in reading and application of reading ability and gaining knowledge through content areas such as social studies and history may be both more difficult to achieve and more important for students to experience if the curriculum is narrowed for lower-achieving readers. Sam Dillon (2006) reports a survey by the Center on Education Policy that "found that since the passage of the federal law (No Child Left Behind), 71 percent of the nation's 15,000 school districts had reduced the hours of instructional time spent on history, music, and other subjects to open up more time for reading and math . . . . Narrowing the curriculum has clearly become a nationwide pattern" (p. A1).

Several letters to the editor following the publication of Dillon's news article provide informative responses to the narrowing of the curriculum and the eliminating or reducing time spent on subjects such as history and social studies. For example, P. David Pearson (2006), a reading educator and the dean of the Graduate School of Education, University of California at Berkeley, expresses his belief that shortchanging these subjects is also harmful for reading. He states: "Reading and writing must always be about something, and the something comes from subject-matter pedagogy—not from more practicing of reading skills. Reading skills are important, but without knowledge, they are pretty useless. We'd all be better off if schools taught reading as a 'tool' to support learning those big ideas found in subject-matter instruction" (p. A22).

Sally K. Chrisman (2006), a seventh-grade reading and drama teacher, echoes Pearson's concerns and beliefs about how reading should include reading in the various subject areas. She states: "If a creative, energetic reading teacher has the autonomy to use the highest quality children's literature and nonfiction in the classroom, then the reading curriculum can include history, science, medicine, geography and all other subjects . . . . Children allowed to have some choice in reading material, to read and discuss great books in the classroom, to find the books' settings on a world map and to dramatize their favorite scenes, can recognize that books are a source of valuable and interesting information on any subject" (p. A22).

These letters show that narrowing of the curriculum makes it more imperative that teachers provide broader, not narrower, reading coverage in their classes. Both E. D. Hirsch, Jr. (2004) and Thomas L. Friedman (2006) emphasize that students in twenty-first-century schools need a broader education that leads to more sophisticated comprehension of content and challenging subjects that develop creative problem solving and innovation. Hirsch expresses concern that many Americans can read but do not comprehend what they read because they lack the cultural literacy background developed through a knowledge of history, literature, art, music, science, and math that is required for comprehension.

Friedman expresses a concern for education that emphasizes rote learning that is unleavened by art, literature, music, and the humanities. He believes that rote learning such as that used in China and India leads to higher standardized test scores but does not develop creativity and innovation. He concludes: "My guess is that we're at the start of a global convergence in education: China and India will try to inspire more creativity in their students. America will get more rigorous in math and science. And this convergence will be a great spur to global growth and innovation. It's a win-win. But some will win more than others—and it will be those who get this balance right the fastest, in the most schools" (p. A21). This right balance, as long as it does not focus only on the rote learning approach used in China and India, is one that teachers should strive for in our public schools.

Balance between Published Reading Programs and Trade Books

One of the major concerns of reading teachers is how to balance the reading program between basal series and trade books. This is a real concern because many schools are investing thousands of dollars in the basal series and expect them to be used by teachers and followed by students. Let us begin with basal series and try to add the balance.

BASAL READING SERIES   **Basal reading series** are the most widely used materials for teaching reading in elementary schools. Chapter 1, "Changing Trends in Reading Education," compared basal reading series published over the past one hundred years. The first series, *Stepping Stones to Literature—A First Reader* (Arnold & Gilbert, 1902) developed the ability to read and understand literature through poetry, various genres of literature, and art interpretation. The second series, *Reading with Phonics* (Hay & Wingo, 1948) focused on phonics instruction, and the materials read by the students were stories written to match the phonics skills being taught. These two series had two very different philosophies about how reading should be taught and the student outcomes related to reading instruction.

The third series, *McGraw-Hill Reading* (2001), is characteristic of the various basal series available in schools today. It also includes a combination of philosophies found in the 1902 basal and in the 1948 basal. Both literary elements and phonics are provided in the series. Newer basal series respond to the concerns of the states, especially in states like California and Texas, in which there are state adoptions. Consequently, the basals may be aligned to state tests. Contemporary basals such as the McGraw-Hill Reading Series include a structured development of reading skills beginning with readiness materials designed to teach sound/symbol relationships, blending sounds, and high-frequency words. The grade-level basals include a reading textbook for each student. These texts include poetry in which students read selections aloud, stories in art in which they look at a painting and answer questions about the painting, a story to be read and discussed, story questions and activities that relate to the story, a section on study skills to accompany the section, and a short comprehension test.

The stories to be read in Unit 1 of the third-grade reader include a Japanese tale, a nonfiction Latino story written in both English and Spanish, two science nonfiction stories, and a science article. There are three units in this basal; they all follow the same format: a poem, stories in art, stories that represent a variety of genres of literature, study questions and activities, study skills, and test power.

Each basal includes a practice workbook with a teacher's edition that provides the answers and a series of "Language Support" and "Extend" materials. For example, the "Language Support for Grade 3" includes lesson plans and masters for worksheets. The "Extend" materials are designed to teach various literary skills such as vocabulary and story comprehension, study skills, and context clues to accompany each story.

Each unit also includes lessons from "A Grammar Practice Book" and a "Spelling Practice Book." The series includes a "Diagnostic/Placement Evaluation" that includes an "Individual Reading Inventory," "a Running Record," "Word Recognition and Placement Tests," "Decoding and Phonics Inventory," "Vocabulary Strategies Inventory," and Comprehension Strategies Inventory." See Table 12.1 for an example of a lesson plan found in "Language Support" to accompany *Grandfather's Journey*, written and illustrated by Allen Say.

TABLE 12.1

Lesson Plan Sample

GRANDFATHER'S JOURNEY pp. 12A-47P
Written and Illustrated by Allen Say
BUILD BACKGROUND FOR LANGUAGE SUPPORT

I. Focus on Reading

Focus on Skills

OBJECTIVE: Analyze character and setting

Alternate Teaching Strategy
Teacher's Edition p. T60

TPR

II. Read the Literature
Vocabulary
journey
surrounded
enormous
astonished
towering
scattered

CONCEPT

nonverbal prompt for active participation

one- or two-word response prompt

Develop Visual Literacy

Point to the people in the painting who are crying and waving. Ask; *What are they doing?* Dramatize crying. Encourage students to pretend to cry. Ask: *How do the people feel?* (sad) Ask, *Why do you think they are sad?* Model looking behind you.

Ask, *Why are the people looking behind them?* If necessary, explain that the people are leaving their homes to find new homes in another country. Help students notice the people's clothing. Ask, *Do you think this picture was painted today or a long time ago? What picture clues help you know that?*

Vocabulary

Print the vocabulary words on the chalkboard. Say each word and have students repeat them after you. Give students a number of objects, such as dominos, blocks, etc., that can be stacked. Ask them to make two towers, one taller than the other. Have them point to the taller of the stacks and say: *This one* is <u>towering</u>. Explain that to *tower* means that it rises high up in the air. Then have them take the objects and make a circle on their desks. Tell them to put one object in the middle and say: *This one* is <u>surrounded</u>. Make sure they understand that to be surrounded means there are things all around it. Have them move the objects all around their desks in random order. Say: *Now they are <u>scattered</u>.* Ask them to show you how to scatter the objects and then have them repeat the sentence. Ask them to work with a partner and build the tallest tower they can using all their objects. As you walk around the room, show great surprise and say: *I am <u>astonished</u> to see such a tall tower!* If a tower falls, show surprise again and say; *I am astonished that your tower fell!* Let students walk around and observe their friends' towers and use the word *astonished*. Finally, ask one student to walk around the room collecting the objects and then say: [student's name] *is going on a <u>journey</u> to collect the blocks.* Have other students ask as he or she walks around the room: *Are you enjoying your journey?* Let students discuss journeys they have taken or where they would like to go.

Evaluate Prior Knowledge

Display pictures of different types of transportation. (boat, car, train, airplane, journeys etc.) Bring in pictures or video of a vacation. Share with students what you did on a recent journey.

Invite students to draw pictures of journeys they would like to take. Encourage them to show where the journey would begin, how they would travel, and where they would go. Have them share and explain their pictures with the class.

Develop Oral Language

Invite students to share their own travel experiences with the class.

- Preproduction: *Show us* (point to class and self) *ways you have traveled by pointing to the pictures.* (Point to pictures of boat, car, and so on.)
- Early production: *Did you have a good trip? Who went with you?*

(Continued)

TABLE 12.1
(Continued)

prompt for short answers to higher-level thinking skills	• Speech emergence: *Name these objects.* (point to pictures of various forms of transportation: train, bus, airplane, car, ship.) *How did you travel on your journey? How did you get to school today? What did you see?*
prompt for detailed answers to higher-level thinking skills	• Intermediate fluency: *How did you feel while you were on your journey? Why did you feel that way? What did you see and do on your journey?*

Guided Reading

Preview and Predict

Share with students that the author of this story tells about his grandfather and the many journeys his grandfather took. Explain that the author talks about his grandfather, grandmother, parents, and eventually himself. Most of this story takes place before the author is born. Tell students: *Grandfather's Journey takes us to many exciting places. Let's see where this story may take us.* Lead students on a picture walk using the story illustrations to reinforce the concept of a journey. Ask questions such as: *Where is Grandfather now? How do you think he is feeling? Whom does he meet on his journey? Where do you think his journey will take him next?* Students needing language support may respond with one-word answers or point to the illustrations.

Objectives

GRAPHIC ORGANIZER
Blackline Master 1

• To reinforce understanding of character and setting
• To reinforce working cooperatively

Materials

One copy of Blackline Master 1 per group of three students; pencils; student copy of *Grandfather's Journey*

Organize students into groups of three, placing students of varying abilities in each group. Emphasize character and setting as you take a second picture walk through *Grandfather's Journey*. Invite groups to look at each illustration and determine the setting of each. On page 17, for example, guide students to see that Grandfather is on a ship. Simplify the story elements for students needing extra language support by asking: *Who is in the picture? Where is he or she?* On the graphic organizer, write the word *ship* under *Setting,* and the word *Grandfather* under *Character.* If necessary, have students help you complete this graphic organizer on the chalkboard or on an overhead.

Reinforce the story elements of character and setting by using this graphic organizer for familiar fairy tales or nursery rhymes. List the setting and/or character and have students complete the chart by filling in the corresponding character/setting. Some examples: brick house and three pigs; Red Riding Hood and Grandmother's house; candy cottage and Hansel and Gretel; Humpty Dumpty and a wall; Jack and Jill and a hill. Students needing language support may draw pictures of characters and settings rather than writing the words. Encourage them to describe their drawings.

III. Build Skills
Comprehension

Objectives

REVIEW STORY ELEMENTS

• To analyze and make inferences about character and setting
• To develop word identification and word meaning

Blackline Master 2

• To practice working cooperatively

TABLE 12.1
(Continued)

Materials

Alternate Teaching Strategy
Teacher's Edition p. T60

One copy of Blackline Master 2 per student; pencils; student copy of *Grandfather's Journey*

Copy the Venn diagram on the chalkboard. Read the words in the word bank aloud with students, demonstrating meanings if necessary. Direct students back to the story. Explain that the story has two settings: California and Japan. Then ask, *Are there mountains in California?* Write or draw *mountains* on the left side of the diagram. Repeat the question, using the right side of the diagram and the setting, Japan. Say, *Both California and Japan have mountains.* Move *mountains* to the center of the diagram. Erase the words and/or drawings in the left and right circles. If necessary, model placing another word, such as *village,* in the diagram. Then organize students into pairs. Encourage them to ask each other the question *Are/Is there _____ in California/Japan?* for each word in the word bank.

INFORMAL ASSESSMENT

Encourage students to compare and contrast the two settings and various characters in the story. Direct students to the illustration on page 24. Ask: *How are these people alike? How are these people different?*

Comprehension

INTRODUCE MAKE PREDICTIONS

Blackline Master 3

Objectives
• To practice making predictions
• To reinforce understanding of character

Materials

Alternate Teaching Strategy
Teacher's Edition p. T62

One copy of Blackline Master 3 per student; crayons or colored pencils

Help students understand making predictions. Tell students: *There is a big gray cloud outside. What will happen next?* (It will rain.) Point to the boy and read aloud his thought bubble. Be sure students understand that the boy is thinking these words. Ask students: *What do you think will happen next?* Encourage students to give simple responses. Then have them draw pictures to show what they think will happen next.

INFORMAL ASSESSMENT

Direct students to the text and illustration on page 30. Ask: *What is happening now? What do you think will happen next?*

Vocabulary Strategy

INTRODUCE COMPOUND WORDS

Blackline Master 4

Objectives
• To identify and define compound words
• To work cooperatively

Materials

Alternate Teaching Strategy
Teacher's Edition p. T63

One copy of Blackline Master 4 per student; pencils

Help students understand the meaning of *grandfather.* Show students that the two words *grand* and *father* are put together to make this new word. Write the words on cards, give one card to each of two students, and have them stand together to show how the two words combine. Pair students needing extra language support with more fluent readers. Read aloud the puzzle pieces and their definitions on the blackline master. If necessary, model combining the second and/or third word and its definition.

INFORMAL ASSESSMENT

Direct students to page 30. Ask them to find a compound word on the page. (song-birds) invite them to guess the word's meaning. (birds that sing songs)

As can be seen by the materials included in this basal series, it is an example of teacher-directed and guided material, and sequenced and prescribed instruction. The teachers' manuals are scripted so teachers have both questions and answers. The materials have advantages, especially for beginning teachers, because teachers do not need to develop their own lessons; the instructional materials are sequenced to provide systematic teaching of reading, and they review the reading skills.

The vast amounts of materials supplied by some basal series, however, require that teachers select only those activities that are appropriate for their students. Beginning teachers often respond to the large amounts of materials available by considering a basal series a total reading program; one that requires no other instructional strategies or materials. One concern about basal reading instruction is, "If teachers perceive basals as total reading programs, they may fail to provide the variety of experiences children need for a balanced program. Basals can never provide all of the reading situations a student needs to encounter" (Burns, Roe, & Smith 2002).

As we look at basal series let us consider some of the following advantages and disadvantages of the basals, as reflected in Table 12.2. If the goal is to develop a balanced reading program, how would you use the basal series but make changes to overcome the disadvantages of the basal series?

TABLE 12.2

Advantages and Disadvantages of a Basal Reading Program for Balanced Reading Instruction

Advantages	Disadvantages
1. Series includes a structured sequence of skills developed through the stories and workbooks.	1. The stories and sequence of skills may not be appropriate for all students.
2. The stories are leveled for reading difficulty that makes grouping by ability groups easy.	2. Students need more than ability groupings in order to make progress.
3. Basal series are developed by reading authorities who use research to support the structure.	3. Teachers are afraid to change the instructional activities developed by experts even if the stories and the activities may not motivate the students in a class.
4. Many of the lessons are designed for teacher-directed instruction.	4. The lessons do not provide opportunities for center-based discovery and individualized learning.
5. The newer basals often integrate the language arts.	5. An inquiry approach to education emphasizes unit teaching and integration of all the content areas.
6. Basals may be aligned to the tests of states that have state-mandated tests and curriculums.	6. The basals may not match the goals and objectives of the school district.

At this point you may wonder if research supports using only a published reading program to teach reading. Richard L. Allington (October-November 2005) answers this question when he concludes:

> No use of any commercial core reading program reliably produces better results than the use of locally developed core reading programs. Indiscriminate use of any core program such that all children in a grade are placed in a single strand, text, or level contradicts everything research and practice has taught us about matching students with curriculum appropriate to their level of development. The same is true for adoption of a single intervention program for struggling readers. Children differ. Struggling readers differ. Any curriculum decision that fails to acknowledge this must be considered unscientific." (p. 18)

BALANCING THE BASAL SERIES WITH TRADE BOOKS AND OTHER READING MATERIALS   It would be impossible to provide the diversity of reading materials or to meet individual interests or to conduct research and inquiry projects if the only materials read were from a basal reading series. The characteristics of the schools in Finland that have the highest literacy rates in the world, reported in Chapter 7 (Alvarez, 2004), would not be possible without expanding the reading curriculum through children's literature. Finnish educators reported three characteristics found in all schools:

1. Teachers read orally to children.
2. Teachers teach the folktales that reflect the culture.
3. All students spend considerable time in the library where they read all types of literature and conduct research using literature.

A teacher conducts a reading lesson for one of the ability groupings in her class.

These characteristics show the importance of balancing the reading program through trade books. Chapter 7 ("Reading, Writing, and Literature in the Content Areas: Kindergarten through Fourth Grades"), Chapter 8 ("Reading, Writing, and Literature in the Content Areas: Fourth through Eighth Grades"), and Chapter 10 ("Literacy Instruction for ELL Students, Multicultural Education, and Students with Special Needs") provide numerous examples of ways to add literature to bring balance to the basal reading program.

A story in a basal series may be a springboard to an expanded study of a culture. For example, the basal series discussed earlier had a Japanese folktale, a Chinese folktale, and a Latino story. Using the multicultural literature and literature strategies developed in Chapter 10, students and teachers can select one of the cultures and conduct an in-depth study of the culture.

The same basal includes a short biography of Benjamin Franklin. Students could read and discuss biographies of Benjamin Franklin such as Jean Fritz's *What's the Big Idea, Ben Franklin?* (1978) which is appropriate for eight-year-old students. A more advanced biography is Milton Meltzer's *Benjamin Franklin: The New American* (1988), which is appropriate for older readers and gives more historical background, uses quotes drawn from Franklin's writings and speeches, and develops a character with both strengths and weaknesses. Candace Fleming's *Ben Franklin's Almanac: Being a True Account of the Good Gentleman's Life* (2003) is modeled after Franklin's *Poor Richard's Almanack* and provides numerous glimpses into Franklin's life. These biographies could be used to add balance to a reading series by allowing students to expand their knowledge through independent reading. This basal reading story could also be expanded into an inquiry study about topics such as Benjamin Franklin's inventions, the literary characteristics of biographies, or biographies of other world leaders who lived during Franklin's time.

The basal concludes with an excerpt from E. B. White's *Charlotte's Web* (1952). This is the perfect time to have students read the rest of the book, either independently or as a class project, and expand their responses to Charlotte, Wilbur, and their adventures on Zuckerman's farm. When reading this book, students frequently identify the importance of friendship as a theme in books. They could read additional books in which friendship is shown as an important animal or human characteristic. An author study of E. B. White could investigate the author as well as other books by him including *Stuart Little* (1945) and *The Trumpet of the Swan* (1970). The basal also presents the illustrator of *Charlotte's Web,* Garth Williams. An artist study could be conducted that focuses on Williams's life and work including illustrations for Laura Ingalls Wilder's *Little House in the Big Woods* (1953) and the other "Little House" books and George Selden's *The Cricket in Times Square* (1960) and *Chester Cricket's Pigeon Ride* (1981).

Studies also show that reading newspapers as part of the curriculum benefits reading. A study conducted by the Newspaper Association of America Foundation and reported in *Reading Today* (February–March 2005) concluded that 62 percent of students who read newspapers as part of the curriculum continued to read newspapers as adults. In contrast, only 38 percent of those students who did not read newspapers in school read newspapers as adults. The study concluded that newspaper reading increases students' interest in the news and local and world political issues. If one of the goals of the reading program is to develop lifelong readers, then including newspapers and other types of journals in the reading program for older readers is also desirable.

Balancing between Prescribed Instruction and Instruction Based on Individual Learners

Two philosophies of reading develop very different instructional approaches (Ruddell 2002). The bottom-up philosophy emphasizes a predetermined scope and sequence in areas such as word analysis and comprehension. This approach is usually a skills-orientated approach that carefully develops and reinforces one skill before another skill is presented. This instruction is carefully prescribed with a heavy emphasis on testing and teaching the skills. This approach is found in many published phonics materials and in some basal series.

In contrast, the top-down philosophy stresses giving attention to skills as the needs arise. This top-down approach is found in many learning approaches labeled whole language. It is also found in individualized reading approaches. Characteristics of an individualized reading approach include (Burns, Roe, & Smith 2002):

1. Students choose materials that interest them.

2. Each child reads materials at his or her own pace.

3. The teacher helps students, individually or in small groups, when the students need a reading strategy such as word recognition or comprehension approach.

4. The teacher keeps records of each student's progress, noting strengths and weaknesses.

5. Teachers schedule student-teacher conferences several times a week to discuss, observe, or assess reading behaviors.

6. Students do independent work at their seats rather than spending most of the time in a group lead by the teacher.

In this type of individualized reading program, the teacher needs access to a wide range of reading materials. In order to have meaningful conferences with students about books read, the teacher needs to have read the books available to the students and developed a list of comprehension questions that could accompany the book. It is also helpful to identify word recognition and comprehension strategies that might help individual students understand the specific book.

Teachers may begin a file of cards they can use to remind themselves of book content and questions they might ask to accompany the book. (As a reminder, also include short answers to the questions.) This literature file can be developed gradually as teachers read and use more and more books. Table 12.3 is an example of a card that could accompany a book.

Balance between Teacher-Guided Instruction and Independent Reading

In teacher-guided instruction the teacher acts as a guide and reinforces skills. During teacher-guided instruction the teacher works with small groups of students who have similar needs. The teacher focuses on the learner and listens for the student responses. The purpose for instruction is to encourage the development of strategies

TABLE 12.3

A Literature Card to Accompany Carl Hiaasen's *Hoot* (2002)

Book Title	*Hoot* by Carl Hiaasen (Knopf, 2002)
Book Summary	Roy Eberthardt, a sixth-grade boy, is unhappy about his move from Montana to Florida until he discovers a purpose that changes his life as well as the lives of some of his classmates. What will happen when a developer wants to build a pancake house on a plot of land that is the home of an endangered owl? This book is filled with environmental issues and carries a strong statement about how a group of kids can make a difference and save the home of one small creature.
Grade Levels	Fourth through eighth.
Questions	*Literal Recognition:* Where does the story take place? What is the sequence of events that led Roy to protest against the land developer? Compare the difference in belief about the environment between Roy and the developer. Describe Roy's character traits that make him fight for the owl's habitat.
	Inference: What should we infer about Roy's character when the author states:
	"They've got permits to bury owls?" Roy asked in disbelief" (p. 156) What do you believe is the theme of the work? What message do you believe the author is trying to express? Think about the class before Roy got many of them involved in the project to save the owl and the class after they succeeded. How do you believe they are different? What made them different after this experience? What character traits does Roy display? What do you believe would have happened if the sixth-grade class had not tried to stop the development? Would the owls have found a new home? Why or why not?
	Evaluation: Do you agree with Roy and his classmates who believe that saving the owl is important? Why or why not? Do you believe that this is a good way for the author to approach the problems related to environmental issues? The author developed both person versus person and person versus society conflicts. Which conflicts do you believe were the most believable? What techniques did the author use to make the conflicts believable?
	Appreciation: How did you respond to the plot and theme of the story? What was your reaction when the class worked together to save the owls? Which of the characters did you feel the closest to? Which of the characters would you like to have as a best friend? Why? How did the author encourage you to visualize the setting? Have you ever felt or known anyone who had an experience like Roy and his classmates?
	Inquiry Ideas
	Search newspapers and other sources for examples of environmental issues. What animals or environments might be endangered? How have groups tried to save the habitats or the environment?

for independent reading. The materials used may be from a basal reading series or literature-based materials. During teacher-guided instruction the teacher:

1. Groups students with similar needs. (These groupings are flexible and change with the needs of the students.)

2. Models the use of various word attack and comprehension strategies.

3. Observes students reading at their instructional reading levels (90–94 percent accuracy). The instructional reading level is found using an informal Reading Inventory.

4. Emphasizes vocabulary development.

5. Directly teaches new strategies.

6. Keeps track of individual reading strengths and weaknesses.

The purpose of teacher-guided reading is the development of independent readers who can read fluently and comprehend reading material. To develop independent readers students need many opportunities to apply their reading strategies using materials they can read with 95–100 percent accuracy. The purpose of independent reading is to encourage students to use effective reading strategies such as summarizing, clarifying, and predicting when they read. To develop independent reading activities the teacher:

1. Provides daily opportunities for students to read materials of their own choosing.

2. Collects a wide variety of materials and various genres of literature written at levels to meet the needs of the students. (The Fry Readability Graph is included at the end of this chapter.)

3. Has conferences with students in which they can discuss their books.

Independent reading is very important at all grade levels. Gay Ivey and Karen Broaddus (2001) surveyed middle school students and asked them what makes them want to read. They concluded: "It is clear that high-engagement reading and language arts classrooms would include time to read, time to listen to teachers read, and access to personally interesting materials" (p. 370).

Balance between Teacher-Directed Instruction and Center-Based Discoveries

Teacher-directed instruction, as the name implies, emphasizes the teaching of specific reading or writing strategies such as how to locate and write main ideas, analyze a selection for theme and point of view, identify points of conflict in a story, and develop characterization in a text. These are strategies, such as locating and developing theme, that most students need help in developing. Consequently, teachers need to teach many of the strategies developed in Chapters 7 and 8 in this text. By first teaching the strategies, students learn to use the strategies in their independent reading and writing.

Richard L. Allington and Patricia M. Cunningham (2002) are adamant about the need for teacher-directed instruction when they argue, "What all children need, and some need more of, is models, explanations, and demonstrations of how reading is accomplished. What most do not need are more assignments without teacher-directed instruction, yet much of the work children do in school is not accompanied by any sort of instructional interaction or demonstration" (p. 46).

Modeling, explaining, and demonstrating are necessary for children learning to read and write. The modeling examples developed in Chapter 6, "Modeling Similes with Lower Elementary Students" and "Modeling Inferencing Characterization with Students in the Upper Grades," are designed to show students how to analyze evidence from a text and to develop understanding for the requirements for effective reasoning. Each of the modeling activities begins with developing background

Listening centers with earphones help students follow the text using prerecorded tapes.

knowledge and then proceeds through a text as the teacher first reads a selection, then asks students questions about the selection. The teacher models the question and answer process by answering the question, providing the evidence used to answer the question, and revealing the thought processes used to reason out the answer. This process models, explains, and demonstrates how the teacher comprehends similes in one example and inferring characterization in the other example. Both modeling examples continue as students join as they listen to or read other examples, answer questions, provide evidence for answers, and explore their reasoning. During the modeling lesson the teacher guides the students to help them explore and use their own thought processes. The teacher explains and demonstrates how to use evidence presented in a text to develop logical answers.

Reading aloud to students is another important modeling activity. Through this activity teachers model fluency in reading and introduce students to a wide variety of stories, share quality literature, develop appreciation for authors, and explore various genres of literature. Because students' listening levels are usually higher than their reading levels, reading aloud to students provides important background knowledge that they might not get from their own reading.

Learning centers provide many opportunities to use and expand on the skills learned during teacher-directed instruction. Learning centers are also used by teachers as a classroom management tool. What happens to the remainder of the class when the teacher meets with students during small group discussions? Will the students take part in meaningless busy work, or will they be actively involved with activities that allow them to expand on the learning presented during group reading instruction?

Michael P. Ford and Michael F. Opitz (2002) provide guidelines for developing successful learning centers that allow students to become independent learners:

1. The students need to be taught how to function independently within the center. For example, do they need to know how to work with others, to use a tape recorder, or to locate materials?

2. Develop activities in the center that encourage students to advance their knowledge about literacy. For example, do they need repeated practice reading a story or to work with a partner who will help them comprehend a story? Do they need to write a response to a story read in the group? To improve oral fluency, do they need to listen to a story read on tape?

3. Make sure that students fully understand the activities by discussing, modeling, and practicing the activities during teacher-directed instruction before students do the activities independently.

4. Make sure the activities can be done independently by the students without interrupting the teacher when he or she is teaching other groups. After the activities in the learning center have been practiced with teacher guidance, make sure they can be performed without teacher guidance.

There are numerous learning centers that may be developed around the various reading strategies developed in this textbook. Table 12.4 presents ideas for learning centers that could accompany the content of each chapter.

TABLE 12.4

Learning Center Ideas to Accompany Each Chapter

Chapter	Learning Center Suggestion
2—Emergent Literacy	Taped stories at a Listening Center that model reading fluency and language development.
	A "Storytelling Center" that includes tapes of storytellers, guidelines for preparing stories, and stories appropriate for storytelling.
4—Phonics and Phonemic Awareness	A "Rhyming Elements Listening Center" that encourages auditory discrimination.
	A Word Family Center that encourages students to add words to a specific family.
	A "Spelling Center" that encourages students to look for and listen for patterns in words.
	A "Spelling Center" that encourages students to write stories using the spelling words taught in class.
5—Vocabulary Development	A "Webbing Vocabulary Center" that allows students to develop and display semantic maps of the vocabularies in the stories they read.
	A "Writing and Vocabulary Center" that encourages the development of individualized dictionaries and vocabulary notebooks. Includes books as models and materials needed for construction.
6—Fluency and Comprehension	A "Little Red Riding Hood Center" to expand interest in the unit. Place the "Independent Projects" and their directions in the center.
	A "Graphic Organizer Center" that encourages students to use and display time lines to show the sequence of material.
	A "Similes Center" that encourages students to use the modeling activity to locate and define additional similes.
	A "Characterization Center" that encourages students to read additional books and locate examples of inferred characterization.
7—Reading, Writing, and Literature in the Content Areas: K–4	A "Literary Genre Center" that focuses on reading and appreciating picture books, folktales, modern fantasy, and so on. Include questions students may use to decide if a book belongs to the genre. Include charts for reporting findings.
	A "Recreational Reading Group Center" where students can go, read, and discuss books they enjoy reading.
	A "Choral Reading or Readers' Theater Center" where students can locate appropriate materials, practice in a group, and practice to present. They might make simple puppets to accompany plays.
8—Reading, Writing, and Literature in the Content Areas: 4–8	An "Analytical Reading Center" in which students apply and discuss Adler and Van Doren's stages for reading a book.
	A "World War II Center" that expands on the unit developed in the chapter. Place the "Additional Activities" within the center such as responding to a biographical character, creating a museum, or sources that help debate an issue.

(Continued)

TABLE 12.4

(Continued)

Chapter	Learning Center Suggestion
9—Reading and Writing Connection	A "Writing Center" that matches the various topics used in a "Writers' Workshop" such as brainstorming ideas, searching for enjoyable linguistic styles in books and using them as models, using wordless books to discover and write story structures, and locating various forms of expository writing and using the forms in informational writing.
10—Literacy Instruction for ELL Students, Multicultural Education, and Students with Special Needs	A "Multicultural Center" that focuses on the culture of the group being studied. Include literature, art, music, artifacts, maps, pictures, and so on.
	An "Author or Artist Center" focusing on the works of one or more of the authors or artists listed in the Multicultural Literature section.
11—Computer-Assisted Instruction in Reading and Writing	A "Technology Center" that includes skill-development software that reinforces one of the reading skills being taught. Could include the guidelines for evaluating software and ask students to use the guidelines to evaluate various examples of software.
12—Putting It All Together	A "Trade Books Center" that extends the content of a basal-reading series such as a folklore center to read additional folktales and expand understanding of folklore or a biography center to expand understanding of biographies.
	An "Independent Reading Center" that includes materials of interest to the students and encourages daily opportunities for students to read materials of their own choosing.

Balance That Integrates Listening, Speaking, Reading, and Writing

This balance may be extended to include the content areas, especially social studies. A unit is one of the ways that such a balance may be developed. Such a unit can also include technology and different types of groupings such as cooperative learning. The following unit exemplifies how one of the learning objectives in social studies, to develop an understanding of the fundamental principles of American democracy, can be developed. This principle emphasizes the importance of the voting process and is important in social studies and history in fourth through eighth grades. It is also one that can be taught through school and local elections as well as national elections.

FOCUS UNIT:
Putting It All Together through a Study of Democracy

OBJECTIVES
1. To use inquiry techniques to enhance learning
2. To incorporate literacy instruction through listening, speaking, reading, writing, and social studies
3. To use technology in a meaningful experience
4. To develop an understanding of the democratic process; to formulate and defend a position
5. To read with comprehension and to evaluate informational literature; to separate fact from opinion
6. To work together in cooperative learning groups

GRADE LEVELS
Fourth through eighth, although some of the books listed could be used with younger students.

MATERIALS
Newspapers, web sites on the election process, and books on the election process. Books include:

Peter W. and Cheryl Shaw Barnes's *Woodrow for President: A Tail of Voting Campaigns and Elections* (1999). This book for younger students follows the life of a mouse as he grows up, registers to vote, runs for town council and later governor, and finally president.

Alice Provensen's *The Buck Stops Here: The Presidents of the United States* (1990)

Jean Fritz's *Shh! We're Writing the Constitution* (1987)

Roxie Munro's *The Inside-Outside Book of Washington, D.C.* (1987)

Milton Meltzer's "Politics—Not Just for Politicians" in James Giblin's *The Century That Was: Reflections on the Last One Hundred Years* (2000)

Richard B. Stolley's *Our Century in Pictures for Young People* (2000)

PROCEDURES
1. Introduce the unit with a quote or situation that reflects the importance of elections and the political process such as this one by Milton Meltzer (2000): "But can we do without politics? Like it or not, it's a powerful force in determining the conditions of life. The decisions of government touch almost every aspect of everyday living. Politics is the activity by which different interests within a city, state, or nation work out compromises in proportion to their influence. It's like a marketplace where social demands are settled by negotiations. A bargain is struck among contending forces. . . .

Our American political system was created by the Founding Fathers when they wrote the Constitution. . . . Under the Constitution, people periodically elect a president and a congress to serve their needs. These officials make the decisions" (pp. 115–116).

2. To begin the inquiry process, have students brainstorm to identify what they know about elections and what questions they would like to investigate. List this information on a chart that can be added to as the inquiry proceeds.

3. Discuss the importance of having the right to vote in a democracy. Share with students that "democracy" means "people's government." Explore the meaning of voting. Share the U.S. history that shows that women and some other groups such as African Americans did not always have the right to vote.

4. To show changes in the right to vote, share books such as *Our Century in Pictures for Young People,* edited by Richard B. Stolley (2000), Penny Colman's "Great Strides: Women in the Twentieth Century" and Walter Dean Myers's "The Changing Concepts of Civil Rights In America," found in Giblin's *The Century That Was* (2000).

5. To help students understand the sequence of history connected with the right to vote, have them divide into cooperative learning groups and use books such as those just listed to draw time lines showing changes in U.S. history. Have each group share their time lines with the rest of the class. Ask them to authenticate their time lines by providing support for the items on the time line. A completed "Voting Time Line" might look like the one shown in Figure 12.1.

6. On a word wall, place vocabulary words that are associated with voting, such as *ballot, candidate, campaign, democracy, endorsed, general election, incumbent, issues, platform, political party,* and *primary.* Next to the words on the word wall have students find examples of how the words are used in newspapers, write defini-

---

FIGURE **12.1**

A Voting Time Line

1776 ● White males over 21 who own property allowed to vote.

1870 ● 15th Amendment—Illegal to keep men from voting because of race.

1848 ● Women's Suffrage Movement—Susan B. Anthohy and Elizabeth Cady Stanton.

1890s ● Poll tax and literacy texts for voting.

1920 ● 19th Amendment—Womens Right to Vote.

1964 ● 24th Amendment ended Poll taxes in national elections.

tions in their own words, and use the words in their own sentences.

7. To develop an understanding of the issues that influence an election and how a party develops a platform, develop an activity such as "The Issues" found in "All About the Election," *Newspapers in Education,* 2004. Have the students count their answers to the issue statements, tally which party their responses are closest to, and write a paragraph about the Lion Party or the Tiger Party's platforms.

8. Have the students select local or national candidates, identify the issues, the candidate's stand on the issue, and mark whether the student agrees or disagrees with the candidate's stand. (This may be done in secret.).

9. Political debates are part of the election process whether running for a school board, a local position, or a state or national position. Students may take part in mock debates in which they research the issues and take the roles of various political candidates.

10. Ask the students to watch local and national television and read newspapers to identify how politicians try to get people to vote for them. Ask students to identify the terms used to depict a party's candidate, such as *effective leader, intelligent, honest, brave, experienced, hardworking, able to work with others.* In contrast, ask them to identify the terms used to depict the opposition candidate. Ask students to find and compare ads paid for by candidates or political parties with news stories about the candidates.

11. To enhance technology, have students search web sites to locate information about the voting process and political parties. This information could be on a "Technology Learning Center." Have them choose one of the following sites, for example, search the site, and report on the information that is available:

Democratic National Committee: www.democrats.org

Republican National Committee: www.rnc.org

Reform Party: www.reformparty.org

Libertarian Party: www/libertarian.org

Green Party: www.greenpartyus.org

The White House: www.whitehouse.gov

U.S. News and World Report:
www.usnews.com/usnews/home.htm

League of Women Voters: www.lwv.org

Information for teaching about the election:

www.atozteacherstuff.com/themes/election

Young Democrats of America: www.yda.org

Young Republican National Federation:
www.youngrepublicans.com

Kids Voting USA: www.kidsvotingusa.org

12. To expand the inquiry process students may select and conduct individual or group research on subjects such as,

The Women's Suffrage Movement: Convention for Women's Rights, Seneca Falls, New York

Biographies of Women Who Made a Difference, for example, Susan B. Anthony and Elizabeth Stanton

Writing and Ratifying the Constitution

The Impact of the Poll Tax and Literacy Tests for Voting

Reflect on Your *Reading*

Why do so many educators advocate a balanced literacy approach? What do you believe the consequences would be for reading education if the curriculum does not include a balance between basal series and trade books; between sequenced, prescribed instruction and instruction based on individual needs of the learners, between teacher-guided instruction and independent reading, between teacher-directed instruction and center-based discoveries; and between listening, speaking, reading, and writing?

Grouping Arrangements for Reading Instruction

The balanced reading recommendations previously discussed are also reflected in the groupings of students for instruction, in the classroom environment, and in room arrangements that accommodate various types of groupings including large group, small group, one-on-one arrangements with the teacher, and learning centers. It is extremely important that these groupings be flexible. It is unfortunate that in some reading classes, students are placed in a reading group according to their abilities and reading levels at the beginning of the year. The needs of the students change. If the teacher uses ongoing assessment, he or she discovers changing reading needs that should be reflected in the various groupings. We will discuss the need for flexibility and transitioning between groups later in this section.

Reading Aloud to Students

Daily reading aloud to students should be a vital part of the reading curriculum at all grade levels. Reading aloud to students may take place as either whole class experiences or in smaller groupings. In the lower elementary grades, teachers may have a location in the room where students sit on the floor or on chairs that are close to the teacher. This close proximity allows the teacher to share illustrations from books and encourages attentive listening by the students. The materials are chosen by the teacher and read with expression that demonstrates fluent reading. The materials are selected at the interest level of the students, but are usually at a higher reading level than students could read independently. The materials should also expose students to well-written literature from different genres.

Reading aloud to students may also be part of smaller ability or interest groupings. Within the smaller groupings, teachers may choose to model reading strategies by pointing out clues to comprehension as the selection is read orally. Some of these reading aloud experiences may be spontaneous as the teacher reads aloud a paragraph with particularly vivid language or shares a poem that relates to the content of the reading lesson.

Various interest groups expand students' literacy.

The materials that are read aloud by the teacher are usually placed in a literature or listening center. As the book is read, the teacher may tape the reading of the book and place it in the listening center so that students can listen to the story or poem again. Or, the books may be placed in a literature center where students can read the stories independently after they listen to the story. They now have background knowledge that lets them read with more experience. The vocabulary, the plot, and the characters are familiar.

Ability Level Groupings

Grouping students by ability **level** is probably the most common reading grouping found in schools. The report of elementary reading instructional practices discussed earlier (Baumann, and colleagues, 2000) showed that the majority of teachers teach in self-contained, heterogeneous classes; use a balanced approach that uses both basals and trade books; and provide explicit instruction in phonic analysis.

A **self-contained, heterogeneous class** means that teachers are teaching students with a wide range of reading abilities. This wide range challenges teachers as they develop instruction that is appropriate for each of the students. Dividing the class into smaller **ability level groups** is one way that teachers have tried to meet the needs of a diverse group. Research suggests, however, that using only ability groupings may be more damaging for lower ability readers than for readers who are reading at or above grade level. Cunningham and Allington (2003) state, "Reading groups based on reading level was a common phenomenon in most elementary classrooms for much of our recent history. Data indicate that children who were placed in the 'low' group almost never moved up to a higher group and that very few of these children ever reached grade level in reading" (p. 135). This conclusion about ability groupings for lower ability readers is supported by a review of the research on grouping instruction for literacy that found that when children are grouped according to reading abilities, low performing students retain low levels of performance (Paratore and Indrisano 2003). These findings indicate that lower ability readers need a balanced reading approach that allows them to be in groupings, such as interest groupings and peer tutoring groups, where they read with students of higher abilities. These findings also suggest the importance of flexible grouping in which students are allowed to change their ability group when their needs change.

The basal reading approaches used by many teachers lend themselves to ability groupings. These materials are leveled according to grade levels and make ability groupings very common. Ability grouping is closely related to the reading assessment strategies discussed in Chapter 3, "Assessment and Evaluation in the Reading and Writing Program." For example, the "Informal Reading Inventory" uses graded reading passages and comprehension checks to identify students' independent, instructional, and frustration levels of reading. These levels can be used for selecting appropriate reading materials and for dividing students into various groupings including ability and interest groupings.

The McGraw-Hill Reading Program discussed earlier includes a "Diagnostic/ Placement Evaluation" for Grades K–3. The results of this test are correlated with the basal series and provide placement recommendations. In addition to comprehension evaluation, there are leveled tests for phonics and vocabulary. The booklet includes "Summary Evaluation Charts" for each grade. The Kindergarten Chart for example, includes scores and teacher notes for beginning reading concepts, word recognition, phonics, and comprehension. By third grade, the summary includes scores and notes for word recognition, vocabulary strategy, and comprehension.

Ability groupings may also take place when teaching phonics and word recognition skills and in spelling instruction. Ability groupings in phonics and word recognition may be of shorter duration as students who need specific instruction in a word recognition strategy are placed together until they have mastered the strategy. Ability groupings for spelling instruction usually cover a longer period of time. Assessment is meaningful when it identifies students' strengths and weaknesses and provides instructional strategies that allow students to make reading gains. But remember to balance the reading instruction to include opportunities for students to read for different purposes and to read with different ability groups, as well as to read a wide range of materials.

Reading Interest Groups

Research has found that students read more and remember more of the content when they are interested in what they are reading. Studies recommend that students have opportunities to read high-interest works of literature (Guthrie, Cox, Anderson, Harris, Mazzoni, & Rach 1998). Consequently, providing materials that students can self-select and then develop **reading interest groups** where they can discuss the materials is a way to include students from different ability levels in a group. Studies that survey student's preferences in reading provide some guidelines about what students, especially those in the middle schools, choose to read. A study of sixth-grade students reading preferences found, for example, that the most preferred materials among sixth graders were scary books and stories, comics and cartoons, magazines about popular culture, and books and magazines about sports. Other popular materials were drawing books, books and magazines about cars and trucks, series books, funny books, and books about animals. Comparisons by genres, income, reading attitude, and achievement found more similarities than differences (Worthy, Moorman, & Turner, 1999).

This list of preferred materials is undoubtedly of the light nature in its requirements for comprehension and understanding literary elements. Fortunately, studies with elementary and middle school students also report that students value the recommendations of teachers and librarians. By reading aloud books and recommending books teachers can influence the books that are chosen by students to read for recreational purposes.

Books chosen to be read and discussed in interest groups may also focus on specific interests of students within the class. Now groups can be organized, usually on a short-term basis, according to specific interests. Students join a group because of the interest, read books that relate to the interest, and discuss the books within the interest group. Interests may correspond with units taught in the class. For example, if the class is learning about weather in science, an interest group might choose to read more about hurricanes, another about tornadoes, or another about the effect of global warming. Animal behaviors might be the focus of an interest group or celebrations associated with a specific holiday. The main criterion for developing the reading associated with the interest groups is a well-stocked library that allows students to explore various topics of interest.

There is currently considerable concern about the reading levels of students in middle school. The *NCTE Inbox* (October 25, 2005) cites recent scores among eighth-grade students that found only 31 percent of the students scored Proficient or higher on the NAEP reading test even though literacy demands are rising. Consequently,

> NCTE (National Council of Teachers of English) supports educators who are striving to meet the needs of middle and secondary level readers. This includes acknowledging that adolescents are already reading in multiple ways and helping these readers grow their competence through engagement with various types of texts, encouraging wide reading for various purposes throughout life. (p. 2)

This call for excellence in literacy instruction again reinforces the need for teaching students to read and comprehend a variety of materials.

Book Clubs

One approach to expanding reading and identifying favorite books is the BBC's "The Big Read" campaign, which sponsored reading clubs and book discussions throughout the United Kingdom. Three quarters of a million votes were cast. The top 10 titles reported in *Reading Today* (February/March 2004) were:

1. J. R. R. Tolkien's *The Lord of the Rings*
2. Jane Austen's *Pride and Prejudice*
3. Philip Pullman's *His Dark Materials*
4. Douglas Adams's *The Hitchhiker's Guide to the Galaxy*
5. J. K. Rowling's *Harry Potter and the Goblet of Fire*
6. Harper Lee's *To Kill a Mockingbird*

7. A. A. Milne's *Winnie the Pooh*
8. George Orwell's *Nineteen Eighty-Four*
9. C. S. Lewis's *The Lion, the Witch, and the Wardrobe*
10. Charlotte Bronte's *Jane Eyre.*

Notice that within this group are award-winning books for children and young adults such as those by Tolkien, Pullman, Rowlings, Milne, and Lewis. Within the top 21 books were also the children's and young adult literature classics, Kenneth Grahame's *The Wind in the Willows* and Louise May Alcott's *Little Women.* The campaign reported that the featured books increased in sales. To learn more about "The Big Read," check the web site: www.bbc.co.uk/arts/bigread.

To organize a book club in your school, select a range of materials that are of interest to students. Members of the book club or the teacher usually select a book that will be read by a specific time and then meet to discuss the book. Libraries and bookstores frequently sponsor book clubs. Schools may support book clubs that encourage students within different grades to read and discuss the books. Summer reading programs may use this type of format. The discussions are quite informal but each student must have read or be reading the book and be ready to discuss the content. These discussions may reflect subjects such as personal responses to the book, what members liked or disliked about the book, memorable moments in the book, how the book relates to their lives, attitudes toward the author, or recommendations about the book. When students are asked, "Who would you recommend read this book and why do you make this recommendation?" teachers discover a great deal about the reading levels and preferences of the class. The discussions in the book clubs are more informal than those used in teacher-directed lessons.

Shared Reading Groups

Shared reading groups are frequently used with children in emergent or early reading stages of development. The purpose of the grouping is to help students become independent readers by providing support for early reading. The materials used in shared reading groups at the kindergarten and first grade are usually big books or enlarged rhymes and poems that the teacher reads while showing the materials to the students. As the reading proceeds, or during multiple readings of the big books, students are encouraged to participate in the reading. The big books allow students to use picture clues, predict what will happen in the story, and develop an understanding that print proceeds from top to bottom and from left to right. During teacher modeling, the teacher points out the reading strategies that he or she uses to read the material. These strategies may include structural analysis as the teacher points out beginning sounds, word families, and context clues. These materials may be placed in a learning center so that students reread the materials, or the materials may be used during partner reading where students with higher reading ability take the role of the teacher. Vocabulary from the reading may be placed on the word wall.

Shared reading is also beneficial at the upper grades. Now teachers use enlarged texts or place the text on an overhead projector and read the text orally. Students may have copies of the text or may read along from the enlarged version. The students participate in the reading and the teacher models various reading strategies. As with younger readers, the approach provides teacher support for student reading. Now students focus on story elements such as setting, conflict, and characters; expand their vocabularies; make connections between background knowledge and new information; and use prediction strategies to develop meaning. Shared reading is especially helpful when developing understanding of poetic elements or when pointing out writing techniques. Shared reading may be used with a basal series when students have particular difficulty understanding a concept or a comprehension technique.

Shared reading is also an excellent strategy to use with English Language Learners (ELL) as the students practice their reading skills and become more proficient in the requirements of the English language. Some of the books listed in Chapter 10 are written in two languages—for example, a shared reading of Diane Gonzales Bertrand's *Uncle Chente's Picnic* (2001) allows teachers and students to share both the Spanish text and the English text. The book includes a full-page illustration on the right side of the text and both English and Spanish text on the opposite page. Books like this allow modeling of both languages. The illustrations provide another source for discussion and comprehension.

Shared reading may be used at the beginning of an inquiry activity in which students need to find information through a variety of nonfiction texts. The teacher shows and discusses the various parts of a book that help students find information: the table of contents; an author's introduction; the index; any visuals that provide information such as graphs, diagrams, photographs, and maps; and a section on further reading. For example, before teaching the "Study of Democracy Unit" presented earlier in this chapter, use a shared reading approach with Richard B. Stolley's *Our Century in Pictures for Young People* (2000). The shared reading experience might include the following examples:

1. Read and discuss the "Table of Contents." Show the students that the text is divided into nine time periods that proceed from "1900–1913: Across the Threshold" to "1993–1999: Our Future.Com." Show and discuss the type of information that will be found in each section including a historical review of the period by a well-known author of children's and young adult literature, a "Turning Point" incident that features a major happening, and a requiem section that highlights people who died during the time period. Ask the students to share how they would use this information in the "Table of Contents" to help them investigate a topic. The teacher also shares how he or she would use this information.

2. Read and discuss the editor's introduction, "Dust Bowls and Other Dreams." Point out the importance of the nearly 400 photographs chosen to tell the story of the century. Show that the introduction gives specific information about the sections of each chapter as found in this quote:

> We have divided the book into nine chapters, nine groups of years. Within
> each chapter is a special section called Turning Point, where we look at a
> major news event—like the discovery of atomic power—and show what it
> meant to the rest of the century. And at the end of each chapter is another
> section called Requiem, in which we tell about some important people
> who died during those years. (Introduction)

3. Because this book is a picture history of the century, share and discuss the importance of careful viewing and reading of the photographs and the captions under the photographs. For example, the "Time Line for Voting" shown in the unit in this chapter includes "The 19th Amendment—Women's Right to Vote." The section for

"1920–1929" includes a photograph of the Suffragettes marching on New York City Hall. The "Turning Point: Closing the Gender Gap" emphasizes the impact of the suffragettes and the passing of the 19th Amendment and how one of the leaders of the movement for voting rights for women, Alice Paul, later worked for gender equality within the United Nations charter and the U.S. Civil Rights Act of 1964. Students can join in the shared reading as they look at the photographs and discuss information that they discover by a careful viewing of the photographs and a reading of the captions.

4.   Share the "Index" and show students how the index may be used to locate information about specific people. For example, to locate information pertaining to voting rights, show "Anthony, Susan B., 21." Page 21 includes a photograph of Anthony and a coin with her picture. Share with students how you could use the caption under her picture to investigate additional information about voting rights and the people who struggled for the rights of women to vote. Read the caption for "Susan B. Anthony, 1820–1906" and discuss the additional information presented about her actions as a champion for female suffrage.

5.   Finally, share information about the editor of this book, Richard B. Stolley. Share information about his background that, for you, makes him a credible and believable editor for this book. (For example, he is currently senior editorial adviser of Time Inc. Previously, he spent 19 years covering events and personalities throughout the world.)

Any informational book may be used as a shared reading example to help students locate and use information found within the text. Folklore is another genre of literature that has informational sources that need to be presented and discussed in a shared reading group. Through a shared reading, show and discuss how retellers of the tales should provide background information about the origin of the tale. Using Virginia Hamilton's *In the Beginning: Creation Stories from around the World* (1988), for example, share with students the important and useful information that Hamilton provides, such as the information about "Spider Ananse Finds Something: Wulbari the Creator," in which she identifies the story's source as the Krachi people of Togo (formerly Togoland) in West Africa. She discusses the importance of Ananse who is a trickster hero found in stories throughout West Africa. She reveals that the rivalry between Ananse and the sky god is a popular storytelling device in which the weak (spider) overcomes the strong (sky god).

Shared reading, for either younger or older students, may be used with small groups or with whole class presentations. It depends on the objective of the reading and the needs and reading levels of the students in the class. Shared readings are almost always important before students do independent work in learning centers. This is one way to help students understand how to read and obtain information from the sources found in the center.

Shared Writing Groups

Shared writing is another approach that provides collaboration between the teacher and the students. The teacher provides support for the writing by modeling and demonstrating how the writing is completed. When involved in shared writing the teacher:

1. Thinks aloud as he or she develops the writing.
2. Focuses on specific skills that are needed by the students and required by the writing.
3. Writes on a large surface or uses technology so that all students can see the process.
4. Models rereading and revising the writing.
5. Discusses the writing with the students.
6. Allows the students to expand on the writing and to read the writing after it is completed.

Like shared reading, shared writing may be accomplished with the total class or with a small group. The group size depends on the level and needs of the students. If the total class needs help with a writing strategy, with punctuation, or with grammar, then it may be used with the whole class. Likewise, if only a few students need to focus on the writing skill, teach a shared writing group when it is needed. This is another important grouping for English language learners. These students benefit from shared writing in which the teacher or another student models the writing process and encourages the students to share their writing.

Partner Reading Groups

Partner reading is another means for balancing instruction and improving comprehension (Fuchs, Fuchs, Mathes, & Simmons, 1997). It may be used within any of the groupings whether the materials are chosen from a basal reading series or texts used for individualized instruction or independent reading groups. The grouping is easily arranged as students work in pairs to help each other read. For partner reading, a stronger reader reads aloud for about five minutes, then the weaker reader reads the same passage. The weaker reader then describes the materials just read. The weaker reader may summarize a passage or predict what will happen next. The students then read the next page and decide whether or not the predictions are correct.

Coaching Groups

There are two terms used in the literature: *coaching groups* and *reading coaches*. Coaching groups are small groups of students who need extra directions in using word attack, vocabulary, or comprehension strategies. Coaching groups are teacher-directed and provide explicit instruction in reading skills. These skills are usually skills presented in an earlier class, but need to be reinforced through extra practice or additional reading strategies. For example, after teaching a lesson on using one of the context clues to identify unknown words, a coaching group might focus on definition clues, comparison clues, summary clues, familiar expression clues, experience clues, or synonym clues. This might be the time to provide more guidance by modeling and demonstrating how the teacher uses these clues to gain comprehension. Many struggling readers need this extra direction. Coaching groups usually take place while the rest of the class pursue independent activities such as working at interest centers or finishing assignments.

Up for Discussion

Readability versus Leveling

Readability is a procedure that uses a formula to measure the difficulty of a book. The readability is usually measured according to the syntactic difficulty and the semantic difficulty of a 100-word passage. The syntactic difficulty of a passage is measured by the length of sentences in the passage. Consequently, the fewer the sentences and the longer the sentences in the passage, the harder the passage is to read. The semantic difficulty is usually measured by the length of words in a passage or the number of syllables in the words. Consequently, the higher the number of syllables in a passage, the more difficult the passage. The argument is that longer words with multiple syllables are usually harder to read than shorter one- or two-syllable words. Readability grade levels of a book may be measured by using a graph such as the one developed by Edward Fry (2002) found in Figure 12.2 for measuring readability.

Leveling, according to Fry (2002), takes into consideration factors related to the structure of the book that may help the reader and, consequently, lower the difficulty level of the book. For example:

1. Is the content familiar to students of that age group?
2. Do the illustrations tell the story or explain the vocabulary?
3. How many words are on a page? How many pages are in the book?
4. Is the book related to teaching methods used in the class?
5. Does the language include repetitious words or phrases?
6. Will the readers' backgrounds and experiences help them understand the text?
7. How will the format (type size, page layout) of the book affect readers' understanding?

To show the differences between using a readability formula and a leveling process, use the graph to judge the readability of the book and then look at the content of the book, especially the illustrations, to decide which is most valuable for selecting books for a classroom. You may decide that both readability formulas and leveling

Discussion of books through puppetry increases both enjoyment for reading and comprehension of texts.

provide the greatest information for helping students read a book. For example, look at the 2004 Caldecott Award book, Mordicai Gerstein's *The Man Who Walked between the Towers* (2003). Using the Fry readability graph the readability of the book is:

	Syllables	Sentences
First hundred words	122	9
Second hundred words	124	7
Third hundred words	133	11.3
Average	126	9.1
Readability on graph:	fourth grade	

Now look at the illustrations that support the text. Many of the multisyllable words are shown in the illustrations, for example, the man riding a *unicycle* as he *juggled* balls and *fiery torches.* The police are shown as they shouted through *bullhorns* and placed *handcuffs* on his wrists. Do you believe that a student would need to have a fourth-grade reading ability to read this text? What should the teacher point out to the students to increase their ability to read and understand the book? This example shows that teaching students to "read" the illustrations can lower the readability of the words in a highly illustrated book.

If the book has no illustrations, however, the readability formula may provide more indicators about the reading level required to read the book. Now, which of the leveling indicators is the most important when selecting the appropriate book or other reading materials and helping students read the material?

FIGURE 12.2

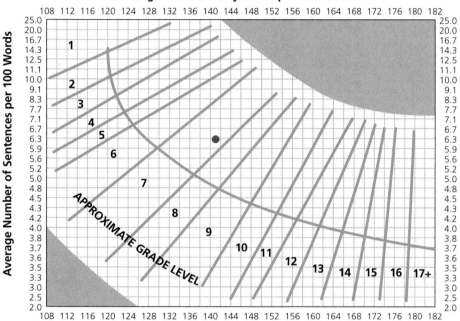

Average Number of Syllables per 100 Words

Directions: Randomly select 3, 100-word passages from a book or article. Plot average number of syllables and average number of sentences per 100 words on graph to determine the grade level of the material. Choose more passages per book if great variability is observed and conclude that the book has uneven readability. Few books will fall in gray area, but when they do, grade level scores are invalid.

Count proper nouns, numerals, and initialization as words. Count a syllable for each symbol. For example, "1945" is 1 word and 4 syllables and "IRA" is 1 word and 3 syllables.

Example:	Syllables	Sentences
First hundred words	124	6.6
Second hundred words	141	5.5
Third hundred words	158	6.8
Average	141	6.3

Readability seventh grade (see dot plotted on graph)

Choose several books or other reading materials that are considered appropriate for a particular grade level. Use the readability graph to identify the readability level of the material. Now look at the same text, but evaluate the text support factors found within the text. How could you use both of these findings to help students have a successful learning experience?

The second term used in the literature is reading coach. The type of reading coach identified by the International Reading Association (IRA) is a reading professional who either comes into the classroom or takes a group of students out of the classroom to work on reading difficulties. The person who conducts this type of instruction is usually a specially trained individual who has an advanced degree in reading. This person may also help the teacher with special reading approaches by modeling instruction with the class or demonstrating assessment and evaluation techniques.

The IRA (*Reading Today,* June/July 2004) states that because of the heavy focus on reading achievement, the role of the reading specialist has changed. Along with the change are a variety of new titles, including "reading coach" or "literacy coach." The IRA identifies the following five key qualifications for reading coaches:

1. They are excellent classroom teachers.

2. They have deep knowledge of the reading processes, acquisition, assessment, and instruction.

3. The have experience in working with teachers to improve the teacher's practice.

4. They are experienced presenters with teacher groups in schools and at professional conferences.

5. They have training that enables them to observe in classrooms and provide feedback to teachers.

The text of the IRA position statement on reading coaches is found at www.reading.org.

Flexibility and Transitioning between Groups

When we visualize each of these groups within the reading curriculum we should not visualize the same students within each group throughout the school year. Many of the groupings such as the reading interest groups, shared reading groups, partner reading groups, and coaching groups allow considerable flexibility as the students have many opportunities to change their groups and work with other students in the class.

The ability groupings associated with most basal-reading instruction are usually the most inflexible because at the beginning of the year, following assessment, the students are divided into ability groupings, read from a basal at their level of reading ability, and complete workbook assignments related to the basal curriculum. Conducting ongoing assessment such as informal reading inventories and running records described in Chapter 3 are crucial for successful ability groupings that are flexible enough to match students' changing needs. When working with students in any of the groupings, teachers should monitor each child's progress and consider changing the child's group when the materials and lessons are either too difficult or too easy for the child.

No matter how teachers name the ability groups, students understand that they are in high, average, or lower ability groups. Consequently, there may be a stigma attached to the child's reading group. Robert B. Ruddell (2002) suggests that: "One way to reduce the negative effects of ability grouping is to alternate basal reading instruction with literature-based instruction, in which students self-select reading groups on the basis of the books they choose to read. This gives them opportunities to cross basal reading group lines" (p. 422). Ruddell also recommends having project groups in which students group according to interests in various projects.

These other groupings allow students to work with students who are not in their ability reading group and to appreciate other types of knowledge and ability. This is especially important when working with ELL students whose language ability may not as yet allow them to be in an upper ability reading group. Their knowledge of a subject or a culture, however, may be superior to that of other students. Chapter 10 discusses the advantages of various types of groupings with ELL students and recommends multicultural literature that may be used during reading instruction and when developing instructional units.

Reflect on Your *Reading*

As you review the various grouping arrangements that you may use in your classroom, remember your own experiences in elementary school. Which types of grouping did your teachers use? How did a specific grouping help or hinder your learning? What are the strengths and weaknesses of each type of grouping?

Organizing the Classroom

The descriptions of effective classrooms found in Chapter 2, "Emergent Literacy, Language Development, and Cognitive Development," emphasized classroom environments that include many books and other reading materials found in inviting book corners, supplies for reading and writing that are easily accessible, displays of students' work, listening centers, writing centers, and other learning centers. A classroom environment that fosters this type of literacy development needs to be organized to accommodate a variety of types of work and groupings. There needs to be a place for reading aloud, where students can be close to the teacher when the teacher reads books, tells stories, or uses big books during shared reading. The organization needs to accommodate large-group instruction, small-group instruction, and independent work in centers.

Most educators would agree that the teacher is the most important element in an effective reading program. Effective classroom organization begins with an assessment of the literacy environment that allows teachers and students to interact with literacy materials, to develop teacher- and student-initiated talk, and to enhance independent learning. An inventory of classroom activities is helpful when developing the classroom organization. For example, look at the items on Table 12.5, "An Inventory of Classroom Activities" and consider how the room might be arranged to accommodate each of the activities.

The philosophy of the classroom is often seen through the organization of the classroom. A traditional classroom that includes mostly teacher-directed activities may have student desks in a row with the teacher's desk at the front. There may be a table where students go for smaller ability groupings. In a heterogeneous classroom, the teacher may have three different ability groupings where the teacher provides daily instruction to one group, while the other groups complete independent work assigned by the teacher. As discussed earlier, students who are not meeting with

These first-grade students are already displaying their love for reading. This love of reading needs to continue if the goal of literacy for life is to occur.

TABLE 12.5

Inventory of Classroom Activities

Classroom Requirements:	Examples:	Organization:
1. Attractive environment that encourages students to read, write, and discover.		
2. Teacher acts as role model for reading by demonstrating reading strategies.		
3. Students share their work in an attractive area where work is respected.		
4. Students take part in groupings that allow them to be discussion leaders.		
5. Teachers develop teacher-directed and teacher-guided instruction.		
6. The classroom encourages students to give personal responses to what they read.		
7. The students have opportunities to do independent work following teacher-directed instruction.		
8. The classroom allows many opportunities for small-group and independent inquiry.		
9. Recreational reading is considered important.		
10. The classroom allows instruction for individual needs.		
11. The classroom is flexible enough for whole class, small group, and individual instruction.		
12. The classroom includes learning centers that are related to the instructional needs of the students.		
13. The classroom encourages the use of technology		
14. Reading is integrated into the total curriculum, including content areas and not just taught during a class designated as "reading."		
15. There is evidence of integrating reading, writing, listening, and speaking.		

the teacher need to be involved in meaningful work. Consequently, the room organization usually includes a library center for individual selection of materials, a computer center to research group or individual projects, and additional tables where students can take part in group projects. There will be numerous bulletin boards for displaying work and blackboards for use by teachers and students. If the class is for young children, there will be a space where the teacher can read orally to the class or to a group. Figure 12.3 illustrates a traditional classroom that may be found in many schools.

A classroom that focuses on learning centers and an inquiry method may look quite different. For example, the elementary school for the International School in Geneva, Switzerland, uses an inquiry method and theme approach throughout the school. When entering the school, visitors and students see a large bulletin board showing the various programs of inquiry being taught in kindergarten through sixth

FIGURE 12.3

Traditional Classroom

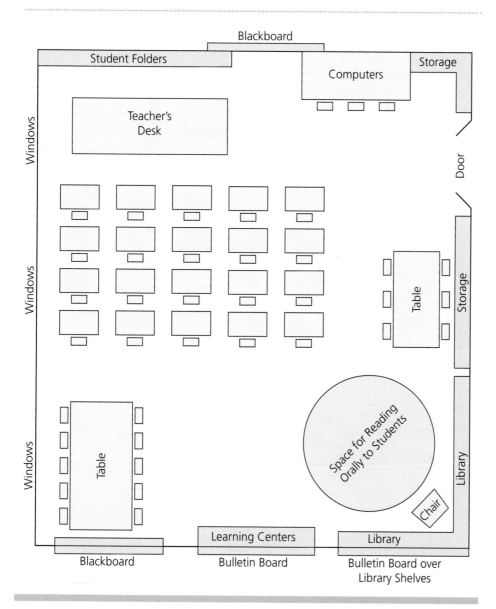

grades. A bulletin board that illustrates a literature selection read by the group provides a colorful introduction to each classroom, as for example a bulletin board of "There Was an Old Woman Who Swallowed a Fly" introducing a second-grade classroom.

The inquiry method requires learning centers and work spaces that encourage students to work together in different-size groups. To meet these needs, the classrooms include several square tables that may be moved together to form larger surfaces when needed. Each table has stools for students. Because the students work at tables rather than having desks with storage areas, each student has a basket in which he or she keeps supplies. A large divided bookshelf stores the baskets when not in use. A colorful class library, several learning centers, and a computer center are around the room. The computer center includes a schedule so that students sign up for use of the three computers found in the room. Every wall surface is covered with examples of students' writings and drawings related to the inquiry subjects. The teacher's desk contains folders for each student where the teacher keeps track of progress and notes suggestions for student teacher and group-teacher conferences. The teacher keeps a rubric for each student that indicates where the student is in developing the inquiry project. Figure 12.4 illustrates a learning center environment.

FIGURE 12.4

Classroom Designed for Inquiry

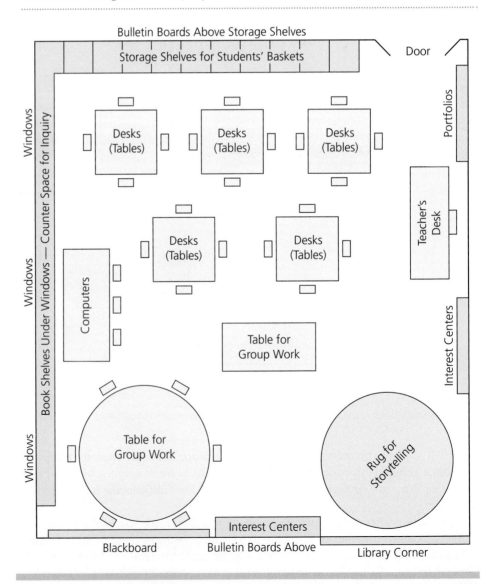

Teachers in this school emphasize their use of different types of groupings. They introduce new subjects and inquiry topics through larger teacher-directed group instruction. They use small group interactions and teacher-guided instruction as students explore their subjects. Many of the groupings include peer teaching and peer-interactions as students help each other investigate their topics. Many of the teachers use writing workshops and the writing process. Now they change the groupings to help students pursue prewriting activities such as brainstorming, writing activities, and revising. The students' finished writing products are published in book form and placed in a center where other students can read the work.

Reflect on Your Reading

Observe the classroom organization in several classes. What types of classroom organization do you discover? What types of reading activities would be encouraged by the classroom organization? Diagram the classroom organization and note the instructional purposes for the organization. If the teacher divides the class into two or three ability groups, how does the teacher organize the class to keep every student involved in learning?

DIFFERENTIATING INSTRUCTION

As teachers put the reading instructional plan together, they face a tremendous task of meeting the instructional needs of all students including average readers, ELL students who require extra help to master the English language, struggling readers and writers who have not mastered appropriate reading skills, and gifted and accelerated students who must be challenged in order to keep their interest and to enhance their developing reading abilities. Michael Winerip (2005) describes a school in New York City that successfully teaches reading to classes that have a high percentage of

Individualized instruction is often essential to help students from different ability groupings.

Spanish-speaking students as well as struggling students who have special reading needs. He describes how the teachers individualize instruction, use team teaching, and "provide extra enrichment for bright students so they stay challenged" (p. A28).

Katherine Riley Mehigan (2005) recommends using a "strategy toolbox" to identify appropriate teaching and learning strategies that can be used in different situations and with different populations and students. Teaching strategies are plans selected and applied by the teacher to help students construct meaning such as teaching students how to develop a story plot structure or brainstorming a vocabulary web. Learning strategies are learner-controlled activities that are selected and applied by the learning in order to construct meaning.

Mehigan maintains that teachers need to have various strategies if they are to choose the best plan of action because they need to

1. consider a variety of strategies for a given lesson
2. experiment with a specific strategy in a variety of instructional situations
3. cue students to the strategy in use
4. Gather data to show that a particular strategy is working for students (p. 561)

She asks teachers to consider what strategies they would use to teach students to complete tasks such as summarize a book, write a paragraph that compares two objects, describe the main character in a book, write an article, or read an article about an unfamiliar topic.

Summary

Most teachers use a balanced approach to reading and literacy, especially as they balance published basal materials and trade books in the classroom. Most basal series include teacher-directed and guided materials and structured, sequenced skill development through stories and workbooks. Teachers use trade books to provide students wider ranges of interesting materials and sources for study.

The balanced approach also provides balance between prescribed instruction as found in many published materials and individualized instruction where students choose materials that interest them, read at their own pace, and are involved in small groups when they need help with reading strategies. Balanced instruction provides balance between teacher-guided instruction and independent reading. For teacher-guided instruction the teacher groups students with similar needs, models the use of various word attack and comprehension strategies, directly teaches new strategies, and keeps track of individual reading strengths and weaknesses. Learning centers provide many opportunities for students to use and expand the reading skills learned during teacher-directed and guided instruction. Balanced instruction also integrates listening, speaking, reading, and writing, and the content areas.

Grouping arrangements in the classroom include large groups, small groups, and individual instruction. Ability level groupings are used in many classes that use a basal reading approach. Reading interest groups are developed around the interests of students rather than ability levels. Book clubs provide opportunities for students to read and discuss books. Shared reading groups are frequently used with children in emergent or early reading stages of development as the teacher and students read large books. In the upper grades, teachers model various reading strategies as the students focus on the text. Partner reading groupings and coaching groups are also valuable, especially for struggling readers. All of the factors for developing effective reading instruction in today's classrooms are also considered when organizing the classroom for instruction. The effective classroom provides opportunities for different types of groupings as well as a classroom environment that demonstrates the power of reading and learning.

Reflect on Your Reading

Think about the various reading strategies we have discussed in this book. What strategies might you use to teach these various tasks to meet the needs of differentiated instruction? How might you modify instruction to meet the needs of ELL students, struggling readers and writers, and students who are gifted and accelerated?

Key Terms

balanced reading, p. 485

basal reading series, p. 488

self-contained, heterogeneous classes, p. 505

ability level groupings, p. 505

reading interest groups, p. 506

shared reading groups, p. 508

readability, p. 512

For authentic classroom videos, online case studies, and grade-level appropriate classroom activities, go to Allyn & Bacon's MyLabSchool.com. You'll find resources related to **Effective Reading Instruction** under several courses, including Reading Methods, Language Arts, Content Area Reading, and Foundations/Intro to Teaching.

Extend Your Reading

1. Choose a grade level example from a basal reading series. Using the themes of the stories or the reading skills developed in the series, develop a list of materials that could be used to provide additional reading during individual or group activities.

2. Choose one of the areas under balanced literacy: (1) balance between published reading programs and trade books; (2) balance between prescribed instruction and instruction based on individual learners; (3) balance between teacher-guided instruction and independent reading; (4) balance between teacher-directed instruction and center-based discoveries; and (5) balance between listening,

speaking, writing, and reading in the content areas. With a group of your peers outline a portion of the reading curriculum that shows how you will balance instruction in that area. Why do you believe that balanced literacy is so important?

3. With a group of your peers, model a shared reading activity. Use either a big book format for emerging literacy or an example that could model and demonstrate a reading strategy for upper grades.

4. As a field-based activity, visit a school and observe the different instructional groupings developed by the teachers. What are the instructional goals of the groupings? How do the teachers use different groupings to balance instruction?

5. Using the information on Table 12.4, choose one of the suggestions for developing a learning center that can accompany the content of this textbook. With a group of your peers, develop a learning center appropriate for a specified grade level.

6. Conduct a research study that focuses on one of the group arrangements for reading instruction. What are the advantages and disadvantages of the grouping? Which students benefit from the grouping? Locate at least two journal articles that discuss the grouping.

7. Using Table 12.3, "A Literature Card to Accompany Carl Hiaasen's *Hoot*" as a model, develop several literature cards that could accompany a book used for individualized or independent reading.

8. Review the models of the reading process and the approaches to reading instruction discussed in Chapter 1. What types of groupings do you believe would be the most effective for the bottom-up model, the top-down model, and the interactive model? Explain why you chose those groupings. What types of groupings do you believe would be the most effective for phonics approaches, sub-skills approaches, whole language approaches, literature-based approaches, and balanced reading approaches? Explain why you chose these groupings.

For Further Reading

1. There are web sites that provide information on balanced literacy, including

    www.earlyliterature.ecsd.net/balanced%20liter acy.htm
    www.sedl.org/reading/topics/balanced.html
    www.sarasota.k12.us/sarasota/balanlitprog .htm
    http://regostratopm.beayton.k12.or.us/lbdb/ default.htm (Leveled book database)
    www.leveledbooks.com/equivalency.htm (Leveled book equivalency chart)

2. Rita M. Bean, Allison L. Swan, & Rebecca Knaub (February 2003), "Reading Specialists in Schools with Exemplary Reading Programs: Functional Versatile, and Prepared," in *The Reading Teacher, 56,* 446–455. The article surveys the role of reading specialists and lists the tasks they accomplish in relation to reading. This article relates to Reading Coaches.

3. Cathy Collins Block, Margaret Oakar, & Nicholas Hurt (April-June 2002), "The Expertise of Literacy Teachers: A Continuum from

Preschool to Grade five," in *Reading Research Quarterly, 37,* 178–206. The article identifies the qualities of teaching expertise that distinguish highly effective instruction at different grade levels.

4. Carla C. Dearman, & Sheila R. Alber (April 2005), "The Changing Face of Education: Teachers Cope with Challenges through Collaboration and Reflective Study," in *The Reading Teacher, 58,* 634–640. The article describes how administrators and teachers meet the needs of students.

5. Beth, Maloch (2002), "Scaffolding Student Talk: One Teacher's Role in Literature Discussion Groups," in *Reading Research Quarterly, 37,* 94–112. Maloch uses a third-grade classroom to describe the relationship between a teacher's role and students' participation in discussion groups.

REFERENCES

Allington, Richard L. (June/July 2005). "The Other Five 'Pillars' of Effective Reading Instruction." *Reading Today,* 22, 3.

Allington, Richard L. (October-November 2005). "NCLB, Reading First, and Whither the Future?" *Reading Today.* 23, 18.

Allington, Richard L., & Cunningham, Patricia M. (2002). *Schools That Work: Where All Children Read and Write,* 2nd ed. Boston: Allyn & Bacon.

Alvarez, Lizette. (19, April 2004). "Suutarila Journal: Educators Flocking to Finland, Land of Literature Children." *New York Times,* p. A4.

Arnold, Sarah Louise, & Gilbert, Charles B. (1902). *Stepping Stones to Literature: A First Reader.* New York: Silver, Burdett.

Baumann, James F., Hoffman, James V., Duffy-Hester, Ann M., & Ro, Jennifer Moon. (July-September 2000). "The First R Yesterday and Today: U.S. Elementary Reading Instruction Practices Reported by Teachers and Administrators." *Reading Research Quarterly,* 35, 338–377.

Burns, Paul C., Roe, Betty D., & Smith, Sandy H. (2002). *Teaching Reading in Today's Elementary Schools,* 8th ed. Boston: Houghton Mifflin.

Chrisman, Sally K. (28 March, 2006). "Reading, Rehashing, 'Rithmetic: To the Editor," p. A22.

Cunningham, Patricia M., & Allington, Richard L. (2003). *Classrooms That Work: They Can All Read and Write,* 3rd ed. Boston: Allyn & Bacon.

Dillon, Sam. (26 March, 2006). "Schools Cut Back Subjects to Push Reading and Math." *New York Times,* pp. 1, 16.

Ford, Michael P., & Opitz, Michael F. (May 2002). "Using Centers to Engage Children During Guided Reading Time: Intensifying Learning Experiences away from the Teacher." *The Reading Teacher,* 55, 710–717.

Friedman, Thomas. (24 March, 2006). "Worried About India's and China's Booms? So Are They." *New York Times.* p. A21.

Fry, Edward. (November 2002). "Readability versus Leveling." *The Reading Teacher,* 56, 286–291.

Fuchs, D., Fuchs, L. S., Mathes, P. G., & Simmons, D. C. (1997). "Peer-Assisted Learning Strategies Making Classrooms More Responsive to Diversity." *American Educational Research Journal,* 34, 174–206.

Gootman, Elissa. (30 September, 2004). "Harlem Kindergartners Receive a Key to the Future." *New York Times,* p. A27.

Guthrie, J. T., Cox, K. E., Anderson, E., Harris, K, Mazzoni, S., & Rach L. (1998). "Principles of Integrated Instruction for Engagement in Reading." *Educational Psychology Review, 10,* 177–198.

Hay, Julie, & Wingo, Charles E. (1948). *Reading with Phonics.* Chicago: Lippincott.

Hirsch, E. D., J. (25 February, 2004). "Many Americans Can Read But Can't Comprehend." *USA Today,* p. A13.

Ivey, Gay, & Broaddus, Karen. (October-December 2001). "'Just Plain Reading': A Survey of What Makes Students Want to Read in Middle School Classrooms." *Reading Research Quarterly,* 56, 350–377.

McGraw-Hill. (2001). *McGraw-Hill Reading.* New York: McGraw-Hill School Division.

Mehigan, Katherine Riley. (March 2005). "The Strategy Toolbox: A Ladder to Strategic Teaching." *The Reading Teacher,* 58, 552–566.

NCTE. (25 October, 2005). "Reading in Middle and High School." *NCTE Inbox.* Urbana, IL: Author.

Newspapers in Education and Great Lakes Higher Education Guaranty Corporation. (2004). "All About the Election." A Supplement for the *Wisconsin State Journal.* Madison, Wisconsin.

Paratore, Jeanne R., & Indrisano, Roselmina. (2003). "Grouping for Instruction in Literacy." In James Flood, Diane Lapp, James R. Squire, & Julie M. Jensen (Eds.), *Handbook of Research on Teaching the English Language Arts*, 2nd ed. Mahwah, NJ: Lawrence Erlbaum, 566–572.

Pearson, P. David. (28 March, 2006). "Reading, Rehashing, 'Rithmetic: To the Editor." *New York Times*, p. A22.

Reading Today. (February-March 2004). "*Lord of the Rings* Tops List of Favorite Books in UK." *Reading Today, 21*, 15.

Reading Today. (February-March 2004). "Making Reading a Priority in Middle Schools." *Reading Today, 21*, 17.

Reading Today. (February-March 2005). "Report Targets Reading in Middle School and High School." *Reading Today, 22*, 23.

Reading Today. (February-March 2005). "Study Finds Link between Newspaper Use in School and Young Adult Readership." *Reading Today, 22*, 35.

Reading Today. (June/July 2004). "Spotlight on Reading Coaches: Position Statement Outlines Roles and Qualifications." *Reading Today, 21*, 1, 3.

Reutzel, D. Ray. (January 1999). "On Balanced Reading." *The Reading Teacher, 52*, 322–324.

Ruddell, Robert. (2002). *Teaching Children to Read and Write,* 3rd ed. Boston: Allyn & Bacon.

Winerip, Michael. (November 2005). "Learning-Disabled Students Blossom in Blended Classes. *New York Times*, p. A28.

Worthy Jo, Moorman, Megan, & Turner, Margo. (January-March 1999). "What Johnny Likes to Read Is Hard to Find in School." *Reading Research Quarterly, 34*, 12–27.

Children's Literature References

Barnes, Peter W., & Barnes, Cheryl Shaw. (1999).*Woodrow for President: A Tale of Voting Campaigns and Elections.* VSP.

Bertrand, Diane Gonzales. (2001). *Uncle Chente's Picnic.* Illustrated by Pauline Rodriguez Howard, Spanish translation by Julia Mercedes Castilla. Arte Publico.

Fleming, Candace. (2003). *Ben Franklin's Almanac: Being a True Account of the Good Gentleman's Life.* Atheneum.

Fritz, Jean. (1987). *Shh! We're Writing the Constitution.* Illustrated by Tomie dePaola. Putnam.

Fritz, Jean. (1978). *What's the Big Idea, Ben Franklin?* Illustrated by Margot Tomes. Coward McCann.

Gerstein, Mordicai. (2003). *The Man Who Walked between the Towers.* Roaring Brook.

Giblin, James Cross, ed. (2000). *The Century That Was: Reflections on the Last One Hundred Years.* Atheneum.

Hamilton, Virginia, retold by. (1988). *In the Beginning: Creation Stories from around the World.* Illustrated by Barry Moser. Harcourt Brace.

Hiaasen, Carl. (2002). *Hoot.* Knopf.

Meltzer, Milton. (1988). *Benjamin Franklin: The New American.* Watts.

Munro, Roxie. (1987). *The Inside-Outside Book of Washington, D.C.* Dutton.

Provensen, Alice. (1990). *The Buck Stops Here: The Presidents of the United States.* HarperCollins.

Selden, George. (1981). *Chester Cricket's Pigeon Ride.* Illustrated by Garth Williams. Farrar, Straus & Giroux.

Selden, George. (1960). *The Cricket in Times Square.* Illustrated by Garth Williams. Farrar, Straus & Giroux.

Stolley, Richard B, ed. (2000). *Our Century in Pictures for Young People.* Photographs from *Life Magazine.* Little, Brown.

White, E. B. (1945). *Stuart Little.* Illustrated by Garth Williams. Harper & Row.

White, E. B. (1952). *Charlotte's Web.* Illustrated by Garth Williams. Harper & Row.

White, E. B. (1970). *The Trumpet of the Swan.* Illustrated by Edward Frascino. Harper & Row.

Wilder, Laura Ingalls. (1932, 1953). *Little House in the Big Woods.* Illustrated by Garth Williams. Harper & Row.

Appendix

International Reading Association (IRA)

Standards for Reading Professionals—Revised 2003

IRA Standard	Chapter and Heading
1: Foundational Knowledge	
1.1 Demonstrate knowledge of psychological, sociological, and linguistic foundations of reading and writing processes and instruction.	1: "Models of the Reading Process"; "Theories of Learning That Relate to Reading Instruction" 2: "Language and Cognitive Development"; "Techniques to Enhance Literacy" 9: "Steps in the Writing Process and Suggestions for Instruction"
1.2 Demonstrate knowledge of reading research and histories of reading.	1–12: All chapters include reading research that supports the instructional strategies developed in each chapter. 1: "Theories of Learning That Relate to Reading Instruction"; "A History of Basal Reading"; "A History of Requirements for Teachers of Reading"
1.3 Demonstrate knowledge of language development and reading acquisition and the variations related to cultural and linguistic diversity.	2: "Characteristics of Language Development in Early Childhood"; "Techniques That Enhance Language Development in Early Elementary Grades" 10: "The Most Effective Programs for Teaching Students Whose First Language Is Not English"
1.4 Demonstrate knowledge of the major components of reading (phonemic awareness, word identification and phonics, vocabulary and background knowledge, fluency, comprehension strategies, and motivation) and how they are integrated in fluent reading.	1–12: All chapters include this topic. Some specific examples follow. 4: "Building Foundations for Reading through Phonemic Awareness"; "Phonics Instruction for Stages of Word Knowledge Development" 5: "Vocabulary Development in the Pre-K through Fourth Grades"; "Vocabulary Development in the Fourth through Eighth Grades" 6: "Using Modeling Techniques"; "Predicting Outcomes to Improve Comprehension"; "Developing Fluency in Reading"
2: Instructional Strategies and Curriculum Materials	
2.1 Use instructional grouping options (individual, small-group, whole-class, and computer-based) as appropriate for accomplishing given purposes.	1: "Grouping and Instructional Techniques" 11: "Using Technology in the Reading Curriculum" 12: "Grouping Arrangements for Reading Instruction"; "Organizing the Classroom"

IRA Standard	Chapter and Heading
2.2 Use a wide range of instructional practices, approaches and methods, including technology-based practices, for learners at different stages of development and from differing cultural and linguistic backgrounds.	1–12: All chapters include this topic. Some specific examples follow. 1: "Models of the Reading Process"; "Approaches for Reading Instruction" 2: "Stages in Language Development and Implications for Reading"; "Stages in Cognitive Development and Implications for Reading" 6: "Using Graphic Organizers"; "Using Modeling Techniques"; "Using Questioning Strategies" 7 and 8: "Teaching Reading and Literature in English/Language Arts, Social Studies, Science, and Art in Kindergarten through Fourth Grades and Fourth through Eighth Grades" 10: "Literacy Instruction for ELL Students and Students with Special Needs" 11: "Research Studies Connecting Reading and Technology"
2.3 Use a wide range of curriculum materials in effective reading instruction for learners at different stages of reading and writing development and from different cultural and linguistic backgrounds.	1–12: All chapters include this topic. Some specific examples follow. 2: Lists of books that match children's language and cognitive development from early elementary grades through middle school 5: "Vocabulary Development in the Content Area Materials" 6: Curricular materials that enhance different levels of comprehension 7 and 8: Literature selections to enhance reading and writing from kindergarten through eighth grades 9: Materials that enhance the development of expressive, imaginative, and expository writing 10: Multicultural literature for studies of Native American, African American, Latino, and Asian Americans

3: Assessment, Diagnosis, and Evaluation

3.1 Use a wide range of assessment tools and practices that range from individual and group standardized tests to individual and group informal classroom assessment strategies, including technology-based assessment tools.	1: "Reading Assessment in the Classroom" 3: "Recommendations for Assessments: Preschool—Age 12"; "Standardized Tests"; "Assessment in the Classroom That Leads to Instructional Planning"; "Informal Tests of Reading"; "Diagnostic Reading Inventories"; "Running Records"; "Miscue Analysis"; "Cloze Assessment"; "Portfolio Assessment"
3.2 Place students along a developmental continuum and identify students' proficiencies and difficulties.	2: Specific characteristics of students as they progress in their language and cognitive development. 3: "Assessment through Observation"; Portfolio Assessment"; "Relating Assessment to Instructional Approaches"; "Recommendations for Assessments: Preschool—Age 12" 4: "Phonics and Stages of Word Knowledge Development"

IRA Standard	Chapter and Heading
3.3 Use assessment information to plan, evaluate, and revise effective instruction that meets the needs of all students, including those at different developmental stages and those from differing cultural and linguistic backgrounds.	1–12: All chapters include sections for differentiated learning that stress adapting instruction for ELL students, struggling readers and writers, and gifted and accelerated readers and writers. Some specific examples follow. 3: "Assessment in the Classroom That Leads to Instructional Planning" 10: Literacy Instruction for Students Whose First Language Is Not English"; "Characteristics of Students with Special Needs in Reading and Approaches for Intervention"; "Intervention Strategies for Specific Special Needs" 12: "Coaching Groups" and "Flexibility and Transitioning between Groups"
3.4 Effectively communicate results of assessments to specific individuals (students, parents, caregivers, colleagues, administrators, policymakers, policy officials, community, etc.).	3: "Relating Assessment to Instructional Approaches"; "Principles of Assessment"; "Recommendations for Assessments: Preschool—Age 12" 10: "Developing Family Support for ELL Students"; "Characteristics of Students with Reading Difficulties and Intervention Strategies"

4: Creating a Literate Environment

IRA Standard	Chapter and Heading
4.1 Use students' interests, reading abilities, and backgrounds as foundations for the reading and writing program.	1–12: All chapters emphasize the importance of interests, reading abilities, and backgrounds. Specific examples follow. 1: "Recreational Reading Groups"; "Ability Groupings"; "Literature Circles" 9: "Expressive Writing and Emergent Literacy"; "Imaginative Writing for Emergent Literacy" 10: "Helping ELL Learners Construct Knowledge"; "Lesson Plan: Developing Background Knowledge and Respect for Cultural Identity" 12: "Reading Interest Groups"; "Book Clubs"; "Balance between Teacher-Guided Instruction and Independent Reading"
4.2 Use a large supply of books, technology-based information, and nonprint materials representing multiple levels, broad interests, and cultural and linguistic backgrounds.	1–12: As shown by the references at the end of each chapter, this text includes lists of a large supply of books including multiple levels, broad interests, and cultural and linguistic backgrounds. 10: "Multicultural Education through Multicultural Literature" 11: "Using Technology in the Reading Curriculum"; "Developing Classrooms for Writing through Technology"; "Writing Software"
4.3 Model reading and writing enthusiastically as valued lifelong activities.	1–12: All chapters stress the main goal for reading and writing instruction is developing literacy for life. 12: Provides guidelines for developing "Balanced Literacy," which encourages teachers to use instruction approaches that integrate listening, speaking, reading, and writing as lifelong activities. "Reading Aloud to Students" is one of the best ways to share a love for reading.

IRA Standard	Chapter and Heading
4.4 Motivate learners to be lifelong readers.	1–12: All chapters stress the need to motivate learners to be lifelong readers. Specific examples follow. 12: "Groupings for Reading Instruction" are especially important because the various groupings such as "Reading Interest Groups" and "Book Clubs" allow students to share a love for reading and motivate their reading.

5: Professional Development

5.1 Display positive dispositions related to reading and the teaching of reading.	1–12: All chapters stress the importance of positive dispositions. Model lesson plans, instructional units, and varied instructional activities provide models for professional development. Activities such as in Chapter 9 "Imaginative Writing through Poetry Appreciation and Writing Workshops" emphasize this skill.
5.2 Continue to pursue the development of professional knowledge and dispositions.	1: "Changing Trends in Literacy Instruction" emphasizes the changes within the teaching profession and the requirement to develop professional knowledge that is influenced by research. "A History of Requirements for Teachers of Reading" shows how education requirements have changed. 3: "Provisions of No Child Left Behind That Relate to Reading Instruction" and "Reactions to No Child Left Behind" provide current impacts on the reading profession. 1–12: All chapters include numerous research-based instructional strategies that allow teachers to continue the development of their professional knowledge.
5.3 Work with colleagues to observe, evaluate, and provide feedback on each other's practice.	12: Chapter includes guidelines for developing "Literacy Instruction That Works."
5.4 Participate in, initiate, implement, and evaluate professional development programs.	1–12: Every chapter includes several "Reflect on Your Reading" activities that ask students to think about and to evaluate various reading programs. Every chapter includes an "Extend Your Reading" feature. Many of these features ask students to initiate, implement, or evaluate reading programs. Each chapter includes a "For Further Reading" feature that stresses how professional educators have increased literacy through professional development programs.

Glossary

ability level groupings Dividing students for instruction according to their measured levels of reading ability.

aesthetic literacy The ability to read or interpret images in order to enjoy, appreciate, and understand them.

aesthetic scanning A search for artistic elements that emphasize such content as line and color.

analytical reading An in-depth reading strategy that applies informed criticism to a book.

appreciation Responding to a text and reacting to the author's use of language.

assessment The gathering of data through formal and informal tests as well as classroom observation in order to understand the reading strengths and weaknesses of the individual student or the total reading program.

assessment related to desired student outcomes Assessment that is closely related to classroom learning and evaluates whether desired learning has taken place.

at-risk students Students with characteristics that make them at risk for reading failure.

auditory awareness Recognizing that different sounds have different meanings.

auditory blending Blending sounds to form words.

auditory discrimination Distinguishing one sound from another.

auditory sequential memory Hearing, remembering, and repeating sounds in sequence.

authentic assessment Evaluating reading while children are taking part in actual classroom reading activities.

authenticating literature Researching the accuracy of literary elements and content in a book, such as setting and facts.

balanced reading approaches Instruction that uses the best aspects of the phonics, whole language, or literature-based approach.

balanced reading Providing opportunities for students to use a variety of strategies and materials to develop reading ability.

basal readers A sequentially developed series of materials designed to teach various components of reading.

basal reading series A published reading series that structures the development of reading skills and includes supplementary materials.

behaviorist theory A learning theory that suggests students can be taught to perform any task successfully if the unit of learning is small enough.

bilingual education Incorporating both the learner's native language and English in instruction.

blends A word formed by combining parts of other words.

bottom–up model A reading process that begins with the sounds of the letter and progresses upward to the meaning of the text.

characterization Studying the development of a character in a book so that readers understand the strengths, weakness, pasts, hopes, and fears of that character.

choral reading Reading verse or other text orally in groups often with alternating lines.

cloze assessment A form of assessment that leaves out words, usually every fifth word in a reading passage, and observes the number of correct words a reader can supply for those missing words.

cognitive development theory of learning A learning theory that suggests changes that occur in children's mental skills development and influence their abilities to learn.

cognitive development Systematic changes in children's mental skills and abilities including reasoning, concepts, and memory.

comprehension The act of understanding what is read, heard, or seen; is considered one of the ultimate goals of reading instruction.

conflict The struggle and action as characters face problems and overcome difficulties.

context clues Using definitions, comparisons, summaries, familiar expressions, experiences, and synonyms to understand a text.

contextual analysis Identifying meanings of unknown words by analyzing the context in which they are written.

culturally diverse classrooms Classrooms with individuals who represent different racial, ethnic, and cultural backgrounds.

diagnosis   The gathering of data and selecting appropriate tests for students, administering tests, and using results of tests to plan appropriate instruction.

differentiated instruction   Modifying instruction when appropriate to meet the different reading needs of students in the classroom.

direct instruction in phonics   Systematic instruction of a phonics principle by the teacher.

educational software programs   Programs designed to teach, test, or extend information in specific areas of the curriculum such as writing, geography, and mathematics.

electronic books   A replacement for paper-based books.

electronic library and resources   Library collections and services that are available to users through online systems.

e-mail   A system of electronic transmission from one location or person to another location or person.

emergent literacy   Basic knowledge or foundations for reading and writing skills in which children learn concepts such as *print has meaning*.

English language learners (ELL)   Students whose native language is not English and receive instruction in English.

English as a second language (ESL)   Language instruction is exclusively in English.

evaluation   Considering test results and making decisions about the effectiveness of the instruction; or, making judgments about the content of a selection.

expository writing   Writing that focuses on facts, ideas, or opinions, and is usually about nonfiction subjects.

expressive vocabulary   The vocabulary needed for speaking and writing.

expressive writing   Writing about personal experiences and feelings.

frustration level   A level of reading difficulty in which a student is unable to read a passage without considerable teacher assistance.

graphic organizers   Use of visual displays such as semantic maps and flow charts.

high-stakes tests   National and state tests that have serious consequences for students, teachers, and schools.

imaginative writing   Original writing by students; is also referred to as creative writing.

independent level   A level of reading difficulty low enough that the reader can progress without teacher assistance.

inference   Going beyond information the author provides and hypothesizing about details, main ideas, and so forth.

informal assessment   A form of assessment that is based on individual student's needs in the classrooms and not based on standardization.

informal reading inventory   A test that is designed to assess individual student's reading abilities and to identify independent, instructional, and frustration levels of reading.

instructional level   A level of difficulty at which the reader can read with understanding with teacher assistance.

interactive model   A reading process that combines the bottom-up (text-based) and top-down (reader-based) models.

intervention   Programs designed to improve the reading abilities of students with special needs.

invented spelling   Students make up their own spellings for words.

language development   The process that allows children to form words, use various meanings for words, and use language to communicate ideas.

language scope and sequence   Breadth and order of coverage of how the components of language are taught.

literacy circle   Groups of students that meet in class to discuss books.

literacy-rich environments   Classrooms where students are surrounded by books and reading materials, art, and stimulation through various interest centers.

literal recognition   Questions that require students to identify information stated in a text.

literary elements   The author's use of plot, characterization, setting, conflict, point of view, and theme to create a believable story.

literature-based approaches   Curricula that emphasize reading and discussing literature, analyzing and criticizing literature, and responding to literature.

longitudinal studies   Studies that evaluate children's language development over a longer period of time in order to identify specific stages in language development.

mental imagery   Visualizing a setting, situation, or character to develop understanding.

miscue analysis A technique in which an examiner evaluates the type of reading errors made and the function of the words that are corrected.

modeling reading and language Reading books orally to children so they hear how language is used in written sources.

modeling Activities in which an adult shows his or her thought processing to students.

multicultural education Education that considers the values, beliefs, and perceptions of various cultural groups and enhances cross-cultural understandings.

No Child Left Behind The legislation that includes provisions for reading standards and accountability.

oral language instruction Providing instruction that emphasizes learning through oral components and listening rather than through printed text and reading.

phonemes The smallest units of sounds in a spoken language.

phonemic awareness An understanding that spoken words are made up of individual sounds and syllables.

phonics Teaching reading using individual sound-symbol relationships.

phonics approaches Instruction that emphasizes the relationships between the sounds of language and the written symbols of language.

plagiarism To use another person's ideas and writings as if they are your own without citing the original source of information.

plot diagramming for vocabulary Relating vocabulary to important instances in a story.

plot The plan of action or sequence of events in the story.

point of view The perspective from which the story is told.

portfolio assessment A collection of student work over a period of time.

prefix A syllable, group of syllables, or word added to the beginning of another word to change its meaning.

readability A measured way to give a reading grade level to materials using sentence length and semantic difficulty.

reader response theory A learning theory that suggests that meaning results when there is an interaction between the reader and the text.

readers' circle Students take turns reading orally and discussing their reading.

readers' theater Students read a script out loud often through a staged performance.

reading aloud Reading appropriate books and other materials out loud to children in order to model reading behaviors and develop interest in topics and responses to books.

reading interest groups Dividing students for instruction according to specific interests in reading.

receptive vocabulary The vocabulary used in reading and listening.

running records An assessment technique in which the teacher notes words read correctly and errors made while a student reads orally.

schema theory A cognitive theory that emphasizes the importance of prior knowledge in the development of reading comprehension.

self-contained, heterogeneous classes Teachers teach all of the subjects to students of different abilities.

semantic feature analysis Associating vocabulary with concepts.

semantic maps The visual display of concepts and vocabulary related to the concepts.

setting Where the story takes place as well as time—past, present, or future.

shared reading Students read along as the teacher reads with fluency.

sociolinguistic theory of learning A learning theory that suggests that learning is the result of interactions and relationships with others.

software programs Programs that link the work of the computer with the needs of the user.

standardized tests A published test constructed by experts and then administered, scored, and interpreted according to a specific criteria.

storytelling Telling stories orally from memory without using printed text for reference.

style The way the author chooses to arrange the words to create the story.

sub-skills approaches Instruction that emphasizes that reading requires the mastery of a specific group of sub-skills.

suffix A syllable, group of syllables, or word added at the end of a word to change its meaning.

symbolism Something that represents another thing by association.

theme The central idea that ties the plot, characterizations, and setting together into a meaningful whole.

time lines Graphic depictions of incidents in history or in a person's life.

top–down model   A reading process where the reader brings his or her own knowledge, culture, and experience to the interpretation of the text.

vocabulary notebooks   Students collect personalized vocabularies that include words and associations that are interesting to them.

Web sites   Identifiable electronic addresses used for locating, gathering, and disseminating information.

webbing   Also known as semantic mapping; a method for visually displaying relationships among vocabulary, ideas and concepts.

whole language approaches   A curriculum that is child-centered and focuses on the learner's processes of reading and writing.

word walls   Bulletin board displays of meaningful words frequently associated with the vocabulary found in a unit of study.

writing process   Prewriting, composing, and revising for a final product.

writing workshops   Sharing and discussing the works of established writers as well as writing and sharing original work in groups.

Index

Note: Page numbers followed by *f* or *t* indicate figures and tables.

A

Ability level groupings
advantages of, 32
basal readers and, 504
defined, 523
disadvantages of, 503–504
flexibility and transitioning between, 512–513
lower ability readers and, 503–504
reading assessment strategies and, 33
Accelerated students. *See* Gifted/accelerated students
Accountability
defining, 101
high standards and, 99
standardized testing and, 93–95
Achievement gap, closing, 99–100
Active learning strategies, 81
Advanced readers, phonics and, 153
Aesthetic literacy
defined, 333, 523
reader response theory of learning and, 23
role of, 333–334
Aesthetic scanning, 334, 523
African American literature
examples of, 426–428
folktales, 277, 426–427
for vocabulary development, 193
African American stereotypes, in literature, 437
Age of the Scholar, The (Costa), 460
Alliteration, as poetic element, 372–373
"The All-White World of Children's Books" (Larrick), 437
Alphabet books
award-winning, 293–294
illustrations in, 293–295
phonemic awareness and, 148–149, 149*t*
with specific themes, 294
Alphabet City (Johnson), 293–294
Analytic approach, to phonics instruction, 151
Analytical reading, 313–315
Anansi Does the Impossible: An Ashanti Tale (Aardema), 426
Ancient History: Lives and Times in

Ancient Egypt, Greece, and the Roman Empire software, 466*t*
Animal Stackers (Belle), 183
Appreciation
defined, 523
stimulation, questions for, 240
Art
evaluation criteria, 334
lessons, using Caldecott books, 296
reading and, 292–296, 333–339
symbolism and, 336–338, 338*t*, 339*t*
time periods of, 191*t*
using to develop book reports, 295–296
vocabulary in, 191*t*
Art and Design in Children's Picture Books (Lacy), 336
Art books, using to teach following directions, 296
Art criticism, 334–335
Art history, 338–339
Artifacts, for storytelling, 62
Artistic elements
lines, 334
reading, 335–336, 335*f*–337*f*
shapes, 334
texture, 334
The Art of Reading: Forty Illustrators Celebrate RIF's 40th Anniversary, 67–68
Asian Americans, literature, 430–431
Assessments
ability level groupings and, 33
annual academic, 99
authentic, 104, 106, 131, 523
in classroom, 7, 35–37
cloze (*see* Cloze assessment)
defined, 96, 523
informal (*see* Informal tests/assessments)
No Child Left Behind (*see* No Child Left Behind)
reading chart for, 110, 112*t*
recommendations, by grade level, 125*t*–127*t*
related to desired student outcomes, 523
relating to instructional approaches, 106–108
through observation, 108–109
Assonance, as poetic element, 373

At-risk students, 408, 523. *See also* Students with special needs
Auditory awareness
activities for, 141–142, 142*t*
defined, 523
types, 142*t*
Auditory blending, 141, 523
Auditory discrimination
of beginning, middle and ending sounds, 146–148, 147*t*
books with rhyming elements for, 143, 143*t*–144*t*
defined, 141, 142–143, 523
poems, 143, 145
types, activities for, 147
Auditory perception, 141
Auditory receptive language, 141
Auditory sequential memory, 141, 523
Authentic assessment, 104, 106, 131, 523
Authenticating literature
defined, 523
example of, 385–386
in social studies and history, 320–321
workshop development, steps for, 384–385
Author summary, as context clue, 195, 197
Autobiographical writing, 382
Automatic reading, of sub-skills, 13
Automatic word recognition, difficulties, intervention strategies for, 443
Award-winning books, writing a critical evaluation for, 386–388
Aztec folklore, 428

B

Background knowledge. *See* Knowledge, prior or background
Bacon, Francis, 5
Balanced reading approaches, 483–502
advantages of, 483–484
assessment of, 108, 109*t*
basal reading series in, 486, 490–491
curriculum narrowing and, 484–485
defined, 160, 523
description of, 11–12, 19*t*, 160
grouping arrangements for (*see* Grouping arrangements)
individualized instruction and, 493

Balanced reading approaches *(Cont.)*
  integrating listening, speaking, reading
    and writing, 498, 499*t*–502*t*
  locally developed core programs, 491
  in middle school, 484
  prescribed instruction and, 493
  "Study of Democracy," 498, 499*t*–
    502*t*
  teacher-guided and center-based
    discoveries in, 495–497
  teacher-guided and independent
    instruction in, 493–495
  trade books in, 491–493
"Barbara Frietchie" (Whittier), 375
Basal reading series (basal readers)
  ability level groupings and, 504
  advantages/disadvantages, 490*t*
  balancing with trade books and other
    reading materials, 491–493
  components of, 486
  defined, 486, 523
  definition of, 24
  examples of, 486
  groups, flexibility and transitioning
    between, 512–513
  history of, 24–32
    Elson Basic Readers, 28–29
    McGraw-Hill reading series, 31–32
    McGuffey Readers, 27–29
    Reading with Phonics, 30
    Silver, Burdett Company, 25–26
  independent reading and, 262
  language support lesson plan, 489*t*–
    491*t*
  philosophy of, 25
  teacher-directed and guided materials,
    490
  trade books, other reading materials
    and, 491–493
Beat the Story-Drum, PumPum (Bryan),
  426
Beginning readers, phonics instruction
  and, 152, 153–154
Beginning sounds, auditory
  discrimination, 146–147, 147*t*
Behaviorist theory of learning, 20, 523
*Ben Franklin's Almanac: Being a True
  Account of the Good Gentleman's
  Life* (Fleming), 492
Benjamin Franklin: The New American
  (Meltzer), 492
*Best Practice: New Standards for
  Teaching and Learning in
  America's Schools* (Zemelman,
  Daniels & Hyde), 218
"The Big Read" Campaign, 505–506
Bilingual education
  advantages of, 409–410

  defined, 523
  selection of programs for, 410
Bill Peet: An Autobiography (Peet), 293
Biographical writing, 382
Biographies
  African American, 427–428
  defined, 274
  examples of, 274
The Birchbark House (Erdrich), 425
Blends, 146–147, 147*t*, 523
Blue's Clues: ABC Time Activities, 474
Blue's Clues: Blue Takes You to School
  software, 466*t*
*The Bone Man: A Native American
  Modoc Tale* (Simms), 424
Book clubs, 505–506
Book evaluations, expository writing
  workshops for, 383–384
Book jackets, creating, 295–296
Bookmatch approach, 298, 299*f*
Book reports, using art for, 295–296
Books. *See also* Literature; *specific book
  titles*
  alphabet (*see* Alphabet books)
  Caldecott award-winning (*see*
    Caldecott award-winning books)
  with color artistic reproductions, 335
  on colors and shapes, 186
  for literacy circles, 276
  narrative poetry, 278
  with opposites illustrations, 187
  parts of, teaching use of, 283–284
  picture (*see* Picture books)
  with repetitive language, 243
  with rhyming elements, 143, 143*t*–
    144*t*
  with school-related vocabularies, 180–
    181
Bottom-up model
  assessment of, 109*t*
  balanced reading approaches and, 11–
    12
  defined, 523
  description of, 8–9, 10*f*
  interactive model and, 217
  phonics approaches and, 12–13, 19*t*
  vs. top-down model, 10*f*, 11, 495
Box Turtle at Long Pond (George),
  290
A Boy, a Dog, a Frog, and a Friend
  (Mercer), 380–381
Brainstorming
  auditory discrimination skills for, 148
  semantic maps for, 224
  for teaching prefixes, 165, 165*t*
Branches, teaching, 166*f*, 167
Buffalo Woman (Goble), 424
Butterflies for Kiri (Falwell), 296

C
Caldecott award-winning books
  alphabet books, 293–294
  art lessons from, 296
  writing a critical evaluation for, 386–
    388
Call It Courage (Sperry), 222
"The Camel's Complaint" (Carryl),
  143, 145
Cause-and-effect relationships,
  inferences of, 239
CD-ROMS, 466–467
Censorship, 344–345
Centering literacy instruction, 160
Ceremony—In the Circle of Life (Deer
  of Autumn), 426
The Ceremony of Innocence
  (Highwater), 426
Certification programs, alternative, 2–3
Characterization
  defined, 263, 523
  developing understanding of, 266
  elements of, 263–264
  impact of illustrations on, 293
Character traits, inferences of, 239
Charlotte's Web (White), 492
Charts, listing daily activities, 366
Chart story, 368–369, 416–417
"Children's Choices," 207–208, 247
Children's literature. *See* Literature
*Child That Books Built: A Life of
  Reading, The* (Spufford), 345
Chinese art, symbolism in, 338, 339*t*
Choral reading
  book selection for, 246
  defined, 246, 279, 523
  guidelines for, 279–280
  of nursery rhymes, lesson plan for,
    280–282
  poems for, 246–247
Chores, daily, charts listing, 366
Chronological order
  of science literature, 290
  time lines and, 229–232, 231*t*
"Cinderella," comparing different
  versions of, 285–288
Citizenship knowledge, cognitive
  development, in fourth grade
  students, 72
Classroom
  activities, inventory of, 513, 514*t*
  culturally diverse, 523
  environment, 49–50
    collaborative, writing workshops
      for, 370
    for whole language approach, 15–16
  labels in, 364–365
  language-rich, 56

organization, 513–517f, 518
philosophy of, 513–514
reading assessment in, 35–37
for reading instruction, 53
Climate, for developing language skills, 47–49
Cloze assessment
advantages of, 122
defined, 523
example of, 107–108, 122–123
Coaching groups, 509, 512
Cognitive development
defined, 523
enhancement of, 51
language development and, 49–50
in lower/early elementary grades
characteristics of, 68, 69t
lesson plan example for, 68, 70–71
for social studies, 71–73
in middle/upper elementary grades, 73
characteristics of, 78t
for social studies, 79, 80t
teaching implications for, 78t
Cognitive development theory of learning, 20–21, 523
Colors, vocabulary dictionaries of, 186–187
Combination approach, 160
Communication media, 460–461
"Community-as-Resource Policy," 81
Comparisons
as context clue, 195, 196–197
inferences of, 239
Comprehension
balanced reading approaches and, 217
cultural literacy background and, 485
defined, 217, 523
development approaches, 232–242
differentiating instruction for, 248–249, 250f, 251
enhancement, technology for, 463–464
graphic organizers, 223–232
improving
outcome prediction, 243–245
through time lines, 229–232, 231t
instruction, for ELL students, 412t, 414–419
as interactive process, 9–10
intervention strategies, 442
learning center activities, 497t
mental imagery and, 221–222
schema theory, 218–219
software programs, evaluation of, 467–468
strategies, 217–218
sub-skills approach and, 14
taxonomy of, 238

vocabulary development and, semantic feature analysis for, 204–205, 206t
Computer-assisted instruction. See also Technology
learning center activities, 498t
Concentration, game of, 148
Concept muraling, 346
Concepts
discussing, for reading aloud, 76
displaying, with semantic maps, 223, 224f
Concrete poems, 374
Conflict
defined, 263, 523
developing understanding of, 265–266
impact of illustrations on, 292
understandings about, 263
Consonant blends, 154
Contemporary literature
African American, 427–428
Asian American, 431
Latino/Hispanic, 429–430
Content areas. See also specific content areas
art (see Art)
English/language arts, developing research skills for, 317–319
expository writing in, 341–342
expressive writing in, 340–341
history (see History)
imaginative writing in, 341
reading and writing connections, 339–346
in grades 4-8, 309–348
learning center activities, 497t
reading in (see also under specific content areas)
guidelines for, 260
social studies (see Social studies)
writing, using books for motivation, 345–346
Content interpretation, for analytical reading, 313
Context clues
defined, 523
lesson plans, 198–202
synonyms, 195, 198
types of, 194–195
vocabulary development and, 203
Contextual analysis, 194–203
author summary and, 197
comparisons and, 196–197
context clues for, 194–195
defined, 194, 523
definitions, illustrations and, 195–196
experience and, 198

familiar expressions and, 197
lesson plans, sample, 198–202
synonyms and, 198
A Corner of the Universe (Martin), 341
Corrected miscue, definition of, 120t
"Create . . ." story activity, for imaginative writing, 368–369
Creation myths, Native American, 423
Creative skills, 14
Creative writing. See Imaginative writing
Criterion-referenced tests, 97
Critical evaluation
of African American literature, 389, 389t–390t
workshop on, 386–389, 389t–390t
Criticism of book, for analytical reading, 313, 315
The Cross of Lead (Crispin), lesson plan, 220–221
Cultural groups. See also specific cultural groups
developing units of study on, 432–433, 433t–434t
Cultural identity, respect for, 418
Culturally diverse classrooms, 523
Culture knowledge. See also specific cultural groups
cognitive development
in eighth grade, 80t
in kindergarten students, 71
in sixth grade, 80t
study, basal reading series and, 492
values and traditions
books on, 228–229
reading about, 21
semantic map, example of, 227, 228f
Curriculum
formulation, questions for, 124
narrowing, 484–485

D
Daily activities, charts for, 366
Dancing Teepees: Poems of American Indian Youths (Sneve), 426
Debating
defending a position for, 393
science topics for, 393–394
Definition, for vocabulary clarification, 195–196
Democracy, study of, 500, 501t–504t
Demonstrating, 495
"Design . . ." story activity, for imaginative writing, 369
Desktop publishing programs, for English Language Learners, 474

Diagnosis
 defined, 96, 524
 intensive level of, 97
 specific levels of, 97
 survey level of, 96
Diagnostic reading inventories, 109–110
Diagnostic tests, development of, 129, 130t
Differentiated instruction
 anecdotal assessment for, 131–132, 131t
 computer-assisted instruction, 474–475
 defined, 39, 524
 for ELL students (see English Language Learners)
 for English/Language arts curriculum, 297–298, 299f
 for gifted and accelerated readers and writers (see Gifted/accelerated students)
 multicultural classrooms and, 39–40
 for struggling readers and writers (see Students with special needs)
 teaching strategies for, 518–519
 for vocabulary development, 207–208
Digraphs, 154
Dinosaur! (Sis), 381
The Dinosaur: Question and Answer Book (Funston), 290
Direct instruction in phonics, 149–151, 524
Directions, following, using art books to teach, 296
Disadvantaged students, failure of schools to educate, consequences for, 99
The Dot (Reynolds), 296
Dragonflies (McLaughlin), 198
Drama/dramatizations
 creative activities, 64–68, 65f, 67t
 for multilingual classrooms, 248
 poetry in, 375
 in teaching reading and writing, 359
Drawing, 51
Drawing from Nature (Arnosky), 296
Dual-language books, 81
Duck for President (Cronin), 369
"Dust Bowls and Other Dreams," 507

E
Early childhood, language development, characteristics of, 54, 55t–56t
Early reading stages, shared reading groups for, 506
EasyBook Deluxe software, 470t

Easy-to-read books, for reading aloud, 59
Economics knowledge, cognitive development and, 71, 72
Educational software programs. See Software programs, educational
Education schools, 1–3
Efferent reading, 23
Ekwall/Shanker Reading Inventory (Fourth Edition), 113, 139
Electronic books, 465–466, 524
Electronic libraries and resources, 465, 524
Electronic publishing, 396
Elementary grades
 language development in (see under Language development)
 lower/early
  best books for, 67t
  cognitive development in, 68, 69t
 middle
  cognitive development in, 73
  language development in, 73, 74t
 upper
  cognitive development in, 73
  language development in, 73, 74t
  shared reading groups for, 506–507
ELL. See English Language Learners
Elson Basic Readers, 28–29
E-mail, 460, 524
Emergent literacy
 assessment through observation, 108–109
 basic understandings in, 50
 creating "best books" lists for, 66–68, 67t
 defined, 49, 524
 developmental accomplishments and, 51, 52t
 environment for, 50–51, 53
 expository writing in, 382–383
 expressive writing and, 364–367
 fostering, 49–50
 imaginative writing for, 367–369
 learning center activities, 497t
 phonics instruction and, 152, 153
 reading behaviors and, 50
 reinforcing with illustrations in alphabet books, 293–295
 shared reading groups for, 506
 writing behaviors and, 50–51
Emporia State University, Kansas, 1–3
Ending sounds, auditory discrimination, 146–148, 147t
English as Second Language (ESL)
 defined, 524
 programs, 409
 program selection issues, 410

reading assessment chart, 110, 112t
English/language arts
 authentication of setting, 315–317
 developing research skills for, 317–319
 differentiating instruction, 297–298, 299f
 illogical spelling and, 137–138
 reading, language scope and sequence for, 312–313
 reading/literature in, 261–282, 312–317
English Language Learners (ELL)
 bilingual programs for, 409–410
 building background knowledge for, 418–419
 cognitive development for social studies, 80–81
 comprehension and fluency instruction for, 248
 computer technology for, 474
 concept muraling for, 346
 defined, 524
 developing family support with, 419
 differentiating instruction, 167
 for English/Language arts curriculum, 297
 ESL programs for, 409
 extending phonemic awareness for, 420
 gifted and accelerated readers and writers, 446
 literacy instruction, learning center activities, 498t
 phonics instruction, 167
 poetry for, 415–416, 444
 reading instruction, guidelines, 412t
 reading-writing connection and, 394–395
 shared reading groups for, 507
 social studies instruction, 80–81
 storytelling activities for, 444
 teaching, effective programs for, 410–420
  general practices, 410
  language experience approach, 416–418
  oral language development, 411, 412t, 413–414
  principles of, 411
  vocabulary development, 411, 413–414
 vocabulary instruction, 207
 whole language approach and, 16
 writing instruction, 394–395
Environment
 classroom (see Classroom, environment)

for emergent literacy, 50–51, 367–368
  creation of, 53
  imaginative writing and, 367–368
  literacy-rich, 53
  school, reading habits and, 291
ESL. *See* English as Second Language
Evaluation, defined, 97, 524
Evaluation questions, 239
Experience
  as context clue, 195, 198
  reading for, 22–23
Expert readers, behaviors for content
  area reading, 217
Explaining, 495
Explanatory writing. *See* Expository
  writing
Explore the World of Thomas Day
  software, 466*t*
Expository writing, 382–394
  in content areas, 341–342
  defined, 365, 382, 524
  in emergent literacy, 382–383
  science topics for, 393–394
  viewpoints in, 393–394
  workshops
    for book evaluations, 383–384
    on critical evaluation or opinion
      articles, 386–389, 389*t*–390*t*
    developing, steps for, 384–385
    on reading and writing opinion
      articles, 390–393
Expression software, 470*t*
Expressive vocabulary, 177, 524
Expressive writing
  in content areas, 340–341
  defined, 524
  description of, 364
  emergent literacy and, 364–367

F
Fact, *vs.* opinion, 391*t*
Familiar expressions, as context clues,
  195, 197
Family drama tales, Native American,
  424
*A Family of Poems: My Favorite Poetry
  for Children* (Kennedy), 370
Family support, with ELL students,
  development of, 419
Fantasy
  facing adversity and, 310
  modern, 272–273
Faraway Worlds (Halpern), 208
Favorite Poem Project web site, 376
Fern's Poetry Club web site, 376
Fiction
  contemporary, 273, 427–428
  historical

African American, 427
Asian American, 430–431
defined, 273
examples of, 273–274
Latino/Hispanic, 429
Native American, 425
reading proficiency for, 6
vs. nonfiction, 284*t*, 2824
Figurative language,
  interpreting/comprehending, 379–
  380
Finland, educational system in, 257–
  259, 260, 491
*First Children: Growing up in the
  White House* (Leiner), 283–284
First Comes Spring (Rockwell), 141–
  142
First-language reading support, for ELL
  students, 412*t*
Fluency
  components of, 244
  development, 244–247
    guided repeated oral reading, 246–
    247
    independent silent reading for, 247
  difficulties, intervention strategies for,
  443
  learning center activities, 497*t*
Focused recreational reading groups,
  277–278
Focus or theme units, 34–35
Folktales (folklore)
  African American, 277, 427
  Asian American, 430
  Aztec and Mayan, 428
  characteristics, 272
  comparing illustrative interpretations
    of, 294–295
  comparing values/beliefs in, 433,
    433*t*–434*t*
  discussion topics/questions, 272
  example of, 272
  for fourth to eighth grades, 190
  Latino, 428–429
  themes, 267–268
  versions of, similarities/differences of,
    284–288
*Food for Thought: The Complete Book
  of Concepts for Growing Minds*
  (Freymann), 383
Foreign-born students, number in U.S.,
  408
Formulation of school curriculum,
  questions for, 124
*The Fossil Girl: Mary Anning's
  Dinosaur Discovery* (Brightone),
  183
Fourth grade students, cognitive

development, in social studies, 72–
  73
Franklin Delano Roosevelt (Freedman),
  time line development from, 229,
  230–232, 231*t*
Freddy in Peril (Reiche), 474
Free Fall (Wiesner), 381
Frequency-of-use approach, in choosing
  spelling words, 162–163, 164*t*
Frog and Toad Are Friends (Lobel), 68,
  70–71
Frustration level, 107, 113, 524
Fry readability graph, 510–511, 511*f*

G
Games
  auditory awareness, 141
  auditory discrimination, 146, 148
Genres, literary. *See* Literary genres
Geography
  knowledge, cognitive development
    and, 71–72, 80*t*
  vocabulary development and, 204
The GEO Reader (Goodman; Sisson;
  Jones), 203–204
Gifted/accelerated students
  comprehension and fluency
    instruction for, 249, 250*f*, 251
  for English/Language arts curriculum,
    298, 299*f*
  English Language Learners as, 446
  phonics instruction for, 169
  reading skills for content areas, 347
  reading-writing connection and, 395
  social studies instruction for, 82–83
  vocabulary instruction, 207–209
  writing process instruction for, 396
Giggle Poetry web site, 376
The Girl Who Loved Wild Horses
  (Goble)
    semantic map, 335–336, 335*f*–337*f*
    symbolism and, 336–338, 338*t*
*Giving Thanks: A Native American
  Good Morning Message* (Swamp),
  426
Goldilocks and the Three Bears (Brett),
  183, 183*f*, 185, 185*f*
Google, 458
Government knowledge, cognitive
  development and, 72, 80*t*
Graded word lists, 113, 114*t*–115*t*
Grammatical function, definition of,
  120*t*
Grandfather's Journey (Say), sample
  lesson plan, 487*t*–489*t*
The Graphic Alphabet (Pelletier), 294
Graphic organizers, 223–232
  defined, 223, 524

Graphic organizers *(Cont.)*
  semantic maps *(see* Semantic maps)
  tiered, drawing conclusions with, 250*f*
  time lines, 229–232, 231*t*, 525
Graphic proximity, definition of, 120*t*
Grouping arrangements, 502–513
  by ability level, 503–504
  book clubs, 505–506
  flexibility and transitioning between, 512–513
  inquiry method and, 518
  partner reading, 278, 509
  by reading interest, 504–505
  shared reading groups, 506–508
  shared writing groups, 508–509
Guided reading and writing, 159–160, 159*f*
Guided repeated oral reading, for fluency development, 246–247
Guji Guji (Chen), 369

H
Haiku, 374
Harlem kindergartners, free college education for, 481–482
"Harry Potter" books
  protests/censorship challenges and, 344–345
  reading habits in Great Britain and, 244
  settings, locating on web sites, 472–473
The Hello, Goodbye Window (Juster), 182
Henry Hikes to Fitchburg (Johnson), 142
Hey Al (Yorinik), 271
High-frequency words, weakness in recognizing, intervention strategies for, 440–442
High-stakes tests
  defined, 98, 524
  raising scores on, 93–95
  role of, 124
Hispanic/Latino culture, web sites on, 436
Historical fiction. *See* Fiction, historical
Historical nonfiction. *See* Nonfiction, historical
History
  art, 338–339
  knowledge
    eighth grade, 80*t*
    fourth grade, 72
    importance to reading, 485
    kindergarten, 71
    second grade, 72
    sixth grade, 80*t*

reading skills development, 319–320
  authenticating literature in, 320–324, 325*t*–328*t*
  point of view and, 328–330
  research, using technology for, 465–466
  time periods, 191*t*
Hitler Youth: Growing Up In Hitler's Shadow (Bartoletti), 196
Holes (Sachar), 243, 310
Hoot (Hiaasen), 494*t*
How the Ostrich Got It's Long Neck (Aardema), 426
How to Read a Book: The Classic Guide to Intelligent Reading (Adler & Van Doren), 313
"How would you . . .?" story activity, for imaginative writing, 369
Humor
  in picture storybooks, 187
  in poetry, 145–146

I
I am Rosa Parks (Parks & Haskins), 445
IBO (International Baccalaureate Organization), 312
Idea circles, 347
"Ideally . . . ?" story activity, for imaginative writing, 369
"If You . . ." story activity, for imaginative writing, 369
Illustration and definition, for vocabulary clarification, 195–196
Illustrations
  in alphabet books, 293–295
  depicting literary elements, 292–293
Illustrators, comparing interpretations of same stories, 294–295
I Love Bugs! (Sturges), 382
Imagery, as poetic element, 373
Imaginative writing
  in content areas, 341
  defined, 364, 524
  developing reading and writing of, additional ideas for, 378–382
  for emergent literacy, 367–369
  motivation, web sites for, 381–382
  poetry appreciation and writing workshops for, 370–382
"Imagine . . ." story activity, for imaginative writing, 369
Immigrants, 408
Inclusion (mainstreaming), 405–406
Independent instruction, balanced with teacher-guided instruction, 493–495, 494*t*
Independent level, 107, 113, 524

Independent reading
  development, activities for, 495
  silent, for fluency development, 247
Index, 508
Individualized reading program, balancing with prescribed instruction, 493
Inference, 238–239, 524
Inflectional suffixes, 165
Informal assessment, defined, 524
Informal reading inventory, 107, 524
Informal tests/assessments
  Cloze assessments, 122–123
  graded word lists, 113, 114*t*
  miscue analysis, 119–122, 120*t*, 121*t*
  portfolio assessment, 123–124
  purpose of, 35
  in reading, 109–113
  reading passage tests, 113, 116*t*, 117
  role of, 124
  running records, 117–118, 119*t*
  sample lesson plan, 128–129
Information, reading for, 22–23
Informational books, 58, 274–275
Inquiry method, classroom organization for, 514–518, 517*f*
Inspiration Software, Education Edition, 470*t*
Inspiration Version 7.5 software, 466*t*
Instant-messaging software, 175–176
Instructional reading level, 107, 113, 524
Instructional strategies/techniques, 358–359. *See also specific teaching strategies*
  ability groupings *(see* Ability level groupings)
  for differentiating instruction, 518–519
  with ELL parents, 419
  focus or theme units, 34–35
  literature circles, 33
  for multicultural literature, 431–436
  recreational reading groups, 34
  Uninterrupted Sustained Silent Reading, 33–34
Integration, of phonics skills into whole language classroom, 159–160, 159*f*
Intensive level of diagnosis, 97
Interactive model of reading process
  defined, 524
  description of, 9–11, 10*f*, 217
  literature-based reading approaches and, 16–17
Interest areas, scientific, nonfiction books on, 289
Intermediate readers, phonics and, 152–153

International Baccalaureate
Organization (IBO), 312
International Reading Association
(IRA), 260
Exemplary Reading Program Award,
486
exemplary reading programs,
components of, 12
reading coaches, qualifications for,
514
standards for reading teachers, 38
International Schools Primary Years
Program, 124, 128
Internet, search engines, 457–459
Interpretive skills, 14
Intervention, defined, 524
*In the Beginning: Creation Stories from
around the World* (Hamilton), 510
Invented spellings
defined, 161, 524
phonics and, 161–162
Inventing, imaginative writing and, 369
"Invent . . ." story activity, for
imaginative writing, 369
IRA. *See* International Reading
Association
ISAT scores, improving, 94, 95
I Spy Fantasy software, 466t
I Wear the Morning Star (Highwater),
426

J
Journals, writing in, 340–341, 364

K
Kid Works Deluxe software, 470t
Kindergarten students
best books for, 67t
cognitive development, in social
studies, 71
dramatic play for, 359
language development in, 54, 55t
KIPP schools, 2–3
Kitten's First Moon, 182
Knowledge
prior or background
as context clue, 195, 198
intervention strategies and, 442–443
schema theory and, 20, 218–219
top-down model and, 9, 10f
structures/frameworks for reading
comprehension, 10

L
Labels, in classroom, 364–365
Language development
cognitive development and, 49–50
defined, 524

in early childhood, characteristics of,
54, 55t–56t
enhancement techniques, for early
elementary grades, 56–68
creative drama, 64–68, 65f, 67t
informal conversations, 57
reading aloud, 58–61
storytelling, 61–63, 63t
in middle/upper elementary grades,
73, 74t
enhancement techniques for, 74–78
instructional implications, 74t
Language experience approach
for ELL students, 416–418
for emergent literacy, 366–367
Language Scope and Sequence, for IBO,
261, 312, 524
Language usage, in poems, 371–373
Latino literature, 428–430
Latino students. *See also* English
Language Learners
developing family support with, 419
motivational activities for, 417
Learning
cognitive development theory of, 20–
21
reader response theory of, 22–24
sociolinguistic theory of, 21–22
Learning centers
activities, balancing with teacher-
guided instruction, 495–497
classroom organization for, 514–518,
517f
developing, 496, 497t–498t
Learning logs, 341
Learning theories, related to reading
instruction, 7, 19–24
Legend Days (Highwater), 426
The Legend of the Bluebonnet
(DePaola), 188, 188f, 189f, 425
Lesson plans
on building language support, 487t–
489t
choral reading of nursery rhymes,
280–282
comprehension, *The Cross of Lead*
(Crispin), 220–221
for cultural identity, respect for, 418
for developing background
knowledge, 418
for *Frog and Toad are Friends*, 68,
70–71
for informal assessment, 128–129
for informal testing, 128–129
modeling technique
for lower grades, 233–235
for upper grades, 236–237
time line development, 230–232, 231t

Leveling, *vs.* readability, 510–511, 511f
*Liberty Kids CD-ROM: The Real
Adventures of the American
Revolution* software, 466t
Limericks, 374
Lincoln: A Photobiography (Freedman),
342–343
Linguistic style, 379–380
The Lion, the Witch, and the Wardrobe
(Lewis), 295
Listen and Write web site, 376
Listening skills
instruction for, 141
for oral language development, 56–57
reading aloud and, 74–75
Literacy approach, balanced. *See*
Balanced reading approaches
Literacy circles, 275–276, 524
Literacy rate, in Finland, 260
Literacy-rich environments, 53, 524
Literal recognition, 238, 524
Literary elements. *See also specific
literary elements*
defined, 524
developing knowledge of, 263–265
developing understanding of, 265–
268, 266f
illustrations of, 292–293
summarizing, semantic mapping for,
268, 269f
Literary genres
biography, 274, 427–428
developing knowledge of, 269–282
examples of, 82–83
fiction (*see* Fiction)
folktales (*see* Folktales (folklore))
historical fiction, 273–274
knowledge development, practice
reading, 275–280
modern fantasy, 272–273
non-fiction informational books, 274–
275
picture books, 270–272
practice readings, 275–280
units of study, 269
Literature. *See also specific literature or
types or literature*
authenticating (*see* Authenticating
literature)
content, teaching for English/language
arts, 262–282
in English/Language arts, 261–282
fiction (*see* Fiction)
literature-based reading approaches,
16–18, 19t
multicultural, 420–437
African American, 426–428
Asian American, 430–431

Literature *(Cont.)*
  instructional strategies for, 431–436
  Latino/Hispanic, 428–430
  Native American, 423–426
  stereotypes in, 437
  nonfiction *(see* Nonfiction)
  for reading aloud, 58–59
  relationship with science, 288
  in science, 288–291
  selection for reading programs, 18
  time periods of, 191*t*
  vocabulary in, 191*t*
  whole language approach and, 15–16
Literature-based approaches, 262
  assessment of, 107–108, 109*t*
  defined, 524
  description of, 16–18, 19*t*
    curriculum, responses encouraged in, 17–18
Literature circles, 33, 415–416
Little Monster at School software program, 474
"Little Red Riding Hood" tale, 224–226, 226*f*, 227*t*
Lizette's Green Sock (Valcky), 369
Logicomathematical ability, 68
Logs, expressive writing in, 364
Longitudinal studies, 54, 524
Loo-Loo, Boo, and Art You Can Do (Roche), 296
Lost in the Barrens (Mowat), 425
Lyric poems, 373

M

Macbeth (Shakespeare), 218–219
Madison, Wisconsin, 47–48
The Magic of Spider Woman (Duncan), 424
Main idea, inferences of, 239
Mainstreaming (inclusion), 405–406
Mandated tests, 35–37
The Man Who Could Call Down Owls (Bunting), 380
The Man Who Walked between the Towers (Gerstein), readability of, 510–511, 511*f*
The Man Who Walked Between the Towers (Lipson), 387, 388
Mayan folklore, 428
Mayer-Johnson symbols, 406–407
McGraw-Hill reading series, 31–32, 486, 504
McGuffey Readers, 27–29, 82–83
Media
  for communication, 460
  for construction, 461
  for expression, 461
  for inquiry, 461

Memory deficiencies, difficulties in organizing materials and, 444
Mental imagery, 221–222, 524
Metaphors, in poetry, 373
Middle sounds, auditory discrimination, 146, 147–148, 147*t*
The Midwife's Apprentice (Cushman), 243–244
Miscue, defined, 120*t*
Miscue analysis, 107, 119–122, 120*t*, 121*t*
  defined, 525
  example of, 121–122, 121*t*
  terminology for, 120*t*
Modeling reading and language activities, 495–496
  defined, 525
  teacher, shared reading groups and, 508
  technique
    concepts, basic, 232–233
    defined, 232
    lesson plans, 233–237
Models of reading process, 6–11, 10*f*
  bottom-up model *(see* Bottom-up model)
  interactive, 9–11, 10*f*
  reading instruction approaches and, 6–7
  top-down model *(see* Top-down model)
Mole's Hill: A Woodland Tale (Ehlert), 424
Motivation for writing
  in content areas
    using newspapers for, 344
    using nonfiction for, 342–343
  imaginative, web sites for, 381–382
Multicultural education
  cross-cultural understanding and, 421–422
  defined, 525
  development, reasons for, 422
  differentiating instruction for, 39–40
  literacy instruction, learning center activities, 498*t*
  as subject for reading classes and content areas, 422–423
  through multicultural literature, 420–437
Multicultural literature, study sequence for, 420–421
Multiculturalism, defined, 422
Multilingual education, differentiating instruction in, 39
Multiracial books, 21–22
Music content area
  African American, books related to, 389*t*

time periods, 191*t*
vocabulary in, 191*t*
My Friend Rabbit (Rohmann), 293
My Puppy is Born (Cole), 290
The Mystery of the Hieroglyphs: The Story of the Rosetta Stone and the Race to Decipher Egyptian Hieroglyphs (Donoughue), 196

N

NAEP. *See* National Assessment of Educational Progress
Nametags, 364
Narrative poems, 278, 373–374
National Assessment Governing Board, 6
National Assessment of Educational Progress (NAEP)
  reading proficiency measures and, 6, 103–104, 105*t*
  state assessments and, 99, 100
National Assessment of Governing Board, 103
National Reading Panel (NRP)
  background/prior knowledge and, 218
  "Five Pillars of Effective Reading Instruction," 483–484
  mental imagery and, 222
  research study connecting reading with computer technology, 461–462
National Spelling Bee, 137–138
National standards, for social studies skills, 79, 80*t*
National tests, role of, 124
Native American culture
  literature on, 283, 420
    contemporary, 426
    nonfiction with historical perspective, 425
    traditional, 423–424
    traditional from several groups, 424–425
  symbolism and figurative language, 76
  traditional values
    books on, 227–228
    semantic map of, 227, 228*f*
NCELA Newsline Bulletin, 408
NCTE Inbox, 505
Newbery award-winning books, writing a critical evaluation for, 386–388
Newspaper articles
  in balanced reading program, 492–493
  for comprehension improvement, 244–245
New York City Teaching Fellows, 2

New York Times, "Best Illustrated Books," 388
Nick Jr. Little Bill Thinks Big software, 466*t*
No Child Left Behind Act
  accountability and, 101
  consequences of, 36–37, 98, 101–102
  curriculum narrowing and, 485
  defined, 525
  emphasis of, 2
  high-stakes testing controversy, 124
  mandated tests and, 35–36
  progressive education and, 2
  reactions to, 100–102
  reading instruction provisions, 98–100
  standardized testing problems and, 94
  teacher quality and, 100
Nonfiction
  biography, 274, 427
  contemporary, African American, 427–428
  historical
    African American, 427
    Asian American, 430–431
    biographies, 427
  with historical perspective
    Latino/Hispanic, 429
    Native Americans, 425
  informational books, 274–275
  reading proficiency for, 6
  for science centers, 289
  using to motivate writing in content areas, 342–343
  vs. fiction, 284*t*, 2824
Non-word miscue, definition of, 120*t*
Norm-referenced tests, purpose of, 97
Notebooks, vocabulary, 185–187
Nursery rhymes, choral reading, lesson plan for, 280–282

O
Observation, in assessment, 108–109
Occupations, literature on, 283
Omnibeasts (Florian), 368–369
One Good Apple: Growing Our Food for the Sake of the Earth (Paladino), 195–196
Opening lines and paragraphs, that hook reader, identifying/modeling of, 378–379
Opinion, *vs.* fact, 391*t*
Opinion articles, reading/writing, 390–393
Opposites, books with illustrations of, 187
Oral debates, 393–394

Oral language
  development
    for ELL students, 411, 412*t*, 413–414
    of ELL students, 81
    informal conversations and, 57
    listening skills for, 56–57
  enhancement of, 56
  instruction, 525
Oral reading
  guided repeated, 246–247
  materials for
    selection of, 58–59
    types of, 58
  for vocabulary acquisition, 182–183
Organizing materials, difficulties in, memory deficiencies and, 444
The Other Side of Truth (Naidoo), 197
Our Century in Pictures for Young People (Stolley), 507–508
Outcomes, inferences of, 239
Outcomes prediction, to improve comprehension, 243–245
Owl Moon (Yolen), 380

P
Paddy Under Water (Goodall), 381
Pantomime, 64, 148
Paragraph summary, 278
Parent-child interaction, school readiness and, 50
Partner reading, 278, 509
Peer-assisted reading, 278
Personal experiences
  emotional, discussions about, 276
  relating vocabulary to, 180–181
Personification, in poetry, 373
Phonemes, 140, 525
Phonemic awareness
  age guidelines, 139
  alphabet books and, 148–149, 149*t*
  assessments, 139
  defined, 140–141, 525
  discrimination problems, intervention strategies for, 440, 441*f*
  for ELL students, 412*t*, 420
  importance of, 139–149
  instruction, 140–141
  learning center activities, 499*t*
  software programs for, 463
  task in, 140
Phonic proximity, definition of, 120*t*
Phonics
  age guidelines, 139
  assessments, 139, 162
  defined, 149, 525
  instruction
    analytic approach, 151

    approaches, 525
    assessment of, 106–107, 109*t*
    beginning readers, 153–154
    description of, 12–13, 19*t*
    direct approach, 149–151, 524
    emergent readers, 152, 153
    learning center activities, 497*t*
    for middle and upper readers (*see* Structural analysis skills)
    software programs for, 463
    spelling and, 160–162
    stages of word knowledge development and, 151–153
    synthetic approach, 151
    transitional readers, 154–159
    for word knowledge development stages, 153–159
  skills
    assessing from student papers, 162
    integration into whole language classroom, 159–160, 159*f*
Physical knowledge, 68
Picnic (McCully), 271, 380
Picture books
  characteristics of, 270–271
  discussion topics/questions, 271–272
  storybooks
    with humor, 187
    for reading aloud, 58–59
    written in English and Spanish, 415
    wordless (*see* Wordless books)
Pictures of Hollis Woods (Giff), 340
A Pipkin of Pepper for the Pumpkin Soup (Cooper), 271, 369
Plagiarism, 471, 525
Plot
  characteristics of, 263
  defined, 263, 525
  development
    in analytical reading, 314
    impact of illustrations on, 292
  structure, developing understanding of, 265, 266*f*
Plot diagrams
  for book structure understanding, 265, 266*f*
  for vocabulary comprehension, 183–184, 183*f*, 184*f*, 525
Poems. *See* Poetry
Poetic elements, 371–373
Poetic writing. *See* Imaginative writing
Poetry
  African American, 427–428
  for auditory discrimination, 143, 145
  bilingual, 394–395
  for choral reading, 246–247
  concrete, 374
  in dramatizations, 375

Poetry *(Cont.)*
  for ELL students, 415–416
  forms of, 373–375
  haiku, 374
  imaginative writing development and, 370–382
  limericks, 374
  lyric, 373
  narrative, 373–374
  opening lines and paragraphs that hook reader, identifying/modeling of, 378–379
  point of view in, 330
  reading aloud, 59
    dramatization for, 61
    to middle/upper elementary grade students, 75
    preparation for, 59
    repetitive language in, 60
    responding to, 60
    rhyming words in, 60
  sharing/discussing, 270
  student's, sharing of, 378
  topics, poets and, 374–375
  writing
    activity for, 376–377
    motivational web sites for, 376
    revision of, 378
    with students, 375–376
    written in two languages, 444
Poetry writing workshops, 370–371
  poetic elements and, 371–373
  progression of poems in, 371, 372t
Poets, 374–375
Point of view, 326–330
  defined, 264, 327, 525
  developing knowledge of, 264–265
  developing understanding of, 268
  first-person, 327
  limited omniscient, 327–328
  objective, 328
  omniscient, 327
  teaching, in social studies/history, 328–330
Poison Dart Frogs (Dewey), 196
Polar Bear Cubs (Matthews), 197
Pollution, smoke from fires and, 215–216
Portfolio assessment, 123–124, 525
The Powderpuff Girls Learning Challenge #2 software, 466t
The Power of the Myth (Campbell), 420
Practice reading, to develop literary genre knowledge, 275–280
Preciseness, of vocabulary, to enhance cognitive development, 191–192, 192t

Prediction relay, 278
Predictions of outcomes, in improving comprehension, 243–245
Prefixes
  defined, 163, 525
  teaching, 163–165, 165t
Preschool children, language development in, 54, 55t
Prewriting stage, 342, 395
Primary Years Program, 53
The Print Shop Deluxe software, 470t
Prior knowledge. *See* Knowledge, prior or background
Progressive education, 2
Prosody, 82
Publishing and sharing stage, of writing process, strategies for struggling readers and writers, 395
Puppets, 146
  for creative drama activities, 64–66
  easy to make, 65f
  paper-bag project, vocabulary instruction and, 180
Purposeful word study, 149–150. *See also* Phonics

Q
Question-and-answer formats, for science literature, 290
Questioning strategies/techniques
  appreciation, 240
  for comprehension development, 238–242
  evaluation, 239
  inference, 238–239
  literal recognition, 238
  during reading, 240–241, 241t
Questions
  aesthetic response, 23
  formulation for research cycle, 317, 318t
  for reader response theory, 23–24

R
Readability
  defined, 510, 525
  vs. leveling, 510–511, 511f
Reader-based model. *See* Top-down model
Reader response theory of learning, 18, 22–24, 525
Readers
  beginning, phonics instruction and, 152, 153–154
  gifted/accelerated (*see* Gifted/accelerated students)
  struggling (*see* Students with special needs)

Readers' and writers workshops, 159f, 160
Readers' circle, 525
Readers' theater, 279, 525
Reading
  applying, 5
  art and (*see* Art, reading and)
  bottom-up model, 139
  connections with writing, 355–397
    in content areas, 339–346
    current attitudes on, 358–360
    importance of, 360
    learning center activities for, 488t
    technology and, 468–470
  in content areas, guidelines for, 260
  in English/Language arts, 261–282
  fluency (*see* Fluency)
  foundations of, 5
  instructional techniques (*see* Instructional strategies/techniques)
  literature in social studies, 282–288
  love for, developing, 260
  prosodic, 82
  relationship with computer technology, 461–462
  in science, 288–291
  skills acquisition
    characteristics for, 73
    stumbling blocks for, 73
  strategies, for computer-based classrooms, 467
  subject area, importance of, 485
  as three-part process, 5
  for vocabulary development, 177–178
  whole language instruction for, 3
Reading aloud
  benefits for struggling readers/writers, 81
  defined, 525
  grouping arrangements for, 504–505
  guidelines for, 60–61
  language development and, 58–61
  for middle/upper elementary grade students, 74–75
  preparation for, 59
  purpose of, 495
  in whole language classroom, 159, 159f
Reading and literacy programs. *See also specific reading and literacy approaches*
  effective, elements of, 484
  exemplary, components of, 12
  long-range goals for, 5
Reading automatic, 246
Reading climate, 47–49
Reading coaches, qualifications for, 512

Reading comprehension. *See* Comprehension
Reading curriculum, technology in, 462–468
Reading education, changing trends in, 24–25
Reading Galaxy software, 465
Reading groups, based on reading levels, 503–504
Reading habits, declining, 291
Reading instruction approaches, 11–18, 19*t*
  balanced, 11–12, 19*t*
  grouping arrangements for, 503–513
  literature-based, 16–18, 19*t*
  philosophy of, classroom organization and, 513–514
  phonics, 12–13, 19*t*
  sub-skills, 13–15, 19*t*
  theories of learning and, 7, 19–24
  whole language, 15–16, 19*t*
Reading interest groups, 504–505, 525
Reading levels, identifying, 110, 112*t*
Reading materials, for ELL students, 412*t*, 414–419
Reading passage tests, 113, 116*t*, 117
Reading process, models of, 6, 7–11
Reading proficiency
  NAEP definition of, 6
  NAEP measures of, 103–104, 105*t*
Reading Recovery program
  modification of, 248–249
  for phonemic discrimination problems, 440
Reading test scores, results of, 98
Reading With Phonics (Hay & Wingo), 30, 488
Reasoning skills
  imaginative/creative, 368–369
  for social studies, 79
Receptive vocabulary, 177, 525
Recreational reading groups, 34, 277–278
Reflective letters, 341
The Remarkable Journey of Prince Jen (Alexander), 243
Repetition, as poetic element, 373
Research
  cycle
    formulation of questions for, 317, 318*t*
    topic selection, 317
  evaluating information for, 319
  plan, 317–318
  presentation or report, 319
  resources, locating and collecting, 318
  sorting information for, 319

synthesizing and organizing information for, 319
  technology for, 465–466
  on writing process, 360–363
Research skills
  development, for content area reading, 317–319
  types of, 383
Retelling
  partner reading and, 278
  of wordless book, 108–109, 110*t*
Revision
  of poetry, 378
  strategies for struggling readers and writers, 395
Rhyme
  books written in, 143, 143*t*–144*t*
  for choral reading, 246
  as poetic element, 371
Rhyming schemes, teaching, 247
Rhyming words
  books/poems with, 148
  matching pictures with, 146, 146*t*
  phonics instruction activities, 154–155
Rhythm
  for choral reading, 246
  as poetic element, 371
Rhythm instruments, sound awareness activities, 142
Role-playing, 359
Roots, teaching, 166*f*, 167
Rosenblatt, Louise, 22
Rote learning approach, 485
Running records, 117–118, 119*t*, 525

S

San Diego Quick Assessment or Graded Word List, 113, 114*t*–115*t*
Say Yes to Education program, 481–482
Scaffolding, for comprehension, 241, 241*t*, 242*f*
Schema, 218
Schema theory
  cognitive theory of learning and, 20
  comprehension and, 218–219
  defined, 218, 525
The School Library Journal, 465
School Library Journal, "best books" listings, 66–67, 67*t*
School readiness, parent-child interaction and, 50
Schools
  environment of (*see also* Classroom, environment)
    reading habits and, 291
  high-poverty/high-performing, reading programs in, 442–443

Science
  curriculum, topics for expository writing and debating, 393–394
  reading and literature in, 288–291
  reading skills development, developing a unit around conservation programs, 331–333
  relationship with literature, 288
Science centers, 288–289
Science literature, analyzing organization of, 289–290
Scribbling, 50–51
Scripps National Spelling Bee, 137–138
Search engines, 457–459, 465
Second grade students, cognitive development, in social studies, 72
Second-language instruction. *See* English as Second Language
Secrets of a Civil War Submarine: Solving the Mysteries of the H.L. Hunley (Walker), 196–197
Secret Writer's Society software, 470*t*
Self-contained, heterogeneous classes, 32, 503, 525
Self-directed reading, 14
Semantic acceptability, 120*t*
Semantic feature analysis, 204–205, 206*t*, 525
Semantic maps (webbing), 223–229
  defined, 525, 526
  to develop interest in a reading unit, 224–226, 226*f*
  in upper grades, 226–229, 228*f*
  displaying concepts with, 223, 224*f*
  of Native American traditional values, 227, 228*f*
  in reading artistic elements, 335–336, 335*f*–337*f*
  for summarizing literary elements, 268, 269*f*
  for vocabulary development
    in grades 4-8, 187–188, 188*f*
    in pre-K to grade 4, 184–185, 185*f*, 186*f*
Sentence expansion techniques, 443
Sentence length, in readability determination, 510–511, 511*f*
Sequel writing, 244
Setting
  defined, 264, 525
  developing knowledge of, 264
  developing understanding of, 266–267
  of story, authentication of, 315–317
"Setting-the-world-in-order" tales, Native American, 423
Shapes, vocabulary dictionaries of, 186–187
Shared reading and writing, 159, 159*f*

Shared reading groups, 506–508, 525
Shared writing groups, 508–509
Sharing, poetry written by student's, 378
Show; Don't Tell! Secrets of Writing (Nobisso), 208
Show and Tell, 57
Silver, Burdett basal reading series, 25–26
Similes, in poetry, 373
Sing a Song of Popcorn: Every Child's Book of Poems (Schenk de Regniers), 283
Sir Gawain and the Loathly Lady (Hastings), 188, 189*f*, 190*f*
Skinner, B.F., 20
Sky Tree: Seeing Science Through Art (Locker), 290
Smoky Night (Bunting), 292
Snow (Shulevitz), 182
Social studies
  cognitive development, in lower/early elementary grades, 71–73
  cognitive development in, 282
  knowledge, importance to reading, 485
  literature, reading of, 282–288
  reading skills development, 319–320
    authenticating literature in, 320–324, 325*t*–328*t*
    point of view and, 326–330
  skills, cognitive development and
    fourth grade, 72–73
    kindergarten, 71
    second grade, 72
    sixth grade, 80*t*
  vocabulary development, 204
Sociolinguistic theory of learning, 21–22, 525
Software programs, educational
  defined, 460, 524, 525
  to enhance phonemic awareness/phonics ability, 462–463
  for reading comprehension, evaluation of, 467–468
  recommendations for, 466*t*
  skill-development, evaluation guidelines, 464*t*
  for vocabulary development, 462–463
  for writing, 470*t*
So Happy (Henkes), 369
Sound-symbol relationships/meanings, 246
"Spache's Spelling Errors Test," 162
Special needs students. *See* Students with special needs
Specific levels of diagnosis, 97

"Spellbinders Program," 61
Spelling
  developmental, stages of, 161–162
  English, as illogical, 137–138
  errors, on student papers, 162
  phonics and, 160–162
Spelling-bee protesters, 137–138
Spelling words, choosing, 162–163
The Spider and the Fly (Howitt; DeTerlizzi), 246, 293
Spiders and Their Web Sites (Facklam), 197
Springboard stories, 77–78
Standardized tests. *See also specific standardized tests*
  common, 96
  defined, 35, 98, 525
  history of, 98
  limitations of, 102–103
  results from, 96–97
  scores, raising, pressure for, 93–95
  vs. diagnostic tests of reading ability, 110
Stanford Achievement Test, 36, 98
Star Boy (Goble), 425
Stars Beneath Your Bed: The Surprising Story of Dust (Sayre), 369
State standardized test scores, raising, pressure for, 93–95
Stepping Stones to Literature—A First Reader (Arnold & Gilbert), 486
Stereotypes, in multicultural literature, 437
Storybook Weaver Deluxe software, 470*t*
The Story of Main Street (Goodall), 381
The Story of Ruby Bridges (Coles), scaffolded reading experience activities, 242*f*
Storytelling
  choosing story for, 62
  defined, 525
  exercises for, 63
  historical tradition of, 61
  for middle/upper elementary grade students, 77
  preparation for, 62, 63*t*
  programs for, 61–62
  sharing methods for, 62–63
Structural analysis skills
  branches, 166*f*, 167
  defined, 163
  prefixes, 163–165, 165*t*
  roots, 166*f*, 167
  suffixes, 165, 166*t*
Students
  gifted and accelerated (*see* Gifted/accelerated students)

learning expectations
  ages five to seven, 261
  ages seven to nine, 261
  papers of
    phonics skills assessment, 162
    spelling errors, 162
  sharing enthusiasm for books, 60
  struggling readers and writers (*see* Students with special needs)
Students with special needs, 437
  characteristics of, 438–439, 439*t*
  combining literature, drama and history, 444–445
  comprehension and fluency instruction for, 248–249
  content area instruction for, 346
  English/Language arts instruction, 297–298
  instructional strategies for, 438–439, 439*t*
  intervention strategies, 438–444, 439*t*
    for automatic word recognition, 443
    for comprehension, 442
    for fluency problems, 443
    for linguistic sophistication, 443
    for phonemic discrimination problems, 440, 441*f*
    for recognizing high-frequency words, 440–442
    for word meanings and background knowledge, 442–443
  literacy instruction, learning center activities, 498*t*
  phonics instruction, 167–169
  reading-writing connection and, 395
  social studies instruction, 81–82
  vocabulary instruction for, 207
  writing process instruction for, 395
"Study of Democracy Unit," 498, 499*t*–502*t*, 507
Study skills, 14
Style
  defined, 264, 525
  developing knowledge of, 264
  developing understanding of, 268
Subject determination, for analytical reading, 313, 314
Sub-skills approaches
  assessment of, 107, 109*t*
  defined, 525
  description of, 13–15, 19*t*
Suffixes, 165, 166*t*, 525
Summary, as context clue, 195, 197
Summation, of literary elements, semantic mapping for, 268, 269*f*
Summer reading lists, 309–311

Supporting details, inferences of, 239
"Suppose . . ." story activity, for imaginative writing, 369
Survey levels of diagnosis, 96
Survey tests. *See* Standardized tests
Sweetgrass (Hudson), 425
Syllables, in readability determination, 512–513, 513*f*
Symbolism
  art and, 336–338, 338*t*
  defined, 525
Synonym, as context clue, 195, 198
Synthetic approach, to phonics instruction, 151

T
Table of contents
  reading/discussing, 507
  teaching use of, 283
The Tale of Despereaux (DiCamillo), 313–315, 340
The Tale of Peter Rabbit, semantic map of, 270*f*
Tales from Shakespeare (Packer), 218–219
Talking with Adventurers (Cummings), 283
The Tarantula Scientist (Montgomery), 196
Teacher-directed instruction, need for, 495
Teacher education programs, 1–2, 38
Teacher-guided instruction balance
  with center-based discoveries, 495–497
  with independent instruction, 493–495, 494*t*
Teachers
  in Finland, 258, 260
  importance of, 513
  provision of reading instruction, 483
  quality of, No Child Left Behind Act and, 100
  of reading, history of requirements for, 7, 37–40
  "teaching to the test," 36, 94
Teach for America, 2
Teaching strategies/techniques. *See* Instructional strategies/techniques; *specific strategies/techniques*
Technology
  in classroom, 457–476
    for reading, research studies on, 461–462
    taxonomy for, 460–461
  enhancement, of reading comprehension, 463–464
  in learning about Latino culture, 436

in reading curriculum, 462–468
reading-writing connection and, 468–470
using to enhance settings for literature, 472–473
Teens at Risk: Opposing Viewpoints (Ojeda), 393
Telephone conversations, 57
Test preparation skills, 94–95
Texas Assessment of Academic Skills, 36
Text messaging, 175–176
Text-based model. *See* Bottom-up model
Texts, related to Pioneer America, 5–6
Theme
  defined, 264, 525
  developing knowledge of, 264, 267–268
  impact of illustrations on, 293
Theme units (focus units), 34–35
Theories of learning, related to reading instruction, 7, 19–24
Theory, *vs.* practice, 2–4
There's Always Pooh and Me (Milne), 246
The Thief Lord (Funke), 315–316, 340
Thinking skills
  imaginative/creative, 368–369
  for social studies, 79
This Land is My Land (Littlechild), 426
Thomas and the Library Lady (Mora), 415
Time Flies (Rohmann), 381
Time lines
  for comprehension improvement, 229–232, 231*t*
  defined, 525
Top-down model
  assessment of, 109*t*
  balanced reading approaches and, 11–12
  defined, 526
  description of, 9, 10*f*
  interactive model and, 217
  vs. bottom-up model, 10*f,* 11, 493
  whole language approaches and, 15
Top Secret: A Handbook of Codes, Ciphers, and Secret Writing (Janecko), 208
Transitional readers
  phonics and, 152
  phonics instruction, 154–159
Two Suns in the Sky (Bat-Ami), point of view in, 328–330
Two-vowel rule, 157
Typographical or format context clues, 194

U
Uncle Chente's Picnic (Bertrand), 507
Uninterrupted Sustained Silent Reading (USSR), 33–34
Unit of study approach
  developing
    on conservation programs, 331–333
    on cultural groups, 432–433, 433*t*–434*t*
  using, 262
Urban students, underachieving, vocabulary development for, 193
USSR (Uninterrupted Sustained Silent Reading), 33–34

V
The Velveteen Rabbit (Williams), 294
Vendela in Venice, 316
Verbs, meaningful, for writing anecdotal records, 131*t*
Viewpoints, in expository writing, 393–394
The Village of Round and Square Houses (Griffalconi), 426
Visualization (mental imagery), 76, 221–222
Vocabulary
  expressive, 177
  precise, to enhance cognitive development, 191–192, 192*t*
  receptive, 177
  rich, value of, 177–178
  school-related, books with, 180–181
Vocabulary development
  building student responsibility for, 202
  in content areas, 203–205, 206*t*
    semantic feature analysis and, 204–205, 206*t*
  context clues and (*see* Context clues)
  differentiating instruction, 207–208
  for ELL students, 411, 413–414
  enhancement of, 177–178
  focus, for reading aloud, 75–76
  in grades 4-8, 187–188, 188*f*–190*f,* 190–193, 192
  guidelines, 178–179
  learning center activities, 497*t*
  in pre-K through fourth grades, 179–187
  reading for, 177–178
  technology for, 462–463
  for underachieving urban students, 193
Vocabulary instruction, 177
  in content areas, 190, 191*t*
  guidelines, 178–179
  objectives, 179

Vocabulary instruction *(Cont.)*
skills teaching, contextual analysis, 194–203
strategies/activities
effectiveness of, 203
identifying words for comprehension, 183–184, 183*f*, 184*f*
individualized dictionaries, 185–187
notebooks, 185–187
oral reading, 182–183
related to personal experience, 180–181
webbing, 187–188, 188*f*
webbing or semantic mapping, 184–185, 185*f*, 186*f*
word walls, 181–182
Vocabulary notebooks, 185–187, 526
Volcano: The Eruption and Healing of Mount St. Helens (Lauber), semantic feature analysis, 206*t*, 2025
Vowels, word families, 154, 155–157

W
The Watsons Go to Birmingham–1963 (Curtis), authentication of, 385–386
Webbing. *See* Semantic maps
Web logs (blogs), 355–357
Web pages, 461
Web sites, 464
book reviews, writing responses to, 468–469
defined, 526
on Hispanic/Latino culture, 436
for motivating imaginative writing, 381–382
for motivating poetry writing, 376
We're Going on a Bear Hunt (Rosen), 243
"What if" incidents, brainstorming, for imaginative writing, 379
What's the Big Idea, Ben Franklin? (Fritz), 492
Where the Buffaloes Begin (Baker), 425
Where the Wild Things Are (Sendak)
descriptions in, 270–271
illustrations in, 292
vocabulary development and, 184, 184*f*, 186, 186*f*
While We Were Out (Lee), 379
Whole language approach

assessment of, 107, 109*t*
characteristics of, 15
defined, 526
description of, 15–16, 19*t*
literacy pyramid, 159, 159*f*
phonics instruction and, 3
Who's in Rabbit's House? (Aardema), 426, 445
Word analysis, in upper grades, 163–169
Word attack, 13, 149–150. *See also* Phonics
Word banks, 153–154
Word boxes, 440, 441*f*
Word decoding techniques, 149–150. *See also* Phonics
Word families, 154, 155–157, 161
Word knowledge development stages. *See also specific developmental stages*
phonics and, 151–153
Wordless books
retelling of, 108–109, 110*t*
story structures in, discovering/using, 380–381
Word meanings, intervention strategies, 442–443
Word recognition skills
enhancement, technology for, 462–463
for middle and upper elementary grades (*see* Structural analysis skills)
Words, high-frequency, 162–163, 164*t*
Word selection, for reading/spelling programs, 162–163
Word walls
defined, 526
for students with special needs in reading, 440–442
for vocabulary development, 181–182
World War II, authenticating literature On, 320–324, 325*t*–328*t*
The Write Connections software, 470*t*
Writers
gifted/accelerated (*see* Gifted/accelerated students)
struggling (*see* Students with special needs)
Writers Studio software, 470*t*
Writing center, 366
Writing classrooms, computer-based, design of, 469–470

Writing process, 361
activities in, 362
assessment of skilled *vs.* unskilled writers during, 361
for compositions, assumptions about, 362
connections with reading, 355–397
in content areas, 339–346
importance of, 360
learning center activities for, 498*t*
technology and, 468–470
in content areas, motivation for
using books for, 345–346
using newspapers for, 344
using nonfiction for, 342–343
defined, 526
first drafts, 363
impact of writing assignments on students, 392
initial research for, 363
instruction
characteristics of, 361
criticisms of, 363
reading-related, 358–360
organization principles for, 359–360
research on, 360–363
role of reading in, 363
selection of activities in, 362–363
software programs for, 470*t*
steps in, 363
strategies, for struggling readers and writers, 395
teaching, standard-based assessments and, 359
testing, multiple-choice tests for, 359
types, related to reading, 363–365
writing/illustrating activity, 382
Writing workshops
defined, 270, 526
expository writing, 383–390
poetry, progression of poems in, 371, 372*t*

Y
Yoko's World of Kindness: Golden Rules for a Happy Classroom (Wells), 369

Z
Zen Shorts (Muth), 271
The Z Was Zapped (Van Allsburg), 243